Encyclopedia of
INTEREST
GROUPS
★ ★ ★ ★ and ★ ★ ★ ★
LOBBYISTS
in the United States

Volume Two

Encyclopedia of INTEREST GROUPS

and

LOBBYISTS

in the United States

Volume Two

IMMANUEL NESS
Brooklyn College, City University of New York

 SHARPE REFERENCE
an imprint of M.E. Sharpe, Inc.

CONTENTS

VOLUME TWO

Section 8. Labor

Introduction 350
Airline Pilots Association 356
American Federation of Labor–Congress
 of Industrial Organizations 359
American Federation of State, County, and
 Municipal Employees 363
American Federation of Teachers 366
American Postal Workers Union 369
Communications Workers of America 372
Hotel Employees and Restaurant
 Employees International Union 375
International Association of
 Fire Fighters 378
International Association of Machinists and
 Aerospace Workers 381
International Brotherhood of
 Electrical Workers 384
International Brotherhood of Teamsters 387
International Union of
 Operating Engineers 390
Laborers International Union of
 North America 393
National Education Association 396
Seafarers International Union of
 North America 399
Service Employees International Union 401
Transport Workers Union of America 404
Union of Needletrades, Industrial,
 and Textile Employees 407
United Automobile Workers 410
United Food and Commercial
 Workers Union 413
United Steelworkers of America 416
United Transportation Union 419

Section 9. Civil and Human Rights

Introduction 422
ACORN (Association of Community
 Organizations for Reform Now) 430
American Civil Liberties Union 433
Anti-Defamation League 435
Freedom House 438
Human Rights Watch 441
League of Women Voters of the United
 States 444
Legal Services Corporation 447
National Coalition for the Homeless 450
National Lawyers Guild 452

Section 10. Political, Religious, and Ideological

Introduction 454
American Conservative Union 460
American Enterprise Institute 463
Americans for Democratic Action 466
Americans for Tax Reform 469
Brookings Institution 472
Cato Institute 475
Center for Public Integrity 477
Center for Responsive Politics 479
Christian Coalition 481
Citizens for a Sound Economy 483

Common Cause 485
Economic Policy Institute 487
Heritage Foundation 490
The Hudson Institute 492
John Birch Society 494
National Council of the Churches of Christ . 496
National Taxpayers Union 498
Public Citizen 500
United States Catholic Conference 502
U.S. Public Interest Research Group 504

Section 11. Single Issue

Introduction 506
Americans United for the Separation of
    Church and State 513
Citizens Flag Alliance 516
Council for a Livable World 518
Handgun Control 521
Mothers Against Drunk Driving 524
National Abortion and Reproduction
    Action League 526
National Committee to Preserve
    Social Security and Medicare 529
National Rifle Association 532
    National Right to Life Committee 536
People for the Ethical Treatment
    of Animals 539
Planned Parenthood Federation
    of America 542
Union of Concerned Scientists 545
U.S. English 547
U.S. Term Limits 550
Zero Population Growth 553

Section 12. Identity

Introduction 555
American Association of Retired Persons 561
American Indian Movement 564
American Legion 567
Congress of Racial Equality 569
Emily's List 572
Human Rights Campaign 575
National Association for the Advancement
    of Colored People 578
National Gay and Lesbian Task Force 581
National Organization for Women 583

Section 13. Foreign

Introduction 586
China 591
Cuban Exiles 594
European Union 597
Israel 600
Japan 603
Mexico 606
Nigeria 609
Russia 611
Taiwan 614
Turkey 616

PART II. POLITICAL ACTION COMMITTEES AND LOBBYISTS: TABLES AND FIGURES

Section 1. Political Action Committees

Introduction 621
Top Agriculture PACs 627
Top Livestock/Poultry PACs 628
Top Dairy PACs 629
Top Tobacco PACs 629
Top Forestry and Paper PACs 629
Top Business PACs 630
Top Food and Beverage PACs 631
Top Retail PACs 632
Top Miscellaneous Services PACs 632
Top Gambling/Recreation/Tourism
    PACs 632
Top Miscellaneous Business PACs 633
Top Construction PACs 633
Top Building Equipment/Materials
    PACs 634
Top Engineering/Architecture PACs 635
Top Contractors and Builders PACs 635
Top Defense PACs 636
Top Electronics/Communications PACs 638
Top Electronic/Computer
    Manufacturing PACs 639
Top Telephone PACs 639
Top TV/Music/Movies PACs 639
Top Telecommunications PACs 640
Top Printing and Publishing PACs 640
Top Energy/Resource PACs 641
Top Oil and Gas PACs 643
Top Mining PACs 644

Top Electric Utility PACs 645
Top Nuclear/Misc. Energy PACs 645
Top Waste Management/Environmental
   Service PACs 645
Top Finance, Insurance, and
   Real Estate PACs 646
Top Commercial Bank PACs 647
Top Savings and Loan/
   Credit Union PACs 648
Top Finance/Credit Company PACs 649
Top Security and Investment PACs 650
Top Insurance PACs 651
Top Accounting PACs 652
Top Real Estate PACs 652
Top Health PACs 653
Top Health Professional PACs 655
Top Hospital/Nursing Home PACs 656
Top Pharmaceutical and Health Product
   PACs 656
Top Democratic/Liberal PACs 657
Top Republican/Conservative PACs 658
Top Women's Issue PACs 659
Top Miscellaneous Human Rights/Identity
   Groups PACs 660
Top Law Firm PACs 661
Top Lobbyist Firm PACs 661
Top Manufacturing PACs 662
Top Chemical Manufacturing PACs 663
Top Steel PACs 663
Top Textile PACs 664
Top Miscellaneous Manufacturing PACs 664
Top Single-Issue PACs 665
Top Pro-Israel PACs 666
Top Environment PACs 667
Top Gun and Gun Control PACs 667
Top Pro-Choice and Pro-Life PACs 667
Top Miscellaneous Single-Issue PACs 667
Top Transport PACs 668
Top Air Transport PACs 669
Top Automobile PACs 670
Top Trucking PACs 670
Top Railroad PACs 670
Top Sea Transport PACs 670
Top Union PACs 671
Top Industrial Union PACs 672
Top Transport Union PACs 673
Top Building Trade Union PACs 674

Top Public Sector Union PACs 674
Top Miscellaneous Union PACs 675
Top Soft-Money Donors, 1997-98
   Election Cycle 676

Section 2. Lobbyists

Introduction 678
Top Banking, Security, and Investment
   Companies Lobbying Expenditures 684
Top Business Associations Lobbying
   Expenditures 685
Top Computer Companies Lobbying
   Expenditures 686
Top Entertainment/Media Institutions
   Lobbying Expenditures 687
Top Government Agencies Lobbying
   Expenditures 688
Top Health Professional Associations
   Lobbying Expenditures 688
Top Insurance Companies Lobbying
   Expenditures 689
Top Oil and Gas Companies Lobbying
   Expenditures 690
Top Pharmaceutical/Health Product
   Companies Lobbying Expenditures 691
Top Single Issue/Identity Groups Lobbying
   Expenditures 692
Top Tobacco Companies Lobbying
   Expenditures 693
Top Corporations/Associations Lobbying
   Expenditures 694
Top Industries—Lobbying
   Expenditures 697
Top Telephone/Utilities Lobbying
   Expenditures 699
Top Transportation Companies
   Lobbying Expenditures 700
Top Lobbying Firms 701
Top Clients of Top Lobbying Firms 703

Contact Information 705

Glossary 719

Bibliography 725

Index 739

Encyclopedia of Interest Groups

and Lobbyists in the United States

SECTION EIGHT
LABOR

The American labor movement is considerably weaker and less effective in advancing the interests of workers than equivalent movements in Western Europe and Canada. In virtually every category of economic security American workers lag behind those in other advanced industrial countries. On average, American workers earn less and work longer hours than workers in countries with stronger labor movements.

Although American workers' conditions lag behind those in other nations, they are not necessarily any less militant or less interested in improving their living standards through collective action. Scholars attribute workers' inferior position in America to the weakness of labor unions to advance their powers with businesses and corporations, possibly because there has never been a major, labor-based political party in the United States. While effective labor-based parties have emerged in the early twentieth century throughout Europe, no equivalent party has formed in the United States.

In Germany, where a strong labor party has emerged, organized labor is viewed as an important arbiter in determining the distribution of government benefits such as healthcare, pensions, and education. Moreover, while industrial democracies in Europe with a history of labor activism have elaborate social safety nets, the American welfare system has always been less extensive, and at the dawn of the twenty-first century is getting even weaker. Significantly, the United States is the only advanced industrial country that has no universal health insurance system that guarantees healthcare as a right to all its citizens.

In the United States, labor unions are often viewed as special interest organizations because, rather than seeking to advance the interests of workers as a whole, unions—much like corporate interests—sometimes lobby government officials to gain special treatment for industries that employ their members. For example, the United Steelworkers and United Auto Workers support tariffs and restrictions on the import of low-cost steel and automobiles that compete with American products and jeopardize the jobs of its members. Unions that represent workers in the public sector frequently seek to gain greater government funding for their industries. But organized labor also seeks to lobby government officials to improve the conditions for all workers in America. These efforts include support for raising the minimum wage, extending unemployment benefits, and support for universal healthcare.

The American organized labor movement historically has worked toward improving employees' relations with employers and supporting government programs that benefit working people. Unions believe that wages and benefits can be improved through bargaining with employers and through influencing government policies that affect workers as a whole. By engaging in political activities unions strive to defend labor through government programs.

RELATIONS WITH EMPLOYERS

Federal, state, and local laws, judicial decisions, and administrative policies regulate and oversee relations between employers and labor unions. Unions that formed at the turn of the twentieth century placed primary attention on improving organized labor's capacity to organize workers and bargain with employers. Samuel Gompers, president (with one brief interruption) of the American Federation of Labor (AFL) from 1886 until his death in 1924 believed that organized labor's primary goal should be advancing labor rights at the workplace, rather than seeking social advancements for workers through the state. Unions affiliated with the AFL—which represented most organized workers in the early twentieth century—struggled to end child labor, attain and enforce the eight-hour day, improve working conditions, and raise poverty wages. Through organizing, membership mobilization, and political action, unions were able to change government law and alleviate sweatshop conditions.

Perhaps the most important goal for organized labor has been the struggle to organize workers into trade unions. Since the early 1800s, many employers have presented obstacles to prevent workers from forming unions. They have resorted to intimidation and union-busting tactics such as dismissing supporters of union organizing campaigns, temporarily raising wages, and actively campaigning against union drives. To combat these tactics, the labor movement worked to create legislation which keeps employers from interfering with workers' right to organize, a law they believe is protected by the U.S. Constitution's First Amendment, which guarantees the right to free association.

The National Labor Relations Act of 1935 (also known as the Wagner Act) proved a milestone in American labor history. It vastly expanded trade unions' legal rights to organize industrial workers, and established procedures for union recognition and collective bargaining. Today, the union movement continues to advocate labor law reform to improve its ability to represent workers.

PRIVATE-SECTOR EMPLOYER RELATIONS

Defending and improving the legal balance of power at the workplace is critical in maintaining unions' ability to survive and grow. Without the right to organize, unions would not have the power to defend workers' rights against employers. Thus, unions are concerned with government policies that bear on their ability to represent workers and collectively bargain with employers. Unions seek to exert influence on the executive, legislative, and judicial levels of government to defend the interests of workers. On the executive level, unions historically have had considerably more influence on and access to Democratic presidents than Republican presidents. As chief executive, the president is in effect the employer of millions of government workers, including hundreds of thousands of union members. In 1981, President Ronald Reagan struck a major blow to labor when he fired thousands of striking air traffic controllers who were employed by the government. The action legitimated the permanent replacement of striking workers in other industries. In the ensuing years, private employers have more frequently engaged in similar actions, crippling the power of the strike as a weapon.

The U.S. president appoints the executive members of the National Labor Relations Board, the agency that oversees labor-management relations. Presidential appointments to the board have great influence over labor's ability to prevent employers from illegally retaliating against workers who support unions. Moreover, the president may make policy directives that assist or undermine unions in organizing. For example, the president has the authority to call for "cooling-off" periods during strikes that have national implications, restricting the union's ability to defend the interests of workers through the strike weapon.

The labor movement also is concerned with legislative policy that affects its ability to organize and defend its members. Pushed through by a Republican Congress, the Taft-Hartley Act of 1947 severely curtailed labor's ability to organize unions by outlawing sympathy strikes and sanctioning open shops that do not require workers who benefit from union contracts to join unions. A major priority for organized labor has been to overturn the law's most anti-union provisions.

The American Federation of Labor-Congress of Industrial Organizations (AFL-CIO), which formed in the merger of 1955, also opposes trade agreements that reduce tariffs for imported goods and jeopardize American jobs. In 1993, the federation was unsuccessful in preventing passage of the North American Free Trade Agreement (NAFTA), an accord with Mexico and Canada that eliminated tariff barriers and exposed American workers to competition from lower-paid laborers. Democratic President Bill Clinton and the Republican Congress supported the agreement. However, four years later labor was successful in preventing the expansion of NAFTA to additional countries in Latin America.

SUPPORT FOR SOCIAL BENEFITS

Since the 1930s, the union movement also has been at the forefront of defending social welfare benefits—government-funded programs that protect Americans from economic calamity and distress due to unemployment, old age, sickness, or destitution. The idea of social welfare is based on the belief that Americans cannot always depend exclusively on earned wages for their livelihood. Programs that have been supported by organized labor are unemployment insurance, Social Security, and universal healthcare, including Medicaid and Medicare. These programs, funded by worker contributions and tax dollars, are common throughout most industrial countries of Europe, North America, and East Asia. The United States, however, differs in that there is no universal healthcare system. The leading advocates for social benefit programs historically have been industrial and service unions that represent lower-paid workers. These unions see government as a key component in protecting the average American working family and reducing economic inequality.

The union movement also has supported government job programs for American workers. Since the 1950s unions representing government workers have grown more rapidly than private-sector unions, whose memberships have declined precipitously since the 1970s. A primary concern for public-sector unions in the last two decades of the twentieth century has been the subcontracting of government jobs to private employers. To defend workers from relentless privatization campaigns that undermine the wages of public-sector workers, unions have advocated living wage initiatives in localities throughout the United States. These campaigns have supported local legislation stipulating that workers employed by private firms that perform government subcontracted work are paid wages that are at least 100 percent above the poverty line. Public-sector unions also are concerned with the growth of workfare initiatives that have replaced decent-paying unionized jobs in the public sector with recipients of government assistance who work in exchange for their welfare check—which often does not even rise to the minimum wage.

Although unions are seeking to organize newly marginalized workers who are subject to government and industrial restructuring, they also are trying to defend government jobs. On state and local levels, public-sector unions frequently mobilize members and lobby governors and state legislatures to maintain and increase government funding for education, healthcare, services, and other programs that rely on public funding.

Government programs that safeguard jobs and income security are of great concern to most unions. The labor movement was a leading supporter of the Family and Medical Leave Act, signed into law in 1993. The law guarantees workers who must take a leave of absence due to catastrophic illness or childbirth the right to return to their jobs. However, this protection is not universal, covering only workers in medium and large companies, and does not provide income support during the worker's absence, as is the custom in most European countries with similar standards of living.

TYPES OF LABOR ORGANIZATIONS IN THE UNITED STATES

Industrial and craft unions represent workers in relations with management, while labor federations represent unionized workers across industry divisions. Local unions join labor federations on the national, state, or regional levels. Although unions and labor federations strive to advance workers' economic and political interests, they differ significantly in their individual objectives and capabilities.

Labor unions. The first labor unions in the United States tended to represent workers who were organized on the basis of craft. In the garment industry, for example, separate unions represented workers in the same company who performed different tasks. However, the growth of large-scale industry tended to homogenize distinct skill categories, and by the 1930s unions began to organize on an industry basis. Rather than organizing specific segments of workers in an industry, unions organized entire factories. Thus, the growth of the steel, automobile, and electronics industries produced a rapid growth of industrial-based unions. Although craft unions continue to represent some workers, most unionized workers today are represented by industrial unions.

Trade unions are structured on the basis of union locals, district councils, and international unions. Union locals generally represent workers in a given city or town, district councils represent workers in the same industry on a regional basis, and internationals usually represent workers in a distinct industry throughout the United States and Canada. Local unions typically organize and negotiate contracts with management on a local or regional level. International unions set policy and administer operations of union locals and bargain with management in industries that are national in scope—such as the airline, automobile, and steel industries.

Labor Federations: AFL-CIO. The AFL-CIO represents virtually all union members on a national basis and coordinates the political activities of 86 national and international industrial and craft unions in the United

States and Canada. Formed in 1955, the AFL-CIO is a federation of diverse unions, seeking to unify organized labor on issues concerning workers. Thus, the organization's aims are less narrow than international unions that have labor market concerns related to their industries.

The president of the AFL-CIO has historically been one of the most politically influential leaders in the United States. In 1995, the AFL-CIO held one of its first contested races for president since its inception as the AFL in 1886. Insurgent international union leaders distressed with the moribund state of the AFL-CIO forced Lane Kirkland from office and elected John Sweeney as the new president of the association. Sweeney promised to support a program to revitalize the labor movement by organizing new members and encouraging the participation of women, minorities, and other groups who were frequently excluded from leadership positions.

OPPONENTS OF ORGANIZED LABOR

Interest groups that represent various segments of private business are the primary source of opposition to the American labor movement. Private business fundamentally opposes any interference by outside entities in their right to run their firms. Thus, many business leaders view labor unions as third-party meddlers who interfere with management decisions and raise the cost of doing business by organizing workers to demand higher wages and benefits. Leading political opponents of organized labor in Washington are the U.S. Chamber of Commerce, the National Association of Manufacturers, and the National Federation of Independent Business—organizations that represent commercial, manufacturing, and business interests. Business organizations contribute to candidates opposing government interference with the private market. For example, business lobbyists generally oppose raising the minimum wage, extending unemployment benefits, and other federal regulations governing labor. Moreover, business interests also oppose eliminating open-shop laws and other obstacles to organizing labor in the United States.

A leading legislative goal of organized labor's opponents in the 1990s has been restricting labor's use of union dues for political purposes. Political opponents of organized labor sponsored such legislation in several states. However, in 1998, a Republican-sponsored referendum calling for restrictions on the use of union dues for political purposes was defeated in California. On the national level, opponents of labor have sponsored legislation to further weaken unions by prohibiting labor organizations from collecting union dues as a condition of employment. The National Right to Work Committee, a leading national opponent of organized labor, is sponsoring the National Right to Work Act, which would greatly restrict unions' ability to function. Right to work laws have severely impeded labor's power in many states of the South and Southwest where corporations have opposed the expansion of labor power. Typically supported by Republicans who oppose labor, right to work laws currently cover about 35 percent of all workers in the United States. Organized labor contends that right to work laws are thinly disguised political efforts to restrict workers' democratic right to organize and defend themselves against management.

Conservative political think tanks are leading opponents of organized labor and oppose government social benefit programs that seek to protect workers' economic status. The Heritage Foundation, a leading right-wing think tank, provides research that exposes union abuses, usually without referring to the benefits that workers gain from union membership. The organization also resolutely opposes minimum wage laws, unemployment insurance, and most government programs that interfere with the functioning of the private market.

LABOR UNIONS' POLITICAL ACTIVITIES

The labor movement employs a wide range of strategies and activities to advance the political and economic status of workers in American society—from social protest, electoral politics, lobbying, and campaign contributions to sympathetic candidates and politicians. Since the election of John Sweeney as president of the AFL-CIO, the union movement has sought to emphasize organizing new members to stem a long period of decline and to reestablish the power of workers. A growing number of AFL-CIO unions have welcomed the new emphasis on organizing and have devoted greater attention, additional staff members, and significantly larger financial resources to recruiting new members.

However, organized labor asserts that if it is to successfully organize many new members, America's restrictive labor law must be reformed. For more than 50 years organized labor has considered labor laws in the United States unfavorable to organizing new members, in part because of Taft-Hartley.

KEY LEGISLATION

American labor law that does not adequately protect workers who seek to join unions is one of the most important factors in accounting for the failure of the labor movement to organize and grow. While workers in the United States have the nominal right to organize and form unions to represent them in bargaining with management over wages and working conditions, in practice, workers face massive obstacles if they wish to organize against the will of employers. The cornerstone of American labor law is the National Labor Relations Act (NLRA), passed in 1935 during the height of the New Deal, that guaranteed organized labor the right to organize workers and represent them against management. The law established the National Labor Relations Board to oversee relations between the two parties. However, the 1947 Taft-Hartley Act, passed over a veto by President Harry S. Truman, significantly eroded the provisions of the NLRA that provided the legal basis for organizing. The act outlawed sympathy strikes, purged Communist leaders who were instrumental in organizing new workers into the labor movement, and permitted the formation of open-shop unions, enabling employers to reduce the power of organized labor in the South where opposition to unions is stronger. Organized labor has sought without success to repeal the most restrictive elements of the Taft-Hartley Act that hinder unions' ability to organize and represent workers. Employers can violate labor law by firing organizers with minimal penalties.

Thus, a central campaign for the AFL-CIO and its member unions is the Right to Organize campaign, devoted to reducing the obstacles to joining unions. The right to organize is considered both a human right and a right to free speech that is curtailed in the United States and many foreign countries where employers freely intimidate workers for supporting unions.

The AFL-CIO and its constituent international unions participate integrally in government policy debates that affect American workers. For example, unions have actively participated in the debate to raise the minimum wage, extend unemployment insurance benefits, protect Social Security, oppose trade legislation that is detrimental to American workers, and defend the use of union dues.

International unions have sought to influence government legislation that directly affects workers in their industries. For example, industrial unions are frequently supportive of legislation placing limits on the import of foreign goods produced by lower-cost producers. But unions also seek to restrict corporate efforts to restructure industrial operations that lower wages, break unions, and jeopardize their members' jobs. Public-sector unions have sought to increase government funding for education, healthcare, and social service programs on a federal, state, and local basis because these expenditures are a major source of revenue that pays for workers in these segments of the economy. Without adequate funding, unions' ability to negotiate with management is curtailed. Trade unions representing service workers are interested in government regulations that may affect the vitality of the industries where their members work.

Unlike many other interest groups, unions do not only engage in campaign contributions to supportive politicians and in lobbying for their interests. Unions also seek to develop the political power of its own members through public education, citizenship classes, voter registration drives, membership mobilization, political rallies, campaign contributions, lobbying, and strikes. International unions have political action committees (PACs) that contribute money to candidates for public office and expend financial resources for media campaigns directed at defending the jobs and livelihood of their members.

IMMANUEL NESS

Bibliography

Aronowitz, Stanley. *From the Ashes of the Old: American Labor and America's Future.* Boston: Houghton Mifflin Company, 1998.

Bronfenbrenner, Kate, Sheldon Friedman, Richard W. Hurd, Rudolph A. Oswald, and Ronald L. Seeber. *Organizing to Win: New Research on Union Strategies.* Ithaca, NY: Cornell University Press, 1998.

Chaison, Gary N. *Union Mergers in Hard Times: The View from Five Countries.* Ithaca, NY: ILR Press, 1996.

Cowie, Jefferson. *Capital Moves: RCA's 70-Year Quest for Cheap Labor.* Ithaca, NY: Cornell University Press, 1999.

Dark, Taylor. *The Unions and the Democrats: An Enduring Alliance.* Ithaca, NY: Cornell University Press, 1998.

Fraser, Steven, and Joshua B. Freeman. *Audacious Democracy: Labor, Intellectuals, and the Social Reconstruction of America.* Boston: Houghton Mifflin Company, 1997.

Freeman, Richard B., and Joel Rogers. *What Workers Want.* Ithaca, NY: Cornell University Press, 1999.

Herzenberg, Stephen A., John A. Alic, and Howard Wial.

New Rules for a New Economy: Employment and Opportunity in Postindustrial America. Ithaca, NY: Cornell University Press, 1998.

Hoerr, John. *We Can't Eat Prestige: The Women Who Organized Harvard*. Philadelphia: Temple University Press, 1997.

Johnston, Paul. *Success While Others Fail: Social Movement Unionism and the Public Workplace*. Ithaca, NY: ILR Press, 1994.

Juravich, Tom, and Kate Bronfenbrenner. *Ravenswood: The Steelworkers' Victory and the Revival of American Labor*. Ithaca, NY: Cornell University Press, 1999.

Kuttner, Robert. *Everything for Sale. The Virtues and Limits of Markets*. New York: Alfred A. Knopf, 1977.

Lichtenstein, Nelson. *The Most Dangerous Man in Detroit: Walter Reuther and the Fate of American Labor*. New York: Basic Books, 1995.

Mantsios, Gregory, ed. *A New Labor Movement for a New Century*. New York: Monthly Review Press, 1998.

Moody, Kim. *Workers in a Lean World: Unions in the International Economy*. London: Verso, 1997.

Ness, Immanuel. *Trade Unions and the Betrayal of the Unemployed*. New York: Garland Publishing, 1998.

Perusek, Glenn, and Kent Worcester, eds. *Trade Union Politics: American Unions and Economic Change: 1960–1990s*. Atlantic Highlands, NJ: Humanities Press, 1995.

Pollin, Robert, and Stephanie Luce. *The Living Wage: Building a Fair Economy*. New York: New Press, 1998.

Schafer, Todd, and Jeff Faux. *Reclaiming Prosperity: A Blueprint for Progressive Economic Reform*. Armonk, NY: M.E. Sharpe, 1996.

Sweeney, John J. *America Needs a Raise: Fighting for Economic Security and Social Justice*. Boston: Houghton Mifflin Company, 1996.

AIRLINE PILOTS ASSOCIATION

Although it represents just 53,000 members—a relatively small figure by comparison to some of its fellow AFL-CIO member unions—the Airline Pilots Association (ALPA) represents nevertheless a powerful voice in Washington, D.C., through its active membership, its large campaign donations, and its influence over one of the most critical industries in contemporary America. Its members—virtually all of whom are pilots and navigators—work for about 50 of the nation's airlines, including some of the largest, such as Delta, Northwest, and United. But because the ALPA has been unable to negotiate a master contract with all the airlines, salaries, benefits, and working conditions vary greatly from airline to airline. Moreover, many of the pilots at the larger carriers—including American, Continental, and Southwest—have individual unions of their own. Still, the ALPA remains the dominant union in the industry and is often looked to for leadership on air travel and pilot issues by the other unions.

The ALPA consists of over 100 locals, usually located at a specific air hub. These locals are then included in pilot groups across the United States and Canada. Each pilot group consists of members working for a specific airline. The pilot groups enjoy considerable autonomy in governing internal affairs and negotiating contracts. Each group is headed by a master executive council, composed of several elected representatives of the group's various locals. Local council representatives also comprise the board of directors for the union as a whole, which sets overall policy. The union's executive board and executive council—elected at biennial meetings—run the day-to-day affairs. The international office—located in suburban Washington, D.C.—is headed by four national officers: president, vice president, secretary, and treasurer.

The ALPA—whose members are among the highest-paid workers in any industry—functions as both a union and a professional organization. Approximately 600 pilots serve on local and national safety committees, and the union donates 20 percent of its dues to support aviation safety. In addition, union representatives are usually granted "interested party" status at major crash sites. Although the union does become involved with broader issues of concern for the labor movement, much of its energy in Washington, D.C., is spent lobbying on airline safety issues, which sometimes include work regulations for pilots.

HISTORY

The ALPA was formed in 1931 by a Boeing Air Transport pilot. The union's early grievances concerned poor working conditions, arbitrary management practices, and wage cuts caused by the Depression. In 1933, Congress passed legislation extending the job security and organizing rights of the Railway Labor Act to the airline industry. This provided a much-needed boost for the fledgling union in negotiating contracts. The ALPA grew slowly in the 1930s and 1940s, but came of age with the booming air transport industry of the 1950s and 1960s.

ACTIVITIES: CURRENT AND FUTURE

The ALPA's lobbying activities in Washington, D.C., concern air safety, which involves working with both Congress and the Federal Aviation Administration (FAA). One of the issues that the ALPA is involved with concerns aging aircraft. The union has strongly pushed the FAA to address the safety and reliability of aging aircraft systems by developing new tests and maintenance standards geared to such aircraft. The union has also been active in the area of air space safety, specifically pushing for a National Civil Aviation Review Commission (NCARC) to investigate the growing density

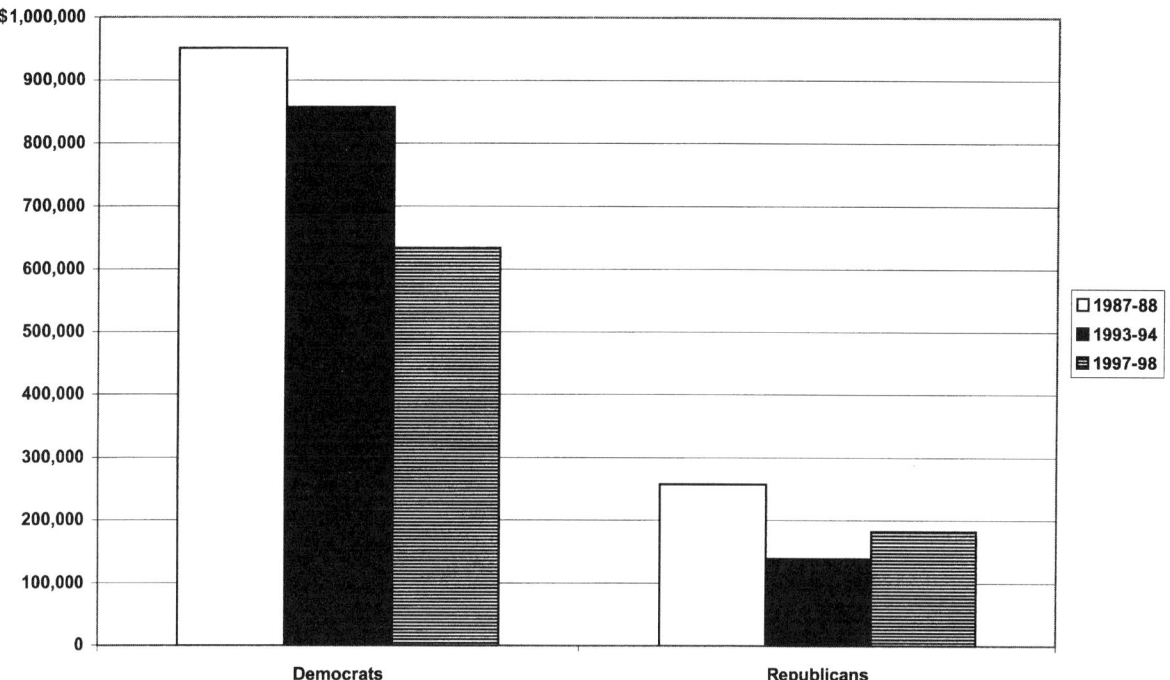

**Airline Pilots Association
Political Action Committee Contributions**

Data derived from official studies available from the Federal Election Commission, Washington, DC, 1987–1998.

of aircraft around major hubs and the distressing number of near collisions in the air. With the report issued in late 1997, the ALPA has been pushing for appropriate legislation to address the concerns raised by the NCARC. Specifically, the ALPA and the report advocate increased funding for the FAA, through cost-based user charges and fuel taxes. In addition, the ALPA would like to see more of the FAA's general revenues devoted to the issue of air space safety.

On a related subject, the union has advocated that Congress push the FAA to take more action on the growing number of runway incursions, in which two aircraft end up on the same landing strip at the same time. As one union official told Congress, "Because the number of incursions has increased each year since 1993, it is vital that we analyze the effectiveness of the measures taken thus far and determine what additional actions are required." The union says the problem has to do with an increase in flights without commensurate development in airport infrastructure, pilot unfamiliarity with airport layouts, and the FAA's lack of leadership on the issue. Moreover, the union has advocated a restriction on what are called "land and hold short" operations (LAHSO), whereby two aircraft operate on separate but intersecting runways. The union advocates the establishment of the recalculation of minimum stopping distances; better runway lighting, marking, and signage; and a ban on LAHSO operations on wet runways. Overall, the union has pushed the FAA to publish more data on flights as a way to assess air safety. But concerned that such data might be used against its members, the ALPA asked that the FAA publish all data cumulatively, so that individual pilots and union members cannot be identified individually.

Overcrowding in the airline industry, as the union understands, is not confined merely to aircraft. Increasingly crowded flights—and extended air time for passengers due to the growing number of hub connections—have produced tensions aboard aircraft and a rise in the number of disruptive passengers. Thus, the union has pushed both Congress and the airlines to do more to combat unpleasant and dangerous situations in which passengers get out of control. The union would like to see tougher prosecution of unruly passengers, both in the United States and abroad, stricter control over deportees transported by air, and the creation of a national database to track incidents and perpetrators.

Concerning pilots as union members, the ALPA has

been cautious in the establishment of emergency boards to deal with pilots' strikes. In the Northwest strike of 1998, for example, the union requested that President Bill Clinton not establish such a board to resolve the dispute. As a union official noted at the time: "Federal government intervention now in the Northwest Airlines matter would prevent workers from exercising their lawful right to strike and would set a very harmful precedent for future labor negotiations. Any federal action in this matter would signal other carriers that they, too, can thwart the collective bargaining process by simply asking the president to intervene."

FINANCIAL FACTS

The ALPA political action committee (ALPA PAC) is one of the largest political action committees of the labor movement—by amount of donation—in the country. During the 1995–1996 election cycle, the Committee on Political Education received $1.15 million and spent $1.1 million. This latter figure includes $822,000 in contributions to candidates and parties—$633,000 to Democrats and $189,000 to Republicans.

The ALPA PAC has been one of the few unions that has seen its receipts, expenditures, and contributions decline significantly between 1987 and 1996. Receipts and expenditures have declined by about 3 percent, while contributions have fallen by 33 percent from $1.5 million to just over $1 million. At the same time, contributions to Democrats have far exceeded those to Republicans, by four to six times as much, but this a comparatively lower ratio than for other unions.

JAMES CIMENT AND IMMANUEL NESS

Bibliography

Hopkins, George. *The Airline Pilots: A Study in Elite Unionism.* Cambridge, MA: Harvard University Press, 1971.

———. *Flying the Line: The First Half Century of the Airline Pilots Association.* Washinton, DC: Airline Pilots Association, 1982.

AMERICAN FEDERATION OF LABOR–CONGRESS OF INDUSTRIAL ORGANIZATIONS

The American Federation of Labor–Congress of Industrial Organizations (AFL-CIO) is the largest association of organized labor in the United States. The organization was founded in 1955 with the merger of the American Federation of Labor (AFL) and the Congress of Industrial Organizations (CIO), the two leading federations of labor in the country. Subsequently, the AFL-CIO has expanded in importance to dominate the labor movement. By the end of the century, virtually all national and international unions in the United States had affiliated with the federation. As a consequence, the AFL-CIO has emerged as the leading federation without any competing organizations.

The AFL-CIO is comprised of 86 national and international unions with members employed in virtually every industry in the United States. While national and international unions tend to address issues in their respective industries, the AFL-CIO tries to unify the diverse interests of organized labor into a single voice. Thus, the AFL-CIO's political concerns tend to mirror the collective interests of the labor movement. These concerns include reforming labor law to enable unions to organize workers, advocating on behalf of government social programs that improve the conditions of workers, and curbing corporate and industrial restructuring that erode labor's bargaining power.

HISTORY

In 1881, leading trade unionists formed the Federation of Organized Trades and Labor Unions of the United States and Canada. Five years later, the organization was officially reorganized into the AFL and quickly emerged as the leading trade union federation in America. Under the leadership of Samuel Gompers, the AFL focused on the defense of the craft unions, which formed the majority of the federation, in opposition to the Knights of Labor, which often favored a more militant and far-reaching strategy of labor mobilization. The AFL opposed the organization of unions on the basis of industrial plant-wide affiliation and encouraged member affiliations on the basis of skill and craft lines, such as construction, printing, and engineering trades. The AFL opposed organization of members on an industrial basis. Gompers and the AFL did not seek to advance labor's standing through government programs but believed that social gains could be achieved exclusively at the workplace. The organization's affiliates therefore sought higher wages and improved working conditions through bargaining with management.

The union movement expanded at the turn of the twentieth century through the recruitment of new industrial workers against aggressive opposition from America's leading corporations and businesses. By 1905, however, in the face of this opposition, union membership stagnated and declined. A new spurt of growth in labor organizing emerged at the end of the First World War as demand for consumer goods and industrial production began to grow. However, by the early 1930s, the failure to organize the growing ranks of unskilled and semiskilled industrial workers reduced the AFL's standing and led to challenges from competing union federations. In 1935, industrial unions affiliated with the Committee for Industrial Organization emerged as a challenger for dominance of the American labor movement. Later renamed the Congress of Industrial Organizations, the CIO expanded rapidly through organizing workers on an industrial basis. Moreover, under the leadership of charismatic president John L. Lewis, the CIO also advocated government social welfare programs to assist working Americans. Leading CIO organizing campaigns were waged in the auto and steel industry. This challenge for leadership by the CIO forced AFL unions to initiate industrial organizing, which also expanded the ranks of the AFL. The period of competition for industrial workers triggered the greatest growth spurt in organizing new unions into the American labor movement.

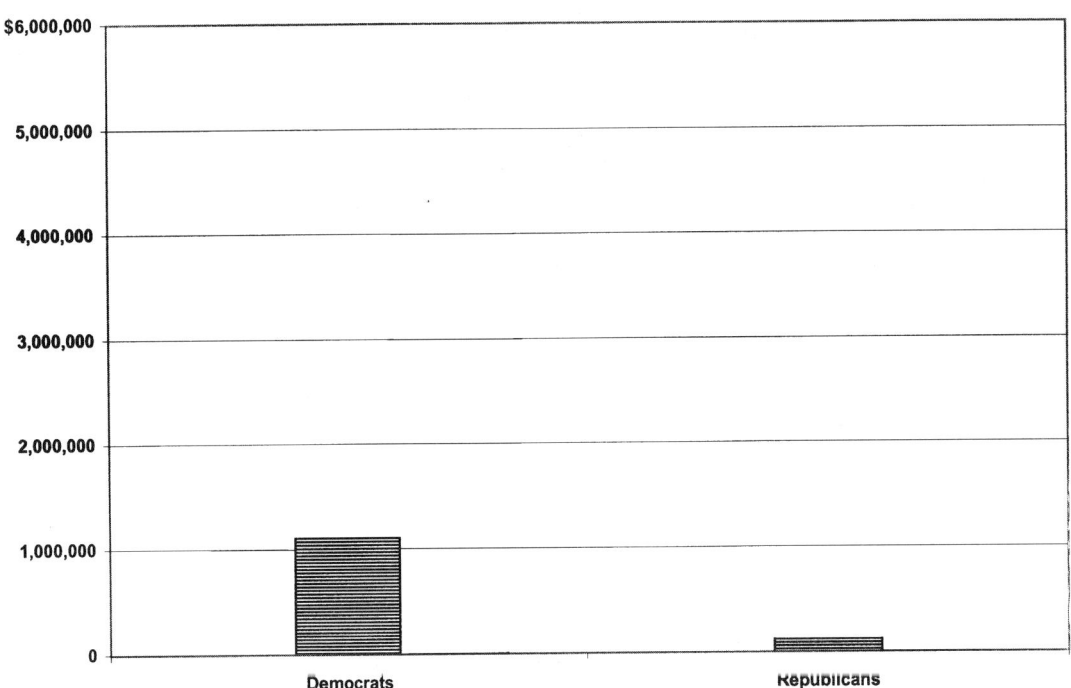

American Federation of Labor–Congress of Industrial Organizations Political Action Committee Contributions, 1997–1998

Data derived from official studies available from the Federal Election Commission, Washington, DC, 1997–1998.

Labor's rapid growth in the 1930s and 1940s contributed to business alarm over the unions' rising influence and the potential for even further labor power. Labor's rise to power also sparked a backlash by anti-labor Republicans in Congress who advocated curbing labor's power to organize, strike, and protest. Against strong Democratic opposition, the Republican-dominated Congress passed the Taft-Hartley Act in 1947, overriding a veto by Democratic president Harry S. Truman. The new law significantly curbed labor's legal ability to organize new workers, rendered sympathy strikes illegal, and purged radicals in the labor movement, including Communist Party members. More than 50 years later, the Taft-Hartley Act remains a major legal impediment in the labor movement's expansion of its ranks of organized workers. AFL-CIO leadership has attempted to influence presidents and lobbied Congress to pass new legislation to change the most serious impediments to organizing.

The AFL and CIO merger in 1955 was intended to expand labor's collective power. For the next 20 years, wages among unionized workers in America grew faster than at any period in the century. Unions represented the vast majority of workers in leading industrial sectors of the economy. Moreover, the organization of public-sector workers into unions continued to sustain trade union membership in the 1960s through the 1980s. However, with the downturn of the American economy in the early 1970s, wages in the manufacturing sector began to stagnate, due in part to growing competition from low-wage producers in the United States and abroad. The domestic and foreign competitive pressure reduced organized labor's ability to command improved wages and working conditions for its workers. Many unions engaged in concessionary bargaining with management and negotiated two-tier wage agreements for workers with seniority and those newly hired.

Internal tensions between rightist and leftist factions in the labor movement kept the federation divided. However, by the 1990s, with the reentry of the Teamsters into the AFL-CIO, most of the leading national and international unions in the United States affiliated with the federation. Despite the consolidation of the federation, however, membership has continued to spiral downward. The percentage of workers belonging to unions declined from about 35 percent in the late 1940s to about 14 percent by the century's close.

Some critics attribute labor's dwindling power to an

orientation toward business unionism, a form of trade unionism that emphasizes servicing the economic and workplace needs of existing members at the expense of organizing new members. In most unions, funds and personnel devoted to organizing dropped to almost nothing. Moreover, in the 1970s and 1980s, a swelling union bureaucracy and concessionary bargaining with management were seen as further impediments to attracting new members. Union membership continued to decline in the 1980s in response to the Reagan administration's failure to enforce labor laws protecting workers' right to organize. In the same period, millions of unionized manufacturing jobs were also lost to foreign competition from lower-wage producers.

By the mid 1990s, recognizing that the AFL-CIO needed to respond more vigorously to government and corporate challenges, leaders of several industrial unions challenged AFL-CIO president Lane Kirkland, who had presided over the federation's decline from 1979 to 1995. Moreover, under Kirkland, the AFL-CIO failed to prevent the ratification of the North American Free Trade Agreement (NAFTA) that threatened to significantly jeopardize American manufacturing jobs. Although Kirkland initially refused calls from a growing number of international unions for his resignation, by early 1995 he resigned and appointed AFL-CIO secretary-treasurer Thomas R. Donahue as the new president. However, key union leaders had already rallied around John Sweeney, then president of the Service Employees International Union, to become the new leader of the federation. The Sweeney slate had the support of the leading industrial unions, and advocated a more aggressive approach to rebuilding the strength of labor in the United States through organizing the unorganized. At the AFL-CIO convention in October 1995, Sweeney was elected as the new president, becoming the first modern challenger for the leadership of the federation to defeat an incumbent president.

ACTIVITIES: CURRENT AND FUTURE

The AFL-CIO uses a wide range of strategies to improve the wages and working conditions for working Americans. Politically, the organization supports candidates running for elected office that are sympathetic to the agenda of the labor movement. The AFL-CIO contributes funds to candidates and mobilizes rank-and-file members to vote for candidates of its choice. The organization lobbies on behalf of issues that concern labor, such as the right to organize, raising the federal minimum wage, lengthening unemployment insurance eligibility periods, and defending Social Security. The AFL-CIO also mobilizes members to rally and demonstrate in support of critical issues. Since the United States does not have a labor party with direct links to the labor movement, the AFL-CIO overwhelmingly supports Democratic candidates, who tend to be more sympathetic than Republicans to labor's position. However, the organization maintains that now it is more careful about which candidates receive funds, because of some who made promises to labor during elections, only to vote against the movement once in office.

The AFL-CIO coordinates its national program on a state and local level through state and regional branches of the organization. The AFL-CIO is decentralized on state and local levels through 50 state federations of labor and more than 600 central labor councils. The independently administered bodies formulate national policy and coordinate state and regional activities. Since 1995, after many decades of dormancy, the AFL-CIO has encouraged state federations and central labor councils to support organizing efforts and actively support the national program to revitalize the labor movement. A number of labor councils have energized the local labor movement through becoming more active in union organizing efforts through educating and mobilizing members.

Perhaps the most important demand of the AFL-CIO in the current era is improving the ability of workers to organize and join unions. Since the early 1980s, nonunion employers typically have resisted union-organizing drives. Moreover, unionized employers have sought to avoid unions through moving to nonunion regions, subcontracting to nonunion firms, and closing unionized operations. Employers frequently fire and discriminate against workers who support unions. Thus, the AFL-CIO believes that existing laws must be enforced and new laws must be enacted that level the playing field between labor and management. In particular, the AFL-CIO believes that the anti-union provisions of the Taft-Hartley Act of 1947 need to be overturned to improve workers' ability to organize into unions.

A key concern for the AFL-CIO is restricting the ability of corporations to evade wage rates and labor laws in the United States by moving production to low-wage countries that have few labor protections. As a result of this practice of shifting production abroad, millions of unionized American workers have lost their jobs in the last two decades. The AFL-CIO and its member organizations believe that the emergence of trade blocs

(NAFTA and other regional associations) and global trade groups (World Trade Organization) that are not subject to democratic control, significantly reduces the ability of American workers to have a say in their economic destiny.

FINANCIAL FACTS

Under Sweeney's leadership, the AFL-CIO has sought to energize the labor movement through encouraging organizing new workers into unions. The AFL-CIO has subsequently devoted significantly increased resources to facilitate new organizing and to help elect politicians who are sympathetic to organized labor and willing to support key legislative goals of the federation. In the 1995–1996 election cycle, the AFL-CIO devoted significant funds to elect Democratic congressional candidates running against Republicans who opposed organized labor's goals. The AFL-CIO devoted $35 million to help elect a Democratic majority to the U.S. Congress.

Although the AFL-CIO dispenses political action committee (PAC) funds to candidates of its choice, the organization also helps to mobilize its membership to vote in key elections. Typically, contributions to Democratic candidates far surpass contributions to Republican candidates. Democratic candidates received 99.7 percent of the AFL-CIO's $1,113,140 in PAC campaign contributions during the 1997–1998 election cycle. Still, under the Sweeney administration, the AFL-CIO has placed greater emphasis on candidate support of labor's legislative goals rather than on party label.

IMMANUEL NESS AND JAMES CIMENT

Bibliography

American Federation of Labor and Congress of Industrial Organizations. *AFL-CIO American Federationist.* Volume 84–present, 1976–present.

———. *One Hundred Years of American Labor, 1881–1981.* Washington, DC: American Federation of Labor and Congress of Industrial Organizations, 1981.

Aronowitz, Stanley. *From the Ashes of the Old.* Boston: Houghton Mifflin Company, 1998.

Fraser, Steven, and Joshua B. Freeman. *Audacious Democracy: Labor, Intellectuals, and the Social Reconstruction of America.* Boston: Houghton Mifflin Company, 1997.

Mort, Jo-Ann. *Not Your Father's Union Movement: Inside the AFL-CIO.* New York: Verso, 1998.

Sweeney, John J. *America Needs a Raise: Fighting for Economic Security and Social Justice.* Boston, MA: Houghton Mifflin Company, 1996.

AMERICAN FEDERATION OF STATE, COUNTY, AND MUNICIPAL EMPLOYEES

As its name implies, the American Federation of State, County, and Municipal Employees (AFSCME)—a member union of the AFL-CIO—represents approximately 1.3 million employees of governmental agencies below the federal level, making it the largest public employee union in the country. AFSCME also includes employees of private hospitals and universities, nonprofit organizations, and public school districts.

Reflecting the diversity of the services offered by government, AFSCME members are arrayed across a broad spectrum of occupations. With 200,000 secretarial and clerical workers, AFSCME is the largest union in this category. Similarly, with 100,000 and 75,000 members employed as social workers and correctional officers respectively, AFSCME is the nation's largest union in these categories as well. Approximately 325,000 healthcare and hospital workers are represented by AFSCME, as are 100,000 largely noninstructional school employees.

AFSCME is the second largest union in the country, representing highway employees, mental health workers, government inspectors, employment counselors, park and recreation workers, and a host of other occupations. AFSCME is organized into more than 3,400 locals, most of which are affiliated with one of the union's 63 councils. Local unions and councils enjoy their own constitutions, elect their own officers, and administer many of their own local services and affairs. The international office is run by a president and secretary-treasurer, elected by convention every four years. Along with 31 vice presidents—chosen at convention on a regional basis—the officers form an executive board, which meets quarterly to determine policy and implement resolutions arrived at by convention vote. In addition, the international office consists of a number of departments, including research, legislative, public policy, political action, fund-raising, legal, organization, education, public relations, and other services.

The legislative department employs a number of full-time lobbyists who meet with Senate and House members to advocate the union's political agenda. At the same time, AFSCME's lobbyists work with federal agencies and the White House to push for regulations and the enforcement of regulations supported by union members. The political action department provides skilled personnel and other resources to help locals organize politically in the electoral and legislative arenas. This includes backing union representatives as delegates to state and national—usually Democratic Party—conventions, as well as grassroots political organizing for candidates and referenda. The union's public policy department conducts research into existing and proposed legislation—research that is then used for collective bargaining or political purposes. Finally, the Public Employees Organized to Promote Legislative Equality (PEOPLE) department represents AFSCME's fund-raising and political donation arm—relying, as per federal law, on voluntary contributions raised by members.

HISTORY

AFSCME's origins go back to Wisconsin in the 1930s, when a number of separate locals representing state employees joined to become a separate department within the American Federation of Government Employees in 1935. The following year, the union was chartered as a member of the American Federation of Labor (AFL). By the time the AFL merged with the Congress of Industrial Organizations (CIO) in 1955, AFSCME represented about 100,000 members. Two years later, the union moved its headquarters from Madison, Wisconsin, to Washington, D.C. In 1978, the 200,000-member Civil Service Employees Association of New York State joined AFSCME, pushing its membership over the 1 million mark.

**American Federation of State, County, and Municipal Employees
Political Action Committee Contributions**

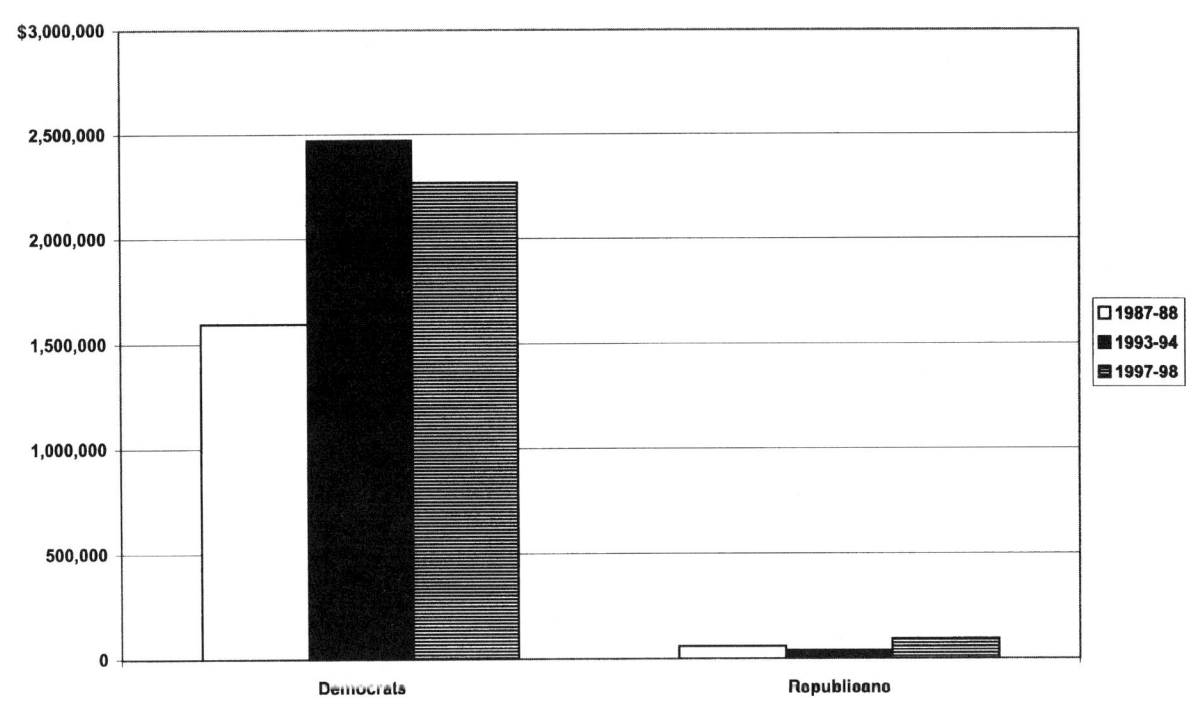

[Bar chart showing PAC contributions with three time periods (1987-88, 1993-94, 1997-98) for Democrats and Republicans. Democrats: approximately $1,600,000 (1987-88), $2,475,000 (1993-94), $2,275,000 (1997-98). Republicans: small amounts near zero for all three periods.]

Data derived from official studies available from the Federal Election Commission, Washington, DC, 1987–1998.

ACTIVITIES: CURRENT AND FUTURE

AFSCME is extremely active in the legislative arena for several reasons. First, because its employees range across so many different occupations and government agencies—as well as private, nonprofit institutions—a variety of issues facing the federal government affect AFSCME members. Second, AFSCME members have a dual interest in government programs and policies, since these affect them as both citizens and employees. Finally, because of its large political war chest, AFSCME often takes the lead in pushing the political and legislative agenda of organized labor overall.

Like most labor unions, AFSCME has had to balance a defensive lobbying approach to block initiatives promoted by members of Congress, many of whom are Republicans, who support anti-organized labor and antigovernmental program initiatives. At the same time, it has tried to work with Democrats in Congress and the White House to push for reforms and new programs that expand government services and protect laboring Americans, particularly those working in the public sector.

Among the initiatives affecting labor and the labor movement overall that AFSCME is working to block are the so-called paycheck deception acts, changes to the 40-hour workweek, promotion of company unions, and Social Security privatization. Paycheck deception first emerged as an issue in 1998 when California placed Proposition 226 on the ballot, a referendum that would have prohibited the use of union dues for lobbying without the prior written consent of individual members. Supporters claimed that workers were "deceived" when union dues were taken out of their paychecks for political purposes. While the measure—which AFSCME and other unions believe would have crippled their lobbying—was defeated, Republican members of Congress have introduced similar measures in the House and Senate.

The Teamwork for Employees and Management Act has also been actively opposed by AFSCME, even though the act would not directly affect AFSCME members. According to unions, the law would overturn the 65-year-old National Labor Relations Act, allowing companies to organize their own unions to counter organizing by independent trade unions. Efforts to amend the Fair Labor Standards Act—mandating overtime pay for most workers who work more than 40 hours in a week—are also being fought by AFSCME. Moreover, AFSCME opposes an effort by House Republicans to deal with the chronic shortfalls in federal funding for unemployment insurance by replacing the 60-year-old partnership between Washington, D.C., and the states with block grants to each of the 50 states. Block grants give states wide discretion in dispersing funds and would, says the union, lead to lower benefits and potential privatization of unemployment insurance. The union is also opposed to Republican attempts to limit Occupational Safety and Health Administration activities by loosening regulations, cutting budgets, and weakening whistle-blower protection.

AFSCME opposes any measure to privatize Social Security, and this for several reasons. First, the union says, despite gloomy political rhetoric the program is not in trouble financially and is not likely to be in the future. Second, it sees privatization as risky and unfair, jeopardizing pensions for workers while enriching Wall Street. Finally, argues AFSCME, privatization undermines the political consensus for a national social security program, in that better-off or more financially astute citizens remove themselves from the program.

AFSCME also opposes measures specifically affecting its own members. High on its agenda is a fight against repeals in labor protection for workers in juvenile justice areas. A House bill that would remove labor protections for state workers whose jobs are funded by federal juvenile justice grants is opposed by the union. In addition, AFSCME is working hard to defeat the push for school vouchers. Here, the dual agenda of AFSCME is most apparent. Opposed to vouchers because of its philosophical commitment to public education, the union also sees in vouchers the undermining of organized labor in public schools, which AFSCME represents.

At the same time, AFSCME is active politically in promoting a number of initiatives that benefit labor and organized labor generally, as well as bills that would aid its own members specifically. Among the former are expanded federal funding for child care, a consumer bill of rights for managed healthcare clients, a higher minimum wage, equal labor rights for workfare employees, and increased training for laid-off workers.

As for measures to help its own members specifically, AFSCME is pushing for bills that would guarantee collective bargaining rights for corrections officers; more protections for police officers charged with noncriminal disciplinary action; a ban on weight-lifting equipment for prisoners—as strengthened inmates allegedly endanger the safety of corrections officers; more federal funding for bulletproof vests for local law-enforcement departments; mandatory testing of prisoners for HIV/AIDS and other communicable diseases—again, as a protection for corrections officers; a program to provide counseling for the families of slain police officers; and a scholarship fund for the children of corrections officers.

FINANCIAL FACTS

According to the union's own records, PEOPLE represents the second-largest political action committee (PAC)—based on donations—of the labor movement and one of the ten largest in the country. During the 1995–1996 election cycle, PEOPLE received over $6 million and spent $4.3 million. Nearly all of the $2.5 million of PEOPLE's political contributions in 1995–1996 was given to Democratic candidates, while only $41,925 went to Republicans. There has been a dramatic increase in PEOPLE's receipts, expenditures, and contributions over the past 10 years. Receipts and expenditures have more than doubled, while contributions have grown more than 25 percent—from $1.658 million in the 1987–1988 election cycle. At the same time, contributions to Democrats have far exceeded those to Republicans—25 to 60 times as much.

JAMES CIMENT AND IMMANUEL NESS

Bibliography

American Federation of State, County, and Municipal Employees. "A Powerful Voice in the Workplace." Washington, DC, n.d. Pamphlet.

Journal of State and Local Government Employees. Vols. 1–45. (1947–1991).

Public Employee. 1992–1999.

AMERICAN FEDERATION OF TEACHERS

The American Federation of Teachers (AFT)—an AFL-CIO member union—consists of some 950,000 educators from elementary school to university levels. In addition, the AFT represents several noninstructional educational professions, including nurses, counselors, and paraprofessionals.

The union—whose membership is expected to climb over the 1 million mark by the year 2000—is organized into three levels. At the bottom are the 2,100 local chapters, representing members in 43 states. The largest of these is the United Federation of Teachers in New York City, with 120,000 members. Locals are generally chartered to represent members employed by a single institution and provide most of the services the union offers, including negotiations with employers, grievance procedures, and other labor-management matters. Members of locals adopt their own constitutions and bylaws, set their own dues, elect their own officers, and hire and direct their own staffs. In addition, local unions elect their own delegates to AFT state and national conventions.

Above the locals are the state federations, which provide locals with services that they could not support on their own. They also serve as a means of communication among locals. State federations are also active in lobbying state governments—an important consideration, given the decentralized school system in the United States.

The national headquarters—located in Washington, D.C.—provides a nationwide system of support for the locals and is active in lobbying the federal government on issues pertaining to education. Delegates establish policy guidelines for the national union at semiannual conventions. They also elect the union's president, its secretary-treasurer, and 38 vice presidents, who are in charge of the different regions, different kinds of members (generally based on instructional levels), and different divisions of the AFT. Altogether, these elected officers form the executive council, which handles the day-to-day activities of the union. At all levels, the AFT sponsors conferences and other events related to education. The AFT's national union includes departments managing the following activities: lobbying, political action, research and technical support, public relations, publications, leadership development and training, professional and workplace issues, organizing and affiliate services, legal defense, human rights, divisional issues, and international relations.

As its name implies, the AFT focuses politically on issues relating to education, including vouchers, privatization, academic standards, teacher accreditation, state takeovers of local school districts and, of course, educational funding, including new school construction.

HISTORY

The AFT was founded in Winnetka, Illinois, in 1916. A group of teachers met to discuss the idea of a national organization that would represent their views, would be independent of existing organizations dominated by school administrators, and would be affiliated with the labor movement. Within the year, delegates from across the United States met to form the union.

From the 1920s to the 1950s, membership fluctuated, depending on organizing efforts, the expanding school system, and the overall economy. A major early problem concerned "yellow dog" contracts, whereby school disticts would prohibit union members from teaching. Many AFT leaders lost their jobs during these years as a result of union activities. Redbaiting—that is, accusing members of Communist proclivities—also damaged the union, despite the fact that the union itself expelled locals with Communist sympathies in 1957. At the same time, it revoked the charters of any local that refused to admit African-American educators.

By 1960, the union had grown to 60,000 members. But its real rise to prominence came later in the decade, when its New York City local spearheaded a strike that

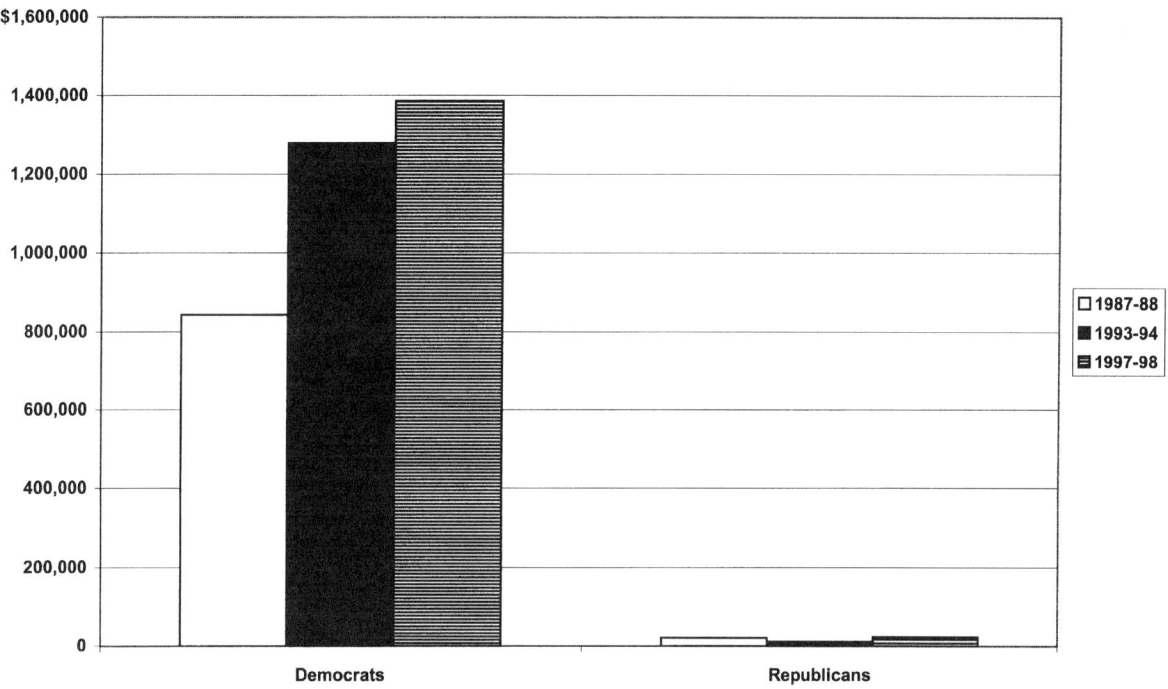

Data derived from official studies available from the Federal Election Commission, Washington, DC, 1987–1998.

won a collective bargaining agreement in the nation's largest school system. By the early 1970s, almost half the teachers in America were engaged in collective bargaining negotiations, though not always under the aegis of the AFT.

ACTIVITIES: CURRENT AND FUTURE

Among the issues that the AFT has been involved with is the reauthorization of Title I of the Elementary and Secondary Education Act (ESEA), specifically efforts to prevent the inclusion of vouchers and block grants in the reauthorization bill. Block grants give states and localities wide discretion in dispersing funds. The AFT protests these moves because it believes that they would take funding away from the schools and school districts that serve the highest concentrations of children from families with limited financial means, which was the intent of the original ESEA. According to union president Sandra Feldman: "The risks with vouchers and block grants are great. Vouchers for a few would come at the expense of the many, and block grants open the door to diverting Title I funds away from poor children. Either way, poor children stand to lose."

The AFT has also been successful in promoting new funding for school construction, including a recent federal program earmarking $145 million for improving low-performing schools in financially impoverished districts. Called the Comprehensive School Reform Demonstration program, it will fund schools to select and adopt whole school reform models, thus demonstrating the models' effectiveness and proving that they can be replicated. Whole school reform is a comprehensive approach to change that involves instruction, assessment, professional development, classroom management, school management, and parent involvement.

At the same time, the AFT virulently opposes school privatization, which includes awarding franchises to private firms, distributing vouchers to citizens who then purchase services from a private for- or nonprofit institution, selling public assets to the private sector, and contracting with private corporations to provide noninstructional services. As the union notes, "AFT members in every constituency are increasingly threatened by privatization and contracting out."

Instead of vouchers, privatization, and other "untested, radical alternatives" to improving public education, the AFT has sponsored a campaign—both in its lobbying efforts in the state capitals and Washington, D.C., and in its general publicity—which uses the slogan "Lessons for Life: Responsibility, Respect, Results." According to the union, the campaign is based on the idea that "other education reforms may work; high standards of conduct and achievement do work—and nothing else can work without them." Essentially, the campaign represents a voluntary effort by school districts, AFT locals, school personnel, and parents to set high standards and results, an effort that does not place mandatory expectations on schools. That is to say, the union opposes rigid testing that seeks to measure educational progress of students. The AFT says that such tests are not an adequate measure of learning and can be used to penalize schools that are performing poorly. Rather than penalties, the union believes these schools should be given more aid to help them improve.

The union has also registered its opposition to talk in Congress about establishing teacher testing, and it has opposed such measures in various states and school districts. The basis of the AFT's opposition to teacher testing is that it circumvents collective bargaining agreements reached between AFT locals and school districts, under the guise of improving the classroom environment. In fact, says the union, such testing of teachers is as meaningless in assessing educational progress as national standards testing for students. Aside from the testing issue, the union has recently lobbied Congress on several other issues relating to teachers as employees, including a campaign to prevent the taxation of public-employee benefits and to maintain the deductibility of state and local taxes from the federal income tax, an issue that, of course, affects virtually all workers in states and localities with income taxes.

FINANCIAL FACTS

The AFT's Committee on Political Education (COPE) represents one of the largest political action committees (PACs) of the labor movement—by amount of donation—in the country. During the 1995–1996 election cycle, COPE received nearly $2.8 million and spent more than $2.6 million. This latter figure includes over $1.6 million in contributions to candidates and parties—$1.6 million to Democrats and $19,750 to Republicans.

There was a dramatic increase in COPE's receipts, expenditures, and contributions in the period between 1987 and 1996. Receipts and expenditures climbed more than 75 percent, while contributions grew from $1.658 million to $2.655 million. At the same time, contributions to Democrats far exceeded those to Republicans, by 40 to 75 times as much.

JAMES CIMENT AND IMMANUEL NESS

Bibliography

American Educator. 1977–1999.

American Federation of Teachers. *AFT Convention Reports.* Washington, DC, 1977–1999.

Berube, Maurice R. *Teacher Politics: The Influence of Unions.* New York: Greenwood Press, 1988.

Mungazi, Dickson A. *Where He Stands: Albert Shanker of the American Federation of Teachers.* Westport, CT: Praeger, 1995.

Murphy, Marjorie. *Blackboard Unions: The AFT and the NEA, 1900–1980.* Ithaca, NY: Cornell University Press, 1990.

AMERICAN POSTAL WORKERS UNION

The American Postal Workers Union (APWU), a member of the AFL-CIO, is the largest union of postal workers in the world, with 366,000 members from every state and territory. This represents an increase of over 100,000 since 1992. Virtually all members of the union are employed by the United States Postal Service (USPS). The APWU is recognized as the collective bargaining agent for postal clerks, motor vehicle service workers, maintenance personnel, and special delivery messengers. In addition, many APWU workers are employed in support services for the USPS, including materiel distribution centers, information service centers, mail equipment shops, and operating services facilities. Finally, the USPS represents a small number of workers in companies contracted by the USPS to haul mail.

Headquartered in Washington, D.C., the APWU has over 2,000 locals throughout the United States. Virtually all members of the union belong to one of these locals, whose officers are directly elected by the members and who conduct most of the day-to-day business. Locals may establish local dues and negotiate local contracts that supplement—but do not contravene—agreements reached by the national office. The locals are distributed across five regions, each with an office in charge of that region.

At the national level, the union's officers include a president, a vice president, a secretary-treasurer, national division officers, and department directors. The union is divided into four craft divisions, including clerical, maintenance, motor vehicle service, and support services. Each of these divisions maintains a force of officers in the field, who deal with locals. In addition, the national union maintains departments responsible for handling different functions and services. These departments are legislative, industrial relations, organization, research and education, human relations, and health plan. Finally, the APWU maintains a lobbying unit known as the Committee on Political Action (COPA), which donates to congressional and presidential candidates.

The top governing body of the APWU is the biennial national convention, though union policy is set by a 12-person executive board. Members of the board include the union president, vice president, and secretary-treasurer, the four craft division heads, the director of industrial relations, and the five regional coordinators.

Because the vast majority of APWU members are employees of the federal government, the union is interested in pensions and healthcare programs provided for federal employees, as well as ensuring that various labor regulations affecting occupation safety and health apply to federal employees. In addition, although it is not immediately affected, the APWU has sided with its fellow unions in opposing fast-track free trade legislation. The most important issue facing the union, however, is the privatization and contracting out of USPS services to private, nonunion shops.

HISTORY

The APWU was formed in 1971 by the merger of five independent postal unions: the United Federation of Postal Clerks, the National Postal Union, the National Association of Post Office and General Service Maintenance Employees, the National Federation of Motor Vehicle Employees, and the National Association of Special Delivery Messengers. The key element behind the merger was the passage of the 1970 Postal Reorganization Act, which effectively turned the United States Post Office, a cabinet-level branch of the federal government, into a semiprivate corporation. Under the act, postal unions were given the right to engage in collective bargaining concerning pay, benefits, and working hours and conditions.

**American Postal Workers Union
Political Action Committee Contributions**

[Bar chart showing PAC contributions to Democrats and Republicans for 1987-88, 1993-94, and 1997-98. Democrats received approximately $835,000 (1987-88), $715,000 (1993-94), and $560,000 (1997-98). Republicans received approximately $60,000 (1987-88), $25,000 (1993-94), and $5,000 (1997-98).]

Data derived from official studies available from the Federal Election Commission, Washington, DC, 1987–1998.

ACTIVITIES: CURRENT AND FUTURE

The APWU's main legislative issue is the Postal Reform Act, which the union adamantly opposes. Under the proposed bill, letters for which the postage exceeded $2 could be carried outside the postal service by private companies. Under current regulations, competitors are required to charge at least double the priority mail rate, which during 1999 stood at $3.20. According to the union, the change could jeopardize as much as $4 billion in annual USPS revenues, thereby undermining the amount of work going to postal workers versus potentially nonunionized employees of private contractors.

In addition, the act would require the postal service to define "universal service"—that is, sufficient postal service to all parts of the United States as required by law. A narrow definition of universal service would mean a further diminishment of USPS business and jobs. Finally, the act would establish an independent study by the National Academy of Public Administration, which would evaluate problems and recommend solutions to the "myriad of employee-management difficulties the Postal Service has faced in recent years." The APWU has made it clear that it opposes any outside interference in the collective bargaining negotiations that occur between itself and the USPS. In defense of its position, the APWU has pointed out that its recent negotiations with the USPS went smoothly and were the first such agreement reached without resort to interest arbitration in over a decade. A related issue concerning the APWU has been the efforts by the USPS to contract out priority mail handling to Emery Worldwide Airlines. The APWU's opposition to this is based on several factors: Postal workers, it claims, are capable of handling the work to be contracted out; the contract will cost the USPS more money than if it handled the service itself; under the original priority mail agreement, all such deliveries were to be handled by the USPS; Emery has proved itself incapable of handling large volumes of packages efficiently and effectively; and most importantly, over 8,000 jobs will be shifted from unionized USPS employees to nonunionized Emery workers by 2005.

In order to block this privatization move, the APWU has won solidarity endorsements from its fellow AFL-CIO members, aired radio advertisements, conducted letter-writing campaigns to the USPS and Congress, and organized pickets and protest marches, along with lobbying the USPS and Congress.

The APWU has also been actively fighting efforts by Congress to reduce the federal government's contribution toward federal employee health insurance, which would result in an increase in employee premiums. Although the APWU recognizes that the premiums paid by its own members would not increase—due to the fact that it negotiates with the semiprivate USPS directly—a premium increase could become an issue in the future.

On the safety front, the APWU supports measures to apply Occupational Safety and Health Administration (OSHA) regulations to postal facilities. Currently, OSHA inspects such facilities but cannot penalize them. The union has been working on a bill to extend OSHA penalties to the USPS while at the same time guaranteeing that small offices in rural areas, which might not meet OSHA requirements, are not closed because of those penalties. Instead, improvements should be made to lift them up to regulations.

Finally, the APWU has actively opposed all surveys conducted by the USPS to ascertain information about employees. The union's opposition is based on privacy issues and on the fact that the USPS could use such information to influence the collective bargaining procedures it conducts with the union.

FINANCIAL FACTS

The APWU maintains a large fund devoted to lobbying and to providing donations to the campaigns of sympathetic congressional and presidential candidates, as well as for party functions. During the 1995–1996 election cycle, COPA received under $1.1 million and spent nearly $1.2 million. This latter figure includes almost $656,000 in contributions to candidates and parties—$628,410 to Democrats and $24,500 to Republicans. For the past 10 years, donations to the Democratic Party have far exceeded contributions to the Republicans—between 15 and 30 times as much.

JAMES CIMENT AND IMMANUEL NESS

Bibliography

The American Postal Worker. 1971–1999.

American Postal Workers Union. "Questions and Answers About the APWU." Washington, DC, n.d. Pamphlet.

Walsh, John. *Labor Struggle in the Post Office: From Selective Lobbying to Collective Bargaining.* Armonk, NY: M.E. Sharpe, 1992.

COMMUNICATIONS WORKERS OF AMERICA

The Communications Workers of America (CWA) is the largest union in the telecommunications industry, with some 630,000 members. Branches of the industry in which members work include manufacturing and construction of telecommunications equipment and infrastructure, telephone, cable, Internet, sound and electronics, media (print and electronic), and electric utilities. In addition, members are employed in the gas utility industry, as well as public service, healthcare, and general manufacturing. Some of the major corporations that have bargaining agreements with the CWA include AT&T, the regional Bell companies, GTE, and the NBC, ABC, and Canadian Broadcasting Corporation television networks.

The CWA—a union affiliated with the AFL-CIO—has more than 1,200 locals in some 10,000 communities across the United States and Canada. It has negotiated over 1,000 bargaining agreements on wages, benefits, and working conditions for its members. Locals enjoy a great deal of independence, while the international office—headquartered in Washington, D.C.—offers help in the form of publicity, legislative affairs, organizing, and bargaining expertise. All local and national officers are elected by vote of the members. While overall policy for the union is set at quadrennial conventions—where national officers are also elected—the union's day-to-day activities are run by an executive board consisting of the president, secretary-treasurer, executive vice president, and the regional vice presidents.

Critical legislative issues for the CWA include those pertaining to the labor movement as a whole, as well as to CWA members specifically. In recent years, the CWA has been involved in struggles over Social Security, Medicare, education, occupational safety and health, organized labor's political rights, overtime, freelance and contract worker pay and benefits, and high-tech and telecommunications concerns.

HISTORY

The CWA's roots go back to the great union-organizing era of the late 1930s. The union was founded as the National Federation of Telephone Workers in 1938, formed out of several dozen autonomous unions—some of which had been founded by telephone companies to preempt organizing by outside groups. The impetus for the creation of the CWA was the 1935 National Labor Relations Act, which outlawed company unions.

During its first decade, the union operated independently, refusing to accept the invitation of the American Federation of Labor (AFL) to become an affiliate of the International Brotherhood of Electrical Workers. Although it resisted similar entreaties by the Congress of Industrial Organizations (CIO), it finally joined the CIO in 1948 and was merged with the Telephone Workers Organizing Committee.

With the growth of the telecommunications industry in the postwar era, the union has grown in numbers and increased its diversity, branching out into the many divisions of the industry. In 1987, the CWA absorbed the 58,000-member International Typographers Union—founded in 1852 and with 410 locals—which is now enrolled in the Printing, Publishing, and Media Workers section of the union. Seven years later, the CWA took in the Newspaper Guild and later the National Association of Broadcast Employees and Technicians.

ACTIVITIES: CURRENT AND FUTURE

As noted above, the CWA's legislative efforts involve issues relating to working people and the labor movement as a whole, as well as issues of direct concern to CWA members. Among the former are Social Se-

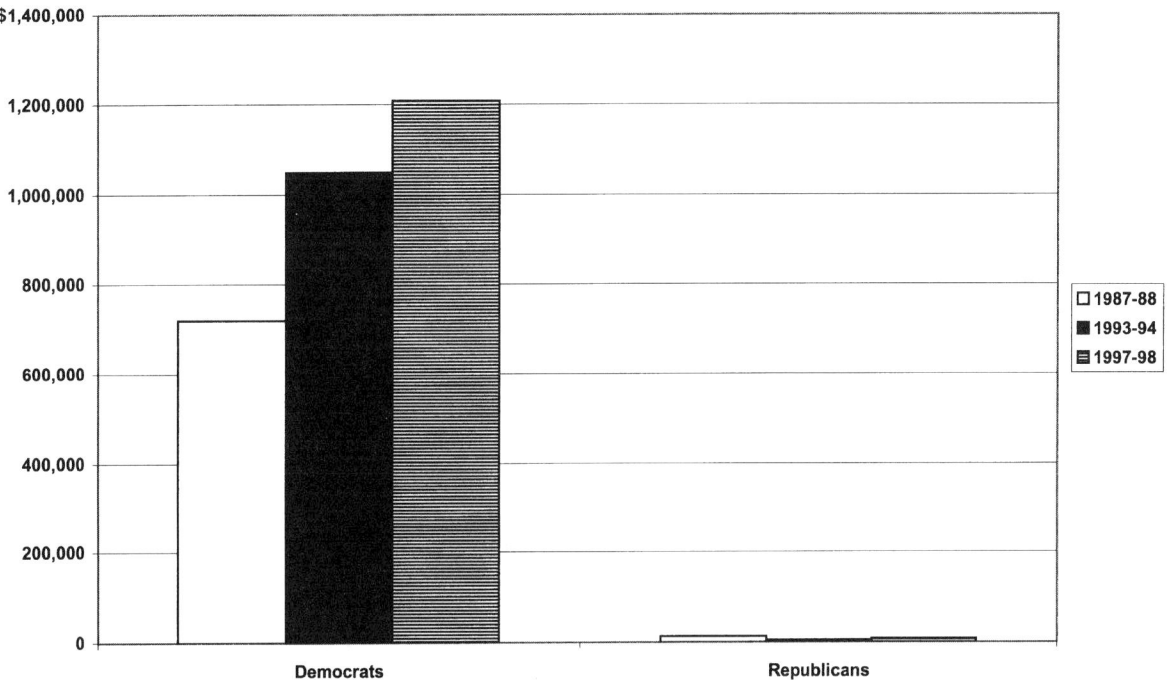

**Communications Workers of America
Political Action Committee Contributions**

Data derived from official studies available from the Federal Election Commission, Washington, DC, 1987–1998.

curity, Medicare, education, the census, occupational safety and health, organized labor's political rights, and overtime.

The CWA supported President Bill Clinton's efforts to set aside most of the current and near-future surpluses from the federal budget in order to guarantee the future of Social Security for the many baby boomers retiring in the first decades of the twenty-first century. At the same time, the union is more wary of talk by Clinton and Congress of privatizing some of the program, fearing that it would jeopardize Social Security payments to many recipients. On Medicare, the CWA also supports Clinton's plan to use budget surpluses to assure the program's viability for the future. In addition, the union has gone on record supporting measures that would allow workers aged 62–65 to buy into the program by paying a base premium now and a deferred premium during their post-65 Medicare enrollment. At the same time, the CWA stands opposed to a Republican initiative—known as the "Medicare Beneficiaries Freedom to Contract Act"—that would allow individuals to contract privately for Medicare services. The union claims this would weaken the overall Medicare program.

On education, the CWA backs measures—first introduced in Texas—offering tax credits for a lifelong learning provision. At the federal level, the union supports the Labor Department's efforts to consolidate some 70 training, vocational, and adult education programs into a "one-stop shopping" educational system that would be funded by block grants to states and localities. On worker issues, the CWA stands opposed to a variety of Republican-inspired initiatives to undermine overtime pay, to subvert union political contributions, to use welfare workers in public-sector employment (thereby undermining union workers), and to compromise occupational safety and health (of particular concern to the union's many members who labor in dangerous and potentially unhealthful sectors of the telecommunications industry, including installation and manufacturing).

On issues of concern to the telecommunications industry and telecommunications workers specifically, the CWA is working with Congress to pass antislamming and anticramming legislation. Slamming is a practice whereby customers find their long-distance service switched from one company to another without their knowledge; cramming involves telephone companies adding for-pay services to a customer without the latter's knowledge. In addition, the union is fighting efforts by members of the software industry to allow exemptions in the immigration laws for technicians. Union leaders say that the industry's claim that there is a shortage of skilled workers is "hogwash" and a "hoax," seeing in this effort a plan to lower pay and undermine union organizing, representation, and bargaining.

Finally, because of the many freelance and contract workers associated with the union's media-based locals, the CWA is adamant in its opposition to recent congressional efforts to pass legislation allowing companies to reclassify freelance and part-time workers as subcontractors, thereby avoiding the requirements of providing benefits and paying contributions to pension plans.

FINANCIAL FACTS

The CWA's political action committee (PAC), the Committee on Political Education Political Contributions Committee, makes contributions to politicians who support legislation beneficial to workers employed in the telephone and communications industry. The PAC also contributes to politicians supporting the goals and objectives of organized labor. During the 1995–1996 election cycle, CWA-COPE PCC received $2.2 million and spent more than $2.3 million. This latter figure includes more than $1.3 million in contributions to candidates and parties—nearly $1.3 million to Democrats and $1,250 to Republicans.

The PAC's receipts, expenditures, and contributions have increased between 1987 and 1996. Receipts and expenditures climbed from nearly $2.15 million in 1987–1988 to just over $2.2 million in 1995–1996. At the same time, contributions to Democrats have far exceeded those to Republicans, by 50 to several hundred times as much.

JAMES CIMENT

Bibliography

Bahr, Morton. *From the Telegraph to the Internet.* Washington, DC: National Press Books, 1998.

Brooks, Thomas R. *Communications Workers of America: The Story of a Union.* New York: Mason/Charter, 1977.

CWA News: Official Journal of the Communications Workers of America. July–1999.

HOTEL EMPLOYEES AND RESTAURANT EMPLOYEES INTERNATIONAL UNION

The Hotel Employees and Restaurant Employees International Union (HERE) represents more than 300,000 workers employed in the hospitality industry in the United States and Canada. The union's members are employed in hotels, motels, restaurants and cafeterias, taverns, cocktail lounges, clubs, casinos and riverboats, hospitals, schools, airports, bus terminals, in-flight preparation services, concession food services, on trains, and in other lodging and food service establishments. The union's members include bellhops, porters, doormen, housemaids, cooks, busboys, waiters, and bartenders. Since the 1950s, membership has stagnated due to union-avoidance efforts by employers, nonunion competition, and lackluster organizing efforts by the union and its member locals. In New York City, as in other major tourist and business centers throughout the United States, union membership in the restaurant industry dwindled to less than 10 percent of the entire regional workforce.

The union's national headquarters is located in Washington, D.C. The national leadership is responsible for coordinating activities between local unions and the international union. These activities include organizing, contract negotiations, research, technological improvements, legislative activities, and communications. The international union communicates with its members through the *Catering Industry Employee,* a national bimonthly publication. The union is led by four key officers: the general president, general secretary-treasurer, director of organization, and general vice president. The four leading officers sit on the general executive board of the international union, along with 14 district vice presidents and 13 vice presidents-at-large, who are elected every five years by delegates to the international convention. The 300,000 members of the union are divided into 14 districts and 118 local unions, ranging in size from several hundred members to the more than 40,000 members in Las Vegas.

In the 1990s, HERE attempted to expand union membership by aggressively organizing new workers and waging sustained campaigns against nonunion employers who undermine local wage and benefit standards set by local unions. The working poor comprise a large proportion of employees in the industry. The union believes that wages and working conditions in the industry can improve through organizing these workers into the union. The union maintains that, on average, members are better paid and enjoy far better working conditions than nonunion individuals performing the same work.

HISTORY

The origins of HERE can be traced to 1866, when German immigrants employed in restaurants and bars in Chicago formed the Bartenders and Waiters Union. In 1891, the diverse hotel and restaurant unions across the United States formally joined the Hotel and Restaurant Employees National Alliance and affiliated with the American Federation of Labor. The union locals typically formed on the basis of craft divisions. Thus, rather than representing the entire hotel and restaurant industry, the union locals represented only bartenders, cooks, waiters, or workers with similar skills. Under the successive leadership of Jere Sullivan, general secretary-treasurer, and Edward Flore, general president, the union grew from fewer than 10,000 members in 1901 to nearly 300,000 members in 1945.

The union has historically concentrated its organizing efforts in tourist and business centers in the United States and Canada that typically attract many travelers and diners. Some of the union organizing highlights in the post–World War II era occurred in Miami, Florida, where a three-year organizing drive between 1954 and 1957 culminated with a 10-year master agreement with the Miami Beach Hotel Association.

Subsequently, the union initiated organizing drives in other leading tourist centers, including Las Vegas, Atlantic City, and New Orleans. Since the mid 1980s,

**Hotel Employees and Restaurant Employees International Union
Political Action Committee Contributions, 1997–1998**

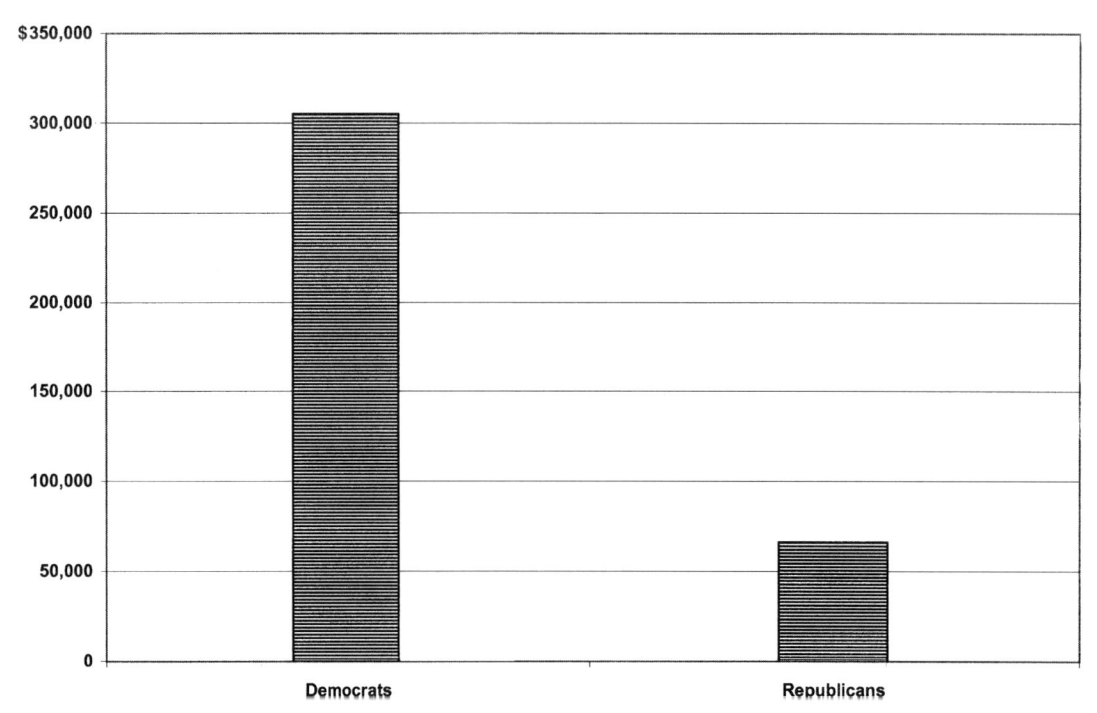

Party	Contributions
Democrats	~305,000
Republicans	~65,000

Data derived from official studies available from the Federal Election Commission, Washington, DC, 1997–1998.

HERE has made a sustained effort in organizing Las Vegas's casino and hotel industry. During the 1980s and 1990s, local union membership in Las Vegas increased by more than 20,000 workers. One of HERE's defining moments in Las Vegas occurred in 1998, when its Culinary Workers Union Local 226 and Bartenders Union Local 165 won a six-and-a-half-year strike that began in 1991 in which not one of the 550 strikers crossed the picket line. In October 1998, the union won an agreement to represent 4,300 workers at the new Bellagio Resort Hotel and Casino in Las Vegas. HERE was instrumental in the drive to unionize the thriving restaurant and hotel industry of New Orleans and to organize for the creation of a local ordinance that would raise the salary of city workers who are employed full time to above the poverty rate.

Following the election of Edward T. Hanley as general president in 1973, HERE initiated a program to consolidate union affiliates that were formed on the basis of craft into broader industrial unions representing workers on a regional basis. Thus, under the new program, the merged locals would represent all workers at a specific establishment. Under Hanley's leadership, HERE also established a strong legislative presence in Washington, D.C. In August 1998, John W. Wilhelm, the chief HERE International Union organizer in the 1980s and 1990s who presided over the rapid growth in the union's membership in Las Vegas, was elected the general president.

ACTIVITIES: CURRENT AND FUTURE

HERE's issues agenda addresses concerns that relate to improving organized labor's capacity to function as a social force in American society and issues pertaining more specifically to the hotel and restaurant industries. Issues of concern to the broader labor movement revolve around reducing the obstacles to the ability to organize members into unions and collectively bargain with management. Reforming labor law that hinders the ability of workers to join unions is at the core of this agenda. HERE has been actively involved in the struggle to enforce the National Labor Relations Act, which allows workers to organize and bargain with management. The union believes that, due to lack of enforcement, labor law has not protected workers' right to organize. Due to the ability of employers to resist unionization, HERE has pursued an agenda to broaden worker power. On a local and regional basis, the union is a primary sponsor of card-recognition agreements with employers. These agreements would ease the ability of prospective members to organize into unions. Employers would be obliged to accept the union's right to negotiate on behalf of workers without going to a contested election. Instead, the union would simply be required to prove that a majority of workers support the union by signing recognition cards.

The union actively lobbies to support raising the minimum wage and is opposed to subminimum wages for youth, which drive down the industry wage and benefit standards. The union also supports the elimination of open-shop laws that allow workers to benefit from a union contract without actually joining. To energize its membership to become involved in politics, the union encourages members to become citizens and register to vote.

In matters related to the hotel and restaurant industry, HERE maintains active boycotts against hotels that are viewed as unfair to workers. In addition, the union is engaged in lobbying efforts to repeal state and local laws that are of concern to members. For example, the union opposes blue laws that ban the sale of alcoholic beverages on Sundays and religious holidays. The union lobbies against the inclusion of tip income for meeting minimum wage standards and supports legislation to repeal an Internal Revenue Service regulation requiring reporting of tips charged to credit cards. The union also opposes federal tax reforms that seek to reduce deductions of business meals and convention expenses because they could also lead to reducing restaurant and hotel expenditures, and therefore jeopardize jobs.

FINANCIAL FACTS

Although HERE is the 15th-largest union in the United States in terms of membership, it devotes considerably fewer resources to federal political action than other unions its size. For example, the American Postal Workers, with 261,000 workers in 1995, expended about five times as much on political action contributions as did HERE. The union's PAC, known as TIP (To Insure Progress), expends about $250,000 per year on the campaigns of political officials. Although TIP contributes to both major parties, the vast majority of its political contributions go to Democratic candidates who are more sympathetic to HERE's political positions such as increasing the minimum wage and other regulations that assist the working poor, who comprise a large share of the union's members.

IMMANUEL NESS AND JAMES CIMENT

Bibliography

Catering Industry Employee (bimonthly publication of the Hotel Employees and Restaurant Employees International Union).

Hotel Employees and Restaurant Employees International Union: www.hereunion.org

INTERNATIONAL ASSOCIATION OF FIRE FIGHTERS

The International Association of Fire Fighters (IAFF)—a union affiliated with the AFL–CIO—represents 151,000 professional firefighters across the United States and Canada. The union includes approximately 2,100 locals, usually based on locale. Locals enjoy a great deal of autonomy within the union and control the elections of their own officers, the negotiations of collective bargaining agreements, and the settlement of local grievances.

The international office, headquartered in Washington, D.C., is divided into several departments, including the office of the president, health and safety, education resources, governmental affairs, emergency medical services, hazardous materials, membership, the Canadian branch office, technical assistance, and communications. Overall, the IAFF helps locals analyze metropolitan budgets to make sure that fire departments and their employees are receiving a fair share of financial resources. In some municipalities, the IAFF offers help defending against efforts to turn city-run fire departments—where employees are paid civil servants—into voluntary or privately run outfits.

The union focuses its legislative and lobbying efforts on issues of concern to working people and the organized labor movement generally, as well as on issues of concern to fire fighters in particular. Among the former issues are Social Security and national collective bargaining rights; the latter issues concern federal funding for fire departments and safety and health regulations.

HISTORY

The origins of the fire fighters' union go back to the civil service battles of the late nineteenth and early twentieth centuries, when professional fire fighters fought to win civil service status. That was the key issue behind the formation of the first such union in Washington, D.C., in 1901. This first effort, however, failed, as internal dissent tore the union apart within two years. The direct antecedent of today's IAFF can be traced to the organization in Pittsburgh in 1903, which still retains distinction as Local Number One. In 1918, the IAFF affiliated itself with the American Federation of Labor and has grown steadily with the expansion and spread of professional fire-fighting systems in cities throughout North America.

ACTIVITIES: CURRENT AND FUTURE

The IAFF lobbies for and contributes to candidates who support a range of issues concerning working people and the labor movement generally, as well as issues directly affecting fire fighters. Several issues overlap both areas.

The first concerns Social Security. While the IAFF is a strong opponent of ongoing efforts to privatize or dismantle Social Security, it also seeks to maintain the current separate pension system for fire fighters. When the Social Security system was created in 1935, public employees were excluded. Fifteen years later, state and local governments received the option of joining the system or not. Fire fighters, however, were explicitly barred from receiving Social Security until 1994. Because of this exclusion, virtually all of them created pension systems of their own, geared to the special needs of fire fighters, many of whom retire early, experience high disability rates, and require extensive healthcare coverage. The IAFF is opposed to current efforts to establish a mandatory, universal Social Security system that would include fire fighters. Their opposition is based on several arguments. First, as noted above, a universal system does not take into account the special retirement, safety, and health needs of fire fighters. Second, because many fire fighters already pay into separate pensions, it would mean an "unfair" 6.2 percent addi-

**International Association of Fire Fighters
Political Action Committee Contributions**

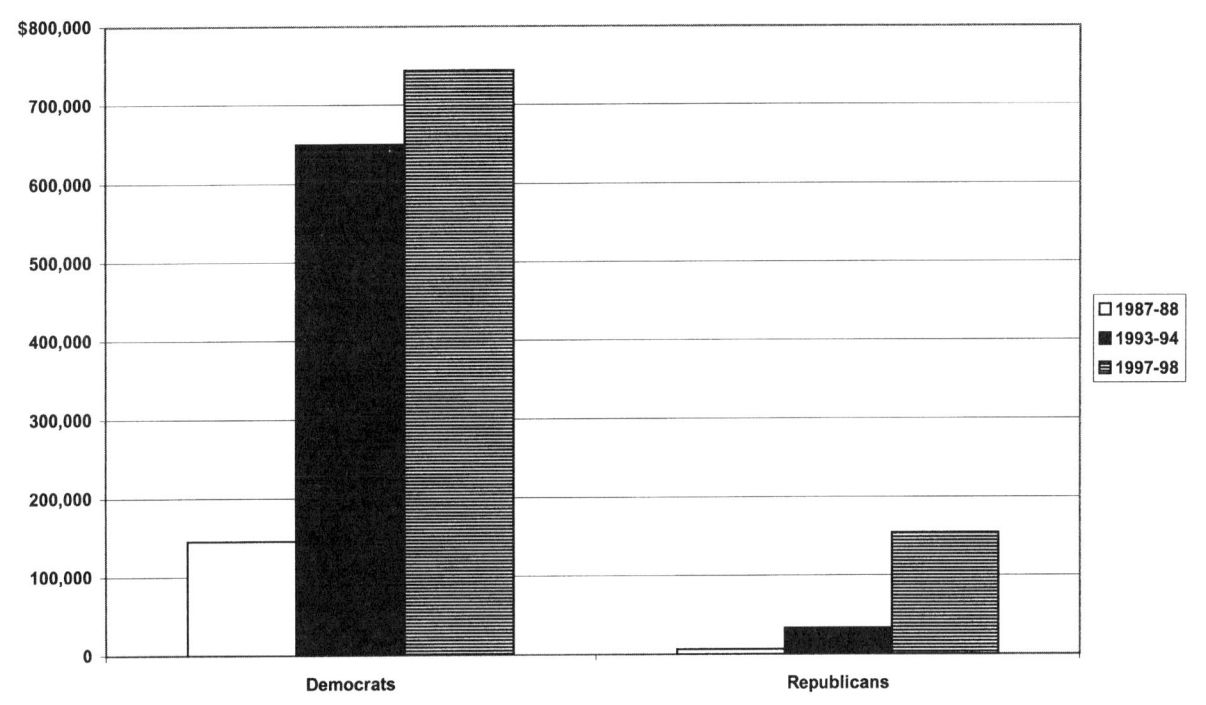

[Bar chart showing contributions to Democrats and Republicans for years 1987-88, 1993-94, and 1997-98. Democrats: approximately $145,000 (1987-88), $650,000 (1993-94), $750,000 (1997-98). Republicans: approximately $10,000 (1987-88), $40,000 (1993-94), $160,000 (1997-98).]

Data derived from official studies available from the Federal Election Commission, Washington, DC, 1987–1998.

tional tax. Finally, requiring financially strapped municipalities to pay the employers' share of Social Security could lead to the layoffs of fire fighters and a diminution of fire departments.

Another concern of both the labor movement generally and fire fighters specifically concerns overtime pay. The 1938 Fair Labor Standards Act (FLSA)—which required employers to establish a 40-hour workweek and overtime pay for additional hours of work—was amended in 1986 to protect state and local government workers, including fire fighters. The 1986 amendments included the stipulation that states and municipalities could not require employees to perform "volunteer" or unpaid work similar to their normal work activities for which they were paid. The prohibition was an appropriate one, says the union, because "this sort of coercion can be so subtle (for example, by rewarding workers who show 'enthusiasm' for their job by 'volunteering') that there is no realistic alternative to an outright ban on performing one's duties for no pay." Recently, the National Volunteer Fire Council and some municipalities have complained that the prohibition makes it difficult to recruit volunteer fire fighters.

Current legislation being considered by Congress would exempt fire fighters and ambulance squad workers from the provisions of the 1986 amendments to the FLSA. The IAFF opposes such an exemption because it believes it undermines the idea of overtime pay and professional firefighting generally.

Related to this, the IAFF supports congressional action to give all public safety employees the right to collectively bargain, a right currently denied to them in 18 states. Although Republican opponents of such a measure argue it would jeopardize public safety, the IAFF disagrees, pointing out that much of what fire fighters bargain for collectively is directly related to improving fire and public safety. On another public safety–related issue, the IAFF is working to persuade Congress to pass legislation requiring all cellular phone networks to be connected to the 911 emergency system.

The IAFF supports the extension of the mandate of the Occupational Safety and Health Administration (OSHA) to cover government workers. Currently, fire fighters are not covered by federal regulations requiring inspections of workplaces and working conditions. While some state governments have adopted OSHA standards for fire brigades, most utilize lesser safety standards. The IAFF favors a consistent national approach to safety on the job for its members. "As [workers in] the nation's most dangerous profession," union officials note, "fire fighters must depend heavily on safe operating procedures and the quality of their protective gear and clothing. Fire fighters deserve universally enforceable minimum safety standards." According to the IAFF, over 1 million fire fighters have been injured and more than 1,000 have died since OSHA was enacted in 1970.

The IAFF is also fighting to overturn a recently passed small-business exemption from certain health and safety regulations. Whereas backers argue that the exemption allows small businesses to avoid unnecessary and burdensome paperwork, the union says that this paperwork includes critical information on hazardous materials. Also concerning this area, the IAFF has been involved in fighting for new legislation on the transport of hazardous materials. The union says it would like to see full operations training for fire fighters dealing with hazardous wastes, rather than "mere awareness-level training," and funding for Operation Respond, a computer software system that provides fire fighters with vital information at the scene of a hazardous material incident. In addition, the IAFF is fighting an effort to exempt the agricultural and chlorine gas industries from regulations requiring posting placards and carrying shipping papers.

FINANCIAL FACTS

The political action committee (PAC) of the IAFF is the International Association of Fire Fighters Interested in Registration and Education (also known as FIRE PAC). One of the largest political action committees of the U.S. labor movement—by amount of donation—FIRE PAC has recently increased contributions to federal candidates. During the 1995–1996 election cycle, FIRE PAC spent $791,000, including $704,000 in contributions to candidates and parties—$631,800 to Democrats and $71,075 to Republicans.

FIRE PAC's receipts, expenditures, and contributions have increased dramatically over the past 10 years. Receipts and expenditures more than tripled, and contributions have quadrupled from $152,000 to $704,000. At the same time, contributions to Democrats have far exceeded those to Republicans, by nine to 24 times as much.

JAMES CIMENT AND IMMANUEL NESS

Bibliography
International Fire Fighter. 1918–1999.

Richardson, George J. *Symbol of Action: A History of the International Association of Fire Fighters, AFL-CIO-CLC.* Washington, DC: International Association of Fire Fighters, 1974.

INTERNATIONAL ASSOCIATION OF MACHINISTS AND AEROSPACE WORKERS

Representing some 534,000 members, the International Association of Machinists and Aerospace Workers (IAMAW) has some 1,565 locals across the United States and Canada. IAMAW members are employed in about 200 basic industries, involving the manufacture of machine tools; the tending of metal-forming equipment; the construction of metal frames for jets, spacecraft, and other aerospace vehicles; and timber work. Headquartered in suburban Washington, D.C., the IAMAW is affiliated with the AFL-CIO and has opened talks with the United Steelworkers of America and the United Auto Workers about possible consolidation by the year 2000.

The IAMAW international office, which sets overall policy for the union and provides support services for the largely autonomous locals, is divided into five regional territories—the western, eastern, midwestern, and southern United States, and Canada. The union is headed by a president and general secretary-treasurer. These two officers, the five regional heads, and two general vice presidents—for headquarters and transportation—make up the executive board that runs the daily affairs of the international office and implements policy established by the delegates at quadrennial conventions. These conventions are also responsible for electing the nine officers.

The union operates a number of divisions. Under the president are divisions handling organizing, bylaws and internal disputes, collective bargaining, communications, community services and retirees, the High Performance Work Organization (a labor-management partnership), aerospace workers, wood and timber workers, human rights, international affairs, legal issues, political and legislative issues, occupational safety and health, strategic resources (largely research services), women's issues, and transportation. Under the general secretary-treasurer are arrayed divisions dealing with personnel, engineering and housekeeping, purchasing, accounting, information systems, and reports.

The IAMAW political department concerns itself with a number of issues affecting working people and the labor movement generally, as well as issues particularly pertinent to its members. Under the former category fall healthcare, occupational safety and health, and union political rights. Issues of special concern to the membership include aircraft safety and forestry, since many members are involved in the timber industry.

HISTORY

The origins of the IAMAW lie in the labor activism of the late nineteenth century, when 19 machinists in Atlanta voted to form a trade union in 1888. The following year, some 34 locals sent delegates to the union's first convention, held in Georgia. By 1891, the union included some 145 locals, including one in Canada. It signed its first collective bargaining agreement with a railroad in 1892 and joined the American Federation of Labor (AFL) three years later. By 1905, when the first apprentices were admitted to membership, the union had grown to 769 locals. Three years later, the union established its metal trades department, and in 1911, women were admitted as members for the first time. In 1915, the union—then known as the International Association of Machinists—won the eight-hour day in many shops, and three years later its membership had grown to 331,000. In 1922, 79,000 railroad machinists joined the union and struck against a wage cut. The loss of that strike reduced membership to 148,000, and it continued to fall during the early years of the Great Depression to just 56,000.

Under the various pro-union labor acts of the administration of President Franklin D. Roosevelt—and because of the growing airplane industry—the union experienced a resurgence to 130,000 members by 1936. Three years later, the union signed its first collective bargaining agreement with the airplane industry. The labor shortage of the Second World War boosted mem-

**International Association of Machinists and Aerospace Workers
Political Action Committee Contributions**

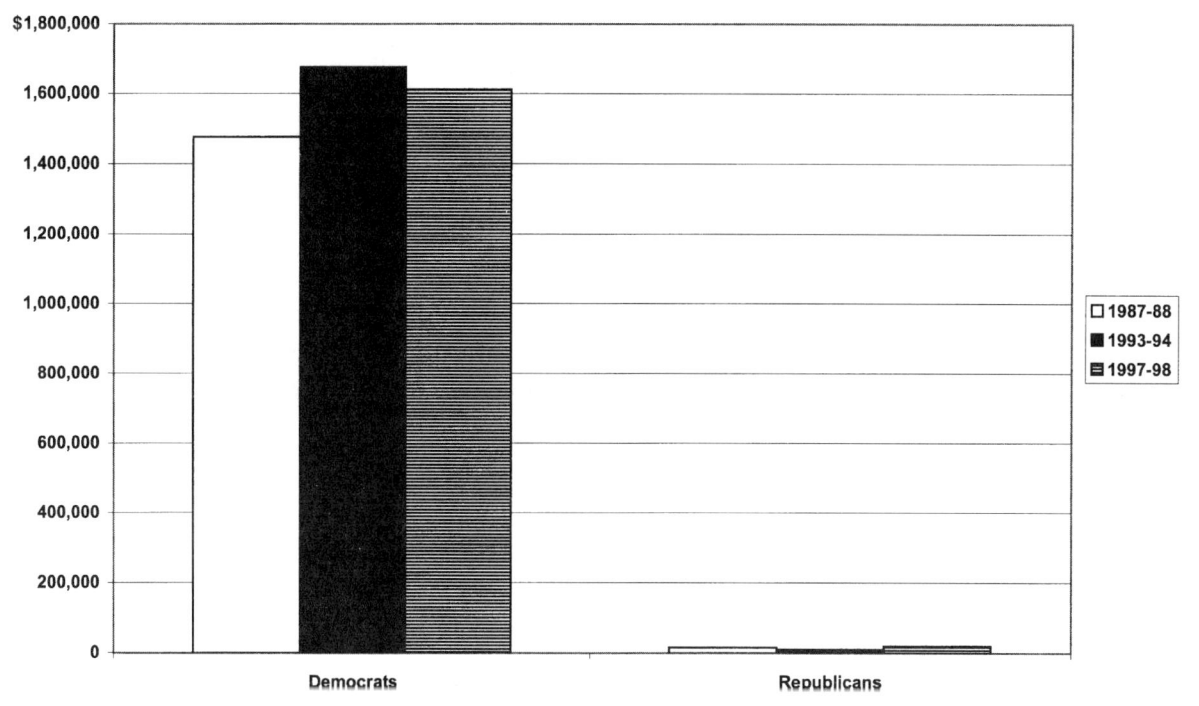

Data derived from official studies available from the Federal Election Commission, Washington, DC, 1987–1998.

bership enormously; by 1944, the union's membership had grown to 776,000. In 1948, the union dropped all race restrictions within its ranks. The booming economy of the 1950s and 1960s—particularly in the aerospace industry—led to a membership peak of approximately 1 million members by 1968. During the 1980s, however, the collapse of many rust-belt industries forced the layoffs of tens of thousands of IAMAW members, and the membership fell to roughly 500,000, where it has remained throughout the 1990s.

ACTIVITIES: CURRENT AND FUTURE

As noted above, the union lobbies Congress and the White House on issues that concern workers generally and IAMAW members specifically. Under the former category of issues, the union has been particularly active in the area of healthcare, an important consideration for many of its members who work in hazardous industries such as timber and machine tools. The IAMAW has placed itself on record as supporting "legally enforceable national standards to assure access to quality healthcare" for all workers. This includes network adequacy, access to specialists, an external appeals process for denied care, information disclosure, and the ability of workers to carry their health insurance from one job to another—an important issue in the volatile industries in which its members labor.

Again, given the hazardous work performed by many of the IAMAW's members, the union has been in the forefront of occupational safety and health issues. The union has made clear its opposition to various Republican-led efforts to cut the budget of the Occupational Safety and Health Administration (OSHA), as well as to allow employers to control review boards on OSHA recommendations. The union believes that this measure would lead to additional secrecy, in which employers could keep information about the reviews out of the public realm. In addition, the union opposes moves to establish a congressional office to oversee OSHA regulation implementation, believing that it would be a tool of labor's political opponents to further gut safety regulations for the workplace, especially in the area of hazardous materials handling.

Moreover, the union is concerned about efforts to

force OSHA to conduct specific company evaluations, rather than industry-wide ones, since it believes this would slow down the fact-finding and implementation process and thus endanger worker safety and health. In general, the union is against the general move to make investigation and enforcement of OSHA regulations more of a voluntary exercise performed by business. Similarly, the union does not like the idea of a move toward more warnings and fewer fines for businesses. Finally, the IAMAW stands opposed to efforts to shift fines from employers to employees in situations where protective-gear regulations are violated, particularly because there are efforts afoot to shift the cost of paying for such gear from employers to employees.

The IAMAW is also concerned that past efforts at the federal level to force unions to win written permission of members to use dues for political purposes will be revived. Specifically, the union cites the 1997 efforts of Senate Majority Leader Trent Lott to kill the campaign finance reform bill by adding such a measure. At the same time, the union has worked against such efforts at the state level as well, including the failed California Proposition 226 in 1998.

On issues of particular concern to members, the IAMAW supports ongoing bipartisan efforts to ensure airline safety by requiring all U.S. aircraft to be repaired and maintained by U.S. workers. The union, of course, supports this move because it ensures more jobs for its members.

The IAMAW has made it clear that it opposes U.S. Forest Service efforts to cut back on road construction for the purposes of timber extraction. Although the union insists that it stands behind preserving the environment, it supports this controversial program—whereby the Forest Service builds taxpayer-subsidized roads that are used by timber companies—and would like to prevent any move to gut its funding. The IAMAW "supports all reasonable efforts to make corporations pay their fair share; however, congressional road construction funding calculations must take into consideration all of the benefits provided by programs under review. The Forest Service forest roads programs allow for timber harvesting activities that directly return funds to the federal government, support tens of thousands of jobs, and help fund public schools and essential public services in timber-dependent communities."

FINANCIAL FACTS

The IAMAW supports well-funded and active lobbying efforts, which donate substantial sums to congressional and presidential campaigns. During the 1995–1996 political cycle, the group's political action committee (PAC), the Machinists Nonpartisan Political League, received nearly $3.7 million and spent $3.6 million. This included almost $2 million in political donations—$1,977,925 to Democrats and only $7,750 to Republicans. In the last 10 years, expenditures have grown from $2.85 million in the 1987–1988 election cycle to $3.6 million in 1995–1996.

JAMES CIMENT AND IMMANUEL NESS

Bibliography

International Association of Machinists Journal. 1995–1999.
The Machinist. Vols. 1–49 (April 4, 1946–1994).
Rodden, Robert G. *The Fighting Machinists: A Century of Struggle.* Washington, DC: Kelly Press, 1984.

INTERNATIONAL BROTHERHOOD OF ELECTRICAL WORKERS

The International Brotherhood of Electrical Workers (IBEW)—a member union of the AFL-CIO—represents approximately 730,000 workers in a variety of industries connected to the communications and electrical industries, primarily working on electrical systems. Industries represented by the IBEW include utility workers at electric power stations; electrical and natural gas lineworkers; residential, commercial, and industrial electrical system installers; electrical installers at missile and aerospace facilities; installers, repair workers, and operators of radio, television, telephone, and cable communications equipment; and railroad electrical repair and maintenance personnel.

In addition, IBEW members labor in the manufacturing of electrical equipment, including batteries, telephones, electric motors, televisions, radios, and household appliances. Major manufacturers where IBEW members work include General Electric, Westinghouse, RCA, GTE, Gould, Rockwell International, Cutler-Hammer, IT&T, AT&T, and Square D. Trade classifications in the union include electrical utilities, the gas industry, the telephone industry, inside electrical workers, the sign industry, electric railroads, electrical manufacturing, the communications industry, the government, and several other trade classifications.

Geographically, the union is organized into 10 regional districts, including one for Canada and one for railroad workers nationally. Structurally, the IBEW consists of the following departments: the several industrial departments listed above, technical assistance, research, media relations, human services, pensions/employee benefits, special projects, safety and health, education, bylaws and appeals, computer services, membership, accounting, and records keeping. The union's political affairs are handled by the IBEW's Committee on Political Education (COPE).

Aside from general union concerns—such as trade, Social Security, and union rights—the IBEW focuses its attention on legislation concerning the utilities industry and federal construction programs.

HISTORY

The origins of the IBEW stretch back to the formation of the National Brotherhood of Electrical Workers and its affiliation with the American Federation of Labor in 1891, making it one of the longest continuously operating unions in America. The first women were admitted to the union the following year, and the union's first journal was published a year after that. In 1895, telephone operators were accepted as members. The union went international with the admission of Canadian workers in 1899, after which the union changed its name to the International Brotherhood of Electrical Workers. In 1971, the IBEW moved to its permanent headquarters in Washington, D.C., and its membership passed the 1 million mark the following year. It dropped below that figure in the 1980s.

ACTIVITIES: CURRENT AND FUTURE

Given the fact that Republicans—with their generally hostile approach to organized labor—control Congress, much of the IBEW's political action has been oriented toward blocking legislation it perceives as hostile to trade unions. Specifically, the IBEW's COPE has been extremely active in lobbying Congress to prevent the passage of fast-track legislation that would allow Congress a yes-or-no vote on trade agreements negotiated by the president and executive branch trade officials. Fast-track legislation would prevent congressional modification of such aggrements—agreements that the IBEW, like other unions, fears would cost American

**International Brotherhood of Electrical Workers
Political Action Committee Contributions**

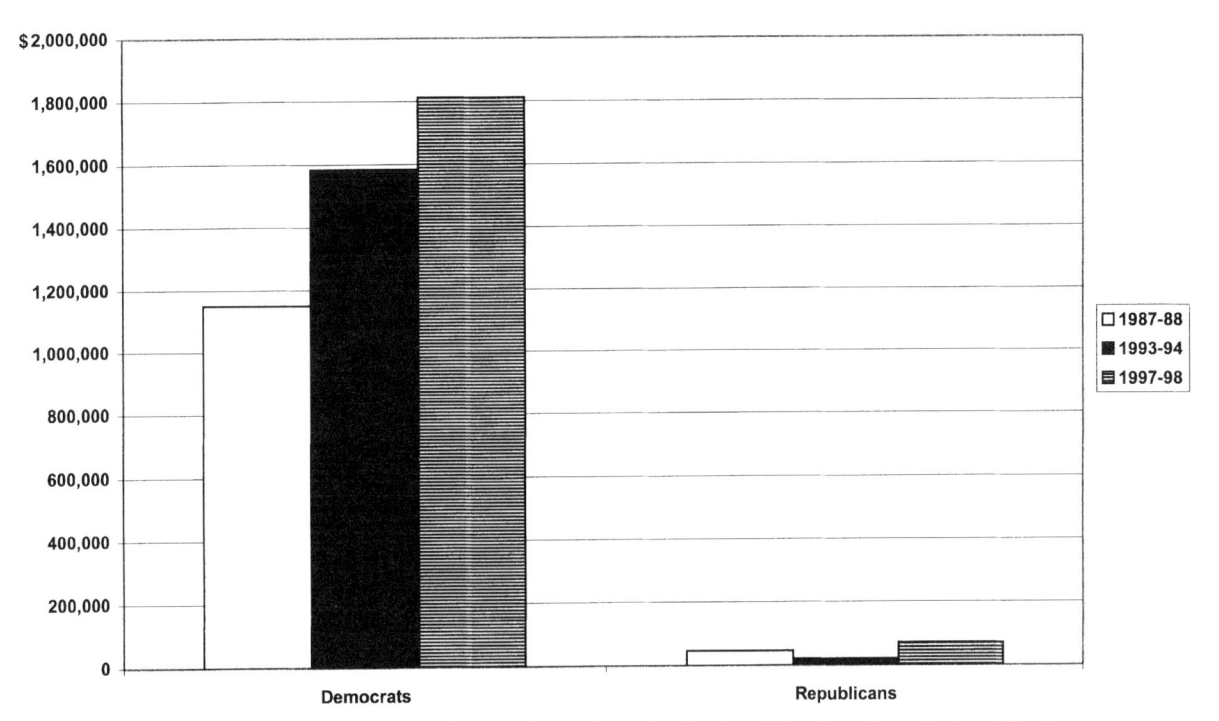

[Bar chart showing PAC contributions for 1987-88, 1993-94, and 1997-98. Democrats received approximately $1,150,000 (1987-88), $1,590,000 (1993-94), and $1,820,000 (1997-98). Republicans received approximately $60,000 (1987-88), $35,000 (1993-94), and $90,000 (1997-98).]

Data derived from official studies available from the Federal Election Commission, Washington, DC, 1987–1998.

workers jobs. This issue is particularly important to the IBEW since many of its members work in the globally competitive electrical manufacturing industry. In addition, and again like other unions, the IBEW stands opposed to Social Security privatization, seeing it as a threat to the national pension system and as a financial windfall to Wall Street securities firms.

With its fellow unions, the IBEW stands opposed to measures that would promote company unions, overthrowing key elements of the National Labor Relations Act of 1935. Under the so-called Truth in Employment Act, employer-supported unions would be permitted even if some workers at a given plant or company were members of independent trade unions. According to the union, "An employee's right to organize is already seriously under attack"; it is not uncommon for many workers to be fired for union activity, employers to hire "union-busting" firms, and companies to force potential IBEW recruits to attend anti-union "education" sessions.

In addition, the IBEW has expressed its opposition to talk of an independent contractors bill contemplated by Republican members of the House and Senate. According to the union, the bill would allow employers to reclassify millions of workers as "independent contractors," thereby avoiding obligations to pay for healthcare, pensions, and other benefits. It also concerns the IBEW because it threatens job security and seniority. According to the IBEW, "When workers are reclassified as 'independent contractors,' it creates a two-tiered workplace in which some workers receive benefits and protections and others, performing exactly the same work, under the same conditions, do not."

Aside from legislation that affects labor and the labor movement generally, COPE has been involved with bills that affect IBEW members in particular. These include changes in the Internal Revenue Service (IRS) code, electricity deregulation, payment protections for subcontractors and suppliers on federal projects, nuclear waste policy, and school construction.

As for the IRS code, there are two components of Section 415 that the IBEW is pushing to change. One concerns rules passed under the 1986 Tax Reform Act. Initially intended to limit early pensions for highly compensated chief executives, it hurts many members of the IBEW who rely on multi-employer pensions. Since many IBEW members work for several employers, they appear to fall under the rule. And because of the danger and arduousness of the work performed by many union members, early retirement is common. Thus, the restrictions limit pension payments, and the IBEW would like to see an exemption made for persons employed in dangerous or arduous industries. A second aspect of the IRS code that the IBEW would like to change concerns "compensation-based limits," which averages income over three consecutive years. Since IBEW members' employment and wages fluctuate so greatly between years, this can have the effect of severely limiting benefits.

The IBEW opposes electricity deregulation. Aside from worries about the safety and reliability of the system under federally mandated deregulation—as well as potential costs to consumers—the union believes that the "cutthroat" competition it will promote is bound to have adverse affects on staffing levels and maintenance programs, the latter endangering worker safety. At the same time, the IBEW is promoting a bill that would require prime contractors on federal construction projects worth more than $2,000 to provide a bond to indemnify all persons supplying labor and materiel to the job. While there are existing rules on the subject, the IBEW would like to see them strengthened.

On nuclear safety, the IBEW would like to see passage of currently debated legislation concerning the establishment of a permanent nuclear waste facility at Yucca Mountain, Nevada. While aware of the dangers of transporting such waste across the United States, the IBEW believes that existing arrangements, in which nuclear waste is stored on the grounds of the facilities that generate it, are dangerous to workers—many of whom are IBEW members who labor in proximity to the temporary storage facilities.

Finally, the IBEW stands behind President Bill Clinton's $4 billion initiative to raise tax-preferred bonds to repair the nation's schools. The IBEW believes that the need is great and that the financing scheme for it is sound. In addition, such school repairs would provide jobs for many IBEW members.

FINANCIAL FACTS

During the 1995–1996 election cycle, the IBEW's COPE received nearly $3.4 million and spent just over $3.4 million. The group contributed $2 million to Democrats and just $46,637 to Republicans. Contributions to Democrats have far exceeded those to Republicans, by 25 to 45 times as much.

There has been a dramatic increase in COPE's receipts, expenditures, and contributions over the past 10 years. Receipts and expenditures have climbed from $2 million to $3.3 million, while contributions have grown from nearly $2.3 million to more than $3.5 million.

JAMES CIMENT AND IMMANUEL NESS

Bibliography
IBEW Journal. 1902–1999.

International Brotherhood of Electrical Workers: History and Structure. Washington, DC: International Brotherhood of Electrical Workers, n.d.

Palladino, Grace. *Dreams of Dignity, Workers of Vision: A History of the International Brotherhood of Electrical Workers.* Washington, DC: International Brotherhood of Electrical Workers, 1991.

INTERNATIONAL BROTHERHOOD OF TEAMSTERS

The International Brotherhood of Teamsters (IBT—or conventionally, the Teamsters), is the third largest union in the country. Based in Washington, D.C., the Teamsters represent more than 1.4 million union members in the United States and Canada. The union has 620 local chapters, 43 joint councils, and 10 state conferences.

The union primarily represents workers in trucking, distribution, and warehousing. However, since its origins in the early twentieth century the Teamsters have expanded to include service (maintenance, laundry, office, department store, cold storage), manufacturing (automobiles), beverage and brewery (soda, nonalcoholic beverages, and beer), building and construction trades, healthcare, and professional workers.

HISTORY

The IBT formed in 1903 with the merger of the Team Drivers International Union and the Teamsters National Union in Niagara Falls, New York. The locals represented workers employed as team drivers who typically distributed goods by horse-drawn carriage. From 1907 to 1952, Daniel J. Tobin, an Irish immigrant and Boston streetcar driver, headed the Teamsters as international president. In 1952, Tobin was succeeded by Dave Beck.

In the late 1950s, following charges of systematic corruption within the international union, the Teamsters drifted from the mainstream of the American labor movement to its margins. The Teamsters were thrown out of the American Federation of Labor–Congress of Industrial Organizations (AFL-CIO) and were not allowed to rejoin until 1987. For many decades, key members of the international leadership of the Teamsters were implicated with organized crime groups. Although the union's leaders were believed to be closely associated with crime figures, many of the union's locals remained crime free.

James R. (Jimmy) Hoffa, perhaps the most well-known union leader in the Teamsters' history, was charged with corruption in 1963. In 1967, Hoffa was convicted of jury tampering and sent to prison. Then in 1977, Hoffa, recently pardoned by President Richard Nixon, disappeared and is believed by many to have been murdered. The union leadership continued to be associated with organized crime figures through the 1970s and 1980s.

For about half a century, the Teamsters were a union dominated by organized crime and corruption until two factors led to its democratic transformation. First, Teamsters for a Democratic Union (TDU), a dissident faction within the union, sought to bring about change through greater democracy and membership participation. From its origin in the mid 1970s, TDU mobilized rank-and-file support for rooting out cronyism and inserting democratic practices into the union's international bylaws. Second, as a result of government investigations throughout the 1970s and 1980s. The federal government charged the Teamsters with violating the Racketeer Influenced and Corrupt Organizations law by associating with organized crime and engaging in corrupt practices. In 1989, Teamster leaders accepted a consent decree that called for the union to be placed under a special court-supervised system of independent overseers, particularly addressing such matters as union structure, elections, and finances.

The Teamsters' bylaws were modified to instill greater democracy through a new provision that allowed members to elect international officers directly. In 1991, Ron Carey, an insurgent union leader, was elected president of the international union with 48.5 percent of the votes. Carey was a dissident leader of a Teamster local in New York City that represented United Parcel Service (UPS) delivery workers. Follow-

**International Brotherhood of Teamsters
Political Action Committee Contributions**

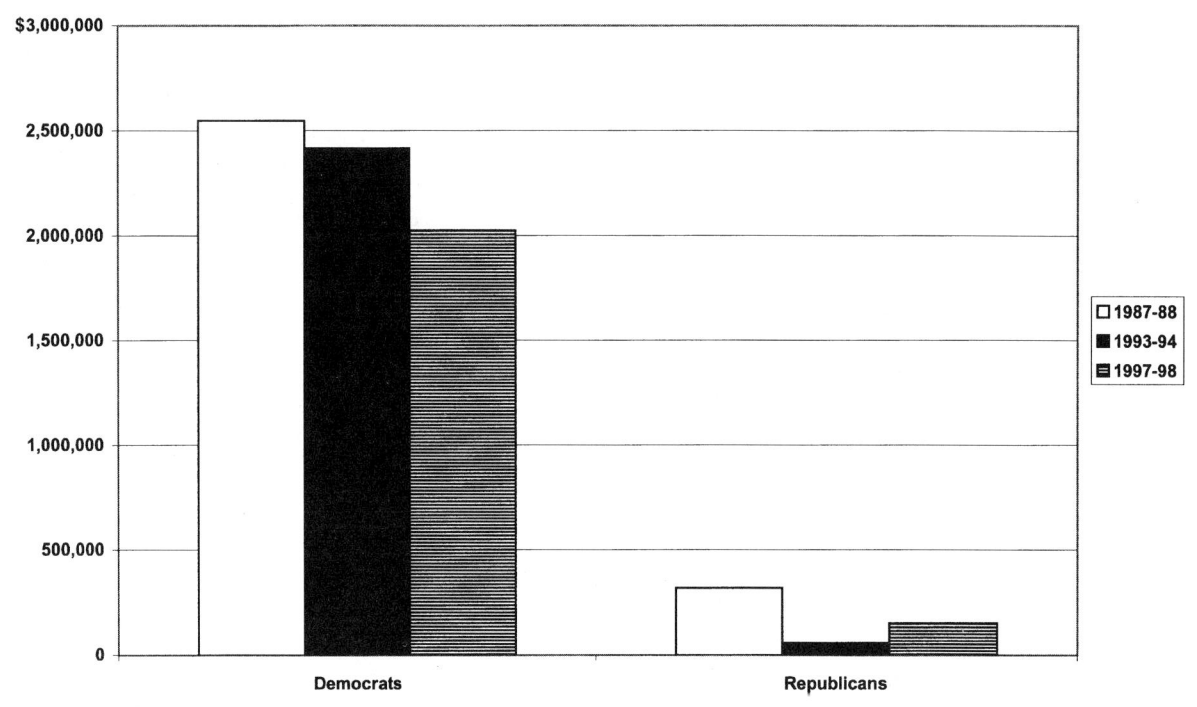

[Bar chart showing PAC contributions to Democrats and Republicans for 1987-88, 1993-94, and 1997-98. Democrats received approximately $2,550,000 (1987-88), $2,400,000 (1993-94), and $2,025,000 (1997-98). Republicans received approximately $300,000 (1987-88), $75,000 (1993-94), and $175,000 (1997-98).]

Data derived from official studies available from the Federal Election Commission, Washington, DC, 1987–1998.

ing his election, Carey pledged to root out corruption in locals and devote greater resources and staff to organize workers into the union. Carey also sought to reverse decades of union concessions to employers that have severely eroded wages and benefits. Perhaps the most important achievement of the Carey administration was the UPS strike in the summer of 1997, when the negotiated agreement provided that the company create 10,000 full-time jobs.

In 1996, James P. Hoffa, the son of Jimmy Hoffa, challenged Ron Carey to the presidency. During the election, Hoffa charged that the Carey administration had misspent resources without serving the needs of the members. And after the election the federal government charged Carey with misuse of union funds to advance his reelection campaign. Amid allegations that contributions were made to Democratic Party operatives in exchange for kickbacks to his own campaign, the election was invalidated by the Justice Department, which ordered a new election. Carey was forced to resign the presidency and banned from running again. In 1999, Hoffa defeated several opponents by a large margin and was elected new president of the union. Hoffa immediately promised to remove any tinge of corruption in the international union and its locals and to support the continuation of democratic elections for international office.

ACTIVITIES: CURRENT AND FUTURE

Teamster president James P. Hoffa promised to be more judicious in supporting candidates for political office than Ron Carey had been. Rather than exclusively supporting Democrats without concrete benefit to the union and its members, Hoffa said the Teamsters would be more vigilant in its political endorsements. Nevertheless, the union continued to criticize Republican legislative efforts. In 1999, the Teamsters opposed Republican efforts to cut taxes, arguing that the proposal was a "bonanza for wealthy Americans." Instead, the Teamsters supported the Democrats' efforts to shore up Social Security.

Primary objectives of the Teamsters are to organize new workers and enhance the economic power of its members. The union contends that deregulation and global trade agreements have significantly eroded the economic security of working families in the United States. Hoffa cites federal reports that demonstrate that U.S. workers' median wages have not caught up to wage levels in 1974. The union supports legislation to enhance the right of workers who seek to improve their economic conditions to organize into unions. Currently, workers who seek to organize into unions without employer approval sometimes face retaliation and intimidation and are fired illegally.

The union is at the forefront of efforts to reduce international and regional competition from low-wage employers seeking to reduce wage costs by shifting operations from the United States. The Teamsters believe that international trade agreements impose restrictions on American business practices and do not take into account labor and human rights conditions in countries producing goods for the American market. The union believes that the World Trade Organization is shifting high-paying jobs to lower-wage markets abroad and lead to lower wages in the United States. In 1999, Hoffa strongly opposed provisions of NAFTA (North American Free Trade Agreement) that allowed Mexican trucks to cross the border into the United States, beginning January 1, 2000. Under the agreement Mexican truck drivers are able to drive to commercial centers within 20 miles of U.S. border cities. The Teamsters believe that opening the border to potentially unsafe Mexican trucks and unqualified Mexican drivers could threaten highway safety standards in the United States. Due to the lower operating costs of Mexican trucking companies, the union believes that if the agreement is implemented, unionized truck drivers face unfair competition and potential layoffs.

Preserving workplace safety and health is an important concern of the Teamsters. In 1999, the union opposed efforts by the U.S. House of Representatives to erode ergonomic standards that seek to protect workers from workplace hazards. For example, the union opposes efforts by the package delivery industry to increase weight limits on goods handled by workers. The union also seeks to advance legislation that improves truck safety.

FINANCIAL FACTS

The Teamsters are among the leading union contributors to politicians for federal office. Although the union's political action committee (PAC) has traditionally contributed the lion's share of its funds to Democrats, under the Carey administration the share of the union's contributions to Democrats increased to an even greater degree. In the 1987–1988 election cycle, only 9 percent of the union's $2.85 million in PAC contributions went to Republicans. But, in the 1993–1994 cycle, the Carey regime gave Republicans only 2 percent of the union's nearly $2.5 million in campaign contributions. Contributions to Republicans rose in the 1997–1998 cycle, but still remained less than half the amount contributed in 1987–1988. In 1999, incoming president James P. Hoffa promised to be more strategic in disbursing campaign contributions to the political campaigns of the two major parties. He indicated that rather than contributing nearly all the union's funds to the Democrats, the union would support Republicans that were sympathetic to the Teamsters' interests.

IMMANUEL NESS

Bibliography

Brill, Steven. *The Teamsters*. New York: Simon & Schuster, 1978.

Crowe, Kenneth C. *Collision: How the Rank and File Took Back the Teamsters*. New York: Charles Scribner's Sons, 1993.

Friedman, Allen. *Power and Greed: Inside the Teamsters Empire of Corruption*. New York: F. Watts, 1989.

International Brotherhood of Teamsters. *The International Teamster*. Vols. 1–51, 1942–1992.

International Brotherhood of Teamsters. *The New Teamster*. Vol. 52. 1992–present.

International Brotherhood of Teamsters: www.ibt.org

La Botz, Dan. *Rank and File Rebellion: Teamsters for a Democratic Union*. New York: Verso, 1990.

Teamsters for a Democratic Union. *Teamster Information Network*. Vol. 1. 1977–present.

Teamsters Research Bulletin. *Harder Work—Lower Pay: What's Happening to American Workers?* April 1995.

Zeller, F. C. Duke. *Devil's Pact: Inside the World of the Teamsters Union*. Secaucus, NJ: Carol Publishing Group, 1996.

INTERNATIONAL UNION OF OPERATING ENGINEERS

The International Union of Operating Engineers (IUOE) represents approximately 400,000 persons in the field of stationary engineering—that is, persons involved in the maintenance, mechanics, and operation of heavy equipment, especially in building construction, but also in highway construction and workers who lay water, power, and sewage lines, and energy pipelines. Most workers are on construction sites but others labor at chemical plants and refineries. Heavy equipment includes front-end loaders, rollers, backhoes, graders, dredges, hoists, drills, pumps, and compressors. According to the union, if it can push, pull, pump, or lift material, and it rolls on tires or crawls on tracks, it falls under the union's jurisdiction. It is the 12th-largest union within the AFL-CIO and the third largest in the Canadian Federation of Labor. The IUOE has signed master work agreements—involving all locals—with several major corporations, including General Electric and Westinghouse.

The union includes approximately 200 locals across North America, which enjoy a great deal of autonomy in running their own affairs, electing their own officers, negotiating agreements, and dealing with employers on grievances and arbitration. The international coordinates affairs of the various locals and provides technical and other services to the locals. It is headed by a president and a secretary-treasurer. These two officers are joined by 11 general vice presidents—each a business manager of a local. Together, the 13 officers form the executive board, which handles the day-to-day affairs of the union. In addition, five business managers serve as international trustees of the union. All officials, as well as overall policy, are voted upon by the delegates at quadrennial conventions. The international office—located in Washington, D.C.—includes departments handling the following: legal, legislative and political, research, senior affairs, civil rights, publications, and media and other affairs.

The IUOE takes a keen legislative interest in a number of issues pertaining to working people and the organized labor movement generally, including Medicare, Social Security, compensation and benefit law, and—because of the hazards involved in the use of heavy machinery—workplace and worksite safety and health. It has also been involved in political efforts around issues of special interest to its own members, especially in the realm of promoting federal construction and cleanup projects.

HISTORY

The origin of the IUOE goes back to a small group of stationary engineers in Chicago, who met to form the National Union of Steam Engineers in 1896. (A steam gauge still figures prominently in the union logo.) At first, the union remained small and growth limited. The largest local had but 40 members and all but one represented workers who possessed the ability to operate dangerous steam boilers. In 1897, Canadian workers began to join the union, and the construction boom around the turn of the century led to the union's expansion. Many members helped rebuild San Francisco after the great earthquake of 1906; others were involved in the construction of the Panama Canal, completed in 1914. In 1912, the union changed its name to the International Union of Steam and Operating Engineers to reflect the growing diversity of its membership. With the switch to internal combustion and electric engines in the 1920s, the word "steam" was dropped from the union's name.

With the passage of the Davis-Bacon Bill of 1931—guaranteeing higher wage rates on federal construction projects—the union was able to weather the Great Depression, though it lost significant membership. During the labor shortages of the World War II era, the union rebounded, joining forces with the Navy Seabies—or engineers—to build bases, airfields, roads, and temporary ports from Europe to the Pacific and on to Korea during the war there. The union's membership, though on a generally downward trend since the 1950s, has

**International Union of Operating Engineers
Political Action Committee Contributions**

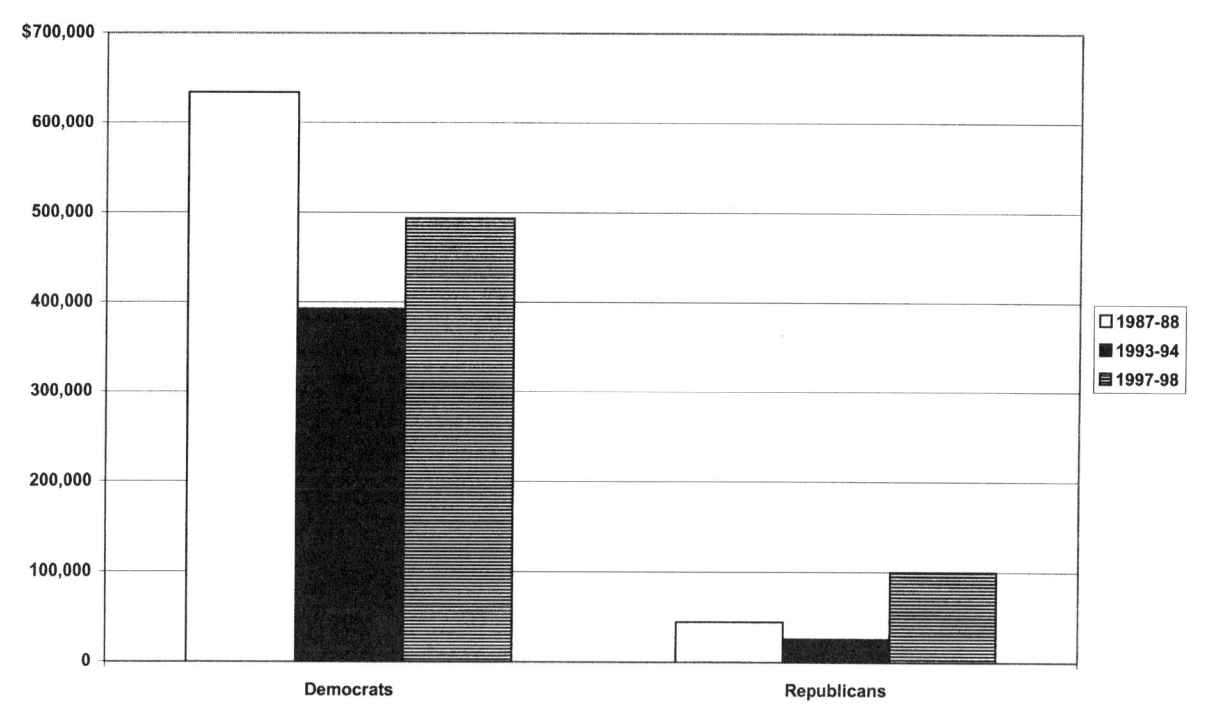

[Bar chart showing PAC contributions to Democrats and Republicans for 1987-88, 1993-94, and 1997-98. Democrats: ~$635,000 (1987-88), ~$390,000 (1993-94), ~$490,000 (1997-98). Republicans: ~$40,000 (1987-88), ~$25,000 (1993-94), ~$95,000 (1997-98).]

Data derived from official studies available from the Federal Election Commission, Washington, DC, 1987–1998.

been represented on the worksites of virtually every major construction project of the postwar era, including Chicago's Sears Tower, Toronto's CN Tower and Sky Dome, and the Alaskan oil pipeline.

ACTIVITIES: CURRENT AND FUTURE

Like other unions, the Operating Engineers have taken an active role in defeating a number of bills that they consider to be antilabor, proposed or introduced in the Republican-dominated Congress of the past few years. Specifically, they have stood against actions that would diminish the right of unions to make political contributions—without winning individual member approval. They have been heavily involved in trying to block efforts to change the nature of overtime compensation from straight time-and-a-half pay to flexible compensation, including time off and/or benefits, seeing in this measure a threat to the salaries of many of its members who often work odd hours on emergency and other construction projects. In addition, the union wants to make sure that Medicare benefits are not cut and that Social Security is preserved for the future and is not privatized in any way in the short term.

At the same time, the union has been active promoting environmental cleanup projects and has fought to enhance the funding and activities of the federal government's Superfund program for hazardous waste, citing both job and environmental concerns for its support. However, on other issues, the union has been at loggerheads with some environmental groups. An active promoter of highway, airport, and pipeline construction, the union has disagreed with environmentalists over the impact of some of these projects. In addition, it has been active in promoting the safe cleanup of asbestos-contaminated worksites and has pursued class-action suits to further its aims.

FINANCIAL FACTS

The IUOE supports well-funded and active lobbying efforts and donates substantial sums to congressional and presidential campaigns. During the 1995–1996 political cycle, the Engineers' Political Education Committee (EPEC) received just over $1 million, but spent over $1.4 million. This included over $500,000 in political donations—$476,200 to Democrats and $27,750 to Republicans. The IUOE, like virtually all other trade unions, has donated far more to Democrats than Republicans, by 15 to 20 times as much.

There has been a substantial upward trend in EPEC donations to political candidates over the past 12 years, although the union significantly lowered its contributions temporarily after the 1992 presidential and congressional campaigns. Between the 1987–1988 and 1995–1996 political cycles, contributions rose approximately 18 percent. Finally, various locals of the IUOE provide significant contributions of their own to congressional and presidential campaigns. For example, in the 1995–1996 election cycle, the top 18 locals contributed a total of approximately $350,000, most of which went to Democratic candidates.

JAMES CIMENT AND IMMANUEL NESS

Bibliography

International Union of Operating Engineers. *Building a Better Tomorrow.* Washington, DC: International Union of Operating Engineers, n.d.

Mangum, Garth. *Union Resilience in Troubled Times: The Story of the Operating Engineers, AFL-CIO, 1960–1993.* Armonk, NY: M.E. Sharpe, 1994.

LABORERS' INTERNATIONAL UNION OF NORTH AMERICA

The Laborers' International Union of North America (LIUNA)—a member of the AFL-CIO—has nearly 750,000 members, largely employed in construction, although the union also represents workers in a variety of industries. These include government employees, healthcare, mail handling, custodial services, shipbuilding, food service, and nonnuclear hazardous waste removal (such as lead and asbestos). Approximately 50,000 members are in Canada, and the rest are in the United States.

With its headquarters in Washington, D.C., LIUNA includes some 650 autonomously operated locals, organized by trade or by geographic region. In addition, each of the locals is affiliated with one of the 61 district councils. Most of the districts are organized along geographic lines, but with ever more diverse occupations represented by the union, an increasing number are organized by occupation. Above the district councils are the 12 regional offices (10 in the United States and two in Canada), which carry out the executive functions of the international and provide services to the locals.

At the top of the organization is the international union, which issues charters for locals and defines the power and jurisdictional areas of the local unions and district councils. The international also develops programs for the union as a whole, in the areas of training, health and safety, and labor-management cooperation. In addition, the international offers services in bargaining, research, public affairs, and legal and political action.

The international is divided into several divisions that manage the various occupational categories represented by members and provide services to union members. These divisions include construction, maintenance and service trades, environmental remediation, international affairs, investments, jurisdiction, legislative, benefits, organizing, public affairs, research and education, community development, defense conversion, health and welfare, pensions, membership assistance, and union privilege (credit union). The two chief officers, elected at convention every five years, are the president and general secretary-treasurer.

While LIUNA is involved in many of the issues that concern the union movement in general—including Social Security privatization and corporate influence in government—it is especially concerned with legislation affecting the construction industry and other issues that directly impinge on its members' well-being. The latter include defense conversion and hazardous waste law.

HISTORY

LIUNA was organized upon the urging of American Federation of Labor (AFL) president Samuel Gompers in 1903. Responding to Gompers's call, some 8,000 laborers met in Washington, D.C., to form the International Hod Carriers and Building Laborers Union of America. The union experienced heavy growth in the 1920s, as the building boom of that decade expanded the industry. In addition, three amalgamations expanded the union's membership. During the 1920s, the International Compressed Air and Foundation Workers, the Tunnel and Subway Constructors International Union, and the International Union of Pavers, Rammermen, Flag Layers, Bridge and Curb Setters, and Sheet Asphalt Pavers affiliated with the Hod Carriers. By the end of the decade, the union had more than 100,000 members.

Although the Great Depression shrank the rolls somewhat, the union expanded enormously during the Second World War, reaching 430,000 members as early as 1942. After the AFL merged with the Congress of Industrial Organizations (CIO) in 1955, a further 60,000 construction workers from the CIO joined the Hod Carriers' ranks. A decade later, the union changed its name to the Laborers' International Union of North America. In 1968, 20,000 members of the Mail Handlers Union joined LIUNA. In 1995, the union signed an oversight agreement with the federal government to root out corruption and implement a reform program.

**Laborers' International Union of North America
Political Action Committee Contributions**

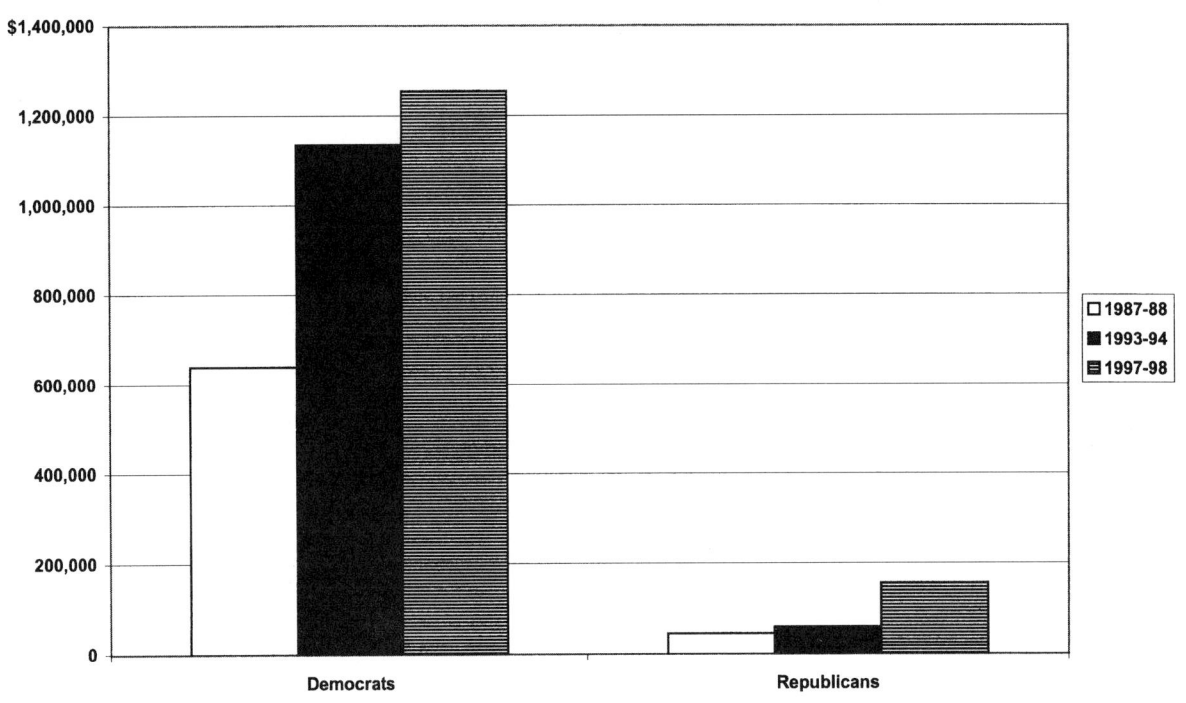

[Bar chart showing PAC contributions to Democrats and Republicans for 1987-88, 1993-94, and 1997-98. Democrats received approximately $640,000 (1987-88), $1,140,000 (1993-94), and $1,260,000 (1997-98). Republicans received approximately $50,000 (1987-88), $70,000 (1993-94), and $170,000 (1997-98).]

Data derived from official studies available from the Federal Election Commission, Washington, DC, 1987–1998.

This action contributed to renewed efforts to organize low-wage workers who had been neglected by the union in past years.

ACTIVITIES: CURRENT AND FUTURE

Among the critical legislative items that LIUNA's Laborers' Political League has been involved with is campaign finance reform. Arguing that donations from corporations and wealthy individuals outstripped those by labor unions by more than eight to one—and that donations by the former have increased 20 times faster than those by the latter—LIUNA supported the McCain-Feingold political finance reform act. More vociferously, they opposed efforts by Majority Leader Trent Lott to kill the bill by adding the "poison pill" amendment, whereby unions would have to obtain written permission of individual members before spending their dues on political action. As the union officials noted, "Meaningful campaign finance reform must address the problem of corporate spending rather than just targeting America's working families. Republicans [spent more than] Democrats by $250 million in the last election (1998), and Senator Lott is trying to protect that advantage by killing real reform. . . . Corporations do not have any check on how they spend money."

Another legislative issue that concerned LIUNA—although more parochial in nature—was Congress's efforts to exempt school construction jobs in the District of Columbia from prevailing wage rules. Helping to defeat the bill, LIUNA saw it as a wedge in which the Republican-controlled Congress could overturn the prevailing wage on other federally funded construction projects. Similarly, LIUNA has been active in overturning rules instituted during the administration of Ronald Reagan that allow for lower-paid helpers on federal construction projects.

LIUNA also stood opposed to a bill promoted in the House and Senate by the United States Chamber of Commerce and the National Association of Manufacturers whereby the Fair Labor Standards Act would be modified to allow for different forms of compensation for overtime. Under the act, overtime pay was set at 50 percent more than regular pay. The legislation would allow certain employers, many in the construction industry, either exemptions from the rule or to pay their employees in comp time—future days off in exchange for working weekends, holidays, or overtime—and other forms of nonmonetary compensation, such as added pensions or health benefits. The union opposes this measure because it gives companies more decision-making power to determine worker pay and puts workers at risk of losing overtime compensation altogether if a company should go bankrupt, a relatively common occurrence in the volatile and seasonal construction industry. The bill would also allow employers to discriminate by rewarding workers who accepted nonmonetary compensation for overtime over those who refused it. Moreover, despite Democratic efforts to exempt construction workers from the bill, LIUNA opposes the legislation as a "bad deal" for all workers.

Another piece of legislation that the union has been fighting is a Republican-sponsored bill that would reclassify many workers—especially in the construction industry—as independent subcontractors, thus jeopardizing the Medicare and unemployment insurance they would be guaranteed as regular employees of prime contractors on federally funded construction projects. According to union officials: "This legislation aggravates an already bad situation. Because of funding cuts and a cumbersome process, the Internal Revenue Service can not adequately enforce the current law, which has led to massive misclassification of workers as independent contractors. Surveys indicate that as many as 20 percent of today's independent contractors were formerly employees of the companies for which they now work as contractors—doing the same work!"

LIUNA also stands opposed to Republican-led efforts to push through changes in the Occupational Safety and Health Administration (OSHA), including measures that would keep OSHA findings secret from workers, allow employers to act as peer reviewers of other employers accused of violating OSHA standards, and add burdensome regulations and rules that would delay implementation of OSHA rules and findings. On organizing, LIUNA is fighting a so-called antisalting bill that would place heavy restrictions on unions sending organizers into nonunion shops.

Finally, while generally supporting the administration of Bill Clinton, the union opposes its efforts to deny funds for highway construction in regions that fail to comply with clear air standards set by the Environmental Protection Agency (EPA). Although LIUNA says that it supports environmental regulations, the union argues that the measure would cost thousands of construction jobs in 634 counties nationwide—according to the EPA's own estimates—and could actually endanger American motorists, since many of the construction projects are necessary for highway safety.

FINANCIAL FACTS

The Laborers' Political League—the union's political action arm—is a major contributor of funds to federal campaigns, both congressional and presidential. During the 1995–1996 election cycle, the Laborers' Political League received $2.5 million and spent nearly $2.4 million. This latter figure includes more than $1.9 million in contributions to candidates and parties—$1.75 million to Democrats and $163,500 to Republicans. Contributions to Democrats have far exceeded those to Republicans, by 12 to 20 times as much, though this multiple is somewhat below that for most trade unions.

There has been a dramatic increase in the Laborers' Political League receipts, expenditures, and contributions over the past 10 years. Receipts and expenditures have climbed 175 percent, while contributions have almost tripled, from $686,000 to $1.9 million.

JAMES CIMENT AND IMMANUEL NESS

Bibliography

Goodman, John F. *Working at the Calling*. Hopkinton, MA: New England Laborers' Labor-Management Cooperation, 1991.

The Laborer. 1947–1999.

Laborers' International Union of North America. "Innovation at Work." Washington, DC: n.d. Pamphlet.

NATIONAL EDUCATION ASSOCIATION

With 2.4 million members, the National Education Association (NEA) is the largest professional employee organization in the United States. Its members include instructors at all levels, as well noninstructional educational staff. In addition, as a professional organization, the NEA includes retired educators, students earning their teaching degrees, and school administrators. Anyone who is employed at a public educational facility is eligible for membership. Though the NEA is the nation's largest union, the organization is not affiliated with the AFL-CIO. However, at the end of the century, the NEA was seriously investigating joining forces with the American Federation of Teachers.

The NEA is organized into four levels: 13,250 locals in all 50 states and Puerto Rico; 50 state organizations (as well as the Asociacion de Maestros in Puerto Rico); six regional branches, and the national union, located in Washington, D.C. The top policy-making body of the NEA is the Representative Assembly, whose 10,000 delegates meet annually. The daily affairs of the union are run by the nine-member executive committee—consisting of the union's president, vice president, secretary-treasurer, and heads of the six regional branches—and the 159-member board of directors. Over 500 staff personnel are employed at the national office.

The national office operates several divisions, including affiliates, audiovisual, classroom issues, Gateway to Education Materials, higher education, legislative action, membership, benefits, foundation issues, New Unionism, press center, publications, Read Across America, retirees, recess issues, the NEA Student Program, locals support, personnel, and technology.

Much of the NEA's campaign contributions and lobbying are geared to support candidates who share educational policy ideas similar to the NEA's and to promote policies that jibe with NEA initiatives. Among these issues are school funding (federal and state), charter schools, vouchers, educational technology, school safety, and school construction, as well as issues connected to teachers as employees.

HISTORY

The NEA is the oldest and largest organization dedicated to public education in the United States. It was founded in 1857 by a group of educators in Philadelphia who said that their organization would serve to "advance the interest of the profession of teaching and to promote the cause of education in the United States." Over the years, the NEA has largely shifted from being a professional organization to a more traditional labor union. Aside from working on issues related to the teaching profession, the union has donated some $70 million to improve public education directly since 1983, when the watershed report on American education—*A Nation at Risk*—was published.

ACTIVITIES: CURRENT AND FUTURE

Along with issues concerning working people and the organized labor movement as a whole—including Social Security privatization—the NEA is actively lobbying Congress on a number of issues concerning students, teachers, and the educational system in the United States.

The NEA advocates reductions in classroom size, as a measure benefiting both teachers and students. Citing a number of studies that show reduced class size leads to better student achievement and lower teacher turnover, the union lobbied Congress to expand and guarantee funding for a national class-size initiative, which would provide pay for 100,000 more teachers through mandatory spending of $12 billion over the next seven years. In addition, the NEA advocates federal legislation to provide tax relief to states and localities so that they can build, repair, and modernize schools. Specifically, on this latter issue, the NEA would like to see Congress

**National Education Association
Political Action Committee Contributions**

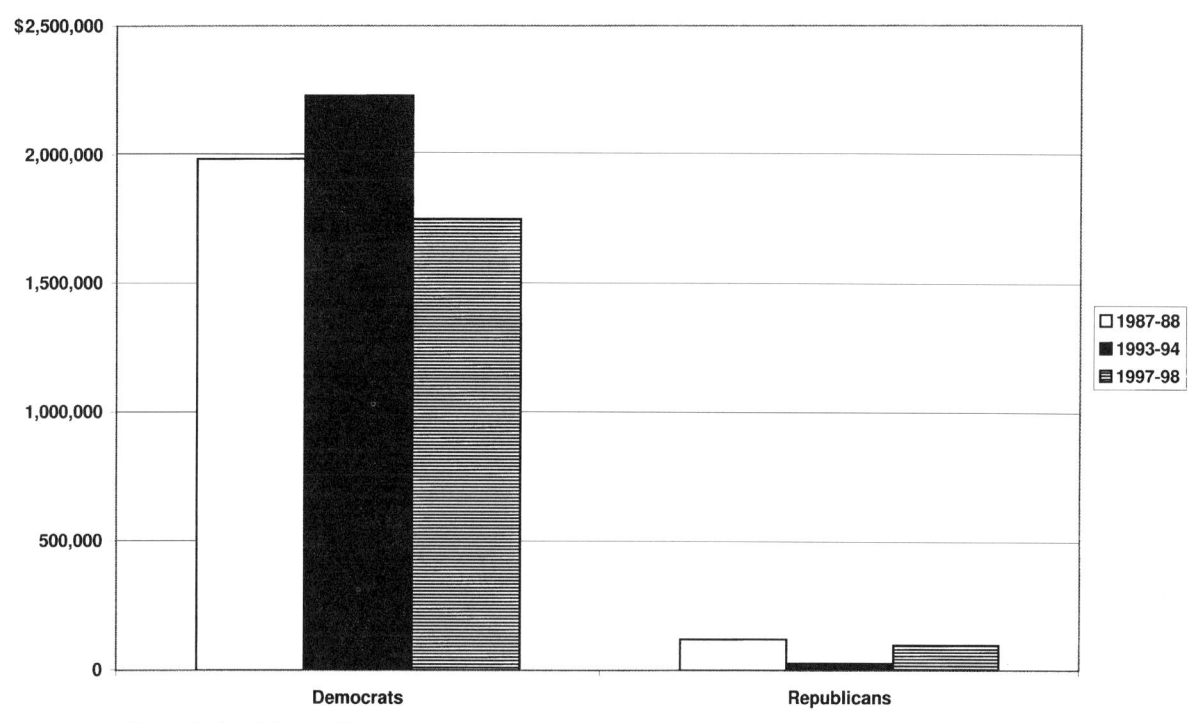

[Bar chart showing contributions to Democrats and Republicans for 1987-88, 1993-94, and 1997-98. Democrats: approximately $2,000,000 (1987-88), $2,250,000 (1993-94), $1,750,000 (1997-98). Republicans: small amounts under $200,000 for all three periods.]

Data derived from official studies available from the Federal Election Commission, Washington, DC, 1987–1998.

pass bond measures to raise $200 billion nationally for school construction and repair, with a special emphasis on inner-city and rural facilities, as well as streamlining the administrative process whereby states and localities obtain federal funding. Similarly, the NEA proposes a number of measures designed to improve the safety of students and teachers. It advocates more funding for school safety and supports the Children's Gun Violence Prevention Act, which seeks to protect children from gun-related violence in schools, communities, and homes.

Noting the importance of new technologies in preparing students for the postindustrial economy, the NEA is lobbying Congress for a host of initiatives designed to introduce new technologies to schools, especially in financially strapped districts. The union wants the federal government to provide tax-based assistance to states and localities for more Internet access, to enlarge libraries, and to provide teacher training in high-technology areas. At the same time, the NEA opposes the introduction of expensive, untried, and ineffective technology to filter content on the Internet. Instead, it would like Congress to encourage schools to implement "acceptable-use" policies to assure proper student use of the Internet.

The NEA supports charter schools—that is, schools with unorthodox or specialized programs designed to draw a diverse array of students from throughout a school district. But the union insists that federal funding for charter schools be used to try to rectify some of the problems connected with this educational innovation, including the propensity of some charter schools to be racially or ethnically unbalanced and to exclude students with disabilities. Thus, the NEA proposes expanding federal funding to charter schools so long as the schools meet the requirements of the Individuals with Disabilities Education Act, enhance accountability, include quality requirements, and provide safeguards against racial and ethnic patterning. It proposes a prohibition on federal start-up grants to for-profit charter schools.

The NEA opposes the shift in federal funding from monies mandated for specific programs—with specific federal requirements attached to them—to general block grants, which leave spending decisions largely up to the states. While supporters of such grants argue that they would allow for more flexibility in meeting local needs, the NEA says that block grants would cause a lack of focus on education, a weakening of accountability, and an inability to measure whether states were meeting national educational standards. Specifically, the NEA stands against proposed changes connected to the reauthorization of the 1965 Elementary and Secondary Education Act (ESEA). The union says that shifting to block grants would undermine the ESEA's original mandate to make sure that more funding goes to schools in impoverished areas, intended to lift them up to national standards. The NEA also believes that students with special educational needs will be shortchanged by block grants, since many of these students attend poorer schools. Ultimately, however, the NEA is against block grants because it sees them as ruses designed to lower funding for education. "The history of block grant proposals," notes the union, "indicates that they weaken our nation's commitment to education." As an alternative, the NEA proposes some changes in federal funding, including allowing states to submit consolidated applications rather than applications for each specific program, waivers for some mandates so long as the underlying purpose of the ESEA is met, and allowing states to include administrative costs in applications for general program funding.

These changes, the union believes, would target specific problems with the ESEA without throwing away the entire program, most of which functions well. At the same time, the union would like to see the ESEA expanded to include more reading programs.

The NEA strongly opposes vouchers as well, both nationally and at the experimental level in Washington, D.C., whose educational system comes under direct congressional scrutiny. The union's opposition to vouchers is based on several factors. First, it says that vouchers shift scarce resources from public schools, where the vast majority of students receive their elementary and secondary education. Second, vouchers are "irresponsible," aiding a small minority of students at the expense of the majority. Third, vouchers do not offer parents choice, since private and parochial schools—the intended beneficiaries of most vouchers—can exclude students for a variety of reasons, selecting only the best performers. Fourth, vouchers encourage "fly-by-night," for-profit schools. Fifth, support for vouchers for parochial schools violates the separation of church and state. And finally, vouchers lead to "double taxation," as parents of students who do not attend private schools pay for those students who do. Parents are thus taxed to support both public and private schools.

FINANCIAL FACTS

The union's political action committee (NEAPAC) is one of the largest political action committees (PACs) of the U.S. labor movement—by amount of donation—and, indeed, is one of the largest PACs in the country overall. During the 1995–1996 election cycle, NEAPAC received nearly $4.8 million and spent over $5 million. This latter figure includes more than $2.3 million in contribution to candidates and parties—$2.3 million to Democrats and only $11,850 to Republicans. Contributions to Democrats have far exceeded those to Republicans, by 15 to over 200 times as much. This became especially marked during the 1990s, as Republicans in Congress were increasingly associated with educational reforms opposed by the NEA.

There has been a dramatic increase in NEAPAC's receipts, expenditures, and contributions over the past 10 years. From 1987–1988 to 1995–1996, receipts and expenditures have climbed from $3.8 million to $4.8 million, while contributions have risen from $3.6 million to over $5 million.

JAMES CIMENT AND IMMANUEL NESS

Bibliography

Berube, Maurice R. *Teacher Politics: The Influence of Unions*. New York: Greenwood Press, 1988.

Murphy, Marjorie. *Blackboard Unions: The AFT and the NEA, 1900–1980*. Ithaca, NY: Cornell University Press, 1990.

National Education Association of the United States. *Handbook*. Washington, DC: National Education Association, 1975–1999.

NEA Today: A Newspaper for Members of the National Education Association. October 1982–1999.

West, Allan M. *The National Education Association: The Power Base for Education*. New York: Free Press, 1980.

SEAFARERS INTERNATIONAL UNION OF NORTH AMERICA

The largest union of maritime workers in the United States, the Seafarers International Union of North America (SIU) represents approximately 80,000 maritime workers, including unlicensed U.S. merchant mariners working on ships plying the Pacific, Atlantic, and Gulf coasts and licensed mariners in the Great Lakes and inland waterway sectors. SIU members are largely employed in three shipboard departments—deck, engine, and steward—and work on a variety of vessels, including commercial containerships and tankers, military support ships, tugboats and barges, passenger ships, gaming vessels, and many more. In addition, SIU members work in the fishing and fish-canning industry, general manufacturing, marine safety, and the public sector.

The SIU—a union affiliated with the AFL-CIO, headquartered in suburban Washington, D.C.—includes a number of affiliated unions, including the Alaska Fish Cannery Workers Union, the Fishermen's Union of America, the Industrial Professional Technical Workers International Union, the International Union of Petroleum and Industrial Workers, the Marine Fireman's Union, the Mortuary Employees Union, the Professional Security Officers Association, the Sailors Union of the Pacific, the Seafarers Commercial Fishermen's Association, the Sugar Workers Union, the United Industrial Workers of North America, and the United Industrial, Service, Transportation, Professional, and Government Workers of North America.

HISTORY

The SIU's roots go back to the formation of the Seafarers Union of the Pacific in 1891—itself formed by the merger of the Coast Seaman's Union and the Steamship Sailor's Protective Association. The union then joined the American Federation of Labor (AFL) as a division of the International Seaman's Union of North America (ISU). But when the ISU left the AFL in 1936 to join the rival and more radical Committee for Industrial Organization—forerunner of the Congress of Industrial Organizations (CIO)—the SIU seceded from the ISU and remained part of the AFL. With the merger of the AFL and the CIO in 1955, the conservative SIU and the more militant National Maritime Union (NMU) found themselves under the same institutional roof. Disputes between the two kept them from merging, and the NMU eventually joined the National Marine Engineers' Beneficial Association, another union affiliated with the AFL-CIO.

ACTIVITIES: CURRENT AND FUTURE

While involved in issues of concern to working people and the labor movement generally, the SIU devotes much of its legislative activity to concerns directly related to the well-being of the maritime industry and its members. Among the efforts of the SIU in recent years was support for an extension of veterans' benefits to include World War II–era merchant mariners.

Concerning the industry itself, the union supports efforts by the administration of President Bill Clinton to establish a "Harbor Services Fund" for the purposes of providing maintenance and upkeep of the nation's ports well into the twenty-first century. The need for such a fund goes back to a recent Supreme Court decision that ruled the once-existing Harbor Maintenance Tax unconstitutional. The new fund would raise $800 million from a new users' fee that would go to dredging, port construction, and installation of new navigation equipment.

Because SIU members labor in an industry in which international competition is inevitable, the union has pushed for legislation designed to protect American workers in the maritime industry. Among the measures supported by the SIU is a bill requiring foreign cruise ships to temporarily fly U.S. flags and hire U.S. crews when sailing in and out of American ports.

The union also backs a recent report to Congress by the Department of Transportation that calls for a series

**Seafarers International Union of North America
Political Action Committee Contributions**

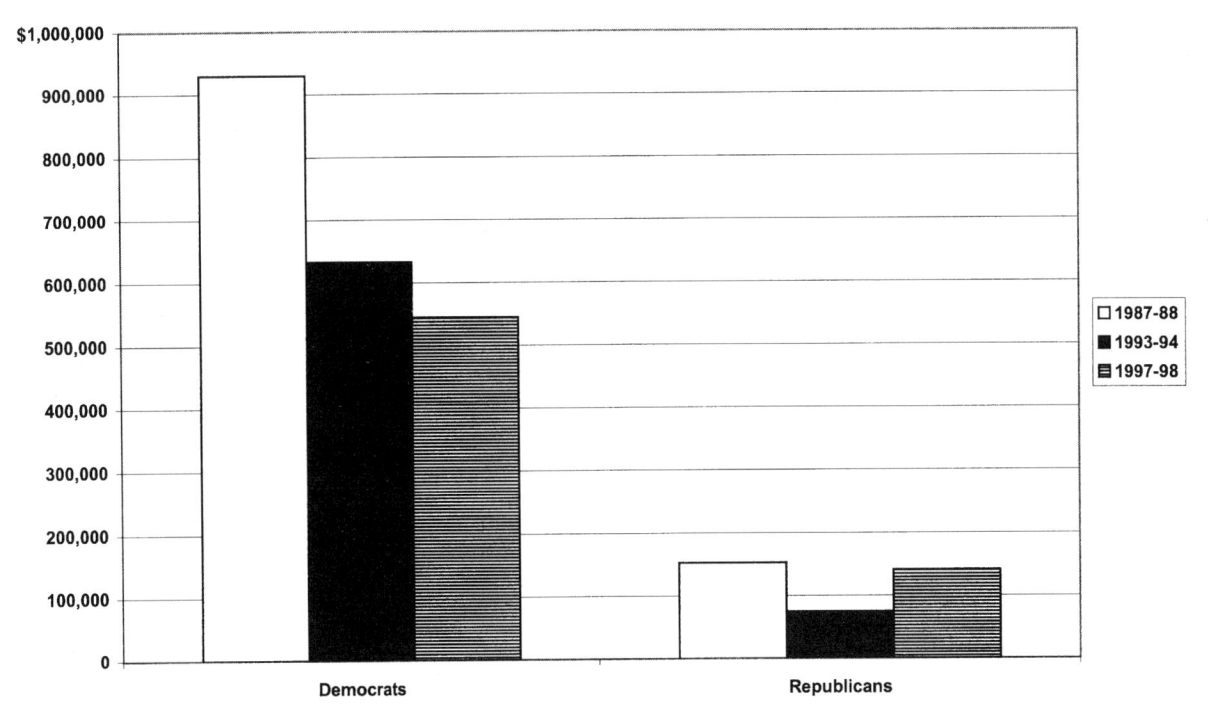

[Bar chart showing PAC contributions to Democrats and Republicans for 1987-88, 1993-94, and 1997-98]

Data derived from official studies available from the Federal Election Commission, Washington, DC, 1987–1998.

of measures to strengthen the U.S.-flag merchant fleet, including continued support for the Maritime Security Program, designed to help fund militarily useful U.S.-flag vessels; continued support for the nation's shipbuilding and ship-repairing industries; continuance of cabotage laws, which require that commodities shipped from one U.S. port to another be transported by U.S.-flag and U.S.-crewed ships; continued support for the Ready Reserve Force of merchant marines; the upgrading of the nation's intramodal transport system, which allows easier transshipment of goods between planes, railroads, trucks, and ships; research into new maritime technologies; and continued government activism in preventing unfair trade practices by foreign shippers.

FINANCIAL FACTS

The Seafarers Political Action Donation Department (SPAD) is one of the largest political action committees (PACs) of the U.S. labor movement—by amount of donation—though its contributions to candidates have dropped significantly over the past dozen years or so. During the 1995–1996 election cycle, SPAD received $1.65 million and spent over $1.6 million. This latter figure includes $736,399 in contribution to candidates and parties—$557,300 to Democrats and $179,099 to Republicans.

SPAD's receipts, expenditures, and contributions increased dramatically over the past 10 years. Receipts and expenditures have climbed 34 percent, while contributions have grown 23 percent, from $1.3 million to $1.6 million. At the same time, contributions to Democrats have exceeded those to Republicans, by three to 10 times as much. Reflecting the basic conservatism of the SIU, this ratio is far lower than for other unions.

JAMES CIMENT

Bibliography
Seafarers Log. 1976–1999.

SERVICE EMPLOYEES INTERNATIONAL UNION

Representing some 1.2 million workers, the Service Employees International Union (SEIU) is one of the largest AFL-CIO unions in the United States. The SEIU, which organizes workers across many industries, is one of the fastest growing unions in the world and is one of the few unions in the United States that experienced growth during the 1980s and 1990s, a period of declining union membership. The SEIU's membership has nearly doubled in the two decades between 1980 and 2000. The union attributes its rapid growth to an aggressive strategy of organizing new workers into the union and successfully negotiating contracts with employers. Part of the SEIU's growth also can be attributed to mergers with independent and unaffiliated unions. Much of this growth took place under the leadership of John Sweeney, who rose from a New York local representing maintenance workers to become president of the international. In 1995, Sweeney, who built his reputation on organizing, defeated Thomas Donahue to become the president of the American Federation of Labor-Congress of Industrial Organizations (AFL-CIO). In 1996, Andrew Stern, the new international president, continued the SEIU's commitment to growth through organizing. Part of this plan included electing a diverse leadership and becoming even more aggressive in the face of corporate and government restructuring that are designed for profitability but neglect the interests of workers and communities.

The union's membership includes doctors, nurses, healthcare workers, clerical workers, engineers, librarians, gas utility workers, lawyers, and janitors. The membership is employed by private employers, nonprofit organizations, and government agencies in the United States and Canada. About 585,000 of the union's members are public employees working in federal, state, county, and municipal governments, and in public schools. Nearly 500,000 of the union's members are healthcare workers employed in hospitals, nursing homes, health maintenance organizations (HMOs) and homecare facilities. Approximately 200,000 of the union's members work as janitors, window cleaners, and security guards. Another 150,000 of the international membership are office workers, including clerical and administrative workers. About 80,000 members are employed at racetracks and sports arenas, and as jewelry and leather goods workers.

The SEIU contends that its members earn significantly higher wages under better working conditions than nonunion workers employed in similar occupations. The international's "Justice for Janitors" campaign has attempted to organize low-wage janitors working under poor conditions in major cities across the United States.

The SEIU is a diverse organization. In 1999, about 58 percent of the union's members were women, and more than one-third are people of color (African Americans, Latinos, Hispanics, Asian Pacific Islanders, Native Americans). Most of the union's members are over 35 years of age, with some 37 percent over 50 years of age. About 32 percent of the union's members earn $35,000 or more per year, 32 percent earn between $25,000 and $35,000, and 36 percent earn under $25,000.

HISTORY

Locals that later formed part of the SEIU were first chartered in the early twentieth century in the Chicago area to represent janitors. A primary objective of the seven unions who formed the original international union was to promote independence among the locals. Local unions continue to have independence in selecting officers, negotiating contracts, and determining priorities. The union is recognized for negotiating contracts that are the best in their regional industries. In 1921, the SEIU received a national charter from the AFL.

The SEIU represents workers employed in diverse occupations across an array of industries. In the 1940s and 1950s, the SEIU was the first union to organize

**Service Employees International Union
Political Action Committee Contributions**

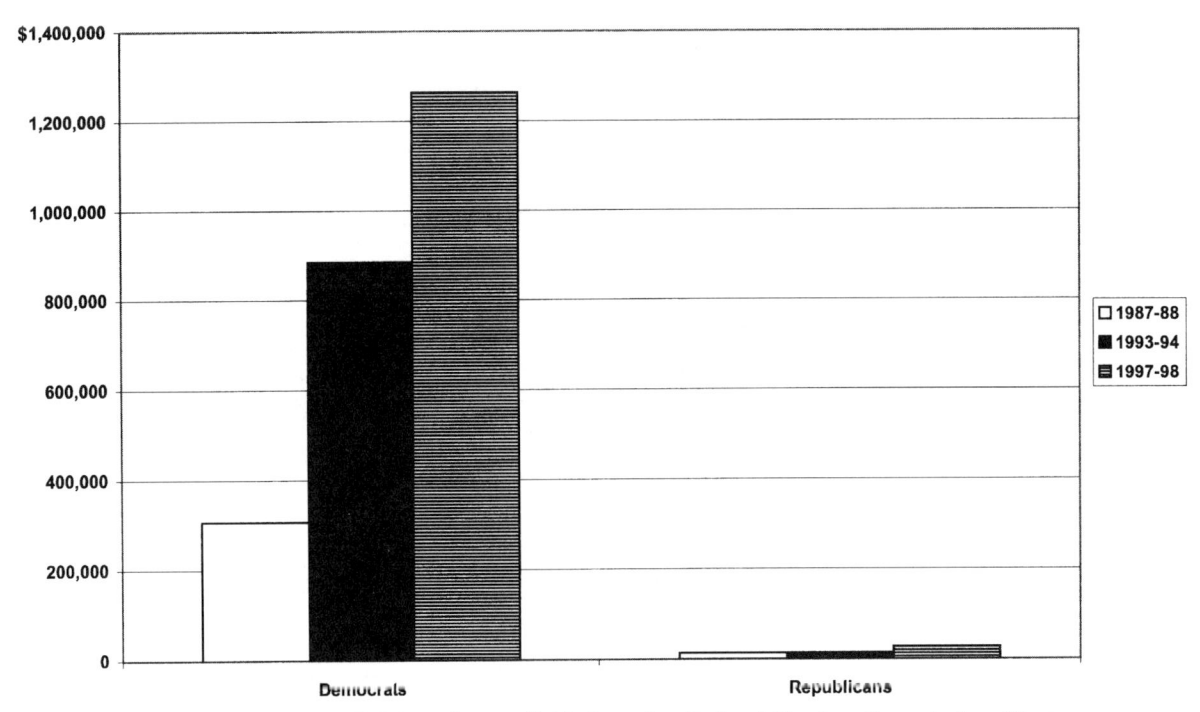

Data derived from official studies available from the Federal Election Commission, Washington, DC, 1987–1998.

hospital and healthcare workers. By the end of the century, the SEIU has grown to become the largest healthcare workers union in the United States, representing some 500,000 members working in hospitals, HMOs, clinics, nursing homes, homecare organizations, and blood banks.

ACTIVITIES: CURRENT AND FUTURE

The SEIU's primary objective in the coming decade is to organize new members into the union to improve the condition of low-wage workers in the service sector. In recent years, the union has launched major drives to organize hospital workers, home healthcare attendants, nursing home workers, and building maintenance workers. Like most other unions, the SEIU supports changing the labor laws to enable workers to organize. The union believes that workers who want to join unions should not be subject to illegal firing and other recriminations.

Unlike most conventional interest groups, the SEIU's political strategy is not directed primarily at lobbying government officials and contributing money to political action committees (PACs). The union does not exclusively engage in campaign contributions and political lobbying. The SEIU also seeks to influence labor policy that bears on union members through mobilizing rank-and-file workers to lobby members of Congress, publicly demonstrate and rally, and vote for politicians that support its members. As the healthcare industry restructures and cuts costs, the SEIU is lobbying and organizing to protect patients' rights and healthcare workers. The union believes that managed care and other changes directed at reducing healthcare costs frequently lead to declining patient access to needed medical care and the erosion of members' job security. The union has formed national and local coalitions with other labor unions and community organizations to advocate on behalf of members.

Through most of its history, the union has fought for racial and gender equality at the workplace to protect many of its members. The union has fought for equal rights and pay equity for women. The union's national policy agenda includes support for national healthcare reform, family and medical leave, and laws that protect the disabled and senior citizens, including defending Social Security. The union also lobbies to support workplace safety and health. In particular the union seeks to increase protections from toxic chemicals, violence, sexual harassment, asbestos, disease, and other hazards that workers face on the job.

FINANCIAL FACTS

The SEIU's contributions to political candidates have increased dramatically in the last decade of the twentieth century, with more than a 400 percent increase between the 1987–1988 and 1997–1998 election cycles—from $320,000 to $1,293,000. The vast majority of the union's PAC funds are contributed to Democratic candidates. In the 1997–1998 election cycle, Democrats received nearly 98 percent of the union's contributions.

IMMANUEL NESS AND JAMES CIMENT

Bibliography

Service Employees International Union. *SEIU Leadership News*. Vols. 1–present. May/June 1968–present.

Service Employees International Union. *Service Employee*. Vols. 16–46. February 1957–December 1986.

Service Employees International Union: www.seiu.org

TRANSPORT WORKERS UNION OF AMERICA

The Transport Workers Union of America (TWUA) represents approximately 100,000 workers in the public bus, train, air transport, and resource distribution industries, the latter primarily involving the installation and repair of natural gas distribution systems. In addition, the union represents local government and university workers, largely in the maintenance field. Major institutions where the TWUA members are employed include Amtrak, Conrail, Port Authority of New York and New Jersey, Columbia University, and Brooklyn Union Gas. Most of the union's members live and work in the northeastern states.

Affiliated with the AFL-CIO and headquartered in New York City, the TWUA has over 100 locals. The union's internal structure consists of three levels: the international office, the industrial divisions, and the local affiliates. The latter are based on type of work performed, employing institution, or geographic location. Locals elect their own officers and have a great deal of latitude in running their own affairs and negotiating their own contracts. The various industrial divisions—handling workers in the employment areas discussed above—offer legal and other help to locals. The international office coordinates the activities of the industrial divisions and assists in local organizing drives, negotiations, and legislative efforts. The top policy-making body of the union is the international convention, held every four years. In addition, the conventions elect the international officers. Between conventions, the policy-making bodies of the union are the international executive council and the international executive board.

The legislative interests of the TWUA range from issues that concern working people and the labor movement generally to issues of particular concern to its own members. The latter include strong support for public transportation development and air safety.

HISTORY

Following several failed efforts to organize transit workers in the New York City metropolitan area in the first two decades of the twentieth century, the TWUA was formed in 1934 to deal with Depression-era attempts by transit companies to cut wages and increase workload. Among the early leaders of the TWUA were subway worker Michael Quill and organizer Douglas McMahon. Early efforts by the union dealt with unsafe working conditions, leading to a successful two-day strike in 1935. More significant was the sit-down strike of 1937, whereby the union forced management to reemploy 600 workers who had been fired because of strike activities. The union's success—and pro-labor federal legislation—brought thousands into its ranks in a few months.

Outside New York City, the union was growing as well, organizing workers in Long Island, Ohio, Nebraska, and New Jersey by 1941. Philadelphia transit workers joined the union in 1944, after a seven-year struggle, followed by Houston workers in 1947 and San Francisco employees in 1950. Brooklyn Gas employees joined in 1941, and maintenance workers at Columbia University signed on two years later. During these same years, the union was expanding into the airline industry, organizing Pan Am and American in the 1940s. In 1954, the TWUA organized a railroad industrial division to deal with metropolitan and national rail systems.

ACTIVITIES: CURRENT AND FUTURE

The TWUA involves itself in the legislative process through lobbying and campaign contributions. It has been active in promoting measures of interest to working people generally or trying to block legislation it

**Transport Workers Union of America
Political Action Committee Contributions**

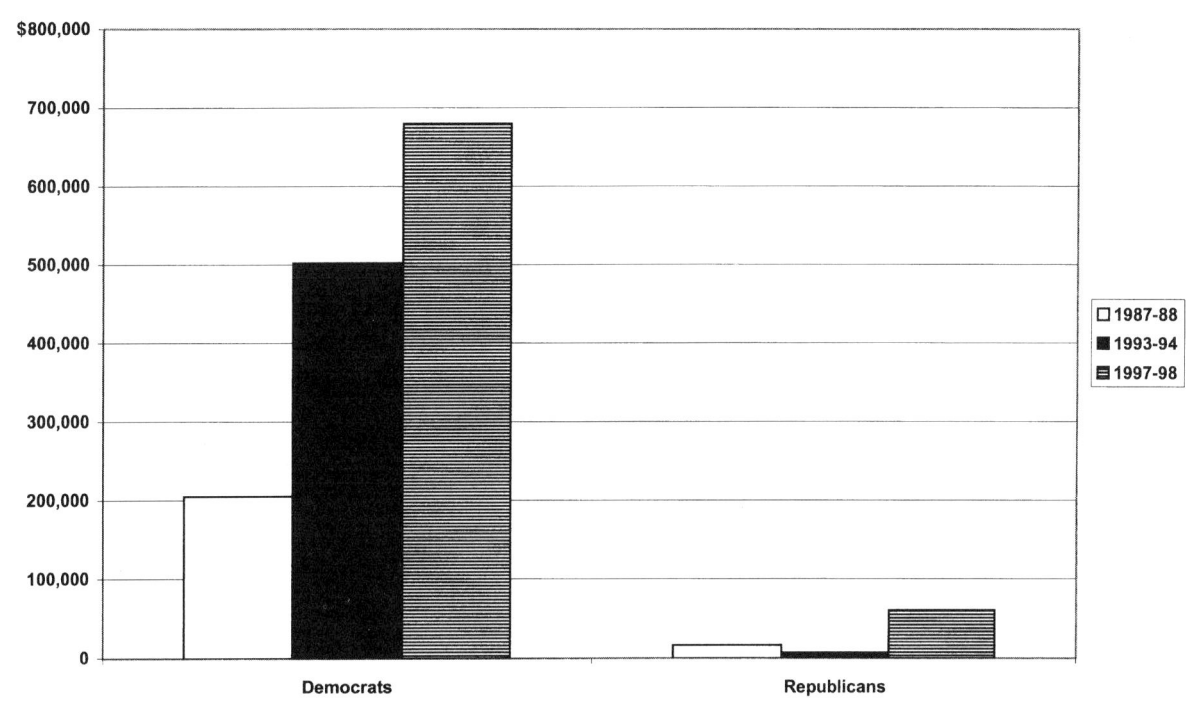

Data derived from official studies available from the Federal Election Commission, Washington, DC, 1987–1998.

deems inimical to working people and the labor movement. For example, it has actively backed legislative efforts to pass a patients' "bill of rights," which guarantees high-quality healthcare for worker-members of health maintenance organizations. At the same time, the union has tried to block Republican efforts to limit the effects of the bill to federally regulated health plans only, eliminating roughly two-thirds of the nation's insured patients. As for uninsured patients, the union supports Democratic efforts to spend $24 billion to provide healthcare for uninsured children. Moreover, it does not see the bill as adequate, citing the fact that up to 60 million persons will be uninsured by 2007, or 25 percent of the nonelderly population. Finally, on healthcare, the union is supporting measures to maintain medical record confidentiality.

The TWUA is also a strong supporter of public education, and has worked actively to get the Public School Excellence Act passed. This bill would reduce class size, rebuild and modernize 5,000 schools across the country, ensure qualified teachers in the classroom, and promote student activities in their local communities. Also on education, the union is backing the Safe Schools Act, which attempts to cut back on violence in schools. For younger children and working families, the union has backed the Child Care Access Act, a comprehensive child-care package that provides tax relief to low- and middle-income families to help them pay for child care.

On pay and pensions, the union has actively supported bills to increase the minimum wage, alleviate the marriage penalty tax, and address the inequalities in pay for women who do equivalent work. The union is also working to pass the Retirement Accessibility, Security, and Portability Act, which would boost pension coverage and make it easier for employers to offer pension benefits. Finally, the union supports President Bill Clinton's plan to devote much of the budget surplus to maintain Social Security, but questions the privatization component of the president's initiative.

Concerning issues that pertain to TWUA members, the union is working to get the Airport Improvement Program Act passed. This act would make the Federal Aviation Association more independent, which the union says would limit political pressure on the agency from the White House and the Department of Transportation. In addition, the bill would make sure that all of the funds collected by federal aviation taxes would go toward aviation concerns, rather than into the general treasury.

On rail transport, the TWUA supports a plan to allow freight transport on Amtrak's northeast passenger tracks. The move—which would save time and money for the freight carriers, thereby making them more competitive with the trucking industry—would also pour money into Amtrak coffers. With many union members employed by Amtrak and Conrail, the issue is of great concern to the TWUA.

FINANCIAL FACTS

The Transport Workers Union Political Contributions Committee (TWUPCC) is one of the largest political action committees (PACs) of the U.S. labor movement by amount of donation. During the 1995–1996 election cycle, TWUPCC received $454,000 and spent $938,000. This latter figure includes $703,000 in contributions to candidates and parties—$631,363 to Democrats and $57,400 to Republicans.

TWUPCC's receipts, expenditures, and contributions have fluctuated over the past 10 years. Although receipts and expenditures have climbed 25 percent, contributions have grown from $222,000 to $703,000. At the same time, contributions to Democrats have far exceeded those to Republicans, by 11 to 70 times as much.

JAMES CIMENT AND IMMANUEL NESS

Bibliography

TWU Express: Official Organ of the Transport Workers Union of America, CIO. December 1948–1999.

UNION OF NEEDLETRADES, INDUSTRIAL, AND TEXTILE EMPLOYEES

The Union of Needletrades, Industrial, and Textile Employees (UNITE) has a membership of roughly 300,000, out of the over 1.8 million workers in the apparel and textile industries of the United States and Canada. Its members work largely in the apparel and textile industries, but a significant minority are scattered across a host of related and unrelated businesses, including auto parts and auto supplies, millinery shops, shoe factories, glove and tanning businesses, bag and packaging plants, and retail shops. In addition, UNITE represents all 7,000 American and Canadian manufacturing workers at Xerox.

Among the more active unions in North America, UNITE includes well over 1,000 locals, all of whom enjoy considerable autonomy in negotiating and electing their own officers. The international headquarters of UNITE—which is affiliated with the AFL-CIO—is located in New York City, America's garment capital. The international office supports its locals with negotiating and bargaining expertise, as well as providing overall organizing strategy and aid and conducting a legislative program in Washington, D.C.

HISTORY

UNITE is a relatively new union, having formed in 1995 through the merger of the 154,000-member Amalgamated Clothing and Textile Workers Union (ACTWU) and the 145,000-member International Ladies' Garment Workers' Union (ILGWU). Despite its recent origins, UNITE—or more precisely, its predecessor unions—has an illustrious history within the labor movement of this country.

The ILGWU was founded in 1900 in New York City, largely by Jewish, Italian, and other European immigrant workers. Major strikes in 1909 and 1910 against shirtwaist and cloak-maker manufacturers, respectively, won important concessions, including the abolition of exploitive home work schemes, establishment of arbitration procedures, and a six-day workweek, all major accomplishments for labor of that era. At the height of labor activism during the Great Depression, ILGWU president David Dubinsky became instrumental in the formation of the industrially oriented Committee for Industrial Organization—predecessor to the Congress of Industrial Organizations (CIO). In 1938, the ILGWU pulled out of the American Federation of Labor (AFL). Despite Dubinsky's work on the CIO, the union opted to become independent. Two years later, it rejoined the AFL.

The ACTWU, meanwhile, had its origins in the formation of the Amalgamated Clothing Workers of America (ACWA) in 1914, after several New York City locals ended their affiliation with the United Garment Workers Union. Famed labor leader Sidney Hillman became the first president of the new union and brought it into the AFL. During the 1920s, the ACWA became a pioneer in the establishment of cooperative housing and banking for union members. The ACWA broke with the AFL in 1938 to join the CIO. In 1976, the ACWA merged with the Textile Workers Union of America to form the ACTWU. By the end of the century, a larger proportion of its members was made up of first- and second-generation female immigrants from Latin America and East Asia.

ACTIVITIES: CURRENT AND FUTURE

Like other unions, UNITE is active in the political arena concerning legislation that affects workers and the union movement as a whole, as well as concerning issues that directly affect its members.

On issues affecting workers generally, UNITE is actively involved with legislation regarding Social Security, Medicare, and tax cuts for the wealthy. On union

**Union of Needletrades, Industrial, and Textile Employees
Political Action Committee Contributions**

[Bar chart showing PAC contributions by election cycle:
- Democrats: 1987-88 ≈ $365,000; 1993-94 ≈ $307,000; 1997-98 ≈ $347,000
- Republicans: 1987-88 ≈ $28,000; 1993-94 ≈ $7,000; 1997-98 ≈ $14,000]

Data derived from official studies available from the Federal Election Commission, Washington, DC, 1987–1998.

matters, UNITE has been working to protect the right of unions to use union dues for political purposes and opposes both budget cuts and fast-track legislation. Concerning its members, the most important item on UNITE's agenda is sweatshop labor.

On Social Security, UNITE is on record as opposing any efforts to privatize the program, seeing in such moves an effort by Wall Street securities firms to gain a windfall in investment. The union also believes that privatization will jeopardize the financial position of Social Security and thereby the retirement pensions of millions of American workers, noting that two-thirds of American workers rely on Social Security for at least 50 percent of their retirement income. They also point out that the program is quite successful as is, with over 90 percent of elderly Americans now living above the poverty line.

UNITE also opposes moves by Congress to raise the eligibility age for Medicare from 65 to 67, saying that "such a move would dramatically increase the number of older Americans without health insurance, including many older workers whose employers have reduced or eliminated health coverage." It also believes that this would hike the cost of retiree health coverage and cause employers to shift more costs to their retirees or drop coverage completely.

UNITE believes that budget surpluses should go toward assuring the financial future of Social Security and Medicare, as well as increasing social spending, rather than being given away in "tax cuts for the wealthy," as Republicans in Congress propose. A recent Senate bill, the union says, "contained big tax breaks for wealthy individuals and corporations—such as capital gains and estate tax reductions—but new meaningful reductions [in benefits] for working families."

UNITE has also been active on three other issues critical to working people: preventing fast-track legislation that would negate the right of Congress to amend economic treaties negotiated by the executive branch, preventing legislation that would allow employers to pay overtime in compensatory time rather than wage-and-a-half monetary compensation, and pushing for a patients' "bill of rights" that would allow customers of health maintenance organizations to have more control over the kinds of treatments and benefits they receive.

On issues of concern to the organized labor movement, UNITE has been active in three areas: assuring the right of unions to use dues for political purposes, fighting budget cuts at the NLRB, and guaranteeing the continuing right of workers to freely organize into unions. On the first issue, the union opposes the so-called paycheck protection act, which would prevent unions from using union dues for political purposes without the written consent of individual members. This legislation would weaken labor's political muscle, UNITE argues, and "further skew the political balance of power in America against working families." Concerning budget cuts at the NLRB, the union notes that this is a favorite target of conservatives in Congress and that, despite a rising number of complaints by workers, the budget has already been cut by 11 percent since 1992, resulting in ever-longer delays in investigations and remedial action. On the right to organize, UNITE opposes recent legislation banning "salting," whereby union members seek jobs in industry for purposes of organizing. UNITE also opposes shifting the costs of labor investigations from employers to the NLRB and laws that would make single bargaining unit organization more difficult. Unions can negotiate more effectively when united in a single bargaining unit rather than separated in multiple units.

Finally, in an issue of special concern to UNITE members, the union has been out front in the struggle to ban the use of sweatshop workers both in the United States and overseas. Currently, says the union, there are no laws on the books in Washington, D.C., requiring corporations to ensure humane working conditions, respect human rights, or pay a living wage. With sweatshops flourishing both in the United States and abroad, the union says, members' wages experience downward pressure and companies are encouraged to shift production from union shops to sweatshops. Because sweatshop conditions mostly occur in subcontractors' shops, UNITE wants Congress to pass legislation that would make the major-label firms more responsible for the conditions of employment in the shops that provide them with subcontracting work. Besides lobbying Congress, UNITE has organized demonstrations and boycotts against companies that are particularly notorious for this practice.

FINANCIAL FACTS

UNITE's Campaign Committee (UNITE-CC) is among the larger political action committees (PACs) of the U.S. labor movement—by amount of donation—though the amount of money it has contributed over the past dozen or so years has fluctuated greatly. During the 1997–1998 election cycle, UNITE-CC received $878,615 and spent more than $817,000. This latter figure includes $364,000 in contributions to candidates and parties, 95 percent of it to Democrats and 4 percent to Republicans. Contributions to Democrats have exceeded those to Republicans, by 13 to 75 times as much.

There has been a slight decrease in UNITE-CC's receipts, expenditures, and contributions over the past 10 years. Receipts and expenditures have fallen 12 percent, while contributions have slipped from $394,000 to $327,000.

JAMES CIMENT AND IMMANUEL NESS

Bibliography

Tyler, Gus. *Look for the Union Label: A History of the International Ladies' Garment Workers' Union.* Armonk, NY: M.E. Sharpe, 1995.

Union of Needletrades, Industrial, and Textile Employees. "The Phony Social Security Crisis." New York, n.d. Pamphlet.

Union of Needletrades, Industrial, and Textile Employees. "Stop Sweatshops." New York, n.d. Pamphlet.

UNITED AUTOMOBILE WORKERS

Officially known as the United Automobile, Aerospace, and Agricultural Implement Workers of America, the United Automobile Workers—usually referred to as the UAW—is one of the most high-profile unions in America, largely as a result of the importance of the automobile industry to the American economy and to the activism and militancy of the union itself. The UAW—a union affiliated with the AFL-CIO—has about 840,000 members, distributed throughout the following industries: 27 percent in motor vehicle parts, 24 percent in motor vehicle assembly, 10 percent working for independent parts suppliers, 4 percent in aerospace, 4 percent in agricultural implements and machinery, 4 percent in civil service, and 27 percent in a host of other industries from healthcare to clerical to education. Virtually all of the major industries in the automotive and agricultural implements sector have UAW employees, including Ford, General Motors, DaimlerChrysler, AMC, International Harvester, and Deere & Company.

The UAW includes 1,430 locals and maintains over 2,300 collective bargaining agreements. The primary units of union self-government and administration, locals are made up of members organized in bargaining units consisting of one or several employers in a given region. If more than one group is involved in a bargaining unit, the local is referred to as an amalgamated local. Each local has an executive board that runs its affairs on a day-to-day basis. With amalgamated locals, decisions are reached at local joint council meetings. Virtually all UAW locals are organized into 12 regions—four of which are in Michigan, two in Ohio, and the remaining six covering the rest of the United States.

For collective bargaining purposes, the union is divided into nine departments: General Motors, Ford, DaimlerChrysler, aerospace, agricultural implements, competitive shops (that is, independent parts suppliers), heavy trucks, transnationals and joint ventures such as GM-Toyota and Ford-Mazda, and skilled trades and technical, office, and professional. In addition, the UAW maintains departments—under the international president—devoted to different activities of the union. These include arbitration, circulation (keeping track of membership), civil rights, community services, retired workers, conservation and resource development, consumer affairs, education, health and safety, information systems, legal, organizing, public relations and publications, recreation and leisure-time activities, research, Social Security, time study and engineering, women's issues, and the Washington, D.C., office (which handles governmental and international affairs and legislation). In addition, the following departments operate under the leadership of the secretary-treasurer's office: accounting, auditing, purchase and supply, strike insurance, and veterans affairs.

The officers of the UAW, which is headquartered in Detroit, include a president, secretary-treasurer, five vice presidents, and 12 regional directors. Collectively, these officers form the international executive board, which handles the day-to-day affairs of the union and implements policies set at the constitutional convention, held every four years. All UAW officers are also elected at these conventions.

HISTORY

The UAW has one of the most illustrious histories in all of the union movement. Founded during the extraordinary burst of organized labor activism in the 1930s, the union dates back to 1934, when several automobile workers unions chartered by the American Federation of Labor (AFL) met in Detroit and organized the National Council of Automobile Workers Unions. The following year, the AFL granted the UAW a charter but, in the tradition of craft unionism, limited the membership to assembly-line workers. Angry with this limitation, the UAW delegates to the second annual convention in 1936 broke away from the AFL to join

**United Automobile Workers
Political Action Committee Contributions**

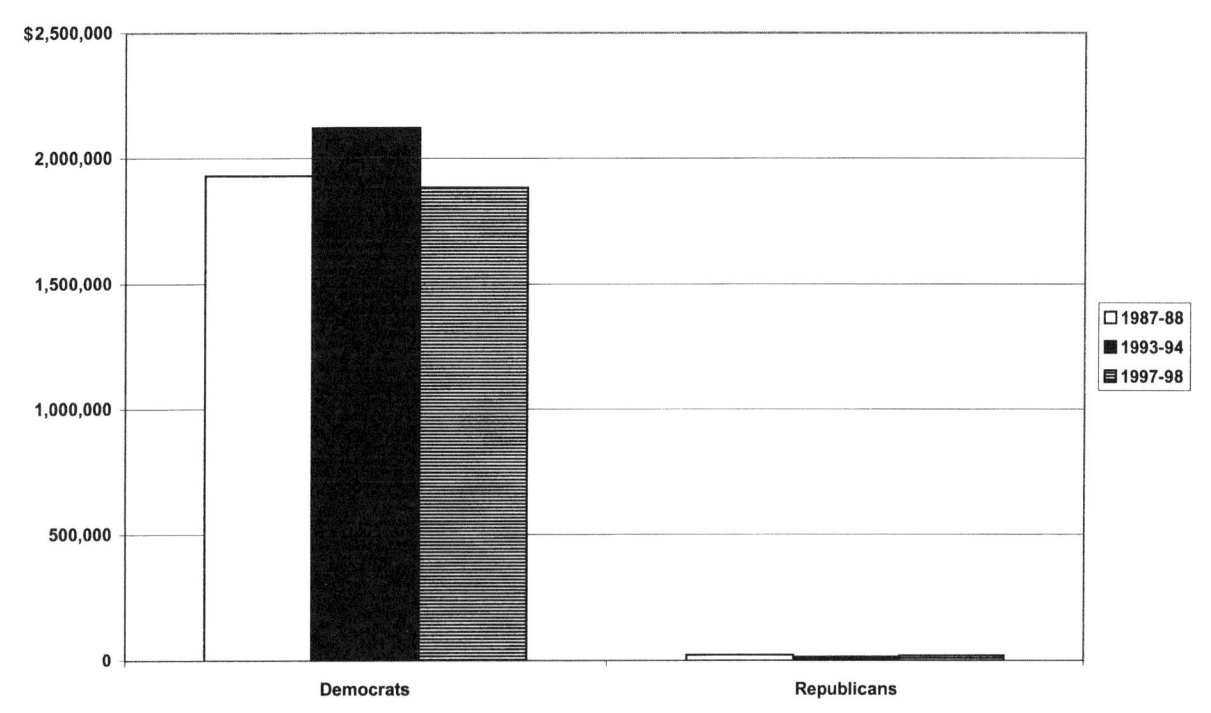

□ 1987-88
■ 1993-94
☰ 1997-98

Data derived from official studies available from the Federal Election Commission, Washington, DC, 1987–1998.

the more radical Committee for Industrial Organization, which was more oriented toward mass organization throughout different industries.

Then began the struggle for employer recognition. In 1937, the UAW struck at Chrysler and General Motors, the latter beginning with a sit-down strike in Flint, where workers refused to leave the factory until management recognized it. Eventually, the union won contracts from both employers. Ford proved a much harder nut to crack, employing all kinds of anti-union tactics, including the hiring of "goons" to violently break up picket lines. With the United States gearing up for the Second World War, the federal government finally put pressure on Ford to recognize the union, which it finally did in 1941.

Following the war, the union engaged in a lengthy strike against General Motors in 1946 over the issue of worker representation on the board of directors. After a devastating multiweek strike, the union backed down, accepting significant wage and benefit increases in lieu of a voice in management. At the same time, the union moved to oust Communists from its ranks during the anti-red hysteria of the period. Walter Reuther, founder and longtime president of the union, also became president of the Congress of Industrial Organizations (CIO) in 1952 and played a major role in the merger of the AFL and CIO in 1955. Political and organizational disagreements with AFL-CIO president George Meany caused Ruether to pull the UAW out of the organization in 1968. The organization later reaffiliated with the AFL-CIO. Reuther died two years later in a plane crash. Seeing its membership diminish with the setbacks to the American automobile industry in the 1970s and 1980s, the UAW began to organize workers outside the industry.

ACTIVITIES: CURRENT AND FUTURE

Because of the diversity of its membership and because it is seen as a trend-setting union on political issues, the UAW's legislative department and Voluntary Community Action Program (VCAP) have been involved in lobbying on a host of issues that affect working Americans generally and the organized labor movement in particular.

Given the global nature of the automobile industry and the fact that the top three automakers have shifted a great number of their assembly facilities to Mexico and other developing countries, the UAW has maintained strong opposition to fast-track legislation that limits the rights of Congress to modify trade treaties negotiated by the president and his trade officials. Indeed, the UAW was key in defeating fast-track legislation in 1997. At the same time, the UAW has supported efforts to prevent undocumented immigrants from entering or staying in the United States, seeing the employment of these persons as potentially leading to lower wages for American workers.

As for federal programs affecting working people, the UAW has made it clear to Congress and the White House that, while it would like to see Social Security and Medicare effectively funded, it does not want either of these programs to undergo any privatization. Moreover, it has actively opposed Republican efforts to cut benefits under the Medicare plan. Ultimately, although the UAW supports paying down the national debt, it does not want this done by sacrificing any of the benefits guaranteed by existing Social Security or Medicare programs. Similarly, the union is actively opposed to the call sounded by some Republicans for a flat tax, seeing in such a change a benefit for wealthier Americans at the expense of persons with more modest incomes. On education, the UAW has actively opposed both vouchers and privatization, seeing both as a threat to the public school system in which many of its members' children receive their education.

The UAW is also involved in legislation dealing with workplace and work-related issues. It has actively opposed the Teamwork for Employees and Management Act, which would overturn the 1935 National Labor Relations Act (NLRA) clause against company unions and change the way overtime is compensated. At the same time, it has opposed Republican efforts to prevent union dues from being used for political action unless members individually approve. This effort, says the union, would undermine organized labor's ability to counter the enormous lobbying efforts of corporate America. At the same time, the UAW opposes efforts to scale back the activities of the Occupational Safety and Health Administration in the areas of inspection and enforcement of workplace regulations. It opposes the so-called SAFE Act, which would establish employer-dominated committees to determine workplace safety—in violation, the union says, of the NLRA.

Finally, because of its large percentage of minority members and its growing number of women members, the UAW has taken an active role in promoting civil rights, including a strong pro–affirmative action position, a strong position on enforcing and expanding protections for women suffering sexual harassment, and advocacy of pay equity for women doing equivalent work in gender-dominated occupations.

FINANCIAL FACTS

The UAW's VCAP represents one of the largest political action committees (PACs) of the labor movement by amount of donation. Indeed, it is one of the largest PACs in Washington, D.C. During the 1995–1996 election cycle, VCAP received $5.1 million and spent nearly $4 million. This latter figure includes $2.5 million in contributions to candidates and parties—$2.4 million to Democrats and $10,975 to Republicans. At the same time, contributions to Democrats far exceeded those to Republicans, by 80 to over 200 times as much.

There has been a dramatic increase in VCAP's receipts, expenditures, and contributions over the past 10 years. Receipts and expenditures have climbed 42 percent, while contributions have grown from $3.1 million to $4 million.

JAMES CIMENT AND IMMANUEL NESS

Bibliography

Asher, Robert, and Ronald Edsforth, with the assistance of Stephen Merlino. *Autowork*. Albany: State University of New York Press, 1995.

Lichtenstein, Nelson. *The Most Dangerous Man in Detroit: Walter Reuther and the Fate of American Labor*. New York: Basic Books, 1995.

United Automobile Workers. *Highlights of the History of Organized Labor and the UAW*. Detroit: United Automobile Workers, 1993.

United Automobile Workers. "UAW Action Program." Detroit, 1998. Pamphlet.

United Automobile Workers. "UAW Resources: A Guide to UAW Services." Detroit, n.d. Pamphlet.

UAW Solidarity. January 1985–1999.

UNITED FOOD AND COMMERCIAL WORKERS INTERNATIONAL UNION

Representing approximately 1 million workers, the United Food and Commercial Workers International Union (UFCW)—a member union of the AFL-CIO—is one of the largest private-sector unions in North America. As its name implies, membership in the union consists mainly of persons working in the food industry. The vast majority of these members work in the food retail industry, largely in the country's major supermarket chains, including Kroger, Safeway, A&P, American Stores, and Giant. In addition, the UFCW represents workers in the meatpacking and food processing industries, including the poultry, beef, fish, frozen vegetable, and condiment industries. These include ConAgra, Swift, Hormel, Heinz, Banquet, Frito-Lay, Kraft, Tyson Foods, Perdue, Butterball, Foster Farms, and Hershey Foods.

Other UFCW members work in a variety of businesses, including healthcare (Kaiser Permanente and Hillhaven), insurance (Prudential, John Hancock, and Metropolitan Life), department stores, garment and textile manufacturing (Levi Strauss, Lee Apparel, and Osh Kosh B'Gosh), fur and leather, shoes, hair care, and distilleries (Molson, Labatt's, Seagram, Jim Beam, Gallo, and Mogen David). Altogether, UFCW workers labor under some 18,000 contracts negotiated by their union.

Headquartered in Washington, D.C., the UFCW has over 500 locals and nine regional offices throughout the United States and Canada. Local unions have responsibility for representing members in negotiating contracts and the administration of collective bargaining agreements. Each local is chartered by the international union, which provides services to, and assures that proper democratic procedures occur, at the local level. The regional offices assist in organizing efforts, negotiating contracts, and coordinating activities among the locals.

The international union is divided into several departments, along with an executive division. The latter consists of the office of the president and the international secretary-treasurer, who oversees four departments: data processing, membership processing, auditing, and accounting. In addition, the international president appoints two officers to oversee organizing and collective bargaining for the nine regions.

Other departments include field services, which supplies to the locals a host of professional and support services related to organizing, collective bargaining, safety and health, education, communications, and research; legislative and political affairs, which deals with political education of members, grassroots political action, voter registration, and lobbying; the Active Ballot Club, which donates money to political campaigns; women's affairs; civil rights and community relations, concerned with minority rights; international and foreign affairs, which coordinates activities with counterpart unions around the world; legal; and personnel and services, providing routine administrative support services for employees of the international, regional offices, and locals.

Finally, aside from representing its own workers, the UFCW has organized the Worker Advocacy Project, which helps nonmembers in the food industry redress grievances through dialogue with employers and, if necessary, legal action.

The UFCW focuses most of its attention on issues concerning labor, the labor movement, and food industries. This includes fighting for higher minimum wage laws, union rights, worker health and safety (a critical issue in the dangerous food-processing industry), and healthcare. With many of its workers in the low-income range, the UFCW has also emphasized a commitment to preserving poverty programs.

HISTORY

The UFCW is a relatively young union, having been formed in 1979 out of a merger of the Retail Clerks International Union and the Amalgamated Meat Cutters and Butcher Workmen of North America, the latter

**United Food and Commercial Workers International Union
Political Action Committee Contributions**

[Bar chart showing PAC contributions for 1987-88, 1993-94, and 1997-98. Democrats received approximately $1,100,000 (1987-88), $1,430,000 (1993-94), and $1,460,000 (1997-98). Republicans received small amounts under $50,000 in each period.]

Data derived from official studies available from the Federal Election Commission, Washington, DC, 1987–1998.

with roots in the late-nineteenth-century union movement. Since that 1979 merger, other unions have joined the UFCW. These include the Barbers, Beauticians, and Allied Industries Associations in 1980; the United Retail Workers in 1981; the Insurance Workers International Union in 1983; the Canadian Brewery, Flour, Cereal, Soft Drink, and Distillery Workers in 1986; the International Union of Life Insurance Agents in 1994; the Retail, Wholesale and Department Store Union in 1994; the United Textile Workers of America in 1995; the Distillery, Wine and Allied Workers in 1995; and the International Chemical Workers Union in 1996. This gradual agglomeration of unions reflects a larger organized labor trend toward union consolidation, even across a diverse spectrum of industries.

ACTIVITIES: CURRENT AND FUTURE

Over the past five years, the UFCW has lobbied Congress (as well as the Canadian Parliament) on a number of critical issues affecting labor and the labor movement.

In the Senate, the UFCW has been active in trying to defeat several bills that it considers deleterious to its members and to the labor movement. The National "Right to Work" Act, the UFCW says, would "destroy labor unions by outlawing any form of collectively bargained union security protection, even when management agrees to it and members vote for it." Specifically, the bill would overturn the section of the National Labor Relations Act of 1935 that gives states the right to determine union security agreements. Union security agreements are more commonly known as "closed-shop" agreements, since they require that all employees of a workplace be members of a union if a majority of those workers vote to join the union in an official certification election. In place of this federal deferment to the states, the National "Right to Work" Act would institute a federal mandate making all such closed-shop agreements illegal in the United States.

Another Senate bill—the Teamwork for Employees and Management Act—has been actively opposed by the UFCW because it would sanction what are popularly known as "employer-controlled" unions. Under the National Labor Relations Act, such unions were effectively banned in the United States. Under the new act, employers would have a right to form such unions, even if an independent union already existed or if employees were in the process of starting or joining an independent union.

Another bill that the UFCW opposed concerned providing the president with "fast-track" power in negotiating economic agreements with foreign countries. (Fast track means that Congress must approve or reject a pact, but cannot revise it.) Implicitly, the defeat of fast track was a defeat of the president's efforts to expand the North American Free Trade Agreement (NAFTA) to include Chile. Like other labor unions, the UFCW sees NAFTA and other such trade agreements as a way to export union jobs to low-wage countries and sidestep laws on wages, worker safety, and environmental protection.

The UFCW has also weighed in on several bills in the Senate—two concerning minimum wage and one concerning healthcare reform. One of the minimum wage acts would allow an exemption for small employers and for workers with less than six months' tenure; the other calls for a simple raise in the minimum wage. The healthcare bill concerns the establishment of medical savings accounts. The UFCW has opposed such accounts since, it said, they "shift costs from employers and insurance companies to workers . . . [and] primarily benefit young, healthy participants at the expense of older people, since young persons' premiums would be substantially lower."

In the House of Representatives, the UFCW was active in opposing several bills, or portions of bills, including legislation intended to prevent the Occupational Safety and Health Administration from investigating and regulating such cumulative trauma disorders as carpal tunnel syndrome, to undermine overtime pay requirements, to allow employers to compensate workers for overtime in nonmonetary ways, to establish medical savings accounts, legislation that would ease federal regulations on nursing homes, to exempt small businesses and short-term employees from the minimum wage, and to permit the continued hiring of foreign nurses on a temporary basis (the UFCW maintains there are enough U.S. nurses to fill any nursing shortage).

Aside from petitioning the Labor Department on matters of organizing, negotiating, and other routine union concerns, the UFCW embarked on a campaign in 1998 to get the Federal Trade Commission (FTC) to investigate Wal-Mart Corporation's "Buy American" advertising program. According to a 180-page report, the use of flags and other patriotic symbols to imply an American source for products sold at the stores is deceptive. The UFCW would like the FTC to investigate and eventually force Wal-Mart to either desist in this allegedly false advertising effort or, better still, to make a policy of actually buying American-made products.

FINANCIAL FACTS

The UFCW supports well-funded and active lobbying efforts, through which it donates substantial sums to congressional and presidential campaigns. During the 1995–1996 political cycle, the Active Ballot Club (ABC) received $3 million and spent nearly $3.2 million. This included $2 million in political donations, of which almost all ($1,993,245) went to Democrats and just $23,050 to Republicans. The UFCW, like virtually all other trade unions, has donated far more to Democrats than to Republicans, by anywhere between 50 and 100 times as much.

There has been a substantial upward trend in ABC donations to political candidates over the past 12 years. Between the 1987–1988 and 1995–1996 political cycles, contributions rose approximately 41 percent. In addition, the Committee on Political Education of the Retail, Wholesale and Department Store Union, a division of the UFCW, has also donated smaller amounts to Democratic candidates. It has also given contributions to Democratic campaigns, largely for get-out-the-vote efforts that encourage supporters to go to the polls.

JAMES CIMENT AND IMMANUEL NESS

Bibliography

UFCW Action. 1979–1999.

United Food and Commercial Workers. "The Professional's Choice." Washington, DC, n.d. Pamphlet.

United Food and Commercial Workers. "UFCW: An Introduction." Washington, DC, n.d. Pamphlet.

United Food and Commercial Workers. "The Voice of Working America." Washington, DC, n.d. Pamphlet.

UNITED STEELWORKERS OF AMERICA

One of the pioneers of twentieth-century industrial unionism, the United Steelworkers of America (USWA) represents approximately 700,000 workers in the steel, aluminum, copper, tin, plastics, rubber, stone, and glass industries. It also represents about 20,000 retail workers in Canada. The union has negotiated approximately 6,300 bargaining agreements that are currently in force. Some 2,600 locals in the United States, Canada, Puerto Rico, and the Virgin Islands are divided into 13 geographic districts, 12 for the United States and its territories and one for Canada, each headed by a director. Locals of the USWA enjoy a great deal of autonomy. Local union officers are elected every three years by their members, and the locals have a great deal of control over grievances, bargaining, health and safety issues, education, civil rights, community service, and volunteer organizing.

The 13 regional directors, the four officers of the international—including the international president, secretary-treasurer, and two vice presidents—the Canadian national director, the executive vice presidents of the rubber plastics division for the United States and for Canada, and the director of the Aluminum, Brick, and Glass division comprise the international executive board, which oversees policy implementation and the day-to-day affairs of the international union, as well as aiding the locals in bargaining, grievances, organizing, and other affairs. These representatives are elected by the members every four years. Much of the union's policy is set at biennial conventions, with delegates chosen by the locals.

Along with the regular divisions that deal with membership, publications and media, legal affairs, legislative and political affairs, organizing, research, and others, the union also includes a special industry conference for the rubber and plastic workers, who were absorbed into the union in 1995.

Although the union's legislative affairs department deals with a host of issues connected to working people and the labor movement generally, the key legislative item it consistently pushes concerns trade, specifically alleged dumping of cheap foreign steel on the American market, which the union wants the federal government to stop.

HISTORY

The origins of the USWA go back to 1876, with the founding of the Amalgamated Association of Iron, Steel, and Tin Workers. After the USWA was founded in Pittsburgh on June 17, 1936—it was originally named the Steel Workers Organizing Committee (SWOC)—it absorbed the Amalgamated. The establishment of the SWOC was part of the national struggle for industrial unions, launched in part by United Mine Workers president John L. Lewis, who believed that the time had come to organize semiskilled and unskilled laborers across entire industries, an idea discounted at the time by the craft-oriented American Federation of Labor. The SWOC became the core union within the Committee for Industrial Organization, founded in 1935. United States Steel, the largest company in the industry, recognized the SWOC as a bargaining agent in 1937.

The organization was a major union from the beginning, changing its name to the United Steel Workers of America in 1942. Two years later, it absorbed the 45,000-member Aluminum Workers of America. In 1967, it took in the 40,000-member International Union of Mine, Mill, and Smelter Workers, which represented copper- and other metalworkers. Over the years, other unions have joined, including the 20,000-member United Stone and Allied Product Workers of America in 1971; District 50, Allied and Technical Workers (a former unit of the United Mine Workers, with 172,000 members) in 1972; the 35,000-member Upholsterers International Union of North America in 1985; the 25,000-member Retail, Wholesale, and Department Store Union of Canada in 1993; the 90,000-

**United Steelworkers of America
Political Action Committee Contributions**

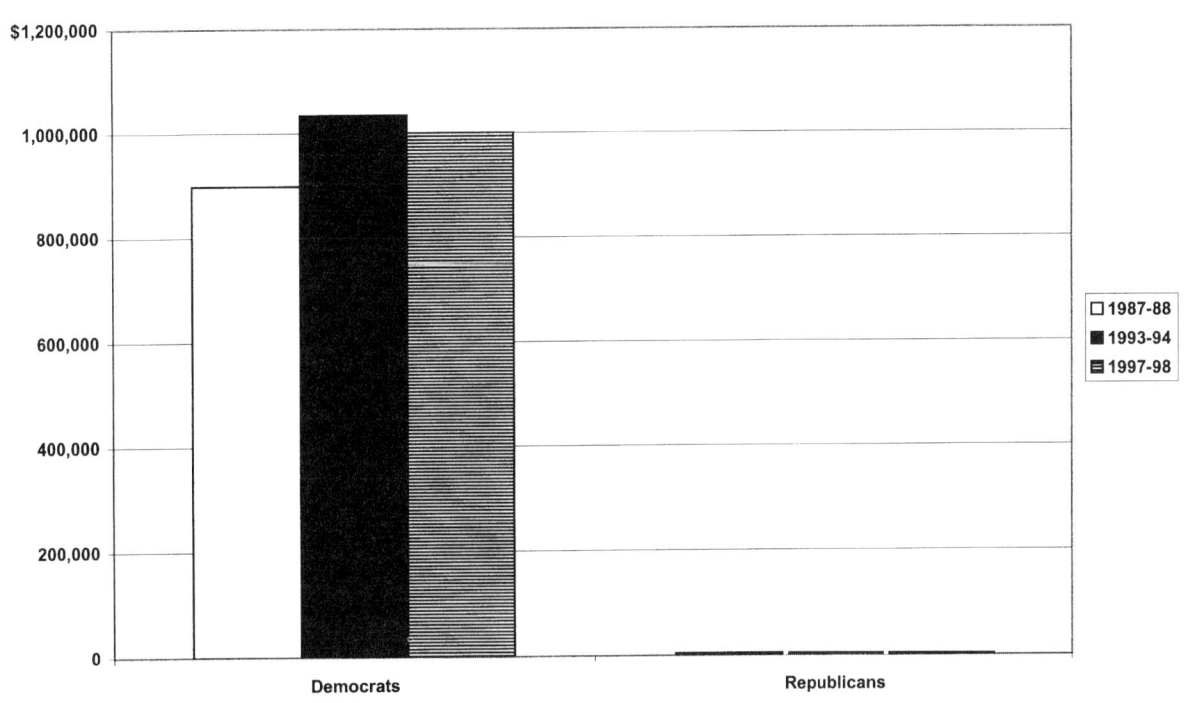

[Bar chart showing contributions to Democrats (approximately $900,000 in 1987-88; $1,040,000 in 1993-94; $1,010,000 in 1997-98) and minimal contributions to Republicans across all three periods.]

Data derived from official studies available from the Federal Election Commission, Washington, DC, 1987–1998.

member United Rubber, Cork, Linoleum, and Plastic Workers of America in 1995; and the 40,000-member Aluminum, Brick, and Glass Workers International Union in 1997.

In 1973, the union and representatives of the major steel companies negotiated the pathbreaking Experimental Negotiating Agreement, designed to eliminate the pattern in which the steel companies would work overtime to build up inventories in preparation for strikes. In exchange for a no-strike clause, the companies agreed to submit unresolved disputes to arbitration. However, the decline of the steel industry in the 1980s saw new stresses placed on the industry, and a major loss of membership in the union.

ACTIVITIES: CURRENT AND FUTURE

As noted above, the number-one issue for the USWA concerns quotas on foreign steel imported into the United States. In years past, the union has worked to get Congress and the president to set quotas on the amount of steel imported from Asia and Brazil, in particular. Recently, the union has expressed growing concern about the import of cheap steel from Russia. The USWA wants the federal government to include Russia in a comprehensive global agreeneent on steel import quotas. According to union officials, "Instead of using his authority to commence a comprehensive agreement by self-initiating a Section 201 filing [that is, the existing legal mandate for such a measure], the President is using it to cut deals country by country, product by product. That simply won't work." The union contends that as many as 20,000 jobs are at stake over Russian imports.

Meanwhile, the union has expressed support for the Commerce Department's determinations—in a joint case filed by the union and American steel companies—concerning alleged dumping of underpriced hot-rolled, flat-rolled, carbon-quality steel products imported from Brazil and Japan. "These preliminary antidumping margins on imports of hot-rolled steel products from Japan and Brazil confirm what we have said about steel dumping in the U.S. market," says the union. "The unfairly traded steel is taking the jobs of American steelworkers and threatening to destroy their communities."

At the same time, the USWA has made its opposition to the North American Free Trade Agreement (NAFTA) known by initiating, along with the Made in the USA Foundation—an institute founded in 1989 and sponsored by a number of unions to support American-made products—a federal lawsuit challenging the constitutionality of the agreement. Specifically, says USWA president George Becker, NAFTA did not receive the constitutionally mandated two-thirds Senate vote. The government maintains that it was not a treaty—which would require such a majority—but an international economic agreement. The USWA opposes NAFTA because it believes it has led to the import of cheap Mexican steel, costing thousands of American steel industry jobs.

FINANCIAL FACTS

The United Steelworkers of America Political Action Fund (USWAPAC) is one of the largest political action committees (PACs) of the U.S. labor movement by amount of donation. During the 1997–1998 election cycle, the USWAPAC received $1.95 million and spent nearly $1.92 million. This latter figure includes $1.1 million in contributions to candidates, 99 percent of it going to Democrats. Contributions to Democrats have far exceeded those to Republicans, by several hundred times as much. Indeed, in some years, the USWAPAC has given no money at all to Republican candidates.

While receipts into the USWAPAC have been relatively stable over the past 12 years, there has been a dramatic increase in its contributions to candidates, reflecting a unionwide trend toward greater participation in the political process at the federal level. While receipts have been increased by just over $100,000, contributions have grown from $1.56 million to $1.92 million.

JAMES CIMENT AND IMMANUEL NESS

Bibliography

Clark, Paul F., Peter Gottlieb, and Donald Kennedy, eds. *Forging a Union of Steel: Philip Murray, SWOC and the United Steelworkers*. Ithaca, NY: International Labor Review Press, 1987.

Steelabor: The Voice of the United Steelworkers of America. January 1979–1999.

United Steelworkers of America. "News from the Steel Workers." Pittsburgh, 1998. Pamphlet.

UNITED TRANSPORTATION UNION

The United Transportation Union (UTU) represents approximately 125,000 active and retired railroad, bus, and mass transit workers in the United States and Canada. Most of its workers are involved in 45 metropolitan and regional, as well as national, transport systems, including Amtrak. Headquartered in Cleveland, the UTU is affiliated with the AFL-CIO and includes more than 700 locals across North America. Most of the union's members are drawn from the operating crafts in the railroad industry, including conductors, brakemen, switchmen, locomotive engineers, hostelers, yardmasters, and ground service personnel. In addition, the union includes some 8,000 workers in the bus industry, including drivers, mechanics, and workers in related occupations. Recently, the UTU moved to merge with the Brotherhood of Locomotive Engineers.

The UTU's international headquarters houses the following departments: bus, general secretary and treasurer, legal, legislative, membership services, public relations, research, tax, Transportation Political Education League (its main lobbying and campaign fund-raising arm), insurance, and yardmasters. The international offers general policies and provides services for the locals, which are largely autonomous. A quadrennial convention helps set overall union policy and elects officers.

As its name implies, the UTU is actively involved in transport issues and is a strong supporter of more funding for rapid transit. Safety is also a primary concern for the union, and it is active in promoting regulations for safer rail transport and highways. Over the years, the UTU was instrumental in the formation of two quasi-public transportation companies—Amtrak and Conrail.

HISTORY

The origins of the UTU go back to the late nineteenth century and the formation of the four main component unions that merged to create the UTU in 1968. The first was the Order of Railway Conductors. This union began when a small group of Illinois Central conductors moved to form a brotherhood in 1868. Ten years later, the brotherhood adopted the name Order of Railway Conductors of America at its convention. In 1907, the union achieved its first major legislative victory, when it helped convince Congress to limit to 16 the number of hours in a day that a conductor could work. It was also instrumental in winning passage of the eight-hour day for railroad workers in 1916. During the Second World War, the union absorbed the Order of Sleeping Car Conductors, and in 1954 the union changed its name to the Order of Railway Conductors and Brakemen to reflect the fact that the union had been accepting the latter as members for over 20 years.

The second component union—the Brotherhood of Locomotive Firemen and Enginemen (BLFE)—began in 1873 in Port Jervis, New York. Within two years, it had 900 members in 31 lodges. The union was briefly led by future Socialist presidential candidate Eugene Debs in the 1880s. Because of the conservative, craft-oriented nature of the union, Debs went on to form the radical American Railway Union, which organized members on an industrial basis. (Rather than representing skilled workers exclusively on the basis of craft, industrial unions organize all workers in a company, irrespective of skill or craft.) Although the BLFE experienced slow but steady growth through the First World War, it lost members in the conservative 1920s and the Depression years of the 1930s.

The largest of the component unions of the UTU—the Brotherhood of Railroad Trainmen (BRT)—was founded in 1883. Within three years, its membership had swollen to 8,000 members in some 244 lodges. Like the other component unions, the BRT was a conservative, craft-oriented union, with a mission to improve the conditions and wages of its members without involving itself in larger politics. In 1933, it began to organize interstate bus workers. It reached its peak mem-

**United Transportation Union
Political Action Committee Contributions**

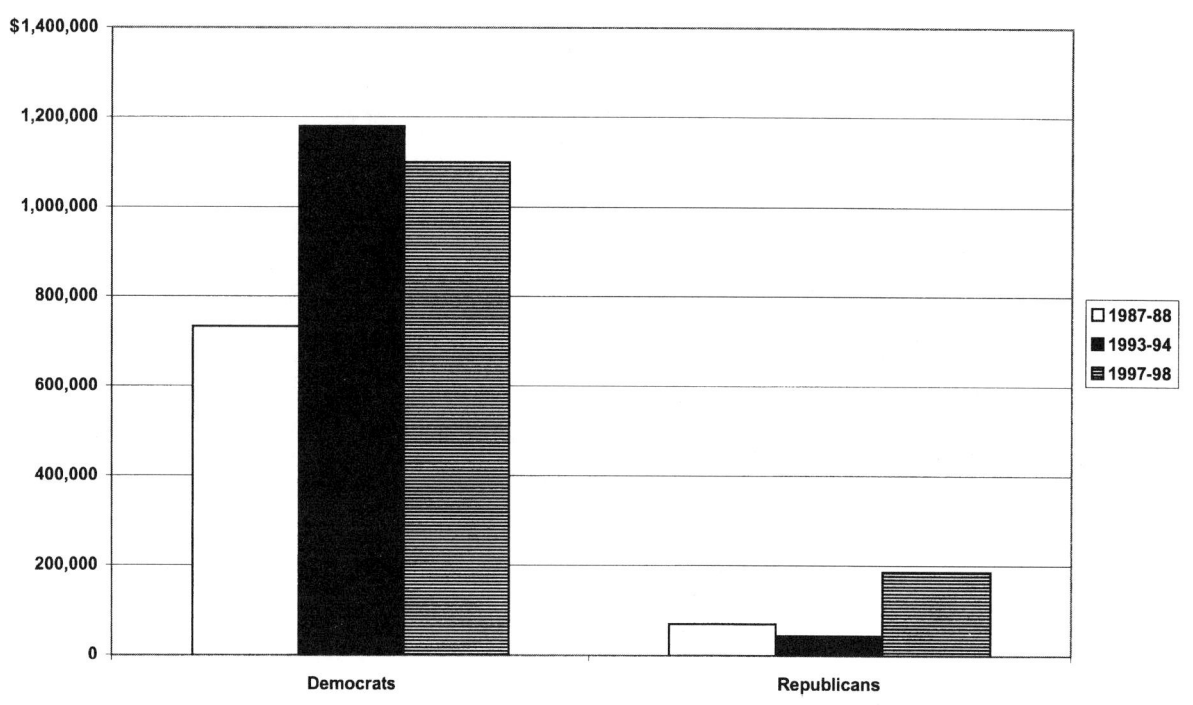

Data derived from official studies available from the Federal Election Commission, Washington, DC, 1987–1998.

bership in 1956, with about 220,000 members. In 1967, it became affiliated with the AFL-CIO. The last and smallest of the component unions of the UTU was the Switchmen's Union of North America, which was formed in Kansas City in 1894.

ACTIVITIES: CURRENT AND FUTURE

Like most other unions, the UTU is involved in a host of legislative issues of concern to working people across America. The UTU is strongly opposed to privatizing Social Security and is against various anti-union measures being pushed by the Republicans in Congress, including measures to limit overtime pay and to block the use of union dues for political activities without the written consent of individual members.

The UTU is also closely monitoring rapid transit funding and has consistently pushed for money to be shifted from support of highways to public transportation. Of particular concern has been the Amtrak Reform and Accountability Act and various Amtrak appropriation bills, all of which involve steep cuts in the national passenger rail transport system. According to the UTU, these actions—which are being led by Republican senators—would affect service, jobs, and especially pensions: "[They] could have a catastrophic effect on our railroad retirement system. The loss of 23,000 people paying into railroad retirement could bankrupt the fund and cause all railroad employees in the United States to have their pensions in jeopardy."

FINANCIAL FACTS

The UTU's Transportation Political Education League (TPEL) represents one of the larger political action committees (PACs) of the U.S. labor movement by amount of donation. During the 1995–1996 election cycle, the TPEL received more than $2.5 million and spent nearly as much. Expenditures during the 1995–1996 cycle included over $1.25 million in contributions to candidates and parties—over $1 million to Democrats and just under $200,000 to Republicans. Contributions to Democrats have far exceeded those to Republicans, six to 30 times as much.

There has been a dramatic increase in TPEL's receipts, expenditures, and contributions over the past 10 years. Receipts and expenditures have climbed about 35 percent, while contributions have increased from $803,835 in 1987–1988 to more than $1.25 million in 1995–1996.

JAMES CIMENT AND IMMANUEL NESS

Bibliography

United Transportation Union. *Constitution*. Cleveland: United Transportation Union, 1995.

United Transportation Union. *Getting a Message to Congress*. Cleveland: United Transportation Union, n.d.

United Transportation Union. *A History of the United Transportation Union and the American Labor Movement*. Cleveland: United Transportation Union, n.d.

United Transportation Union. *Transportation Occupation Handbook*. Cleveland: United Transportation Union, n.d.

UTU News. 1969–1999.

SECTION NINE
CIVIL AND HUMAN RIGHTS

For as long as there have been elected officials and policy-making institutions in American society, there have been interest groups seeking influence. As early as 1757, groups of merchants sought to influence George Washington's bid for office by trading liquor for votes. Thirty-one years later, James Madison penned the classic "Federalist No. 10," which addressed how a well-devised government can and should "break and control the violence of faction." During the next century, agricultural and labor organizations were formed in an effort to protect the economic bedrock of the nation and those who provide it, and professional associations began to proliferate. The event that galvanized and served to forecast the future power of organized interests, however, was the 1896 presidential election of William McKinley. In that contest, McKinley, a Republican, shored up the support of corporate America while his opponent, William Jennings Bryan, procured the support of labor and agricultural groups. Outspending Bryan 20-to-1, McKinley easily secured the White House.

Despite early attempts to control the influence of interests groups (most notably, the 1907 Tilman Act, a campaign finance law), it was clear by the turn of the century that organization was the key to influence and access in American government. Equally clear, however, was the advantage held by financially secure organizations. As Kay Lehman-Scholzman and John Tierney demonstrate in their 1986 book, *Organized Interests and American Democracy,* corporate, trade, and business interest groups have historically eclipsed all other categories. What this means is that the majority of these interest groups have had the organizational capacity, financial security, and—importantly—legitimacy in the eyes of government to protect and expand their interests. Civil, economic, and human rights groups, on the other hand, have historically been marginalized. Shut out from the political system, economically disenfranchised, and incapable of effectively organizing, such groups found it difficult to articulate, much less pursue, an agenda. What further distinguishes these latter groups from all others is that they have endeavored to change attitudes and behavior to end discrimination. As such, civil, economic, and human rights interest groups have struggled to establish and articulate their interests. The great difficulty facing such groups is that they have had to battle a culture that attaches a great value to capitalism, majority rule, and the status quo.

CIVIL RIGHTS, ECONOMIC RIGHTS, AND HUMAN RIGHTS INTEREST GROUPS

This section profiles nine organizations and is divided among civil rights, economic rights, and human rights groups. The civil rights groups selected for inclusion in this anthology include the American Civil Liberties Union (ACLU), the Anti-Defamation League (ADL), and the League of Women Voters (LWV). The economic groups include the Association of Community Organizations for Reform Now (ACORN), Legal Services Corporation (LSC), and the National Coalition for the Homeless. The human rights organizations are Freedom House, Human Rights Watch (HRW), and the National Lawyers Guild (NLG).

The two questions that merit immediate attention are (1) Why are these three categories of groups unified under one section? and (2) Why are these nine groups in particular useful to our understanding of interest group activities? The answer to the first question is that civil, economic, and human rights groups share a commitment to establishing a foundation for the protection of fundamental rights. Whereas civil rights groups typically operate on a domestic-policy plane, human rights groups seek to further similar rights globally. These rights generally include free speech, free press, and assembly rights; ethnic, racial, labor, and religious rights; as well as a host of sociopolitical rights, including governmental benefits, welfare, and freedom from exploitation. Importantly, one of the common denominators of the underrepresentation, exploitation, and denial of rights such groups seek to prevent is economic discrimination. Thus, economic interest groups are not meant to include those organizations representing corporate interests, but those representing the economic underclass. Economic interest groups exist, therefore, to provide a voice for the poor and the powerless, whose members disproportionately overlap other characteristics (e.g., ethnic, sexual, and racial) of "minority" groups broadly defined. In short, the logical interconnection here is that civil and economic rights are human rights.

The answer to the second question is more complex if for no other reason than that it runs the risk of revealing the sin of omission. The nine groups profiled in this section are by no means the only ones relevant to inquiry. They do, however, nicely represent the balance of unity and diversity that characterizes civil, economic, and human rights organizations.

The civil rights organizations, for example, share as their common denominator a commitment to securing equal protection under the law for persons and groups subjected to discriminatory governmental policies. The bases of discrimination relevant to these groups are generally the same as have been relevant to American civil rights law: ethnic, racial, religious, and sexual discrimination. What separates civil rights as a category from identity groups in particular, though, is the democratic equivalence between rights. The American Civil Liberties Union, for example, deliberately avoids issue or group favoritism; rather, it seeks to establish and protect the basic civil liberties and civil rights of even the most controversial groups in American society (e.g., the Ku Klux Klan and neo-Nazis). In a similar fashion the Anti-Defamation League has become a champion of a variety of marginalized groups and issues despite its primary dedication to eradicating anti-Semitism. Importantly, such groups as the Anti-Defamation League recognize the interconnectedness of rights—that it is difficult and not particularly relevant to separate ethnic and religious discrimination. More useful, the organization believes, is an approach that advances the cause of both ethnic and religious tolerance for the population of the country as a whole. By contrast, the League of Women Voters is, by definition, gender-specific. Although it was built on the foundation of the suffrage movement, the league has become increasingly sensitive to the need for a gender-neutral approach to women's rights. Absent the galvanizing force of institutionalized sex discrimination pervasive prior to ratification of the Nineteenth Amendment, for example, the league has become more broadly committed to participatory democracy. This was apparent in the group's support for the National Voter Registration Act (the so-called Motor Voter Bill) and in its present commitment to children's welfare, gun control, campaign finance reform, and healthcare reform.

The economic rights interest groups included in this section represent two national organizations that began as grassroots movements and one that was created by the government in order to provide a legal voice for the economic underclass. Although the literature on "economic" interest groups is large, the literature pertaining to "economic *rights*" is relatively sparse. While business, corporate, and labor groups share space under the rubric of the former, the latter concept is dedicated, in many respects, to what author Michael Harrington termed "the other America" in his book by the same name (*The Other America*, 1962). This "other" America has, by virtue of its financial status, been systematically denied property rights, government benefits, voting rights, legal representation, and political representation. The purpose of ACORN, the National Coalition for the Homeless, and the Legal Services Corporation has been to establish and protect such rights as fundamental. The great difficulty, however, is that these rights have been pushed so far to the periphery of American politics that even the most basic acts of conventional political activity—voting, organizing, letter writing—are difficult to accomplish. And with the prevalent attitude of "blaming the victim" in American society, there is rather little public or political support for the impoverished. Unlike race, gender, and ethnicity, the common argument is that individuals can do something about being poor, thereby absolving the government of responsibility for economic inequality. Consequently, while the government does fund the Legal Services Corporation's efforts to provide legal representation in civil legal proceedings, ACORN has frequently had to engage in nonconventional political action in order to present its case, while the National Coalition for the Homeless enlists both currently and formerly homeless persons in its mission to attract attention to the plight of the economic underclass.

Finally, the human rights organizations include three

groups committed to social and political rights worldwide. Unlike Amnesty International (founded and headquartered in London, England), which is, perhaps, the most recognizable human rights group, Freedom House, Human Rights Watch, and the National Lawyers Guild are all American interest groups. The distinguishing characteristic of these interest groups is that they are not group specific, but issue specific. Their efforts involve domestic politics, but their major cause is to effect change globally. First and foremost, these changes involve the observance of basic human rights. To the National Lawyers Guild and Human Rights Watch, this entails research, pressure, and the utilization of legal machinery to hold those who violate civil and political rights accountable. To Freedom House, human rights are furthered not only through humanitarian and social justice campaigns, but through the creation of free market economies throughout the world. As the entries in this section illustrate, the core issues of human rights remain largely invariant while the methods of operation and policy priorities of different organizations tend to vary.

HISTORICAL CONTEXT

Although "Federalist No. 10" and even the most recent federal elections leave the impression that interest groups are a ubiquitous element of American politics, it must be understood that such groups do not simply and spontaneously spring into existence. On the contrary, as political scientist David Truman observed almost 40 years ago, there are events that trigger the creation and behavior of groups. And, as more contemporary scholars have argued, in addition to responding to a disturbance in the social and political system, it is necessary to develop leadership. The significance of leadership is that it serves to unify, coordinate, and motivate members of a group to articulate and accomplish a goal. In three instances in particular, the relationship between leadership, clout, and success can be attributed in no small part to the charisma, determination, and diligence of the organizations' founders. ACORN, for example, was originally planned to be a local extension of the then-powerful National Welfare Rights Organization. Under Wade Rathke, the Little Rock, Arkansas, division successfully overcame key gaps in class, race, and economic status in order to create the economic and social justice organization then known as the Arkansas Community Organization for Reform Now. On the civil rights front, in 1913, Sigmound Livingston formed the Anti-Defamation League by dedicating two members of his law office staff and $2,000 in the aftermath of the lynching of Leo Frank in Marietta, Georgia. Frank, a Jew, was wrongly accused of killing a 14-year-old girl, and taken from jail by an angry mob who hanged him after his sentence was commuted to life in prison. Within the first years of its existence, the Anti-Defamation League successfully lobbied the White House to delete anti-Semitic language in military training manuals. It persuaded Henry Ford to cease publication of *The Protocols of the Elders of Zion,* an anti-Semitic Russian publication based on European stereotypes of Jewish people cultivated since medieval times. The publication was run in serial form in the *Dearborn Independent*. Ford later publicly apologized. Extending into the realm of human rights, Eleanor Roosevelt was instrumental in the founding and operations of Freedom House in 1941. Just as her profound commitment to genuine democracy prompted her support for women's rights, thereby making her the League of Women Voters' most prominent member, it also engaged her in the movement to support democratization abroad. Specifically, with Freedom House, Eleanor Roosevelt was committed to American leadership in promoting democracy, economic (free market) reform, and respect for human rights wherever tyranny from the far left and the far right was perceived to exist. Due in no small part to Roosevelt's stellar reputation and political connections, the organization has gathered accolades and support from luminaries ranging from Winston Churchill to President Bill Clinton.

While historical events and notable individuals can do much to stimulate support for an organization's activities, they alone are insufficient for long-term success. The political and social systems must create an environment conducive to the acquisition of interest group goals. For rights-based groups, this environment emerged during the 1960s and 1970s. The reasons for this are twofold. First, the civil rights movement was salient throughout the 1950s and 1960s. During this time period, community activism, civil disobedience, and social movements were viewed as necessary avenues for social change. Because such actions occurred in the streets rather than in the election booths, American society was confronted with a flurry of activities structured around a single theme: civil rights and social justice. By entering the discursive terrain, rights groups became a more potent force to be reckoned with. Second, the doctrinal changes in judicial decisions and civil rights legislation during the 1950s and 1960s provided the legal foundation for groups to identify and fight for rights. Importantly, many of the major legal changes of the time owe their origin to interest group action. Therefore, it should come as no surprise that, although all three of the economic rights groups profiled in this section emerged since 1970, only one human rights group and none of the civil rights groups profiled in this section emerged since the 1960s. Indeed, a deliberate attempt has been made in this section to profile the most durable and groundbreaking organizations—the ones that created the opportunity for others to emerge.

By fighting the legal, political, and social systems and winning, a variety of interest groups created space for new groups to address old problems. The ACLU, for example, was founded in 1920 as a public interest law firm dedicated exclusively to civil liberties and civil rights cases. At that time, the federal and state governments had a poor reputation for protecting such rights. Even the United States Supreme Court at the time devalued individual and group rights in pursuit of economic due process. This hostile environment created the social need for an organization such as the ACLU. Based on the notion that the courts are, in theory, the guardians of individual rights and that the Constitution articulates and demands respect for such rights, the ACLU began what would become the most prolific judicial track record of any interest group in history.

In a similar fashion, the National Lawyers Guild was formed in 1936 as an alternative to the all-white, generally antilabor American Bar Association. As the nation's first integrated bar association, it basically sought to expand ACLU-type activities worldwide. By addressing racial, ethnic, and economic discrimination in America and abroad (including participation in the Nuremberg trials), the National Lawyers Guild also became the nation's first human rights interest group.

The economic rights groups, however, did not flourish until the 1960s and 1970s. Although the Supreme Court was deeply interested in economic issues during the first 30 years of the twentieth century, it was not particularly interested in discrimination against the economic underclass. In many respects, indigents constituted the expendable segment of society—they were powerless and poorly organized, and seldom participated in politics. In the strategic environment that defined politics, it was unwise for politicians to represent them. In a capitalist society, it was generally acceptable to ignore them. Since the civil rights movement of the 1960s, however, it has become increasingly clear that discrimination has an economic dimension. This reality, coupled with Michael Harrington's *The Other America*, compelled American government and society to address its commitment to social welfare. An important consequence of this critical introspection was the creation of the Legal Services Corporation.

While grassroots economic rights organizations had to struggle to gain exposure, acceptance, and influence, the Legal Services Corporation was created by the government in 1974 in order to provide civil legal protection and assistance to those who, according to national poverty guidelines, could not afford adequate legal services. The Legal Services Corporation is a restricted organization: it is almost exclusively judicial in nature, limited to civil claims, dependent upon the Congress for annual appropriations, and particularly susceptible to partisan transformations in government. Despite these restrictions, the Legal Services Corporation presently manages a $300 million budget. Conversely, ACORN, with 120,000 members and offices nationwide, and the National Coalition for the Homeless—both of which came into existence in order to represent the interests of the economic underclass—rely on private support to finance their operations. As such, their activities are more broadly based and, indeed, often include nonconventional political activity such as rallies, demonstrations, and the like.

THE CURRENT CONTEXT

Membership and Money

In their book, *Interest Groups in American Campaigns: The New Face of Electioneering* (1999), political scientists Mark Rozell and Clyde Wilcox delineate the strategic context of interest group activities. Based on legal restrictions, resources, and the goals of organizations, there exists an opportunity structure for interest groups to influence the political process. Although legal restrictions such as lobbying activity, political action committee (PAC) activity, and fidelity to Internal Revenue Service (IRS) tax status apply to all groups without prejudice, it is more difficult for civil, economic, and human rights interest groups to form because of their relatively disadvantaged resource base. Specifically, groups that represent the poor, such as the National Coalition for the Homeless, have a considerably smaller resource base than, say, the American Medical Association.

In addition to the disparity that exists in raw dollar amounts, the methods by which "rights-based" interest groups procure and spend money deviates substantially from professional groups as well. Whereas professional interest groups routinely maintain PACs to raise and spend money for political campaigns, rights-based interest groups rely primarily on individual contributions and grants to finance nonelectoral campaigns. Of course, a broad membership base means more individual contributions. As such, an organization's first order of business is gathering members. The core of support for such groups stems from the social movements that spawned the groups' existence in the first place; therefore, most groups maintain a cadre of extremely loyal and dedicated members. The extension of that inner circle, however, then includes those with the most to give in terms of ideological support, but typically the least to give in terms of financial support. The premium, therefore, is placed upon developing methods of reaching out to individuals who support—both ideologically and financially—the organization.

Regarding such outreach efforts, the one strategy common to these interest groups is that they all maintain a stellar commitment to the development of educational programs. Ranging from Internet sites to pamphlets, books, and public lectures, the cornerstone of their activities is information. While information is necessary in pursuit of policy goals, it is also vitally important to the quest for members, who, in turn, finance the operations of the organizations. Given that only one group included in this section maintains a leadership PAC, and only one is government financed, the significance of membership drives, public education campaigns, and grassroots activities cannot be overstated.

The citizen-centered character of these groups is reflected by their financial and tax status. Five of the interest groups included in this analysis are 501(c)(3) nonprofit organizations; two are 501(c)(4) (organizations that are engaged in public service and are therefore not taxed) with 501(c)(3) foundations; one is a 501(c)(4) organization with an affiliated leadership PAC; and another is a government corporation. As a government corporation, the Legal Services Corporation receives most of its money (minus some matching dollars from state and local grants) from congressional appropriations. Its budget for fiscal year 1999—$300 million—eclipses those of other rights-based interest groups. The ACLU, for example, maintains 275,000 active members and has an operating budget of $37 million. Human Rights Watch and Freedom House have fewer individual members, but still maintain multimillion-dollar budgets that reflect substantial contributions from charitable causes and prominent foundations. The National Lawyers Guild's 5,000 members contribute to the organization's budget through a graduated dues program. With consideration given to the type of law practiced and the level of accomplishment in the legal community, individual members basically pay dues on the basis of their ability to do so. Still other groups, such as the National Coalition for the Homeless, operate on an annual budget of only $500,000. With a membership list that actually includes segments of the homeless population, and with individual contributions accounting for 51 percent of the organization's total budget, the reasons for seeking foundation grants and corporate contributions are obvious.

The Institutional Capacity to Achieve Goals

Money and membership are obviously a significant part of an interest group's resource base. But equally important to a group's survival and effectiveness are the less easily quantifiable resources of skill, experience, organization, and specialization of labor. All told, a resource base accounts for what interest groups do and how well they do it.

The interest groups included in this section are all highly professionalized. With the exception of the Legal Services Corporation, whose officers are appointed by the president and confirmed by the Senate, each group is governed by a board of directors and managed internally by officers. Furthermore, each organization maintains a permanent, professional staff reflecting substantive and regional expertise, plus a number of affiliates. Organizations such as the ACLU and the National Lawyer's Guild, for example, maintain professional staffs including attorneys, but a substantial amount of their work is done through attorneys affiliated with—but not permanently employed by—the organization. Organizations such as Freedom House and Human Rights Watch maintain a similar division of labor, matching expertise to issues internationally. As such, many of the internationally oriented interest groups rely on coordinated activities among linguistic, scholarly, and legal experts operating in the field, in research divisions, and in public awareness campaigns.

All of the organizations maintain regional offices, with civil and economic rights interest groups operating almost exclusively on the domestic front, while human rights groups operate internationally. The National Coalition for the Homeless, ACORN, the ACLU, the Legal Services Corporation, and the League of Women Voters operate between 269 (LSC) and 1,100 (LWV) state and local organizations nationwide, while the Anti-Defamation League operates 30 satellite offices, including divisions in Jerusalem and Vienna, outside its New York headquarters. Although the ADL is a national civil rights interest group, its mission of identifying and ending ethnic discrimination in general and anti-Semitism in particular has taken on an international agenda. Conversely, the economic rights interest groups operate at the grassroots level throughout the country. The NCH and ACORN operate 600 and 500 state and local chapters, respectively, and seek to coordinate common activities among regional divisions. While regional divisions inevitably favor their own communities' issues, they do routinely participate in massive voter registration drives, "get out the vote" drives, and demonstrations.

In the realm of human rights, Freedom House and Human Rights Watch both maintain U.S. headquarters and a number of international headquarters. Given its historically central/eastern European focus and its goal of stimulating democracy and free-market economic development abroad, Freedom House currently operates divisions in Bucharest, Budapest, and Kiev. Human Rights Watch, on the other hand, currently operates in 10 locations, including New York, Washington, D.C., Brussels, Hong Kong, London, Los Angeles, Moscow, Rio de Janeiro, Saigon, and Tbilisi. Both Freedom House and Human Rights Watch maintain a number of regional and substantive divisions as well. These substantive divisions include, but are not limited to, religious persecution, the rights of women and children, academic freedom, the freedom of information, and the proliferation of hate groups.

ISSUES, ACTIVITIES, STRATEGIES, AND GOALS

What distinguishes the individual organizations featured in this section are the methods by which they seek to accomplish their goals. However, there are certain activities common to all groups. All of the groups included in this section maintain Internet sites in order to attract new members and inform existing ones of their current activities. For the same general purpose, all produce and distribute pamphlets, press releases, and issue-specific informational materials. Such materials range from the generic "who we are and what we do" pamphlets to well-developed and highly respected scholarly publications and official government documents.

Among the most notable publications produced by rights-based groups are those developed by Freedom House. In addition to a host of issue-specific periodicals (*Freedom Monitor, The First Freedom,* and *NGO News,* for example), Freedom House also publishes two major, original research books: *Freedom in the World* and *Nations in Transition*. Both books are widely read by academics, activists, and government officials; indeed, *Freedom in the World* has become a primary reference book for the Department of Immigration and Naturalization Services.

In a similar fashion, both the Anti-Defamation League and the ACLU publish a variety of books on subjects ranging from right-wing extremism (e.g., *Danger on the Right,* by the ADL) to contemporary applications of individual rights (e.g., the ACLU's 21-part *Rights Of . . .* series). Most closely associated with the government, however, is the Legal Services Corporation (LSC). While the LSC produces a number of informative publications designed to increase awareness of its services, it is also responsible for drafting the government's eligibility requirements for civil legal assistance. Based upon federal poverty guidelines, the LSC report essentially defines eligibility for the services it provides.

Aside from the common practice of developing and distributing written documents, interest group activities diverge according to skill differentials and political clout. In many respects, this means that groups have discovered what they do best and have channeled considerable energy toward those methods. As such, the civil rights and economic rights interest group strategies in particular lend themselves to categorization. As the entries that follow indicate, different groups employ different combinations of means, including public advocacy, legislative/executive pressure, and/or unconventional policy behavior.

The model of judicial activity is manifest in the operations of the ACLU. Since its inception in 1920, the ACLU has participated in at least one major constitutional case per year. Just as the NAACP-Legal Defense Fund noticed that the concreteness and finality of judicial decisions can ultimately compel an otherwise reluctant government to enforce civil rights, the ACLU has successfully utilized the courts as agents of political change. By filing *amicus curiae* briefs, sponsoring cases, and developing test cases, the ACLU has defined itself as a "judicial" interest group. Indeed, aside from the Department of Justice, no other organization or agency has appeared more frequently before the United States Supreme Court than the ACLU.

Among the Court's sibling institutions, civil rights and economic rights interest groups routinely apply pressure by developing model legislation, participating in issue-advocacy campaigns, providing congressional testimony, and influencing elections through voter registration and participation. Not only has the Anti-Defamation League successfully pressured the White House to address early evidence of anti-Semitism, but it has been a visible force in the movement to create and impose hate-crimes laws. It also provides valuable information regarding American foreign policy in the Middle East. Likewise, Freedom House has kept the attention of politicos on both sides of the partisan continuum by testifying on the status of human rights worldwide, the opening (and closing) of media and economic markets, and the furtherance of free-market capitalism. Still other groups, such as the League of Women Voters, the National Coalition for the Homeless, and ACORN, have been active in organizing grassroots support for voter initiatives such as the National Voter Registration Act (the Motor Voter Bill). In their respective spheres, the National Coalition for the Homeless provided the public leadership necessary to secure passage of the Stewart B. McKinney Homelessness Assistance Act in 1987; the League of Women Voters championed the Sheppard-Towner Act of 1921, which provided federal aid for maternal and infant healthcare; and ACORN successfully negotiated a $10 million partnership with NationsBank for low-income home-buyers assistance.

In the realm of nonconventional activity, organizations such as the National Lawyers Guild and ACORN have found it necessary to address certain issues in public. During the 1980s, both groups found it necessary to advocate resistance to a variety of Reagan-Bush policies. ACORN, for example, claimed fame by organizing the creation of "Reagan Ranches," demonstrations that involved approximately 15,000 ACORN activists setting up and settling in tents in 35 cities. The ranches were supposed to symbolize the homelessness presumed to result from President Reagan's effort to increase military spending and decrease social spending. One ranch was set up at the Republican Convention in Dallas, Texas, in 1984. The NLG also supplemented its conventional activities (defending affirmative action policies and operating its National Immigration Project, for example) by aggressively counteracting increasingly restrictive Reagan-Bush civil rights policies, the U.S. intervention in Nicaragua, and discriminatory immigration policies.

CONCLUSION

Among the nine interest groups profiled in this section, one issue that rises to the surface is the impact of the partisan composition of government on interest group fortunes. While all of the groups in this section clearly grew out of a climate largely inhospitable to their claims, their success and failure is in no small way attributable to the receptiveness of government. ACORN, for example, experienced great frustration with the Reagan and Bush presidencies, both of which minimized the significance of poverty in America, as evidenced by their policies and programs. In President Bill Clinton, ACORN has found an administration (and Department of Housing and Urban Development leadership) more sympathetic to its cause.

In a similar fashion, the Legal Services Corporation, although created by a bipartisan effort of Congress, has had to tread lightly since the election of a Republican Congress in 1994. As the entry on the LSC in this section indicates, Congress in 1996 substantially modified (via restrictions) the rules of the game governing the provision of Legal Services Corporation services. Since Congress holds not only the power of the purse but also the power to create and dissolve agencies, the LSC has had to pay dutiful attention to the 1996 rule changes.

The implication of this is that the future of civil rights, economic rights, and human rights interest groups may depend less on internal commitment than on social and political tolerance. These groups depend in large part on a system's dedication to benevolent, humanitarian concerns. When such concerns lose political favor, the groups rapidly become expendable. Although such circumstances provide the breeding ground for social movements and renewed interest group activity, they also reveal the unfortunate state of affairs that necessitates their existence.

BRIAN SMENTKOWSKI

Bibliography

Cigler, Allan J., and Burdett A. Loomis. *Interest Group Politics*, 3d ed. Washington, DC: Congressional Quarterly, 1991.

Craig, Barbara Hinkson, and David O'Brien. *Abortion and American Politics*. Chatham, NJ: Chatham House, 1993.

Epstein, Lee. *Contemplating Courts*. Washington, DC: Congressional Quarterly, 1996.

Epstein, Lee, and Thomas Walker. *Constitutional Law for a Changing America*. Washington, DC: Congressional Quarterly, 1997.

Harrington, Michael. *The Other America*. New York: Simon and Schuster, 1997.

Herrnson, Paul S., Ronald G. Shaiko, and Clyde Wilcox. *The Interest Group Connection*. Chatham, NJ: Chatham House, 1998.

Lehman-Scholzman, Kay, and John T. Tierney. *Organized Interests and American Democracy.* New York: Harper and Row, 1986.

Madison, James. "Federalist No. 10." In James Madison, Alexander Hamilton, and John Jay. *The Federalist Papers,* 2d ed. Roy F. Fairfield, ed. Baltimore: Johns Hopkins University Press, 1981.

Rozell, Mark J., and Clyde Wilcox. *Interest Groups in American Campaigns: The New Face of Electioneering.* Washington, DC: Congressional Quarterly, 1999.

ACORN

The Association of Community Organizations for Reform Now (ACORN) maintains its headquarters in Washington, D.C. In addition, it maintains 500 neighborhood chapters in 30 cities, and has a membership in excess of 120,000 individuals and families. Originally an offshoot of the National Welfare Rights Organization, ACORN was created in 1970 as a regional affiliate dedicated to the cause of social and economic justice. Since its inception, ACORN has represented low- to moderate-income families. Its primary areas of interest include community reinvestment and housing development (through its affiliates, ACORN Housing Corporation and ACORN Community Land Association), economic opportunity, school reform, union support, and voter registration and participation drives. Firmly rooted in the social movement and community activism spirit of the 1960s, ACORN's initial activities involved coalition building, grassroots organizing, and gaining or influencing control of local government. As the organization's institutional capacity increased, it became more active in lobbying, national electoral politics, providing congressional testimony, and—when necessary—organizing demonstrations.

HISTORY

Originally labeled the Arkansas Community Organizations for Reform Now, ACORN was created in Little Rock in 1970 in an attempt to further the cause of the National Welfare Rights Organization (NWRO). Although the NWRO was a central force of the 1960s social justice movement, with 170 branch divisions in 60 U.S. cities by 1966, as a single organization it was incapable of unifying and managing a nationwide campaign on behalf of low- to moderate-income families. In light of this reality, the NWRO sought to establish a network of organizations equally dedicated to social and economic justice. To this end, NWRO organizer Wade Rathke assumed the responsibility of establishing in Little Rock a network of diverse groups (including middle-class, conservative, southern whites) that would support the NWRO's cause. It is in this spirit of creating a genuine social movement that ACORN was begun.

Through ACORN, Rathke succeeded in founding a movement that united races and neighborhoods, and bridged the gap between welfare recipients and working people. The group's early work focused on providing basic human needs—clothing, furniture, and food—to the indigent and disenfranchised. Beyond the common needs of welfare recipients and workers, ACORN mobilized efforts to provide free lunches for schoolchildren and to address labor movement concerns, veterans' rights, and availability of hospital care. In many respects, it was the organization's attempt to do too much that led to an early fracture in its membership. Specifically, welfare rights members who felt betrayed by the organization's increasingly broad mission withdrew from ACORN in order to maintain single-issue representation. Shortly thereafter, ACORN diversified along clearly established boundaries, with the Vietnam Veterans' Organizing Committee (VVOC) and the Unemployed Workers' Organizing Committee (UWOC) operating in spheres of relative autonomy.

ACORN's major activities are diverse and time specific. In the early 1970s, ACORN established itself as a powerful organization based upon the successful "Save the City" campaign in Little Rock, Arkansas, which addressed working-class concerns that neighborhoods were being destroyed by poorly designed traffic patterns and "block busting" (breaking up of existing neighborhoods) by unethical real estate agencies. From there, the organization began to grow geographically: with six regional offices in Arkansas, ACORN was able to successfully address statewide problems. In 1970, ACORN challenged and ultimately gained a victory over the Arkansas Power and Light Company's plan to build a coal-burning power plant in White Bluff, Arkansas. In 1972, ACORN entered electoral politics through its political action committee's (PAC) decision to officially back two candidates for the Little Rock school board. In 1974, 250 ACORN members ran as candidates for the Pulaski County Quorum Court—a 467-member, citizen-based local legislature—and 195 won election. Although they were incapable of directly altering politics, they have been credited with laying the foundation for strict adherence to democratic procedures in the Quorum Court.

From the mid 1970s through the 1980s, ACORN became an increasingly prevalent and political organization. With new branches in Texas and South Dakota, the organization elected its first associate executive board and president, Steve McDonald, in December 1975. In 1978, ACORN held its first national convention in Memphis, Tennessee, coinciding with the National Democratic Party's "mini-convention" conference. Upon completion of a nine-point "People's Platform," ACORN members marched on the Democratic Party conference and demanded a meeting with President Jimmy Carter. Denied that meeting, ACORN conducted a demonstration in the street in order to make its presence—and the interests of low- to moderate-income families—known.

By 1980, ACORN operated branches in 20 states, drafted the ACORN 80 Plan and revised the People's Platform. With platform planks including energy, healthcare, taxes, housing, community development, wages, and rural concerns, these plans represented proposals for changes in the Democratic Party. Signed onto by the United Auto Workers, the International Association of Machinists, the AFL-CIO, and a variety of Democratic state and local parties, the new People's Platform could not be ignored by national party leaders. Indeed, 42 ACORN members served as Democratic delegates and alternates at the convention. On the Republican front, ACORN members testified before the Platform Committee and organized tours of destitute Detroit communities for Republican delegates. The goal was to draw attention to the plight of the economic underclass and flex the organization's growing political muscle.

The great value of ACORN 80 and the ACORN Commission, created at the Democratic Convention, was not so much that they transformed the lives of the downtrodden (they did not), but that they established their place on the discursive terrain and in the halls of government. By 1980 ACORN had over 30,000 members representing virtually every section of the country. Unfortunately for the organization, the Ronald Reagan years were troubling for ACORN. In many respects, ACORN represented exactly the opposite of the Reagan revolution. During that time, wealth flowed upwardly rather than downwardly, and the cultural mantra was individualism, not socialism. Shut out from access to the White House, ACORN participated in less-conventional modes of political action, chiefly by establishing "Reagan Ranches" in over 35 cities in order to protest the Reagan administration's priorities and policies. The ranches were demonstrations that involved approximately 15,000 ACORN activists setting up and settling in tents to symbolize homelessness presumed to result from President Reagan's effort to increase military spending at the expense of social spending. With a more hospitable audience in Congress, ACORN members testified before a Congressional committee about the housing crisis, and staged its ultimate protest by creating a Reagan Ranch at the Republican Convention in Dallas in 1984. Part protest, part voter registration drive, the event involved 15,000 Dallas voters.

During the Reagan years, ACORN strengthened its PAC (APAC) and, through its support of Jesse Jackson in the primaries, gained political ties, experience, and clout in national electoral politics. As was true with the majority of civil rights, economic rights, and human rights organizations that spanned the decades, the social movement spirit that gave rise to ACORN had faded. As the 1980s led into the 1990s, the premium was placed upon organization and professionalization. To this end, ACORN maintained an association with the Rainbow Coalition, the United Labor Union became its official labor organizing arm, and the ACORN Housing Corporation was created.

With the transition from the 1980s to the 1990s, and with shifting partisan composition of Congress and the presidency, ACORN has had to modify its strategies. In President Bill Clinton and Housing and Urban Development (HUD) Secretary Henry Cisneros, ACORN found allies interested in the plight of the lower and middle classes. With the election of a Republican Congress in 1994, however, the organization realized that the institution holding the power of the purse would be disinclined to create or protect ACORN's interests. Consequently, it has redoubled its efforts on the presidency, HUD, and local communities, and in educational missions.

ACTIVITIES: CURRENT AND FUTURE

Since the 1990s, ACORN has dedicated much of its energy toward the issue of affordable housing. Ranging from radical demonstrations, such as a two-day takeover of the House Banking Committee hearing room, to mainstream attempts to influence HUD to designate thousands of homes to low- to moderate-income people that would otherwise have been won at auction by wealthy bidders, ACORN's activities represented the divergent avenues of influence it cultivated during the Reagan years. It has diversified its efforts, however, to address the issues of health, public safety, education, representation, and workers' rights in recent years. With the election of a Democratic president, ACORN became increasingly involved in the National Voter Registration Act (the so-called Motor Voter Act), Project Vote, lobbying HUD Secretary Henry Cisneros to prevent interference with the ACORN Tenant Union, and negotiating a $10 million partnership between ACORN and NationsBank for below-market mortgages to low-income home buyers. Most recently, the organization has engaged in educational missions, including a much publicized conference regarding education reform in Hempstead, N.Y., and in research, such as its study of the lending records of financial institutions in 15 metropolitan areas in 1997. These projects continue today.

As presently articulated, ACORN is committed to organizing the unorganized and maintaining a commitment to social and economic justice at the grassroots level. Aside from increasing the availability of affordable housing and stimulating community reinvestment, ACORN is committed to curbing campaign finances and improving the quality of education in the public school system.

FINANCIAL FACTS

ACORN is a nonprofit, non-tax-exempt organization. Funding for its annual budget is derived from membership dues, grassroots funding, and foundation grants. A nonpartisan but liberal organization, it maintains a PAC (APAC). During the 1995-1996 election cycle, the organization tabulated $43,043 in receipts, $34,111 in expenditures, and $6,250 in contributions. APAC's 1999 year-end Report of Receipts and Disbursements reveals that for the period from November 24, 1998, until December 31, 1998, APAC had $337,739.28 on hand at the beginning of the time period, $2,570.41 in total receipts, and $636.06 in total disbursements, leaving APAC with $339,673.63 in cash on hand at the end of the reporting period.

BRIAN SMENTKOWSKI

Bibliography

ACORN's 25-Year History: www.acorn.org

Federal Elections Commission. *Report of Receipts and Disbursements,* 1999.

DeAngelis, James J. *Public Interest Profiles,* 1998-99. CQ Foundation for Public Affairs. Washington, DC: Congressional Quarterly, 1998.

Greider, William, "The Hard Fight Against Soft Money." *Rolling Stone,* June 6, 1997.

AMERICAN CIVIL LIBERTIES UNION

The American Civil Liberties Union (ACLU) maintains national headquarters in New York City, a legislative office in Washington, D.C., and 53 affiliate offices (one in each state, plus three local chapters). The permanent staff consists of 105 professionals and 45 support staff members, not including affiliates. The organization is regulated by an 82-member board of directors and has been headed by Ira Glasser, executive director, since 1978. There are 275,000 dues-paying members of the ACLU.

The ACLU represents a cause, not particular groups. The cause is "to preserve, defend, and expand application of the constitutional guarantees and freedoms set forth in the Bill of Rights." As such, its main areas of interest include civil liberties and civil rights in general, and—in recent years—affirmative action, gay rights, and privacy rights in particular. Its primary method of operation is litigation, although it remains active in advertising, research, legislative monitoring, grassroots organizing, and sponsoring educational programs.

HISTORY

The ACLU was created as a nonpartisan organization in 1920. Founded by Roger Baldwin, Crystal Eastman, and Albert DeSilver, the ACLU was the first public interest law firm dedicated exclusively to compelling governmental compliance with the liberties articulated in the Bill of Rights. At the time of its founding, both the state and federal governments had a poor reputation for protecting the rights of racial, ethnic, sexual, religious, and political minorities. Indeed, the Supreme Court had not yet, at the time, upheld a First Amendment free speech claim, and the doctrine of selective incorporation of constitutional rights under the Fourteenth Amendment's due process clause was barely on the horizon. Within the first five years of its existence, the ACLU fought the infamous Palmer Raids, which sought to identify and purge American socialists, and secured the services of Clarence Darrow to defend John T. Scopes for teaching the theory of evolution to students in the legendary Scopes monkey case. In each decade since its inception, the ACLU has provided legal counsel for, or filed *amicus curiae* briefs in, landmark cases such as *Gitlow v. New York* (1925), *Hague v. CIO* (1939), *West Virginia v. Barnette* (1943), *Brown v. Board of Education* (1954), *Gideon v. Wainwright* (1963), *Roe v. Wade* (1973), *Texas v. Johnson* (1989), and *Romer v. Evans* (1996). Indeed, in a pamphlet called "77 Years, 77 Victories," the ACLU identifies at least one major case per year in which the organization participated in some capacity.

Working with a cadre of more than 2,000 volunteer attorneys, the ACLU has handled approximately 6,000 cases per year in recent years. Throughout its history it has balanced its dedication to constitutional rights among a variety of issue areas. As such it has successfully argued some of the nation's most important cases on behalf of the labor movement, the rights of the criminally accused, speech rights, the free exercise of religion, racial and ethnic minorities, women's rights, privacy, and procreative freedom. Aside from the Department of Justice, the ACLU has appeared before the U.S. Supreme Court more frequently than any other organization.

In addition to its involvement in court cases, the ACLU has also engaged in lobbying activities. Coordinated through the Washington-based legislative office, the ACLU has spearheaded opposition to the nomination of Robert Bork to the Supreme Court, has lobbied against rolling back affirmative action laws and the freedom of symbolic speech, and has pressured both the legislative and executive branches of government to reassess their operations respecting immigration and legal aliens' rights (the latter of which are coordinated through the ACLU's Immigration and Aliens' Rights Task Force).

ACTIVITIES: CURRENT AND FUTURE

The ACLU maintains a presence in the courts, in the capital, in public, and in cyberspace. It is best known for its litigation on behalf of marginalized and disenfranchised individuals and groups. Presently, the ACLU staff is involved in thousands of cases nationwide and at all levels of the judicial hierarchy. Among its main and affiliated offices, the ACLU receives thousands of requests for legal representation daily. In selecting cases, it seeks to represent persons and groups whose cases may serve as precedents for all others similarly affected under the law. In recent history, this has meant that the ACLU has provided legal representation for unpopular groups such as American Nazis and the Ku Klux Klan—*not* for the purposes of defending their views, but for protecting their constitutional rights.

From its legislative office in Washington, ACLU lobbyists research and track bills, create and recommend model legislation, and testify before Congress in attempts to influence the creation and passage of legislation that preserves or enhances, but never restricts, individual rights. The ACLU is also active in public education and grassroots activities. Its efforts are facilitated through the publication of reports, brochures, books, and videos. Presently, the ACLU lists 21 separate publications as part of the *Rights Of . . .* series; eight shorter publications ranging from *The Case Against the Death Penalty* to *Fighting Police Abuse: A Community Action Manual;* at least a dozen issue-specific briefing papers; and 24 recommended books by or about the ACLU and the issues to which it is committed. With the advent of the Internet, the ACLU has created and maintains a web page, titled the Freedom Network (www.aclu.org), which provides up-to-date information on organizational activities, conferences, research, and resources, and "Constitution Hall," available through America OnLine at keyword: aclu.

The future of the ACLU appears secure. Not only the original but the leading public interest law firm dedicated to civil liberties and civil rights law, the ACLU maintains a steady course with its membership, volunteer staff, operating budget, and activities. While it anticipates no changes in organization and operations, it continues to diversify the issues it represents. Largely a function of issue salience, legislative priorities, and temporally fixed acts of discrimination, the ACLU's agenda manages to create space for "new" categories of cases. Among the current concerns predicted to be of great importance in the near future are affirmative action, gay and lesbian rights, abortion regulation, the right to privacy involving individuals and information, government regulation of the Internet, religious intolerance, and censorship of unpopular ideas. Among the new ideas for tackling such issues are the development of instructional materials for young readers and the production of manuals for campus organizing. Based upon the premise that a more educated and tolerant younger generation may grow up to create fewer laws that discriminate against citizens, thereby negating the need for constitutional challenges to such laws, the ACLU has created the Ask Sybil Liberties series to address pressing concerns from a student's perspective.

FINANCIAL FACTS

The ACLU is a nonprofit organization with 501(c)(4) IRS tax status. Its affiliate, the ACLU Foundation, is identified by the Internal Revenue Service as a 501(c)(3) organization. The ACLU's budget for 1997-1998 equaled $35 million, and was increased to $37 million for the 1999 fiscal year. The ACLU receives no financial support from the government; its primary funding sources are private organizations and individuals. There are no political action committees (PACs) associated with the ACLU.

BRIAN SMENTKOWSKI

Bibliography

"Guardian of Liberty: American Civil Liberties Union." ACLU Briefing Paper no. 1.

"77 Years, 77 Great Victories." ACLU informational material: www.aclu.org

Tolley, H. 1990. "Interest Group Litigation to Enforce Human Rights." *Political Science Quarterly* 105, no. 4 (Winter 1990).

ANTI-DEFAMATION LEAGUE

The Anti-Defamation League (ADL) maintains headquarters in New York and operates a network of 30 regional and satellite offices located throughout the United States and in Jerusalem and Vienna. The organization is committed to fighting organized intolerance and bigotry in general, and anti-Semitism in particular. In addition, its areas of interest include combating racism, extremism, and hate crimes, and diverse work on political and security issues in Israel, Holocaust remembrance, and educational programs. The ADL is headed by Abraham H. Foxman, national director, and a nine-member national commission, plus a six-member national executive committee. Its affiliates include the Anti-Defamation League Foundation; Leon and Marilyn Klinghoffer Memorial Foundation of the Anti-Defamation League, Braun Holocaust Institute, Jewish Foundation for Christian Rescuers/ADL, Hidden Child Foundation/ADL, William and Naomi Gorowitz Institute on Terrorism and Extremism, and ADL: A World of Difference Institute. The Anti-Defamation League consists of 200 professionals and approximately 200 support staff members.

HISTORY

Founded in 1913 by Sigmound Livingston, the Anti-Defamation League was created to stem the tide of anti-Semitism that culminated in the lynching of Leo Frank in Marietta, Georgia. Frank, a Jew, was wrongly accused of killing a 14-year-old girl, and sentenced to death. When his sentence was commuted to life in prison, an angry mob took him from jail and hanged him. To Livingston and the Jewish community at large, this episode was but one manifestation of a growing anti-Semitic ideology that relegated Jews to subhuman status. As an attorney, Livingston donated the services of two staff members of his Chicago law office to efforts to appeal to reason, humanity, and the law in order to halt the defamation of the Jewish people.

Beginning with modest support from the Independent Order of B'nai B'rith and culminating in what is now the most recognizable opponent of anti-Semitism, each decade since the founding of the Anti-Defamation League has experienced a defining moment. In its first 10 years the ADL pressured President Woodrow Wilson to recall military training manuals that mischaracterized Jews. The ADL also pressed Wilson to join former presidents William Howard Taft and Theodore Roosevelt in compelling Henry Ford to halt publication and publicly apologize for circulating *The Protocols of the Elders of Zion,* a Russian anti-Semitic publication based on European stereotypes of the Jewish people cultivated since medieval times, in his newspaper. In 1930, the ADL experienced its first major organizational change. It expanded its staff and began the fact-finding operation that has become a cumulative clearinghouse of information on extremism. With the Nazi Party's ascent to power and the Second World War, the ADL fought bigotry in the United States, chiefly against the German-American Bund (an organization of devoutly pro-Nazi ethnic Germans living in the United States), and instituted a successful "crack the quota" campaign against discriminatory housing, employment, and education laws. In 1948, in the case of *McCullum v. Board of Education,* the ADL filed its first church-state *amicus curiae* brief to the U.S. Supreme Court, and has filed one in virtually every such dispute thereafter.

During the late 1940s and 1950s, the ADL established its position on U.S. foreign policy regarding the newly created state of Israel, while on the domestic front it attacked racism by assisting a journalist to infiltrate the Ku Klux Klan in order to provide information to the ADL, which would ultimately be reported in the press and to the police. Another defining moment in civil rights history found the ADL filing *amicus curiae* briefs in *Brown v. Board of Education* and setting up regional divisions in order to assist in the implementation of the

Supreme Court's ruling in that case. The civil rights agenda dominated the organization's attention well into the 1960s, galvanizing support for the Civil Rights Act and the Voting Rights Act.

During the 1960s and 1970s, the ADL stimulated American support for Israel in the wake of the Six-Day War and then again in the wake of the Yom Kippur War. The ADL also became the first Jewish organization to address right-wing extremism with the publication of *Danger on the Right*. This research tradition continued with an ADL-commissioned analysis of anti-Semitism in America. This effort resulted in several scholarly publications, portions of which were presented before the Vatican II Council. The presentation of this work succeeded in opening a dialogue between Christians and Jews, and ultimately laid the foundation for the ADL's continuing efforts to promote interfaith relations. In 1977, one of the first Holocaust awareness programs was created by the ADL.

During the 1980s and 1990s, the Braun Holocaust Institute became active in Holocaust remembrance and educational events. It addressed intolerance on campuses by writing and distributing materials on extremism, and tackled the emerging trend of revisionist history by developing an advertising campaign (and even conducting on-site counseling) aimed at delineating free speech and hate speech. The educational mission was enhanced with the creation of ADL: A World of Difference Institute and the Children of the Dream program, the former a television project aimed at young children in Israel, and the latter an American-Ethiopian-Israeli "shared experiences" project.

ACTIVITIES: CURRENT AND FUTURE

While the ADL is chiefly dedicated to the struggle against anti-Semitism, it has, in recent years, expanded its commitment to the fight for civil liberties, children's welfare, and interfaith relations, while fighting against extremism, hate crimes, and terrorism. In addition to the host of new issues and phenomena addressed by the ADL, its methods of operation have changed as well. The ADL maintains an informative web page (www.adl.org) and uses the Internet as both an educational device and a vehicle to identify and monitor hate groups.

The ADL is a well-established, professionalized organization; as such it has considerable clout in Congress—where it frequently provides testimony on ethnic and religious discrimination—within human rights circles, and in society in general. The ADL's reputation has been cultivated through its popular Holocaust remembrance and educational forums, its clearinghouse of information regarding the operation of extremist groups, and its advocacy of civil liberties.

Currently, the ADL is a leading advocate of hate crimes prevention and punishment legislation. It participated in the first White House Conference on Hate Crimes in December 1997, where it presented a program, Hate Crimes: ADL Blueprint for Action, and continues to present models of satisfactory legislation. In 1999, the ADL published *1999 Hate Crimes Laws* and produced a number of training programs, videos, and community-organizing materials used to detect and deter such crimes. The ADL's Legislative Action Center also provides a steady stream of pressure chiefly through advertising and writings in opposition to school voucher systems and the increased incidence of racial, ethnic, religious, and political extremism. Specifically, the ADL maintains a public awareness campaign regarding (a) laws that obfuscate the line separating church and state, (b) the activities of the neo-Nazi alliance (through programs stemming from the ADL's publication, *Explosion of Hate*), (c) vigilante and militia groups (based upon its book, *Vigilante Justice*), and (d) the Council of Conservative Citizens. Activities coordinated through the Braun Holocaust Institute continue to sensitize the world to the significance of anti-Semitism and human rights, and ADL: A World of Difference Institute presently promotes the value of tolerance through Israel's Education Television channel and its cable television Children's Channel. On the Internet, the ADL is committed to monitoring and countering the messages of white supremacist groups as well as pseudoscholarly Holocaust analysts and revisionist historians who deny that the Holocaust took place.

Most recently, the ADL has encountered some negative publicity from segments of both the African-American and Jewish communities. While the ADL is committed to a broad application of civil liberties and civil rights, it did take exception to some of the rallying points of the Million-Man March as well as statements made by Nation of Islam leader Louis Farrakhan. The ADL maintains that the foundation for civil liberties and civil rights is tolerance, and that specific anti-Semitic statements made during the Million-Man March and by Farrakhan represented an important difference in the quest for constitutionally protected rights. Within the Jewish community, a December 4, 1998, *Wall Street*

Journal op-ed by ADL director Abraham H. Foxman drew fire by delineating the "dangers" of restitution for the Holocaust. Because the Jewish community is by no means an entirely homogeneous group, Foxman's argument that adding dollar values to the Holocaust detracts from the uniqueness and significance of the phenomenon was met with some internal resistance. There appears to have been no long-term damage to the organization, and its leadership and operations remain unaltered.

Although the commitment of the ADL remains constant, the number of directions and means to address them are expected to expand. In the future, the ADL's technological capacity will certainly increase, thereby permitting more fruitful and productive investigations of the proliferation and impact of hate groups on the Internet and in wider society. The roots of this endeavor already exist through the ADL's Terrorism on the Internet series and international terrorism research. The ADL's Legislative Action Center is also expected to continue its research of legal solutions to hate-related crimes, and is expected to continue drafting model legislation for hate-crimes law. On this latter enterprise, the ADL is likely to find itself in different company than on past initiatives. Although certain civil liberties groups remain opposed to legal codes that distinguish between "crimes" and "hate crimes," the ADL is committed to laws dedicated to identifying and punishing criminal acts predicated upon racial, ethnic, and religious intolerance.

FINANCIAL FACTS

The ADL is a nonprofit organization with 501(c)(3) Internal Revenue Service (IRS) tax status. Its operations are funded by private contributions. For the 1999 fiscal year, the ADL's budget totaled $46 million. A nonpartisan, nonlobbying organization, the ADL is unaffiliated with political action committees (PACs) and does not participate in organized attempts to influence election outcomes.

BRIAN SMENTKOWSKI

Bibliography

Anti-Defamation League: www.adl.org

DeAngelis, James J. *Public Interest Profiles, 1998-1999.* CQ Foundation for Public Affairs. Washington, DC: Congressional Quarterly, 1998.

Foxman, Abraham H. *Wall Street Journal,* December 4, 1998, op-ed.

FREEDOM HOUSE

Although it merged with the National Forum Foundation (NFF) on July 1, 1997, the organization is still officially recognized as Freedom House. Freedom House is based in Washington, D.C., and New York City, and it operates satellite offices in Bucharest, Budapest, and Kiev. The organization has seven officers, including James S. Denton, executive director, Adrian Karatnycky, president, and Bette Bao Lord, chairman. The activities of the organization are overseen by a 35-member board of trustees. The board of trustees includes prominent (primarily conservative) former government officials, leading scholars, journalists, business leaders, and free-market activists. Among members of the board are Zbigniew Brzezinski, Steve Forbes, Samuel Huntington, Jeane J. Kirkpatrick, P.J. O'Rourke, and Wendell L. Willkie II. In addition to the officers and board members, Freedom House maintains a staff of 40 permanent members.

Freedom House does not represent any one category of persons; rather, it seeks to promote its version of democracy, civil liberties, and civil rights throughout the world. As such, it monitors human rights conditions, sponsors public education campaigns, and provides training for efforts to promote free market economic reform. Its most well-known and highly regarded work includes testimony before Congress, field work (including internships and international professional exchange programs), and the publication of *Freedom in the World,* a well-respected and widely read annual assessment of the state of freedom in every country.

HISTORY

Freedom House was founded in 1941 by Eleanor Roosevelt and Wendell Willkie as a nonpartisan proponent of democracy and a staunch opponent of dictatorships representing both the far right and the far left. The reason for its existence was not simply the notion that democracy should flourish worldwide, but that American leadership in international affairs is essential to that effort. Based upon the belief that respect for human rights constitutes the foundation of democratic government, Freedom House's advocacy role spans the decades through support for the Marshall Plan and NATO, the American civil rights movement, the Polish Solidarity movement, and efforts to halt acts of genocide in Bosnia and Rwanda, for example.

Freedom House's commitment to civil rights, economic rights, and democratization exist in practice as well as in spirit. The organization's board of trustees has historically provided a balance between scholars, writers, leaders of business, and former senior government officials representing all segments of the ideological and partisan continuum. It is this mixture of leadership that has provided a sense of direction with regard to the organization's efforts to open media markets, economic markets, and the political process in general.

As the significance of educational initiatives has become more obvious and prevalent, so too have been the organization's publications, conferences, and field work. In an effort to facilitate the organization's operations, Freedom House and the NFF joined forces on July 1, 1997. Retaining the name "Freedom House," the merger allowed two groups who share a common commitment to contribute their strength to a single, unified goal. Under the terms of the merger, former NFF president Jim Denton assumed responsibility for daily operations, publications, finance, and administration, while former Freedom House president Adrian Karatnycky retained his title and assumed responsibility for the organization's public profile, media outreach, fundraising, and research. The ultimate goal was to consolidate programs in an attempt to stimulate advances in advocacy, education, research, and training.

Since its creation, Freedom House has received considerable support from governments, politicians, and human rights advocates. Specifically, its leading publication, *Freedom in the World,* is standard issue in Immigration and Naturalization Service offices. Along with *Nations in Transition, Freedom in the World* ranks among the primary sources that sensitize governments to the state of rights worldwide. As such, Freedom House has received accolades from such luminaries as Winston Churchill, Ambassador Kirkpatrick, Senators Daniel Patrick Moynihan and Bob Dole, President Bill Clinton, John Cardinal O'Connor, and USAID administrator Brian Atwood, among others.

ACTIVITIES: CURRENT AND FUTURE

The current activities of Freedom House range from a continuation of several of its most significant research enterprises to charting new territory in the protection of religious liberty in general, and Christianity in particular, throughout the world. Specifically, with its merger with NFF, new opportunities to enhance democratization have been open to Freedom House since 1997. Since that year, the merger produced a regional exchange program (REF) designed to provide nongovernmental organization staff members with the opportunity to form coalitions and become more instrumental agents of democratization and reform. Freedom House also has extended its reach into the private sector. With its recently launched corporate support regional initiative, Freedom House has embarked on an effort to explore partnerships between nonprofit and business sectors in central and eastern Europe in an attempt to facilitate the development of democratic governments and free market economies.

Most recently, Freedom House has been a leader in bringing the subject of Christian persecution to center stage. Through publications such as *The First Freedom,* published monthly by the organization's Center for Religious Freedom, Freedom House has provided up-to-date analyses of anti-Christian persecution in China, the Sudan, and Egypt, and has encouraged political action ranging from a boycott of Chinese-made Christmas ornaments to supporting the American government's adoption of the International Religious Freedom Act. Paul Marshall, a senior fellow at Freedom House, has spent much of the past year not only writing but lecturing on the subject of religious freedom and international affairs at various forums, conferences, and universities.

In addition to its profound commitment to religious liberty, Freedom House has also contributed new knowledge on the subject of press and media law throughout the world. Ranging from state-specific action in Romania to a comparative analysis of media restrictions in 43 countries, Freedom House presently is committed to drawing attention to the significance—and the absence—of a free press in young democracies.

Finally, Freedom House remains active in research and publishing. In addition to annual editions of *Freedom in the World,* it has also published *Nations in Transition,* as well as a spate of periodicals including *Freedom Monitor* and *The First Freedom,* and a variety of research reports. Among its newest endeavors is *NGO News: A Regional Newsletter for Non-Governmental Organizations.*

Freedom House's future involves continued publication of such standards *as Freedom in the World, Nations in Transition, Freedom Review,* and *The First Freedom,* as well as a major effort to expand its Visiting Fellow program and the American Volunteers in International Development program. It also opposes the current Cuban government through the Cuba Democracy project, and continues to train Romanian officials and communications personnel on opening both the economic and media markets. Finally, with the publication of *NGO News,* Freedom House is signaling its interest in providing regional organizations with the knowledge and assistance necessary to solve regional problems. While this is not a departure from the organization's commitment to establishing its version of democracy throughout the world, it is a clear statement that American leadership, though necessary and important, is insufficient to solve current and future dilemmas in international affairs.

FINANCIAL FACTS

Freedom House is a nonprofit organization. Its primary sources of funding are grants and private financial donations that are tax-deductible under section 501(c)(3) of the Internal Revenue Service code. Major contributors include the Lynde and Harry Bradley Foundation, Byrne foundation, Carthage Foundation, Eurasia Foundation, Ford Foundation, Freedom Forum, Grace Foundation, Inc., Lilly Endowment, Inc., LWH Family Foundation, National Endowment for Democracy, Pew Charitable Trusts, Sarah Scaife Foundation,

Schloss Family Foundation, Smith Richardson Foundation, Inc., Soros Foundation, Unilever United States Foundation, Inc., U.S. Agency for International Development, and U.S. Information Agency. The revenue collected from these sources covers the cost of its publications, public education tasks, international research programs, conferences, fieldwork, and related activities. Freedom House is a nonpartisan, nonlobbying organization; as such, it maintains no political action committees (PACs) and does not contribute to political campaigns.

BRIAN SMENTKOWSI

Bibliography

"Freedom House and National Forum Foundation Join Forces." *Freedom Monitor* 13, no. 2 (Fall 1997): www.freedomhouse.org

Personal interviews with, and materials received from, Lisa L. Davis, Director, RIGHTS Program.

HUMAN RIGHTS WATCH

Human Rights Watch (HRW) operates headquarters in New York and Washington, with regional branches and chapters in Brussels, Hong Kong, London, Los Angeles, Moscow, Rio de Janeiro, Saigon, and Tbilisi. The organization maintains a permanent staff of 127 members, plus 20 to 30 interns, divided among nine committees. The executive committee consists of Kenneth Roth, executive director, Susan Osnos, assistant director, Jennifer Gaboury, executive assistant, and Justine Hanson, associate. The activities of the organization are overseen by a 34-member board of directors.

In addition to its American headquarters, HRW operates regional divisions representing Africa, the Americas, Asia, Europe, Central Asia, Middle East and Northern Africa; three substantive divisions—Arms division, Children's Rights division, and Women's Rights division; and Human Rights Watch California. There are 7,000 individual members associated with HRW.

HRW is dedicated to advancing the human rights of persons and groups throughout the world. To this end it investigates and exposes human rights violations and seeks to hold violators accountable for their actions. While its longstanding areas of interest include the furtherance of human rights and the punishment of perpetrators in general, its present agenda addresses such timely issues as children's rights (including the use of children as soldiers and exploited labor), women's rights, academic freedom and free expression, prison conditions, political violence, and crimes against humanity in such places as Bosnia, Indonesia, and Rwanda.

HISTORY

HRW was founded in 1978. At the time, the organization was known as Helsinki Watch, which later became Human Rights Watch/Helsinki. Based upon a call for assistance from local groups in Moscow, Warsaw, and Prague and charged with the responsibility of monitoring compliance with the Helsinki accord, HRW was begun. Shortly thereafter, Americas Watch (now Human Rights Watch/Americas) was established as a response to Reagan administration foreign policy that consistently tolerated human rights violations by right-wing governments, while deploring those of left-wing governments. By 1987, the regional organizations began to be folded into the divisions of what is now simply called Human Rights Watch.

Since its creation, HRW's greatest success has been its research and publication on human rights issues. To date, it has published more than 1,000 reports on over 100 countries worldwide. Most of the reports are state-specific, and many have a substantive theme (e.g., "Russia—Too Little, Too Late: State Response of Violence Against Women"). Through the years these works have included books commonly read by activists, policy makers, academicians, students, and journalists.

Although HRW ranks among the most recognizable organizations worldwide, it has endured setbacks. Recently, board member Bruce Klatsky offered to resign his post after it was discovered that the corporation he heads (Phillips-Van Heusen) closed down the company's only unionized factory in late 1998. Ordinarily, a decision to close a plant would not merit such attention, but the motivations (allegations of union busting) merited attention from an organization dedicated to workers' rights. And since the factory was located in Guatemala, where human rights violations are rampant and HRW maintains a keen interest in the operation of *maquiladoras* (apparel factories), the closing of the only unionized *maquiladora* was at variance with the organization's mission statement and professional commitment.

ACTIVITIES: CURRENT AND FUTURE

The precursor to solving problems is the careful identification of them. As such, HRW is, first and foremost, a research organization. With teams of linguistic, legal, and scholarly professionals and local volunteers stationed around the world, HRW is dedicated to identifying potential problems rather than simply reacting to them. Upon verification of atrocities or exploitation, the organization attempts to employ conventional legal machinery and propaganda to halt abuse. In its current work on executions, torture, detention, discrimination, and genocide, HRW applies standards (many relating to the Universal Declaration of Human Rights) that have been accepted as universally applicable to the protection of civil and political rights in international law. To this end, HRW has been at the forefront of the movement to establish the International Criminal Court, which would be capable of conducting trials of alleged violators.

Like many human rights organizations (e.g., Freedom House), HRW believes that Western leadership and intervention are necessary to compel compliance with international law. However, whereas many organizations see the problem with compliance to international law as a local or regional problem, HRW is quick to note that many of the problems in using formal legal machinery and regimes to solve human rights problems come from the West, not those against which the West may be compared. Specifically, HRW has isolated as problematic the tendency of Western states to express a preference for economic prosperity over human rights commitments. By ranking economic development above human rights, the pursuit of the former often comes at the expense of the latter. As such, governments may open their markets, but close down avenues of expression, dissent, and access. In its commitment to human rights alone (which includes economic, political, and social justice), HRW stands apart from organizations such as Freedom House, whose mission includes a three-part plan to stimulate and support democratization, free-market economies, and human rights.

With Western nations reluctant in all but the most severe cases to employ the machinery of the legal community, HRW remains committed to publicity as a primary tool for drawing attention to a government and compelling political change. This is the case in present labor disputes involving *maquiladoras* in Latin America, the abduction and enslavement of children in Uganda, and human rights violations in Asia. With the capture of dictator Augusto Pinochet of Chile, allegations of war crimes and crimes against humanity in Yugoslavia, and recent allegations of genocide in Bosnia and Rwanda, HRW insists on the application of the rule of law in criminal trials against perpetrators.

The future of HRW appears secure due, in no small part, to the atrocities that define the conclusion to the century. The NATO airstrikes against Serbia in 1999 were precipitated by the disclosure of information regarding human rights violations and genocide in Bosnia provided by (among others) HRW. Regardless of the military endeavor, HRW remains committed not only to the termination of such atrocities, but to holding Serb leadership responsible for its actions against ethnic Albanians. In a broader sense it is committed to Arrest Now, its campaign to apprehend war criminals in the former Yugoslavia, and the establishment of the International Criminal Court. On other fronts, it remains committed to the abolition of land mines, the forced trafficking of young women, and sex discrimination in Mexican factories, as well as a legal conclusion to Pinochet's extradition.

As the United States's largest and best-known human rights organization, HRW intends to diversify the methods it uses to reach audiences. To this end it has added to its traditional methods of operation (coalition forming, research, and litigation) a host of awards programs, fellowships, international activities and film festivals, and internships. Similar to other organizations, HRW has made extensive use of its World Wide Web domain, www.hrw.org, as a vessel for providing up-to-date information on developments throughout the world as well as within the organization.

FINANCIAL FACTS

HRW is a nonprofit organization. Its primary sources of funding are grants and private financial donations that are tax-deductible under section 501(c)(3) of the Internal Revenue Service code. A breakdown of contributions and contributors reveals that during the mid to late 1990s, 22 separate individuals or foundations provided contributions exceeding $100,000, while 48 donated between $25,000 and $99,999. An additional 52 donors contributed between $10,000 and $24,999, and at least 79 donated between $5,000 and $9,999. The contributors represent an eclectic mix, ranging from the

Ford Foundation (a $100,000+ contributor) to the Dr. Seuss Foundation and major television networks. Recent budget figures indicate that HRW maintains a budget in excess of $14.3 million. A nonpartisan organization, HRW maintains no political action committees (PACs) and does not contribute to political campaigns.

BRIAN SMENTKOWSKI

Bibliography

Human Rights Watch: www.hrw.org

DeAngelis, James J. *Public Interest Profiles, 1998-1999.* CQ Foundation for Public Affairs. Washington, DC: Congressional Quarterly, 1998.

Raymond, John. "Human Rights Watch Member Offers Resignation." *New Amsterdam News,* March 11, 1999.

LEAGUE OF WOMEN VOTERS OF THE UNITED STATES

The League of Women Voters of the United States (LWV) "encourages the informed and active participation of citizens in government and influences public policy through education and advocacy." In order to achieve the league's ultimate goal of involving all citizens in electoral democracy, this diverse, nonpartisan organization utilizes a variety of methods. Included among, but not limited to, these methods of operation are advertisements; awards programs; coalition forming; conferences and seminars; congressional testimony; grassroots organizing; initiative/referendum campaigns; legislative/regulatory monitoring; litigation; lobbying; media outreach; polling and research; voter registration drives; and sponsoring debates, forums, and community dialogue programs.

The LWV is comprised of more than 150,000 active individual members throughout its 50 state and local leagues. A strictly nonpartisan organization, the LWV supports or opposes issues, not candidates or political parties. With a total of 1,100 separate local leagues, the LWV is capable of influencing politics at the national, state, and local levels.

Headquartered in Washington, D.C., the LWV is supported by a staff of 51, including 30 professionals and 21 support staff members, plus 3 interns. The current executive director is Jane Gruenebaum, who was formerly the deputy director of the Center for Public Policy Education at the Brookings Institution.

HISTORY

The roots of the LWV are directly linked to the women's suffrage movement. In fact, the league was founded on February 14, 1920—six months prior to the passage of the Nineteenth Amendment, granting women the right to vote—at the Chicago convention of the National American Woman Suffrage Association (NAWSA). The NAWSA had been created in 1890 by uniting the National Woman Suffrage Association, which had worked toward the goal of a women's suffrage amendment to the U.S. Constitution, and the American Woman Suffrage Association, which targeted state-level suffrage amendments. Carrie Chapman Catt is credited with reorganizing the NAWSA's 2 million members into the League of Women Voters.

The passage of the Nineteenth Amendment was viewed by the league as the beginning, not the end, of its commitment to enhancing democratic participation. Although initially viewed as a single-issue organization, the league sees itself as an agent of change in helping to "finish the fight" for women's rights in particular and fair democratic procedures in general. This is done chiefly through a variety of educational and interactive programs.

According to literature produced by the LWV, the organization's hardest-won battle was also its first legislative victory—the passage of the Sheppard-Towner Act in 1921, which provided federal aid for maternal and infant healthcare. In addition to providing funds for maternal and children's programs, the passage of this act also offered evidence that the "league's grassroots lobbying and coalition building were effective legislative tools."

The league has continued to pursue multiple issues throughout its history. There are, however, specific issues that can be associated with specific time periods. In the 1940s, the league was a staunch supporter of international peace building through the promotion of international organizations such as the United Nations. In the 1950s, then-league president Percy Maxim Lee testified against Senator Joseph McCarthy's abuse of Congressional investigative powers for the Senate Subcommittee on Constitutional Rights. It was also during this decade that the League of Women Voters Education Fund was established, with the purpose of increasing citizen understanding of major public policy issues and promoting citizen involvement in government decision making. In order to fulfill this goal, the fund has conducted research and produced numerous publications on a wide range of topics, including the environment, as well as social, international, and government issues.

Throughout the 1960s and 1970s the league would identify itself as a "foe of discrimination" in education, employment, and housing, and members were strong supporters in the civil and womens' rights movements. During the 1970s, the league vigorously pursued the ratification of the Equal Rights Amendment, which, ironically, it had opposed in 1921 for fear of adversely affecting labor laws. In 1976, the league sponsored its first presidential debate, between Jimmy Carter and Gerald Ford. It should be noted, however, that this debate followed a tradition of furnishing voter information that can be traced back to 1928, when the league sponsored the first national radio broadcast of a candidate forum entitled "Meet the Candidates."

During the 1970s and 1980s the league focused its attention on environmental regulation, halting the arms race, and furthering the cause of equality of opportunity. During the 1990s, the league's attention was drawn primarily to the desire to end all remaining obstacles to voter registration, which culminated in the passage in 1993 of the National Voter Registration Act (also called the Motor Voter Act), which was intended to help enfranchise millions of American citizens by making voter registration more uniform and accessible. In addition, the league has placed a great deal of emphasis on the need for campaign finance reform. The focuses and intents of this objective are numerous, not the least of which is the need to open new opportunities to elective office for women and minorities, thus making government truly representative.

ACTIVITIES: CURRENT AND FUTURE

Currently, the LWV is concentrating on a number of broad-reaching issues in its pursuit of advocating, informing, and activating the participation of all citizens in government. Included among the league's current concerns is campaign finance reform, which, according to the league, would allow candidates to compete more equitably for public office. Other issues the league is currently pursuing include children's welfare through the promotion of policies and programs that provide for "the well-being, development, and safety of all children"; environmental issues such as resource management, environmental protection, and pollution control; gun control; healthcare; and minimizing all remaining obstacles to voter registration and participation for all American citizens. In addition to these goals, the league is interested in the debate over school vouchers; the need to conduct a fair and accurate census in 2000 (of specific concern is the underrepresentation of racial minorities, the poor, and inner-city residents and how this ultimately translates into underrepresentation in government); and promoting "the league's nonpartisan, grassroots approach to citizen involvement in democratic politics" to newly democratizing regions of the world.

From its roots in the women's suffrage movement to its activist role as a committed fighter for child labor laws, the protection of civil rights for all, and equal pay for women, to the current desire to promote campaign finance reform, overhauling the U.S. healthcare system, and "making democracy work," the LWV has had a rich and interesting history. Its future, however, appears to be less certain. Since its founding—and especially since 1970—the number of active members has dropped precipitously. The league is thus faced with the dilemma of how to expand its base support group.

In order to combat the organization's dwindling numbers, the league is increasingly emphasizing diversity. Through this commitment, the LWV is reaching out to a wide variety of individuals, and by embracing diversity the league may be able to overcome the stereotype of being "just" a women's organization. The league is aware that women's organizations as a whole are facing many new challenges, such as the erroneous perceptions that women have truly achieved social, political, and economic equality; that as more women are working outside the home they have less time to dedicate to volunteer organizations; and that there currently seems to be a lack of any one galvanizing issue (e.g., abortion rights or the ratification of the Equal Rights Amendment) that can bring and hold women together. Consequently, these traditional "women's groups" are having to expand their bases, and the promotion of diversity (social, sexual, ethnic, and age-related) is one way to accomplish this goal. Nonetheless, the LWV continues to play an important role as a political—but not partisan—catalyst in this country by reconnecting citizens with their governments.

FINANCIAL FACTS

The LWV's fiscal year 1999 budget totaled $2.62 million. This nonprofit, nonpartisan organization receives contributions from a number of sources including corporations, foundations, unions, and individual members. In fact, member payments account for 48 percent of the league's funding source. Additionally, direct mail contributions comprise 32 percent; nationally recruited members account for 8 percent; and investment income represents 5 percent. The LWV is classified as a 501(c)(4) organization under the Internal Revenue Service code. It maintains no political action committee (PAC), but does maintain one affiliate, the League of Women Voters Education Fund (LWVEF), which is classified as a 501(c)(3) organization under the Internal Revenue Service code, thus allowing it to accept tax-deductible contributions. The combined expenditures of the national offices of the LWV and the LWVEF are approximately $5.5 million.

BRIAN SMENTKOWSKI AND KATHRYN BETH ADKINS

Bibliography

Duskin, Meg. "Census 2000 Doesn't Add Up." *National Voter* 48, no. 3 (March/April 1999).

DeAngelis, James J. *Public Interest Profiles,* 1998–1999. CQ Foundation for Public Affairs. Washington, DC: Congressional Quarterly, 1998.

Impact on Issues, 1998–2000, LWV National Program: www.lwv.org

LEGAL SERVICES CORPORATION

The Legal Services Corporation (LSC) is a private, nonprofit corporation created by Congress in order to ensure equal access to the legal system for those who could not otherwise afford it. With headquarters in Washington, D.C., the corporation is headed by an 11-member board of directors. All board members are appointed by the president and confirmed by the Senate. The board is, by law, bipartisan, with no more than six members representing the same political party. John McKay is presently president of the LSC.

Operating under the authority of the board of directors are two separate divisions: an office of inspector general and an office of the president. The latter oversees the operations of eight additional offices, including, but not limited to, offices of general counsel, governmental and public affairs, program operations, and information technology.

The LSC itself does not provide legal services; rather, independent local programs that successfully compete for grants execute the LSC's operations. As of 1997, the LSC funded 269 local programs, effectively representing all congressional districts and territories. Native Americans and migrant workers have special areas dedicated to their claims.

Each of the LSC-funded local programs is governed by its own board of directors. The rules for local board membership require that a majority of each board shall be appointed by the local bar association, and that one-third of the members be client representatives appointed by client groups. Staff members are hired by the local board executive director, who is hired by the board. In accordance with established congressional parameters, each board has autonomy in selecting cases.

HISTORY

The LSC was created by Congress in 1974. Coming on the heels of Michael Harrington's now-classic book, *The Other America,* which called attention to the plight of the economic underclass in the United States. The enabling legislation represented a bipartisan effort by Congress and easily won the support of President Richard M. Nixon. The primary concern of the legislative and executive branches of government was that the judiciary should be open to all parties, regardless of economic status. Since *Gideon v. Wainwright* (1963), the right of indigents to legal counsel in criminal cases has been recognized, but no such provision applied to civil matters. Since many of America's poor require legal assistance in order to realize certain basic rights and to guard themselves against discrimination in housing and employment, for example, the LSC was designed to address the civil legal needs of the poor by providing efficient, effective, civil legal assistance. There is still no right of the indigent to legal council in civil cases, but the LSC grants provide some access to counsel.

While the mission of the LSC has remained unchanged, as a corporation of the government it has had to contend with certain political realities. Chief among them is the impact of alternating partisan control of Congress. For the majority of the postwar era, the Democratic Party has held control of the House of Representatives and, therefore, has had primary control over the power of the purse. Given the party's overall support for social welfare programs, the House provided a relatively hospitable environment for the LSC. With the election of a Republican majority in 1994, however, the climate began to change. Specifically, in 1996, Congress imposed a variety of new restrictions on the operation of the LSC. Reflecting the new majority's attitude toward the poor and what it perceived to be expensive exploitation of the judicial system, the 1996 rules prohibited class-action lawsuits; challenges to welfare reform; rule-making, lobbying, and litigation on behalf of prisoners; representation in eviction cases involving allegations of drug use; and representation of certain immigrants. The LSC was also required to adopt a new system of competing for grants. Moreover, the new approach was designed to ensure greater efficiency and effectiveness of LSC-funded legal services.

At risk of losing its federal funding, the LSC rigorously enforces the new rules and restrictions. As such it has not been financially penalized with the partisan transformation of the Congress—only procedurally restricted. Its budget continues to increase modestly with annual appropriations, and the House Appropriations Committee, while challenging the organization, has not abandoned the primary cause for which the LSC was established.

ACTIVITIES: CURRENT AND FUTURE

Although the LSC does not engage in lobbying per se, it does seek to influence appropriations decisions. On March 3, 1999, for example, the LSC appeared before the House Appropriations Committee to request a $340 million budget for the year 2000. The $40 million in additional funds (based upon its $300 million budget for fiscal year 1998–1999) has been defined as necessary for the continuation of existing grant programs and the addition of new initiatives.

In addition to making its annual budget requests and presentations before Congress, the LSC also schedules public hearings on various proposals, programs, and rules. In April 1999, for example, the LSC issued a Federal Register Notice of a public hearing on the subject of when certain immigrants must be present in the United States in order to qualify for legal assistance from LSC-funded programs. The hearing relates to a study undertaken by a recently appointed LSC special panel on legal assistance to eligible immigrants, which is itself a product of the increased demand for civil, human, and economic rights groups to respond to changes in immigration law and aliens' rights.

April 1999 was the effective date of new income eligibility requirements for LSC assistance. Pursuant to a legal requirement that the LSC establish maximum income levels for individuals eligible for legal assistance, the LSC amended its standards in order to reflect recent changes in federal poverty guidelines issued by the Department of Health and Human Services. Designed to equal 125 percent of the poverty guidelines, the LSC's report ("CFR Part 1611 Eligibility") documents the maximum income for families ranging in size from one to eight members, with special instructions for families exceeding the upper size parameter.

Aside from these largely administrative initiatives, the LSC is currently exploring new methods of availing itself not only to independent programs seeking grants, but also to eligible individuals who need legal assistance. Among the most innovative endeavors has been the creation of a site on the World Wide Web. Located at www.ltsi.net/lsc/html, the corporation's web site has succeeded in advertising the LSC's services and establishing interaction among clients, personnel, and grant recipients. More importantly, perhaps, the web site informs the general public of the LSC's current priorities. These priorities include a substantial emphasis on family law, fair housing, government benefits, and consumer affairs.

Although the fortunes of the LSC are ultimately determined by Congress and, in particular, the prevailing ideology of the institution, the LSC has generally maintained the bipartisan support for its mission that prevailed at the time of its founding in 1974. In a report by LSC President John McKay in a March 3, 1999, appearance before a House Appropriations Committee, the bipartisan tone was apparent as only one substantive criticism was raised regarding audits conducted by the Office of the Inspector General. The balance of the meeting was spent identifying and addressing the unmet goals of the previous year as well as goals for future operations.

On the operational front, the LSC has identified six general goals for fiscal years 1998–2003. These goals include strengthening its legal services delivery system, ensuring compliance with legal restrictions (i.e., the 1996 rules changes), enhancing the quality of services to clients, expanding services through partnerships and initiatives financed by federal funds, expanding its commitment to equal access to justice, and maximizing efficiency and productivity of the corporation's internal operations.

The LSC's substantive goals for the immediate future are twofold. The corporation is dedicated to initiatives directed at assisting the victims of domestic violence and meeting the legal needs of children (an estimated $298 million would be dedicated to these causes), in addition to its longstanding commitment to the elderly and those at risk of being evicted from their homes. Second, the LSC intends to dedicate an additional $13 million in fiscal year 2000 to grants for programs designed to expand technological services and client self-help.

FINANCIAL FACTS

The LSC receives 100 percent of its funding from Congress. For the present fiscal year, the LSC maintains a budget of $300 million. Because of its unique status and relationship with the federal government, the LSC is unaffiliated with political action committees (PACs) and does not seek to influence the outcome of political campaigns and elections.

Although appropriations by Congress finance the operation of the LSC, local programs are permitted to supplement their LSC grants with additional funding from various sources. Local programs may, for example, seek to procure additional funds from state and local governments, IOLTA (Interest on Lawyer Trust Accounts) programs, federal agencies, bar associations, and financial contributions from individuals, foundations, corporations, and charitable organizations.

BRIAN SMENTKOWSKI

Bibliography

Legal Services Corporation: www.ltsi.net/lsc.html

NATIONAL COALITION FOR THE HOMELESS

The National Coalition for the Homeless (NCH) is based in Washington, D.C. Mary Ann Gleason is the organization's executive director, and there is a 42-member board of directors including service providers, organizers, and academics. Approximately 31 percent of the board are homeless or formerly homeless men and women. In addition to the executive director and the board members, the NCH maintains a staff of seven members.

The NCH seeks to be an advocate for poor and homeless individuals in the United States. There are currently 600 organizations and 1,000 individuals who are members of the NCH. Some of the methods of operation for the organization include forming coalitions, hosting conferences and seminars, providing Congressional testimony, lobbying, and publishing *Safety Network,* a semimonthly newsletter.

HISTORY

The NCH was founded in 1982 by a coalition of local and state organizations whose primary mission was to end homelessness. Since then, the NCH has committed itself to increasing public awareness of homelessness and lobbying to influence public policy. The NCH's web site lists updated legislative alerts that deal with homelessness-related legislation.

The NCH sponsors many different projects ranging from educational programs to annual events. The National Homeless Civil Rights Organizing Project began to protect the civil rights of people who are homeless. The National Welfare Monitoring and Advocacy Partnership supports the monitoring of welfare at the local level. The Street Newspaper project was an undertaking by the staff at the NCH who assembled information on street newspapers that have been been written, produced, and/or distributed by homeless people. The Educational Rights project increases awareness about the educational rights of homeless children. These are a few of the many projects and efforts the NCH has worked on since 1982.

ACTIVITIES: CURRENT AND FUTURE

In keeping with its mission to end homelessness, the NCH engages in policy advocacy, public education, and grassroots organizing. With regard to policy advocacy, in 1987 the NCH provided leadership to pass the Stewart B. McKinney Homelessness Assistance Act, which was the first, and so far only, major federal legislative response to homelessness. Since the passage of the McKinney Act, the NCH has continued to ensure that billions of dollars are made available for McKinney programs such as education for homeless children and emergency shelter grants.

Public education is of vital importance to the NCH. The staff provides fact sheets, reports, and workshops to thousands of people each year, including the general public, community groups, and the media. The NCH serves as a national clearinghouse for information regarding homelessness and its library is the largest holding of its kind. The library provides research on homelessness and poverty—government reports, case studies, conference reports, evaluations, and more. The NCH also maintains a vast database on research, and members of the staff constantly respond to inquiries.

The NCH is continually organizing grassroots efforts across the country. It has developed dozens of local and state coalitions that have contributed to such efforts as the You Don't Need a Home to Vote campaign and the National Homeless Person's Memorial Day, which takes place every year on December 21. The NCH works to empower homeless people through these nationwide efforts because the organization believes that their voices are vital to the public policy debate.

Current concerns for the NCH include, but are not limited to, gaining access to holistic healthcare; locating affordable, quality housing; education; civil rights; welfare reform; and income maintenance. The NCH has a number of publications that are obtainable through the organization. Facts sheets are available on various aspects of homelessness, including employment, addiction disorders, and domestic violence. A few of the numerous publications include *The 1997 Empowerment Directory*; *Addiction on the Streets: Homelessness and Substance Abuse in America*; *Broken Lives: Denial of Education to Homeless Children*; and *A Directory of National, State, and Local Homeless and Housing Advocacy Organizations*.

The NCH's future activities include continuing to increase public awareness of the prevalence of homelessness and providing information to the general public, agencies, and legislators. In May 1999, the NCH hosted the National Summit on Homelessness in Washington, D.C., to discuss ways of combating homelessness in the twenty-first century. The NCH will continue its education projects, as well as promoting federal legislative priorities that include issues such as health, education, income, and civil rights.

The NCH will continue to host and promote conferences across the country that deal with the many issues associated with homelessness. The organization makes a special effort to ensure that people know that they can make a difference in the fight against homelessness. Whether it be working at a shelter or contributing clothes, money, or food, the NCH operates according to the premise that the only way that homelessness will be eradicated is if society as a whole contributes.

FINANCIAL FACTS

The NCH is a nonprofit organization. Its funding is derived from individual donations, the Combined Federal campaign, foundation grants, and telemarketing. Of the total budget, individual donations make up 51 percent, foundation grants make up 20 percent, corporate donations are 12 percent, membership dues are 11 percent, and publications and conferences each make up 3 percent. Its annual budget averages approximately $500,000, which helps to cover the cost of its educational projects, annual events, special campaigns, and publications. The NCH engages in lobbying to advocate policy; however, it does not contribute to individual political campaigns.

BRIAN SMENTKOWSKI AND THERESA HAUG

Bibliography

DeAngelis, James J. *Public Interest Profiles, 1998-1999*. CQ Foundation for Public Affairs. Washington, DC: Congressional Quarterly, 1998.

National Coalition for the Homeless: www.nch.ari.net

NATIONAL LAWYERS GUILD

The National Lawyers Guild (NLG) is the only public interest bar organization consisting of members who are active in virtually every area of civil and human rights practice. Headquartered in New York and operating 200 chapters nationwide, the NLG is actively engaged in the movement for social and economic justice. It is headed by a four-member national executive committee led by Karen Jo Koonan, president, six vice presidents, and eight regional vice presidents. A sophisticated organization, it maintains eight national executive committees, including the Economic Rights Task Force; the international committee; and the Corporations, the Constitution, and Human Rights committees. Its operations are facilitated through a total of 21 NLG committees, projects, and task forces. With more than 5,000 registered members and several thousand associates, the NLG Membership Network coordinates the acquisition of legal representation and the organization of movements for social change.

HISTORY

The NLG's creation occurred at an informal meeting of lawyers on December 1, 1936, at New York's City Club. The group discussed the formation of a progressive, multiracial bar organization that could serve as an alternative to the all-white and generally antilabor American Bar Association. Two months later, the NLG emerged as both the nation's first integrated bar association and the first human rights organization.

In its first decades, the NLG's main method of operation was organization. Operating in an area where racial and economic discrimination converge, the NLG organized support for the New Deal and industrial unions, as well as opposition to poll taxes and racial discrimination. In the aftermath of the Second World War, guild members participated in the Nuremberg trials, the founding of the United Nations, and investigations of race riots. During the 1950s, the NLG dedicated its legal skills to the defense of labor leaders, political activists, and dissidents accused of being un-American. Indeed, at the height of McCarthyism, the NLG was the only legal organization that did not require anti-Communist oaths of its members.

During the 1960s, the NLG experienced one of its most important organizational changes. In its effort to organize massive assistance to the southern civil rights movement, it created the Committee to Aid Southern Lawyers. This not only began the NLG's era of developing specialized committees to deal with particular sociolegal issues, but also demonstrated the organization's willingness and ability to adapt to new problems and methods of solving them. This was continued in the 1970s when the NLG defended draft resisters and antiwar activists in the United States and in Indochina, began its Prison Law project in support of prisoners' rights, and established legal defense teams for defendants from the siege at Wounded Knee and the Attica Prison uprising.

During the 1980s and 1990s, the NLG became increasingly active in advocating resistance to Reagan/Bush–era civil rights policy initiatives, U.S. intervention in Nicaragua, and discriminatory immigration policies. It organized and defended cases demanding affirmative action in law schools while its National Immigration Project served as a leader in providing defense and issue advocacy for legal aliens and immigrants.

ACTIVITIES: CURRENT AND FUTURE

During the 1990s, educational initiatives have become the NLG's main method of operation. Through its writings, training seminars, and educational programs, the organization has been at the forefront of the labor and workforce movement, and is a major advocate of immigrant and prisoners' rights.

With the publication of a 190-page manual, "Speaking Up for Affirmative Action," the NLG's Bay Area Affirmative Action Committee has been engaged in an educational program designed to protect affirmative action policies and to facilitate their implementation nationwide, although an immediate concern has been to address California's special circumstances emanating from Proposition 209, which eliminates affirmative action requirements. The manual provides statistical information on race and gender discrimination, and also includes a substantive analysis of the impact of weak and absent affirmative action policies in schools and the workplace. The manual has also become the foundation for a number of public education initiatives, including practical information on organizing local affirmative action speaker's bureaus.

The NLG also runs a National Immigration Project, which investigates discriminatory policies, provides legal challenges to such policies, and publishes a number of works dedicated to stemming the anti-immigration tide. These works include, but are not limited to, the NLG's quarterly *Immigration Newsletter,* its *Brief Bank Index,* and a number of books published by West Group on immigration law and naturalization.

The Prison Law project, which was reestablished in 1993, provides a formal mechanism for jailhouse lawyers to work with the NLG. The purpose of this enterprise is to establish a legal commitment to the premise that human rights should be viewed as more important than property rights. More pragmatically, the NLG is presently establishing a prisoners' rights education program, as well as a public education program about prison and criminal law issues. Part of this mission is to advocate the adoption of policies and laws that accommodate the work of jailhouse lawyers.

As is the case with most human rights organizations, the NLG is expected to monitor the proliferation and conduct of hate groups on the Internet and in society generally. The organization remains committed to eradicating race, sex, and economic discrimination, and is in the process of charting new paths to address the various new manifestations of discrimination that have begun to emerge. These new challenges are, and will continue to be, evident in state and federal affirmative action policy changes, in the growing intolerance toward the economic underclass, and in efforts on behalf of gay and lesbian rights. The NLG has issued a call, in fact, for a rededication to progressive legal work. Since its inception in 1936 the NLG has been committed to bringing together "all those who regard adjustments to new conditions as more important than the veneration of precedent" (www.nlg.org). Its concern for the future is that law schools are training status quo–oriented public interest lawyers, rather than progressive, innovative lawyers who will use the law to change—rather than blindly serve—politics and government.

FINANCIAL FACTS

The NLG is a nonprofit organization whose foundation maintains 501(c)(3) tax status. Its annual budgets are funded by individual contributions, foundation support, and personal membership dues. The membership dues themselves are structured according to income and legal status (e.g., law school students, practicing attorneys, and jailhouse lawyers all pay different membership rates). None of the organization's activities is financed by government grants. A nonlobbying organization, the NLG does not operate a political action committee (PAC) and does not participate in or finance electoral campaigns.

BRIAN SMENTKOWSKI

Bibliography

The National Lawyers Guild: www.nlg.org; informational materials forwarded upon request. National Lawyers Guild, 126 University Place, 5th Floor, NY, NY 10003.

Tolley, H. "Interest Group Litigation to Enforce Human Rights." *Political Science Quarterly* 105, no. 4 (Winter 1990): 617-639.

SECTION TEN
POLITICAL, RELIGIOUS, AND IDEOLOGICAL

Political, ideological, and religious interest groups represent political interests from across the ideological spectrum, from the far right to the left. Some were founded early in the twentieth century and have long records of political activism and influence. Most were founded during the wave of interest group formation that emerged after the 1960s. Some of the groups are nonmembership groups, as in the case of "think tanks" that focus on putting research and policy analyses into the hands of decision makers. Other groups draw their strength from a large and active membership that can be mobilized to bring pressure on elected officials. These membership bases are diverse, representing some of the traditionally active segments of the population with higher incomes and education but including more recently mobilized populations, for example, people who favor prayer in schools and oppose abortion rights. The financial resources of these groups run the gamut as well, from contributor-dependent groups with annual budgets of less than $100,000 to corporate- and foundation-backed groups with annual budgets as high as $50 million.

These groups are actively engaged in efforts to shape policies that affect every major political issue on the national agenda. These are groups that focus on international trade issues, national security and military issues, and other foreign policy issues. Almost all the groups are involved in domestic, economic, and budget issues, including tax reform, entitlement reform, the costs and benefits of economic regulation, and reducing the national debt. Many groups are concerned with social issues such as education, welfare policies, affirmative action, crime, and drug abuse. Many are engaged in cultural or "values" issues related to family concerns, pornography, domestic violence, homosexuality, school prayer, and abortion. Political issues such as campaign finance reform, term limits, and ethics in government are also on some of their agendas.

These groups make use of virtually every tactic in the arsenal of pressure groups, including direct lobbying, grassroots mobilization, and media and public relations activities. Most are technologically sophisticated, relying on new technologies for influence and fund-raising. Almost all of the groups have a site on the World Wide Web, many of them elaborate, some of them award-winning and even regarded as path-breaking.

AREAS OF INTEREST

Interest groups have existed throughout American history. James Madison pointed out in the 1780s that their causes are "sown in the nature of man." The social and economic climate in the United States, with its racially, ethnically, and culturally diverse population and competing economic interests, has also been hospitable to the formation of interest groups. The political structure in the United States has opened the door to the formation of a vigorous interest group system by providing many access points for those who seek to influence public policies. Although there is a long history of interest group activity, all the groups covered in this section are of relatively recent origin, having been founded in the twentieth century and, in fact, most were founded in the last four decades of the century.

The Brookings Institution is the oldest think tank. It was founded in 1916 to support research and reform in the area of efficiency and economy in government during the Progressive Era, when expertise and rationality were the watchwords of government and industry. Americans for Democratic Action and the John Birch Society were founded in the early days of the Cold War and their missions are a reflection of the tensions of the time. Liberal academics, intellectuals, and politicians founded Americans for Democratic Action in 1947 to promote a liberal political agenda without the "taint" of communist influence. The John Birch Society was created as an anti-communist organization in 1958 by Robert Welch, a candy manufacturer who was convinced that an international communist conspiracy that included President Dwight Eisenhower had infiltrated the American government. All the other groups were founded after 1960 during what scholars regard as one of the great waves of interest-group formation in American history.

The 1960s saw a surge in the number of interest groups engaged in the political process, a surge that has continued for three decades and more. This expansion of groups came not only among traditional economic groups (such as business and trade associations) but also among public-interest citizen groups focusing on consumer protection or government ethics, for example, and political and religious groups focusing on a range of contentious issues, including what are considered the fundamental values of American society and culture. The proliferation of interest groups was accompanied by a centralization of group headquarters in Washington, D.C., as groups and their lobbyists took up permanent residence in the nation's capital to plead their causes. It was also accompanied by a growing technological sophistication, with many groups developing elaborate systems for soliciting and communicating with members, mobilizing pressure on policy makers, and honing their messages for specific targets. A long-term trend toward higher levels of education provided an expanded pool of potential recruits.

A number of changes in the social, economic, and political climate contributed to the decades-long surge in interest group activity and to the particular mix of political and ideological interests that have been activated. In the 1960s and 1970s, the national government created or expanded major government programs in social welfare, education, and healthcare. It also passed new regulatory legislation in the areas of civil rights, consumer protection, and occupational health and safety. This greatly expanded role of government served as an impetus for the growth in the number of interest groups. New government agencies helped organize service providers or program beneficiaries to press for continued government action. Ideological opponents of expanded government organized, forming the American Conservative Union, the National Taxpayers Union, and the Cato Institute. Business opponents of new regulation and new taxes pumped money into organizations such as the Heritage Foundation and, later, Citizens for a Sound Economy, to press the case against bigger government. A "tax revolt" in the late 1970s generated new energy for organized action to reduce the level of taxation. Supporters of more aggressive government regulation to protect consumers and the environment also organized, including Citizen Action, Public Citizen, and the U.S. Public Interest Research Group.

The increase in interest group activity also flowed from the social and cultural upheaval of the 1960s that carried into the 1970s. This was a period of social protest that challenged established practices and authorities, demanded more accountability from political leaders, and legitimated new grassroots political tactics. The civil rights movement and the anti-Vietnam War movements were among the most visible elements of the new activism, but protest and social ferment emerged in various segments of society. Even the hierarchy of the Roman Catholic Church endorsed greater social and political engagement after Vatican II in 1965. The social protest movements also brought new demands for the recognition of rights for blacks, women, Hispanics, American Indians, prisoners, the mentally ill, the homeless, and gay men and lesbians. These demands added to the momentum of group formation.

By the late 1970s, a backlash began to emerge from the widening role of government and a sense among some segments of the population that government programs undermined traditional values and institutions, gave too much support to minorities, and were too expensive to operate. The election of President Ronald Reagan in 1980 was one element in a conservative tide in the 1980s that contributed to new vigor in political organizing by conservatives and corporations. Conservative groups such as Americans for Tax Reform supported the Reagan administration's efforts to cut taxes and shrink social programs. Liberal groups critical of the Reagan administration's economic policies and their impact on minorities and the poor also organized, including the National Coalition for the Homeless and the Economic Policy Institute. The late 1970s also marked the beginning of the political mobilization of religious conservatives. The emergence of the "electronic church" brought large television audiences to evangelical ministers and religious entrepreneurs such as Jerry Falwell, Pat Robertson, and Jim Bakker. The Christian school movement, formed out of the resistance to racial integration as well as out of a reaction to secular trends in public schools and public life, also brought together a potential political constituency. The tax treatment of religious schools and the regulatory treatment of religious broadcasters, combined with increasingly prominent social issues such as abortion, school prayer, and family breakdown brought religious conservatives into the political arena through groups such as Moral Majority, Christian Voice, and one of the largest and most influential, the Christian Coalition, founded in 1989.

The decades since the 1960s also witnessed efforts by presidential administrations, elected officials, and interest groups to alter the legal terrain to support friendly interests and to undermine opposing groups. Tax code provisions regarding deductions for contributions to interest groups or for lobbying expenses, subsidies of postal rates for nonprofit groups, and rules for the registration and regulation of lobbyists influence those groups that thrive and those that struggle. The Reagan administration undertook a conscious effort to defund the left and mobilize its conservative allies, to restrict government funds that assisted political organizing by advocates of government programs or to challenge the tax-exempt status of its critics. The Clinton administration has evidently pursued similar tactics against groups that opposed its policies.

Finally, the creation and maintenance of interest groups require large amounts of capital. Many of the newly formed interest groups have been able to sustain their activities by developing new sources of funding outside their immediate membership. Political entrepreneurs and patrons of political action, including wealthy individuals, corporations, private foundations, and government agencies, have been willing to back groups supportive of their interests. Conservative think tanks have been especially successful at attracting the financial support necessary to build influential institutions and infrastructures. According to the National Committee for Responsive Philanthropy (NCRP), the top 20 conservative think tanks, including the Heritage Foundation, the American Enterprise Institute, and the Cato Institute, spent $158 million in 1996. These think tanks have relied upon wealthy benefactors such as the Koch family (Kansas oil billionaires), conservative foundations such as the John M. Olin Foundation, and corporations and businesses such as Amway to build sophisticated political advocacy machines. The NCRP estimates that overall spending by conservative think tanks will have exceeded $1 billion in the last decade of the twentieth century.

TYPES OF ORGANIZATIONS

Interest groups can be categorized in several ways. Some scholars group them according to the kind of interest they represent (economic or social, for example), whether they are open to all persons for membership or are restricted by occupational affiliation, or whether they are for-profit or nonprofit entities. Most of the groups in this section fall into one of two categories: citizen groups or think tanks. Citizen groups claim to represent a general, public interest and do not restrict membership on the basis of occupational or professional affiliation. Think tanks are private research-oriented groups that analyze public policy issues and advocate policy alternatives. Some citizen groups and think tanks are explicit about their political leanings and ideological commitments, such as the liberal Americans for Democratic Action, the conservative American Conservative Union, and the libertarian Cato Institute. Other groups insist that their interest is the public's interest, but most can also be placed on the ideological spectrum; for example, Public Citizen and Common Cause are regarded as liberal interest groups, whereas Citizens for a Sound Economy and Americans for Tax Reform are regarded as conservative interest groups.

Some of the groups do not offer membership. Think tanks such as the Brookings Institution and the American Enterprise Institute employ scholars, researchers, and other professional staff, and focus primarily on publishing policy analyses and disseminating the results among policy-makers and the public. Some of these "nonmember" interest groups solicit contributions from sponsors or patrons and provide newsletters, publications, discounts, or other benefits to contributors. Other groups are explicitly member organizations: members pay dues in exchange for various benefits.

Some of the membership groups are fairly small. The John Birch Society has a membership of around 40,000, and Americans for Democratic Action has about 60,000 members. Many of the groups report membership in the hundreds of thousands, although most are below 300,000. The Christian Coalition claims almost 2 million members. Some of the groups have other organizations as members. These organizations have memberships that do not necessarily join or support the interest group. For example, the National Council of Churches represents some 52 million members who have not necessarily expressed support for the group's advocacy agenda.

Studies have shown that most Americans do not join interest groups. Those who do share the demographic characteristics of those most likely to vote: higher education and higher income. Unlike voting, though, joining a group carries more obvious costs, and interest group membership has an even more pronounced upper-status skew than voting. However, there are exceptions to the upper-class tilt of interest group membership. Populist groups with an anti-elitist, anti-establishment message have historically drawn support from lower-status citizens. In recent decades, this has been especially true of conservative groups whose emphasis has been on the threats to traditional values and institutions posed by the secular and economic developments of modern life promoted by "the establishment." The John Birch Society, with its ultrapatriotism and aggressive defense of traditional morality, has drawn support from lower-income, less-educated, often rural citizens. The more recent religious conservative movement, sometimes referred to as the "Christian Right" and reflected in such groups as the Christian Coalition, has also been successful at mobilizing lower-status citizens. Aggressive and sophisticated direct-mail solicitation techniques have garnered conservative populist groups (and candidates) large amounts of money in small contributions from a large donor base. There is also some evidence that the religious right has made inroads into the more well-off, more-educated suburban population in the last decade.

The groups in this section have budgets that run from fairly modest, such as the $600,000 annual budget of Americans for Democratic Action, to very robust, such as the $43 million annual budget of the Heritage Foundation. Most of the groups in this section have annual budgets that exceed $1 million, some have multi-million-dollar budgets, and a handful, including the Heritage Foundation, the Brookings Institution, American Enterprise Institute, Common Cause, and the Christian Coalition, have annual budgets that exceed $10 million. The sources of revenue vary from group to group, as does the mix of revenue sources.

The main sources of income for these groups are contributions or dues from individuals, grants from charitable foundations, contributions from corporations, and grants from government agencies. Some receive income from investments, many receive income from the sale of publications, and some receive income from renting member or contributor lists to other groups. Many foundations support the research and organizing activities of interest groups, sometimes without regard to the political leanings of the group. Some foundations are clearly patrons of conservative groups, including the Sarah Scaife Foundation, the John M. Olin Foundation, the David H. Koch Charitable Foundation, Lynde and Harry Bradley Foundation, Smith-Richardson Foundation, and Adolph Coors Foundation. Others are typically supporters of liberal groups, including the Florence and John Schumann Foundation, John D. and Catherine T. MacArthur Foundation, Henry J. Kaiser Family Foundation, Joyce Foundation, and Charles Stewart Mott Foundation.

CURRENT ISSUES

Political, ideological, and religious interest groups attempt to influence public opinion and policy regarding virtually every issue on the national agenda. None of these groups confines its efforts to a single issue.

The general principles, as well as the detailed policies of international affairs issues, draw the attention of most of the groups in this section. Liberal groups, such as Americans for Democratic Action, have pressed the case for American foreign policies that emphasize human rights, economic assistance to underdeveloped countries, arms control, global environmental regulation, and support for international organizations such as the United Nations. Conservative groups, such as the Heritage Foundation, have argued for policies that clearly define and advance America's own vital interests, provide maximum military power and technology, including a missile defense system, and limit economic assistance to countries that are not supportive of American interests and values. They are skeptical of global treaties and international organizations. The libertarian Cato Institute has argued for peaceful trade relations with all nations and entangling alliances with none. It has opposed most U.S. engagement abroad that involves covert or overt efforts to change or coerce other governments. The John Birch Society is fearful of a global conspiracy to create a one-world totalitarian government and has identified enemies of America in virtually every spot around the globe, enemies that should be guarded against rather than traded with.

On international trade issues, liberals such as Americans for Democratic Action or the U.S. Catholic Conference have argued for basing normal trade relations on the human rights and labor practices of the country in question. Conservatives such as Citizens for a Sound Economy have argued that free markets, and therefore free trade, benefit citizens in all countries over the long run.

Domestic economic issues have also engaged almost all of these interest groups. Liberal groups—including the Economic Policy Institute, Public Citizen, Citizen

Action, and Americans for Democratic Action—have pushed for an active government role in regulating corporate action to protect consumers against hazardous products, employees against hazards in the workplace, and citizens against hazards in the environment. They have pressed for greater funding for social welfare programs that provide food, education, housing, and healthcare assistance to low-income citizens. They have pressed for progressive income taxes that shift more of the tax burden to the wealthy and corporations.

Conservatives, including Americans for Tax Reform, the American Conservative Union, the National Taxpayers Union, and Citizens for a Sound Economy, have lobbied for lower and flatter tax rates, less government regulation in the areas of education, healthcare, the environment, the workplace, and product safety, and less government social spending overall. Plans to reduce government regulation and spending include proposals to privatize all or part of the Social Security and Medicare programs. Conservative groups have also favored balancing the federal budget. Some support the passage of a balanced budget constitutional amendment.

Social issues are the concern of many of these groups. On abortion, religious groups such as the U.S. Catholic Conference and the Christian Coalition join with conservative groups such as the John Birch Society to support efforts to criminalize most abortions. The libertarian Cato Institute joins with liberals such as Americans for Democratic Action to oppose legal restrictions on abortion. Some of the conservative groups that are focused on taxes and economic regulation studiously avoid the issue. The Christian Coalition joins with the Cato Institute and conservatives in opposition to gun control, while the U.S. Catholic Conference and the National Council of Churches join with liberals to support tighter legal restrictions on gun access and possession. The issues of gay rights, pornography, the death penalty, child care, and media depictions of sex and violence also concern many of these groups, with the ideological line-ups sometimes unpredictable.

Political issues such as term limits and campaign finance reform are also the focus of public education and lobbying efforts by many of these groups. Campaign finance and the relationship between special interests and politicians are especially the concern of Common Cause, Public Citizen, the Center for Public Integrity, and the Center for Responsive Politics. Some groups, especially the John Birch Society, aggressively pushed for the impeachment and removal of President Bill Clinton. Others, especially Americans for Democratic Action, were critical of the impeachment.

TYPES OF ACTIVITIES

Despite differences in the kinds of interest groups represented here, all engage in a range of efforts designed to influence public debate and political decisions regarding public policies. The types of activities they engage in, however, are shaped by government regulations.

Most of the groups in this section are designated as tax-exempt organizations under Section 501(c)(3) of the Internal Revenue code, which stipulates that they may engage in educational activities but may not lobby for or against legislation. In some cases, however, 501(c)(3) organizations may spend 15 percent to 20 percent of their expenses on lobbying without paying a penalty. Other groups in this section are tax-exempt organizations under Section 501(c)(4) of the Internal Revenue code, and they are allowed to lobby for or against legislation that will promote the general welfare but not benefit one single industry. There has always been a fine line between educational activities and lobbying, and groups have battled the Internal Revenue Service (IRS) over where the line falls. In 1999, the IRS ruled that certain Christian Coalition activities crossed into partisan activity, and it revoked the group's tax-exempt status, forcing it to reorganize as a for-profit, partisan lobbying group. Some political groups do engage in lobbying and also make contributions to political candidates.

Although most of these groups do not technically engage in lobbying and do not make contributions to candidates for public office, many still enter the electoral process. Several maintain and publish "scorecards" of the voting records of members of Congress, rating them on how often they vote the "correct" way on issues of importance to the group. The scorecards of the American Conservative Union and Americans for Democratic Action have become widely accepted measures of the political ideology of members of Congress. The Christian Coalition also publishes scorecards on the voting records of members of congress and distributes millions of these in churches across the country at election time.

Most of the groups publish policy analyses and positions on advocacy for sale or distribution. Think tanks such as American Enterprise Institute, Cato Institute, and the Brookings Institution have extensive publications, including scholarly monographs, trade books, and research reports. The John Birch Society runs a large-scale publishing operation, American Opinion Books, that publishes books and pamphlets that are distributed through a chain of book outlets run by the society. Most of these groups also publish newsletters or magazines with information on issues and legislation for members or financial supporters.

Citizens for a Sound Economy is one of several of the groups that maintains a professional field staff to train volunteers across the country in organizing, media tactics, and public education techniques. The group, along with others, organizes state and local chapters to educate citizens and conduct letter-writing and phone campaigns, and it supports them with products and services that include position papers, videos, and bumper stickers.

Common Cause, Public Citizen, the Center for Responsive Politics, the Heritage Foundation, the Cato Institute, the American Enterprise Institute, and many of the other groups also devote a significant effort to influencing the public debate in the media. Staff analysts, economists, and spokespersons write op-ed articles and appear on radio and television public affairs shows. They are available as speakers for local civic groups and colleges. Many of the groups organize seminars, conferences, and workshops, some of them overseas, to discuss issues of concern and to advance their point of view. These groups also target members of Congress and their staffs for "educational" activities, holding briefings, providing analyses, and drafting legislation and speeches. The Heritage Foundation and Citizens for a Sound Economy have been especially influential, forging close ties to the Republican congressional leadership in the 1990s.

Finally, almost all of the groups in this section maintain a site on the World Wide Web. Some of them are extensive and sophisticated. Many provide access to an extensive archive of policy reports and analysis. Issue briefings, legislative updates, links to other organizations, and recommendations for action are common on these sites. Some provide direct links to the offices of members of Congress, allowing visitors to e-mail their representatives and senators.

RAYMOND B. WRABLEY, JR.

Bibliography

Berry, Jeffrey M. *The Interest Group Society,* 2d ed. Boston: Scott, Foresman/Little, Brown, 1989.

Callahan, David. *$1 Billion for Ideas: Conservative Think Tanks in the 1990s.* Washington, DC: National Committee for Responsive Philanthropy, 1999.

Cigler, Allan, and Burdett Loomis, eds. *Interest Group Politics,* 4th ed. Washington, DC: Congressional Quarterly Press, 1994.

Edsall, Thomas B., and Mary D. Edsall. *Chain Reaction: The Impact of Race, Rights, and Taxes on American Politics.* New York: W.W. Norton, 1992.

Herrnson, Paul, Ronald Shaiko, and Clyde Wilcox, eds. *The Interest Group Connection: Electioneering, Lobbying, and Policymaking in Washington.* New York: Chatham House, 1998.

Hrebenar, Ronald J. *Interest Group Politics in America.* Armonk, NY: M.E. Sharpe, 1997.

Walker, Jack L. "The Origins and Maintenance of Interest Groups in America." *American Political Science Review* 77, no. 2 (June 1983): 390–406.

AMERICAN CONSERVATIVE UNION

The American Conservative Union (ACU) is the nation's oldest conservative lobbying organization. Founded in 1964 and headquartered in northern Virginia, the ACU's Statement of Principles lays out its strong support for capitalism, the doctrine of original intent of the framers of the Constitution, traditional moral values, and a strong national defense. Its mission is to communicate and advance the goals and principles of conservatism through one multi-issue, umbrella organization. With 500,000 members nationwide, the ACU engages in lobbying and public education activities on a wide range of issues.

The ACU devotes a significant amount of effort to mobilizing its members and supporters to influence the decisions made in Congress. Its recently launched site on the World Wide Web allows members to sign up for the ACU's e-mail service, Infonet, and receive memos, news releases, commentaries published by ACU leaders, and sample letters to Congress on key legislation. The site also allows visitors to join the ACU, register for conferences, access published materials, and do research on their representatives and senators. The ACU Ratings of Congress are archived back to 1971 on the site. These ratings give members of Congress a score based on how they voted on important issues throughout the year. The ACU rating is a widely accepted measure of the political ideology of representatives.

The ACU also collaborates with other groups in coalitions to mobilize the public on various issues and has even joined with liberal groups like Americans for Democratic Action when they share a common position. They have organized town meetings to help spread the conservative viewpoint. A media bureau provides the public and the media with information and commentary and an ACU speakers bureau provides community and civic groups with orators for their events. The ACU also publishes legislative guides for members of Congress and their staffs that provide conservative policy analysis and proposals. It also produces television and newspaper advertisements, and audio and video documentaries on various issues.

Since 1974, the ACU has hosted the annual Conservative Political Action Conference, where thousands of conservative leaders and activists meet to discuss current issues and policies. The conference has become one of the more prominent and prestigious events within the conservative movement and has attracted high-profile speakers and participants like Ronald Reagan, George Bush, Dan Quayle, Bob Dole, and Newt Gingrich.

HISTORY

The ACU was founded in 1964 by prominent conservatives, including Frank Meyer, John Ashbrook, William F. Buckley, L. Brent Bozell, and Robert Bauman. Its mission was to provide unified leadership to the conservative movement, mold public opinion, and stimulate responsible political action. In 1965, under the leadership of William Rusher, the ACU mounted a successful drive to expand its membership and create state affiliates. It also launched a lobbying and publication effort in the 1960s, and backed the election of Richard Nixon and Spiro Agnew in 1968. In 1970, the ACU created the Conservative Victory Fund, one of the first conservative campaign war chests to support political candidates. In 1971 it began to publish the ACU ratings of members of Congress. The ACU eventually became critical of what it perceived to be a liberal drift in the Nixon administration, and it endorsed ACU founder John Ashbrook's bid for the 1972 Republican presidential nomination. In 1974, the ACU sponsored the first Conservative Political Action Conference to help train, inform, and inspire conservative activists. The ACU was unsuccessful in its effort to help Ronald

**American Conservative Union
Political Action Committee Contributions**

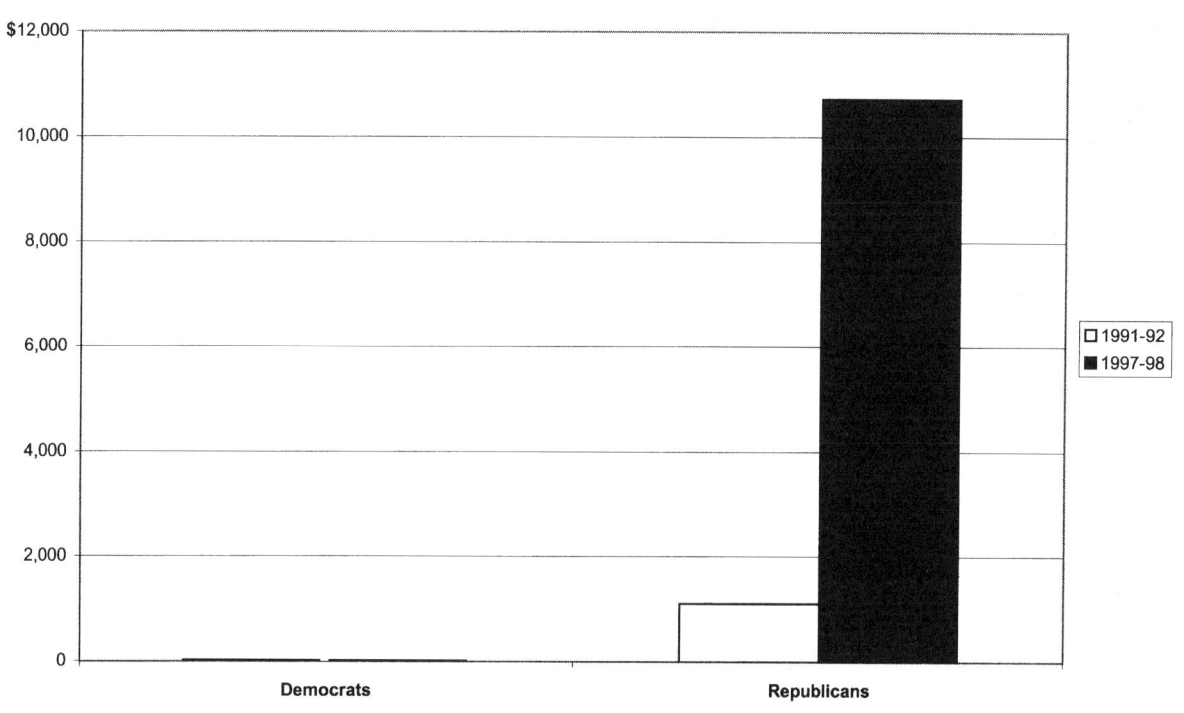

Data derived from official studies available from the Federal Election Commission, Washington, DC, 1991–1998.

Reagan win the Republican presidential nomination in 1976.

The ACU incorporated as a nonprofit organization in 1979. Financial difficulties plagued the organization throughout the 1980s, as it competed with emerging conservative groups for money and members. The election of Democrat Bill Clinton in 1992 prompted a resurgence in support and the ACU's membership reached an all-time high in 1994. It was able to purchase a permanent headquarters in Alexandria, Virginia, in 1994 and its political action committee, ACU PAC was able to support many conservative candidates.

ACTIVITIES: CURRENT AND FUTURE

The ACU lobbies Congress on a range of issues. As the self-proclaimed "conservative voice in Washington," the ACU has pushed for a balanced budget, lower taxes, less government regulation, less spending on social programs, more spending on the military, and stronger support for traditional moral values. Recently, the ACU supported the Tax Code Termination Act, which would have abolished the current tax code by a certain date. According to the ACU, this would open the way for a new tax system with lower and flatter rates. The group lobbied against increases in the minimum wage, arguing that the minimum wage law is a "job killer" because it would force employers who could not afford to raise wages to lay off workers.

The ACU has opposed the most prominent campaign finance reform proposals and instead has supported reforms that would abolish campaign contribution limits, terminate public financing of presidential elections, and strengthen disclosure and reporting requirements.

The ACU has supported various proposals for school choice, including school vouchers and tax-free educational savings accounts. It has also supported a ban on racial and gender preferences in federal contracting and hiring, claiming that such programs are the antithesis of civil rights. It has been in the forefront of the effort to pass a national ban on a late-term abortion procedure that critics call partial-birth abortion. The ACU has lobbied to abolish the National Endowment for the Arts, claiming that it subsidizes "pornographic, blasphemous, and extremist political 'art.'"

The ACU pressed Congress to reject the Comprehensive Test Ban Treaty backed by the Clinton administration, arguing that the treaty would do irreparable damage to the U.S. nuclear weapons program and national security. It has supported abandoning the Anti-Ballistic Missile Treaty and constructing a missile defense system. The ACU lobbied for rejection of the Chemical Weapons Treaty signed by President Clinton, and opposed the Kyoto Protocols which aims to reduce greenhouse gas emissions worldwide. Those pacts, the ACU argued, would weaken the U.S. military and limit American autonomy. The ACU has also pushed for tighter restrictions on U.S. commercial activities and trade with China.

FINANCIAL FACTS

ACU PAC, the political action committee of the American Conservative Union, has given increasing sums to the campaign coffers of Republican candidates for Congress over the past decade, although these amounts remain relatively modest. In the 1991–1992 cycle, ACU PAC gave a little over $1,000 to Republican candidates for Congress; during the 1997–1998 election cycle, that figure had climbed to just over $10,000. Given its conservative ideological predilections, the American Conservative Union gives no money to the campaigns of Democratic candidates for Congress.

RAYMOND B. WRABLEY, JR.

Bibliography

"American Conservative Union." *Human Events,* vol. 50, no. 12, April 1, 1994, p. 10.

American Conservative Union website: www.conservative.org

Crawford, Alan. *Thunder on the Right: The "New Right" and the Politics of Resentment.* New York: Pantheon Books, 1980.

Wilcox, Derk Arend. *The Right Guide: A Guide to Conservative and Right-of-Center Organizations.* Ann Arbor, MI: Economics America, Inc., 1997.

AMERICAN ENTERPRISE INSTITUTE

The American Enterprise Institute for Public Policy Research (AEI) is one of the largest and most respected think tanks in the United States. Founded in 1943 and based in Washington, D.C., AEI sponsors original research on government policy, the American economy, and American politics. It is a tax-exempt, nonpartisan organization, although it is recognized as one of the preeminent conservative think tanks in the nation's capital. Its self-proclaimed mission is to preserve and strengthen the foundations of freedom—limited government, private enterprise, vital cultural and political institutions, and a strong foreign policy and national defense. It employs a resident faculty of scholars and fellows and supports more than 100 adjunct scholars at universities and policy institutes throughout the United States and abroad. Its staff of scholars and writers includes prominent conservative academics and politicians.

AEI engages in a wide range of activities that are designed to influence public policy debates in the United States. Among its most important efforts is its book-publishing program. The AEI Press produces volumes by leading policy-makers and scholars on economics, foreign affairs, politics, and culture. Among its more provocative publications in recent years were *The Bell Curve,* by Charles Murray and Richard Herrnstein, and *The End of Racism,* by Dinesh D'Souza.

AEI also maintains an active government relations program, communicating its research findings and proposals to members of Congress and their staffs, officials and staff from the executive branch, federal judges, and state and local officials. AEI scholars testify regularly before congressional committees. The organization also holds numerous briefings each year for government officials and AEI events often feature presentations by government leaders. A survey of congressional aides and journalists by *Mediaweek* found AEI to be among the most influential think tanks in Washington, D.C.

AEI also provides support to numerous journalists and commentators whose columns appear in leading newspapers or who appear regularly on television news programs promoting AEI's point of view. The work of AEI scholars is cited more frequently in newspapers and newsmagazines than that of their peers at other research institutes. AEI also organizes nearly 200 seminars, conferences, lectures, and briefings each year. At its well-attended annual dinner in Washington, D.C., AEI presents the Frances Boyer Award to an individual who has made notable intellectual or practical contributions to American society.

AEI publishes a bimonthly magazine of politics, business, and culture, titled *The American Enterprise.* It also maintains a comprehensive site on the World Wide Web, where visitors can access a wide array of policy analyses and commentary, including audio files.

HISTORY

AEI was founded in 1943 by Lewis H. Brown, chairman of the Johns-Manville Corporation, to promote free market ideas. Its financial support came almost exclusively from corporations and business-minded individuals. In 1954, William J. Baroody, Sr., became its executive vice president, at a time when AEI had four full-time employees and an annual budget of $85,000. Baroody developed AEI, becoming its president in 1962. Shortly thereafter its name was changed to the American Enterprise Institute for Public Policy Research.

Baroody was a key advisor to Senator Barry Goldwater during his 1964 presidential campaign and AEI was criticized as being a "cover" for political activities. By the early 1970s, Baroody had hired a public relations firm to promote AEI, begun a series of videotaped forums on current topics, and aggressively sought to broaden support for AEI beyond the business community. AEI grew dramatically, employing a staff of over 100, with a budget of $6 million. It launched a number of new periodicals, including *Regulation* and *Public Opinion,* and hired a number of former Nixon administration officials as fellows, including William Simon and Robert Bork. In 1977, former President Gerald Ford was named AEI's first "distinguished fellow."

AEI was aggressive in promoting its research among members of Congress and in the early 1980s gained influence in the Reagan White House, as a number of AEI fellows won appointments in the administration. It also began an effort to move to the ideological center, hiring a number of Democrats as staffers. In the mid 1980s, under the leadership of William J. Baroody, Jr., AEI fell upon hard times, suffering from budget deficits and poor management, and with conservative money shifting to newly formed conservative competitors, partly in response to AEI's move to the center. In 1986, Baroody was forced out as president of AEI and was replaced by Christopher C. DeMuth. DeMuth instituted a series of budget and staff cuts, sold off several publications, and initiated an aggressive fund-raising effort, including an "associates program" to solicit support from individuals.

In the 1990s, AEI was able to bring on board high-profile academics and former government officials, which contributed to its success in attracting more foundation and corporate support. It has been able to expand its presence in academe, the media, and the halls of government, and to solidify its reputation in the Washington policy community.

ACTIVITIES: CURRENT AND FUTURE

AEI does not take an institutional position on policies and legislation, but it supports hundreds of scholars, writers, and journalists who research and comment on virtually every domestic and foreign policy issue and who support a wide range of policy proposals. Its research "shop" is divided into economic policy studies, foreign and defense policy studies, and social and political studies. These broad areas include hundreds of specific policy areas, such as business and enterprise, markets, trade, the environment, federalism, culture, religion, and the family. Although AEI scholars take positions that cover a broader swath of the ideological spectrum than do the more conservative Heritage Foundation or the more ideologically pure libertarian Cato Institute, conservative policy prescriptions clearly dominate. AEI writers have generally been hostile to the policies of the Clinton administration.

In the area of economics, AEI scholars generally advocate lower taxes, less regulation, less government spending on social programs, and entitlement reforms that rely on privatization. In the area of national defense, AEI scholars have generally argued for more defense spending, development of a missile defense system, a robust definition and defense of U.S. national interests, and skepticism about the role and effectiveness of the United Nations. AEI analysts have been critical of what they perceive to be liberal dominance in the educational system, criticizing especially the emphasis on diversity and multiculturalism. They have argued for more discipline and parental control, a traditional curriculum with traditional instructional methods, and experimentation with school vouchers. AEI scholars have been critical of affirmative action in education and in the workplace. Policies that strengthen the two-parent family have won support from AEI writers, as have policies that encourage traditional morality and discourage "alternative" lifestyles. In each of these areas, a range of views is expressed by various authors and commentators related to AEI.

FINANCIAL FACTS

AEI had revenue of $19.6 million in 1998, excluding investment activity. The bulk of its revenue has been from contributions and gifts from foundations (42 percent), corporations (28 percent), and individuals (23 percent). Conference fees, publication sales, and miscellaneous sources account for 7 percent of revenue. The John M. Olin Foundation, Lynde and Harry Bradley Foundation, Smith Richardson Foundation, and Sarah Scaife Foundation are among the numerous foundations to provide support to AEI. AEI does not accept contract research.

In 1998, AEI spent $15.3 million. Most of the spending (60 percent) supported its economic, social, political, foreign, and defense policy studies. Marketing, management, and administrative support accounted for 24 percent of expenditures, publications 11 percent, and conferences 5 percent.

AEI is a tax-exempt organization under Section 501(c)(3) of the Internal Revenue code, which means that contributions to AEI are tax deductible for contributors who itemize on their tax returns. Its 501(c)(3) status allows AEI to engage in public education activities but bars it from lobbying for or against particular legislation. It does not make contributions to political candidates.

RAYMOND B. WRABLEY, JR.

Bibliography

AEI: www.aei.org

American Enterprise Institute for Public Policy Research, Annual Report 1999, Washington, D.C.

Lanouette, William J. "The Shadow Cabinets—Changing Thenselves as They Try to Change Policy." *National Journal* 10, no. 8 (February 25, 1978): 296–300.

Mundy, Alicia. "Tanks for the Quotes." *Mediaweek,* July 1, 1996, pp. 16–19.

AMERICANS FOR DEMOCRATIC ACTION

Americans for Democratic Action (ADA) is an independent, liberal, political organization founded in 1947 by prominent liberal academics, activists, and politicians, including former First Lady Eleanor Roosevelt, economist John Kenneth Galbraith, historian Arthur Schlesinger, Jr., theologian Reinhold Niebuhr, and former Vice President Hubert Humphrey. ADA is based in Washington, D.C., but also has close to two dozen state and local chapters nationwide, with approximately 60,000 members. Youth for Democratic Action (YDA) is the "under-30" arm of the ADA and is active in organizing on college campuses and in communities to promote a liberal political agenda.

ADA provides information and support to thousands of activists seeking to lobby Congress and the president and gives liberal values a public voice through appearances on talk radio and television, in public forums, and through electronic activism via the Internet. ADA's *Annual Voting Record,* a scorecard rating of the voting records of members of Congress, has been published since 1947 and has become a widely accepted standard measure of the political ideology of members of Congress. *ADAction News & Notes* is published every week that Congress is in session and gives liberal activists a legislative update on crucial votes. ADA also publishes a quarterly magazine, *ADA Today,* and researches, publishes, and disseminates special reports and policy briefs on national issues.

Throughout its history, ADA has taken a lead in lobbying for civil rights, labor rights, minimum wage, nuclear arms control, women's rights, and national health insurance. Its political action committee (PAC), ADA PAC, makes political contributions to liberal candidates for federal office.

HISTORY

ADA was founded in 1947 out of the remnants of the Union for Democratic Action (UDA), which was started in 1941 by dissident socialists who had split from the Socialist Party over its isolationism. The UDA was one of the few progressive political organizations in the 1940s that excluded Communists from membership, calling communism and fascism equal threats to democracy. Its membership and budget were dwarfed by other progressive organizations that included Communists and that had joined in a popular front to oppose fascism. In January 1947 the UDA met in Washington, D.C., at a conference organized by James Loeb, Jr., UDA's executive secretary. At that conference, the organization's name was changed to Americans for Democratic Action, and it attracted the support of prominent liberal and labor leaders. Its statement of principles included "insuring decent levels of health, nutrition, shelter, and education; civil liberties for all Americans regardless of race, color, creed, or sex; full support for the United Nations; and rejection of association with communists."

In 1947, ADA backed the Truman Doctrine to contain communism, along with the Marshall Plan to help rebuild Europe, in the face of criticism by other progressive organizations. ADA competed with other organizations on the left, especially those loyal to former Vice President Henry Wallace, for the support of liberals and labor. In 1948, ADA successfully pushed the Democratic Party to adopt a civil rights plank in the party platform. After the 1948 elections, ADA emerged as a significant voice in American politics and in the Democratic Party for anti-Communist liberalism. It became a target of conservative critics for its advocacy of liberal politics. Vice President Richard Nixon referred to it as the "red ADA." ADA was also criticized by such prominent leftists as sociologist C. Wright Mills, for its "pragmatic gradualism." In the 1960 presidential election, ADA gave lukewarm support to John Kennedy, having preferred Hubert Humphrey for the Democratic nomination. After the election, however, President Kennedy drew generously on ADA for appointments

**Americans for Democratic Action
Political Action Committee Contributions**

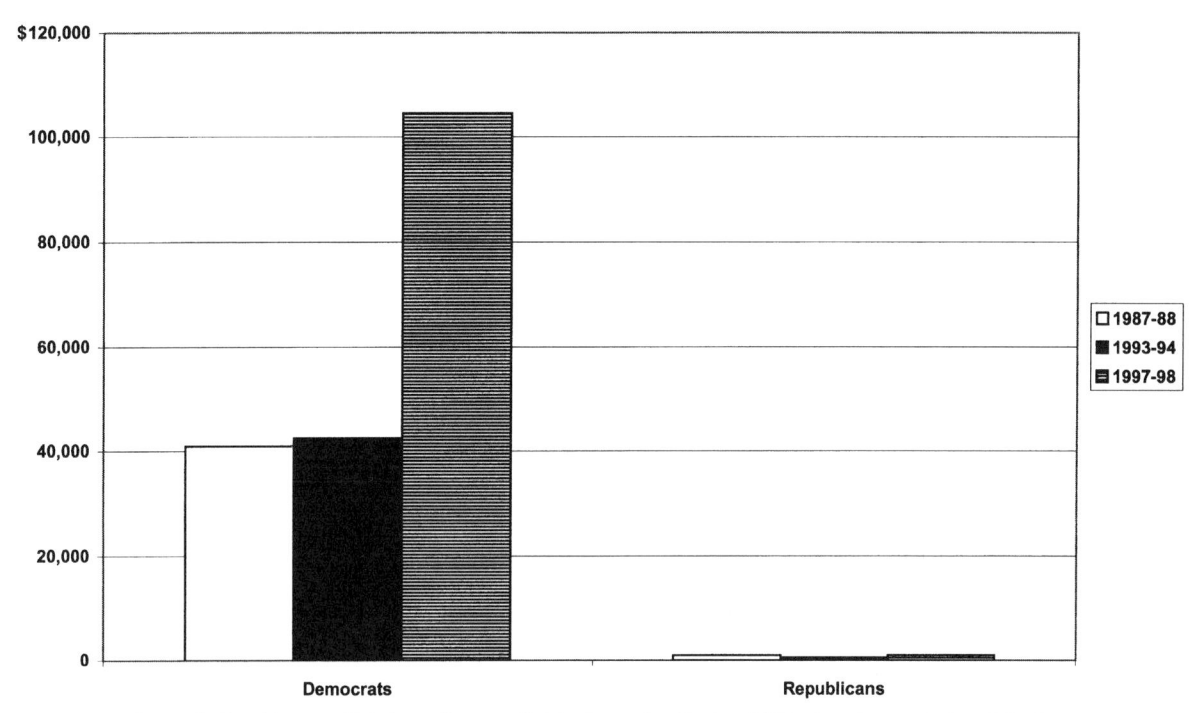

Data derived from official studies available from the Federal Election Commission, Washington, DC, 1987–1998.

in his administration, including ADA members Theodore Sorensen, Harris Wofford, Abraham Ribicoff, and Archibald Cox.

ADA was heavily involved in lobbying for the passage of the 1964 Civil Rights Act and in supporting President Johnson's "War on Poverty." By the late 1960s, the Vietnam War began to split the traditional Cold War liberals from a younger generation of reform liberals, steeped in the civil rights movement and skeptical of Cold War rhetoric and hardline anti-Soviet politics. By the end of the 1960s, the antiwar, reform liberals, disillusioned with the moderation and pragmatism of the Democrats and the old ADA leadership, gained the upper hand within ADA.

In the 1970s, ADA's positions on foreign policy shifted focus from east-west conflict and Communist containment, to north-south dialogue and addressing "the needs of the poorest countries." ADA's economic positions shifted to the left, emphasizing "democratic" control of economic organizations. Prominent socialist Michael Harrington was elected to the ADA national board. ADA criticized President Jimmy Carter's moderation and in 1980 supported Massachusetts Senator Edward Kennedy's unsuccessful challenge to Carter for the Democratic nomination. After a divisive debate, ADA endorsed Carter in 1980 over ADA founding-member turned conservative Ronald Reagan. Reagan's election, and the conservative ascendance of the 1980s left the ADA at an ebb of political influence.

ACTIVITIES: CURRENT AND FUTURE

For over 50 years, ADA has been an influential voice in liberal politics and in the left wing of the Democratic Party. Its lobbying and organizing and its connection to Democratic presidents and members of Congress have given ADA a role in the passage of legislation on civil rights, welfare, healthcare, and arms control. At the end of the 1990s, ADA continued to lobby for liberal legislation and against much of the legislative agenda of the Republican-controlled Congress. ADA's agenda for the 106th Congress (1999–2000) includes support for increasing the minimum wage, campaign finance reform, a single-payer national health insurance system, abortion rights, and affirmative action. ADA opposes funding a missile defense system and supports cuts in the military budget. ADA has taken a position opposing privatization experiments with Social Security and instead has proposed an increase in the wages that are covered by the payroll tax. It has also called for tax reform that would make the federal income tax more progressive by increasing taxes on corporations and the top 20 percent of income earners. According to ADA, this would help generate revenue for more domestic spending, including the hiring of more public school teachers and the construction of new schools.

ADA also took a formal position opposing the impeachment of President Bill Clinton in 1998, asserting that the evidence did not support a bipartisan finding of "high crimes and misdemeanors" and that the impeachment was a partisan challenge to the constitutional separation of powers. ADA also opposed the renewal of the independent counsel law that establishes legal and prosecutorial oversight of the president.

ADA's lobbying effort in the late 1990s included the building of a constituent lobby network that recruits citizen lobbyists to lobby their own members of Congress. ADA notifies the members of this network of pending votes by phone, mail, fax, or e-mail. In 1999, Votenet named ADA's web site an "outstanding political web site."

FINANCIAL FACTS

In 1997, ADA's total revenue was $681,000, with expenses of $650,000. Much of its revenue came from membership dues ($236,000). Other income came from various programs, list rental, publications and subscriptions, and gifts and grants from individuals and foundations. Expenses were primarily for program services.

ADA is a tax-exempt organization under Section 501(c)(4) of the Internal Revenue code, making it a nonprofit organization that allows it to lobby for or against specific legislation if such legislation promotes the social welfare and not a specific industry. Individuals may not deduct contributions to ADA.

The ADA also maintains a political action committee (PAC) that donates to the campaigns of liberal—usually Democratic Party—candidates. Over the years, these donations have risen dramatically, from $42,000 in the 1987–1988 election cycle to $105,551 in the 1997–1998 election cycle.

RAYMOND B. WRABLEY, JR.

Bibliography

Americans for Democratic Action Web site:www.adaction.org

Brock, Clifton. *Americans for Democratic Action: Its Role in National Politics*. Washington, DC: Public Affairs Press, 1962.

Gillon, Steven. *Politics and Vision: The ADA and American Liberalism, 1947–1985*. New York: Oxford University Press, 1987.

Wilcox, Derk Arend, ed. *The Left Guide: A Guide to Left-of-Center Organizations*. Ann Arbor, MI: Economics America, 1996.

AMERICANS FOR TAX REFORM

Americans for Tax Reform (ATR) is a nonprofit organization of over 80,000 taxpayers and taxpayer advocacy groups who oppose all tax increases at the federal and state levels. It serves as a clearinghouse for the grassroots taxpayers' movement by working with approximately 800 state- and county-level groups. ATR is affiliated with the research and education organization, Americans for Tax Reform Foundation. Founded in 1985, ATR is based in Washington, D.C. The group's ultimate goal is to cut government costs by one-half.

ATR promotes its small-government agenda through a broad array of political and educational activities. It devotes a significant amount of money to lobbying Congress and educating the public on tax and budget issues. Since 1986, ATR has sponsored the Taxpayer Protection Pledge, a written promise by legislators and candidates to oppose any effort to increase taxes on individuals and businesses. ATR also sponsors the calculation of "Cost of Government Day," which highlights how much time Americans spend working just to pay taxes. Cost of Government Day, ATR claims, marks the day that Americans stop working to pay their annual federal and state taxes and get to keep their income for themselves. ATR also rates members of Congress on the basis of their votes on tax and budget issues and gives them such awards as "Friends of the Taxpayer" or "Taxpayer Villains." ATR's Ronald Reagan Legacy Project campaigns to honor the former president by having at least one notable public landmark in each state named after him. Among its successes are the renaming of Washington's National Airport and Florida's turnpike system.

ATR also runs the K Street Project, which reports on the political affiliation, employment background, and political donations of members of Washington's premier lobbying firms, trade associations, and high-tech companies. The report is a compilation of Federal Election Commission filings for each individual's political contributions to candidates, parties, and political action committees (PACs) that are overwhelmingly partisan. ATR also hosts a Wednesday, invitation-only gathering of activists, policy analysts, candidates, journalists, and elected officials to discuss upcoming bills and initiatives and to organize and raise money for grassroots political efforts. Representatives from such groups as the National Rifle Association, Cato Institute, Christian Coalition, Heritage Foundation, and U.S. Term Limits regularly attend. ATR maintains a comprehensive web site that provides access to its reports, ratings, and press releases, and shows visitors how to join or contribute to ATR.

HISTORY

ATR was founded by Grover Norquist in 1985 at the suggestion of Reagan administration officials eager to organize grassroots support for the president's 1986 tax simplification legislation. Norquist graduated from Harvard in 1978 with a degree in economics and later earned an MBA from Harvard Business School. In the early 1980s he worked to reinvigorate the national College Republicans organization along with another young activist, Ralph Reed, who later headed the Christian Coalition. Before founding ATR, Norquist worked for the U.S. Chamber of Commerce, National Taxpayers Union, Republican National Committee, and Reagan administration. He has earned a reputation as an effective, assertive, and zealous conservative activist.

ATR quickly gained attention for its aggressive effort to persuade political candidates to sign its Taxpayer Protection Pledge. Many in the ATR believe that Senator Bob Dole's refusal to sign the pledge in 1988 damaged his chances for the Republican presidential nomination. In the early 1990s, ATR helped organize the Leave Us Alone Coalition, bringing together such groups as big business, small business owners, farmers,

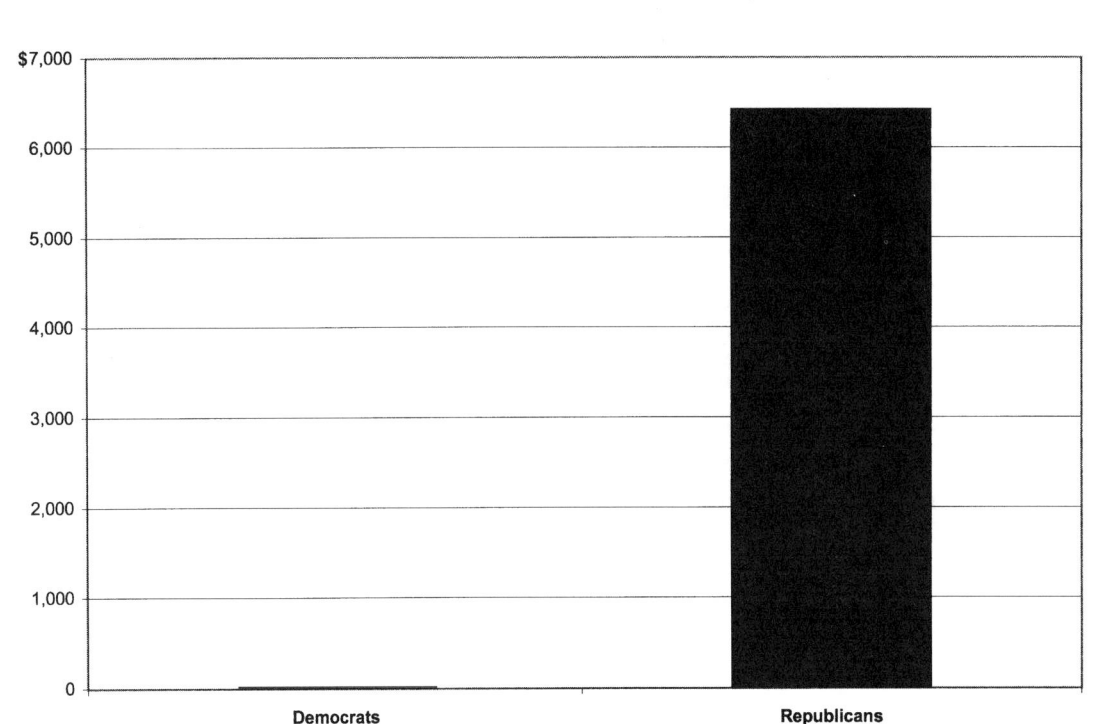

**Americans for Tax Reform
Political Action Committee Contributions, 1995–1996**

[Bar chart: Democrats ≈ $0; Republicans ≈ $6,400]

Data derived from official studies available from the Federal Election Commission, Washington, DC, 1987–1998.

gun owners, and the Christian Right to fight government regulation. ATR played an important role in the 1994 election that led to the first Republican majority in the House of Representatives in 40 years. Norquist became an unofficial advisor to Speaker of the House Newt Gingrich and maintained close relations with him throughout his speakership.

ACTIVITIES: CURRENT AND FUTURE

ATR lobbies and organizes around a wide range of issues, with the goal of reducing taxes and government spending and regulation. According to Norquist, "If you privatize Social Security, if you voucherize education, if you sell $270 billion worth of airports and wastewater treatment plants, eliminate welfare, and so on, you can get the federal government, state government, and local government [down] to basically half of its present level of costs."

ATR has pushed a Social Security reform proposal that would allow workers to put Social Security contributions into private savings accounts. They have argued that not only is the Social Security system headed for insolvency, but it limits freedom and provides a poor return on a worker's investment. ATR has also promoted medical savings accounts as a way to bring down medical costs and reduce the role of government in the healthcare industry. ATR has supported school choice and voucher programs that would allow parents to use tax money to reduce the costs of the private or public school of their choice.

ATR has led the fight against a value-added tax (VAT), a proposed national sales tax that would replace the income tax. ATR argues that a VAT hides the costs of government from taxpayers. The organization has supported a flat income tax. ATR has also opposed recent plans to tax sales made on the Internet. ATR has opposed the Kyoto Protocol on global warming signed by President Bill Clinton, arguing that it would reduce economic growth and increase energy taxes. ATR has actively promoted the balanced budget amendment to the U.S. Constitution, which would mandate a supermajority vote in Congress to raise taxes. ATR has also spearheaded the "Paycheck Protection Act," which would prohibit unions from using union dues for political purposes without the explicit approval of union members.

At the end of the 1990s, ATR persuaded all candidates for the Republican presidential nomination to sign the Taxpayer Protection Pledge. This demonstrates the influence that ATR has achieved in Republican Party politics.

FINANCIAL FACTS

ATR has an annual budget of about $8 million, almost all of it received from contributions and grants. In 1996 ATR received a controversial contribution from the Republican National Committee, of $4.6 million, which was used to finance a television advertising campaign designed to help GOP candidates in the last weeks of the campaign.

ATR is a nonprofit 501(c)(4) lobbying organization. Contributions to ATR are not tax deductible; this status allows the group to lobby for or against legislation. The American Tax Reform Foundation is a 501(c)(3) research and educational organization. It does not engage in lobbying, and contributions to the foundation are tax deductible.

ATR also maintains an entirely separate political action committee that donates modest sums of money to conservative Republican candidates. In the 1995–1996 election cycle, the ATR political action committee gave roughly $6,400 to Republican candidates.

RAYMOND B. WRABLEY, JR.

Bibliography
Americans for Tax Reform: www.atr.org
Carlson, Tucker. "What I Sold at the Revolution: Grover Norquist Joins the Club," *The New Republic*, June 9, 1997.

BROOKINGS INSTITUTION

The Brookings Institution is a private, nonprofit think tank dedicated to improving the performance of American institutions by analyzing emerging public policy problems and offering practical solutions to them in books, reports, and articles that are available to policy-makers, experts, and the general public. Founded in 1916 and based in Washington, D.C., Brookings is one of the oldest, largest, and most respected public policy research organizations in the United States. It employs a staff of over 200, including dozens of resident scholars who conduct research on economics, government, foreign policy, and the social sciences. Long regarded as the preeminent liberal think tank in Washington, Brookings has recently established its credentials as a centrist policy organization and is currently led by a Republican and former Bush administration official, Michael Armacost.

A major part of Brookings's efforts to shape public policy debates is its book-publishing program. Its fellows conduct such programs as research in economic studies, foreign policy studies, and government studies. Their research is published by the Brookings Institution Press, which also publishes the books of outside scholars and distributes the books of several other nonprofit research organizations from the United States and abroad. Brookings also publishes two highly acclaimed journals, *Brookings Papers on Economic Activity: Macroeconomics* and *Brookings Papers on Economic Activity: Microeconomics*. *Brookings Review* is the institution's quarterly journal and is intended to make Brookings's research and policy proposals available to a wide audience. Brookings recently launched three new annual journals on international trade, education, and financial services.

Brookings also conducts a vigorous education and outreach program. At forums in Washington and in other cities and in partnership with other organizations, Brookings sponsors conferences, special briefings, policy debates, and town meetings to present research on policy issues in a timely manner. Some of its conferences are offered online through videoconferencing technologies. Brookings's outreach activities include the Brookings National Issues forum, the Brookings Policymaker series, Brookings Briefings for the Foreign Press, *Brookings Policy Brief Series,* and the *Brookings Quarterly Newsletter*. The Brookings Center for Public Policy Education conducts educational programs for leaders in business and government. Seven other policy centers, including a joint center with the American Enterprise Institute, conduct research and educational programs on a range of policy issues. A comprehensive and interactive site on the World Wide Web also helps Brookings reach a wide audience with its policy analysis and prescriptions.

HISTORY

Robert S. Brookings founded the Brookings Institution as the Institute for Government Research in 1916. Brookings made a fortune in timber and mining by the age of 30, and later became a civic leader and philanthropist and served on the War Industries Board during the First World War. In 1927, he merged the Institute for Government Research with two of his other creations, the Institute of Economics and the Robert Brookings Graduate School, to create the Brookings Institution. Its purpose was to conduct and foster research and education in economics, government administration, and the political and social sciences generally. In its early days, the Brookings Institution was regarded as a bastion of conservatism, and it depended on industry groups for support. In the 1930s, many of its scholars were critical of President Franklin Roosevelt and his social program called the New Deal, although it played a role in the creation of the Marshall Plan after the Second World War. In the 1940s, Brookings built an endowment, freeing it from dependence on any special interest, and hired a staff capable of conducting nonpartisan research on public policy.

In the 1960s, Brookings developed a reputation as an activist, left-of-center think tank, as it helped shape the social and economic policies of the Kennedy and Johnson administrations. Its liberalism was less welcomed by the Nixon administration, as Watergate dirty tricksters unsuccessfully plotted to firebomb the institution. Brookings provided experts to help staff the Carter administration in the 1970s and provided a haven for Democrats in exile as Republicans controlled the White House in the 1980s. By the mid 1980s, Brookings began to reposition itself as a centrist, bipartisan policy organization able to offer policy analysis and advice to both parties. This was especially true in the 1990s, as Brookings attracted officials from former Republican administrations. Brookings president Michael Armacost remarked that "with a Democratic President and Republican Congress, most of the solutions to public problems that will pass muster politically are going to be in the center." Brookings has also made an effort in the 1990s to move away from its more aloof, long-range research focus and to more aggressively engage in policy debates by getting timely policy briefs quickly into the hands of journalists and policy-makers.

ACTIVITIES: CURRENT AND FUTURE

Although Brookings does not take an institutional position on issues, its scholars routinely analyze and address a comprehensive array of domestic social and economic policies, as well as foreign policies. Brookings publishes a highly respected volume of policy analysis and prescription called *Setting National Priorities*. Its *Policy Briefs* and the op-ed columns of its scholars also stake out positions on numerous issues.

In the 1999 debate over the projected budget surplus, several Brookings scholars argued against the large tax cuts proposed by the Republican congressional leaders. They have taken a position more in line with President Bill Clinton's, arguing that much of the surplus ought to be devoted to providing long-term repairs to Social Security and Medicare. Some have argued for lifting the stringent spending caps imposed in the most recent balanced budget legislation. They have argued for boosting public investment on infrastructure, such as highways and sewer systems. They have urged greater spending on education, targeted especially to early childhood programs aimed at low-income children. Also in the area of education, several Brookings papers have argued for national standards for achievement, measured by national tests. Teacher competency and testing have also been advocated, as have various versions of school choice and competition.

Some Brookings papers have argued that the defense budget needs modest increases focused on unit readiness, including increased spending for salaries, spare parts, and maintenance. They have been critical of the Pentagon's requests for large budget increases, arguing that they are not necessary in an era when the United States faces no major rivals.

A Brookings paper makes the case for experimenting with market-based solutions to environmental problems, and for more flexible regulations than those traditionally found in environmental legislation and the directives issued by the Environmental Protection Agency. Some scholars have also argued for passage of a global treaty to reduce greenhouse emissions, with a provision that richer countries pay poor countries to reduce their emissions.

Brookings scholars have typically taken positions in favor of an active global role for the United States, including a diplomatic and security role in promoting the Middle East peace process and a military role in suppressing ethnic violence in Kosovo, a province in the former Yugoslavia. Brookings writers have generally taken a position in favor of free trade, supporting the admission of China to the World Trade Organization and criticizing unilateral economic sanctions on nations with poor human rights records.

FINANCIAL FACTS

Brookings's budget exceeds $20 million annually. Gifts and grants from foundations, corporations, and individuals account for 35 percent of operating revenue. Support from its endowment provides 32 percent of operating revenue. Remaining funds comes from its Center for Public Policy Education seminars and conferences (16 percent), book publication and sales (9 percent), government support for research (4 percent), and miscellaneous revenue sources (4 percent). Brookings has an endowment of $167 million, larger than that of any other think tank. Foundations providing support to Brookings include the William and Flora Hewlett Foundation and the Rockefeller Foundation.

Research and associated costs for its economic studies, foreign policy studies, and government studies programs account for 62 percent of Brookings's expenditures. Costs associated with conferences and seminars sponsored by the Center for Public Policy Education account for 17 percent of expenditures; printing, marketing and distribution of Brookings books and publications receive 13 percent of expenditures; development and public affairs take 5 percent; and communications account for 3 percent.

Brookings is a tax-exempt organization under Section 501(c)(3) of the Internal Revenue code. Under this statute, it may engage in public education activities but it may not directly lobby for or against specific legislation. Brookings does not make contributions to candidates for public office.

RAYMOND B. WRABLEY, JR.

Bibliography

Brookings Institution: www.brook.edu

Critchlow, Donald T. *The Brookings Institution, 1916–1952: Expertise and the Public Interest in a Democratic Society*. DeKalb: Northern Illinois University Press, 1985.

Saunders, Charles. *The Brookings Institution: A Fifty-Year History*. Washington, DC: The Brookings Institution.

Solomon, Burt. "Ferment at Brookings." *National Journal* 29, no. 42 (October 18, 1997): 2080–2089.

Wilcox, Derk Arend. *The Left Guide: A Guide to Left-of-Center Organizations*. Ann Arbor, MI: Economics America, 1996.

CATO INSTITUTE

The Cato Institute is a nonpartisan public policy research foundation based in Washington, D.C., It is the preeminent libertarian think tank in the United States, with 73 employees and 60 adjunct scholars, many of them internationally prominent advocates for free markets and limited government. Libertarians argue for the priority of individual liberty over other values, and they oppose most government regulation of the marketplace or individual choices. Cato has an extensive publications program, publishing books, monographs, and shorter studies that analyze public policy issues from a libertarian perspective and advocates policies aimed at eliminating government intervention in economic, social, and cultural life as much as possible. It also sponsors major public policy conferences and publishes the *Cato Journal,* the quarterly magazine *Regulation,* and a bimonthly newsletter, *Cato Policy Report.*

The Cato Institute undertakes significant public education activities through its publications, conferences, and web site. Its scholars and staff also actively seek to influence public opinion through op-ed columns in national newspapers and television appearances. In 1994, Cato scholars appeared on more than 100 television and radio shows criticizing President Bill Clinton's healthcare plan.

HISTORY

The Cato Institute was founded in 1977 by Edward H. Crane and Charles G. Koch. Crane was a financial analyst and vice president of Alliance Capital Management Corporation. He had been a student activist at the University of California at Berkeley in the 1960s and was later a leader of the Libertarian Party. Koch was a multimillionaire oil company owner from Wichita, Kansas. The Institute is named for *Cato's Letters,* libertarian pamphlets circulated during the colonial period that helped shape the philosophical foundation of the Declaration of Independence and the American Revolution. Crane and Koch founded the Cato Institute to broaden public policy debates to include options more consistent with the principles of limited government, individual liberty, and peace. The institute describes its philosophy as libertarianism or "market liberalism" and "combines an appreciation for entrepreneurship, the market process, and lower taxes with strict respect for civil liberties and skepticism about the benefits of both the welfare state and foreign military adventurism."

In 1978, the institute launched a daily public affairs radio program, *Byline,* which was broadcast in more than 260 cities. It also began publishing classic manuscripts by authors such as the conservative free-market scholar Friedrich A. Hayek, along with policy reports and monographs on public policy issues like Social Security and healthcare. In 1981, the first issue of *The Cato Journal* was published. This scholarly journal has been published three times a year since.

In 1982, the Cato Institute published a volume of essays by Hayek, Milton Friedman, Ludwig von Mises, Michael Polanyi, and others, called *Solidarity with Liberty,* and smuggled it into Poland in an act that was denounced by the Polish embassy. In 1985, the institute had copies of its Russian-language collection of essays, *Friedman and Hayek on Freedom,* smuggled into the Soviet Union. In 1988, Cato sponsored the first free-market conference in China since the Communist takeover. In 1995, it published the first in a series of Cato Handbooks for Congress, detailing a program to reduce government spending, regulation, and power. It also launched a web site that has won the Four-Star Magellan award for excellence.

ACTIVITIES: CURRENT AND FUTURE

In the years since its inception, Cato's authors and speakers have tackled such issues as immigration, occupational licensing, education and school choice, drugs, welfare, trade, environmental policy, and foreign policy. The Cato Institute has also sponsored conferences on these issues with renowned scholars and policy makers in Washington, D.C., and in cities around the world. These conferences are now broadcast live on the World Wide Web and archived for on-demand viewing.

Cato has argued that "the immense body of [government] regulations" is the greatest threat to American prosperity. Cato scholars claim that consumer interests would most effectively be protected by a "regulatory rollback" that relies on the incentive forces of the market to create competitive markets and to provide consumers with information. This position has been elaborated in policy proposals that would scrap much of the existing regulation in favor of policies that take advantage of market incentives, private property rights, and privatization. In the area of monetary policy, Cato has explored alternatives to government control of money and banking. In education, Cato has been a leading advocate for school choice and voucher initiatives, charter schools, and other experiments with privatization and deregulation.

Cato's ideology and issue positions have been the basis for a sometimes contentious relationship with other conservative political organizations over the years. Its free-market economic positions critical of government regulation, spending, and taxes have won it support and influence among conservatives. Its economic theories and arguments were influential in the Reagan administration as well as with the Republican congressional majority elected in 1994. Its libertarian positions on "social issues"—support for gay rights and drug legalization, and opposition to censorship of pornography, for example—have earned it the condemnation of traditional conservative groups. The Cato Institute has also taken isolationist foreign policy positions, opposing "entangling alliances" abroad (warned of by President George Washington in his Farewell Address), U.S. military intervention in the Middle East and Bosnia, and U.S. intelligence activities during the Cold War. Its opposition to U.S. military action during the Persian Gulf crisis almost cost it the support of conservative foundations. It also took a position opposing NATO's military action in Kosovo in the former Yugoslavia in 1999.

At the end of the 1990s, the Cato Institute continued to maintain a visible presence among Washington, D.C., think tanks and to exercise influence among conservative policy-makers, including those in the Republican congressional majority. The *Cato Handbook for Congress,* published in 1997, represents a comprehensive (550 pages) libertarian program for reform of virtually every government program. Despite its newfound access and influence, Cato's president, Edward H. Crane, sees a unique role for the organization: "The traditional think tanks see themselves as government's helper. We see ourselves as government's adversary."

FINANCIAL FACTS

In 1998, the Cato Institute had a budget of $12 million. The bulk of its revenue comes from foundations, including the Sarah Scaife Foundation and John M. Olin Foundation, as well as from businesses and individuals. A smaller percentage of revenue comes from the sale of publications, conference registration fees, mailing list rentals, royalties, and interest income. It accepts no government funding.

Cato's largest expenditure is the production and distribution of its publications. It also has significant expenditures on its conferences and forums.

As a tax-exempt educational foundation under Section 501(c)(3) of the Internal Revenue code, Cato is generally prohibited from direct lobbying for or against specific legislation, although it may publish nonpartisan analysis as part of its educational activities. Contributions to Cato are considered charitable donations and are deductible for taxpayers who itemize.

RAYMOND B. WRABLEY, JR.

Bibliography

Cato Institute. *Cato Handbook for Congress: 105th Congress.* Washington, DC: Cato Institute, 1997.

Cato Institute: www.cato.org

Wilcox, Derk Arend. *The Right Guide: A Guide to Conservative and Right-of-Center Organizations.* Ann Arbor, MI: Economics America, 1997.

CENTER FOR PUBLIC INTEGRITY

The Center for Public Integrity (CPI) is a nonprofit, nonpartisan, tax-exempt educational organization created to analyze and report in depth on important national issues. Founded in 1989 and based in Washington, D.C., CPI has been called "a watchdog in the corridors of power" for its investigative reports on ethics-related issues in politics and government. While the center is independent and has criticized alleged influence peddling in both major parties, it is generally regarded as a liberal public interest group. Only recently has it become a membership organization. It now has about 5,000 members.

With a small group of investigative reporters, CPI focuses less on individual cases of ethical misconduct and more on the overall effects of what it considers widespread unethical behavior in campaign financing and lobbying. Since its inception, the center has examined and disseminated a wide array of information in more than 30 published CPI reports. By writing and issuing reports and studies, writing articles to be published in various newspapers and magazines, and breaking national stories via television, the center believes it can help make government officials more accountable for their actions. Its experienced and reputable journalists produce reporting that is relied upon or cited by national news organizations.

Since 1994, the center has published a monthly newsletter, *The Public i*, which makes public the results of its investigations. In 1997, the center launched a new project, the International Consortium of Investigative Journalists (ICIJ), a network of the world's premier investigative reporters. ICIJ extends the center's investigative approach to issues of international concern. It also gives the ICIJ Award for Outstanding International Investigative Reporting, a prize worth $20,000. CPI maintains a comprehensive site on the World Wide Web.

HISTORY

The Center for Public Integrity was founded in 1989 by Charles Lewis, a former producer at *60 Minutes*, who had also worked at CBS News and ABC News. Lewis earned a B.A. degree in political science from the University of Delaware and a master's degree from the Johns Hopkins School of Advanced International Studies. He had twice received Emmy nominations in the Outstanding Investigative Reporting category. In the late 1980s Lewis grew frustrated that "America's best and brightest reporters" too often were not investigating "the country's biggest, most important stories." He saw a need for insightful, analytic studies of the systemic and structural problems of Washington's "mercenary culture." To pursue such studies he founded CPI.

The center's first study, "America's Frontline Trade Officials," a 90,000-word report released in 1990, analyzed the activities of some of the personnel at the Office of the U.S. Trade Representative. The report noted that 47 percent of former senior trade officials, or their firms, had registered as foreign agents for overseas companies or governments. During the 1996 presidential campaign, CPI broke the story of the Lincoln bedroom scandal, wherein hundreds of Clinton campaign contributors were invited to spend the night at the White House. For reporting this story, *The Public i* won the Society of Professional Journalists' 1996 Sigma Delta Chi Award for Public Service in Newsletter Journalism. Another CPI report revealed that Larry Pratt, a co-chair of Patrick Buchanan's campaign committee, had spoken at meetings attended by white supremacists from the Aryan Nations and the Christian Identity Movement. Buchanan immediately placed Pratt on leave from the campaign.

ACTIVITIES: CURRENT AND FUTURE

The CPI has focused its investigations on ethics and public integrity in public service. It has reported extensively on the "revolving door"—the exchange of personnel between government and lobbying groups—arguing that former officials are frequently hired by special interests to lobby their former agencies. The center has also argued that Americans' privacy is being compromised and invaded as sensitive financial and personal data are collected, bought, and sold by thousands of companies. According to the center, legislation aimed at curbing various kinds of invasion of privacy have been killed in Congress at the behest of corporate interests. One CPI report argues that problems in airline safety have not been remedied as "Congress has repeatedly put the economic interests of the airline ahead of safety concerns." Another report asserts that meatpacking continues to be one of the most dangerous professions and that the number of disease-producing agents in the nation's food supply is growing, but "Congress continues to protect the food industry instead of the public health." A similar argument is made in reports about pesticides and toxic wastes.

The root of the problem, according to the center, is the influence of money in Congress. In "The Buying of Congress," the center argues: "Too frequently, on the most important public-policy issues of our time, at critical forks in the road between the broad public interest of the American people and the narrow, economic agenda of a few vested interests, Congress has taken the wrong path. That wrong path, more often than not, is illuminated by flashing, neon-green dollar signs." "The Buying of the President" raises similar issues regarding the presidency and presidential candidates. As a leading source of data and analysis about campaign contributions and lobbying, the Center for Public Integrity has been used by advocates of campaign finance reform, lobbying reform, conflict-of-interest disclosure, and other ethics-in-government campaigns.

FINANCIAL FACTS

In 1998, CPI had revenue of about $2 million, almost all of it from grants and contributions, with smaller amounts from program services revenue, publications sales, editorial consulting, and interest on savings. Foundations that have supported the center include the Ford Foundation, Joyce Foundation, John D. and Catherine T. MacArthur Foundation, and Florence and John Schumann Foundation. The center does not accept contributions from corporations, labor unions, or governments.

CPI's expenses in 1998 were approximately $2.1 million, most of which was devoted to program services and, in smaller amounts, to administration and fundraising. The center is a tax-exempt organization under Section 501(c)(3) of the Internal Revenue code. It does not take formal positions on legislation and does not engage in lobbying.

RAYMOND B. WRABLEY, JR.

Bibliography

Center for Public Integrity: www.publicintegrity.org

Lewis, Charles. "The Need for a Center for Public Integrity," *Social Studies*, October 1998.

CENTER FOR RESPONSIVE POLITICS

The Center for Responsive Politics (CRP) is a nonprofit, nonpartisan research organization founded to analyze the role that money plays in American politics and, more specifically, in Congress. Established in 1983 and based in Washington, D.C., CRP is a nonmembership organization with a staff numbering around 11. The center conducts computer-based research on campaign finance issues for the news media, academics, activists, and other observers of Congress. Former Executive Director Ellen Miller said CRP intends to be a "one-stop shopping center on money and politics."

CRP's Open Secrets project uses sophisticated computer-assisted analysis to track over 200,000 political action committee (PAC) contributions and over 800,000 individual contributions made to congressional and presidential candidates. These contributions are matched with the economic and ideological interests of the contributors in order to establish patterns of money and influence in federal campaigns.

The center also publishes *Capital Eye*, a bimonthly eight-page newsletter that provides substantive articles on the role of money in American politics. It is aimed at a readership of journalists and activists. CRP maintains a National Library on Money and Politics that houses sophisticated databases that make it possible to examine correlations between campaign contributions and lawmakers' legislative records. The library responds to hundreds of individual requests for studies on money in politics from journalists, public interest groups, educators, activists, and other researchers. For information and arguments regarding political reform proposals journalists and advocates have relied on CRP reports and analyses and books like *Open Secrets: The Encyclopedia of Congressional Money and Politics*.

As part of their work of providing commentary and analysis for news organizations, CRP has developed regular consulting ties with CNN and other media outlets, including Congressional Quarterly and the *Wall Street Journal*. CRP also hosts seminars and conferences. Many CRP databases can be accessed at its site on the World Wide Web. The site allows visitors to look up campaign finance information by categories like soft money, political action committees, donors, lobbyists, and politicians. Visitors can also subscribe to a Money and Politics alert that is e-mailed every Monday, highlighting special-interest legislation on Capitol Hill and who is giving money to whom.

HISTORY

The CRP was created in 1983 by former senators Hugh Scott (R-PA) and Frank Church (D-ID). In 1991, the center merged with the National Library on Money and Politics, a group founded by Philip Stern, a campaign-finance-reform advocate and author of *The Best Congress Money Can Buy*. Also in 1991, the center launched FEC Watch, the only independent watchdog observing the operations of the Federal Election Commission. In 1994, the center launched its newsletter, *Capital Eye*. For most of its history the CRP has been led by Ellen Miller, a former staffer in both the House of Representatives and the Senate. Miller resigned from the CRP in 1999 and was succeeded by Larry Makinson.

ACTIVITIES: CURRENT AND FUTURE

CRP has focused its analysis and educational activities on political contributions from individuals and special interests to political candidates and officials. It compiles an extensive database on political contributions that also includes information on interest groups' expenditures and lobbying. Recent studies on patterns of special interest contributions focus on the National Rifle Association, professional sports teams, and high-tech companies. Other studies reveal favors to members of Congress from corporations and pressure groups. CRP has also documented efforts by congressional leaders and their PACs to circumvent campaign finance laws, as well as a lack of vigorous FEC enforcement.

CRP does not lobby or take formal positions on specific legislation. However, an implication of its research and educational activities is that campaign finance and lobbying systems in the United States allow special interests to buy undue influence in the policy-making process. Its information and analyses have provided ammunition for those who advocate campaign finance reform, lobbying reform, and stronger ethics-in-government laws.

FINANCIAL FACTS

The CRP has an annual budget of $1.2 million. Besides contributions from individuals, the center has received funding from the Carnegie Corporation, Ford Foundation, Joyce Foundation, Pew Charitable Trusts, and Florence and John Schumann Foundation.

CRP is a tax-exempt organization under Section 501(c)(3) of the Internal Revenue code. Its tax-exempt status bars it from lobbying on specific legislation. Contributions to CRP are tax deductible.

RAYMOND B. WRABLEY, JR.

Bibliography

Center for Responsive Politics: www.crp.org

Stone, Peter H. "Tracker on the Political Money Trail," *The National Journal*, November 13, 1993.

CHRISTIAN COALITION

The Christian Coalition is a citizen action organization that promotes Christian values in government. Founded in 1989 and based in Chesapeake, Virginia, the Christian Coalition has about 1.5 million members and 1,500 local chapters in all 50 states. It is one of the largest political organizations of Christian conservatives and, in the mid 1990s, was widely recognized as one of the more powerful conservative interest groups, with influence especially in the Republican Party.

The Christian Coalition is committed to "pro-family activism" aimed at influencing public policy at all levels of government. One of its most visible forms of political action is its publication and distribution of Voter Guides and Scorecards that set forth candidates' positions on various issues of interest to the Christian Coalition, including abortion, education, pornography, taxes, and gay rights. Tens of millions of these guides, customized for local elections, are distributed primarily through churches. The Christian Coalition and its local chapters also mobilize supporters at election time through mailings and phone calls.

The Christian Coalition also maintains a lobbying staff in Washington, D.C., and devotes a significant portion of its efforts to lobbying Congress. Out of hundreds of lobby groups, a study by the Center for Responsive Politics ranked the Christian Coalition thirteenth in lobbying expenditures ($7.9 million) in 1997, just behind Blue Cross/Blue Shield. The Christian Coalition mobilizes its members and supporters as part of its grassroots lobbying efforts, using "Action Alert" postcards, phone calls, and e-mail. It also conducts training seminars to teach lobbying skills to citizen lobbyists and local organizations. Its annual "Road to Victory" national conference attracts thousands of conservative activists, along with prominent politicians, candidates, and celebrities. The Christian Coalition also runs a program that provides money to inner-city churches that minister to at-risk youth.

The Christian Coalition publishes several newsletters, including *Religious Rights Watch*. Its Legislative Scorecards, policy position statements, and announcements of events are available on its comprehensive web site.

In 1996, the Federal Election Commission sued the Christian Coalition, charging that it was effectively acting as an arm of the Republican Party without reporting its political spending, a position rejected by a federal court in 1999. Also in 1999, the Internal Revenue Service (IRS) ruled that the Christian Coalition is not entitled to tax-exempt status because it engages in partisan political activity.

HISTORY

The Christian Coalition was founded in 1989 by businessman and evangelist Pat Robertson. In the aftermath of his 1988 bid for the Republican presidential nomination, Robertson had been urged by supporters to take advantage of the mobilization of Christian conservatives who had backed his campaign. At a meeting in Atlanta that included Dr. James Kennedy, Beverly LaHaye, and Ralph Reed, the decision was made to create the Christian Coalition. They decided to base the organization in Chesapeake, Virginia, to avoid being drawn into what they perceived as the insider politics of Washington, D.C. Reed was given responsibility for building the organization. Using the list of Robertson's campaign contributors, Reed was able to solicit money and members and begin to create local organizations. The Christian Coalition attracted national attention when it bought full page ads in the *Washington Post*, *New York Times*, and *USA Today* denouncing the National Endowment for the Arts and warning members of Congress that they would risk the wrath of religious conservatives if they continued to fund it. The Christian Coalition offered critical support for the reelection of Senator Jesse Helms (R-NC) in 1990 and the nomination of Clarence Thomas to the Supreme Court in 1991. It was also successful in recruiting and supporting conservative candidates at the local level, especially in school board races.

Membership in the Christian Coalition doubled after the election of Bill Clinton as president in 1992. By 1994 it had over 1 million members and a budget of $12 million and was regarded as one of the more powerful political organizations of religious activists. It acquired influence especially within Republican Party politics. In 1994 the Christian Coalition backed the Republican "Contract with America" and helped the party win control of both houses. In 1997, Reed left the Christian Coalition to form his own political consulting business, and by the late 1990s, the Christian Coalition's fortunes had shifted. It had lost hundreds of thousands of members, its income was down, and senior staff members had quit. Its influence had waned and it was forced to reorganize after the IRS revoked its tax-exempt status, finding it had engaged in pro-Republican partisan activities prohibited by the Internal Revenue code.

ACTIVITIES: CURRENT AND FUTURE

The Christian Coalition lobbies on a broad range of issues. Arguing that human life begins at conception, it has been persistent in its efforts to extend full legal protections to the unborn. It has supported a constitutional amendment to prohibit abortions. It has also condemned the Supreme Court's rulings in favor of abortion rights and has worked to pass restrictions on abortions and federal funding of a late-term abortion procedure that critics call a partial-birth abortion.

The organization has also pressed for education reform, seeking to give maximum control over education to parents and local communities. It has opposed national education standards and national testing of students or schools. It has supported school choice proposals, including tuition vouchers, education savings accounts, tuition tax credits, and charter schools.

The Christian Coalition has argued that federal courts have misinterpreted the First Amendment in requiring strict separation of church and state. It has lobbied for voluntary prayer in public schools and has supported other public expressions of religious faith. It has also taken a position on campaign finance reform, opposing many of the prominent proposals to impose tighter restrictions on campaign contributions and spending. The Christian Coalition favors lifting restrictions on contributions and spending, while requiring greater public disclosure and reporting of campaign finance activities.

The Christian Coalition has supported restrictions on pornography and opposed legislation to give civil rights protections to homosexuals. It has called for the abolition of the National Endowment for the Arts, arguing that government should not play a role in subsidizing the arts, especially art that is offensive to certain segments of society. It has also called for an end to government sponsorship of gambling, and has favored tax cuts and laws to give more protection to victims of crime. It supported the impeachment of President Bill Clinton and condemned his acquittal by the Senate as a "mockery of our nation's long history of equal justice under law."

FINANCIAL FACTS

The Christian Coalition has an annual budget of over $15 million. Over 90 percent of its revenue comes from contributors, with other revenue coming from program services and other miscellaneous sources. Its biggest expenditure is on "legislative affairs," which covers lobbying activities.

In response to the IRS ruling that revoked its tax-exempt status, the Christian Coalition announced in 1999 that it was splitting into two new organizations. Christian Coalition International will be a not-for-profit, taxable corporation that will have the ability to form a political action committee (PAC) to raise and distribute funds directly to candidates. The other organization, Christian Coalition of America, will be a 501(c)(4) tax-exempt organization that will conduct nonpartisan get-out-the-vote efforts and distribute voter education materials.

RAYMOND B. WRABLEY, JR.

Bibliography

Christian Coalition: www.cc.org

Martin, William. *With God on Our Side: The Rise of the Religious Right in America.* New York: Broadway Books, 1996.

Watson, Justin. *The Christian Coalition: Dreams of Restoration, Demands for Recognition.* New York: St. Martin's Press, 1997.

CITIZENS FOR A SOUND ECONOMY

Citizens for a Sound Economy (CSE) is a nonpartisan think tank and grassroots political organization that advocates market-based solutions to public policy problems. Based in Washington, D.C., CSE also has nine state chapters and claims a membership of 250,000. Through a broad range of lobbying activities and grassroots mobilization efforts, CSE promotes an agenda of less government, lower taxes, and less regulation. With heavy financial backing from the business community, CSE has seen its budget and influence swell in the 1990s. It maintains close ties with the Republican congressional leadership, and *Roll Call* magazine has ranked CSE among the top five most influential lobby groups.

CSE devotes a significant amount of effort to producing and disseminating educational materials as part of an aggressive campaign to influence public policy debates from the grass roots. It seeks out individuals who want to get involved in public policy debates; trains them in organizing, media tactics, and public education techniques; and supports them with products and services, including position papers, videos, bumper stickers, buttons, and t-shirts. It runs an e-mail campaign to inform members about issues that are important to CSE, instructs them on effective letter-writing techniques, provides sample letters, and links members to their congressional offices. CSE also employs policy analysts and economists who brief congressional aides, write op-ed articles, and appear on radio and television news shows. CSE publishes a bimonthly newsletter for members, the *CSE Sentinel,* which provides updates and educational information on CSE campaigns and issues.

Citizens for a Sound Economy Foundation (CSEF) is CSE's research and education division and has been home to some of the nation's top fiscal conservatives, including former Reagan administration budget director James Miller III.

CSE also has a "Key Vote" program that tracks the votes of members of Congress on issues of importance to CSE. A scorecard at the end of each congressional session is regarded as a gauge of members' adherence to free market principles, and a Jefferson Award is given to members who vote with CSE on at least 80 percent of the key votes.

HISTORY

CSE was founded in 1984 by Richard H. Fink, a fiscally conservative economics professor at George Mason University with connections to the Koch family, oil industry billionaires and founders of several charitable foundations, who have pumped millions of dollars into conservative causes and organizations. Fink became CSE's first president. He had previously established the Center for the Study of Market Processes at George Mason, with the financial backing of David and Charles Koch. David Koch was the Libertarian Party vice presidential candidate in 1980.

CSE promoted free market economic principles and quickly became influential in public policy debates, especially within the Reagan administration. CSE economists were influential advisors in the 1987 privatization of Conrail.

In 1994, CSE demonstrated its political clout with its $5 million campaign to defeat President Bill Clinton's proposed healthcare reforms. It has gained influence in the states on fiscal and regulatory issues and has established a number of state chapters.

ACTIVITIES: CURRENT AND FUTURE

CSE is involved in a wide range of policy issues as part of its goal of reducing the role and scope of government. It has been especially active recently on environmental issues. CSE has opposed the enforcement of new clean air standards issued by the Environmental Protection Agency, arguing that they will increase government control and costs to businesses without realizing promised benefits. It has also opposed ratification of the

Global Warming Treaty, which aims to reduce greenhouse gas emissions, on grounds that the treaty is one-sided, costly, and likely to lead to tax increases.

In 1997, CSE unsuccessfully opposed the Balanced Budget Act, claiming that it actually slowed progress toward a balanced federal budget by increasing spending and creating new entitlements. The Citizens for a Sound Economy Foundation has taken a lead in promoting tax simplification and fairness, partly through its "Scrap the Code Tour," which features a debate over the merits of the flat tax versus a national sales tax. CSE has also promoted Social Security reform, advocating a version of privatization that would allow individuals to invest a portion of their Social Security taxes in private retirement accounts. CSE has opposed healthcare reform proposals that mandate specific insurance practices or coverage.

CSE has also promoted the reform of liability laws to reduce what it calls "frivolous" lawsuits and "outrageous" settlements. In the area of trade, CSE has advocated tariff reductions, normal trade relations with China, and, generally, free-trade arrangements. CSE has also been active on the issues of public utility deregulation, insurance reform, and the reform of the Food and Drug Administration. With the backing of businesses and trade associations, CSE has been able to promote its issue agenda through persistent lobbying, massive advertising campaigns, and a grassroots operation that generates tens of thousands of phone calls and letters to policy-makers.

FINANCIAL FACTS

In 1997, CSE had revenue of $9.2 million, of which businesses contributed 68 percent. Koch Industries, an oil and natural gas conglomerate that has backed many conservative causes, has been an especially important contributor. Trade associations, including the American Petroleum Institute and the National Association of Manufacturers, contributed 12 percent, and individuals contributed 15 percent. Other sources of revenue included interest on investments, publication sales, and conference fees. Expenditures in 1997 were $8.6 million, 91 percent of it devoted to research and educational activities. In 1997 the CSEF had $5.2 million in revenues and $4.3 million in expenditures.

CSE is a tax-exempt organization under Section 501 (c)(4) of the Internal Revenue code, which stipulates that contributions to CSE are not deductible, and it is allowed under the law to lobby for or against specific legislation, but only if it is to promote the social welfare. CSEF is a 501 (c)(3) tax-exempt organization that is generally prohibited from direct lobbying for or against specific legislation, although it may publish nonpartisan analyses as part of its educational activities. Contributions to CSEF are considered charitable donations and are deductible for taxpayers who itemize. Neither CSE nor CSEF participates in local, state, or federal elections. The two related organizations maintain separate boards of directors, bank accounts, and financial statements.

RAYMOND B. WRABLEY, JR.

Bibliography

"Citizens for a Sound Economy." *Human Events,* September 22, 1995, pp. 18–19.

Citizens for a Sound Economy 1997 Annual Report.

Citizens for a Sound Economy: www.cse.org

Stone, Peter H. "Grass-Roots Goliath," *National Journal,* July 13, 1996, pp. 1529–1533.

COMMON CAUSE

Common Cause is a nonprofit, nonpartisan interest group whose goals include ensuring open, honest, and accountable government at the national, state, and local levels. Founded in 1970 and based in Washington, D.C., Common Cause has approximately 200,000 members nationwide, with members and volunteers in every state. Common Cause employs a staff of 50 people at its national headquarters and approximately 60 staff members in state offices. They are assisted by hundreds of volunteers and interns. Common Cause is one of the oldest and largest "citizen lobbies" and is regarded as one of the most influential liberal public interest groups. A national governing board, elected by the membership to three-year terms, determines and oversees Common Cause's issue, organizational, and financial activities.

Common Cause is registered with Congress as a formal lobbying group and focuses its efforts on lobbying Congress on issues of campaign finance, open government, freedom of information, waste in government, civil rights, and congressional reform, among others. With a staff of several dozen seasoned political veterans, Common Cause lobbies members of Congress in Washington and in their home districts. A sophisticated communications network between Washington and congressional districts that includes telephone chains, telegrams, and e-mail alerts allows Common Cause to mobilize thousands of volunteers to contact their representatives on Capitol Hill. Common Cause also does extensive research on issues of concern to its members and provides information and analysis to members of Congress and their staffs. Common Cause staffers sit in on bill-drafting sessions to bring added pressure on representatives. They also publicize their research and positions through newspaper columns, press conferences, letters to the editor, and speeches to community groups. Common Cause relies on an extensive network of volunteers nationwide to undertake these activities in communities and media across the country. Television and newspaper advertisements are also used. Common Cause regularly publishes investigative studies on the effects of money in politics and reports on a variety of integrity-in-government issues. It also publishes a magazine, *Common Cause,* and often joins with other groups in coalitions to mobilize citizens or to lobby Congress.

Common Cause maintains a site on the World Wide Web that allows visitors to contact their representatives, read news and reports on current issues, find data on campaign finance issues, or sign up for CauseNet, Common Cause's e-mail alert network.

HISTORY

Common Cause was founded in 1970 by John Gardner as a "nationwide, independent, nonpartisan organization for Americans who want to help in the rebuilding of the nation." At the time, Gardner was the chairman of the Urban Coalition Action Council and had previously served as president of the Carnegie Foundation and as a cabinet member in the Johnson administration. Within a year, more than 100,000 people had joined Common Cause as it launched a grassroots effort to end the Vietnam War, reform the campaign finance system, pass the Equal Rights Amendment, and lower the voting age to 18. During the 1970s, Common Cause was involved in the successful efforts to pass campaign finance reform legislation, establish an independent counsel to investigate wrongdoing in the executive branch, open congressional meetings to the public, and pass legislation restricting gifts and fees from special interests to elected officials. Over the next two decades, Common Cause achieved prominence as a public watchdog, especially regarding the secrecy of government proceedings and the flow of special-interest money to politicians. It was led by a succession of high-profile presidents, including Archibald Cox, Fred Werthheimer, and Ann McBride.

Common Cause has consistently drawn its leadership and membership from the better-educated, higher-income groups. Critics have called it elitist and radical in pushing too hard to eliminate the traditional political give-and-take that is said to make the system function smoothly. Supporters have praised it as a voice and force for the average citizen against the money and power of well-heeled lobbies.

ACTIVITIES: CURRENT AND FUTURE

Common Cause has lobbied Congress and rallied its members on numerous domestic and foreign policy issues. One of its highest priorities has been reform of the existing campaign finance system that it believes is corrupt and makes officials less responsive to voters than to special interests. It supports a ban on "soft money" (the unregulated contributions to political parties by corporations, unions, and individuals), along with spending limits and more stringent public disclosure requirements. Common Cause has also pressed for stronger ethics and conflict-of-interest laws that require financial disclosure for public officials, restrictions on the acceptance of gifts, and limits on post-employment activities of former public officials. Common Cause has also made a priority of pushing for more open government, with government records readily available to the public, and full disclosure by lobbyists of their activities and expenses.

Common Cause has had a record of activism in the area of civil rights, pressing for full political rights for those who have suffered from discrimination. It pushed President Bill Clinton to eliminate the ban on military service for gay men and lesbians. Common Cause also argued for cutting "corporate welfare," the subsidies given to businesses, and protecting the progressivity of the income tax.

Common Cause opposed U.S. participation in the Gulf War and has opposed funding a missile defense system. It has called for reducing the levels of military spending, especially on nuclear weapons.

FINANCIAL FACTS

Common Cause has an annual budget of over $10 million. About 90 percent of its revenue comes from member dues and contributions, most of it in amounts of $100 or less. Other sources of revenue include sales of publications, interest on savings, and mailing-list rentals. It accepts no government or foundation grants and does not accept monetary contributions from corporations or labor unions in excess of $100 in a calendar year.

Common Cause spends most of its budget on its programs, especially its lobbying programs that include monitoring government activity, communicating with legislators, and publicizing its positions at the national and state levels. Other expenditures include program development and management, as well as policy formation and litigation. Common Cause does not make contributions to political parties or candidates for public office.

Common Cause is recognized as a nonprofit, tax-exempt organization under Section 501(c)(4) of the Internal Revenue code. As a full-time lobbying organization, it is not considered a charitable organization, and contributions to Common Cause are not tax deductible.

RAYMOND B. WRABLEY, JR.

Bibliography

Common Cause: www.commoncause.org

Hrebenar, Ronald J. *Interest Group Politics in America,* 3d ed. Armonk, NY: M.E. Sharpe, 1997.

ECONOMIC POLICY INSTITUTE

The Economic Policy Institute (EPI) is a nonprofit think tank whose mission is to provide high-quality research and education in order to promote a prosperous, fair, and sustainable economy. Founded in 1986, EPI is based in Washington, D.C., and employs a staff of approximately 35, with 11 Ph.D.-level researchers. EPI is nonpartisan, but it is regarded as one of the prominent liberal think tanks in Washington, focusing its research on the economic condition of low- and middle-income Americans and receiving some of its financial support from labor unions. It advocates a range of traditional economic policies, including increased government spending on social programs. It employs or supports several well-known liberal economists and has established a reputation as one of the main progressive alternatives to the conservative think tanks that have exercised great influence in economic policy debates in recent decades. It is one of the most frequently cited sources in the media on issues of poverty, living standards, and work issues.

EPI devotes significant effort to producing and disseminating analyses of the impact of economic trends and policies on low-income families. Its flagship book, *The State of Working America,* is published biennially, most recently in 1999. It is a comprehensive study of the living standards of working Americans and includes a significant amount of economic data. EPI publishes other books, as well as issue briefs, briefing papers, reports, and working papers that are available for sale. *EPI Journal,* a collection of issue perspectives and updates on EPI activities, has been published three times a year since 1990.

EPI also engages in public outreach and popular education activities as part of its effort to influence policy debates and decisions. Its reports, papers, and press releases are circulated to hundreds of journalists in the print and electronic media, and its staffers appear on radio and television news shows. In 1997, EPI's work was cited over 3,000 times in the print media, and EPI staff had over 200 radio and television appearances. In addition, EPI economists wrote op-ed pieces for numerous newspapers across the country.

EPI organizes conferences, and its staffers participate in other sponsored conferences. In 1997, its conference, *Restoring Broadly Shared Prosperity,* was televised by C-SPAN. It also provides information to elected officials. Its work has been cited by President Bill Clinton's labor secretary, Alexis Herman, and members of Congress, including Representative David Bonior (D-MI) and Senator Edward Kennedy (D-MA).

EPI maintains a site on the World Wide Web. It includes up-to-date economic data, charts, and graphs in its *DataZone* and a weekly critique of articles in the *New York Times* and the *Washington Post* in a section called *Reading Between the Lines*. The site was chosen as a Dow Jones Select Site because "it provides exceptional value" to its readers.

HISTORY

EPI was founded in 1986 by Jeff Faux, the current president of EPI; economist Barry Bluestone of the University of Massachusetts; Robert Kuttner, columnist for *Business Week* and *Newsweek* and the editor of *The American Prospect;* Ray Marshall, former U.S. labor secretary and professor at the Lyndon B. Johnson School of Public Affairs; Robert Reich, former labor secretary and professor at Brandeis University; and economist Lester Thurow of the Massachusetts Institute of Technology Sloan School of Management. These founders, liberal academics and activists, believed that as conservative money poured into think tanks and universities in the 1980s there was a need for serious, progressive economic analysis to fill a vacuum that existed in political debate. Their response was to create an organization that would focus on the economic conditions of low-income Americans while adhering to strict standards of sound, objective research and analysis.

EPI challenged the ideological and economic analysis and policies of the Reagan administration and later the Bush administration. Its early research, published in *The State of Working America,* pointed out adverse trends in income stagnation and the increasing economic squeeze on working families. EPI argued, against the dominant political and economic trends of the 1980s, that government could play a constructive role in increasing productivity and stimulating economic growth. It developed the capacity to compile economic data and analysis and to distribute it quickly to provide journalists, labor leaders, and politicians with the evidence and arguments to challenge the conservative Reagan and Bush administrations.

By the 1990s, EPI had developed a reputation for sound analysis and rapid response that gave it a strong presence among progressive activists in the nation's capital and in the states. Its publications, such as *The State of Working America,* and its staffers, including founder Jeff Faux, were relied upon to provide a liberal response to conservative think tanks and media. Although the Clinton administration has been more receptive to the agenda and analyses of EPI, the administration's centrist budget and trade policies have come under criticism by EPI.

ACTIVITIES: CURRENT AND FUTURE

EPI engages in efforts to educate the public and policy makers about the living standards, working conditions, and limited economic opportunities for the lower class, minorities, and the poor. EPI has criticized policies that it believes favor the rich over the poor, and has advocated policies that provide assistance and opportunity to the economically disadvantaged.

EPI has been on the side of labor in arguing against free-trade policies and agreements—such as the North American Free Trade Agreement (NAFTA)—that, from its perspective, force American workers to compete against repressed, low-wage workers in Central and South America. It was at the forefront of efforts to block NAFTA and the General Agreement on Tariffs and Trade. It has opposed extending normal trade relations to China or admitting China to the World Trade Organization. It has been critical of U.S. support for the International Monetary Fund (IMF) on grounds that the IMF protects multinational banks but not average working people in debtor countries. EPI has supported the imposition of quotas on foreign steel imports, arguing that illegal dumping by foreign steel producers threatens a domestic steel industry that has made great gains in efficiency and contributed to the nation's growth and prosperity in the 1990s.

EPI has also pressed for increased government spending in education, job training, public transportation, and research and development, claiming that this type of public investment in physical infrastructure and human capital will make for a more broadly shared economic prosperity. According to EPI, the projected budget surpluses make it easier to expand government social investment. EPI has argued against using budget surpluses for tax cuts. It has also opposed proposals to devote large portions of the projected surplus to Social Security. According to EPI, Social Security can be protected by raising the caps on earnings subject to the Social Security tax and by increasing the payroll tax. It has opposed proposals to privatize parts of Social Security or Medicare.

EPI has been consistent in supporting an increase in the minimum wage. It has also argued that stringent environmental regulation and economic growth are compatible policy goals. While EPI has become a dependable source of information and analysis for liberal activists, conservatives have criticized it for misrepresenting or misinterpreting economic trends and developments.

FINANCIAL FACTS

EPI has a budget of about $3 million. An overwhelming majority of its revenue (95 percent) comes from gifts or grants from individuals, foundations, businesses, and labor unions. Grants in recent years have come from the Henry J. Kaiser Institute, Carnegie Corporation, Rockefeller Foundation, and Ploughshares Fund. Government grants account for 4 percent of revenue and the remaining revenue comes from the sale of publications and interest on savings and investments. EPI does not accept contract research.

EPI's research, publications, and education activities account for a large majority of its expenses. Other expenses include management and administration, as well as fund-raising.

EPI is a tax-exempt organization under Section 501(c)(3) of the Internal Revenue code. Under this code, contributions to EPI are tax deductible for contributors who itemize. Its tax-exempt status allows EPI to engage in educational activities but bars it from direct lobbying for or against a particular piece of legislation.

RAYMOND B. WRABLEY, JR.

Bibliography

Bartel, Richard D. "EPI Links Economic Growth with Economic Justice," *Challenge* 35, no. 1 (January/February 1992): 13–23.

EPI 1997 Annual Report. Washington, DC: 1997.

EPI: www.epinet.org

HERITAGE FOUNDATION

The Heritage Foundation is a conservative think tank whose mission is to formulate and promote public policies based on the principles of free enterprise, limited government, individual freedom, traditional American values, and a strong national defense. Founded in 1973, the Heritage Foundation has become one of the nation's largest public policy research organizations and one of the best-connected, most influential conservative organizations in national politics. According to an editorial in the *Washington Times,* "The rise of conservatism in Washington and the rise of the Heritage Foundation are linked together like strands of DNA."

The Heritage Foundation employs a staff of over 160. It engages in a wide array of research, public education, and political organizing activities. The foundation's educational activities include articulating and disseminating conservative policy analyses through publications, lectures, briefings for policy-makers, and commentary in the print and electronic media. The Heritage Foundation has published over 3,000 books, monographs, and policy studies since its inception. Its bimonthly magazine, *Policy Review,* seeks to "monitor conservative ideology as it moves from the realm of theory to the world of practical politics." It presents the works of prominent academics and conservative intellectuals and activists addressing a broad spectrum of public policy issues.

The Heritage Foundation hosts lectures by U.S. and foreign political leaders and sponsors panel discussions and seminars on major policy issues. Recent lecturers include House Majority Leader Richard Armey (R-TX), former British Prime Minister Margaret Thatcher, and Supreme Court Justice Clarence Thomas. Conferences and seminars cover such topics as Social Security reform, missile defense, and family and cultural issues.

Member of Congress are the foundation's primary audience. It has a sophisticated government relations operation that seeks to advance conservative positions in the legislative process. In 1998, all congressional candidates received the foundation's *Issues 98: The Candidate's Briefing Book,* a 600-page summary and analysis of key issues and policy recommendations. The foundation's Center for Data Analysis "scores" legislative proposals using advanced econometric modeling techniques that offer members of Congress data alternatives to those available from the Congressional Budget Office or the Office of Management and Budget. The Heritage Foundation also hosts luncheon briefings for congressional press secretaries, helps congressional committees identify conservative experts who could testify on major policy questions, and helps translate conservative themes into legislative proposals.

Its aggressive public relations efforts make the Heritage Foundation the single most frequently quoted conservative think tank in America, according to a survey by FAIR, a liberal media watchdog group. Through its op-ed program, more than 150 articles written by Heritage experts appeared in major national and local newspapers in 1998. Its experts also appeared on all of the major news and public affairs shows on cable and broadcast television stations. Major conservative radio hosts frequently rely on the Heritage Foundation for the information and analyses it supplies.

ACTIVITIES: CURRENT AND FUTURE

The Heritage Foundation's mission of promoting free enterprise, traditional values, and a strong defense has led it to address a comprehensive set of policy issues. It has opposed tax increases, made the case for indexing the tax code to protect against "bracket creep," supported the Reagan administration's "supply side" tax cuts, argued for the repeal of the death tax, and supported tax reform that would institute a flat tax.

It has also argued for free trade and supported the North American Free Trade Agreement (NAFTA) and the General Agreement on Tariffs and Trade. It has argued for expanding NAFTA to include Chile and has made the case for maintaining normal trade relations with China.

The Heritage Foundation has been a long-time advocate of a robust defense budget and the doctrine of peace through strength. It has pushed for increased defense spending, arguing that recent budget trends have weakened U.S. defense capabilities. It has argued that the 1972 Anti-Ballistic Missile Treaty is legally null and void and has supported the building of a missile defense system. The foundation has supported U.S. efforts to topple anti-American governments in Nicaragua in the 1980s and in Iraq in the 1990s. It has also been critical of what it perceives as subordination of U.S. interests in the United Nations.

The foundation has been a supporter of Social Security reform proposals that would allow citizens to invest in alternative private retirement plans. It has also supported market-oriented reforms of Medicare and other health insurance regulations. Market-oriented reforms that rely on privatization and competition have also been supported in other areas, including environmental protection and education.

The Heritage Foundation has argued that government social and economic policies have contributed to a breakdown of the role of the family in creating responsible citizens, workers, and neighbors. It has made the case that marriage and religious faith are central to addressing various social problems, including drug use, school violence, and poverty. In general, the foundation advocates a range of policies that it claims would reinforce traditional values and institutions.

FINANCIAL FACTS

The Heritage Foundation reported income of $43.8 million in 1998. A large percentage is from contributions by individuals (61 percent), foundations (26 percent), and businesses (4 percent). The foundation attracted large contributions from individuals, foundations, and corporations that have traditionally supported conservative causes, including contributions of more $100,000 from the Amway Corporation, Joseph Coors, Pfizer, Inc., the John M. Olin Foundation, and the Sarah Scaife Foundation, among others. More than 200,000 other contributors make the Heritage Foundation the most broadly supported think tank in America. It accepts no government funding and performs no contract work. Other sources of income include revenue from the sale of publications and from investments. In 1998, it launched a massive Leadership for America campaign designed to raise $85 million, a goal it expected to fulfill before the end of 1999.

Almost half of the foundation's spending goes to marketing its ideas and proposals, with 25 percent of expenditures devoted to educational programs and 18 percent to media and government relations. Research receives 41 percent of spending, fund-raising receives 13 percent, and management and administration receive 3 percent.

The Heritage Foundation is a tax-exempt public policy research organization operating under section 501(c)(3) of the Internal Revenue code. Under this statute, contributions to the foundation are tax deductible.

RAYMOND B. WRABLEY, JR.

Bibliography

Edwards, Lee. *The Power of Ideas: The Heritage Foundation at 25 Years*. Ottawa, IL: Jameson Books, 1997.

The Heritage Foundation 1998 Annual Report.

The Heritage Foundation: www.heritage.org

Wilcox, Derk Arend. *The Right Guide: A Guide to Conservative and Right-of-Center Organizations*. Ann Arbor, MI: Economics America, 1997.

HUDSON INSTITUTE

The Hudson Institute is a nonprofit public policy research organization that forecasts trends and develops solutions for government, businesses, and the public. Founded in New York City in 1961, the Hudson Institute is now based in Indianapolis, Indiana, and has more than 70 researchers and employees at eight offices worldwide, including Washington, D.C., Montreal, Canada, and Brussels, Belgium. The institute is nonpartisan and does not explicitly advocate a political ideology. It claims to hold a "futurist orientation" as well as optimism about technology and its role in solving problems. However, its ardent support for free-market solutions and its emphasis on traditional and religious values in public life make the institute one of the more prominent conservative think tanks.

The Hudson Institute publishes policy research and analysis on a wide range of issues, including agriculture, crime, education, the environment, healthcare, national security, trade, and labor. It supports policy centers focused on welfare, global food issues, workforce development, the digital future, and Central European and Eurasian studies. The Hudson Institute also sponsors domestic and international conferences and symposia, and its researchers and staff members engage in public policy discussions through newspaper editorials and feature articles, press conferences, participation in radio and television programs, and briefings and presentations for government and industry.

The Hudson Institute hosts various annual award dinners to honor individuals who have made significant contributions in American public policy. Award recipients in recent years include former Vice President Dan Quayle, former senator and presidential candidate Barry Goldwater, former president Ronald Reagan, and former secretary of state Henry Kissinger.

The institute publishes a quarterly review of its activities, *Vision*, as well as a quarterly magazine of articles, *American Outlook*. It also maintains a comprehensive web site.

HISTORY

The Hudson Institute was founded in 1961 by Herman Kahn, with Max Singer and Oscar Ruebhausen. Kahn was a physicist and consultant on military strategy. His arguments—that nuclear war would differ in degree but not type from past wars, that it would not annihilate civilization, and that strong civil defense measures could alleviate its effects—had made him a controversial figure. The Hudson Institute was conceived as a research organization "dedicated to thinking about the future from a contrarian point of view." Donald Brennan was named the institute's first president.

In 1962, the Hudson Institute published Kahn's *On Thermonuclear War*, which examined in detail the consequences of nuclear proliferation. The Hudson Institute quickly began to organize seminars, studies, and research projects on various issues. Throughout the 1960s and 1970s, it received funding and grants from various sources to study trends and policies relating to the environment, economic development, the Japanese economy, national defense, healthcare, gambling, and education. The institute also published several more books by Kahn, including *The Emerging Japanese Superstate* (1970) and *The Next 200 Years* (1976).

In 1976, the Hudson Institute opened an office in Montreal, Canada. In 1943, a year after the death of Herman Kahn, the Hudson Institute moved its headquarters to Indianapolis University–Purdue University at its Indianapolis campus. In 1986, it relocated to a turn-of-the-century mansion in Indianapolis, which was named the Herman Kahn Center. In the late 1980s and early 1990s, the Hudson Institute created several policy centers, including the Center for Global Food Issues and the Competitiveness Center, chaired by former Vice President Dan Quayle. It also became home to the Education Excellence Center and, in 1994, undertook a major project with the state of Wisconsin, "Wisconsin Works," to revamp the state's welfare system.

In 1997, Herbert London, John M. Olin Professor of Humanities at New York University, became the Hudson Institute's president. A quarterly magazine devoted to the study of the future, *American Outlook,* was established in 1998.

ACTIVITIES: CURRENT AND FUTURE

Hudson Institute researchers and staffers have examined and addressed a vast array of issues during its history. In the 1970s, the Hudson Institute was a leading critic of the environmental movement's emphasis on the limits to growth. In the 1980s, it argued that natural sources of acidification were at least as damaging to the environment as industrial pollutants. In the 1990s, it published *Saving the Planet with Pesticides and Plastic,* a study describing the environmental benefits of high-yield agriculture.

The Hudson Institute has taken a long-term interest in forecasting developments in Asian economies, especially in Japan. In the 1960s, it predicted that Japan's economic development would ultimately make the country an economic rival for the United States. Various Hudson Institute studies, including *The Japanese Challenge* (1979) and *The Competition: Dealing with Japan* (1985), continued this focus.

The Hudson Institute has also focused on education. In 1984, it published Herbert London's criticism of how schools teach about the future, *Why Are They Lying to Our Children?* Its evaluation of the nation's educational practices was published in Robert Probst's *Response and Analysis: Teaching Literature in Junior and Senior High Schools* (1988). The Hudson Institute's Center for Education and Employment explores the relationship between education, training, and employment. The institute was central in the creation of the Modern Red School House program, which seeks to "reinvent the virtues of the little red school house in the modern context."

Among the Hudson Institute's most recent projects is a collaboration with the U.S. Chamber of Commerce called "The Next Agenda," the purpose of which is to find solutions for upcoming post–Cold War problems. The Institute's emphasis continues to be on the virtues of free enterprise, free trade, a strong national defense, and the restoration of traditional community networks and values.

FINANCIAL FACTS

In 1997, the Hudson Institute had revenues of just under $7 million and expenses of $7.3 million. Most of the revenue (69 percent) was derived from restricted grants and contracts. Unrestricted grants and donations made up 23 percent of the revenue. The Sarah Scaife Foundation, John M. Olin Foundation, and Pew Charitable Trusts were among the supporters. Other sources of income included interest and income from endowment and government contracts, including contracts with the Department of Defense, Department of Justice, and city of Indianapolis. An aggressive new membership initiative was established in 1997 to solicit contributions from individuals, small businesses, corporations, and foundations.

Most of the Hudson Institute's expenses (85 percent) were devoted to its public-policy research activities. The institute is a tax-exempt organization under Section 501(c)(3) of the Internal Revenue code. As such, it is prohibited from lobbying for or against specific legislation, although it may publish nonpartisan policy analysis as part of its educational activities. Contributions to the Hudson Institute are tax deductible.

RAYMOND B. WRABLEY, JR.

Bibliography

"The Face of the Future: 1997 Annual Report." Indianapolis: Hudson Institute, 1998.

Hudson Institute: www.hudson.org

JOHN BIRCH SOCIETY

The John Birch Society (JBS) is a political organization that seeks to educate Americans about constitutional and religious values, and to organize political action to resist perceived threats to those values. Founded in 1958 by Robert Welch in order to remove Communist influences from American government, the JBS became an influential organization among conservatives especially concerned about the spread of communism and various alleged conspiracies to subvert American values and institutions.

The JBS is organized into local chapters, with a membership of at least 40,000. Professional field coordinators assist local organizations to disseminate information and to organize political activities to influence policy decisions. Members receive the monthly *JBS Bulletin* with information and perspectives on political issues, along with recommendations for programs of action for immediate and long-range attention. Letter-writing campaigns, literature distribution, and petition drives are among the techniques used to reach the public and to influence legislators. The JBS does not endorse, finance, or recruit candidates for political office, emphasizing educational activities and the "mighty power of the pen."

The JBS also maintains a speakers bureau that provides orators for service clubs, schools, public forums, and radio and television shows. It organizes seminars on important political issues and produces video and audio programs for sale or for use by local chapters. The JBS also runs a large-scale publishing operation, American Opinion Books, which produces hundreds of books and pamphlets that are available through a JBS chain of book outlets. A biweekly magazine of articles and opinions, *The New American,* is published by a JBS-affiliated corporation.

The Robert Welch University (RWU), formerly the John Birch University, is also affiliated with JBS. It offers summer camp courses from an "Americanist" perspective, with titles such as "Our Godly Heritage," "Global Tyranny: The United Nations," and "Exposing the Media Bias." RWU houses a 30,000-volume library and publishes books through its own RWU Press. The goal of the RWU is to develop a four-year, degree-granting college of liberal arts.

HISTORY

The JBS was founded in 1958 in Belmont, Massachusetts, by Robert Welch. An executive for a large candy manufacturer and a former director of the National Association of Manufacturers, Welch had become convinced that an international conspiracy was creating a worldwide totalitarian government. He identified President Dwight Eisenhower, among other prominent American political and military leaders, as a member of an international Communist conspiracy.

Welch created the JBS as an anti-collectivist, anti-Communist organization dedicated to defending both Judeo-Christian values and a capitalist, constitutional republic against the conspiracy. The JBS was founded as a hierarchical organization under the direction of Welch's personal leadership. The society was named for John Birch, a Baptist missionary and American intelligence officer killed by the Communist government in China, becoming America's first Cold War casualty, according to Welch.

In 1959, 40 local JBS chapters were formed in ten states. Among their first activities was to protest the visit to the United States of Soviet leader Nikita Khrushchev. In 1961, the JBS organized the Movement to Impeach Earl Warren, the liberal Chief Justice of the United States. The JBS began attracting national attention, much of which was criticism for its excessive anti-Communist zealotry and conspiracy mongering.

In the 1960s, membership in the JBS grew rapidly and included some members of Congress. It was persistent in its efforts to expose a Communist influence in the U.S. government and in 1965, created TACT (Truth About Civil Turmoil) to expose alleged Communist influence in the civil rights movement. It also launched a weekly magazine, *The Review of the News*. In 1966, JBS TRAIN (To Restore American Independence Now) committees were organized to press for U.S. withdrawal from the United Nations. In the late 1960s, the JBS focused organizational energy on a campaign to restore traditional morality.

In the 1970s, the JBS was among the opponents of the Equal Rights Amendment, and it organized efforts to stop the treaty to give control of the Panama Canal to Panama. It also launched a program called TRIM (Tax Reform Immediately) to promote lower taxes.

In 1983, Robert Welch turned over the chairmanship of the JBS to Representative Larry McDonald (D-GA). McDonald was killed later that year in the crash of Korean Air Lines flight 007. Robert Welch died in 1985, the same year that the weekly magazine, *The Review of the News*, was merged with the monthly journal, *American Opinion*, to form *The New American*. In 1989, the JBS moved its headquarters to Appleton, Wisconsin. In the 1990s, the JBS continued to focus its efforts on exposing an alleged conspiracy of "insiders" who, according to the JBS, constitute an evil global organization intent on creating a "new world order" under totalitarian rule. The JBS celebrated its 40th anniversary in 1998.

ACTIVITIES: CURRENT AND FUTURE

The JBS was founded as an anti-Communist organization, based on the belief that Communists were conspiring to undermine American values and institutions. Its focus has been primarily on opposing communism abroad and all its perceived manifestations in the United States. This effort has included a defense of private enterprise and traditional morality, and opposition to many modern government programs. More recently, it has focused on a broader conspiracy of global "insiders" who, according to the JBS, use communism as one tool in an effort to subvert the United States. The JBS has sought to expose alleged Communist infiltration of the U.S. government and various social reform movements. It has been active in the opposition to legal abortion and gun control and has supported tax cuts. It has vigorously opposed United Nations activities and has long called for United States withdrawal from the United Nations. The JBS has opposed the effort to limit the terms of members of Congress on the grounds that political problems are related less to the amount of time spent in office than to poor performance in public office. The JBS has also devoted significant effort to oppose a new constitutional convention that would add a balanced budget amendment to the Constitution. It has argued that the actual intent for such a convention would be to make radical changes in the Constitution. The JBS was one of the earliest organizations to call for the impeachment of President Bill Clinton, accusing him of treason by accepting "bribes" from the Communist government in China in exchange for access to U.S. national security secrets. The JBS has also described the NATO military operation in Kosovo in the former Yugoslavia as a cynical effort to advance the cause of global government.

Although membership in the JBS is below what it was at its peak, its publications have influenced debate on numerous issues, and it has won praise from some prominent politicians.

FINANCIAL FACTS

The JBS budget figures are not made available to the public. However, according to its 1998 Annual Report to members, the JBS derives revenue from two primary sources. A portion of its revenue comes from business transactions (literature sales, including sales through American Opinion Books of close to $1 million annually, subscriptions and advertising in *The New American*, etc.). Contributions (member dues, monthly donations, one-time gifts, etc.) make up 75 percent of revenue. Other sources of revenue include bequests from the estates of deceased members.

Expenditures are made for paying officers and field staff, publishing the *JBS Bulletin*, developing TRIM Bulletins, speaker tours, and legislative monitoring. The JBS is a nonprofit entity, but has never sought the Internal Revenue Service tax code 501(c)(3) nonprofit designation. The RWU is a 501(c)(3) nonprofit organization under the Internal Revenue code, for which contributions are tax deductible. The JBS owns all the stock of American Opinion Publishing, Inc., a for-profit corporation, and is the majority shareholder in Western Islands, another for-profit book-publishing firm.

RAYMOND B. WRABLEY, JR.

Bibliography

John Birch Society: www.jbs.org

Forster, Arnold, and Benjamin Epstein. *Danger on the Right*. New York: Random House, 1964.

Stone, Barbara S. "The John Birch Society: A Profile." *Journal of Politics* 36 (February 1974).

NATIONAL COUNCIL OF THE CHURCHES OF CHRIST

The National Council of the Churches of Christ in the USA, also known as the National Council of Churches (NCC), is the primary national expression of the movement for Christian unity in the United States. The NCC's member communions—thirty-five Protestant, Orthodox, and Anglican church bodies—work together on a wide range of activities that aim to further Christian unity and serve people throughout the world.

Founded in 1950 and headquartered in New York City, the NCC has been described as "the most influential spokesman for mainline Protestant churches in America." The organization, which has a staff of about 350, wields economic, political, and intellectual influence in shaping and implementing public policy. Some 52 million Christians belong to churches that are NCC members, although not all support the group's political agenda, which is generally regarded as liberal. Many Christians have organized other groups that advocate more conservative positions.

The NCC operates a variety of offices and agencies that are involved in public policy issues. The Church World Service (CWS) works with local agencies, often Christian councils, to provide emergency relief and long-range development assistance around the globe. Its emergency aid goes to victims of famine, war, and natural disasters such as hurricanes. Its Immigration and Refugee Program assists with the resettlement of refugees. The CWS, along with Lutheran World Relief and the National Catholic Welfare Program created the Christian Rural Overseas Program (CROP), a joint community hunger appeal. CROP has organized Friendship Food Trains and Friendship Food Ships to gather and deliver food contributions to relieve hunger. The CWS has used radio spots to communicate its message; for example, one recent radio message was recorded by Archbishop Desmond Tutu of South Africa on the Kosovo crisis.

NCC officials testify before Congress on various public policy issues. They also issue press statements and reports on social justice issues and urge federal officials to take specific actions on policy questions. The NCC's Friendship Press publishes educational resources on issues of concern. A recent World Wide Web publication, a "Web book," dealt with Cuba. The NCC's sophisticated web site includes calendars of events, texts of press releases, and links to various offices and educational resources.

In 1996 the NCC joined with Catholic leaders to establish the Joseph Cardinal Bernadin Common Ground Award, a prize named for the late Chicago archbishop. The award recognizes "persons whose lives have shown dedication to the unity of people." The NCC also publishes the New Revised Standard Version of the Bible.

HISTORY

The NCC was founded in 1950 in Cleveland, Ohio, by mainline Protestant churches seeking common ground in dealing with the religious and cultural challenges of the postwar world. Twelve previously existing ecumenical agencies were merged as part of the creation of the NCC. Early on, the group supported many liberal programs and causes, including Social Security, unemployment insurance, minimum wage laws, regulation of business, collective bargaining rights, and civil rights. It also backed the Korean War and NATO.

In the 1960s and 1970s, the NCC's political efforts reflected the upheaval of the times. It embraced the antiwar movement and supported affirmative action and school integration through busing. In the 1980s, the NCC consistently criticized the Reagan administration's domestic and foreign policies. It opposed cuts in social welfare programs and increases in the defense budget. In the 1990s, the NCC reached out to develop new interfaith ties with American Muslims, evangelical Protestants, and Roman Catholics. Its overtures to the

National Association of Evangelicals marked a new dialogue between the theologically conservative evangelicals and the more theologically liberal NCC.

In 1991, Joan Brown Campbell became the first ordained woman minister to serve as NCC general secretary, the group's top staff position. Her term expired at the end of 1999. The term of NCC President Craig B. Anderson also expired, and he was succeeded by Andrew Young, former representative and mayor of Atlanta.

ACTIVITIES: CURRENT AND FUTURE

The NCC addresses a wide range of religious and political issues in numerous ways. Its general assembly resolutions aim to influence opinions within member congregations as well as among the broader public. In many instances, the various ministries and offices are engaged in educational activities and programs that reflect the NCC philosophy. Most member churches take positions that support activism on behalf of the poor and disadvantaged. This has led the NCC toward activism for "social justice" at home and for peace, economic development, and human rights abroad.

The NCC has consistently supported full funding of government social welfare programs. In 1995, the NCC urged President Bill Clinton to veto Republican-sponsored budget cuts, saying, "We name them for what they are, an assault on those least able to defend themselves in order to reach self-imposed budget goals that include tax breaks for the more fortunate." The NCC has pressed for continued protection of Social Security, Medicare, Medicaid, food stamps, and other government-assistance programs.

The NCC has also taken a strong position in support of public education, arguing that many of the most vulnerable children in society depend on public schools. It has opposed the school voucher movement that would allow tax money to subsidize the costs of private religious schools. Arguing that "public funds should be used for public purposes," the NCC has advocated increased spending to reduce class size and modernize public school facilities.

The NCC has supported the environmental movement, arguing, "human beings are called to care for the earth." It has undertaken an educational and advocacy effort that includes public service announcements, and has endorsed the Kyoto Protocol on global warming.

A senior NCC official recently took a controversial position supporting a Planned Parenthood sex-education kit that failed to condemn abortion or homosexuality. The NCC backs civil rights for homosexuals and has denounced violence against gay men and lesbians. Another controversial position taken by the NCC urges the release of Leonard Peltier, a Native American imprisoned since 1977 for the murder of two FBI agents. Peltier maintains his innocence, and Amnesty International, the worldwide human rights group, regards him as a political prisoner.

The NCC has also supported economic and humanitarian assistance in poor countries. It favored economic sanctions against South Africa to help end apartheid, as well as sanctions against Iraq as an alternative to the Gulf War. In other instances it has questioned the use of sanctions because of the serious hardship such measures create for the civilian population.

FINANCIAL FACTS

The NCC has an annual budget of $60 million. It receives income from congregations and denominational headquarters, as well as from public appeals to churches, individuals, and foundations. In the 1990s it faced financial duress that required it to cut back on expenditures for programming and staff. In 1994, the NCC lost $8 million from bad investments.

RAYMOND B. WRABLEY, JR.

Bibliography

Billingsley, K. L. *From Mainline to Sideline: The Social Witness of the NCC.* Washington, DC: Ethics and Public Policy Center, 1990.

NATIONAL TAXPAYERS UNION

The National Taxpayers Union (NTU) is a grassroots organization that lobbies for lower taxes and less government spending. Founded in 1969 and based in the Virginia suburbs of Washington, D.C., the NTU has 300,000 members in all 50 states. It has been called the "grandaddy" of tax revolt organizations. Its affiliated educational research organization, the National Taxpayers Union Foundation (NTUF), was founded in 1977 and conducts research on issues that concern taxpayers. The NTU and the NTUF are nonpartisan organizations whose positions are frequently consistent with those of Republican officials, although they are critical of Republicans who support tax increases or increases in government spending.

The NTU pursues its agenda of lower taxes and less government through lobbying, public education, and public relations campaigns. The NTU and the NTUF maintain a large library of statistics on items such as the federal debt and deficit, the distribution of taxes by wealth, the total tax burden on a typical family, comparisons of state and local tax rates, and past and projected growth of Social Security and Medicare spending. It conducts and compiles research on the effects of raising and lowering taxes, the impact of subsidies and corporate welfare, the cost to taxpayers of various interest groups' agendas in Congress, and the effect of various tax and entitlement reform proposals. The NTU analysts help local activists determine the costs and benefits of government projects in their regions.

Since 1979, the NTU has conducted an annual Rating of Congress that shows how often each lawmaker voted to reduce or control taxes, spending, debt, and regulation. The NTUF's Vote Tally and Bill Tally systems provide cost information for every significant piece of spending legislation before Congress and assign running cost tallies to lawmakers based on what they vote for or sponsor. The NTU also maintains a comprehensive database of pension estimates for members of Congress and for former and current presidents. They also maintain data on House office expenditures.

The NTU analysts and staff members lobby Congress and state legislatures on tax and spending legislation. They also appear on radio and television news programs and are interviewed by the press. They maintain a database of over 900 citizen activists and organizations across the country that can be enlisted to provide media commentary or speakers on local tax issues. The NTUF publishes the *Chartbook on Entitlements*, which analyzes the long-term problems of major entitlement programs and advocates solutions to those problems. It also regularly publishes issue briefs and policy papers on a wide range of topics of interest to taxpayers. Assistance is also given to NTU members in their efforts to become effective citizen lobbyists. Much of the research, analysis, and advocacy produced by the NTU and the NTUF is available on a comprehensive site maintained by the group on the World Wide Web. The NTU publishes *Dollars and Sense*, a magazine for members, six times a year, and the NTUF publishes *Capital Ideas,* a magazine for contributors.

HISTORY

The NTU was founded in 1969 by James D. Davidson, a 22-year-old political science graduate student at the University of Maryland, who had worked for the Nixon campaign. He formed the NTU to defend "the poor, neglected taxpayer" in policy debates. The NTU scored an early victory when it helped defeat the Nixon administration's proposal to build a costly supersonic transport like the Concorde. In 1975, NTU initiated the campaign for a balanced-budget amendment, which has been a continuous part of the group's agenda. In 1979, the NTU played a key role in the successful effort in California to pass Proposition 13, a tax-cutting initiative. In the early 1980s, President Ronald Reagan shared many of the NTU's goals and credited its lobbying effort for helping to pass tax cut and income tax indexing proposals.

The NTU's persistent lobbying for tax cuts and its constant scrutiny of government spending programs have brought it into conflict with conservatives on several occasions. The NTU has even joined with liberal groups to promote cuts in military spending and anti-environmental corporate subsidies. Liberals, however, have criticized the NTU, claiming that its rating methods distort the voting records of members of Congress.

ACTIVITIES: CURRENT AND FUTURE

The NTU focuses on issues of taxes and spending at the federal as well as state levels. It has played a leading role in the effort to pass a constitutional amendment to require a balanced budget. The NTU has also supported an amendment that would make it more difficult for Congress to increase taxes. It constantly scrutinizes proposed legislation and criticizes spending proposals that it regards as wasteful, unnecessary, or inefficient. It played a role in stopping high-profile federal research projects such as the superconducting super collider, the advanced liquid metal reactor, and the advanced solid rocket motor. It has published analyses and criticism of the spending agendas of the League of Women Voters, the National Education Association, and the American Association of Retired Persons.

The NTU has advocated the elimination of various government bureaucracies and the reining in of others. It fought for a Taxpayers Bill of Rights that would include protections against "abuses" by the Internal Revenue Service. It fought to reduce the costs of Congress, opposing both congressional pay increases and the rising administrative costs of congressional offices.

The NTU has been an advocate of Social Security and Medicare reforms. It has supported proposals to privatize both of these programs through personal and medical savings accounts. The NTU has advocated other spending cuts, such as eliminating the space station, closing military bases, and ending subsidies for corporations and low-income citizens. The NTU supports a tax reform proposal that would replace all federal income, payroll, and capital gains taxes with a national sales tax.

FINANCIAL FACTS

In 1998, the NTU had revenue of $2.5 million, almost all of which came in contributions and grants from individuals, businesses, and foundations. Its expenses in 1998 totaled approximately $2.8 million, with most going to program services, including research and public education, publications, and lobbying. Management, fund-raising, and other supporting services accounted for other expenses. The NTU is a tax-exempt organization under Section 501(c)(4) of the Internal Revenue code. Contributions to the organization are not tax deductible.

The NTUF had revenues of $3.2 million in 1998. Most of the revenue came in grants and contributions from individuals, businesses, and foundations. Over the years it has received grants from the John M. Olin Foundation, Sarah Scaife Foundation, and William H. Donner Foundation, among others. Some revenue also came from investments. The NTUF had expenses of $2.7 million. Public education, research, conferences, and fund-raising were among the expenditures. The NTUF is a tax-exempt organization under Section 501(c)(3) of the Internal Revenue code. It may engage in public education activities but may not lobby for or against specific legislation. Contributions to NTUF are tax deductible.

RAYMOND B. WRABLEY, JR.

Bibliography

McWilliams, Rita. "The Best and the Worst of Public Interest Groups: From Lifting Up the Poor to Shaking Down the Elderly." *Washington Monthly*, March 1988, pp. 19-29.

National Taxpayers Union and National Taxpayers Union Foundation Financial Statements, 1998.

National Taxpayers Union: www.ntu.org

PUBLIC CITIZEN

Public Citizen is a nonprofit, nonpartisan, member-supported interest group that lobbies on behalf of issues related to consumer and workplace safety, environmental protection, safe energy sources, campaign finance reform, and ethics in government. It was founded by consumer advocate Ralph Nader in 1971 and is based in Washington, D.C. With about 150,000 members, Public Citizen is one of the most prominent liberal public interest groups formed during the period of social and political activism in the late 1960s and early 1970s. It is organized into six divisions: Congress Watch, the Health Research Group, the Litigation Group, the Critical Mass Energy Project, Global Trade Watch, and Buyers Up.

Public Citizen is one of a handful of public interest groups that pioneered many of the techniques used in contemporary grassroots lobbying. It organizes citizen pressure on members of Congress through letter writing, fax, e-mail, and telephone campaigns. It provides advice and assistance to citizens and local groups on public education activities and lobbying legislators, and joins with other national and local groups in grassroots coalitions. Its researchers prepare reports and fact sheets on issues of concern to its members. Its staffers organize press conferences, appear on television and radio news programs, write newspaper columns, and reach out to editorial boards to secure favorable press coverage of their issues and activities. Public Citizen's attorneys bring lawsuits in state and federal courts on behalf of citizens to force or block action on issues of concern and assist other lawyers on cases before the Supreme Court. Public Citizen's most influential effort in influencing policy is its relationship with members of Congress, especially liberal Democrats. Public Citizen has developed a reputation for providing credible information and expertise to counter the information provided by corporate lobbyists. Its experts testify before Congress and federal agencies and provide legal analysis and strategic advice to help pass or block legislation.

Public Citizen maintains a sophisticated site on the World Wide Web that includes action alerts that help citizens make informed inquiries or comments to members of Congress on a range of issues. It also contains a comprehensive list of reports and publications that are available for purchase as well as full texts or excerpts from numerous Public Citizen publications. The site also has an abbreviated online version of *Public Citizen News*, the bimonthly membership newsletter of articles and editorials. Other regular Public Citizen publications include *Health Letter* and *Critical Mass Bulletin*.

Public Citizen Foundation is the tax-exempt affiliate of Public Citizen that provides research and litigation on issues pertaining to the environment, consumer affairs, organized labor, public health, corporate responsibility, and occupational safety.

HISTORY

Public Citizen was founded in 1971 by Ralph Nader. Nader had gained public attention in 1965 with the publication of his best-selling book, *Unsafe at Any Speed*, an exposé of the dangers in the operation of the Chevrolet Corvair. He quickly gained a reputation as an anticorporate consumer crusader and founded a number of public interest groups. Public Citizen became the umbrella group to raise and distribute funds to various other Nader projects. The Health Research Group was created in 1971 by Nader and Dr. Sidney Wolfe to promote research-based, systemwide changes in healthcare policy as well as to provide advice concerning drugs, medical devices, doctors and hospitals, and occupational health. The Litigation Group was created in 1972 as a public interest law firm litigating in the area of health, safety, and consumer rights. Congress Watch was created as the lobbying arm of Public Citizen by Joan Claybrook in 1973 to push for legislation on workplace safety, consumer protection, and open government. The Critical Mass Energy Project was created in 1974 to promote renewable energy and energy efficiency technologies and as a watchdog on nuclear safety issues. Global Trade Watch is the division created to promote government and corporate accountability, along with consumer and environmental protection, by engaging in research and advocacy in the field of international trade and investment. In 1983, Buyers Up was created to help consumers pool their buying power and save money on home heating oil.

In its early years, Public Citizen relied on a collection of young lawyers and activists to pursue an "investigate-expose-lobby-lawsuit" strategy of attack. Pursuing a broad agenda and exploiting the activist political climate of Washington in the 1970s, Public Citizen achieved prominence in the public interest movement and exercised influence in a number of policy areas, forcing drug companies to withdraw dangerous drugs from the market, requiring health-warning labels on various products, pushing for the passage of community right-to-know laws, and helping to kill funding for a proposed plutonium breeder reactor at Clinch River, Tennessee.

By the 1990s, businesses had effectively organized to counter the successes of Public Citizen and other public interest groups. The era of government and social activism had ended, and there was less money and public support for the kinds of social or regulatory programs supported by Public Citizen. Some critics argued that Public Citizen represented middle-class activists who were insensitive to the economic costs of government regulations. Even supporters worried that Nader and his projects had spread themselves too thin. However, Public Citizen remains active and influential on a range of issues, supporting the successful Supreme Court case to overturn the Line Item Veto Act in 1997 and, more recently, blocking congressional efforts to weaken environmental and consumer protection regulations.

ACTIVITIES: CURRENT AND FUTURE

Public Citizen remains active in analyzing, publicizing, and lobbying in many policy areas. It has pushed for campaign finance reform, claiming that monied interests control the agenda in Congress because they control campaign purse strings. Public Citizen has long favored public financing of all federal campaigns, but it has supported the more limited proposals to ban "soft money" (that is, unregulated contributions made to political parties as opposed to contributions made directly to candidates) and to enhance disclosure and enforcement. Public Citizen has also supported reform of the Independent Counsel Act, a law that Public Citizen pushed for in the 1970s. In addition, Public Citizen has advocated a number of reforms to protect investigators of executive branch wrongdoing from political pressures.

Public Citizen has also been an advocate for cuts in corporate welfare, that is, the corporate tax breaks, subsidies, and incentives that amount to public welfare for corporations. It has also opposed recent congressional efforts to "roll back" government regulations, arguing that antiregulatory extremists are seeking to weaken environmental, health, and safety laws. Public Citizen has also criticized congressional efforts to reach an agreement with the tobacco industry to limit its liability in lawsuits in exchange for a lump sum payment to the federal or state governments for healthcare costs related to tobacco use. It has generally been a critic of civil justice reform proposals that would limit the liability of companies in lawsuits brought against them for damages caused by their products.

Public Citizen has also opposed free trade accords, including the North American Free Trade Agreement and the General Agreement on Tariffs and Trade, charging that these pacts allow corporations to evade environmental, health, safety, and labor regulations and that they cost American jobs. Public Citizen addresses a great many issues in healthcare, product liability, government ethics, and energy generation.

FINANCIAL FACTS

Public Citizen has an annual budget of about $10 million. The largest source of revenue is gifts and grants from foundations, businesses, and individuals. Another large source of revenue is the sale of publications. Other sources include court-awarded attorney's fees, mailing-list rentals, income from the Buyers Up program, and other miscellaneous sources. Major expenses include research, publication and distribution of publications, fund-raising, and staff support.

Public Citizen is recognized as a tax-exempt organization under Section 501(c)(4) of the Internal Revenue code. This designation allows Public Citizen to lobby for legislation that promotes the general social welfare, but contributions to Public Citizen are not tax deductible.

RAYMOND B. WRABLEY, JR.

Bibliography

Hrebenar, Ronald J. *Interest Group Politics in America,* 3d ed. Armonk, NY: M.E. Sharpe, 1997.

Public Citizen: www.citizen.org

UNITED STATES CATHOLIC CONFERENCE

The United States Catholic Conference (USCC) is the public policy agency of the American Catholic hierarchy. It is a civil, nonprofit organization incorporated in Washington, D.C. The USCC consists of five committees: Communications, Education, Campaign for Human Development, Domestic Policy, and International Policy. These committees consist of clergy and religious and lay people who develop policy and programs for approval by an administrative board and the body of bishops. The positions taken on political issues by the USCC, especially on federal budget and social welfare issues, are generally consistent with the positions of liberal interest groups.

The USCC, through its various departments, engages in a wide array of activities aimed at applying Catholic social teaching to major contemporary domestic and international issues that have significant moral and human dimensions. The Department of Social Development and World Peace advocates for the poor and disadvantaged, and for justice and peace, while helping build the capacity of the Church to act effectively in defense of human life, human dignity, and human rights. The USCC's Office of Domestic Social Development coordinates USCC policy on major national issues including healthcare, welfare reform, poverty, civil rights, housing, homelessness, and labor. The Office of International Justice and Peace also engages in similar development and advocacy activities in the areas of human rights, religious liberty, peace and disarmament, foreign assistance, and religious and ethnic conflicts. The Department of Social Development and World Peace sends out a bimonthly "issue mailing" to subscribers with information and materials to assist social justice activists.

The USCC also operates the U.S. Catholic Church's antipoverty program, the Campaign for Human Development (CHD). The CHD raises funds through a nationwide, parish-level collection and provides grants to low-income groups for projects such as job creation, improvement of work conditions, crime fighting, school reform, and assistance for the elderly. The CHD distributes approximately $8 million in grants annually. The Department of Communications provides reviews of movies, videos, and television shows and runs the Catholic News Service, an international wire service for Catholic newspapers worldwide. The Office of Government Liaison represents the bishops before Congress on a wide variety of public policy issues. It coordinates and directs the legislative activities of the USCC staff and other Church personnel in order to influence the actions of Congress.

The USCC, with the National Council of Catholic Bishops (NCCB), operates Publishing and Promotion Services, which publishes approximately 50 books, videos, and electronic compact disc products each year. Topics covered on the titles range from issues such as politics, violence, and substance abuse to sources of religious education. The USCC/NCCB also maintain a comprehensive web site that includes a broad range of information, position papers, and press releases.

HISTORY

The USCC was established by the American Catholic hierarchy in 1966, but it has its origins in the National Catholic War Council. The National Catholic War Council was created at the urging of James Cardinal Gibbons of Baltimore to enable Catholics to contribute funds and commit personnel to meet the spiritual and recreational needs of U.S. servicepersons during the First World War. The council demonstrated the value of episcopal collaboration at the national level and, with the encouragement of Pope Benedict XV's call for Catholics to work for peace and social justice, led the hierarchy to establish the National Catholic Welfare Council (NCWC) in 1919. The NCWC included the bishops in its annual meeting. A second entity, the NCWC, Inc., consisted of the bishops working through their staffs in the areas of education, immigration, and social action. Both of these organizations were headquartered in Washington, D.C. They served the Church in the United States until 1966, when the hierarchy voted to establish the NCCB and the USCC.

The NCCB is a canonical entity made up exclusively of bishops. Through the NCCB, the bishops attend to Church-related affairs in the United States. In the USCC, the bishops collaborate with other Catholics to address broader issues that concern the Church as part of the larger society. By the 1990s, the USCC had established an elaborate organization of departments and committees that develop positions and programs on issues of concern to the bishops, and present those positions in the public policy process.

ACTIVITIES: CURRENT AND FUTURE

The USCC takes an interest in virtually every domestic and international policy issue on the national agenda. It has taken public positions over the years on issues relating to the nature of the U.S. economic system, disarmament, healthcare, economic inequality, education, and abortion. Its Legislative Program for the 106th Congress includes proposals on numerous issues. It calls for adequate funding for programs that serve the poor, including housing programs for the elderly and people with AIDS, nutrition programs, and healthcare programs. It criticizes proposals to cut spending on social programs. It calls for an increase in the minimum wage and for indexing the minimum wage to the cost of living. The USCC has supported reforms to preserve Social Security, with an emphasis on maintaining the redistributive properties of the program that ensure that the return to the poorest is greater than that to the wealthiest. It also has supported healthcare reform that would guarantee universal access to affordable healthcare. The USCC has also supported expansion of the Family and Medical Leave Act.

The USCC has supported gun control, including the requirement of child safety locks on handguns. It has consistently opposed the death penalty. It has taken the lead in promoting education reforms that include "school choice" provisions that would provide tax vouchers or credits for families that send children to private or religious schools. The USCC has also been at the forefront of anti-abortion lobbying efforts to ban tax subsidies for abortions, deny aid to international family planning organizations that support abortion, prevent importation or sale of chemical abortifacients, ban human cloning, and to prohibit research using fetal tissue.

The USCC has supported U.S. economic and humanitarian assistance to foreign countries. It has been critical of the tight economic sanctions maintained against Cuba, calling for an immediate end to the ban on the sale of food and medicine in Cuba. It has supported U.S. ratification of various recently negotiated international treaties, including those that would ban the use of landmines (the Ottawa Treaty) and ban nuclear testing (the Comprehensive Test Ban Treaty). It has been favorable toward the Kyoto Protocol that would reduce global greenhouse gas emissions. The USCC has called for more liberal immigration policies and has championed human rights as a central element in U.S. foreign policy.

FINANCIAL FACTS

As a nonprofit organization, the USCC does not have a political action committee (PAC) and is prohibited by the Internal Revenue Service from contributing to electoral campaigns.

RAYMOND B. WRABLEY, JR.

Bibliography
United States Catholic Conference: www.nccbuscc.org

U.S. PUBLIC INTEREST RESEARCH GROUP

The United States Public Interest Research Group (US PIRG) calls itself a "watchdog for the public interest in the nation's capital." Founded in 1983 and headquartered in Washington, D.C., US PIRG has a staff of 20 and claims a membership of 1 million. It also has organizations in 22 states and on more than 100 college campuses. With origins in the liberal consumer and public interest movement of the 1970s, US PIRG focuses its grassroots organizing, advocacy, and litigation efforts on such issues as product safety, environmental protection, public health, consumer protection, and special interest influence in government. An affiliated organization, US PIRG Education Fund (US PIRGEF), is its research and education arm. In 1997, US PIRGEF published 16 national studies and exposés on threats to the environment, consumer rights, and democracy. It also conducted workshops to train citizens in the skills that enhance their ability to influence public policy. US PIRGEF also participates in a workplace giving campaign through Earthshare.

US PIRG engages in a wide range of advocacy and educational activities. It distributes a Congressional Scorecard, which rates members of Congress according to their voting records on key public interest issues. In 1997, over 1 million scorecards were distributed in 282 congressional districts. US PIRG's quarterly newsletter, *Citizen Agenda*, reports on its investigations and other PIRG activities. Staff attorneys bring lawsuits to protect consumers and punish corporate abuses. Other PIRG staffers attend congressional hearings, monitor legislation, and lobby Congress. They also provide information and analysis for the media, appear on public affairs programs, testify before Congress, and write op-ed columns. In coalition with other groups like the Sierra Club, the Natural Resources Defense Council, and the American Lung Association, US PIRG organizes grassroots campaigns to bring pressure on elected officials.

In 1997, US PIRG upgraded its presence on the World Wide Web. Its site provides visitors with instant access to more than a dozen US PIRG reports and consumer surveys, as well as US PIRG's Congressional Scorecards. An automatic e-mail consumer alert allows subscribers to receive periodic alerts on pressing consumer issues. Links on the site allow visitors to access information provided by other public interest and environmental groups.

HISTORY

US PIRG was created by the state PIRGs in 1983 to advocate for the public interest in the nation's capital. The first state PIRGs were set up in 1971 by Ralph Nader, who had made a name for himself in the 1960s with his exposé of the safety problems of General Motors' Chevrolet Corvair. Nader has founded many consumer groups, including Public Citizen. The early organizing of the PIRGs was based on college campuses with the idea that students would pool their financial resources to fund research on issues of interest and importance to the public. The PIRG would be a form of participatory democracy through which students would play a larger role in public affairs. By the end of the 1970s, there were 120 PIRG chapters in 25 states.

The funding method for the campus PIRGs has long generated controversy. Organizers succeeded in persuading many universities to enroll all undergraduates in the campus PIRG through a "negative checkoff" mechanism. When students paid tuition, a fee for PIRG membership was automatically assessed. Students could later request that the money be refunded. Opposition over the years, on grounds that PIRG's tactics were deceptive or coercive, led to changes that reduced funding for the PIRGs.

The state PIRGs undertook many successful organizing and lobbying activities in the states in the 1970s and often joined with other consumer and environmental groups to promote the public-interest agenda. In the 1980s, the creation of US PIRG allowed the public-interest movement to bolster its research and advocacy capabilities nationally. US PIRG also attracted foundation support and a large enough membership to become one of the more liberal and effective public interest lobbies.

ACTIVITIES: CURRENT AND FUTURE

One of US PIRG's major concerns is what it regards as abuses by big business that receive protection from government while harming consumers. US PIRG argues that, without a vigilant watchdog, government officials cater to the special interests that finance their campaigns. PIRG consumer advocates investigate unsafe business practices and publicly name unsafe products. In recent years, PIRG exposés have focused on dangerous toys, lax antitheft protection for debit cards, excessive bank fees, and identity theft and anti-consumer practices by rent-to-own businesses, credit bureaus, and airlines.

Another major focus of PIRG lobbying has been the health threat posed by pollution. In 1997, PIRG teamed with other environmental groups to press for tough, new limits on smog and soot. It mobilized citizens to testify at Environmental Protection Agency hearings and helped gather 250,000 signatures on a petition delivered to President Bill Clinton and Congress. It participated in a "Tombstone Tour" that featured a 10-foot tombstone to commemorate the 15,000 Americans it claimed air pollution would kill in 1997. It also lobbied to strengthen the Endangered Species Act and to oppose congressional efforts to weaken the Superfund toxic-waste cleanup law. US PIRG opposed a law that would allow the shipment of radioactive wastes on highways and rail lines, sought to cut government subsidies for polluters, and lobbied for increased support for clean energy alternatives.

US PIRG has also been a leading advocate of political reforms to reduce the role of special-interest money in political campaigns, supporting various state and federal campaign-finance reform efforts.

FINANCIAL FACTS

US PIRG and US PIRGEF have a combined annual budget of over $600,000. About 80 percent of its revenues come from contributions by individuals and foundations, with lesser amounts from state PIRG contributions and other revenue. Foundations that have provided support include the Rockefeller Family Fund, Tom Creek Foundation, and Pew Charitable Trusts. Most of PIRG's expenses cover program services, and about 10 percent goes to fund-raising.

US PIRG is a tax-exempt organization covered by Section 501(c)(4) of the Internal Revenue code. It is allowed to engage in direct lobbying, and contributions are not tax deductible. Contributions to US PIRGEF, a 501(c)(3) organization, are tax deductible.

RAYMOND B. WRABLEY, JR.

Bibliography
State PIRGs: www.igc.org/pirg/
US PIRG Annual Report to Members, 1997.

SECTION ELEVEN
SINGLE ISSUE

Single-issue interest groups are political interest groups that form around one issue, or perhaps several related issues. More often than not, they are concerned with social rather than economic issues. Many, although not all, believe intensely in the righteousness of their cause and would be willing to use militant, confrontational means to achieve their ends. Almost since the beginning of America's modern democratic system, single-issue groups have been major players on our national stage. Some single-issue groups have had a lasting decisive effect on public policy, while others have come and gone without leaving much of a trace.

In 1794, with the American Republic not even a decade old, one of the first single-issue groups made its mark. In 1791, Congress had passed an excise tax on whiskey to help pay off the nation's debt. Small farmers in rural areas, who produced and consumed vast amounts of whiskey, were not pleased. In a move later referred to as the Whiskey Rebellion, farmers attacked federal collectors who tried to enforce the tax. In July 1794, 500 men attacked and burned the home of the regional tax collector in western Pennsylvania. The following month, President George Washington issued a proclamation ordering the rebels to return home and called up the militia from four of the neighboring states. After Washington ordered 13,000 troops into the area, the farmers returned to their homes, offering no resistance. Two of the rebel ringleaders were convicted of treason but later pardoned by the president. Troops occupied the area and enforced the collection of the tax. However, many single-issue, antitax groups, to this day, cite the reasons behind the Whiskey Rebellion—excessive taxation and overbearing government—as being as repugnant now as they were in the past.

THE ABOLITIONIST MOVEMENT: FROM EXTREME TO MAINSTREAM

Most historians see the beginnings of modern democracy in America as starting in the late 1820s during the presidency of Andrew Jackson. Then, the rigid property qualifications required for voting by white males were dropped, and elections were no longer the exclusive exercise of wealthy, white property owners.

Almost immediately after that change, the New England Anti-Slavery Society, dedicated to ending slavery, was founded in 1831. The Liberty Party, also dedicated to ending slavery, was born in 1839, and the more mainstream abolitionist group—the Free Soil Party—was organized in 1848. These parties were seen as radical splinter groups well outside the mainstream of political thought, with little chance of influencing public policy. However, several events and trends helped the abolitionists move from the extreme to the mainstream. Those events and trends included the bloody struggles between pro- and antislavery forces in the Kansas and Nebraska territories, the Fugitive Slave Law allowing slave owners to capture runaway slaves, and northern industry's view of slavery as a source of cheap labor that would give southern industry an unfair, competitive advantage.

In 1856, the newly formed Republican Party, with General John Frémont as its candidate, ran on an antislavery expansion platform. In 1860, Republican Abraham Lincoln also ran on the platform of admitting no new slave states to the Union. His position on this issue was a key factor behind the outbreak of the Civil War. Even though Lincoln issued the Emancipation Proclamation in 1863, freeing the slaves, the famous abolitionist leader Wendell Phillips proclaimed that Lincoln could not have grown on the slavery issue "without us watering him." It is hard to see how the political climate would have changed over the decades, allowing passage of a constitutional amendment banning slavery, without the agitation of an intense—and some would say over-zealous—single-interest group, the abolitionists.

THE "KNOW-NOTHING" PARTY: IMMIGRANTS NOT WELCOME

However, the abolitionists were not the only single-interest group trying to put a stamp on public policy in the mid 1800s. In the 1840s and 1850s the "Know-Nothing" Party was a force to be reckoned with. The party was originally founded as the Secret Order of the Star Spangled Banner. Their business meetings were conducted in private, and it was said all of their members were instructed to answer "I know nothing" when asked about those meetings. They managed to convince many that Catholic immigrants were polluting the white Anglo-Saxon Protestant base of the country. Outspokenly anti-immigrant, they were dedicated to keeping "lesser breeds" out of America and to making sure that the nation kept its white Protestant base intact and unsoiled. They held that no alien should be granted citizenship for 21 years, no foreign-born person should be allowed to hold office, and the number of new immigrants allowed to enter the nation should be drastically reduced, especially Catholic immigrants. "America for Americans" was one of their slogans.

Know-Nothing forces were believed to be responsible for the dynamiting of Catholic churches and other assorted acts of violence. However, this single-issue group was a powerful political force in the 1840s and 1850s. They elected a number of governors and congressmen in several states. In 1856, the Know-Nothings nominated ex-President Millard Fillmore, who gained some 25 percent of the vote in a three-way race. But as the issues of slavery and preserving the union came to a head, the Know-Nothings' anti-immigrant platform lost its appeal. The party split on the slavery issue and soon was no longer a serious political force. One of Lincoln's more famous quotes about the Know-Nothings read, "As a nation, we began by declaring 'all men are created equal.' We now read it 'all men are created equal, except Negroes.' When the Know-Nothings get control, it will read, 'All men are created equal except Negroes and foreigners and Catholics.'"

FREE SILVER—THE "COWBIRD" OF THE REFORM MOVEMENT?

Another intensely committed, but ultimately unsuccessful, single-issue group that left its mark on the political scene was the Free Silver movement. Its members believed that the gold standard favored lenders over debtors and helped ensure that the big banks on the eastern seaboard would dominate the economy. They favored adopting the free and unlimited coinage of silver at a ratio of 16 ounces of silver to one ounce of gold. This new silver standard, it was argued, would increase the flow of money in the economy and help hard-pressed midwestern farmers to pay off their debts and ease their cash-flow problems.

The rising third-party group, the Populists, adopted a free silver plank in their 1892 platform. Then, in 1893, a depression rocked the country. The economic hardships strained the splits in the country between debtors and creditors, dirt-poor farmers and well-off industrialists, between the allied agrarian West and South and the industrial East. When the Republican Party met in 1896, it came out foursquare for the gold standard, declaring it must be preserved. A group of pro-silver western Republicans walked out of the convention and founded the National Silver Party, which would later endorse the Democratic nominee for president, William Jennings Bryan. The Democratic Party snubbed its pro-gold standard-bearer, President Grover Cleveland, and nominated pro-silver Democrat Bryan. In a famous speech at the convention, Bryan roused delegates to a fever pitch by declaring ". . . having behind us the producing masses of this nation and the world, supported by the commercial interests, the laboring interests, and the toilers everywhere, we will answer their demand for the gold standard by saying to them: You shall not press down upon the brow of labor this crown of thorns, you shall not crucify mankind upon a cross of gold."

A position that had been held only a few years ago by a fringe, single-issue group was now part of the political mainstream. Yet there were those at the time who deplored their success in making free silver the leading issue for the Democrats and Populists and, in doing so, harming both parties. Reformer Henry Demarest Lloyd complained: "Free silver is the cowbird of the Reform movement. It waits until the nest has been built by the labor and sacrifices of others, and then laid its eggs in it, pushing out the others which lie smashed on the ground. It is now flying around while we are expected to do the incubating."

The other "eggs" that Lloyd believed had been pushed aside by the free silver movement included calls for a graduated income tax, public works to fight unemployment, stricter antimonopoly laws, and public ownership of the railroads. When Bryan and his populist allies lost in 1896 to Republican James McKinley, the free silver movement collapsed. The gold standard remained in place for the next 40 years until the Great Depression. Many believed that the overreliance of the Democrats on the issue of free silver hurt them with the broader public.

SUFFRAGISTS AND FEMINISTS

There have been similar criticisms aimed at the single-issue groups supporting women's suffrage—their right to the ballot box. In 1848, the first convention dealing with the issue of women's rights was called to order in Seneca Falls, New York. The document it produced was broad-based. Not only did it call for giving women voting rights, but it also addressed related areas of social and economic deprivations—the fact that women had few rights in wage and property matters, no rights in divorce proceedings, no equal opportunity in employment, and no access to advanced education. In the nineteenth and early twentieth centuries, energies were for the most part focused on winning the right to vote. Wyoming was the first state to grant women that right, in 1890, after which the movement for women's suffrage gathered momentum. In 1893, Colorado gave women the right to vote. Idaho followed suit in 1896. After a pause of a decade, more and more states recognized women's rights in the voting booth. In 1920, the Nineteenth Amendment to the Constitution was ratified into law, giving all American women the same voting rights as men. On the surface it would seem that the single-issue groups had achieved an unqualified success. However, the criticism expressed by social reformers about the free silver movement's single-minded focus on their goal hurting broader social causes was heard by leaders in the women's movement at the turn of the century. Emma Goldman, the famous radical social activist said:

> Our modern fetish is universal suffrage.... The women of Australia and New Zealand can vote, and help make laws. Are labor conditions better there....?
> The history of the political activities of man proves that they have given him absolutely nothing that he could not have achieved in a more direct, less costly, and more lasting manner. As a matter of fact, every inch of ground he has gained through a constant fight, a ceaseless struggle for self-assertion, and not through suffrage. There is no reason whatever to assume that woman, in her climb to emancipation, has been, or will be, helped by the ballot.

Helen Keller, writing to a suffragist in England, echoed Goldman's thoughts:

> Our democracy is but a name. We vote? But what does it mean? It means that we chose between two bodies of real, though not avowed, autocrats. We chose between Tweedledum and Tweedledee. You ask for votes for women. What good can votes do when ten-elevenths of the land of Great Britain belongs to 200,000 and only one-eleventh of the land belongs to the rest of the 40,000,000. Have your men with their millions of votes freed themselves from this injustice?

The Nineteenth Amendment was ratified just in time for women to vote in the 1920 election. That election saw Warren Harding become president, one of the more conservative presidents of the twentieth century.

THE PROHIBITIONISTS—VICTIMS OF THEIR OWN SUCCESS?

The prohibitionists, a highly successful single-issue group, campaigned during the 1800s against the manufacture, sale, and consumption of alcoholic beverages. The Prohibition Party, founded in 1869, embraced many issues beyond prohibition, including the right of women to vote, the direct election of president and vice president, a reduction in transportation rates, and less restrictive immigration policies. After several poor performances at the polls, however, the Prohibition Party dropped all other issues and focused on the evils of drink. Sure enough, the party polled a much larger vote in the 1884 and 1892 elections. By 1919, prohibition activists, working through the structures of the two parties, convinced 37 of the 48 states to ratify the Eighteenth Amendment, banning the manufacture, sale, and consumption of alcoholic beverages. Not satisfied with this success, some of the more zealous advocates wanted to press for a worldwide prohibition, but national prohibition turned out to be such a failure in practice that it was repealed in 1933.

AMERICA FIRST: KEEPING THE UNITED STATES OUT OF WORLD WAR II

The threat of world war looming ever larger in the late 1930s gave rise to one of the most powerful single-issue groups ever active in American politics. On September 4, 1940, the America First Committee announced its formation, with national headquarters in Chicago. Its original statement of principles was very narrowly focused and straightforward:

1. The United States must build an impregnable defense for America.
2. No foreign power, nor group of powers, can successfully attack a prepared America.
3. American democracy can only be preserved by keeping out of the European War.
4. "Aid short of war" weakens national defense at home and threatens to involve America in war abroad.

Although most of the American people probably agreed with the committee that American troops not participate in the European war, polls showed that the public still wanted to supply England with the arms and tools it needed to fight Nazi Germany. Nevertheless, the America First Committee became a powerful influence, especially in the Midwest. By December 1941, it had 450 chapters and subchapters and about 850,000 members. Its prime mover and most active speaker was the popular hero-aviator, Charles Lindbergh. The committee had the active support of powerful senators and corporate chairmen. In 1940, President Franklin Roosevelt, in an effort to boost military preparedness, pushed a bill extending the term of military service beyond one year. It passed the House over the opposition of America First and other isolationist groups by a single vote.

But Japan's attack on Pearl Harbor and Hitler's declaration of war against the United States cut the ground out from under the isolationist movement. The country rallied behind the war effort, and the America First Committee ceased to be a serious political force.

TILTING AT WINDMILLS: THE 1968 "DUMP JOHNSON" MOVEMENT

One of the most spectacularly successful single-issue groups, "Dump Johnson" in 1968, overcame what most thought were impossible odds. In 1964, Lyndon Johnson was elected president by one of the largest landslides in political history, defeating Senator Barry Goldwater. In 1964 and 1965, he signed into law landmark social legislation, including the Voting Rights Act, the Medicare Act, and the Civil Rights Act. But from 1965 onward, he increased U.S. military involvement in the Vietnam War. As American casualties climbed from the hundreds into the thousands, with no victory in sight, the war became steadily more unpopular with the American people. Virtually all of the political experts—except one—thought it would be impossible to deny a powerful sitting president his own party's nomination in 1968.

Allard K. Lowenstein was a veteran political activist and organizer. He had been involved in many liberal causes, including registering blacks to vote in Mississippi and lobbying against South Africa's Apartheid government. Because the Vietnam War was so unpopular with the American people, he believed a movement to block Johnson's reelection could be mounted. He organized like-minded activists into an informal "Dump Johnson" campaign, recruiting support from such antiwar and liberal groups as the Americans for Democratic Action and Students Against Nuclear Extermination to go on record in support of a peace candidate if Johnson did not change his war policies. The movement was made up of Democratic Party activists who believed that Johnson had lied to them in the 1964 election when he pledged not to expand the war. They also believed that the increased spending for the war came at the expense of badly needed social programs. Lowenstein also convinced the National Students Association to organize an "alternative candidate task force." He aggressively recruited idealistic college students to join his movement. He organized lists of friendly contacts and raised money from those seeking to end the war. Later that year, several Democratic Party leaders signed on. Across the nation, Lowenstein helped nurture his movement through rallies, fund-raisers, and networking. At the end of the year, "Dump Johnson" got what it needed most—a candidate. Senator Eugene McCarthy of Minnesota declared he would run against Lyndon Johnson in the presidential primaries on a Vietnam peace plank.

With the New Hampshire primary coming in March 1968, the outlook for the "Dump Johnson" movement looked bleak. McCarthy was not an inspiring candidate and trailed Johnson badly in the polls. But a few key events turned things around. The Communists launched the Tet Offensive in Vietnam in February, causing high American casualties and new doubts about

Johnson's war policies. An army of clean-cut college students who went "clean for Gene" invaded New Hampshire and, in March, McCarthy captured 42 percent of the vote to Johnson's 48 percent. Bigger shocks were yet to come.

On March 31, Johnson announced he was no longer a candidate for president and dropped out of the race. Most political observers saw Lowenstein's success in putting together a mainstream movement that defeated a powerful sitting president as a remarkable achievement. What was deemed "impossible" had come to pass. Although "Dump Johnson" succeeded in its immediate goal of denying Johnson reelection, it failed in its broader goal of electing an antiwar president. When antiwar candidate Robert Kennedy was assassinated in June 1968, after winning the California primary, the Democratic Party leadership saw to it that pro-war candidate and sitting Vice President Hubert Humphrey received the nomination. Humphrey received the nomination despite the fact that he had not run in any of the primary elections that year, and that almost 70 percent of all voters in the spring Democratic primaries had voted for peace candidates Kennedy or McCarthy. In the fall, voters were faced with a choice of Vietnam hawks Richard Nixon, George Wallace, or Humphrey. Nixon went on to win in November by a narrow margin. Some members of the antiwar and "Dump Johnson" movements took comfort in the fact that, upon taking office, Nixon steadily pulled American troops out of the war, slowly shifting the burden of the ground fighting to the South Vietnamese army.

PROPOSITION 13 AND THE ANTITAX MOVEMENT—TIDAL WAVE OUT OF CALIFORNIA

In 1978, few would have predicted that California would set the pace for a national tax revolt. After all, in 1973, popular Governor Ronald Reagan pressed for a tax-limiting measure that went down to defeat by a wide margin, even though his side had widely outspent the opposition. The leader of the antitax movement, Howard Jarvis, was a fringe political figure. He was the head of a small antitax group in the state and had trouble getting a decent turnout at his community meetings. Nevertheless, Jarvis pressed ahead with his proposed ballot initiative to roll back property taxes by more than 50 percent. His measure, Proposition 13, produced instant opposition from the AFL-CIO and the California Chamber of Commerce, among others. His ballot issue foes outspent him by a wide margin, to no avail. A few weeks before the vote in June 1978, tax assessment bills were mailed out to homeowners all across the state. In many cases, those assessments showed huge increases in the property tax burden. In the June election, Proposition 13 passed by an almost 2–1 margin. Angry voters turned out in record numbers to vent their rage at the high property taxes. Other antitax groups around the nation had been pushing ballot issues, limiting or rolling back state and local taxes. After Proposition 13 passed in June, those measures received an unmistakable boost. Of the 16 measures on the state ballots in 1978, either cutting taxes or limiting spending, more than three-quarters of them passed.

When Jarvis addressed Congress in 1978, he was treated as a hero by the Republican Party. Lowering taxes and shrinking big government became the mainstays of Reagan's presidential election campaign in 1980. In 1981, President Reagan signed the Kemp-Roth tax bill into law, radically cutting the income tax rate in America. After 1981, the tax-limitation movement seemed to lose some of its momentum. Other issues came to the fore, and the deep recession of 1982 underlined, in the minds of many voters, the need for some government spending. But the antitax movement was a victim of its own success. Once federal income and local property taxes were limited or cut, the American people wanted to move on to other issues. However, the spectacular success of this movement can hardly be denied. Many political observers believe that without Proposition 13's passing in 1978, Reagan and the Republican Party would not have swept into power in 1980.

FREEZING THE ARMS RACE: A GLASS HALF FULL OR HALF EMPTY?

With the election of Ronald Reagan in 1980, tensions between the United States and the Soviet Union deteriorated. Reagan pushed a major increase in the defense budget in 1981 and talked of "winnable" nuclear wars. The increased tension between the two superpowers and the increased public fear of a nuclear war gave rise to another single-issue group, the Nuclear Freeze Movement.

The Freeze was a grassroots collection of citizens groups with offices in St. Louis and New York. The Freeze platform called for a halt to the nuclear arms race and "a mutual freeze on the testing, production and development of all nuclear warheads, missiles and delivery systems." The ultimate goal of the peace activists supporting the nuclear freeze movement was to reduce the nuclear weapons stockpiles of both the United States and USSR. "Freezing" the number of weapons where they were was seen as only a first step toward their total elimination.

Between 1979 and 1982, Freeze organizers helped put nuclear freeze initiatives on the ballot in 25 states and in 62 towns and cities. The nuclear freeze resolutions passed in 24 of the 25 states and in 59 of 62 towns and cities where they were on the ballot. Of the voters who had the chance to vote on the Freeze measures across the nation, 63 percent voted "Yes." However, the Freeze initiatives were nonbinding. They did not have the force of law and were just a measure of public opinion. In 1983, Congress passed a nonbinding "sense of Congress" resolution endorsing the idea of eliminating nuclear weapons. That vote would probably not have been possible without the strong grassroots showing of the Freeze campaign across the nation. But, like the state and local ballot initiatives, the congressional vote did not carry the force of law. The same Congress that voted for a nonbinding resolution to eliminate nuclear weapons later voted for binding laws and spending bills that increased the nuclear arsenal. In 1987, the Nuclear Freeze movement ceased to exist as a separate organization—having merged with another peace group. However, when Vice President George Bush felt the need to remind voters that it was not "those Freeze folks" who brought about some limited federal steps to hold the line on nuclear weapon expansion, many in the Freeze movement believed they had received a backhanded compliment. Ever since the collapse of the Soviet Union in 1991, there have been no major cuts in America's defense budget. To many, this is the clearest sign of the ultimate failure of the Freeze movement.

BRINGING DOWN APARTHEID: DIVESTMENT AND DISINVESTMENT

During the years of the Cold War between the United States and Soviet Union, America supported many governments based on their firm stand against communism, without regard to how they treated their own people. For many Americans, one of the worst examples of this policy was United States' support of the South African government, which used the Apartheid system to hold down and abuse the black majority. In the mid 1960s, a group of citizen activists decided to do something about the situation. Because Congress was unwilling to curtail corporate investments in a nation governed through repression, these activists decided to target American financial and industrial corporations having major investments in South Africa. Their strategy was to contact investors with big blocks of stock in these businesses and persuade them to let management know that they would divest, or sell off their stocks, unless the companies pulled out of South Africa, or disinvested from the Apartheid regime. At first, the South African activists received little support. They tried to organize church groups with stocks in companies or students at universities that owned stocks in different businesses, and tried to get them to attend shareholders meetings, threatening total divestment of their stock unless there was a disinvestment from South Africa. These activists were usually met with a wall of skepticism. Management believed that disinvesting from South Africa would not solve any problems. They believed some other business would just come along to fill in the gap. Disinvesting, many reasoned, would mean only that these companies would give up any leverage in influencing events in South Africa and would be an empty public gesture.

During the late 1960s and early 1970s, divestment activists began organizing with college students, organizing churches with large stock holdings, and labor unions who were upset at how South Africa treated its labor unions and workers. Slowly, the movement gathered momentum. Eventually the leaders of hundreds of elite institutions, from religious groups, such as the United Church of Christ, to huge charities, such as the Ford Foundation, to Harvard University, began to question the morality of investing in companies operating in South Africa. During the late 1970s, many students protested their college's investment in corporations that did business in South Africa. "Divest Now!" became a popular chant in more and more schools across the country. Organizers became increasingly active in convincing state and local governments to divest funds in firms that did business with Apartheid. In 1979, the city of Berkeley, California, voted to divest all city holdings in companies that invested in South Africa. By 1982, three cities (Philadelphia, Wilmington, Delaware, and Grand Rapids, Michigan) and three states (Connecticut, Michigan, and Massachusetts) had approved the divestment of more than $250 million in public monies. New York State followed in the mid 1980s. Many large corporations, responding both to increased public pressure in the United States and to increasing turmoil in South Africa, voluntarily shut down their operations in that country. From January 1, 1986, to April 30, 1988, 114 American companies disinvested from South Africa. Those firms included Control Data, Dow Chemical, Eastman Kodak, Exxon, Ford, General Electric, Goodyear, Johnson Controls, Merck, Newmont Mining, and Unisys.

As the 1980s progressed, and violence and instability inside South Africa became increasingly worse, the divestment movement won the day, as Congress, in 1986, overrode President Reagan's veto and imposed economic sanctions on South Africa. The Apartheid system eventually collapsed and free elections were held in the country in 1994. South Africa's new president and anti-Apartheid fighter Nelson Mandela publicly credited the divestment movement with helping to bring about the overthrow of Apartheid.

Throughout our history, some single-issue groups have had spectacular successes, and others, spectacular failures. But win, lose, or draw, as long as there are heated issues that stir the nation's passions, these single-issue groups will continue to have a role in our political system.

GLENN DAIGON

Bibliography

Batchelor, John Calvin. *Ain't You Glad You Joined the Republicans?* New York: Henry Holt, 1996.

Chafe, William H. *Never Stop Running—Allard S. Lowenstein and the Struggle to Save American Liberalism.* New York: Basic Books, 1993.

Cole, Wayne S. *Charles A. Lindbergh and the Battle Against American Intervention in World War II.* New York: Harcourt Brace Jovanovich, 1974.

Leone, Bruno. *The Women's Rights Movement—Viewpoints.* San Diego: Greenhaven Press, 1996.

Loeb, Raul Rogat. *Hope in Hard Times—America's Peace Movement in the Reagan Era.* Lexington, MA: Lexington Books, 1987.

Massie, Robert Kinloch. *Loosing the Bonds—The United States and South Africa in the Apartheid Years.* New York: Doubleday, 1994.

Slaughter, Thomas P. *The Whiskey Rebellion: Frontier Epilogue to the American Revolution.* New York: Oxford University Press, 1986.

Zinn, Howard. *A People's History of the United States, 1492–Present.* New York: HarperPerennial, 1995.

AMERICANS UNITED FOR THE SEPARATION OF CHURCH AND STATE

Americans United for the Separation of Church and State (AU) is a national organization of 60,000 members dedicated to keeping the boundaries between church and state activity separate. Its headquarters is in Washington, D.C., and it has 115 local chapters across the nation. AU is run by a 15-member executive board; those board members are nominated by a committee and then ratified by the general membership at the organization's annual meeting.

The organization encourages political involvement by its members to advance its issue agenda. It does this through legislative action alerts, a monthly newsletter, and books. The organization's national headquarters houses the following departments: executive, field services, legal, legislative, state legislative, development, and financial.

HISTORY

Americans United for the Separation of Church and State was originally founded in 1947. Its original title was Protestants and Other Americans United for the Separation of Church and State. The idea for the organization started with a group of civic and religious leaders concerned about the dangers to religious freedom in the nation. The original founders were also worried about the tensions between Protestants and Catholics in the United States after the end of the Second World War and wanted to avoid the bitter religious conflicts that had torn apart many other countries.

The group's first big test came in 1951, when President Harry Truman announced his decision to send General Mark Clark to the Vatican as an official U.S. ambassador. AU objected on the grounds that a government that separates church and state and guarantees personal and religious freedom to all and preferential treatment to no one ought not to single out one church, or one church/state entity, for recognition. The group argued that if the United States was going to take this action, then to be consistent it would also have to exchange diplomatic officials with the Archbishop of Canterbury, the Patriarch of Constantinople, the World Council of Churches, and so forth. Many believed the main reason Truman took this step was to curry favor with Catholic voters in the 1952 elections.

AU sponsored letter-writing campaigns to Congress and organized mass rallies against the move around the nation. In early 1952, General Clark asked President Truman to withdraw his name from consideration, and the president announced that he would not send another name to Capitol Hill. During the rest of the 1950s, the big issues that the organization was involved with were censorship, "captive schools," and Catholic hospitals. Also, AU fought pressure by Catholic groups to ban the showing of a film about Martin Luther on Chicago television.

In the mid 1950s, AU went to court to stop public "captive schools" from being run by religious orders. In some rural communities, many of the taxpayer-supported schools were being run as parochial schools in all but name. Many of the teachers were nuns who signed over tax-supported salaries to their religious orders. In some of the schools, the Mother Superior acted as principal and hired only teachers they deemed religiously acceptable. Books and course material were strongly slanted toward one faith. AU found the same type of captive schools being run by Protestants. In rural Kentucky districts, the United Presbyterian Women's Missionary Society completely ran the school buildings and the courses taught. The courts ultimately ruled in favor of the AU and ordered the respective boards of education from these school districts to stop distributing religious books and literature on school grounds, to stop keeping religious periodicals in the school library, and to stop spending public funds for religious purposes.

AU also opposed any public funding of sectarian hospitals. The group argued that, although, for example, many Catholic hospitals provided fine medical care to millions of people, they still operated under a medical code that forbade birth control information. The group believed there could be potential for many problems in funding hospitals where the members of religious orders could dictate medical policy to doctors, even in the operating room. AU was ultimately unsuccessful in its efforts to block funding for sectarian hospitals.

In the 1960 presidential election, church/state separation issues moved to the forefront as John F. Kennedy attempted to become America's first Catholic president. Many openly questioned whether a Catholic could be independent from church leadership. Kennedy publicly opposed aid to parochial schools, pledged independence from religious leaders in all decision making, and would not oppose birth control programs. After Kennedy won the 1960 election, many in AU believed he had one of the strongest records on church/state separation issues.

In 1961, Kennedy pushed legislation to expand federal aid programs to public education. He steadfastly refused the demands by the U.S. Catholic Conference that parochial schools be included in all federal aid programs. AU strongly supported Kennedy's efforts to target federal aid to public, nonreligious, schools only. Ultimately, Kennedy's bill died by one vote in the House.

On the other hand, AU strongly opposed the Higher Education Facilities Act, which provided public funds for construction at church-based colleges. The measure passed Congress and was signed into law in 1964. In 1965, President Lyndon Johnson proposed the Elementary and Secondary School Act, which allowed for public funding for parochial schools. It too passed Congress and was signed into law by the president.

During the 1970s, AU vigorously opposed the "prayer amendment" that would allow prayer in public schools. It helped lobby against the "Wylie Amendment," which would have permitted "nondenominational prayer" in all public buildings. The measure was defeated on the House floor in 1971. During that same year, the Supreme Court upheld lower court decisions to strike down laws in Pennsylvania and Rhode Island to provide tax aid to parochial schools. AU was involved in bringing those cases before the High Court; most considered this court ruling to be a landmark decision.

Frank J. Sorauf, Dean of the College of Liberal Arts at the University of Minnesota, published a book in 1976 entitled *The Wall of Separation: The Constitutional Politics of Church and State*. He analyzed 67 decisions by high-level federal courts on church and state separation issues. Sorauf concluded that AU was involved in 51 of these 67 important cases.

AU activities were not restricted to lobbying Congress or the state legislatures, or filing legal briefs in court to challenge laws it believed were illegal. In the 1970s, the organization became involved in coalitions opposed to ballot initiatives, which, if passed, would have led to direct or indirect public aid to church-related education. The voters easily defeated these initiatives placed on the state ballots of Idaho, Oregon, Maryland, Nebraska, Michigan, and Missouri.

During the 1980s and 1990s, the group took many of the religious right's political actions to court, believing that they crossed the line of church/state separation. One action that AU and others opposed was the Christian Coalition's distribution of voter education pamphlets in churches before election day. To date, AU is still active in pursuing individual church groups and church associations for illegal and inappropriate political activity. In the spring of 1999, the Internal Revenue Service (IRS) revoked the Christian Coalition's tax-exempt status, stating it was a partisan political group. AU had provided the IRS evidence documenting the Christian Coalition's partisan political activities.

ACTIVITIES: CURRENT AND FUTURE

AU has seen its mission as protecting the separation between church and state as mandated in the First Amendment to the Constitution. The organization cites the First Amendment, which specifies that "Congress shall make no law respecting an establishment of religion, or prohibiting the free exercise thereof." Toward that end, the organization is currently involved in many battles at the federal, state, and local levels.

At the federal level, the group is fighting to block a bill, Charitable Choice, that would allow church institutions to receive federal money to run social services and health-benefits programs for the government. AU is also opposing a bill, the Education Savings Account and School Excellence Act, that would use public money for parochial elementary and secondary schools. Also at the federal level, the organization is working to stop passage of a constitutional amendment to outlaw flag burning, and is opposing parental rights legislation and the American Heritage Act, promoting the use of religious materials in public schools.

At the state level, AU will be going to court to have

Florida's far-reaching, newly passed school voucher program thrown out as being unconstitutional. AU is working to convince legislatures in Texas, California, Michigan, and Illinois not to pass similar voucher programs. In states around the nation, AU is working to block bills requiring prayer in school, tax exemption for leased religious property, and tuition tax credits for private and church-run schools. The organization has opposed zealous religious groups such as the Moral Majority from aggressively pursuing partisan politics. In 1999, AU accused a New York church of partisan electioneering in 1992. The IRS revoked the church's tax-exempt status, and that action was upheld in the federal courts.

FINANCIAL FACTS

Under the IRS tax code, AU is designated 501(c)(3), that is, it exists as a not-for-profit organization and is prohibited from making campaign contributions to candidates for federal elected office.

GLENN DAIGON

Bibliography

Americans United for the Separation of Church and State: www.au.org

Archer, Glenn, and Albert Menendez. *The Dream Lives On: The Story of Glenn L. Archer and Americans United.* Washington, DC: Robert B. Luce, 1982.

CITIZENS FLAG ALLIANCE

The Citizens Flag Alliance, Inc. (CFA) is a coalition of organizations, most of which are national in scope, that have come together for one reason: to persuade the United States Congress to propose a constitutional amendment to protect the flag from physical desecration and to send the amendment to the states for ratification.

More than 135 organizations make up the CFA, with a membership totaling 20 million. Organized in every state, the individual, nonorganization-affiliated membership is 200,000. Membership is open to fraternal, ethnic, civic, and veteran organizations, corporations, and businesses by application. There is no membership fee, but it is expected that member organizations would have the endorsement of the governing body. It is also expected that member organizations would promote the flag protection amendment among their members and the public, and it would allow the publication of their names as member organizations of the CFA. It is expected that they participate in the CFA's legislative activities and grassroots lobbying efforts. Some of the groups that belong to the CFA include the Moose, the Elks, and the Knights of Columbus. The American Legion is the organization that is the founder of, and driving force behind, the CFA. Much of the organization's funding originates with the American Legion, and the CFA uses American Legion's Washington, D.C., staffers and office space to help them lobby for passage of the flag protection amendment.

The CFA is run by a 20-member board of directors, of which only one, the chairman, is paid. The rest of the board consists of officials of the coalition of organizations that make up the CFA. The organization hires private firms to do its lobbying work in Washington, D.C., and relies on its individual organizations to get the word out to their grassroots members to help press its agenda at the state and federal levels. The organization also communicates with its diverse base through legislative action alerts and a monthly newsletter. CFA has used numerous methods of rallying its members in support of the flag protection amendment. Those methods have included mass rallies in Washington, intense advertising campaigns in the states of key lawmakers before crucial votes, legislative alerts urging members to write their senators and representatives in support of the flag protection amendment, and voter education projects informing members how their lawmakers have voted on the flag protection amendment. The headquarters for the CFA is located in Indianapolis, Indiana, and operates out of a facility owned by the American Legion.

HISTORY

In the summer of 1984, 48 states and the federal government had laws on the books making it a crime to desecrate or abuse the flag. In Dallas, Texas, Gregory Johnson marched from the Republican convention being held in Dallas to the steps of Dallas City Hall and burned an American flag. He was arrested, charged, tried, and convicted of violating a Texas law that made desecration of the U.S. flag a crime. Five years later, that decision was appealed all the way to the Supreme Court. In a 5–4 vote, the High Court ruled that Johnson had been denied his free speech rights and ruled the Texas flag desecration law unconstitutional. That decision swept away all the other 47 state laws as well as the federal statute.

Congress responded by passing the Flag Protection Act of 1989. Within a matter of days, the act was struck down by another 5–4 Supreme Court vote. In the fall of that year, the American Legion adopted a resolution at their convention seeking passage of a flag protection amendment to the Constitution. The following year the flag protection amendment came up for a vote in Congress. Neither the Senate nor the House was able to muster the two-thirds majority needed for passage.

In May 1994, the American Legion decided to create

a broad-based organization, the Citizens Flag Alliance, to help get the flag protection amendment passed. In June 1995, the amendment cleared the House by a vote of 312–120, but failed by a three-vote margin to get the two-thirds majority required in the Senate. The final vote was 63 senators in favor, 36 opposed. In 1997, the flag protection amendment was brought up again. It passed by a vote of 310–114 in the House, but the Senate never voted on the amendment, killing it for a second time. On June 24, 1999, the House voted to pass the flag protection amendment, 305–124.

ACTIVITIES: CURRENT AND FUTURE

The focus of this organization is passage of a simple, 18-word constitutional amendment overruling the Supreme Court decision stating that flag burning was freedom of speech protected by the Constitution: "The Congress shall have the power to prohibit the physical desecration of the flag of the United States." The CFA states that the American flag is more than just a piece of cloth. It believes it is a symbol of our nation's pride and that desecrating or abusing this symbol would dishonor the memories of all those who died or were wounded in service to our country. The CFA believes the flag to be a unique symbol that represents the ideals on which America was founded and is a symbol of all the common values, traditions, and principles that bind our diverse nation together, and it should be respected accordingly.

Even opponents of the measure concede that its sheer simplicity makes it hard to oppose. Senator Robert Kerrey of Nebraska commented, "It's too difficult for people running for office to oppose in a 30-second sound bite. The measure seems so reasonable on its face."

Opponents have tried to use the argument that, although the amendment sounds reasonable on paper, it would be impossible to enforce in reality. Former Senator John Glenn raised the point that the words *flag* and *desecration* are hard to define, and unless defined by the courts, would simply raise more questions than answers. Glenn asked: "How . . . do we know what is prosecuted under this amendment? If a mechanic is lying on his back in a flag T-shirt, which is dirty and sweaty, is that desecration? If someone is wearing a pair of flag boxer shorts, is that desecration?"

Massachusetts Democratic Senator Edward Kennedy wondered why we should limit the issue to just flag burning. "What will we do if someone burns the Declaration of Independence or the Constitution of the United States?" Other opponents of the measure said it would trivialize the Constitution by creating a solution for a problem that doesn't exist in the first place. Senator John Chafee of Rhode Island said that the Congressional Research Service could find only 41 instances of flag desecration from 1995 to 1999, or only an average of eight a year. Others argue that the amendment violates the spirit of freedom of expression, one of the very principles the flag is meant to symbolize. Senator Glenn stated, "It is a hollow victory to protect the symbol while chipping away at the freedoms themselves."

The CFA lobbyists counter these arguments, declaring that the flag is such a unique symbol of American values that it should be placed in a judicial category to exempt it from free speech. They also argue that just as no one has the free speech to joke about bombs at airports or to stand naked in major thoroughfares, neither should people be allowed to burn the most visible symbol of our nation. Flag protection amendment backer and Arizona Senator John McCain declared, "American blood has been shed all over the world for the American flag. . . . I believe it deserves respect."

In 1999, General Norman Schwarzkopf made a public statement in favor of the flag protection amendment. He said: "I regard legal protections for our flag as an absolute necessity and a matter of critical importance to our nation. The American flag, far from a mere symbol or a piece of cloth, is an embodiment of our hopes, freedoms, and unity. The flag is our national identity."

FINANCIAL FACTS

The CFA is designated 501(c)(3) by the Internal Revenue Service, that is, not-for-profit. It is therefore prohibited from making campaign contributions to candidates for federal elected office.

GLENN DAIGON

Bibliography
Citizens Flag Alliance: www.cfa-inc.org
Goodman, Y.R. "Flag Law on the Front Burner." *Legal Times,* May 10, 1999.

COUNCIL FOR A LIVABLE WORLD

The Council for a Livable World (CLW) has over 100,000 members in all 50 states. Its members are organized on an at-large basis; CLW has no formal state chapters. The organization's goal is to rid the world of weapons of mass destruction and to cut excessive military spending. It employs a staff of lobbyists in Washington, D.C., to lobby the U.S. Senate on such issues as the Strategic Defense Initiative ("Star Wars") and the Chemical Weapons Treaty. The council also has a research staff that prepares one- or two-page fact sheets as well as lengthy briefing books to advocate the organization's stands on the issues of the day. CLW is run by a 23-member board of directors; the directors are nominated by the president of the group. CLW communicates with its membership through action alerts, newsletters, and profiles of political candidates seeking the group's endorsement. The organization has 15 full-time staff members.

Since its inception in 1962, the council claims that it has helped elect 80 U.S. senators. CLW asserts that the organization's high-profile endorsements and its political action committee's (PAC) campaign contributions have made the difference in close races. Some of the other ways CLW tries to shape the political agenda in Washington include:

Raising the visibility of issues with Congress. CLW lobbyists provide information to senators and representatives on key issues and alert them to upcoming votes.

Finding a leader on the issues. CLW lobbyists encourage and support leadership in Congress on issues of importance to the organization. For example, CLW worked with senators Carl Levin and Jeff Bingaman and others on Star Wars and START III.

Building coalitions. CLW tries to build bipartisan, broad-based coalitions inside and outside Congress on key issues. CLW helped to circulate letters endorsing prompt action on START II, a letter signed by 36 senators.

Ensuring that the administration is engaged in the issue. CLW worked closely with the Clinton administration to seek its lobbying assistance on both START II and National Ballistic Missile Defense.

Working with the media. Lobbyists work hard to make sure that important arms control stories are reported to the public in an accurate, objective manner.

Running editorial campaigns. Media campaigns consist of first sending background materials and arguments on major legislation and upcoming votes to generate news stories and editorials. These campaigns are usually targeted in the districts or home states of key members. The second phase consists of sending packets of editorials to those legislators to show broad-based support or opposition on a key issue.

Running grassroots campaigns. These campaigns consist of mobilizing citizens to write letters to their members of Congress. These campaigns try to generate hundreds of letters to key legislators in order to have a maximum impact. CLW alerts its grassroots base by Legislative Action Alerts through the mail.

Running television or radio ads on an issue. CLW tries to target funds for media ads in districts of undecided members of Congress before an upcoming vote.

Campaign fund-raising or working on behalf of a candidate. CLW tries to influence elections by dispensing millions of dollars in PAC contributions, and mobilizing campaign workers to get out the vote for endorsed candidates.

In 1980, CLW's board of directors incorporated the Council for a Livable World Education Fund as a separate organization to educate the public about the dangers of the arms race and peaceful alternatives. In 1982, CLW organized the political action committee, PeacePAC, to help elect candidates to the House of Representatives. CLW claims that since its start, PeacePAC has helped more than 70 members of Congress get elected. CLW also claims that in the last several years, PeacePAC has contributed more to House candidates in critical races than all other peace political action committees combined. After the Gulf War, CLW's board of directors decided to create two new programs to work against arms sales to other governments and to build support for U.N. peacekeeping operations.

HISTORY

To combat the menace of nuclear war, physicist Leo Szilard founded the Council for a Livable World in 1962. The organization's motto, "To Eliminate Weapons of Mass Destruction" has been its consistent theme for more than 35 years. Over time, the council has been in the front lines, either opposing the building of new weapons systems or pushing for treaties that limit the number of existing weapons. Some of the campaigns the council has waged have included

- support of the 1962 Nuclear Test Ban Treaty;
- the fight against the Anti-Ballistic missile system in 1969;
- support of the SALT I and SALT II treaties during the early 1970s limiting the nuclear weapons arsenals of the United States and the Soviet Union;
- limiting deployment of the MX missile and B-2 bomber in the 1970s and 1980s;
- support of the Chemical Weapons Convention, banning biological weapons and terminating chemical weapons production; and
- support of the 1992 Nuclear Testing Moratorium and the 1993 Limited Test Ban Treaty.

In 1996, a CLW report cited waste in Pentagon projects. Among the examples cited were construction of a third golf course at Andrews Air Force Base; a money-losing dairy herd at the U.S. Naval Academy; a Pentagon-leased hotel in Orlando, Florida, that loses $27 million a year; and a door hinge for the C-17 airplane that costs $2,187. "Unfortunately, these examples are only the tip of the iceberg," the report stated.

ACTIVITIES: CURRENT AND FUTURE

The organization has listed its priority issues and objectives in a particularly straightforward manner. The top priorities for CLW include the following:

Senate approval of the Comprehensive Test Ban Treaty. President Bill Clinton joined world leaders in signing the Comprehensive Test Ban Treaty in 1996. The treaty bans all nuclear testing and sets up a strict monitoring system to enforce the ban. The U.S. Senate has yet to ratify the treaty.

Protection of the Anti-Ballistic Missile Treaty (ABM) from Republican attack and blocking deployment of national missile defense. CLW believes that only by staying with the ABM Treaty and blocking new spending for anti-missile defense systems can deep cuts in U.S. and Russian nuclear weapons be achieved.

Further deep cuts in nuclear weapons, either through negotiation or "going-it-alone." CLW believes that the United States should drastically cut back on the number of nuclear weapons. If the United States can't accomplish this through a treaty with the Russians, then CLW believes our country should "go-it-alone" and cut back our own stockpile to no more than 1,000 deployed weapons.

CLW outlines its next three priorities:

Deep cuts in military spending. CLW believes that closing unneeded military bases, eliminating pork-barrel military spending, stopping "gold-plated" weapons systems, and cutting U.S. troop levels would save the taxpayers millions of dollars in nonessential military spending.

Payment of the U.S. debt to the United Nations. CLW asserts that unless the United States pays off its $1 billion debt to the U.N., it will lose its vote in the U.N. General Assembly starting in the year 2000.

Full funding of the program to help Russia dismantle its nuclear weapons complex. An act sponsored by Indiana Senator Richard Lugar and former Georgia Senator Sam Nunn granted about $440 million to the states of the former Soviet Union to assist them in dismantling and securing their nuclear weapons stockpile. CLW strongly supports this act.

**Council for a Livable World
Political Action Committee Contributions**

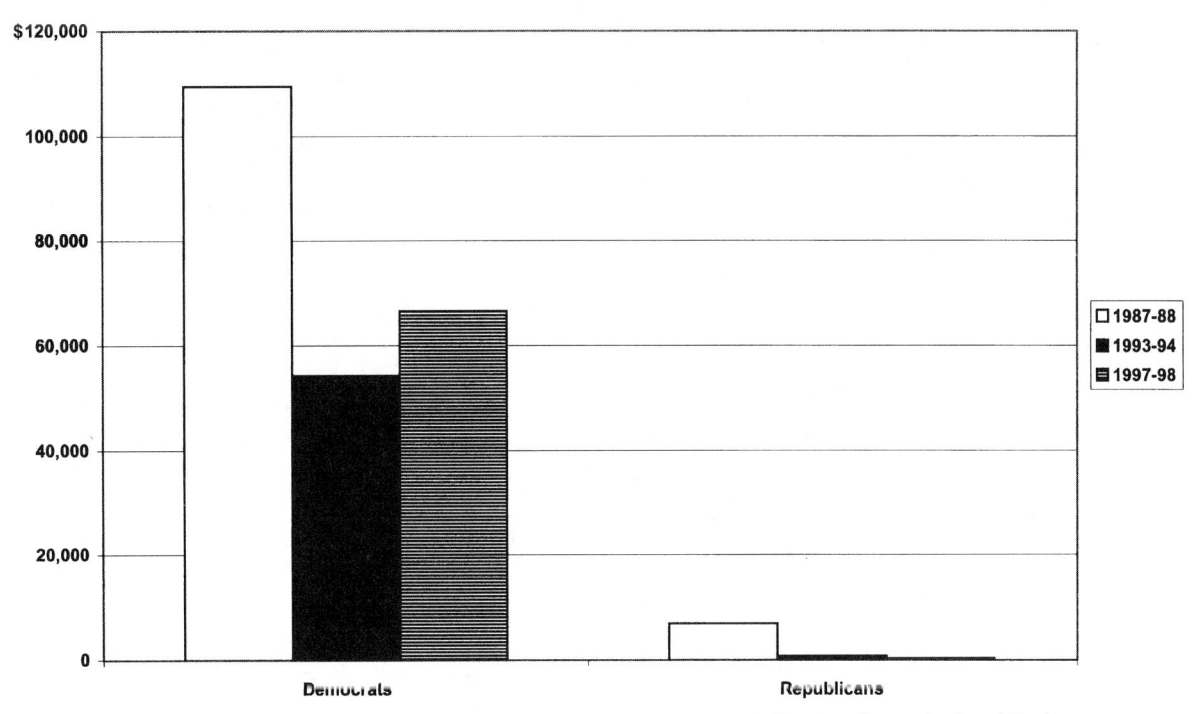

```
$120,000

100,000

 80,000

 60,000                                    □ 1987-88
                                           ■ 1993-94
 40,000                                    ☰ 1997-98

 20,000

      0
         Democrats              Republicans
```

Data derived from official studies available from the Federal Election Commission, Washington, DC, 1987–1998.

Other issues that have the attention of CLW include:

Rejection of further enlargement of NATO. CLW believes that expanding NATO will only create new divisions in Europe.

A new push to ban U.S. use of land mines. CLW will lobby the Clinton administration to sign the international treaty banning the production, use, and stockpiling of land mines. The Clinton administration came out against the treaty.

Strengthening the Biological Weapons Convention. The 1972 Convention negotiated by President Richard Nixon bans worldwide biological weapons. CLW supports current negotiations to strengthen verification procedures for the treaty.

CLW wants the United States to drop its insistence on the right to use nuclear weapons first in a conventional conflict and to abandon its threat to use nuclear weapons in retaliation for the use of chemical or biological weapons.

FINANCIAL FACTS

From the 1987–1988 election cycle to the 1995–1996 election cycle, there has been a decrease in CLW's PAC receipts, expenditures, and contributions. Receipts declined by nearly $300,000, from about $950,000 in the 1987–1988 election cycle to about $650,000 in 1995–1996. At the same time, contributions to the senatorial campaigns of Democrats have far exceeded those of Republicans; in no cycle did the Democrats get less than 90 percent of PAC contributions. Receipts, expenditures, and contributions to candidates for the U.S. House of Representatives through the PeacePAC also declined between the 1987–1988 election cycle to the 1995–1996 cycle. At the same time, contributions to Democrats have far exceeded those of Republicans; in no cycle did the Democrats get less than 95 percent of PAC contributions.

GLENN DAIGON

Bibliography

Council for a Livable World: www.clw.org

HANDGUN CONTROL, INC.

Handgun Control, Inc. (HCI) is a nonprofit lobbying group with over 400,000 members. The organization is run by a 27-member board of trustees who are chosen from a list of candidates sent to the entire membership by the organization's nominating committee. The list contains information on each candidate's background and his or her public policy objectives for the group. The organization is split into two affiliates: Handgun Control, Inc., that consists of the organization's management, federal legislative/public policy, communications, finance/administration, development, and state legislative/public outreach departments. The second, the Center to Prevent Handgun Violence, is an affiliate of Handgun Control, Inc., and was founded in 1985. It consists of the organization's legal action/research department as well as an education department. The organization's headquarters are in Washington, D.C., and it has field offices in San Diego, Sacramento, and Los Angeles. It has a staff of 60.

HISTORY

Handgun Control, Inc., was founded by Dr. Mark Bonnisky, a victim of gun violence in 1974. Later that year, N. T. Shields joined Dr. Bonnisky, having lost his son to a serial killer in San Francisco. Both men became dedicated to the movement to strengthen the regulation of guns.

In 1985, four years after almost losing her husband in the attempted assassination of President Ronald Reagan, Sarah Brady, wife of Reagan's press secretary James Brady, joined Handgun Control, Inc., and currently serves as its chair. In 1986, HCI began a national campaign to pass the Brady Bill, which required a background check on any intended handgun purchaser and a five-day waiting period before the purchase of a handgun. In 1993, after a seven-year effort, President Bill Clinton signed the Brady Bill into law. During 1994, HCI lobbied heavily to support the assault weapons ban provision of the Violent Crime Control and Law Enforcement Act. The assault weapons ban made illegal the import and manufacture in the United States of semiautomatic weapons with multiple assault weapons features and high-capacity ammunition magazines. The ban passed in the House of Representatives that year by a margin of one vote. The organization turned back several attempts by politicians to weaken or repeal the ban.

In the wake of school-yard shootings in Arkansas, Oregon, and Colorado, public opinion may be shifting even further in favor of tougher gun control laws. In 1999, Congress, with the full support of Handgun Control, Inc. lobbyists, came close to passing measures to ban imported, high-capacity ammunition clips, to require background checks for buyers at gun shows, and to raise the minimum age for purchasing guns from 18 to 21.

ACTIVITIES: CURRENT AND FUTURE

The organization sees the passage of the Brady Bill and the Assault Weapons Ban at the federal level as only the start of their efforts to modernize gun regulations. In 1998, it unsuccessfully tried to get the Senate to pass legislation that would have required the manufacture of childproof handguns. It will continue to push for passage of this measure. HCI has introduced legislation to make the five-day waiting period of the Brady Bill permanent. It has introduced a bill to more strictly regulate the sale of guns at trade shows—which the organization believes provide loopholes whereby gun manufacturers can get around tighter regulations elsewhere. Legislation has been drafted in Congress to prohibit the purchase of more than one handgun a month, which has the enthusiastic support of HCI. A bill to prohibit the possession

**Handgun Control, Inc.
Political Action Committee Contributions**

[Bar chart showing PAC contributions to Democrats and Republicans across three election cycles: 1987-88, 1993-94, and 1997-98. Democrats received approximately $203,000 (1987-88), $233,000 (1993-94), and $138,000 (1997-98). Republicans received approximately $10,000 (1987-88), $36,000 (1993-94), and $10,000 (1997-98).]

Data derived from official studies available from the Federal Election Commission, Washington, DC, 1987–1998.

or transfer of "junk guns" also has HCI's active backing. Legislation at the federal level to prohibit the transfer of a handgun to, or the possession of a handgun by, an individual under the age of 21 is high on the organization's list of important bills to pass.

At the state level the organization is no less active. Here is just a sample of the bills that HCI is trying to pass:

- **California**
  Bill to ban assault weapons and ammo magazines over 10 rounds;
  Bill to require child safety locks to be sold with all firearms;
  Bill to limit purchases to one handgun per month;
  Bill to ban Saturday Night Specials;
- **Florida**
  Bills introduced to close gun-show loopholes in four counties;
- **Louisiana**
  Opposed bill to prevent cities from suing gun manufacturers for damages due to negligence;
- **Missouri**
  Opposed ballot referendum to allow citizens to carry concealed weapons (successful in helping to defeat the measure 52 percent to 48 percent);
- **Minnesota**
  Opposed bill to allow citizens to carry concealed weapons;
- **Pennsylvania**
  Supported bill to limit gun purchases to one a month

One radically new approach that Handgun Control, Inc. is trying in its efforts to tighten gun restrictions is the judicial system. On October 30, 1998, New Orleans became the first city to sue the gun industry. Two weeks later, Chicago followed with a similar lawsuit. Since then, a host of cities and counties have filed suit, including Miami-Dade County, Florida; Bridgeport, Connecticut; Atlanta, Georgia; Cleveland and Cincinnati, Ohio; and Detroit/Wayne County, Michigan.

Some of the lawsuits assail the industry's failure to design and market safer guns that cannot be fired by children and unauthorized users. Those filed by other cities attack the industry's negligent distribution of guns, which aids gun trafficking and crime. The lawsuits are modeled after the public lawsuits brought against the tobacco industry. Handgun Control, Inc., through its legal division, joined with those cities filing suit against the gun industry. In February 1999, a New York City jury returned the first-ever verdict holding gun manufacturers liable for criminal misuse of one of their handguns. If more verdicts are returned holding the gun industry liable for how their products are used, that may ultimately have a greater impact on the industry than the passage of new federal and state laws.

FINANCIAL FACTS

Handgun Control's political action committee (PAC), Handgun Control Voter Education Fund, has been consistently active over the last few electoral cycles. During the 1997–1998 cycle, it received $90,755 in receipts and spent $178,430. This latter figure includes $146,114 in contributions to candidates and parties, $136,614 to Democrats and $9,500 to Republicans.

In the 1992 elections, receipts exceeded $1.1 million and spent about $940,000. At the same time, contributions to Democrats far exceeded those to Republicans, by a factor of more than 10 to 1.

GLENN DAIGON

Bibliography

Davidson, Osha Gray. *Under Fire: The NRA & the Battle for Gun Control*. New York: Henry Holt, 1993.

Handgun Control, Inc.: www.handguncontrol.org

MOTHERS AGAINST DRUNK DRIVING

Mothers Against Drunk Driving (MADD) is a grassroots citizens group made up of victims of drunk-driving crashes and concerned citizens. Headquartered in Irving, Texas, the group has 3.2 million members and a professional staff of 317. The organization is run by a 25-member board of directors, all volunteers. New board members are nominated by a nominating committee and then voted on by the full board. MADD has more than 600 affiliates, including local chapters, community action teams, and state offices. The national office communicates with its affiliates and grassroots members through weekly mailings and action alerts. The headquarters conducts training sessions and holds an annual conference. MADD's national office has departments that include field services, human resources, legal, marketing and resource development, public policy, public relations, victim services, and youth programs.

HISTORY

MADD got its start in 1980, when a 13-year-old girl was killed by a hit-and-run driver. The driver had been involved in another hit-and-run accident two days earlier and was free on bail. What originally started as a campaign by a handful of mothers to save their children from drunk drivers has mushroomed over the years into a group with millions of members and active chapters in New Zealand, Canada, Australia, and Great Britain. The organization's original title was Mothers Against Drunk Drivers.

MADD's first important break as an organization came in 1982, when President Ronald Reagan announced a presidential task force on drunk driving and invited MADD to serve on it. By the end of the year, MADD had grown to over 100 chapters. In 1983, NBC produced a made-for-television movie about MADD, and the organization received other significant media attention. In 1984, MADD got its first important national legislative win when legislation was signed into law setting 21 as the national minimum drinking age. That same year MADD opened its first international chapter in Canada.

In 1986, the organization established a Victim Assistance Institute to train volunteers on how to support victims of drunk driving and how to serve as their advocates in the criminal justice system. The following year, MADD set up a national hotline to provide support for victims of drunk driving. In 1988, MADD won another important legislative victory with the passage of the Omnibus Anti-Drug Abuse Act. Included in this bill was an amendment to extend to all victims of DWI the same compensation rights offered to victims of other crimes. Also adopted was the Alcohol Beverage Labeling Act, requiring warnings on alcohol containers.

In 1990, MADD filed a brief with the U.S. Supreme Court supporting the constitutionality of sobriety checkpoints. The Court ruled in favor of the checkpoints. That same year, MADD unveiled its "20 by 2000" plan to reduce the proportion of alcohol-related traffic fatalities by 20 percent by the year 2000. In 1991, the organization scored more national legislative wins with the passage of the Intermodel Surface Transportation Efficiency Act and the Transportation Employee Testing Safety Act. The first law encourages states to pass tougher DUI programs. The second law requires alcohol as well as drug testing of transportation employees in safety-sensitive jobs. That same year, MADD sponsored a Gallup survey of public attitudes toward drunk driving and released its first annual Rating the States survey on the status of state and federal efforts against drunk driving.

The 1993 Fatal Accident Reporting System Statistics revealed that alcohol-related traffic deaths dropped from the previous year to a 30-year low. The National Highway Transportation Safety Administration credits MADD's efforts, along with tougher safety laws. Two years later, MADD participated in the secretary of transportation's Summit on Highway Safety. The organization announced a goal of reducing alcohol-related traffic fatalities to 11,000 or fewer by the year 2005. MADD also began offering public policy seminars to train state public policy liaisons in DUI issues and legislative how-to techniques.

Over the years, the group has had its share of controversies. In 1994, its founder, Candy Lightner, was hired as a lobbyist for a trade group representing restaurants and breweries. In her new role, she was active in lobbying against a law lowering the acceptable blood alcohol content (BAC) from .10 to .08, a law strongly supported by her former organization. Lightner headed MADD from its founding in 1980 to 1985, when the board stripped her of her office after she inquired about getting a $10,000 bonus on top of her $75,000 salary.

That same year, MADD was criticized by both the Better Business Bureau and the National Charities Bureau for spending too much time on fund-raising and too little time on program development. Roughly 10 years later, the national office of MADD came into conflict with its local chapters over control of money raised. Some chapters broke away from the national office to form separate organizations; the Michigan MADD chapter settled a suit it filed against the national office.

In 1998, MADD suffered a major defeat when legislation was defeated in Congress that would have lowered the BAC standard from .10 to .08. MADD and an alliance of consumer groups could not overcome the lobbying power of the liquor industry and restaurant associations. However, in recent years, MADD helped back lobbying efforts in five states that resulted in the lowering of the legal BAC from .10 to .08.

ACTIVITIES: CURRENT AND FUTURE

MADD has aggressively pursued an agenda that works to reduce the number of accident-related fatalities and to offer support to drunk-driving victims. They have done this both by lobbying in Congress and the state legislatures as an issues advocacy group from the outside, and by working with key agencies from the inside on public relations and community outreach programs.

MADD has lobbied the Congress and states to lower the legal blood alcohol content level from .10 to .08. The organization firmly believes that lowering the acceptable level would save many lives and serious injuries on the nation's highways each year. MADD also advocates confiscating vehicles or vehicle license plates from habitual impaired drivers. MADD is pressing for adoption of laws requiring mandatory jail sentences for repeat offenders and the development of special minimum security facilities for incarceration of convicted DWI/DUI offenders—facilities that include assessment and treatment while incarcerated.

MADD is on record as supporting ignition interlock devices installed in the cars of convicted drunk drivers. The ignition interlock system forces the driver to breathe into a small device near the dashboard that resembles a cell phone. If there is a trace of alcohol on the driver's breath, the device automatically prevents the car from starting. MADD has lobbied for laws allowing victims of alcohol-related traffic crashes to sue bars and servers who have provided alcohol to those intoxicated drivers. MADD has called on the hospitality industry to voluntarily end all "happy hours." The organization has endorsed alcohol warning labels, an increase in taxes on alcoholic beverages, and a constitutional amendment to protect the rights of victims of drunk driving in the criminal justice process. MADD also supports compensation for victims of drunk driving, pre-employment alcohol testing, sobriety checkpoints, and DWI tracking systems.

FINANCIAL FACTS

MADD is a 501(c)(3) not-for-profit organization according to the federal tax code and is prohibited from making campaign contributions to candidates for federal elected office.

GLENN DAIGON

Bibliography

Lewin, Tamer, "Founder of Anti-Drunk-Driving Campaign Now Lobbies for Breweries." *New York Times,* June 15, 1994.
"MADD Settles Suit Filed by Its Michigan Chapter." *Wall Street Journal,* June 16, 1996.
Mothers Against Drunk Driving: www.madd.org
Sadoff, Micky. *America Gets MADD! Mothers Against Drunk Driving.* Irvington, TX: MADD, 1990.

NATIONAL ABORTION AND REPRODUCTIVE RIGHTS ACTION LEAGUE

The National Abortion and Reproductive Rights Action League (NARAL) is a grassroots membership organization of over 500,000 dedicated to preserving the choice of abortion as a constitutional right. With local chapters in over 30 states, NARAL educates Americans, supports pro-choice candidates, and advocates pro-choice legislation at both the state and federal levels. It is governed by a board of directors whose membership ranges between 30 and 40 individuals. Each director is nominated by a nominating committee, and then a national ballot is mailed out to all NARAL members for the final decision. NARAL's work is divided among three organizations:

NARAL, Inc., a 501(c)(4) nonprofit organization, works through the political system to create effective reproductive choices for all Americans and uses sophisticated political strategy, as well as extensive grassroots organizing and lobbying to advance the pro-choice agenda.

NARAL-PAC, a political action committee (PAC), is the driving force behind the organization's efforts to elect pro-choice candidates. NARAL-PAC uses efforts such as get-out-the-vote drives and paid advertising to elect its favored candidates.

The NARAL Foundation, classified by the Internal Revenue Service tax code as a 501(c)(3) charitable organization, was founded in 1977. It supports in-depth research and legal work, publishes policy reports, mounts public education campaigns and provides leadership training for grassroots activists.

The organization's national office houses departments handling the following activities: executive leadership, communications/marketing, constituency development, finance/administration, government relations, legal/research, and political.

HISTORY

Founded in 1969, NARAL was originally the National Association for the Repeal of Abortion Laws. It formed after the 1967 conference of the National Organization for Women, which included on its eight-item agenda the right of women to control their reproductive lives. NARAL scored its first victory in 1970 when the New York State legislature passed, and Governor Nelson Rockefeller signed into law, a bill repealing the state's abortion codes, which for the first time gave women the right to choose abortion under certain circumstances. NARAL had similar successes in the early 1970s in liberalizing abortion laws in Alaska and Hawaii.

With the Supreme Court's 1973 *Roe v. Wade* decision effectively throwing out all state laws banning women from having abortion in the first trimester, the political dynamics of the issue shifted. NARAL changed its name from National Association for the Repeal of Abortion Laws to National Abortion and Reproductive Rights Action League to reflect the new reality. In one fell swoop, the Court's decision had accomplished the organization's goal of repealing state laws that banned a woman's right to choose abortion. But the organization had a new mission now—protecting that right from counterattack by right-to-life groups.

In 1976, Congress approved the Hyde Amendment, barring any Medicaid funding for abortions. Many argued that this would force women who could not afford abortions to bear unwanted children. Abortion clinics became targets of violence over the years and doctors who have performed abortions have been murdered. While right-to-life groups have been unsuccessful in passing a constitutional amendment overturning *Roe v. Wade* and making abortion a crime, they have been successful at the state level in passing bills that require teenagers to obtain parental notification before having an abortion. In some states, right-to-life groups have also succeeded in banning "partial birth" abortions and requiring a 24-hour waiting period before an abortion can be performed on a patient. "Partial birth" abortions, otherwise known as dilation and extraction procedures, are abortions performed late in pregnancy. NARAL had some success with the

**National Abortion and Reproductive Rights Action League
Political Action Committee Contributions**

- 1987-88
- 1993-94
- 1997-98

Data derived from official studies available from the Federal Election Commission, Washington, DC, 1987–1998.

election of ally Bill Clinton in 1992. In 1993, after strong NARAL backing, Clinton issued five executive orders that:

- overturned the ban on funding for federal clinics that provided counseling on abortion;
- directed the FDA to promote the testing and licensing of the French abortion pill, RU-486;
- renewed the funding for fetal tissue research;
- lifted the ban on privately funded abortions in military hospitals;
- lifted the condition of U.S. foreign family planning aid that abortion services not be provided.

Again with strong NARAL backing, President Clinton signed the federal clinic protection law that guaranteed safe access to abortion clinics by those who made the abortion choice; however, in 1994, the election of Republicans at both the federal and state levels resulted in a major setback for NARAL's agenda.

NARAL estimates that anti-choice forces have enough votes in 90 percent of state legislatures to pass restrictive legislation and 70 percent of governors have signed (or would be willing to sign) restrictive legislation, responding to increased anti-abortion representation in state governments. Overall, NARAL believes that anti-choice forces have been successful in chipping away at or rolling back the right of women to choose abortion.

ACTIVITIES: CURRENT AND FUTURE

At the federal level, NARAL was in the forefront of the successful fight to sustain President Clinton's veto of the Partial Birth Abortion Ban. They have also lobbied hard against the Child Custody Protection Act. This would make it a federal offense to transport a minor across state lines if this action circumvents the applications of a state law requiring parental approval of a minor's abortion.

NARAL has also strongly supported the Family Planning and Choice Act of 1997. This bill would increase funding for contraceptive services at federal clinics, require private health insurance companies to provide coverage of contraceptives, and further promote the testing and development of the French abortion pill, RU-486.

At the state level, NARAL has been forced to adopt a more defensive role. The organization has lobbied over half-a-dozen state legislatures to stop the passage of laws banning "partial birth" abortions. Some 28 states already have laws on the books banning "partial birth" abortions. It has successfully lobbied against requiring a 24-hour waiting period for women seeking abortions in Arkansas. By the end of 1998, 19 states had laws requiring women to wait a specific time period for an abortion after receiving required state lectures on the issue. NARAL has lobbied states to include contraceptive coverage in their health insurance plans. The organization has also pressed for passage of state laws against clinic violence and harassment, and for public funding for abortion. The organization has fought against legislation requiring parental consent for teenagers choosing to have an abortion. As of the end of 1998, 39 states had passed laws requiring parental consent laws.

FINANCIAL FACTS

NARAL's political action committee (NARAL-PAC) has been consistently active in recent elections. During the 1997–1998 cycle, NARAL-PAC received $1,038,075 in receipts and spent $1,062,984. This latter figure includes $299,255 to candidates and parties, $271,700 to Democrats and $27,555 to Republicans. From the late 1980s to the late 1990s, there were ups and downs in NARAL-PAC's receipts, expenditures, and contributions. Between 1988 and 1992, receipts and expenditures increased more than sixfold, only to go down again in the next few elections to their former levels. At the same time, contributions to Democrats have far exceeded those to Republicans, by a factor of almost 10 to 1.

GLENN DAIGON

Bibliography

Gorney, Cynthia. *Articles of Faith*. New York: Simon and Schuster, 1998.

National Abortion and Reproductive Rights Action League: www.naral.org

NATIONAL COMMITTEE TO PRESERVE SOCIAL SECURITY AND MEDICARE

The National Committee to Preserve Social Security and Medicare (NCPSSM) is a grassroots senior citizens advocacy and education association. The group is the second largest senior citizens advocacy group in the nation. It consists of 5.5 million members, with headquarters located in Washington, D.C. The organization has a paid staff of 71. A 16-member executive board administers the NCPSSM and a nominating committee selects each potential board member. The general membership then votes on the nominees through a ballot in the March/April issue of the organization's magazine.

The national headquarters has a Grassroots Outreach Services Department to keep in touch with its members. The department's mission is to:

- coordinate and implement the organization's legislative and political agenda among members and senior advocates at the local, regional, and state levels;
- maintain a network of informed members, activists, and opinion leaders;
- respond to members' inquiries and concerns via phone, letters, and electronic mail;
- support efforts that increase awareness of retirement and other aging issues and expand opportunities for seniors to act on their own behalf.

The Grassroots Outreach Services department is divided into two parts. The Grassroots regional coordinators division does much of its work in the field. Duties include assisting members to lobby elected officials, serving as liaisons with members in the field, addressing seniors' needs and concerns, and working with agencies for the aging organizations, and community groups in planning briefings and seminars on issues of importance to seniors.

Member services representatives are called on to respond to letters and phone calls, deliver petitions to members of Congress on important legislation, and continuously update the organization's database of members. Other departments in NCPSSM's national office in Washington include lobbying, government relations, minority affairs, volunteer coordination, and publications.

HISTORY

NCPSSM was conceived and created by fundraisers. A conservative direct-mail business, Butcher-Forde, incorporated NCPSSM in 1982 as a nonprofit, tax-exempt foundation. Butcher-Forde had supported the tax-cutting measure, Proposition 13, in California in 1978. The organization signed on James Roosevelt, son of the late President Franklin Roosevelt, as a consultant. In 1983, the organization sent out fund-raising letters to seniors claiming that Congress was cutting Social Security benefits to allocate more money for illegal aliens. Other fund-raising letters went out to the elderly asking for contributions to build a Franklin Delano Roosevelt Memorial Social Security and Medicare building. One particularly controversial fund-raising letter, signed by James Roosevelt, stated, "My father started Social Security. Now we must act to save Social Security and Medicare. . . . Never in the 51 years since my father, Franklin Delano Roosevelt, started the Social Security system, have there been such threats to Social Security and Medicare benefits." The letter went on to request a $10 contribution, without which the elderly may soon "face a crippling, financial hardship."

A public hearing on the committee's mail practices was called by Congress in the mid 1980s. Senator Jay Rockefeller derided NCPSSM's practices as "a fundraising scam that degrades the Roosevelt name." Postal inspectors and the Justice Department forced the organization to stop making its mailings look like official government documents. The Social Security

Administration stopped NCPSSM from offering, for 10 dollars, to do an analysis of individual's retirement benefits, a service that is provided for free by the Social Security Administration. The organization made the list of *Washington Monthly*'s worst public interest groups, for using misleading mailings to bilk senior citizens. In 1987, NCPSSM hired 13 lobbyists. Many believe this was done to counter criticism that the organization was just a front for a direct-mail fundraising business.

It was not too long before NCPSSM's more aggressive involvement in public policy lobbying made itself felt. In 1989, one year after Congress passed legislation setting up a catastrophic health insurance program, Congress received a flood of postcards from angry seniors, upset about the high taxes required to pay for the program. The mail blitz was directed by NCPSSM, and that year Congress voted to repeal the program. The organization lobbied on behalf of "notch babies," born between 1917 and 1921, who they claimed were getting short shrift on Social Security benefits. In the early 1990s, the organization came out against President Bill Clinton's health insurance program, although it is on record as supporting national health insurance. NCPSSM portrays itself as a watchdog on behalf of the elderly against conniving politicians who plan to abuse the Social Security and Medicare programs and benefit levels.

ACTIVITIES: CURRENT AND FUTURE

The organization's whole reason for existing is to preserve the Social Security and Medicare programs and to ensure that they serve the needs of senior citizens. NCPSSM had laid out its broad goals in a very straightforward manner through a series of position papers. The group is totally opposed to the privatization of Social Security. The organization believes that diverting payroll taxes into private accounts would mean that current workers would end up paying more money for lower benefits. It believes that the risk would be shifted to individual workers instead of being spread out over the entire workforce. NCPSSM believes Social Security does face financial problems and needs shoring up, but it prefers President Clinton's plan to use the budget surplus to accomplish that goal rather than setting up private accounts.

NCPSSM favors expanding the Medicare program to cover prescription drugs and preventive care while limiting out-of-pocket costs. The Supplemental Security Income program (SSI) is the social welfare program providing cash assistance to the aged, blind, and disabled, and is funded by general revenues, not by the Social Security Trust Funds. NCPSSM supports increasing the SSI benefit level above the poverty line, increasing the staffing of the program to handle cases more quickly, and allowing SSI recipients to own more assets.

Some recent legislative battles NCPSSM has waged in Congress are consistent with the organization's stated goals. In 1999, the group supported a resolution in the House of Representatives declaring that the current problems facing Social Security are manageable and that radical solutions, such as using the Social Security system to fund private retirement accounts, are not necessary. NCPSSM joined other groups in opposing a proposed Medicare reform plan that would have increased premiums, deductibles, and copayments; increased the eligibility age; and instituted a 10 percent home health copayment. The group supported the idea of creating a seniors-only Consumer Price Index, on which Social Security's cost-of-living adjustments would be based. The point is that since seniors spend more on health care, they have a higher cost of living, which would be reflected in both this new index and cost-of-living adjustments to Social Security benefits.

On the issue of long-term care, NCPSSM supports a strong public program to provide the basic security for individuals of all ages who need long-term care. The organization believes that goals can be met through a combination of private long-term insurance with federal standards to protect consumers, public programs, and the inclusion of long-term care benefits in any reform of the Medicare program.

Another important issue for the group is ensuring that widows are eligible for the same Social Security benefits as their husbands. Toward that end, NCPSSM supports legislation providing two-thirds of a couple's combined benefits to a surviving spouse, removing limitations on disabled widow benefits, and counting up to 10 care-giver years and five additional years toward special minimum benefits.

FINANCIAL FACTS

NCPSSM's political action committee (PAC) has been active in federal elections. For the 1997–1998 election cycle, The National Committee to Preserve Social Security PAC received $1,853,740 in receipts and spent $1,839,753. The latter figure includes $670,688 in contributions to candidates and parties, $534,057 to Democrats and $134,189 to Republicans. Between the 1987–1988 election cycle and the 1995–1996 election cycle, receipts declined from $4.5 million to $2.3 million, while expenditures declined commensurately from $4 million to $2.2 million. At the same time, contributions to Democrats have exceeded those for Republicans by a factor of better than 3 to 1.

GLENN DAIGON

Bibliography

Lindeman, Bard. "A Famous Son, An Old Game." *50 Plus,* June 1988.

McWilliam, Rita. "The Best and Worst of the Public Interest Groups." *The Washington Monthly,* March 1988.

National Committee to Preserve Social Security and Medicare: www.ncpssm.org

NATIONAL RIFLE ASSOCIATION

The National Rifle Association (NRA) consists of over 3 million dues-paying members nationwide, including target shooters, hunters, gun collectors, gunsmiths, police officers, and others interested in firearms. The organization promotes rifle, pistol, and shotgun shooting; hunting; gun collecting; home firearm safety; and wildlife conservation. The NRA encourages civilian marksmanship, educates police firearm instructors, maintains national and international records of shooting competitions, and sponsors teams to compete in world championships.

The NRA is governed by a board of directors that consists of 75 NRA members who are elected by mail ballot sent to the membership of the association. Each board member is entitled to a vote. One additional board member is elected at the organization's annual meeting. The right to hold the office of director is limited to NRA lifetime members who have attained an age of 18 years and are citizens of the United States. Directors are elected for a term of three years, with the exception of the director elected at the annual meeting of members, who serves a one-year term. The terms of office of one-third of the board expire each year. Members of the board are nominated from the general membership either by recommendation to the nominating committee or by petition of at least 250 members.

The NRA is a national organization with affiliates and club members in all 50 states. Leaders encourage members to write, e-mail, and fax opinions to the national office. Because so much of the money that sustains the organization comes from member dues, the NRA's leadership feels a special need to listen to its members. The national office solicits advice from the members about which candidates to back, takes public opinion polls of the membership, and issues federal and state legislative action bulletins alerting members about upcoming bills that impact their right to bear arms.

The national headquarters is located in Fairfax, Virginia. There is a federal affairs office in Washington, D.C., that houses lobbyists, and a state and local affairs office in Sacramento, California. The size of the total staff is 400. National headquarters in Washington, D.C., houses the following departments: competition, education and training, field services, hunting and conservation, the Institute of Legislative Action, law enforcement assistance, and public affairs.

HISTORY

The NRA was founded in New York City in 1871 by ex-military men with the purpose of training the National Guard to be sharpshooters. Civil War General Ambrose Burnside was listed as the first president. With the aid of General Burnside, the New York state legislature passed legislation in 1872 setting aside $25,000 to buy 100 acres on Long Island to be developed into a rifle range. The NRA gained prominence in 1874 when it sponsored an international shooting competition. In that competition, the NRA's Amateur Rifle Club upset the heavily favored, world champion Irish Rifle Association.

Although there was a downturn in public interest in gunnery shooting tournaments in the late 1800s, the NRA's popularity bounced back after the turn of the century. The Boer War in South Africa highlighted the importance of good marksmanship. In 1903, Congress created the National Board for the Promotion of Rifle Practice to build ranges for civilian use and to promote them. In 1905, Congress passed Public Law 149 authorizing the sale of surplus military firearms and ammunition—at cost—to rifle clubs that were sponsored by the National Rifle Association. In 1912, Congress began funding the annual NRA shooting matches. After World War II, due to the interest of returning soldiers in firearms, NRA membership tripled. The NRA began to put a greater emphasis on hunting to respond to the interests of their new members.

Because gun control laws were weak and scarce, the

NRA did not have much of a lobbying presence in Washington, D.C. All of that changed after Lee Harvey Oswald was alleged to have shot President John F. Kennedy with a high-powered rifle in 1963, and Congress passed the Gun Control Act of 1968. The law barred mail-order and interstate shipments of firearms and ammunition and instituted a wide range of restrictions and regulations that frustrated gun owners and dealers. By 1977, NRA membership had grown to 1 million; that number had climbed to 2.6 million by 1983. In 1980, for the first time in its history, the NRA endorsed and actively supported a presidential candidate, in this case, Ronald Reagan. Reagan became the first American president to address the organization at their annual convention in 1983. In 1986, the NRA was seen as the lobbying group most responsible for passage of the McClure-Volkmer Act. This bill repealed many of the restrictions placed on gun owners by the 1968 Gun Control Act, and observers see this time as the high-water mark for the NRA's power. A story in the *New York Times* referred to the gun lobby as "the most persistent and resourceful of the single-issue groups."

As gun control advocates became better organized and received more popular support in the face of horrendous shooting sprees around the country, the NRA began to suffer more and more defeats. In 1988, Maryland voters passed a ballot initiative banning the sale of "Saturday night specials." That same year, Congress passed, and President Reagan signed into law, a measure that banned hard-to-detect plastic guns, over NRA opposition. For the NRA, 1993 and 1994 were the worst years yet, with gun control advocates able to pass legislation requiring a five-day waiting period for new gun owners (the Brady Bill) and banning certain semi-automatic weapons. In 1994, the Republican Party took control of both the House and Senate, and many believed that the reason the Democrats suffered so badly at the polls was the backlash against the new gun control laws that they had passed. Some Republicans believe that, without the NRA's massive financial contributions and get-out-the-vote efforts, they would not have been nearly as successful as they were. Despite having their Republican allies back in control of Congress, the NRA failed in their efforts to overturn the ban on semi-automatic weapons.

To prevent further passage of gun control measures, the NRA has taken the line that more efforts should be made to enforce current gun control laws and actively prosecute violators of existing laws rather than pass additional regulations. NRA officials point to the success of "Project Exile" in Richmond, Virginia. Under that program, Richmond police officials and Virginia troopers can immediately initiate federal prosecution if a person is arrested who has a gun and is a "convicted felon (state or federal), drug user or addict, a fugitive who has fled another state, or is under indictment for a felony." When an officer makes an arrest and one of these crimes is involved, the officer calls the 24-hour pager number to determine whether a federal law may have been broken before initiating prosecution. The U.S. Attorney reports that publicity is essential to the program's success. More than 15,000 business cards printed with the slogan "An illegal gun gets you five years in federal prison" were distributed, and the slogan was widely circulated in the media. According to the NRA, six months after Project Exile was implemented in Richmond, the city's homicide rate was cut in half. The NRA is touting this program as a successful example of reducing gun violence. It faults the Clinton administration for pressing for new controls on guns rather than just enforcing the current federal laws on the books. The NRA has urged expansion of Project Exile on a national scale.

Whether this tactic will be successful for the NRA remains to be seen. With the school-yard shootings in Oregon, Arkansas, and Colorado, the political tide may be moving against the NRA. In the late spring of 1999 the House of Representatives defeated new gun control laws, suggesting that the NRA has weathered the storm. However, there are some definite danger signs for the organization.

Since the Colorado school shootings, public opinion polls have consistently shown greater public support for more gun control laws. Some GOP candidates for president were breaking ranks and calling for additional restrictions. Even some trade groups representing gun dealers, manufacturers, and distributors have endorsed new restrictions on gun ownership, leaving the NRA alone in its opposition to these measures.

In the past, these trade groups have presented a united front with the NRA against new control measures. But in 1999, those same trade groups believed themselves vulnerable to lawsuits filed by gun violence victims. Many of them see public support of laws requiring safety locks for guns as one way to make themselves less vulnerable to negligence lawsuits.

New Jersey Democratic senator and party leader Robert Torricelli warned, "No force on earth can stop this [senators' votes on gun control restrictions] now from becoming a central issue in the 2000 elections debate." Whether the NRA has the strength to ride out the storm in the wake of school-yard killings will be decided in the next few years.

**National Rifle Association
Political Action Committee Contributions**

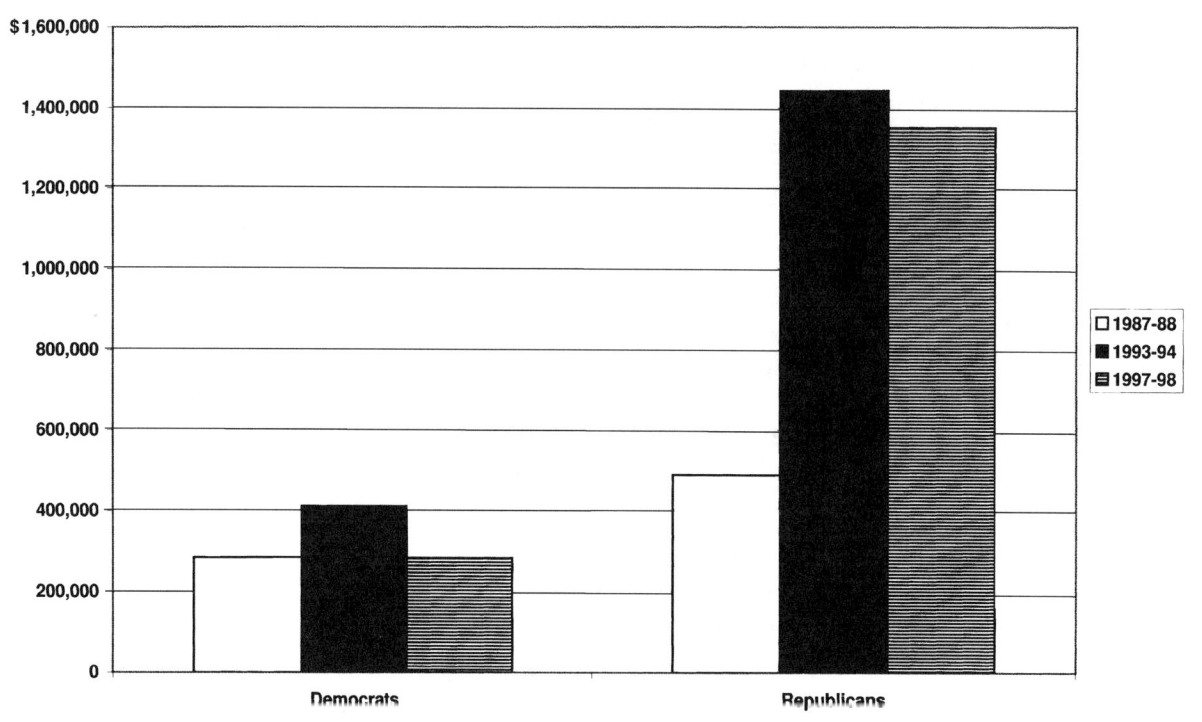

[Bar chart showing PAC contributions to Democrats and Republicans for 1987-88, 1993-94, and 1997-98. Democrats received approximately $280,000 (1987-88), $410,000 (1993-94), and $280,000 (1997-98). Republicans received approximately $485,000 (1987-88), $1,440,000 (1993-94), and $1,350,000 (1997-98).]

Data derived from official studies available from the Federal Election Commission, Washington, DC, 1987–1998.

ACTIVITIES: CURRENT AND FUTURE

The defining purpose behind the NRA's involvement in politics has been to defend the Second Amendment, the right to bear arms. This has meant that the organization has become involved in a whole range of issues and legislation at the federal, state, and even local level, whenever it feels that its Second Amendment rights have been threatened. In 1998, the NRA successfully lobbied Congress to defeat a bill requiring "childproof" locks on new guns. In the state of Georgia, it successfully persuaded the legislature and governor to enact a law that would ban cities in Georgia from suing gun manufacturers for liability in gun deaths. This bill was in response to a New York City jury's holding gun manufacturers liable for gun deaths, and mayors of several large cities bringing forward suits against gun manufacturers in hopes of getting similar verdicts. By the spring of 1999, nine other states had laws similar to Georgia's on the books. The NRA has also pressed for passage of laws that would give citizens the right to carry concealed weapons. It has been successful in its efforts; by the end of 1998, more than 30 states had laws that give citizens the right to carry concealed weapons. The one exception has been the state of Missouri. In 1999, citizens voted down an NRA-backed initiative giving them the right to carry concealed weapons. In the aftermath of the Colorado school shootings, the NRA withdrew from consideration concealed weapons bills it was planning to press ahead with in several state legislatures.

The NRA has also been active lobbying at the state level against legislation that would restrict gun purchases to one a month, bills that would outlaw new forms of semi-automatic weapons, and laws that would limit the size of ammunition clips. Since the Colorado shooting, the NRA has been put on the defensive. Michigan shelved a concealed weapons bill, and gun control measures are advancing in California, Oregon, Connecticut, and New Jersey.

FINANCIAL FACTS

The NRA's political action committee (PAC), NRA Political Victory Fund, is one of the largest in the nation.

During the 1997–1998 election cycle, it received $7,773,471 in contributions and spent $7,978,499, significantly higher than the $3.7 million in receipts and $4.7 million in contributions during the 1987–1988 election cycle. Expenditures in 1997–1998 include $1,633,211 in contributions to candidates and parties, $238,200 to Democrats and $1,350,011 to Republicans. Between the 1987–1988 and 1995–1996 election cycles, receipts and expenditures climbed 67 percent, while contributions more than doubled from $772,756 to $1,633,211. At the same time, political contributions to Republicans far exceeded those to Democrats by a factor of better than 3 to 1.

GLENN DAIGON

Bibliography

Cigler, Allan J., and Burdett A. Loomis. *Interest Group Politics,* 5th ed. Washington, DC: Congressional Quarterly, 1998.

Davidson, Osha Gray. *Under Fire: The NRA and the Battle for Gun Control.* New York: Henry Holt, 1993.

National Rifle Association: www.nra.org

NATIONAL RIGHT TO LIFE COMMITTEE

The National Right to Life Committee (NRLC) is the nation's largest pro-life group, with affiliates in all 50 states and approximately 3,000 local chapters nationwide. Each state elects a member to the NRLC board of directors, the governing body of the NRLC. Three additional at-large board members are chosen by a national ballot mailed out to all NRLC members. Over the years, the NRLC has cultivated different outreach programs aimed at specific groups. One of those outreach programs, National Teens for Life (NTL), was started in 1985. NTL sends speakers to high schools and youth groups, and has volunteers for crisis pregnancy centers and peer counseling. It has members in all 50 states and holds its own convention during the summer months in conjunction with the National Right to Life Convention.

Black Americans for Life (BAL) is another outreach program sponsored by NRLC. As its name suggests, it targets members of the black community to support the NRLC's agenda. On more than one occasion, NRLC spokespersons and supporters have likened abortion to a racist form of birth control.

The Hispanic Outreach program of the NRLC strives to unite Hispanic Americans from all over the United States into the pro-life movement. NRLC views the Hispanic community as important because Hispanics will make up nearly 25 percent of the population in the next century. The organization also believes that, because many of these people come from cultures where abortion is illegal, the right-to-life viewpoint has a natural venue that it might not have with other ethnic groups.

American Victims of Abortion (AVA) is another outreach effort by the NRLC. It involves abortion "victims" using their own personal experiences with abortion to spread the right-to-life message. The NRLC national office in Washington includes departments handling the following areas: communications, development, education, federal legislation, financial services, medical ethics, news, state legislation, state organizational development, and voter identification.

HISTORY

The National Right to Life Committee came into being virtually within days of the Supreme Court's 1973 *Roe v. Wade* decision overturning state laws that banned abortion. Their statement of purpose was very direct and simple:

> The purpose of the National Right to Life Committee, Inc., is to engage in educational, charitable, scientific and political activities and projects, or purposes, including specifically, but not limited to, the following:
> 1. To promote respect for worth and dignity of all human life, including the life of the unborn child from the time of fertilization.
> 2. To promote, encourage and sponsor such mandatory and statutory measures which will provide protection of human life before and after birth, particularly for the defenseless, the incompetent, the impaired and the incapacitated.

Literally within days of the *Roe v. Wade* decision, the NRLC's friends in Congress were drafting a constitutional amendment to ban all abortions. Passage of this amendment became the centerpiece of the NRLC's early years.

The National Right to Life organization began to make its mark in 1976, when it helped to pass the Hyde Amendment, barring all Medicaid funds for abortion. Then, in 1978, the NRLC poured money and volunteers into the Iowa race for U.S. Senate. The liberal, pro-choice, Democratic incumbent, Dick Clark, was supposed to be the easy winner, but he lost by a narrow margin to Republican Roger Jepsen, a supporter of the Human Life Amendment. Even Clark admitted publicly

**National Right to Life Committee
Political Action Committee Contributions**

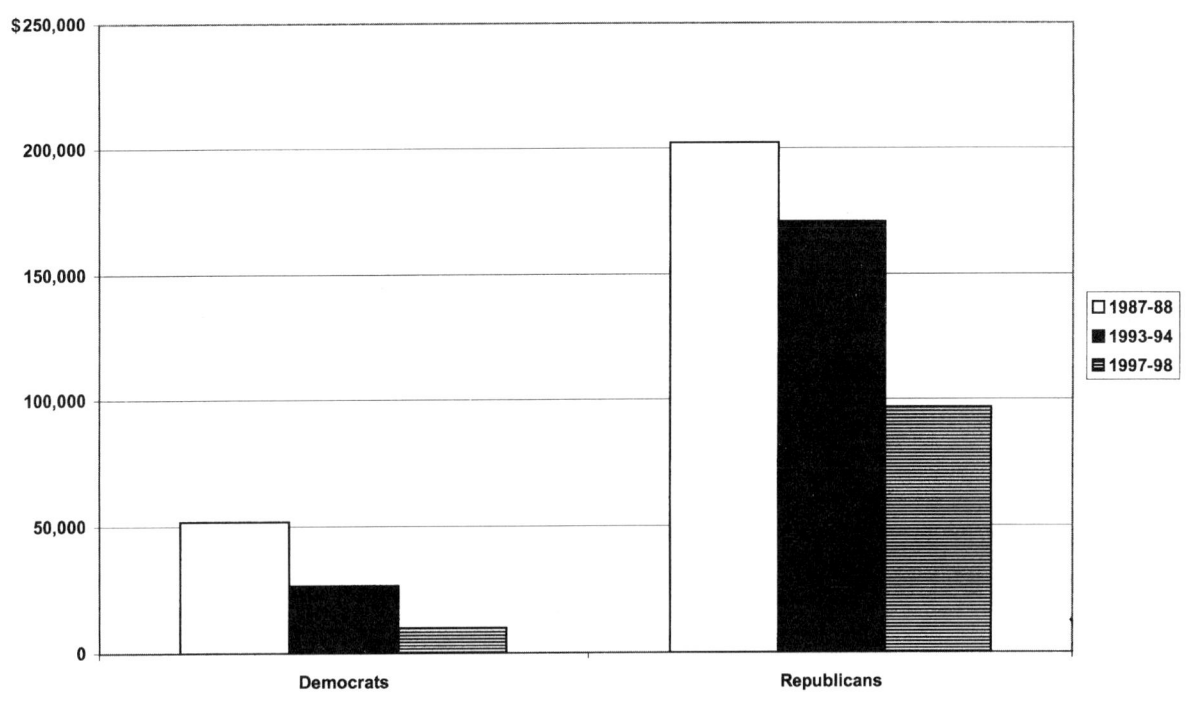

[Bar chart showing contributions to Democrats and Republicans for years 1987-88, 1993-94, and 1997-98. Democrats received approximately $52,000 (1987-88), $27,000 (1993-94), and $10,000 (1997-98). Republicans received approximately $203,000 (1987-88), $172,000 (1993-94), and $99,000 (1997-98).]

Data derived from official studies available from the Federal Election Commission, Washington, DC, 1987–1998.

that the National Right to Life movement had made a decisive difference.

The 1980 election went even better for the National Right to Life Committee. Not only did it help elect a pro-life president, Ronald Reagan, but it also replaced four pro-choice incumbent senators with four Human Life Amendment supporters, as well as electing many supporters to the House of Representatives. An election banner in the organization's newsletter, *National Right to Life News,* read, "Prolife Gain: President, 10 Senators and More." Many believe that the organization had its best chance ever to successfully pass the Human Life Amendment through Congress and to get the states to ratify it to the Constitution, following the momentum provided by the 1980 elections. However, the NRLC became badly divided over tactics. Some in the movement supported an amendment to the Constitution outlawing abortion; others supported a simple bill banning abortion as the best way to overturn the Supreme Court decision. The result was that neither a Human Life Amendment nor bill made it through Congress.

The NRLC was more successful in getting President Reagan to appoint pro-life justices to the Supreme Court. As the decade wore on, these justices began to tip the balance. In decisions such as *Webster v. Reproductive Health Services* and *Hodgson v. Minnesota,* access to abortions became more restricted. These decisions seemed to energize the pro-choice forces, as they actively helped winning candidates who pledged to appoint pro-choice judges. The committee viewed President Bill Clinton and the Democratic Party as hopelessly pro-choice, and it worked hard to elect the tidal wave of Republicans who swept in at the national and local levels in 1994. It used its electoral success to further restrict abortion rights, with the passage of numerous laws requiring teenagers seeking abortions to first get parental approval and a 24-hour waiting period for women seeking abortions in some states.

The "partial birth" abortion issue has popular support, and the committee has successfully passed laws outlawing it in many states; however, the committee's ultimate goal of outlawing abortion seems as distant as ever. "Partial birth" abortion is a procedure known as dilation and extraction, or abortions performed late in pregnancy. Anti-abortion activist and one-time presidential candidate Pat Robertson stated: "There's no way we are going to pass a constitutional amendment on abortion. It's not going to happen. . . . I think the protection of the life of the unborn and protection of the life of the elderly should be a noble goal that we are going to strive toward one day. . . . But in terms of practical politics an incremental goal is much more effective." Many political observers would find that statement to be a very realistic view on what the anti-abortion movement can and cannot do in the near future.

ACTIVITIES: CURRENT AND FUTURE

The National Right to Life Committee is actively pursuing its agenda at the federal and state levels. At the federal level, the committee has a majority of its supporters on the issue of banning "partial birth" abortions. However, it did not have the two-thirds majority to override the president's veto in the 1990s. The committee has also pledged to seek $85 million for a national Women's and Children's Resources Act. The act is a grant program for women seeking alternatives to abortion such as maternity homes and adoption services. The NRLC will also lobby Congress to close the loopholes in the law passed by Congress in 1995, banning the use of federal tax dollars to support medical experiments that involve the killing or harming of living human embryos. This act overturned a 1993 executive order of President Clinton's, permitting federal tax dollars for such purposes. The Child Custody Act is another priority of the NRLC. It would make it a federal offense to transport a minor across state lines for an abortion if this action is taken to avoid a state law requiring parental involvement in a minor's abortion. The NRLC also has pledged to stop the McCain-Feingold campaign finance bill, believing that it restricts the ability of citizens' groups to bring their cases to the voting public.

At the local level, the NRLC plans to pursue the same agenda that it has been successful in pursuing in the past. In 1999, bills banning "partial birth" abortion have been introduced in a number of state legislatures, and bills have been introduced requiring 24-hour waiting periods, requiring schools to teach abstinence, and blocking insurance coverage of contraceptives in states throughout the country. In the fall elections of 1998, two states had ballot measures that would have banned "partial birth" abortions. The measures, heavily backed by the NRLC, were voted down. A Colorado ballot measure supporting parental notification for abortion passed.

FINANCIAL FACTS

The NRLC's political action committee (PAC) has been active in the last decade of the twentieth century. During the 1997–1998 election cycle, it received $1,455,355 in receipts and spent $1,548,625. This latter figure includes $106,934 in contributions to candidates and parties, with $10,000 to Democrats and $96,934 to Republicans. NRLC PAC receipts and expenditures peaked in the 1995–1996 election cycle, when receipts totaled nearly $2.5 million and expenditures rose to over $2.2 million. In the 1997–1998 cycle, receipts and expenditures returned to levels of the cycle in 1987–1988. At the same time, contributions to Republicans have far exceeded those to Democrats by a factor of roughly 8 to 1.

GLENN DAIGON

Bibliography

Gorney, Cynthia. *Articles of Faith*. New York: Simon & Schuster, 1998.

National Right to Life Committee: www.nrlc.org

PEOPLE FOR THE ETHICAL TREATMENT OF ANIMALS

People for the Ethical Treatment of Animals (PETA) has over 600,000 members and a full-time staff of 100. Its headquarters are located in Norfolk, Virginia, and it has membership offices in San Francisco, London, and Rome. A three-person board of directors runs the organization. Its national office in Norfolk houses the following departments: public relations, human resources, research and investigations, education, and international grassroots campaigns.

HISTORY

PETA was originally founded in 1980 on the principle that animals are not ours to eat, wear, experiment with, or use for entertainment. PETA cofounder Alex Pacheco started the ball rolling on the organization's first big campaign when he discovered inhumane treatment of laboratory monkeys at the National Institute of Health's research facilities in Silver Spring, Maryland. This resulted in the first arrest and conviction of an animal experimenter in the United States on charges of cruelty to animals, the first confiscation of abused laboratory animals, and the first U.S. Supreme Court victory for animals in laboratories.

Over the years, PETA has used a wide range of tactics to achieve its mission. Those tactics include public education, cruelty investigations, research, animal rescue, legislation, special events, celebrity involvement, and direct action. For example, PETA released investigators' photographs and videotaped footage taken inside Carolina Biological Supply Company, the nation's largest biological supply house. PETA documented animals being removed from gas chambers and injected with formaldehyde without being checked for vital signs, as well as cats and rats struggling during embalming and employees spitting on animals. The company was charged by the U.S. Department of Agriculture with violations of the Animal Welfare Act.

Another investigation resulted in a videotaping of Las Vegas entertainer Bobby Berosini beating orangutans with a metal rod. The U.S. Department of the Interior revoked Berosini's captive-bred wildlife permit. Another PETA videotape of the treatment of primates at the University of Pennsylvania head injury laboratory resulted in government fines and the end of primate use there. PETA's undercover investigation of a huge contract testing laboratory in Philadelphia and the subsequent campaign led to cosmetics company Benneton's permanent ban on the use of animal tests. Other leading cosmetics companies, such as Avon, Revlon, and Estée Lauder, followed suit. L'Oréal, the world's largest cosmetics manufacturer, yielded after PETA's four-year international campaign. Gillette announced a moratorium on animal tests after PETA's 10-year campaign. PETA now lists more than 550 cosmetics companies that do not test products on animals.

PETA's campaigns have targeted other large corporations as well. The organization convinced Mobil, Texaco, Pennzoil, Shell, and other oil companies to cover their exhaust stacks after showing how millions of birds and other bats become trapped in the shafts and burned alive. In 1994, Calvin Klein announced it would stop marketing furs. Many believe the decision was a result of PETA activists invading Mr. Klein's offices earlier that year, spray-painting "kills animals" on the company emblem, and putting stickers on the walls reading "fur hurts." Klein met with members of the group who showed him a film of animals being killed to provide furs. Observers believe the company made this decision to avoid more bad public relations. PETA had convinced top models Naomi Campbell, Christie Turlington, and Tatjana Patitz to pose for a series of antifur ads. Other designers who decided against furs include Giorgio Armani, Christian La Croix, Bill Blass, Carolina Herrera, and Norma Kamali.

In fact, over the years, PETA has aggressively recruited celebrities to promote its cause. The organization completed two animal rights albums, *Animal Liberation* and *Tame Yourself,* featuring artists such as Chrissie Hynde, Indigo Girls, Michael Stipe, and Belinda Carlisle. PETA also held several "Rock against Fur" benefit concerts featuring the B-52s, k.d. lang, and others. The group received pledges from filmmakers Oliver Stone, Martin Scorsese, and Rob Reiner to keep fur off movie sets. PETA and actress Alicia Silverstone launched a national "Cut Out Dissection" campaign, educating students about their rights to alternatives to dissecting animals in the classroom.

ACTIVITIES: CURRENT AND FUTURE

In addition to targeting specific companies and facilities, PETA has a broad issue agenda. For example, PETA state chapters in Arkansas and Louisiana are advocating an excise tax on meat, poultry, and fish. The tax is modeled after the tax on cigarettes, and PETA argues that Americans spend at least $123 billion a year to treat hypertension, heart disease, stroke, cancer, obesity, and other diseases related directly to meat consumption. "In addition to saving countless animals' lives," said PETA president Ingrid Newkirk, "a meat tax could be used as insurance for health problems that America's meat-eaters face later in life."

In Illinois, PETA is pressing the legislature for adoption of the Illinois Dissection Alternatives Act, which would require that all students be allowed to choose alternatives to dissection without being penalized or forced to drop the class in which it is scheduled. In Washington, D.C., PETA is pressing Congress for the adoption of a bill to prohibit the interstate transport of birds for fighting purposes. This bill is meant to put an end to cockfighting, where two or more roosters are outfitted with razor-sharp spurs and placed in a pit to fight to the death.

In 1999, PETA supporters drenched Gucci designer Tom Ford with a bucket of tomato juice amidst accusations of "Shame on you Tom Ford! Stop using fur!" Ford was about to give a keynote address at a CEO summit being held at the Ritz Carlton Laguna Niguel hotel. The designer is one of the top targets for PETA and other animal rights activists because he has refused their appeals to stop using fur. Some of the organization's other current campaigns include:

Procter & Gamble. PETA is urging consumers to boycott this company because it tests its products on animals to determine the safety of cosmetics and household products. PETA asserts that many animals needlessly suffer and die in these painful tests. PETA is urging consumers to boycott Procter & Gamble in favor of cosmetic companies that have pledged not to conduct animal testing. The group has also staged direct actions and protests targeting the company.

Fur. PETA has urged citizens to write letters to four major stores (Macy's, Bloomingdale's, Neiman Marcus, and Saks Fifth Avenue) urging them to close their fur salons on the grounds of cruelty to animals and consumer fraud.

Circuses/animals in entertainment. PETA is urging citizens to boycott circuses that use animals and attend only those with human performers, such as the Cirque du Soleil or the Pickle Family Circus.

Premarin. A public relations campaign against the use of Premarin, a drug made from slaughtered horses used for estrogen-replacement therapy. The organization believes that if women knew the origins of this drug, they would use alternatives.

Fishing. PETA urges its members not to fish on the grounds of cruelty to animals and is encouraging other alternative outdoor activities to fishing. The organization has literature outlining how fishing is painful to fish and how commercial fishing is depleting the ocean's fish population.

College campaigns. PETA has compiled a list of issues for college students to work on as well as a list of suggested tactics for running effective campaigns.

Just for activists. A "how-to" list for activists; tips on effective lobbying, research, and letter writing.

Consumer products. PETA has put together a listing of companies that do and do not test their products on animals.

Health charities. A listing of health charities that test on animals and those that do not. PETA is conducting an active campaign to discourage people from giving to charities that conduct animal tests.

Animal experimentation. PETA has put together literature on some companies and laboratories that the organization believes do needlessly cruel and unnecessary experimentation on animals. The organization has also put together an action plan on how concerned citizens can stop this experimentation.

Companion animals. A list of tips on humane treatment of pets and how to research cruelty to animals by stores that sell pets.

Wildlife. PETA has documented what it believes are some of the more inhumane campaigns to exterminate wildlife.

Vegetarianism. An aggressive education campaign is being mounted by the group to promote the benefits of vegetarianism to the average consumer.

FINANCIAL FACTS

PETA is designated a 501(c)(3) not-for-profit organization and is prohibited from making campaign contributions to federal candidates for elected office.

GLENN DAIGON

Bibliography

People for the Ethical Treatment of Animals: www.peta-online.org

Spindler, Amy. "Calvin Klein Will Stop Making Furs." *New York Times,* February 11, 1994.

PLANNED PARENTHOOD FEDERATION OF AMERICA

Planned Parenthood Federation of America (PPFA) is a leader in the field of making voluntary fertility regulation—including contraception, abortion, and voluntary sterilization—available and accessible to all. Its headquarters is in New York City, and the organization has a full-time staff of 10,961. Planned Parenthood Federation of America operates more than 900 centers that provide medically supervised reproductive health services and educational programs.

It is estimated that 10 percent of all abortions in the United States are performed at Planned Parenthood clinics. PPFA conducts extensive biomedical, socioeconomic, and demographic research studies, and develops appropriate training, information, and education programs to increase knowledge of human sexuality and reproduction.

HISTORY

The roots of the Planned Parenthood Federation go back to before U.S. entry into the First World War. In 1916, social activist Margaret Sanger and her sister Ethel Byrne, both nurses, along with a third woman, Fania Mindel, opened the first birth control clinic in Brooklyn, New York. All three were arrested under New York State's Comstock laws, which forbid the dissemination of birth control information. The Comstock laws had been passed by Congress and nearly every state in the 1870s. The laws defined contraceptive information and materials as "obscene" and forbade their distribution.

The 1920s saw the first, fitful steps being taken by the family planning movement. In 1921, the first American Birth Control Conference was held in New York City and resulted in the founding, the following year, of the American Birth Control League. During the meeting, Sanger was arrested for attempting to address a mass meeting on birth control. In 1923, Sanger opened the Birth Control Clinic Research Bureau in New York for the purpose of dispensing contraceptives to women, under the supervision of a licensed physician. By 1925, the Sanger clinic on Fifth Avenue had served 1,655 women. In 1926, as president of the American Birth Control League, Sanger helped organize the first World Population Conference in Geneva, Switzerland. She later took steps toward developing a permanent organization, the Population Union, for the study of population problems. In 1929, the Birth Control Clinic Research Bureau was raided by New York City police. Physicians and nurses were arrested, and clinic supplies and confidential records were seized. The defendants were later discharged, but the birth control issue made headlines all over the country.

During the next decade, the family planning movement continued to grow. In 1935, the American Birth Control League held a mass meeting in New York City. In 1937, the American Medical Association officially recognized birth control as an integral part of medical practice and education. In 1939, the American Birth Control League and the Clinical Research Bureau merged to form the Birth Control Federation of America.

The 1940s saw the formation of PPFA as an organization. In 1942, Planned Parenthood Federation of America was adopted as the new, more comprehensive name for the Birth Control Federation of America. Contraceptive services were made available in 218 Planned Parenthood clinics across the nation. In 1947, six Protestant physicians were dismissed from the staffs of three Roman Catholic hospitals in Connecticut for refusing to withdraw from the "Committee of 100," a group of doctors who supported a birth control bill that would overturn the Comstock laws. In 1948, representatives from more than 20 nations attended the International Conference on Population and World Resources in Relation to the Family. The conference led to the formation of the International Planned Parenthood Committee. The 1960s saw the acceleration of

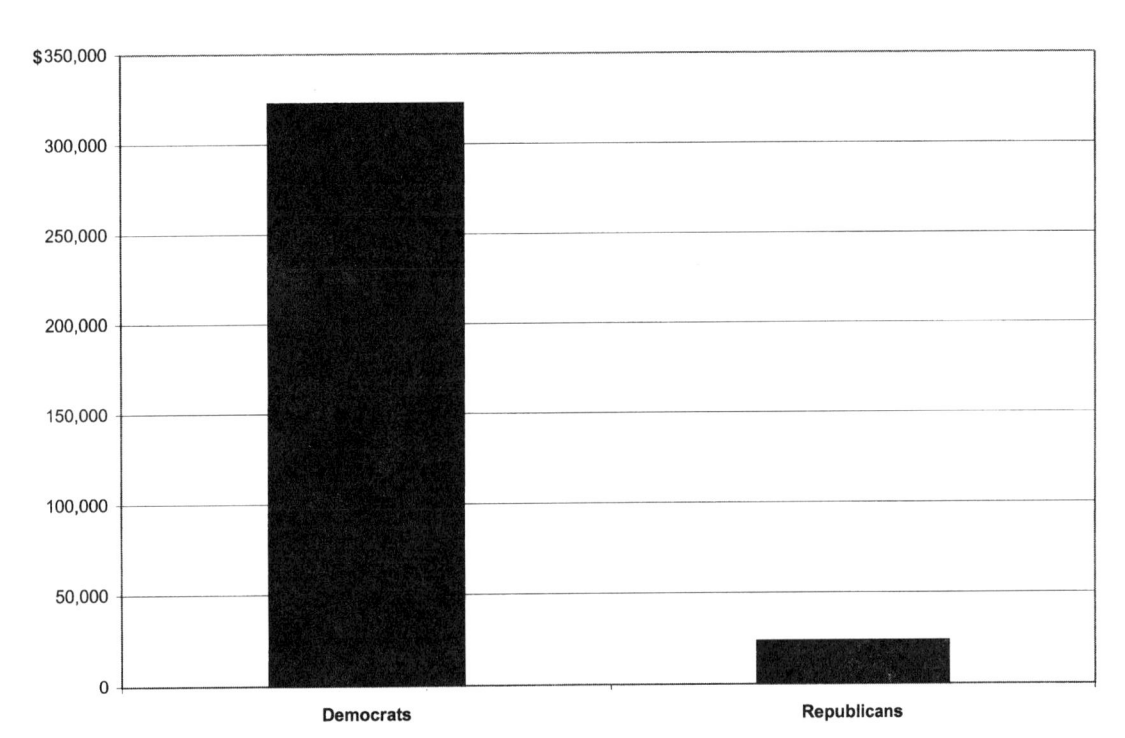

**Planned Parenthood
Political Action Committee Contributions, 1997–1998**

Data derived from official studies available from the Federal Election Commission, Washington, DC, 1997–1998.

major changes in national and international family planning policy. In 1963, the U.N. General Assembly approved a resolution on population growth and economic development. Congress amended a foreign aid bill to authorize funds for research into the problems of population growth. In 1965, the Supreme Court ruled that Connecticut's law prohibiting the use of birth control by married couples was unconstitutional. As a result, 10 states liberalized their family planning laws and began to provide tax-funded, family planning services. In 1968, Planned Parenthood membership approved policies that recognized abortion and sterilization as legitimate medical procedures, the ultimate decision resting with the individual and her physician.

The 1970s saw even more sweeping change. In 1971, Congress repealed most of the Comstock laws. That same year, Planned Parenthood established its own international program, Family Planning International Assistance (FPIA). FPIA soon became the largest non–U.S. government provider of family planning services to millions of women and men in developing countries. By 1972, over 2.5 million patients were served by U.S. family planning clinics, an increase of 200 percent since 1968. In 1973, the Supreme Court struck down state laws prohibiting abortion in the *Roe v. Wade* case. In the 1976 Supreme Court case, *Planned Parenthood of Central Missouri v. Danforth,* the U.S. Supreme Court struck down state requirements for parental and spousal consent for abortion and set aside a state prohibition against saline-induced abortions.

With the election of Ronald Reagan as president in 1980, the family planning movement went on the defensive. In 1982, Planned Parenthood, the National Abortion Reproductive Rights Action League, and other pro-choice activists successfully blocked passage of the Hatch Human Life Federalism Amendment. That same year, in *Planned Parenthood of Kansas City v. Ashcroft,* the Supreme Court found that states cannot require hospitalization for abortions after the first trimester.

However, in the late 1980s and early 1990s, the Supreme Court upheld more restrictive state abortion laws. In the 1992 case, *Planned Parenthood of Southeastern Pennsylvania v. Casey,* the Supreme Court upheld state laws requiring a 24-hour waiting period before an abortion is performed and stipulations that minors obtain parental consent for abortion services.

ACTIVITIES: CURRENT AND FUTURE

Planned Parenthood believes in the fundamental right of the individual to manage her own fertility regardless of marital status, race, sexual orientation, age, national origin, ethnicity, or residence. Toward that end, the organization has become active in a whole range of issues. Their action agenda for Congress and the states includes the following:

- **Increasing services that prevent unintended pregnancy.** PPFA is working to accomplish this goal by lobbying for legislation expanding federal funding for family planning programs, guaranteeing insurance coverage for contraceptives, and expanding federal funding for contraceptive research as well as for sexual education programs.
- **Improving the quality of reproductive health care.** PPFA is working to meet this goal by supporting legislation guaranteeing a patient's right to know about her doctor's medical advice. The group also supports bills that would require all insurers to allow women direct access to gynecological providers and would ensure patient confidentiality by protecting the privacy of healthcare information.
- **Ensuring access to abortion.** PPFA supports legislation to increase federal funding for the enforcement of the Freedom of Access to Clinic Entrances Act. The group also supports the FDA approval of the French abortion pill, RU-486.

FINANCIAL FACTS

In 1996, PPFA formed a political action committee (PAC), which first became active during the 1997–1998 election cycle. During that cycle, the Planned Parenthood Action Fund received $704,641 and spent $359,408. This latter includes $346,757 in contributions to candidates and parties, $323,007 to Democrats and $23,715 to Republicans.

GLENN DAIGON

Bibliography

Planned Parenthood Federation of America: www.plannedparenthood.org

UNION OF CONCERNED SCIENTISTS

The Union of Concerned Scientists (UCS) is a nonprofit organization dedicated to promoting environmentally friendly technology. It conducts research on energy policy, global environmental problems, transportation, and biotechnology arms control. UCS also distributes research results to the public and assists members and the public in presenting their views before government agencies and the courts. The organization conducts public education programs including nationwide events, television and radio appearances, speaking engagements, and speakers' bureaus. UCS sponsors annual national education campaigns and sees itself as forging a partnership between scientists and informed citizens to secure changes in government policy, corporate behavior, and people's actions to achieve its goals. It uses a combination of scientific analysis, policy development, and citizen advocacy to make sure that new technology is developed along what it believes to be environmentally friendly lines. From its national headquarters in Cambridge, Massachusetts, and its offices in Washington, D.C., and Berkeley, California, UCS seeks to influence government policy at the local, state, federal, and international levels. The USC is governed by an 11-member board of directors chosen by a nominating committee.

Scientists on the staff carry out technical analysis. The results of the analysis are brought to the attention of the public and policy makers through the work of public outreach, media, and legislative departments. In addition, UCS offers two nationwide activist networks—the Scientists Action Network and the Concerned Citizens Action Network—for individuals wishing to become more involved in UCS's work. Members participate in educational and advocacy programs.

UCS employs a full-time staff of 40 and has 80,000 contributing sponsors. The organization's national headquarters in Cambridge includes the following departments: government relations, communications, and executive. Most of the other departments are organized along the project category that UCS is currently working on.

HISTORY

UCS was founded in 1969 by a group of faculty and students at the Massachusetts Institute of Technology. As a single-issue group focused on developing technology that does no harm to the environment, UCS has taken on a wide range of projects. The group had its roots in the late 1960s movement to promote the Anti-Ballistic Missile Treaty. Technical analysis of the treaty was the mainstay of the group's arms control work. Through the years, it continued to use its technical skills to highlight the defects in more complicated weapons systems such as the Strategic Defense Initiative ("Star Wars") in the 1980s and the B-2 Stealth Bomber program in the 1990s. From the 1970s and through the 1990s, the group has advocated switching away from the use of polluting fossil fuels such as oil and coal. UCS advocated an energy program that favored renewable energy sources such as solar and geothermal, and pressed for safer nuclear power plants and changes in people's transportation patterns.

In 1992, the organization's research staff conducted an in-depth study of the potential for solar, wind, and biomass technology to supply power in the Midwest, an area that relies heavily on dirty coal. It then estimated the costs of developing these resources and worked up case studies in which they could be practically applied. It also researched the employment impact its model would have on the area and what government action needed to be taken to enable this new technology to compete in the marketplace. When UCS released its report in 1993, members worked with legislators and utility executives to turn the report's recommendations into concrete action.

Since the early 1970s, UCS has worked to ensure

the safety of nuclear power plants. Its nuclear safety program monitors the activities of the Nuclear Regulatory Commission and alerts the public to major risks. These efforts recently led to the shutdown of two unsafe nuclear plants—one in Massachusetts, the other in Oregon. UCS has also been involved over the years in several international coalitions, including the International Climate Network and the International Network of Engineers and Scientists for Global Responsibility.

ACTIVITIES: CURRENT AND FUTURE

Even though UCS is a single-issue group focused on developing scientific technology that is friendly to the environment, the range of issues that tie in with the organization's goal is quite broad. One look at the projects that UCS is working on currently is enough to drive that point home. UCS completed a study in 1999 that showed that the nuclear power industry was not taking the safety steps to ensure that another Three Mile Island accident wouldn't happen. Another UCS research project completed in January 1999 found that the United States could increase the share of electricity generated from renewable resources (wind, solar plants, and geothermal) to about 10 times the current level over the next 20 years and still see a 13 percent decrease in the price of electricity.

UCS has been very active in transportation issues as well. The organization announced in 1998 that it was working with General Motors and Green Mountain Energy to install a new charging station for electric cars that supplies 100 percent renewable power. UCS has worked for passage in the California legislature of several bills that would spur the development and purchase of electric cars.

UCS has also played a very active role in arms control debates. It published a study of the proposed national missile defense system. UCS found that "this Star Wars sequel is a flop. Even if it is 'technologically possible' to deploy a national missile defense, the system will not work against a real world missile threat." Over the years, UCS has developed a detailed agenda for reducing and dismantling nuclear warheads, strengthening the Treaty on Non-Proliferation of Nuclear Weapons, and increasing the U.N. Security Council's role in enforcing the treaty and peacekeeping. UCS has also marshaled scientific evidence against the effectiveness of the Strategic Defense Initiative ("Star Wars") and the B-2 Bomber.

FINANCIAL FACTS

The Union of Concerned Scientists is a (501)(c)(3) not-for-profit organization and is not allowed to contribute to partisan political campaigns.

GLENN DAIGON

Bibliography

Union of Concerned Scientists: www.ucsusa.org

Wager, Janet S., "Union of Concerned Scientists." *Environment Magazine,* May 1994.

U.S. ENGLISH

U.S. English is the leading citizens' group dedicated to making English the official language of government in the United States. It has 1.2 million members nationwide and a staff of 18. U.S. English is run by a three-member board of directors nominated for their positions by members of the previous board. The organization has two major divisions, U.S. English, Inc., and U.S. English Foundation, Inc. U.S. English, Inc., is the legislative organization, working at the state and federal levels to pass legislation to make English the official language of government and to reform bilingual education. The U.S. English Foundation, Inc., has several missions. They include helping to improve the teaching of English, studying language policy and its effects around the world, and raising the public awareness through the media about the importance of a common language. The U.S. English Foundation also maintains a database of ESL (English as a Second Language) classes across the nation. It maintains contact with its membership through legislative action alerts and newsletters. Its Washington, D.C., headquarters houses the following departments: communications/media, development, legislative/government relations, and accounting.

HISTORY

U.S. English was founded by the late California Republican Senator S.I. Hayakawa in 1983. The organization's goal is to have English declared the official language of government so that all government business would be conducted in English. It is the largest national, nonpartisan, nonprofit citizens' action group trying to make English the official language of government. The organization has been active at both the state and federal levels in trying to achieve its mission. U.S. English has been active in many of the campaigns that established English as the official language in 25 states. The organization is working in several more states, in hopes of raising that total number. U.S. English was heavily involved in supporting Proposition 227, the "English for Children" initiative that was approved by California voters in 1998. This initiative will phase out current bilingual education programs in California public schools.

In August 1996, U.S. English helped pass House Resolution 123, the Bill Emerson English Empowerment Act of 1996, in the House of Representatives by a vote of 259–169. This legislation declared English the official language of government so that most official government business would be conducted solely in English. The Senate failed to pass the measure.

Another legislative priority for the organization is the passage of the English Language Fluency Act. This bill would require that all federally funded English language instruction programs be reviewed every two years to examine their effectiveness. This bill would also eliminate the current federal requirement that 75 percent of all bilingual education funding go to programs that use native language instruction. The legislation would ensure that parents are given notification that their children have been identified as needing specialized English language instruction and guarantee them the right to determine whether they want their children enrolled in the program. This bill passed the House in 1998 and as of this writing was still awaiting action by the Senate.

ACTIVITIES: CURRENT AND FUTURE

U.S. English firmly believes that having English as the official language of government is essential and beneficial for all citizens in America. The organization believes that, by providing a common means of communication, it unites all Americans, who now speak more than 329 languages. U.S. English also believes that it encourages

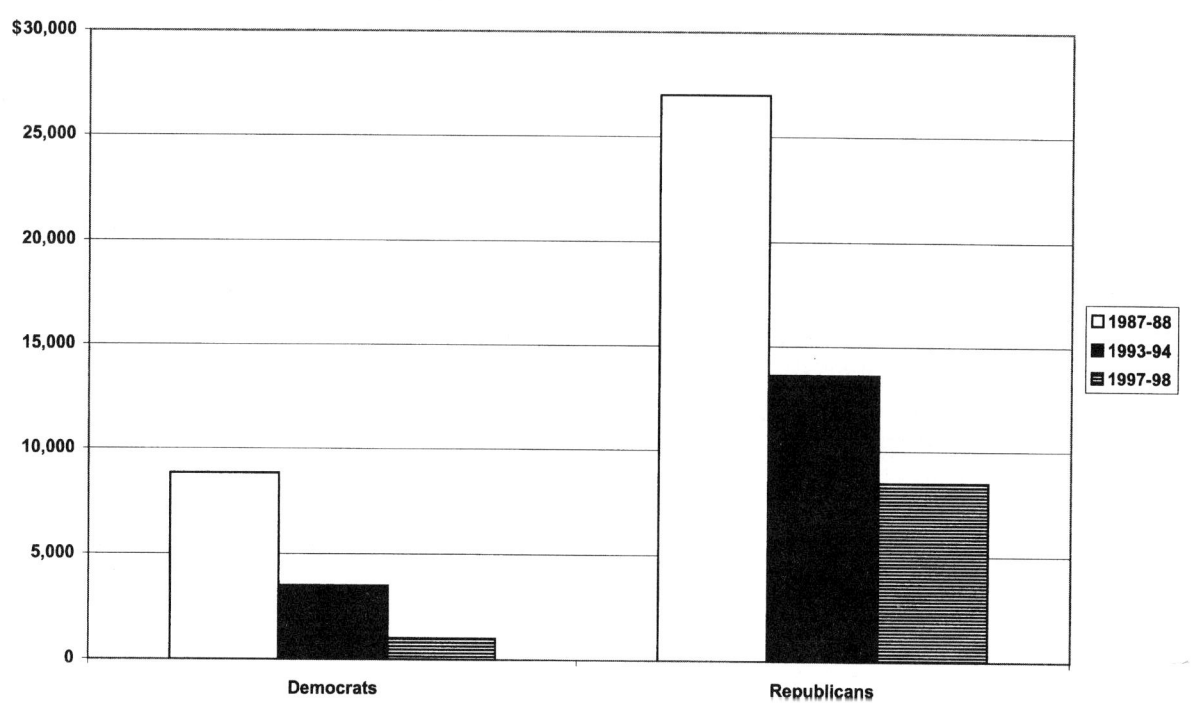

**U.S. English
Political Action Committee Contributions**

[Bar chart showing PAC contributions to Democrats and Republicans for election cycles 1987-88, 1993-94, and 1997-98. Democrats: approximately $9,000 (1987-88), $3,500 (1993-94), $1,000 (1997-98). Republicans: approximately $27,000 (1987-88), $13,500 (1993-94), $8,500 (1997-98).]

Data derived from official studies available from the Federal Election Commission, Washington, DC, 1987–1998.

immigrants to learn English much more quickly. The organization supports the reform of bilingual education to favor those programs that are English-intensive, short-term, and transitional. It has been sharply critical of some bilingual programs that they view as not English-intensive enough and ineffective in bringing immigrants into the mainstream of American society.

To bolster their arguments, U.S. English likes to point to the problems of other countries who have not adopted one official language. The examples of Canada and India are cited by the organization in making their case for English as the official language for the United States. In 1969, Canada officially adopted a bilingual system, putting the French language and English language on equal footing. U.S. English claims it costs the Canadian government, at the federal level, $1.3 million a day to duplicate services, forms, and other communications in a second language. According to the organization, a mere five years after Canada's bilingual status was established, the province of Quebec adopted French as its only language. U.S. English claims that this policy has threatened national Canadian unity. It says that some of the symptoms include Toronto baseball fans jeering when the national anthem is broadcast in French, Quebec officials making it illegal for store owners to post signs in English, and English-speaking Canadians defiling the Quebecois flag. Recent ballot initiatives on whether Quebec should become an independent country have added fuel to the fire for those who argue that bilingualism leads to national disunity.

India is another example cited by U.S. English of the dangers of not having one official language. There are more than 12 languages spoken on the Indian subcontinent. Because there is no official language, people in different regions often cannot understand one another. The inability of government officials to communicate swiftly and efficiently, U.S. English says, can lead to paralysis. The group further argues that divisiveness and chaos have resulted when governments have granted official status to multiple languages in such countries as Belgium, South Africa, Sri Lanka, and Afghanistan. U.S. English points to signs of the same thing happening in this country, citing the following examples:

- In 1994, the Internal Revenue Service printed and distributed 500,000 copies of tax form 1040 in

Spanish. The total cost was $118,000, and only 718 were returned.
- California offers driver's license exams in 30 different languages, New York in 23, and Michigan in 20. In all, 38 states currently offer the exam in languages other than English.
- The Los Angeles City Council prints all its public notices in six foreign languages in addition to English, doubling its budget to $1 million.
- The U.S. Postal Service has printed 1 million brochures designed to help clerks communicate with customers in nine languages, which will be distributed nationwide.
- The Social Security Administration is hiring more bilingual staff in an effort to "dramatically reduce reliance on the middlemen in developing claims of non-English-speaking applicants."

The organization does not see itself as anti-immigrant or antidiversity. In fact, it sees its efforts as being squarely in the interests of newcomers to this country. U.S. English points to studies done by the U.S. Labor Department showing that immigrants learn English faster when there is less native language support around them. The group also points to census data showing that immigrant income rises about 30 percent as a result of learning English. U.S. English maintains that only by encouraging immigrants to learn English can they truly enjoy the economic opportunities available to them in this country. The organization believes passage of H.R. 123 declaring English the official language of the United States the best means to achieve that end. The organization is working to reintroduce the measure in the next session of Congress.

Another legislative issue in which U.S. English has been actively involved, and one that will most likely come up again in the near future is the issue of Puerto Rican statehood. The organization strongly criticized the House of Representatives in 1998 when it voted to allow the island to hold a plebiscite on the issue. U.S. English Chairman/CEO Mauro Mujica declared: "Swallowing up a Latin American nation is a recipe for disaster. Less than 25 percent of the Puerto Rican population speak English and only 16 percent consider themselves American. This is after 100 years of association with the United States. In the rush to grant statehood, we could be creating our own Quebec." Mujica continued: "The United States is an English-speaking country. Just as immigrants to the United States are expected to speak English, a new state is to become an English-speaking state. Congress has the power to require Puerto Rico to adopt English as a condition of statehood. They put language requirements on Louisiana, Oklahoma, New Mexico, and Arizona. Why should Puerto Rico be any different? If the people of Puerto Rico want to preserve their language and culture, statehood is not an option."

FINANCIAL FACTS

The U.S. English political action committee (PAC) has given decreasingly small sums of money to federal candidates over the years. In the 1987–1988 election cycle, the organization donated approximately $35,000 to candidates for Congress, with over three-quarters going to Republicans. By the 1997–1998 election cycle, however, the total amount donated to candidates for Congress had dropped to under $10,000, with about 80 percent going to Republicans.

GLENN DAIGON

Bibliography

De la Pena, Fernando. *Democracy or Babel? The Case for Official U.S. English*. Washington, DC: U.S. English, 1991.

U.S. English: www.us-english.org

U.S. TERM LIMITS

U.S. Term Limits (USTL) is run by a 12-person board of directors. Its national office is located in Washington, D.C., with field offices in Spokane, Washington, and Denver, Colorado. A third field office is slated to be opened in Georgia or Florida. USTL supports its affiliates in the states through information research, voter education, and outreach programs as well as independent financial expenditures for issue advertisements in selected congressional races.

HISTORY

The organization's history goes back to 1990. In that year, the research group Citizens for Congressional Reform (CCR) was founded. It was almost the sole source of the funding behind a very far-reaching term limits initiative on the ballot in Washington State. That initiative went down to defeat. A short time later, some term limits opponents in Michigan filed a complaint questioning a list of donors submitted by CCR; the group soon disbanded after that complaint.

However, a wealthy New York businessman, Howard Rich, took over the disbanded group and changed its name to U.S. Term Limits. By anyone's measure, USTL's first few years were spectacularly successful. In 1992, its first year of operation under new direction, USTL donated at least $1.8 million to various term limits campaigns. Ballot initiatives limiting the terms of state and federal officeholders appeared before the voters in 14 states and were easily approved in 13. Presidential candidate Ross Perot made term limits a big issue in his strong race for the White House that year. In 1994, USTL helped put term limits before the voters in eight states and the District of Columbia. D.C. voters and the voters in seven of the eight states passed term limit measures. That same year, the Republican Party gained control of Congress by using it as an issue against the Democratic majority. Republicans even included a term limits pledge in their famous "Contract with America."

After 1994, the term limits movement lost momentum. The Supreme Court ruled term limits on members of Congress and senators to be unconstitutional, throwing out the results of many ballot initiatives. The Republican majority refused to pass a term limits bill, despite many repeated tries. Many believed that when the Republican Party was in the minority it didn't have much to lose by advocating limits. Once it gained a narrow majority, it wasn't going to do anything to jeopardize its hold on Congress. In fact, some of the Republican—and Democratic—House candidates who ran and won on the issue in 1994 of staying in office no more than three terms (six years) are having second thoughts about keeping their pledges.

USTL continues to believe that, despite some recent setbacks, it has been the overall winner in the last eight years on this issue. It cites the fact that the courts have upheld the constitutionality of term limits for state and local officeholders, even though they struck down limits for Congress. It cites statistics showing that, prior to 1992, fewer than 300 cities and towns had term limits. Today, over 3,000 have adopted term limits, including New York, Los Angeles, San Francisco, and Washington, D.C. USTL also points out that, prior to 1992, only 29 governors and no state legislatures were term limited. Today, there are now 39 governors and 19 state legislatures that are term limited, including California, Florida, Michigan, and Missouri. Overall, USTL has felt that its efforts have been successful over the last eight years.

ACTIVITIES: CURRENT AND FUTURE

After the success of U.S. Term Limits in 1992 and 1994 in passing term limits ballot issues at the local and state levels, and the organization's failure in the GOP Congress and in the courts to enact term limits for federal officeholders, the organization has launched a new campaign, the Term Limits Declaration. The declaration asks each candidate for the U.S. Congress to pledge himself or herself to limit service to no more than three terms in the House and two terms in the Senate. USTL plans on heavily publicizing, during the 2000 elections, which candidates did and did not take the term limits pledge. USTL has publicly targeted candidates running in 2000 who broke their three-term pledge.

Term Limits Declaration

I commit to be a citizen legislator, not a career politician, and therefore declare and pledge to the citizens of my state and district: I will not serve in the United States House of Representatives for more than 3 two-year terms.

Printed Name of Candidate _____

Signature of Candidate _____

Signature of Witness _____

Date _____

District/State _____

Only congressional service after 1998 will be considered when calculating service for the purposes of this declaration. Service in office for one-half a term shall be deemed service for a full term unless the legislator is elected to fill an unexpired term.
CITIZEN LEGISLATORS. NOT CAREER POLITICIANS.

USTL is planning to place initiatives on the ballot in California, Colorado, and Florida that would allow self-limiting candidates to inform voters of their self-limit pledges. USTL would do this by placing the statement "Signed Term Limits Pledge to serve no more than 3 terms in the U.S. House" next to candidates' names on primary and general election ballots. Voters then would see in writing on the ballot which candidates signed USTL's Term Limits Pledge and which ones did not. The organization believes that once that difference is spelled out clearly to the voters those candidates who signed the pledge should have an easy time winning. This will help the organization meet its stated goal of replacing professional politicians with "citizen legislators."

FINANCIAL FACTS

In 1992, term limits committees in 14 states raised $5.9 million. Eighty percent of that money, or $4.7 million, came from four term limits groups and 624 donors of $600 or more. The 624 donors supplied $2.5 million of the $4.7 million. Of the remaining $2.2 million, U.S. Term Limits supplied $1.8 million (roughly 30 percent of the total $5.9 million spent), with the three remaining smaller term limits groups supplying $400,000. In 1994, USTL donated at least $1.8 million to various term limits campaigns. Campaigns in Alaska, Colorado, Idaho, Maine, Massachusetts, Nebraska, Nevada, and Utah were all financed by USTL. The following is a selective state-by-state breakdown of financial expenditures to advance term limits initiatives:

- In Alaska, almost all of the $40,000 spent by term limits advocates came from USTL to pass a statewide ballot issue limiting terms for politicians.
- In Idaho, USTL contributed $66,000 of the $82,000 raised on behalf of the term limits ballot issue.
- In Maine, USTL donated $163,500 of the $171,000 raised.
- In Nebraska, USTL provided $219,000 of the $256,000 spent on the term limits ballot issue.
- In Nevada, USTL donated $40,000 of the $153,000 spent to pass the term limits ballot measure.
- In Utah, a total of $169,000 was raised to pass a term limits initiative, $32,000 of it coming from USTL.
- In Colorado, $97,400 was raised to pass a term-

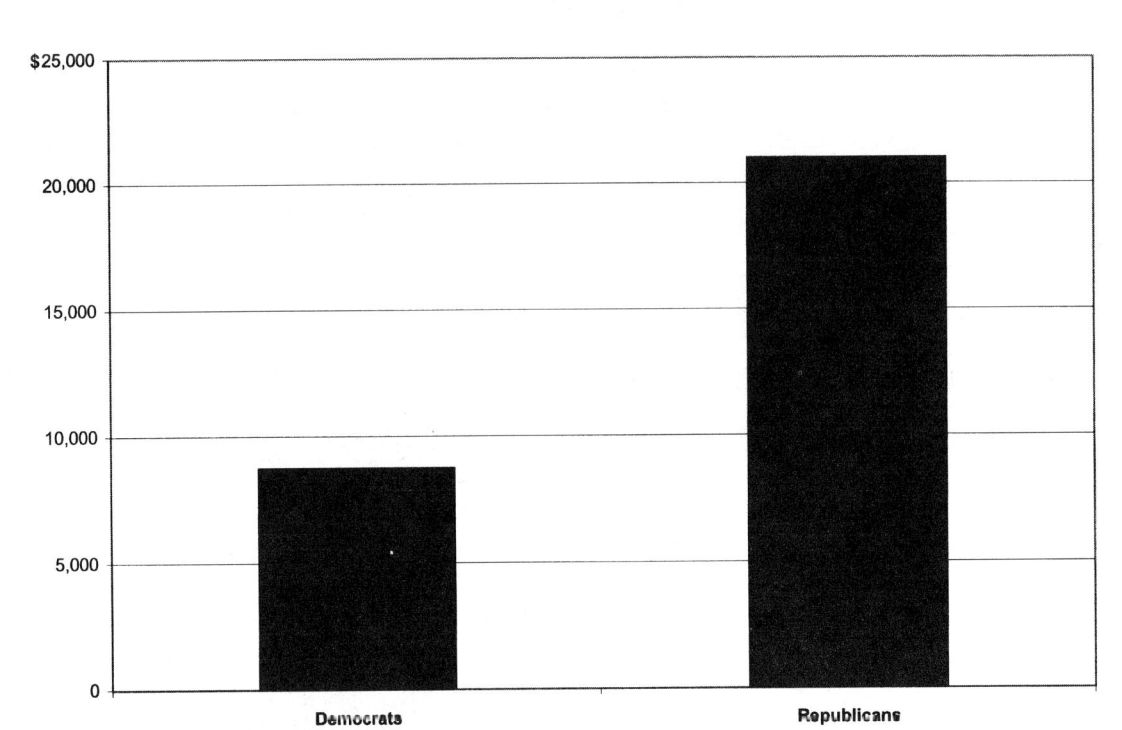

**U.S. Term Limits
Political Action Committee Contributions, 1997–1998**

Democrats	Republicans
~$8,800	~$21,200

Data derived from official studies available from the Federal Election Commission, Washington, DC, 1997–1998.

limiting ballot initiative, with $83,000 coming from USTL.

All told, USTL raised 70 percent of the $1.4 million raised to pass 1994 term limits initiatives on state ballots around the nation.

GLENN DAIGON

Bibliography

Kamber, Victor. *Giving Up on Democracy: Why Term Limits Are Bad for America.* Washington, DC: Regnery, 1995.

U.S. Term Limits: www.ustermlimits.org

Young, Amy. "The Money Behind the Movement." *Common Cause Magazine,* Summer 1993.

ZERO POPULATION GROWTH

Zero Population Growth (ZPG) is an education and advocacy group with its headquarters located in Washington, D.C., and a field office located in Sacramento, California. It has 20 chapters around the nation and over 50,000 dues-paying members. A 16-member board of directors runs ZPG, each of whom is nominated by recommendations from individual people or groups.

The national headquarters is active in lobbying Congress on both national and international population and reproductive rights issues. Much of this effort is accomplished through the ZPG Activist Network—a coalition of ZPG members, staff, and chapters that work together on population issues. Network members are kept abreast of important issues through timely "alerts" as well as the organization's bimonthly newspaper, The ZPG Reporter. Legislative alerts and "letters to the editor" are some of the tools that the Network uses to keep the grassroots membership involved.

ZPG's Population Education Network coordinates over 250 teacher training workshops each year as well as publishing classroom texts aimed at grades K–12. One of the Population Education Network's most successful efforts has been the Population Education Trainers Network. Staffers under this program were trained in workshops on how to incorporate environmental and population issues into the classroom. The number of workshops increased to 165 in 1998. Since 1975, the program has helped more than 1 million students learn about population issues.

ZPG also has a very active Speakers Network program. Started in 1991, the program has volunteer members present ZPG's message to community and civic groups, school classes, and college students and others interested in learning about the impact of population growth. To date, hundreds of presentations have been made to groups across the country.

ZPG's national headquarters in Washington, D.C., houses departments that handle the following activities: outreach and communications, population education, membership development, communications, government relations, field and outreach, and finance and administration.

HISTORY

The roots of ZPG go back over 30 years to the publication of the best-selling book, The Population Bomb. Encouraged by the book's popularity, the author Paul Ehrlich, together with lawyer Charles Bower and academic Charles Remington, founded ZPG in 1968. ZPG worked to show the link between overpopulation, falling living standards, and environmental destruction. Using bumper stickers, posters, public service announcements, and magazine advertisements, ZPG sought to change the country's attitudes toward family size. Some of their catchier slogans included, "The pill in time saves nine!" "This line is too long. Join ZPG!" and "Just have two." By 1972, the organization had 35,000 members.

After 1970, legislative change in population-related fields came very quickly. Congress repealed the Comstock laws, which blocked the distribution of contraceptives. In 1973, the Supreme Court legalized abortion. Environmental and energy issues became important to the average American. ZPG realized that its narrowly focused message "stop at two" needed to be updated to keep up with the rapidly changing times. ZPG joined forces with pro-choice legislation to lobby Congress and the states to protect a woman's right to choose. The group also works with cities to implement growth plans that avoid urban sprawl and suburban overcrowding.

ZPG feels that it deserves a big share of the credit for the change in the U.S. fertility rate. In the early 1960s, the rate was 3.4 children per woman; it had decreased to 1.8 by 1975. The time it would take for the U.S. population to double increased by 14 years between 1968 and 1975.

ZPG's classroom programs try to link population and environmental quality. Cofounder Paul Ehrlich, stated: "Solving the population problem will only buy you a ticket to solve the other problems. It won't solve them in itself."

In the 1990s ZPG continued to lobby both the federal and state governments on their traditional bread-and-butter issues such as securing funding for family planning programs and requiring population studies to be part of the school curriculum. But ZPG has also become involved in a broad range of issues such as protecting a woman's right to choose, addressing the root causes of Third World immigration to the United States, and pushing for equal rights for women. The organization believes all of these problems are connected to overpopulation and need to be addressed.

ACTIVITIES: CURRENT AND FUTURE

ZPG has had one constant mission over the years: to bring the human population and its activities back into balance with earth's resources and activities. Toward that one goal, ZPG has defined its main mission as the adoption of public policies that slow population growth to a more manageable level. On a broad basis, ZPG has backed measures such as a national population policy, access to safe and affordable contraceptives, reproductive choice, school-based sex education and health services programs, voluntary family planning programs, and funding for international family planning programs.

ZPG's legislative goals are in sync with its stated policy mission. Most recently, ZPG has supported efforts in Congress to restore U.S. funding to the United Nations Population Fund. ZPG has backed proposals in Congress to limit suburban sprawl in the United States—"smart growth" legislation that would channel new growth to existing developed areas. At the state level, ZPG has backed legislation introduced in 24 states that would require coverage of prescription contraceptives by health insurers. ZPG has supported repealing the Hyde Amendment, which bars public Medicaid funding from paying for abortions for women who cannot afford them. In the 1997–1998 session of Congress, ZPG lobbied heavily around prochoice issues. The organization supported repealing the law that prohibits female military personnel overseas from obtaining abortions with their own funds at military hospitals. It opposed a bill to prevent international family planning providers that offer abortion services or participate in discussing abortion as an option from receiving any U.S. population funding. This provision was known as the Global Gag Rule. ZPG also opposed an amendment to prohibit the Food and Drug Administration from using federal funds to test, develop, or approve any drug for chemically induced abortions.

In the 1997–1998 Congress, ZPG supported a law that would have prohibited the Office of Personnel Management, the personnel office for federal employees, from entering into a contract with a health care provider that excludes prescription contraceptive drugs. It blocked an amendment that would have required parental notification or written consent before minors could obtain contraception services from federally funded planning clinics.

FINANCIAL FACTS

Zero Population Growth is designated a 501(c)(3) not-for-profit organization and cannot contribute to candidates running for federal political office.

GLENN DAIGON

Bibliography
Sherman, Dianne. "Zero Population Growth." *Environment Magazine,* November 1993.
Zero Population Growth: www.zpg.org

SECTION TWELVE
IDENTITY

Identity groups are citizen groups that often have cut across traditional and ideological lines emphasizing group rights or individual rights, with protection on the basis of some group characteristic. Over the past 30 years, traditional class-based or economic interest groups have been joined, in what has been termed an "explosion," by interest groups that either have had a sole noneconomic focus or have had mixed noneconomic emphases with the traditional economic focus. Citizen groups, formed from the social movements of the 1960s—most notably the civil rights and feminist movements but also the general drive toward post-materialism and quality of life issues—began to dot the political landscape in the United States and elsewhere. Civil rights, human rights, ideological, religious rights, environmental, and other groups appeared during the 1960s to lobby government, stage protests, and engage in advocacy and service on behalf of either their members or for the general citizenry (both national and international). Still, citizen groups in total comprise less than 10 percent of all interest groups officially registered in the United States and, though they have the ability to stage large-scale protest, are generally less well funded and powerful than the traditional economically based interest groups (though exceptions are notable to this general rule).

IDENTITY GROUPS DEFINED

Collective identity movements are broad. They range from ethnic groups (racial, linguistic, or other), feminist groups, the elderly, veterans, and even smokers or nonsmokers. Group, or collective, identity is a crucial variable in understanding particular types of political behavior. Identity politics can be based either on a self-help or isolationist orientation (potentially either a conservative or radical orientation) or on egalitarian social, economic, or political policies achieved through integrative politics (a traditional liberal orientation). Identity groups, though their critics might suggest otherwise, do not fit neatly into a liberal or conservative categorization; they cut across different types of interest groups and the liberal-conservative spectrum.

Identity politics is based upon a shared group identity or a shared sense of common interests that may be based upon historical, experiential, or some other form of solidarity. Claus Offe, an expert on collective action and identity politics, has termed collective identity as based on a "shared definition of the field of opportunity and constraints . . . [and the] unity is a result rather than a point of departure." Identities are not constant and may either be self-selected or societally determined; the importance of identity may either increase or decrease over time, and identities may be contradictory or create tensions either for individuals, since one may have numerous and conflicting identities (for example, an African American lesbian possesses three distinct identities), or between groups and organizations that share similar identity classification. These identities may be ascribed—those that are essentially unchangeable such as ethnicity, language, gender, or sexual orientation. They may also be "assigned identities," which may be based on individual beliefs or sentiments on an issue. Identity politics, at its core, attempts to change power relationships between groups and to achieve group gains, which may be economic, political, or social in scope.

Often, though not always, identity politics represents a challenge between out-groups, or marginalized actors, such as feminist, minority, or gay organizations, and dominant actors. These marginalized groups seek to change the nature of the relationship between themselves and the dominant group, either through accommodation or through separation. Struggle is central to many forms of identity politics and often involves grassroots or nontraditional forms of activity such as protest behavior, civil disobedience, and (in rare circumstances) violence. These grassroots movements have often formed in order to counter governmental discrimination; thus, they operated outside the traditional policy arena and rejected the governmental sphere in favor of identity as the organizing vehicle to achieve their individual and group goals.

Identity groups that are liberal in their orientation seek to develop strategies for negotiation and inclusion within the existing policy framework to supplement their challenging behavior. Over time, demonstrations are supplemented by traditional direct lobbying activity by organizations as they adapt to changing political and social circumstances. Many scholars suggest that groups that begin with challenging behavior are often moderated in their mode of operation by successes in the political arena. Identity politics has neither inherently negative nor positive political effects on society. Negative effects of extreme identity politics are plentiful; for example, one can look to the recent crises in the Balkans as an example of extreme identity politics having destructive effects. Others have noted that identity politics has been influential in changing society, aiding countries in their achievement of democratic goals of liberty and equality in the United States and elsewhere.

GROUPS PROFILED: DIVERSITY OF IDENTITY GROUPS

In this section of the anthology, nine identity groups are profiled in exploring the range and scope of identity interest groups. They were selected due to the variance of the groups, their goals, strategies, and resources, and their success in the policy arena.

Two groups profiled are African American civil rights organizations. The National Association for the Advancement of Colored People (NAACP) is the oldest African-American civil rights organization. Founded in 1909, the NAACP has maintained throughout its history nonviolent and multiracial advocacy strategies. It has had numerous successes, especially during the civil rights era of the 1950s and 1960s; it was at the forefront of changes in educational access, voting rights, civil rights protections, and affirmative action legislation. The Congress of Racial Equality (CORE), conversely, is an African-American civil rights organization that has changed its orientation from its nonviolent origins to an armed orientation, to a conservative self-help strategy since the 1970s. Comprising two of the "Big Four" civil rights organizations, the NAACP and CORE represent two different orientations and strategies and suggest that identity groups do not fit neatly into a liberal or conservative (or even a radical) label.

Two gay rights organizations, the National Gay and Lesbian Task Force (NGLTF) and the Human Rights Campaign (HRC) are profiled. Both groups represent gay and lesbian concerns and are liberal and mainstream in their orientation and strategies as opposed to more radicalized gay organizations, such as Outrage! They are traditional civil rights organizations emphasizing equal treatment under the law for gays and lesbians (along with bisexuals and transgendered citizens). However, although they are similar in goals, unlike the two African-American groups profiled, they differ in their strategies. Both organizations are nominally national in their orientation; the HRC, however, directs most of its activity at the national level and congressional campaigns and lobbying, whereas the NGLTF emphasizes state and local strategies.

Two feminist organizations are profiled, Emily's List and the National Organization for Women (NOW). While both agree on many political issues, especially the protection of reproductive rights, which is central to both groups' missions, they seek achievement of goals through different means. NOW, founded in 1966, is a full-service organization that engages in advocacy, litigation, grassroots lobbying, direct lobbying of members of Congress, and, through a separate political action committee (PAC), providing campaign funds to candidates who share its political philosophy regardless of gender. Emily's List, founded more recently in 1985, reflects a changing political orientation among feminists. Emily's List places its efforts solely on providing campaign funds to pro-choice Democratic women to increase the number of women legislators and executives. Thus, while agreeing on goals, it, like the NGLTF and the HRC, differs on the methods of operation.

A seventh group profiled is the American Indian Movement (AIM). AIM is an excellent example of a new social movement that grew up against the backdrop of the civil rights and antiwar movements of the 1960s. In its early years, AIM engaged in national and armed protest against the American government and has sought self-help policies and changes in federal policies toward Native Americans. The organization has shifted its emphasis from national politics over the past 30 years to locally based strategies and ceases to be influential at the national level with the exception of isolated cases.

Two "assigned" identity groups are profiled. The

American Legion is a veterans' organization that campaigns for "patriotic" issues and for the rights of veterans in employment and medical care. It is a large and broad-based organization that is somewhat conservative in its orientation and engages in both direct lobbying as well as service to its constituents and to youth. The American Association of Retired Persons (AARP), one of America's most successful lobbying groups, coalesces around the shared characteristic of age. Its emphasis is on service to its membership and to lobbying efforts to protect the rights of the elderly, including Social Security and Medicare.

The profiled groups have some similar and some different issues that they have stressed. The gay, feminist, and ethnic groups have demanded equal treatment under the law, protection against police brutality, employment nondiscrimination, and general civil rights protections. They have been interested in providing services to members in order to aid in economic and social advancement (this latter point is especially true of the feminist and minority organizations). The American Legion and the AARP have focused almost entirely on membership-driven activities and the provision of services, although the American Legion has expanded its scope to include service and programs aimed at nonmembers, especially the young.

The organizations vary in terms of their size and influence. Although for some groups, precise membership figures are impossible to determine, the American Indian Movement is a relatively small organization with limited financial means reflecting the marginalized status of Native Americans. The African-American groups have maintained significant membership levels, with the NAACP's 500,000 members dwarfing its rival, CORE. The HRC maintains a significant membership level of 250,000, while NOW also counts an active membership of approximately 250,000. The largest organizations are the two "assigned" identity groups: the American Legion comprises a membership of 3 million while the AARP's membership tops 33 million.

Although membership levels are not necessarily an indicator of success, the larger organizations generally have significant budgets that aid in organizing, in providing services, and in lobbying governmental officials. The AARP's $450 million budget enables it to maintain nearly two dozen lobbyists and a think tank. In comparison, the American Legion maintains a significant budget of over $60 million, which has aided its lobbying efforts and given the organization the ability to provide essential services to its members. The other organizations maintain significantly smaller budgets; for example, the HRC has a budget of $15 million, while the NGLTF has a budget of $3.6 million.

Most of the groups (with the exception of Emily's List, which is explicitly partisan) are nonpartisan in orientation. Three of the groups—Emily's List, NOW, and the HRC—maintain PACs providing campaign funds to candidates. And although they are technically non-partisan, the groups' contributions have gone mostly, almost solely, to Democratic candidates. Emily's List has emerged as one of the strongest financial political organizations, with members contributing over $7 million to candidates in 1998. The HRC contributed nearly $1 million through its PAC, while NOW's PAC is relatively small, contributing less than $200,000 during the 1997–1998 election cycle. In addition to political contributions, almost all of the organizations conduct voter registration drives in some form. Emily's List, for example, has spent $10 million on a voter registration and turnout campaign.

Most identity groups, as most citizen groups, are classified by the Federal Election Commission (FEC) as 501(c)(3) organizations. This status denotes that the group advocates positions but does not lobby Congress; this enables contributions made to the group to be tax-deductible. In order to ensure the tax-deductibility of contributions, which encourages citizens to contribute more, most citizen groups do not formally endorse candidates for office though they do utilize their budgets to highlight differences between candidates with no formal endorsement. Those organizations with PACs (such as the HRC, Emily's List, and NOW) maintain a 501(c)(4) PAC, which enables the PAC to make endorsements and engage in partisan politics. In fact, in keeping with a trend in American politics, some of the most powerful lobbying groups in the United States do not maintain PACs, such as the AARP, which is the most powerful of the identity groups.

AREAS OF INTEREST

Many of these organizations were born in the 1960s or 1970s or increased in strength during the progressivism of the era. Throughout much of the century, identity politics focused on the plight of African Americans in the United States. Although the NAACP was created in the early part of this century, its major successes came during the 1950s and 1960s. The success of the African-American civil rights movement suggested a ripe political and social environment for the creation and successful entry of new and diverse groups. Feminist organizations, such as NOW, began to emerge to represent a voice for women.

Spurred by the success of the women's and African-American civil rights movements, gay organizations began to dot the political landscape after the 1969 Stonewall Riots in Greenwich Village in New York. The NGLTF was born in 1973 as part of the broader-based effort to enhance civil rights protections for gays and lesbians and other marginalized groups. Quickly, new organizations were founded as well, and by the mid 1980s numerous gay organizations were created—such as the Human Rights Campaign, among others.

The American Indian Movement was also born in the struggle for civil rights in the 1960s. Labeled the "Black Panther Party" of Native Americans, AIM focused not on integration and individual rights protections—an emphasis of NOW, the NGLTF, and the NAACP—but rather on group rights and group identity. It sought sovereignty for the Native Nations either by negotiations with the federal government or through armed protest. While they have, in the words of one observer, "mellowed" since their founding, AIM still maintains a separatist philosophy.

The American Legion is the second oldest of the groups profiled, with its founding in 1919. It originated in the aftermath of the First World War to lobby on behalf of soldiers reentering society after their war service. It perceived an important bond inherent in military service and sought to utilize this commonality to lobby for beneficial policies and to engage in education and advocacy. The AARP was founded in the 1950s and was reflective of the growing elderly population in the United States. As life expectancy has increased, AARP has sought protections of both retirees and the working elderly.

The interests of the organizations are diverse. The marginalized groups (African American, gay, and feminist) have emphasized affirmative action protections along with employment/educational protections. In addition, feminist organizations have sought to protect reproductive rights, while all three have sought protection against violence; in the case of women, NOW's emphasis has generally been on domestic violence against women, whereas African American and gay organizations have emphasized protection from police brutality and hate crimes, especially salient in the wake of the dragging death of James Byrd, Jr., an African American male, in Texas, and the sadistic murder of an openly gay college student in Wyoming (Matthew Shepard).

The political context for these organizations is quite complex at the end of the twentieth century. For African American, feminist, and gay organizations, they have sought increasing civil rights protections through affirmative action policies, stricter enforcement of laws on the books, or, in the case of gays and lesbians, new statutes to protect against discrimination. The political climate in the United States is relatively good for gays and lesbians. Tolerance among the public has increased and, for women and African Americans, enormous strides and gains were made in the past 30 years. Coupling these facts with the election of a sympathetic figure, Bill Clinton, to the White House in 1992 suggests that a favorable climate was created for either protections or advancements.

The picture, however, is murkier. First, with the election of the Republican Congress in 1994, emphasizing traditional family values, there have been policies perceived to be unfriendly toward all three groups (as well as the AARP); and devolution has changed the battleground from Washington to the states and made the struggle 50 battles rather than one. Second, there has been a political backlash against affirmative action and policies created in the 1960s and 1970s to protect women and minorities, as well as against what conservatives have labeled the "special rights" agenda of gay and lesbian organizations. Especially in the states, but in the Republican Party generally, there has been an attack on prior gains, forcing NOW and the NAACP into fighting a rear-guard battle to protect their victories rather than pushing for new policies. Thus, numerous ballot measures have sought to eliminate affirmative action, laws have sought to curtail reproductive rights, and initiatives in some states, such as Colorado, have targeted gay and lesbian protections or sought to overturn them after their passage. Thus, while President Clinton supports many issues central to the NAACP, NOW, the NGLTF, and the HRC, an unfriendly Congressional and state environment has limited the ability of these organizations to realize political success.

For groups such as the AARP, the climate is also complex, although the AARP has been singularly successful in maintaining its power in Washington. Politicians tread lightly when suggesting reform of Medicare or Social Security due to the clout of the AARP. While proposed changes would suggest a struggle for the AARP, in fact it has been successful in blunting reforms and ensuring that both Democrats and Republicans will seek AARP support before proposing overhauls. Thus, although change may be in the offing for these two programs, the support and power of the AARP in

Washington ensures that they will be central to the reform process.

TYPES OF ACTIVITIES

Identity groups are diverse in their scope as well as their activities. They participate in traditional lobbying and campaigning, grassroots lobbying activities, public education, and the provision of services.

Traditional lobbying strategies take two important forms for identity groups. First, they engage in direct lobbying of legislators, executives, and government agencies on policy. They provide congressional testimony, aid in the writing of legislation, conduct studies, and provide information to members of Congress. They also produce ratings of members of Congress on key issues to show their voting record. The American Legion is pivotal in influencing governmental agency decisions; it is the only veterans' group with membership staffing the federal government Veterans Administration insurance centers. Some groups expend considerable resources on this type of lobbying activity; the AARP estimates it spends $6 million on lobbying, whereas the American Legion spends nearly $250,000. A think tank supplements this activity for the AARP and the NGLTF, and many other organizations staff full-time experienced lobbyists.

Second, the HRC, NOW, and Emily's List maintain PACs. These committees provide essential funds to candidates and to political parties. Emily's List, in enhancing its political clout, successfully utilized a fundraising technique known as bundling—a strategy to circumvent FEC regulations on PACs. FEC rules limit PAC contributions to candidates to $5,000; Emily's List bundles individual contributions of its members to candidates by having members write checks to candidates (it publishes a list of those preferred) and send the checks to Emily's List, which then forwards the checks to the candidate. This strategy has been extremely successful, and other organizations have used Emily's List as a model.

Although traditional lobbying activity has been important, grassroots pressure tactics are central to marginalized groups' activity. The NAACP and CORE initiated nonviolent protest strategies; gay organizations, African-American groups, and women's groups have utilized large-scale demonstrations such as NOW's 1992 pro-choice rally, which brought 750,000 to Capitol Hill, and the proposed Millennium March on Washington, D.C., cosponsored by the HRC. Additionally, these groups have used letter-writing campaigns and other grassroots efforts that have become technologically sophisticated with the creation of the Internet. For example, the HRC and NOW each maintain an Internet mailing list that provides "action alerts" to members to encourage immediate activity. These activities have been essential in mobilizing their constituencies. AIM has been unique among these nine groups in utilizing grassroots armed protest to seek redress of grievances.

Public education is an essential strategy for identity groups. They have sought, through such activities as media outreach and sponsorship of forums, to articulate the positions of the organizations. The HRC has even sponsored a program called OutVote, which was a convention to put gay and lesbian issues in the limelight.

Service-related activities for members and nonmembers have been at the core of activities of many groups. AIM has sponsored a Legal Rights Center to provide its members with legal advice; the NAACP has sponsored numerous programs, such as ACT-SO, to encourage excellence in technology and science among African American youths; CORE hosts a "boot camp" to rehabilitate troubled youths and sponsors Project Independence, designed to help single mothers to break welfare dependency; the AARP sponsors numerous programs aimed at breast cancer detection, employment, and other activities to protect the elderly; and the American Legion sponsors the Boy Scouts and spends an additional $5 million on youth-related programs. Although just a sample, these activities reflect the diversity of activities of these organizations.

MICHAEL LEVY

Bibliography

Aronowitz, Stanley. *The Politics of Identity: Class, Culture, and Social Movements*. New York: Routledge, 1992.

Keys, David. "Collective Identity Theory of Social Movements: Development of African American Consciousness and the Congress of Racial Equality, 1942–66." Master's thesis, University of Missouri-Columbia, 1994.

Offe, Claus. "New Social Movements: Challenging the Boundaries of Institutional Politics." *Social Research* 52, no. 4 (1985).

Rajchman, John, ed. *The Identity in Question*. New York: Routledge, 1995.

Riessman, Frank, and Timothy Bay. "The Politics of Self-Help." *Social Policy* 23, no. 2 (1993).

Ross, Jeffrey et al., eds. *The Mobilization of Collective Identity: A Comparative Perspective*. Lanham, MD: University Press of America, 1980.

Rozell, Mark, and Clyde Wilcox. *Interest Groups in American Campaigns*. Washington, DC: Congressional Quarterly, 1999.

Slagle, Anthony. "In Defense of Queer Nation: From Identity Politics to a Politics of Difference." *Western Journal of Communication* 59, no. 2 (1995): 85–103.

Taylor, V., and N. Whittier. "Collective Identity in Social Movement Communities: Lesbian Feminist Mobilization." In *Frontiers in Social Movement Theory*. Edited by Morris and Mueller. New Haven: Yale University Press, 1992.

AMERICAN ASSOCIATION OF RETIRED PERSONS

A nonprofit organization established in 1958 to serve the interests and welfare of individuals aged 50 and older, the American Association of Retired Persons (AARP) is headquartered in Washington, D.C. AARP has been at the forefront in providing goods and services for retired persons as well as lobbying governmental agencies on behalf of both retired persons and the working elderly over age 50. Through education, lobbying activities, and the provision of services, AARP seeks to meet the wide array of needs of America's growing elderly population. AARP is a mass-membership organization of approximately 33 million people, which represents approximately 20 percent of America's registered voters, and is both nonprofit and nonpartisan. Membership is open to anyone age 50 or over and costs $8 per year. Classified by the Internal Revenue Service 501(c)(4), it endorses no candidates for office and does not maintain a political action committee (PAC) for electoral advocacy efforts; rather, it focuses its efforts on lobbying. Supporting the organization is a staff numbering nearly 2,000 individuals. AARP has five regional offices and 25 state offices, along with 3,700 chapters; it employs 19 staff lobbyists (135 people are employed on the lobbying/public affairs staff) and maintains a 32-scholar think tank.

AARP is headed by Horace Deets, who is considered a major player in American politics on issues affecting those age 50 and over and on general budgetary issues. AARP has been characterized as the "most feared lobby in Washington" (*Fortune* magazine) and "America's most powerful lobby" (*Nation* magazine); it has been included in *Fortune* magazine's listing of America's most powerful interest groups, and had a ranking of number one in both 1997 and 1998. AARP is a pivotal player in negotiations and debate over reforming Medicare and Social Security.

HISTORY

Formed in 1958 by retired educator Dr. Ethel Percy Andrus, the organization has expanded in size from its humble beginnings. AARP engages in a series of major activities and has numerous publications to aid and educate its members. Among its many areas of interests and activities, AARP holds seminars, produces tapes, engages in media outreach, organizes volunteer programs such as 55 Alive, provides presentations for employers, provides training through "Experience for Hire," and provides tax information.

AARP has had numerous successes in the policy arena and is courted by politicians on all issues affecting elderly Americans. For example, President Bill Clinton sought the aid of AARP in 1998–1999 to protect against a Republican-inspired tax cut, in order to boost and maintain Medicare and Social Security. However, while the organization's successes are numerous, one major defeat for AARP was the repeal of Medicare Catastrophic Coverage in 1989.

Through its Public Policy Institute and other organization endeavors, AARP produces a bimonthly magazine called *Modern Maturity* and a monthly *AARP Bulletin,* which goes out to over 20 million households in America and provides information on such issues as Social Security, Medicare, managed care, and other important issues.

ACTIVITIES: CURRENT AND FUTURE

AARP's efforts include a variety of methods in order to advocate on behalf of its members. The organization pursues goals at the local, state, and national levels and maintains that its primary areas of concern are information and education, community service, advocacy, and member services.

Among its information and education functions, AARP funds gerontology research and broadcasts weekly radio talk shows in both English and Spanish. Through its network of chapters and volunteers, the organization provides such extensive community service programs as "Money After 50, "55 Alive/Mature Driving," and "Connections for Independent Living." It advocates on numerous issues for older Americans, such as Medicare, Medicaid, Social Security, age discrimination, and fraud. Further, it provides such services to its members as discounts on insurance, mail-order prescription services, and legal services, among other benefits.

Through the AARP at the Local Level program, AARP volunteers serve the community through education, advocacy, and community service activities. Additionally, the organization has a Department of State Legislation, which coordinates state activities and helps to prioritize and organize the group's goals for each individual state. AARP also provides technical assistance to volunteers at the state and local levels.

Nationally, AARP's efforts are run by a Federal Affairs department, which, aided by the Public Policy Institute, engages in lobbying activity along with the AARP Washington staff and the National Legislative Council. Members of the organization regularly meet with individual legislators and provide testimony before committees on Capitol Hill.

In addition to these efforts, AARP receives nearly $75 million per annum from the federal government in grants to finance programs aimed at aiding older Americans in finding employment. These programs include the Senior Community Service Employment program and the Senior Environmental Employment program, along with programs such as Early Detection and Control of Breast Cancer, the National Legal Assistance Support Project, and Americans with Disabilities: Accessibility for Older Persons, which supports older Americans in the areas of consumer education, health, and financial security.

Educationally, AARP maintains a nonpartisan voter education program called "AARP/VOTE," through which the organization educates voters and candidates about issues facing older Americans in order to provide this group with an adequate voice in the electoral process. Although AARP/VOTE does not endorse any candidate for office, it does host debates that allow its members and the general public to obtain information on the candidates' positions on issues. And even though AARP does not formally endorse candidates for office, the group has been a popular target of conservative groups and has been labeled as liberal by publications such as the *National Review*. While AARP rejects being labeled liberal, *Forbes* magazine has argued that its "activist, liberal staff" regularly ignores the conservative views of its members, and the *National Review* has said that the AARP is the "best friend of big, dumb government." The National Taxpayers Union and other conservative organizations have attacked AARP policies as being liberal and not solely limited to advocating for benefits for elderly citizens. In attacking the organization, conservatives have pointed out AARP's support for higher gas taxes and AIDS research, as well as opposition to Clarence Thomas's appointment to the Supreme Court.

In the future, AARP will seek to maintain its current status as one of America's most powerful lobbying organizations and interest groups. Given the graying of America's population and the fact that 50 percent of Americans aged over 50 are members, this provides the opportunity for AARP to grow in both size and clout at the ballot box. While it would be hyperbole to suggest that the group could expand its power much further, it is certainly not an exaggeration to say that AARP's influence is not likely to wane in the long-term future of American lobbying, and its efforts and support for or opposition to reforms in healthcare policy will be a significant factor in policy change in those areas of competence and interest for AARP.

FINANCIAL FACTS

AARP's interests are wide and it pursues its goals at the national, state, and local levels. Its interests include providing its members with economic security, protection against age discrimination, consumer protection, long-term care, employment rights, and protection for Social Security and Medicare.

AARP has total operating revenues of approximately $450 million and operating expenses of nearly $375 million. Since it does not maintain a political action committee (PAC) and concentrates its activities on lobbying and other efforts, the organization provides no formal support to either Democrats or Republicans. However, organizational lobbying expenses amount to over $6 million, according to AARP figures. Supported primarily through membership dues, AARP also receives a substantial amount of its funding from investments, the sale of publications, and group insurance administrative allowances. Of these amounts, more than $30 million per annum comes from royalty income (3 percent of all purchases through Prudential Insurance), combined with over $150 million from membership dues.

MICHAEL LEVY

Bibliography

AARP. "Where We Stand," February 2, 1999: www.aarp.org/where.html

Birnbaum, Jeffrey. "Washington's Second Most Powerful Man." *Time,* May 12, 1997.

DeAngelis, James, ed. *Public Interest Profiles, 1998–99.* CQ Foundation for Public Affairs. Washington, DC: Congressional Quarterly, 1998.

McArdle, Thomas. "Golden Oldies: American Association of Retired Persons' Liberalism." *National Review* 47, no. 4 (1995).

Morris, Charles. *The AARP: America's Most Powerful Lobby and the Clash of Generations.* New York: Times Books, 1996.

AMERICAN INDIAN MOVEMENT

The American Indian Movement (AIM) was formed in 1968 in Minneapolis, Minnesota, and maintains its headquarters in Minneapolis with chapters in numerous urban centers in the United States and in Indian Nations (reservations). Its founding by Dennis Banks, George Mitchell, Vernon Bellecourt, and Clyde Bellecourt helped to bring the demands of Native Americans to the forefront, and AIM was the central actor and organizer of Indian protest during the 1970s. It was organized to give voice to the claims of Native Americans. The organization has spent much of its 30-year history articulating the demands of Native Americans and pursuing policies to protect their rights as guaranteed by the U.S. government in treaties, the Constitution, and laws. Although no count of members exists, AIM generally has consisted of youth from the reservations, cities, and universities and is much stronger at the local level than as a cohesive national organization.

AIM is not a typical American interest group and can be classified rightly as a new social movement founded during the turbulent and progressive 1960s. It has pursued its strategies through two primary means. First, it has sought litigation and has filed suit against the federal government in order to ensure that Native Americans' rights are adequately protected. Second, it has pursued community organization and grassroots protest in order to gain publicity and influence the policy process. While not totally eschewing traditional lobbying, most of its activities are grassroots and locally oriented, though that was not true in the early years of AIM.

AIM's philosophy is described by the organization as based on self-determination and rooted in "traditional spirituality, culture, language, and history." AIM heavily emphasizes spirituality, as well as an inherent connection of all Indian people regardless of nation. Under the leadership of NeeGawNwayWeeDun (Clyde Bellecourt), AIM has sought to serve the interests and needs of the Indian communities.

HISTORY

AIM formed in 1968 and quickly rose to both national and international prominence. In what has largely been an urban protest movement, AIM sought to combat discrimination and police brutality. It has been labeled an "indigenous version of the Black Panther Party" and received large amounts of publicity and media attention in the 1968–1974 period. Unlike traditional civil rights organizations, it differed on the goals of the movement. Integration was not a goal of AIM, and individual rights were not the emphasis; rather, group preservation and group rights were the cornerstone of AIM. When the organization was founded, it focused on the War on Poverty policies initiated by President Lyndon Johnson to ensure that the program targeted Native Americans. In its early years, the organization focused on small and local demonstrations that didn't require coordination between the various chapters that sprouted up after its foundation.

After a few years of protests, it was decided at its national conference in 1971 that the organization would need to build an indigenous organization to address the issues of education, health, and police brutality against Native Americans. By 1972, AIM organized, along with disparate Indian organizations, a caravan, known as the Trail of Broken Treaties, which brought Native American representatives to Washington to lobby the U.S. Department of the Interior and put claims and demands before President Richard Nixon. It was AIM's first attempt at a major national protest and brought approximately 1,000 Native Americans to Washington. Among its 20 demands put forward in 1972, which are still relevant nearly 30 years later, were a restoration of treaty making, formation of a commission to create new treaties with better terms for America's indigenous population, a review of treaty violations, restoration of 110 million acres of land taken away from Native Americans, federal protection for offenses against Indians, abolition of the Bureau of Indian Affairs, creation of a new office of federal Indian relations, Indian religious freedom, and national Indian voting. These, among other demands, were put forward as AIM's agenda before the American public.

ACTIVITIES: CURRENT AND FUTURE

In addition to its support for these policies, AIM has a long and distinguished record on promoting the rights of Native Americans. In 1968, AIM established the Minneapolis Patrol, which addressed the issue of police brutality; it developed a Legal Rights Center in 1970, which assists Indians facing legal problems and has helped 20,000 Indians in their legal representations; it developed schools for Indian children to combat the high drop-out rate among Native Americans; it established a news organization (MIGIZI) to provide information on and about Native Americans; it promoted a walk from California to Washington to protest anti-Indian legislation; it has developed an industrialization center to combat unemployment; and it helped organize a coalition on racism in sports and the media to address the use of Indian mascots in sports. This is just a brief sampling of some of the diverse activities sponsored by AIM.

Whereas AIM has been a mainstay of the Native American community in promoting native rights, the organization received its most publicity during the 1970s for its protest behavior, much of which shapes the way AIM is viewed by most Americans even today. In November 1969, AIM participated in an Indian occupation of Alcatraz Island. This high-profile activity etched AIM in the media, and it remained there through the Alcatraz incident and after U.S. government forces, armed with handguns, shotguns, M-1 30-caliber carbines, and other weapons, stormed Alcatraz and retook the island in June 1971.

From its founding, AIM was a grassroots protest organization that emphasized, along with local concerns, national issues. One of AIM's earliest protests came on Thanksgiving Day in 1970 when its members protested Thanksgiving celebrations by "seizing the Mayflower II." This event sought to stir Indian activism. In addition, it also held an "antibirthday" party on Mount Rushmore on the Fourth of July, along with other highly visible protest activities.

Perhaps, however, AIM is best known for its armed activity. In 1973, it took over Wounded Knee on the Pine Ridge reservation in South Dakota. The tribal president, Richard Wilson, was in the process of transferring a strip of uranium-rich land to the Interior Department. The Indians resisted, prompting the federal government to dispatch marshals; in response to the federal activity, the local Native Americans, the Oglala, sought AIM's help. In March 1973, the Indian occupiers of Wounded Knee proclaimed sovereignty according to the Laramie Treaty of 1868, and the siege ended 71 days later. The siege saw the deaths of AIM members (approximately 60), the injury of dozens more, and the disappearance of others. The battle, according to AIM, was totally unprovoked, and the federal government committed numerous atrocities and murders, including the murder of Oglala leader Pedro Bissonette, who AIM claims was unarmed. In spite of numerous witnesses claiming police brutality, no formal charges were ever filed.

After Wounded Knee, two leaders, Dennis Banks and Russell Means, were tried for their part in the siege at Wounded Knee. The trial, which gained significant national attention, was used by defense attorney William Kunstler to launch an attack on the federal government and as evidence that highlighted the unmet treaty obligations of the U.S. government

For many observers, the most visible figure of AIM has been Leonard Peltier. During a shoot-out with federal agents at Wounded Knee, two marshals were killed. Peltier's trials, marked by suppressed evidence and some inconsistencies, resulted in his incarceration; he is currently serving two life sentences for those murders. Human rights and left-wing political organizations have viewed him as a cause célèbre and a political prisoner and have sought new trials and clemency.

Following the Wounded Knee sieges, AIM shifted its attention from national issues to local issues and local problems. In 1982, Dennis Banks called a national meeting of AIM in San Francisco to recreate a national organization. This meeting was attended by approximately 250 people; although some agreements were reached, AIM has not reestablished a strong national organization and remains largely chapter- and locally based. Since its heyday in the 1970s, the group has "mellowed" in its approach and emphasizes less high-profile activities to continue its mission. The locally based strategies are likely to continue in the absence of a defining national cause.

FINANCIAL FACTS

As a charitable, nonprofit organization, the American Indian Movement does not engage in official lobbying of federal and state government officials.

MICHAEL LEVY

Bibliography

Churchill, Ward. "A Force, Briefly, to Be Reckoned With." *The Progressive,* June 1997.

Johnson, Troy. "Roots of Contemporary Native American Activism." *American Indian Culture and Research Journal* 20, no. 2 (1996).

Kennedy, Michael. "The Law and Native Americans." *Boston Globe,* November 20, 1997.

Waterman, Laura, and Elaine Salinas. "A Brief History of the AIM," February 2, 1999: www.tdi.net/Ishgooda/aimhist1.htm

AMERICAN LEGION

The American Legion is a "patriotic, mutual-help, war-time" veterans organization headquartered in Indianapolis, Indiana. Representing veterans who served on "honorable federal active duty" in the First and Second World Wars, the Korean War, the Vietnam War, Lebanon, Grenada, Panama (Operation Just Cause), and the Persian Gulf (Operation Desert Shield/Storm), the organization's membership totals nearly 3 million in 15,000 posts worldwide. Each post is organized into a larger department; there are 55 departments representing each state, Washington, D.C., Puerto Rico, France, Mexico, and the Philippines. In addition to the legion's nearly 3 million members, it maintains two affiliated groups. The American Legion Auxiliary comprises 1 million members; membership is open to wives and daughters of American Legion members. The Sons of the American Legion is open to the sons of American Legion members and contains an additional 200,000 members.

The American Legion's interests can be subdivided into a variety of categories, including Americanism, children and youth, legislative goals and initiatives, upholding and defending the Constitution through advocating policies aimed at national security and foreign relations, the economic security of veterans, and veterans affairs and rehabilitation issues. While its activities are broad in scope, the American Legion largely works to uphold policies that support veterans and promote traditional American ideals, values, and patriotism.

HISTORY

Founded in 1919, the American Legion is the largest veterans organization in the world. It seeks to maintain the "basics" of its founding, which include veterans' rehabilitation, Americanism, child welfare, and national security. The organization was founded in order to be the chief advocate of veterans. Its original meetings took place in early 1919 in "introductory" conventions in Paris and St. Louis and determined that a goal of the organization would be volunteerism. The American Legion's first national convention occurred in November 1919 in Minneapolis.

The American Legion has been instrumental in lobbying activities related to veterans issues. One of the most successful moments for the legion was the 1944 passage of the G.I. Bill. The legion was pivotal in lobbying both for its writing and its passage. The bill, which the organization counts as a major innovation, assisted in the reentry of soldiers after the end of the Second World War. The legion has expended considerable energy on helping veterans take advantage of the opportunities the bill provided.

Through the years, the organization has developed a highly skilled process of creating mandates, which has helped put numerous laws on the statute books that seek to support and protect the rights of its members. This process occurs for both federal and state legislation and aids the organization in influencing policy-making.

The organization has been highly successful in its lobbying activities and maintains an active profile. Currently, the legion is lobbying for a G.I. Bill of Health and has called for an inquiry into Gulf War illness, including a criminal investigation of missing chemical-detection logs that could show whether U.S. troops were exposed to Iraqi chemical weapons during Operation Desert Storm.

ACTIVITIES: CURRENT AND FUTURE

In order to promote its priorities, the American Legion is active in grassroots and direct-lobbying activities. These activities are numerous and, in fact, one can think of the American Legion as an umbrella organization with numerous components, each contributing to the group. The following is just a sampling of the numerous and diverse activities of the American Legion.

To protect the flag, the American Legion convened the first National Flag Conference in 1923 and drafted a U.S. Flag Code, which served as a set of guidelines on the use of the flag and was adopted by Congress in 1942. Since the *Texas v. Johnson* (1989) Supreme Court decision, the organization has sought a constitutional amendment allowing the states and federal government to enact legislation protecting the flag. In this effort, in 1994 the American Legion founded the Citizens Flag Alliance to work for a constitutional amendment.

To promote patriotism and education, the American Legion is also active in elementary and secondary education by providing medals, educational assistance, scholarships, sporting activities, and contests, as well as sponsoring the Boy Scouts organization. The American Legion is firmly committed to enhancing educational opportunities for children and to imbuing that education with a sense of Americanism. Although the legion focuses much of its activities on veterans, it also has strong youth programs—spending over $5 million on programs for the young on such things as teen suicide, drugs, immunization, and the like.

The legion also focuses on national security issues, especially those related to foreign affairs, supporting a policy it labels "democratic activism." Democratic activism promotes democratic values overseas and supports policies aimed at promoting a strong defense, free and fair trade, and aid to developing nations.

As a veterans organization, the American Legion lobbies and supports job preference for its members for jobs for which they are qualified. Including members who served during periods of conflict, along with members who are disabled, the legion argues that members are entitled to "extra consideration" and seeks to provide opportunities for them.

Given the legion's efforts to aid veterans, some of its most highly visible activities are in the area of veterans affairs and veterans health. The Veterans Affairs and Rehabilitation Commission oversees programs provided by the Department of Veteran Affairs, and the legion is the only veterans organization with membership staffing at the insurance centers of the federal government Veterans Administration.

As a lobbying group, the legion is organized into a Legislative division and a National Legislative Commission. The Legislative division is headquartered in Washington, D.C., and performs such activities as preparing material for congressional hearings, scheduling experts to testify in Congress, helping to prepare bills, and analyzing bills and their effects on veterans. The National Legislative Commission petitions Congress for legislation in which the American Legion is interested.

Current activities, thus, can be summarized into four main categories: the legion seeks to protect the flag from desecration, promote a G.I. Bill of Health, promote a strong national defense, and promote good citizenship. These activities are pursued through both grassroots and direct-lobbying activities.

Given recent military ventures, along with the Vietnam era veterans, the legion's prominence is likely to continue and its membership is likely to grow. Its contacts in Washington and its representation at Veterans Administration insurance centers ensure its continued impact on policy. It is likely to have a continued interest in Gulf War illness, and it will likely continue to focus on flag desecration, along with its emphasis on veteran-related issues.

FINANCIAL FACTS

The national annual budget of the American Legion is approximately $64 million. It maintains no political action committee (PAC) and is a nonpartisan organization that does not endorse particular candidates for office. However, while nonpartisan, it does engage in a variety of advocacy and lobbying activities. Its overall lobbying budget for 1997 was $240,000, according to the group's internal figures.

MICHAEL LEVY

Bibliography

American Legion. "The American Legion: Who We Are," April 9, 1999: www.legion.org/backfact.htm

Rumer, Thomas. *The American Legion: An Official History*. New York: M. Evans, 1990.

CONGRESS OF RACIAL EQUALITY

Headquartered in New York City, the Congress of Racial Equality (CORE) is one of the nation's oldest civil rights organizations and is included as one of the "Big Four" African-American civil rights groups. Founded to champion "true" equality, CORE has gone through some distinct historical periods, moving from an initiator of nonviolent protest strategies to gain civil rights advances, to an advocate of armed struggle, to an organization whose leader, Roy Innis, has been profiled positively by the conservative publication *National Review*. The organization is open to African Americans and non-African Americans, and is governed by its national headquarters along with scores of local affiliates and chapters throughout the United States, Africa, Central America, and the Caribbean. While membership figures are sketchy, the organization claims to have over 100,000 members organized in its over 100 chapters.

According to its mission statement, CORE seeks individual self-determination, allowing individuals to make their own decisions without undue interference from those who disagree or oppose them. Its emphasis currently is on self-governance to achieve equality regardless of race, creed, sex, age, disability, religion, or ethnic background. The organization seeks to identify and expose acts of racism and discrimination both in the public and private arenas.

HISTORY

CORE's history, including changes in its mission/tactics/strategies, is quite diverse and fascinating. Originally called the Committee on Racial Equality, the organization was formed in 1942 and adopted its current name in 1944. Unlike some civil rights organizations, CORE pursued the use of nonviolent protest behavior to achieve its goals. In fact, it was the first organization committed to nonviolent challenges to segregation; its original mission statement claimed that "CORE has one method: interracial, nonviolent direct action."

Founded by James Farmer, who in 1993 received the U.S. Medal of Freedom from President Bill Clinton, the organization's activities were inspired in large measure by Indian protest leader Mahatma Gandhi. Its membership was multiracial and its membership and leadership in the early era was largely white and middle class. Indicative of its activities, during the early 1960s, CORE led pickets at city and federally funded projects demanding the hiring of African-American workers.

By the 1960s, CORE's methods and mission began to change substantially. It expanded its membership, which began to include large numbers of African Americans and more radicalized workers, farmers, and youths. By 1964, the organization was largely African American and it began to distance itself from its nonviolent past. By 1966, CORE endorsed armed self-defense as a tactic to win the struggle for civil rights. At its 1966 national convention, delegates voted to eliminate adherence to nonviolence as a protest strategy.

By the 1970s, CORE began to emphasize "self-determination" and "equal opportunity" as a means of achieving its goals. Its national chairman since 1968, Roy Innis was transformed politically during the early 1970s from a political radical to a policy conservative, and CORE's activities reflect a self-help conservative ideology. Focusing on the agenda of self-help during the 1970s and 1980s, CORE emphasized voter registration to elect African Americans to office and established cooperatives to help African-American businesses keep their wealth in the black community.

During the 1980s, CORE faced problems related to its fundraising. CORE was accused by New York State of illegal fundraising, misusing $500,000, and misrepresentation in seeking contributions. While admitting no guilt, CORE settled with New York State. In the 1990s, CORE had been associated with American conservatives. Ward Connerly, leader of the movement to end affirmative action programs in California, spoke glowingly of Innis. The organization lent its support to increased gun ownership among blacks, and supported the authoritarian regime of Sani Abacha in Nigeria. Innis also consistently attended National Rifle Association and Christian Coalition meetings. *National Review*, a conservative publication, praised CORE for its deviance from the civil rights establishment and the organization's efforts to emphasize community self-help.

Under Innis' leadership, CORE has been the target of and has targeted many traditional civil rights groups. When Betty Shabazz, Malcolm X's widow, was buried, Innis was not invited to participate in the service. CORE strongly endorsed Clarence Thomas's nomination to the Supreme Court, although he was already at odds with most civil rights organizations because of his conservative politics and the sexual harassment lawsuit brought against him. In 1998, after years as a Democrat, Innis joined the Libertarian Party and has been suggested as a mayoral candidate in New York City under the Libertarian banner, a position he sought in the 1980s as a Democrat when he tried to unseat New York City's first African-American mayor, David Dinkins. Innis has been a very controversial figure throughout his tenure as head of CORE. He participated in the first live "fisticuffs" on television in 1988 on the Morton Downey Jr. show when he pushed the Reverend Al Sharpton because Sharpton interrupted him. During President Bill Clinton's impeachment trial, CORE lambasted the Republicans for "kowtowing" to the media and expressed anger that the behavior of the president went unpunished. Thus, CORE has separated itself from the mainstream civil rights establishment. Symbolic of its outsider status was its invitation in 1998 to radio host Bob Grant, who has been called an anti-Semite and a racist, to its 14th Martin Luther King Jr. Ambassadorial Reception and Awards dinner. However, it is important to note that CORE has continued to deplore violence and discrimination against African Americans and has spoken quite forcefully on police brutality and hate crimes, such as the dragging death of James Byrd Jr. in Jasper, Texas.

ACTIVITIES: CURRENT AND FUTURE

CORE focuses much of its activity around service programs for the African-American community. Generally not a direct-lobbying organization, CORE does not maintain a political action committee (PAC). Its current activities include maintaining a legal defense fund, immigration assistance, a complaints department, an Internet watch group, a civil rights "boot camp," and Project Independence.

Project Independence is typical of CORE's current approach to problem-solving within the African-American community. Arguing that welfare dependency needs to be broken, CORE's Project Independence seeks to provide worker training and welfare-to-work assistance. Drawing on what it sees as a lack of skills among youth in inner cities, the program targets the unemployed, especially young single mothers who are on welfare assistance. Knowing that not everyone can be helped with its limited resources, it has targeted "welfare mothers" in order to break the cycle of dependency through training and creating partnerships with the private sector to instill a work ethic. After receiving training, CORE provides career counseling and advice on interviewing and preparing resumes, and hosts job fairs. The $1,500 per trainee cost, CORE claims, is 80 percent effective.

In addition, its boot camp seeks to rehabilitate youths. The CORE Youth Boot Camp is open to whites and blacks and, in one of its more high-profile cases, attempted the rehabilitation of five white youths who had written racist statements in their graduation yearbook.

As long as it is led by Innis, one should expect CORE's emphasis to be on self help. Recently, CORE has consistently argued against affirmative action, busing, gun control, and "political correctness." Innis has argued that the main problem facing black society is internal and related to black-on-black crime, drugs, and a lack of discipline and values. Programs aimed at solving these problems are likely to be central to CORE's agenda. Its alienation from mainstream civil rights organizations such as the NAACP and the Urban League is likely to continue for the foreseeable future, with polls suggesting that most blacks view CORE and Innis unfavorably, while most whites have a favorable view of both CORE and Innis. Its support in the African-American community is not likely to increase in the foreseeable future, though its support in Republican and conservative organizations is likely to increase, making CORE the voice of conservative black America.

FINANCIAL FACTS

CORE does not give money to politicians, because it is a nonprofit organization. As a registered federal non-profit organization, CORE is prohibited from contributing funds to political campaigns. However, the organization lobbies members of Congress on behalf of policies and legislation that it supports.

MICHAEL LEVY

Bibliography

CORE. "Congress of Racial Equality": www.core-online.org

Keys, David. "Collective Identity Theory of Social Movements: Development of African American Consciousness and the Congress of Racial Equality, 1942–66." Master's thesis, University of Missouri-Columbia, 1994.

Lieberman, Alan. "Up from Liberalism." *National Review*, March 1, 1993, pp. 26–28.

Meier, A., and E. Rudwick. *CORE: A Study in the Civil Rights Movement, 1942–1968*. New York: Oxford University Press, 1973.

Packer, George. "A Tale of Two Movements." *The Nation*, December 14, 1998, pp. 19–24.

EMILY'S LIST

Founded in 1985, Emily's List is headquartered in Washington, D.C. Created to help elect pro-choice Democratic women to state and national office, Emily's List has become one of the most powerful political fund-raising machines in the less than two decades since its founding.

Members contribute at least $100 to Emily's List and pledge to contribute $100 to at least two candidates over a two-year period. Emily's List identifies and recommends to its members electable pro-choice candidates. It then asks members to make checks (averaging $90) directly payable to candidates and to send those checks to Emily's List, which then forwards these contributions to the candidates, thereby maximizing its members' power. This practice, known as bundling, involves a process whereby a third party makes a contribution to a candidate on the "suggestion" of a political action committee (PAC), thus allowing the donors to circumvent the $5,000 PAC contribution spending limit. Thus, official Federal Election Commission (FEC) figures actually underplay the group's clout. The PAC of Emily's List, according to analysts, is more like a "clearinghouse" for members rather than a traditional PAC. In 1996, Emily's List coordinated contribution of approximately $6.7 million to candidates through bundled donations.

Although Emily's List is not alone in utilizing the practice of bundling, it has been among the most successful. When Congress debated campaign finance, bundling became a major issue, and Emily's List was successful in getting an exemption included in the House legislation to allow groups that didn't lobby to continue to bundle contributions. The change in the legislation was considered an indicator of this organization's political clout on Capitol Hill.

HISTORY

Emily's List was founded in 1985 by Ellen Malcolm, along with two dozen of her friends, in order to create an association of donors to enable female candidates to wage viable campaigns. The acronym EMILY stands for "Early Money Is Like Yeast" (i.e., early money makes the "dough" rise). Founded to elect pro-choice Democratic women candidates, the organization focused (and continues to focus) on campaign fund raising and engages in no lobbying activities on Capitol Hill.

When the organization was founded in 1985, it engineered a new style of campaigning by bundling campaign contributions. It started slowly by raising $350,000 for two Senate candidates in 1986 (Barbara Mikulski and Harriett Woods) and helped to elect Mikulski. Its membership rolls totaled just over 1,000 in 1986.

By 1988, its membership roster had increased to 2,000 members and it oversaw contributions of $650,000 to female candidates, becoming the largest resource for female candidates in the country. During 1990, it raised $1.5 million and had a membership of 3,500. During the 1992 election season, it grew dramatically: it ended 1992 with 23,701 members and coordinated contributions of more than $6.2 million dollars. The growth is attributed to the growing political awareness of women as well as the Clarence Thomas hearings on Capitol Hill.

By 1996, the group began to expand its impact. It grew to 45,000 members and began to widen its scope to include the Women Vote! movement, as well as building a consulting infrastructure to enable women to wage effective campaigns. During the 1996 campaign, the Democratic National Committee included Emily's List as the first women's group on the steering committee. As part of the steering committee, Emily's List helped to coordinate Democratic national strategy. Its 1998 election activities helped to elect seven new pro-choice women to the House and a new female senator. Through its entire brief history, it has maintained its mission and increased its impact, becoming one of the most powerful and feared political fund-raising machines.

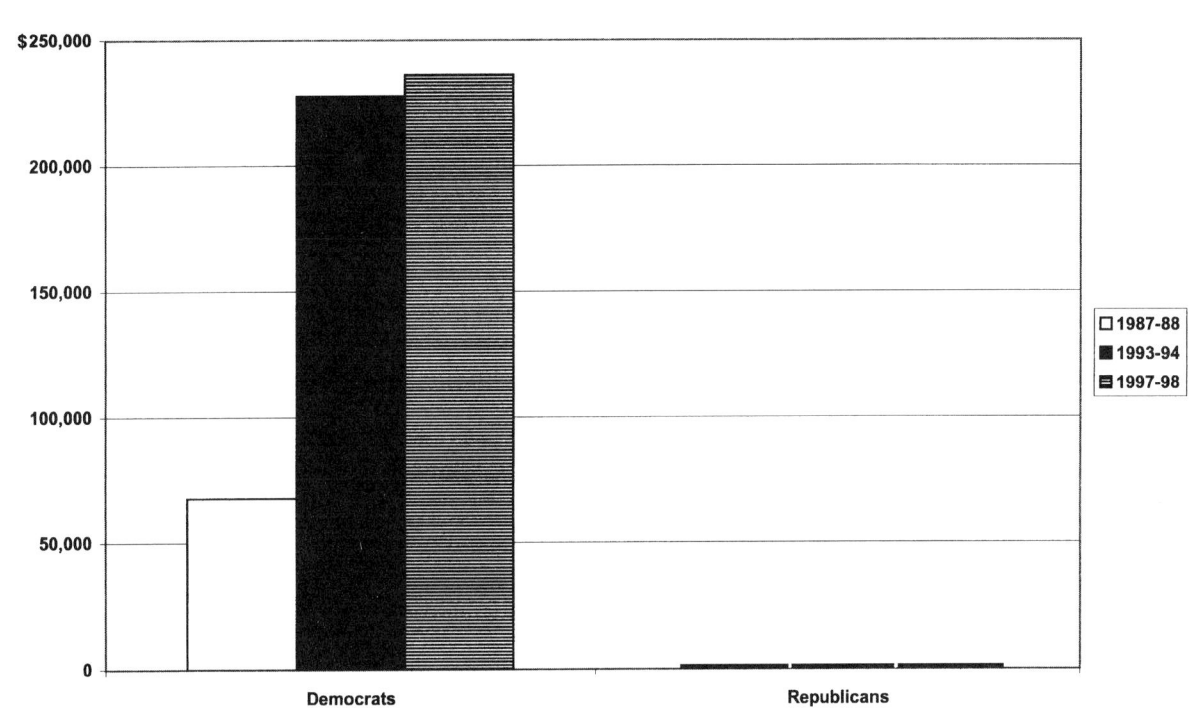

**Emily's List
Political Action Committee Contributions**

[Bar chart showing PAC contributions for election cycles 1987-88, 1993-94, and 1997-98. Democrats received approximately $68,000 (1987-88), $228,000 (1993-94), and $238,000 (1997-98). Republicans received negligible amounts across all three cycles.]

Data derived from official studies available from the Federal Election Commission, Washington, DC, 1987–1998.

ACTIVITIES: CURRENT AND FUTURE

While electing pro-choice Democratic women is the main goal of Emily's List, its activities include more than simple fund raising. Emily's List performs a variety of activities to support this goal. In aiding female candidates in building strong winning campaigns, the organization seeks to mobilize female voters. Emily's List also conducts recruitment in order to find potential female candidates, gathers research, and provides campaign training and technical assistance through its organization infrastructure.

In trying to elect female candidates, the organization focuses not only on candidate recruitment, but also on voter turnout. Emily's List created "Women Vote!," which has spent nearly $10 million to mobilize Democratic female voters across the United States. Its stated goal is to increase the turnout of women to "counter religious extremist organizing" and to help Democrats up and down the ballot. Emily's List also conducts educational programs to empower its members. During the 1997–1998 electoral cycle, the Women Vote! campaign helped to target female voters by sending out nearly 8 million letters and placing over 3 million phone calls to women in order to encourage voter turnout.

Emily's List also spent approximately $2 million helping female candidates build strong campaigns. It holds training seminars for potential candidates and helps to provide individuals with the technical expertise to fill such jobs as fundraisers, managers, researchers, and press secretaries, thereby encouraging women to be involved in all phases of the campaign process and assisting women to mount effective campaigns.

Emily's List has been highly successful in promoting the candidacies of Democratic pro-choice women, and it is credited with helping to elect seven senators, nearly 50 members of the House, and three governors. Before its creation there had been no Democratic women elected to the Senate on their own, virtually no woman had been elected governor of a large state, and female representation among Democrats in the House was declining. Although Emily's List alone is not responsible for the victories, its campaign cash along with its expertise have provided a critical influx of aid to potential female candidates in both primaries and general elections.

Its success and influence cannot be overstated. One result is that Emily's List organizations have popped up in both the United Kingdom and Australia. Further, Republican women have organized a Susan B. Anthony political action committee (PAC) in order to help elect their pro-life representatives. Thus, its impact has been important in influencing organizations aimed at electing female candidates in both the United States and in English-speaking democracies.

Emily's List is an example of an organization created to fill a niche and to focus on a limited goal, that of electing pro-choice Democratic women. Although it began slowly, it picked up force through the highly publicized Clarence Thomas hearings and has increased its clout. Its strength is likely to continue in the near future, with its success based on how many women it can help elect. Thus far, its track record has been very successful.

FINANCIAL FACTS

In direct contributions to candidates, Emily's List gave approximately $230,000 in the 1997–1998 election cycle. However, by bundling contributions from its roster of nearly 50,000 members who pay $100 to join, Emily's List is a financial powerhouse that provides enormous sums of money. In 1998 alone the organization coordinated contributions of more than $7.5 million to help fund critical activities and provide a campaign advantage for pro-choice Democratic candidates. For the 1997–1998 election cycle, Emily's List raised approximately $15 million and had a budget of approximately $22 million in 1998. With expenditures of almost $14 million, Emily's List has been active and successful in aiding female candidates. The organization invests approximately 30 percent of its budget on fund-raising for candidates and other operating expenses, including the employment of over 20 people, direct-mailing efforts, and its telemarketing strategies.

The organization not only raised record amounts of money in 1998, but contributors to Emily's List comprised the largest group of contributors to candidates for national office. Contributions from Emily's List and its members have been labeled "critical" by recipients.

MICHAEL LEVY

Bibliography

Emily's List. "Pro-choice Democratic Women Candidates: Emily's List," February 17, 1999: www.emilyslist.org

Kranish, Michael. "Women with Wallets." *Boston Globe,* May 25, 1997.

Stanton, Robert. "Big Money PACs." *Headway* 19, no. 5 (1997).

White, Ben. "PACs Raise Record $359 Million, Then Spend It Quickly." *Washington Post,* October 12, 1998.

HUMAN RIGHTS CAMPAIGN

The Human Rights Campaign (HRC) is the country's largest gay and lesbian political organization. Headquartered in Washington, D.C., the organization represents the gay and lesbian community's interests in attempting to guarantee basic human rights and equality for gays and lesbians specifically and all Americans generally.

With a membership roster of 250,000 members, the HRC's staff numbers more than 60. The staff engages in lobbying activities, campaigning, and promoting gay and lesbian political issues. Its budget, nearly $15 million, most of which is funded through the collection of membership dues, affords the organization the ability to expend considerable resources on lobbying, as well as other activities.

HISTORY

Founded in 1980, the Human Rights Campaign has become a major player on the political stage in the movement for achieving equality for gay and lesbian citizens, both in federal law and in the states, though most of its activity focuses on national issues and congressional lobbying. Its mission statement includes commitments to legislative and social goals. For recent Congresses, its goals have included protecting gays and lesbians from job discrimination (Employment Nondiscrimination Act); advocating hate crimes legislation, which gathered strength in the wake of the murder of Matthew Shepard, an openly gay student in Wyoming; promoting policies aimed at combating AIDS; and waging a rearguard campaign against anti-gay legislative and ballot measures, such as those in Colorado, Hawaii, Maine, and other states. Headed by Elizabeth Birch, who serves as the organization's executive director, the HRC maintains a presence in both lobbying and educating members of Congress on gay- and lesbian-related issues, as well as AIDS and other health-related issues.

ACTIVITIES: CURRENT AND FUTURE

Activities can be grouped into six main categories: lobbying Congress, contributing to candidates for office, issue-oriented political campaigning, sponsorship of the National Coming Out Project, training and mobilizing at the grassroots level, and educating the public. In pursuing its goals, the HRC engages in a diversity of activities that include, among other activities, campaign contributions, congressional testimony, grassroots activities such as Field Action Networks and Speak Out Action Grams, polling, lobbying, voter registration, media outreach, research, and training. To provide information, the HRC also produces a quarterly newsletter (*HRC Quarterly*) and a weekly e-mail newsletter (*HRC News*) along with the publication of resource guides (including the *Resource Guide to Coming Out* and *LAWbriefs*).

The HRC participates actively in lobbying activities. It has worked, since its founding, to advance gay and lesbian equality in Congress through helping to draft legislation and lobbying for fair policy. As part of its congressional lobbying, the organization produces ratings of members of Congress on gay- and lesbian-related issues and seeks to organize grassroots efforts through constituency advocacy. In order to pursue these goals, the HRC maintains an action network that notifies members what action they can take to influence legislation and members of Congress. Further, the HRC profiles members of the House and Senate on gay- and lesbian-related issues and urges action based on that information.

Although advancement of gay and lesbian political equality has been relatively slow, the organization has participated actively and aided in the passage of several important pieces of legislation. Counted among its successes are increases in AIDS funding; the passage of the Ryan White Comprehensive AIDS Resources Emer-

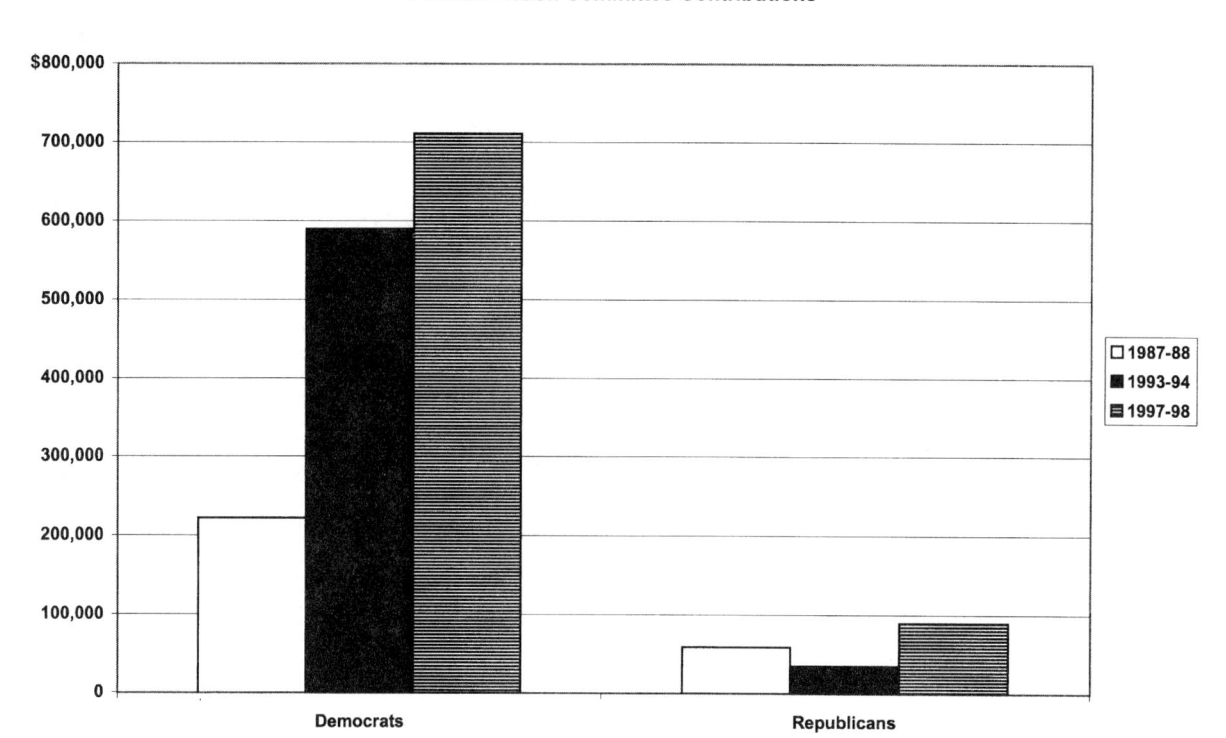

**Human Rights Campaign
Political Action Committee Contributions**

[Bar chart showing PAC contributions to Democrats and Republicans for three election cycles: 1987–88, 1993–94, and 1997–98. Democrats received approximately $220,000 (1987–88), $585,000 (1993–94), and $710,000 (1997–98). Republicans received approximately $55,000 (1987–88), $30,000 (1993–94), and $85,000 (1997–98).]

Data derived from official studies available from the Federal Election Commission, Washington, DC, 1987–1998.

gency Act; the Americans with Disability Act, which classified AIDS sufferers as a protected class; the Hate Crimes Statistics and Hate Crimes Sentencing Enhancement Acts (though hate crimes against gays and lesbians are not included as federal statute); and programs to increase research for health-related issues such as breast and cervical cancer.

One of the HRC's main activities is providing resources and aid to favorable candidates and attempting to defeat candidates unfavorable to gay and lesbian political issues. Its Human Rights Campaign political action committee (PAC) has raised considerable resources and targets races where financial support could prove critical. Through a field action network, the HRC not only provides financial backing, but also attempts to organize volunteers in House and Senate campaigns and educates candidates on gay- and lesbian-related issues.

Political campaigning is a cornerstone of HRC activity. The HRC seeks to register gay-friendly voters and targets races in which openly gay and lesbian candidates are seeking elective office. The HRC also sponsors two unique campaigning events. First, the HRC hosted in 1998 an OutVote Convention, which put the gay and lesbian equality agenda on the political landscape. Speakers at OutVote included Jesse Jackson, Democratic National Committee chair Roy Romer, AFL-CIO chief John Sweeney, and Congresswoman Cynthia McKinney. This high-profile event also featured a dinner that was attended by Vice President Al Gore. Past dinners have also featured President Bill Clinton, who became the first president to speak at a national gay and lesbian organization's function. Second, the HRC also sponsors a youth college, which trains individuals on how to campaign effectively. Its graduates enter the political campaigns of viable candidates and are active within gay organizations to aid in the effective articulation of gay- and lesbian-related issues. In 1996, 25 graduates worked on campaigns in 11 states.

A main priority of the HRC is the National Coming Out Day project. Begun in 1988, the National Coming Out Day project seeks to provide an environment in which gays and lesbians feel comfortable in outing themselves to coworkers and friends in order to promote honesty and openness.

One further recent priority of the HRC has been the Ray of Light project. The Ray of Light project seeks to counter the Ex-Gay movement, which seeks to "reform" gays and lesbians through ministry. The HRC provides information and has maintained a high profile to combat both this movement and politicians who endorse the Ex-Gay movement's views. The HRC is also a cosponsor of the Millennium March on Washington, a stance that has come under fire from other gay rights organizations such as the National Gay and Lesbian Task Force, which sees the march as an improper use of community resources.

Chief activities of the HRC have included battling anti-gay ballot measures. The HRC helped to fund the defeat of such measures in Oregon and Idaho in 1994 and Maine in 1995, and was the largest contributor to the challenge of Colorado's Amendment 2, which banned laws protecting homosexuals from discrimination. The HRC also conducts polling on gay and lesbian political issues and uses the information from those surveys to plan its lobbying and policy strategies.

The future of the HRC looks bright. Over the past few years, its budget has increased and its clout has grown as tolerance of gays and lesbians increases. The organization has made inroads into the policy community and within the Clinton White House. Its future success is tied to the success of Democrats both in the Congress and in the Oval Office. As such, a successful bid for the presidency by Al Gore would provide continuity for the organization and enhance its political power; conversely, Republican success in the 2000 presidential election would signal a decrease in legislative success, although it could enhance mobilization efforts.

FINANCIAL FACTS

In the 1998 election cycle, the HRC's PAC raised over $1 million and expended over $900,000 on candidates.

Given its emphasis on gay and lesbian political issues, and the political stances of the Democratic National Committee and the Republican National Committee, the bulk of the group's disbursements go to Democratic candidates. From January 1, 1997, to January 1, 1999, the HRC contributed $817,271 to Democratic candidates and $82,500 to Republican candidates. In addition to candidate expenditures, the HRC also contributed $27,000 to political parties and $88,100 to other political action committees. For the 1997–1998 election cycle, the HRC targeted nearly 200 House and Senate races and focused on five Senate races (Carol Moseley-Braun, Barbara Boxer, Russ Feingold, Harry Reid, and Patty Murray). It attempted to elect three openly gay Democrats to the House, including Christine Kehoe, Margarethe Cammermeyer, and Tammy Baldwin (elected as the first openly gay member of the House of Representatives). The HRC endorsed 194 candidates in 1998, including 178 Democrats, 15 Republicans, and one independent. Overall, HRC-backed candidates have done fairly well in the electoral arena, winning 83 percent of races in the 1996 election cycle and 90 percent in 1998. Among its controversial endorsements was the backing of Republican Alfonse D'Amato in New York's Senate campaign over Charles Schumer. While direct expenditures are important, HRC members also helped raise over $1.5 million for candidates.

MICHAEL LEVY

Bibliography

Bull, Chris. "The Power Brokers." *Advocate,* June 23, 1998.

DeAngelis, James, ed. *Public Interest Profiles, 1998–99.* CQ Foundation for Public Affairs. Washington, DC: Congressional Quarterly, 1998.

Human Rights Campaign: www.hrcusa.org

Stanhope, Victoria. "Where to Now? The Gay Rights Movement." *Off Our Backs,* December 6, 1996.

NATIONAL ASSOCIATION FOR THE ADVANCEMENT OF COLORED PEOPLE

The National Association for the Advancement of Colored People (NAACP) is a civil rights organization headquartered in Baltimore, Maryland, that campaigns for the political, educational, social, and economic equality of minorities.

With a membership of approximately 500,000 members and 2,200 branches in the United States, Germany, and Japan, the NAACP seeks to eliminate racial prejudice. Among its 500,000 members are 67,000 youth members organized in 120 college chapters and 450 youth councils. The organization is split into seven regions and is managed nationally by a 64-member board of directors. The NAACP is the country's oldest and largest civil rights group.

The NAACP seeks to achieve its goals through nonviolent strategies. It utilizes a variety of methods to achieve its goals, relying on the press, initiatives, the courts, and legal and moral persuasion to curtail and reduce racial discrimination and hostility in the United States.

HISTORY

The NAACP was founded on February 12, 1909—the 100th anniversary of Abraham Lincoln's birth—by black and white citizens who sought political equality and freedom for African Americans specifically and for minority citizens generally. Support for the organization came from black and white professionals including W.E.B. Du Bois and Ida Wells-Barnett. Throughout its history, the NAACP has focused on litigation and grassroots organizing for resolving discrimination. Court decisions in cases litigated by the NAACP beginning in 1910 gradually eliminated *de jure* (by lawful title) segregation in the United States on such issues as grandfather clauses, restrictive covenants, and integrated communities, among other issues.

Since its founding, the NAACP has engaged in a variety of efforts aimed at securing freedoms for the African-American community by sponsoring demonstrations, marches, and political lobbying to agitate for peaceful change. In 1919, the NAACP published a report on lynching in the United States that helped to expose the level of lynching activity in the South. As lynchings decreased, the NAACP shifted efforts during the Great Depression to focus on economic protection and police brutality, lobbying against racial discrimination in New Deal legislation.

After the Second World War, the NAACP engaged in litigation aimed at voter registration and education. The NAACP successfully litigated the landmark 1954 case, *Brown v. Board of Education of Topeka, Kansas,* which ended *de jure* segregation in U.S. public schools. Through protests and other activities, the organization helped usher in reforms on civil rights throughout the 1950s and 1960s.

In order to build coalitions, the NAACP created the Leadership Conference on Civil Rights to expand the scope of the struggle. Its successes include the Civil Rights Act, the Voting Rights Act, and the Fair Housing Act. Although the organization was always seeking to eliminate discrimination, over time the focus has changed from emphasizing advocacy to a more service-oriented strategy.

Recently, the NAACP experienced hard times. It was mired in a $4 million debt, it faced charges of corruption and scandal, and it was fighting an image of irrelevance as an organization. With the selection of Kweisi Mfume, who left a congressional seat to take over the ailing organization, the NAACP sought to reverse its downward slide. Under Mfume, along with Julian Bond, the chairman of the board, the NAACP has sought to return to its original mission: emphasizing equal rights and discrimination.

When Mfume and Bond began their tenure in the NAACP, the activities of the organization were 25 percent advocacy and 75 percent service. The percentages are slowly changing in favor of advocacy. However, the

NAACP will not abandon its commitment to service; rather, it will farm out these endeavors to other organizations.

ACTIVITIES: CURRENT AND FUTURE

The areas of interest of the NAACP are diverse and include affirmative action, hate crimes, foreign policy (especially related to sub-Saharan Africa and the Caribbean), desegregation, employment, and education.

Headed by the former head of the Black Congressional Caucus, Kweisi Mfume, the organization engages in numerous activities and sponsors scores of programs. Among these is ACT-SO (Academic, Cultural, Technological, and Scientific Olympics), which seeks to encourage African-American high school students to excel in science. The NAACP national office also develops and implements programs related to veteran affairs, education, health, economic development, employment, religion, and voter education, and it has a youth and college division. The Washington office focuses on lobbying members of Congress and executive agencies on civil rights issues.

Some samples of activities and programs include the NAACP's Legal Affairs department, which provides legal advice and representation to its more than 2,000 affiliates. The department directly litigates civil rights cases, provides free legal assistance to people suffering civil rights violations, and files *amicus curiae* briefs on behalf of cases in state and federal court. The Fair Share program, initiated in the 1980s to encourage the economic advancement of African Americans, targets companies, negotiates goals, and monitors compliance. Since its creation in 1981, the program has been successful in helping African Americans receive $1 billion in contracts annually and has generated scores of African-American owned businesses. The NAACP's Education Division seeks to encourage excellence among black students and examines issues related to education, including charter schools, voucher systems, school choice, testing procedures, and desegregation. The NAACP also publishes *Crisis Magazine,* which explores the African-American movement, key issues, and debates within the African-American community.

Thus, the NAACP engages in a wide array of activities, including direct-lobbying efforts in Washington and grassroots activities such as educational programs and advocacy on behalf of the African American community. In carrying out its activities, the NAACP advertises; engages in coalition-forming with like-minded groups; holds demonstrations; arranges for congressional testimony; engages in litigation, lobbying, and media outreach; offers scholarships; and promotes voter registration. These activities, among others, encourage greater participation of African Americans in politics and seek to enhance economic and social development in the African-American community.

The NAACP is at a crossroads. During its heyday in the 1950s and 1960s, it was successful in lobbying for civil rights reform in education and politics and was pivotal in the civil rights movement. The NAACP has sought, in the aftermath of its success, to find an organizational rationale. The crisis in the NAACP in the 1970s and 1980s was, according to some analysts, historical and philosophical, and the NAACP became a victim of its success. The successes of affirmative action and the various civil rights legislation have come under assault in the 1980s and 1990s. School desegregation is being challenged, and affirmative action is being eliminated or at least questioned. As a result, defense of affirmative action is the top priority of the NAACP, and the organization heavily funded a campaign to defeat anti-affirmative action measures in California and Washington State.

In addition to defending affirmative action, the NAACP has also fought in favor of hate crimes legislation, an area made especially salient after the dragging death of James Byrd Jr. in Jasper, Texas. It has also fought corporate discrimination (in such high-profile cases involving Texaco and Denny's); combated police brutality; and worked at registering voters and trying to curb gun violence. On this latter point, the NAACP has considered suing gun manufacturers for damages due to excessive gun violence in predominantly African-American areas.

Although the organization appeared to be a dinosaur and to be losing its influence and standing as the dominant civil rights organization for African Americans, Mfume has turned it around. Fund-raising has increased significantly and the financial health of the organization has returned. In 1998, its revenues outpaced expenditures by over $1 million, thus reversing the debt inherited by Mfume and Bond. Over the next few years, one should expect that advocacy activities will increase and that the defense of affirmative action and educational programs will continue to dominate internal debate and external advocacy. Rearguard battles fighting attempts to eliminate affirmative action and the threat of its irrelevance as an organization will likely continue to dominate the NAACP's agenda as other African-American organizations, such as Louis Farrakhan's Nation of

Islam, seek to supplant the NAACP as the chief voice of African Americans.

MICHAEL LEVY

Bibliography

DeAngelis, James, ed. *Public Interest Profiles, 1998–99.* CQ Foundation for Public Affairs. Washington: Congressional Quarterly, 1998.

Millner, D. "20 Years Then and Now—1970–1990." *The Black Collegian* 21, no. 3 (1991).

NAACP. "Welcome to the NAACP Homepage": www.naacp.org

Ovington, Mary White. 1999, 1914. "How the NAACP Began": www.naacp.org/about/history.html

Packer, George. "A Tale of Two Movements." *Nation,* December 14, 1998.

NATIONAL GAY AND LESBIAN TASK FORCE

While most other major national gay organizations, including the rival Human Rights Campaign, emphasize influencing the legislative process on Capitol Hill, the National Gay and Lesbian Task Force (NGLTF) has focused much of its attention and efforts at the state and local levels. Under the leadership of its executive director Kerry Lobel, the NGLTF has sought to be a voice for disadvantaged communities and to build "an unpretentious organization" that engages in grassroots organizing and advocacy. It acts as a lobbying and educational organization for full gay and lesbian civil rights and equality and seeks to create a society in which gays, lesbians, bisexuals, and transgendered individuals can live openly and without fear of attack and discrimination. Its main goal, thus, is to eliminate prejudice and anti-gay attacks and discrimination.

The NGLTF maintains a wide variety of interests and has battled numerous causes over the years. Its main activities are related to combating anti-gay violence, battling anti-gay ballot initiatives locally and at the state level, and advocating antidiscrimination legislation, the repeal of sodomy laws, HIV legislation, and reform of the U.S. healthcare system.

HISTORY

Founded in 1973, the NGLTF is the oldest national gay and lesbian civil rights organization in the United States. The organization was founded as part of the movement to advocate for social justice and diversity. Headquartered in the heart of the Adams Morgan district in Washington, D.C., and with offices in Boston and San Jose and a policy institute in New York City, the NGLTF has been at the forefront of major battles involving the rights of lesbians, gays, bisexuals, and transgendered individuals. The organization maintains a permanent staff of 20.

Since 1987, the organization has sponsored an annual Creating Change conference. This conference generally brings together between 1,000 and 2,000 gay activists from across the country and emphasizes coalition-building, state and local organizing skills, and motivation for activities.

ACTIVITIES: CURRENT AND FUTURE

The NGLTF engages in a wide array of activities and sponsorship of programs. One of its major programs for 1999 was the Equality Begins at Home campaign, which emphasized the political challenges facing the gay and lesbian community in the states. The goals of the campaign were to enhance state organizations and their capabilities of advancing gay and lesbian causes at the state level. The NGLTF argued that such an emphasis was essential, given the changing political landscape in the 1990s with the election of the Republican Congress in 1994, along with major gains by Republicans in statehouses and governors' mansions across the country and their stress on state and local control.

The NGLTF's Policy Institute produces information, research, policy analysis, and publications for the NGLTF. Created in 1994, the think tank, headquartered in New York City, seeks to link academe, activists, and policy makers through the publication of research papers, the development of policy proposals, and the development of strategies to advance gay, lesbian, bisexual, and transgender equality. In 1998 alone it published numerous reports, including *Income Inflation: The Myth of Affluence Among Gay, Lesbian, and Bisexual Americans; Calculated Compassion: How the Ex-Gay Movement Serves the Right's Attack on Democracy; Capital Gains and Losses: A State by State Review of Gay, Lesbian, Bisexual, Transgender, and HIV/AIDS-Related Legislation in 1998;* and *Out and Voting: The Gay, Lesbian, and Bisexual Vote* in *Congressional House Elections 1990–96*. The Policy Institute, thus, is the organization's main educational link and is responsible for crafting the background upon which it bases its strategies.

The Policy Institute also carries out surveys of public attitudes toward gays and lesbians. One study, released in 1998, showed a rise in tolerance of gays and lesbians, although the same study also showed majority disapproval of homosexuality. The NGLTF's Public Information Department maintains a clearinghouse for the gay and lesbian community and the media and produces newsletters and other publications.

The NGLTF has been at the forefront on HIV/AIDS-related issues. In 1997, for example, it backed the U.S. Conference of Mayors' resolution urging state and local health officials to support needle exchange in order to combat the spread of HIV/AIDS.

Especially in the wake of the murder of Matthew Shepard, an openly gay student in Wyoming, a chief area of concern for the NGLTF has been hate crimes legislation and the reporting of hate crimes statistics. It consistently and actively has supported the inclusion of gays, lesbians, bisexuals, and transgender individuals in hate crimes protections. Arguing that the laws are valuable since they create an environment in which society shows it will not tolerate discrimination, the NGLTF has fought for both federal and state hate crimes laws. An additional priority for the NGLTF has been the elimination of sodomy statutes at the state level.

Among other projects and initiatives of the NGLTF are the Anti-Violence project, which collects and releases information about gay-bashing incidents; the Privacy/Civil Rights project, which seeks repeal of anti-sodomy laws; the Campus project, which offers aid for students, faculty, and staff on campuses in their quest for equal treatment; and the Lesbian and Gay Families project, which attempts to guarantee legal recognition and protection for gay families.

Another current concern of the NGLTF is same-gender marriage rights. In the wake of state court decisions that influenced numerous states and the national government to adopt Defense of Marriage acts in order to limit the definition of marriage to a union between a man and woman, the NGLTF has been outspoken in advocating equal marriage rights for gays and lesbians. It has filed *amicus curiae* briefs in several cases.

The NGLTF has been a successful gay organization since its creation nearly 30 years ago. Though dwarfed in size by the larger and rival Human Rights Campaign (HRC), which sought to merge the two groups into the HRC's own programs, the NGLTF maintains a distinctive role through its Policy Institute and its emphasis on state and local politics, as opposed to the HRC's national emphasis. Its emphasis in the future will likely be a continuation of its current efforts and will include the abolition of sodomy laws, marriage and domestic partner benefits (sure to be a central issue in the first decade of 2000), hate crimes legislation, and HIV/AIDS-related issues. Given the increase in contributions and the NGLTF's budget in 1999, along with the increasing openness and activism of America's gay and lesbian community, one can expect the organization to grow in both size and influence over the next few years. However, its success is dependent upon Democratic success in upcoming congressional, presidential, and state and local campaigns. Should the Republicans capture the White House in 2000, one should expect the NGLTF's influence to diminish significantly, although this could yield increasing activism from an energized constituency.

FINANCIAL FACTS

In contrast to the Human Rights Campaign, the NGLTF's budget is quite modest. Its 1999 operating budget was $3.6 million, a 30 percent increase over 1998 figures. Much of the increase, which occurred for many gay rights organizations, was attributed to the rise in anti-gay activities symbolized by the killing of Matthew Shepard; Senate Majority Leader Trent Lott's remarks equating homosexuals with kleptomaniacs; and the Ex-Gay campaign, which seeks to "reform" gays and lesbians through ministry.

MICHAEL LEVY

Bibliography

"An Unlikely Cash Cow." *Advocate,* March 30, 1999.
Brown, Jessica. "Creating Change Offers Activists Opportunities for Organizing, Infighting." *Off Our Backs,* January 1999: 10–11.
Bull, Chris. "The Power Brokers." *Advocate,* June 23, 1998.
DeAngelis, James, ed. *Public Interest Profiles, 1998–99.* CQ Foundation for Public Affairs. Washington, DC: Congressional Quarterly, 1998.
NGLTF. "Welcome to the National Gay and Lesbian Taskforce On-Line": www.ngltf.org

NATIONAL ORGANIZATION FOR WOMEN

Headquartered in Washington, D.C., the National Organization for Women (NOW) was founded to bring women full equality and privileges in the United States and to provide an equal partnership between men and women. Representing women's rights, NOW is a nonprofit organization that boasts a membership of 500,000, with 250,000 active members organized into nearly 550 chapters in all 50 states and the District of Columbia. These figures make NOW the largest feminist rights organization in the United States.

The national organization is staffed by 30 full-time employees, along with interns and volunteers. Its chief areas of interest are to eliminate discrimination against women in all sectors of society, but especially in employment settings, schools, and the justice system; to end domestic violence and other forms of violence against women; to ensure access to abortion; to end sexism (along with racism and homophobia); and to promote equality in the United States.

NOW maintains a political action committee (PAC). NOW/PAC is nonpartisan, although its campaign contributions tilt heavily in favor of Democratic candidates. Though feminist in orientation, NOW provides funding to male and female candidates who satisfy their criteria for support. These criteria include support for abortion rights, support for civil rights (including gay, lesbian, and racial), ending violence against women, support for an Equal Rights Amendment (ERA), affirmative action, and nonpunitive welfare-to-work policies.

HISTORY

NOW was founded in 1966 by 28 women attending the Third National Conference of the Commission on the Status of Women. The purpose of the commission was to explore areas in which women were discriminated against and to encourage the full and equal participation of women in politics and economics. Arguing that there was no civil rights organization on behalf of women, NOW was created to be the chief advocate for women's rights during the civil rights era. Among its original founders were Betty Friedan, who was the organization's first president, and Rev. Pauli Murray, who co-wrote NOW's original mission statement. That mission statement sought equality of women with men, to move the women's movement beyond words, and to engage in direct action in order to secure women's rights. Some of NOW's earliest activities concerned women in poverty, reproductive rights, the image of women in the media, educational access, legal and political rights, and equal opportunity in employment. Thus, while some additional issues have appeared over the past 30 years, NOW has been consistent in pursuing its earliest objectives and seeking to maintain its policy gains.

Over its history, NOW has engaged in both traditional and nontraditional methods to pursue its goals. In order to gain media coverage, NOW has organized mass marches, engaged in civil disobedience, held rallies, and picketed. Over the past 30 years, some of its demonstrations have included an Equal Rights Amendment rally in 1978 that drew 100,000, a pro-choice rally in 1992 that drew 750,000, and a more recent demonstration to combat violence against women that drew 250,000 to Washington.

Among its earliest concerns was the Equal Rights Amendment. NOW engaged in a series of high-profile events along with significant lobbying. Although the ERA was not passed, NOW was successful in lobbying Congress to extend the deadline for ratification by three years and spurred the creation of its PAC to raise money on behalf of candidates who support the ERA.

Over time, NOW has continued its quest for the ERA and has dedicated itself to preserving the *Roe v. Wade* decision, which guaranteed abortion access to women. With the election of Ronald Reagan as presi-

**National Organization for Women
Political Action Committee Contributions, 1987–1988**

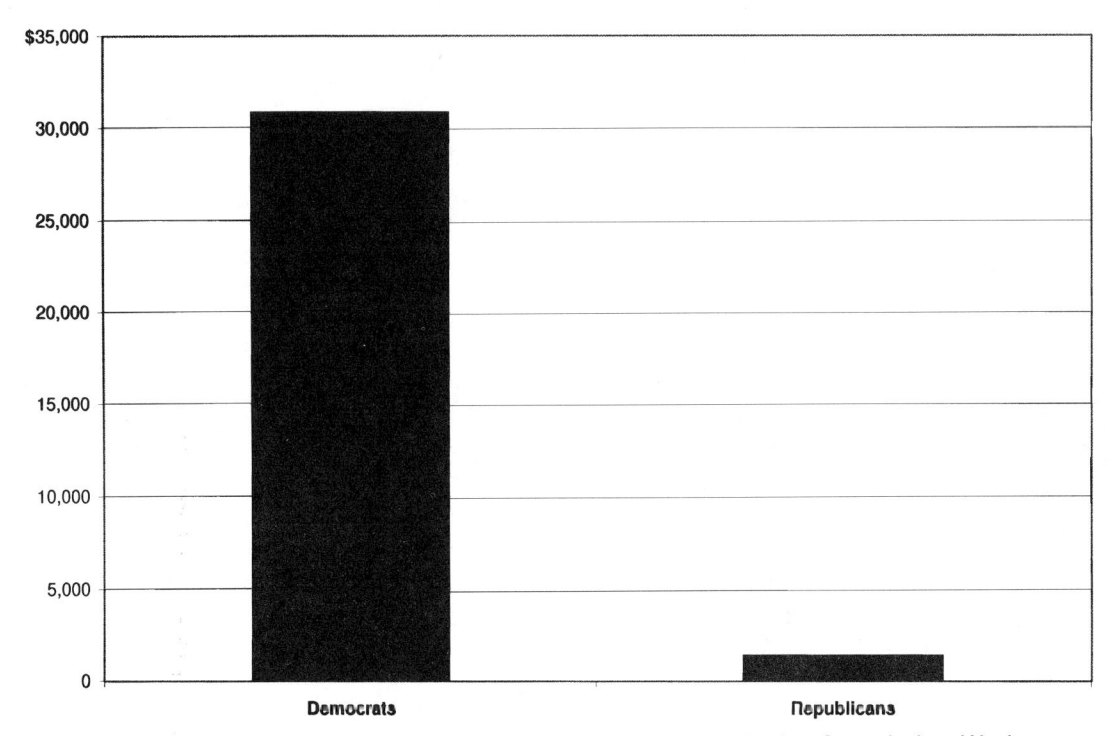

[Bar chart showing Democrats received approximately $31,000 and Republicans received approximately $1,500]

Data derived from official studies available from the Federal Election Commission, Washington, DC, 1987–1988.

dent in 1980, NOW began to turn its attention to the federal courts, establishing a Court Watch project to monitor appointments. In that vein, NOW has consistently fought judges who are unfriendly to women's rights and was pivotal in mobilizing against Clarence Thomas in his Senate Judiciary Committee hearings.

More recently, NOW has focused its attention on fighting rearguard battles to maintain abortion rights and affirmative action. Like other civil rights organizations, it has, in some ways, been a victim of its own success. With the exception of the ERA, NOW secured many of its earliest goals, including reproductive rights protections, affirmative action, and funding for programs related to women in college (Title IX). During the Reagan/Bush years, many of the successes came under attack, with abortion access being increasingly restricted and affirmative action debated and eliminated in some areas (such as the passage of Proposition 209 in California). NOW's vigilance in fighting reversals in these policies, along with other feminist organizations, has dominated much of its recent activities.

Although it has been a strong supporter of harassment laws, NOW, along with other feminist organizations, came under fire from conservatives when it stood by President Bill Clinton during the impeachment debate in 1998–1999. Patricia Ireland, along with past-president Betty Friedan, organized grassroots efforts to express opposition to impeachment and removal and utilized the issue to encourage citizens to vote against the president's opponents, citing partisan politics rather than a conversion by the Republicans to support for women's rights.

ACTIVITIES: CURRENT AND FUTURE

NOW's official priorities are equal rights, economic equality, abortion rights, civil rights, lesbian rights, and ending violence against women. Its current activities concern these priorities. NOW supports efforts to maintain access to abortion, birth control, and related information, and lobbies against efforts to regulate and curtail abortion access, including a constitutional amendment. It has litigated cases in order to ensure that women entering health clinics providing abortion services are not harassed. It has challenged pro-life groups to combat clinic violence in the wake of murders of abortion providers. It has sought to mobilize pro-choice advocates against regulations such as the Teen Endangerment Act, which would make it a crime for someone to accompany a minor across state lines to obtain abortion services.

NOW is a strong supporter of affirmative action policies for women and has rallied in favor of judges and federal appointees who uphold affirmative action. It is a strong supporter of domestic and hate crimes legislation, urging stronger methods of prosecution.

NOW has issued statements and lobbied Congress on behalf of women in other countries. Recent concerns have included treatment of women in Afghanistan by the Taliban, the Muslim fundamentalist group, and sponsoring the Convention on the Elimination of All Forms of Discrimination Against Women. In addition to these issues, NOW's current activities include lesbian rights, economic equality, combating racism, advocating on behalf of women in the military, and creating a positive employment atmosphere for women.

Under the leadership of Patricia Ireland, president since 1991, NOW has continued its efforts in both traditional direct lobbying and grassroots activity. NOW, as other traditional lobbying organizations, maintains close contacts with legislators favorable to feminism and seeks to influence the substance of policies and to encourage the development of friendly policies. In pursuing its objectives, NOW produces action alerts, holds news conferences, holds demonstrations such as the 1996 March to Fight the Right in San Francisco to defend affirmative action, engages in boycotts, publishes voter guides (including an award-winning Internet voting guide), litigates cases, and publishes the *National NOW Times* to inform its members about current concerns and how they can become involved in influencing policy. Thus, its nonlobbying activities are diverse and include organizing and mobilizing, educational efforts, and advocating on behalf of women.

NOW's future activities are likely to revolve around a continued rearguard battle in the areas of affirmative action and abortion rights. The likelihood of success cannot be gauged in these areas, but NOW will expend considerable resources to support candidates with like-minded views. While NOW will continue for the foreseeable future as the largest women's rights organization, judging from contributions, the organization has not witnessed a growth (partially due to the growth in other feminist groups) in support and is not likely to increase its influence without the return of a Democratic Congress. In that vein, NOW established a Victory 2000 campaign to elect 2,000 feminists by 2000.

FINANCIAL FACTS

During the 1998 election season, NOW/PAC raised approximately $160,000 and disbursed a similar amount. It contributed $80,385 to Democratic candidates and $46 to an Independent candidate. NOW/PAC contributions represent a significant drop from its high in 1991–1992. The Clarence Thomas judicial hearings spurred contributions to feminist organizations. NOW's 1992 contributions to Democrats totaled $287,638, whereas Republicans were provided with $26,000 in support.

MICHAEL LEVY

Bibliography

Carabillo, Toni. *The Feminist Chronicles, 1953–1993*. Los Angeles: Woman Graphic, 1993.

DeAngelis, James, ed. *Public Interest Profiles, 1998–99*. CQ Foundation for Public Affairs. Washington, DC: Congressional Quarterly, 1998.

NOW. "National Organization for Women": www.now.org

Zuckerman, Edward, ed. *The Almanac of Federal PACs: 1998–99*. Arlington, VA: Amward, 1998.

SECTION THIRTEEN
FOREIGN

Foreign governments have promoted their interests in the United States since the 1800s. As the United States became a great power, its actions (or lack of involvement) in foreign policy had greater impact on other countries. As the American economy grew stronger relative to other nations, for example, its trade policies became more significant to their welfare. Thus, the growth of United States power in the world increases the incentives of foreign governments to attempt to influence the design of American foreign policy. In the 1990s the United States has remained the world's most powerful nation, as determined by economic and military measures as well as by cultural influence. For the near future, foreign governments will have reason to continue their lobbying efforts.

The lobbying activities of foreign governments received intense media attention after the 1996 elections, with the discovery that Chinese nationals had illegally contributed to both Democratic and Republican candidates. The investigation of these contributions failed to discover a direct link to the Chinese government to a plot to take over the American foreign–policy making process. Nevertheless, questions were openly asked regarding American vulnerability to attempts by foreign governments to buy influence. This concerned many Americans despite the fact that most of the organizations that lobby on behalf of foreign entities do so for international businesses; however, this often serves the interests of foreign governments as well. Moreover, it is becoming increasingly popular for foreign governments to hire outside counsel to pursue their own interests directly. Given the perception by policy makers that most voters pay little attention to foreign-policy decision making, critics of foreign government interest groups fear that pressure from these lobbies could lead policy makers to develop a foreign policy that would fail to serve the American national interest.

In fact, contrary to the fears expressed by some during the China lobby scandal, interest groups that focus on foreign policy are greatly outnumbered by domestic organizations. Foreign government lobbies in the form of registered political action committees (PACs) contributed over $2 million to 1990 congressional campaigns. Though not an inconsequential amount, this is dwarfed by the $678 million contributed by domestic PACs. Although the number of interest groups that focus on foreign affairs has increased in the 1990s, it has been matched by the growth of interest groups that lobby for domestic interests.

There are several types of organizations used by foreign governments. One is ethnic lobbies: for some countries, hyphenated Americans with an interest in promoting the well-being of their mother country are a source of influence over policy makers in Washington. Another set of venues used by foreign governments directly to represent their interests are public relations firms and law firms. In some cases, the interest groups of international businesses also pursue the interests of foreign governments. Most commonly, however, foreign governments lobby through their embassies: these are not defined as formal interest groups, yet they actively lobby for their national interests. In fact, the difference between diplomacy and lobbying is fuzzy. Thus, it is difficult to measure precisely how much is being spent by foreign governments on lobbying. In addition, one indirect means for governments to influence policy is by funding academic departments and academic research in the hope that this will shape discussions of foreign policy among elite policy makers.

In the post–Cold War era, one common fear of foreign governments is the possibility of a resurgence of American isolationism. For various reasons, foreign governments do not wish to see an American withdrawal from international politics. One major goal of much of their lobbying involves access to American money. Foreign aid, most-favored-nation (MFN) trade status, American investments, trade arrangements, and investment opportunities in the United States constitute the bulk of foreign governments' interests. Another goal of some lobbies is to obtain military assistance and security guarantees in the form of arms sales and defense arrangements. Immigration policy is another issue that affects foreign governments. In some cases, the goal of foreign government lobbies is a negative one: to avoid sanctions or admonition for a questionable human rights record. It should be noted that some of the most important goals of a foreign government are those for which it cannot directly lobby; for example, China is happy about American troop reductions in Asia. Generally, such policies affect the economic strength, political stability, and national security of other states.

Foreign governments focus their lobbying efforts on Congress, federal and state agencies (particularly the State Department), White House liaisons, governors, and local governments where foreign firms want to locate. Many foreign governments find America's decentralized and vast government structure conducive to the pursuit of their interests. They also attempt to influence the media and American public opinion in general.

AREAS OF INTEREST

Foreign governments have lobbied in America for over two centuries. One early instance of this activity involved Daniel Webster, who was retained in the 1840s by the wealthy Lord Ashburton of England. Ashburton gave Webster "secret service" funds to shape public opinion, and Webster negotiated a treaty favorable to the British. This stirred some criticism; however, it was not until 1938 that activities of foreign lobbies were regulated. In response to fascist and Nazi propaganda circulating in the United States, Congress passed the Foreign Agents Registration Act. This act required anyone who represented a foreign government or individual to register with the Department of Justice. With the rise of the Cold War, some lobbies concentrated on maintaining a security relationship with the United States. In the 1940s and the 1950s, Europeans lobbied for the Marshall Plan, and during decolonization newly independent states appealed for foreign aid. In the early 1970s, when the American economy began to falter, foreign governments lobbied against protectionist trade legislation.

Occasionally the activities of foreign government lobbies have led to political scandals. By law foreign citizens are prohibited from giving money to American campaigns, although ethnic lobbies and American subsidiaries of foreign businesses are allowed to do so. In 1976 the *Washington Post* reported that South Korean agents, led by businessman and socialite Tongsun Park, tried to bribe U.S. officials and buy influence among journalists in order to sustain a favorable legislative climate for South Korean interests. The *Post* discovered spending between $500,000 and $1 million annually on cash and gifts to members of Congress; three members of Congress were reprimanded, and one former member was sent to prison.

More recent scandals include reports after the 1996 election that illegal campaign contributions were made by Chinese citizens to both parties: the Democrats had to return $3 million. These contributions had the purpose of maintaining MFN status with the United States. The investigation into the source of these contributions eventually fizzled, but the fact that foreign nationals had illegally contributed to American campaigns has made the subject of foreign government interest groups a controversial one.

CURRENT CONTEXT

In the post–Cold War era there has been considerable uncertainty about the international environment and America's proper role within the world. The United States remains a superpower, and its actions continue to affect other nations. This has led to an increase in lobbying activity on the part of foreign governments; while still outnumbered by domestic lobbies, the number of organizations formed or hired to promote the interests of foreign governments has risen steadily since the mid 1960s.

Reductions in military spending are leading to pressures to reduce or withdraw U.S. troops abroad. At the same time, American involvement in multilateral organizations such as the United Nations and the North Atlantic Treaty Organization (NATO) promotes continued American interest in issues of international security. On the economic front, while the strong economy of the 1990s has reduced tensions about the trade deficit, affected industries still lobby for protectionist trade policies.

It is very difficult to determine the efficacy of the lobbying of foreign governments. Direct links between lobbying and policy results are hard to prove. Furthermore, the distinction between lobbying activity and diplomacy is difficult to determine. Generally, however, foreign governments are more effective when lobbying on noncrisis issues, or issues defined as "low politics," such as economic matters. In the "high politics" area of security, foreign government lobbies are successful only if their interests mesh with the perceived interests of the United States. They are also more likely to succeed when lobbying for issues that are less visible or salient to the public at large.

Overall, the results are mixed. Foreign aid is not a popular topic in American political discourse, and attempts by the Republican-controlled Congress to reduce it are common. Military spending was also reduced in the 1990s, and the United States reduced many of its overseas commitments. At the same time, however, the United States has not returned to a "fortress America" isolationist foreign policy. It continues to be an active member of international organizations and to play a powerful role in influencing the decisions of multilateral institutions such as the World Bank and NATO. To the extent that the United States remains active in international politics, policy makers will be confronted with foreign-policy decisions. In many cases the power of foreign government lobbies is in their role as information providers; if a member of Congress is relatively uninterested in foreign affairs, an effective lobby can sway an otherwise uncommitted policy maker to support the interests of its client.

TYPES OF ORGANIZATIONS

The most important organization that lobbies for a foreign government is its own embassy. It is commonplace for embassy personnel to visit members of Congress, congressional staff members, and White House staff members to promote their interests. These embassies are able to promote their government's interests directly. The other type of lobbying that is used by foreign governments is to hire public relations firms and law firms. All of the foreign governments that hire these firms are required by law to disclose this information; these organizations for 1999 are listed in the appendix to this article.

More common, but less directly focused on a country's national interest, are lobbies for foreign businesses. In the case of some countries, such as Japan, these lobbies are an important part of their overall lobbying power.

Less common, but in some cases more effective, are ethnic lobbies, which are composed of Americans loyal to their mother country. As American citizens, members of ethnic lobbies may legally contribute to political campaigns. Countries that are able to sustain the loyalty of American ethnics benefit from the efforts of ethnic lobbies to promote the interests of their mother country. The classic example of this is Israel, which has 75 ethnic lobbies, including the powerful American-Israel Political Action Committee (AIPAC). However, not every ethnic group in the United States has a strong lobbying presence in Washington. Groups that are unsure of their status within the larger society and fearful of the disdain that their activities might generate may be constrained from active involvement: some argue that this is a partial explanation for the absence of a strong Asian ethnic lobby. Furthermore, some ethnic lobbies focus more on improving conditions for their group within the United States, rather than pursuing preferences in foreign policy; for example, the Mexican-American Legal Defense and Education Fund works primarily to improve conditions for Mexican Americans within the United States.

CURRENT ISSUES

For many countries the United States is their number-one trade partner; for many others the volume of trade with the United States has increased rapidly in recent years. Consequently, one issue that continues to be important is keeping American markets open to imports. In the 1990s one major goal is the establishment of free-trade zones in order to offer foreign governments greater protection from protectionist pressures within America.

Immigration restrictions are another important issue. In 1996 Congress passed new restrictions on immigration that made entry into the United States much tougher. This action upset groups representing Mexico and Cuban exiles, which depend on immigration as an outlet for domestic pressures or to promote change within their mother country. Generally, foreign governments are interested in promoting a more positive image of immigration.

For some ethnic lobbies, issues that generate organized responses are moral and humanitarian concerns, such as imposing sanctions on a nation or regime that is acting against the interests of the mother country. These policy preferences can conflict with official arguments and policies that stress the primacy of strategic considerations as the most important rationale for foreign policy. After Turkey's invasion of Cyprus the

Greek-American lobby worked for an embargo on arms sales to Turkey, despite Turkey's strategic location and its status as a NATO member.

Another issue for many foreign governments is American involvement in international organizations. Many states think that ultimately, given America's relative power capabilities, the decisions of multilateral groups ultimately reflect American preferences. One particular issue is America's unpaid debt to the United Nations (UN), which was $1.6 billion in 1999; some foreign governments argue that if the United States wants to continue to have voting rights in the UN, this debt should be paid. However, this is proving to be a difficult issue, as Congress continues to resist arranging for repayment while arguing that the UN needs to enact internal reforms before it will do so. American participation in UN peacekeeping missions and the conditions for such participation are issues of concern to foreign governments. Another issue of concern regarding U.S. participation in international organizations is American support for the expansion of NATO. Foreign governments are divided on the wisdom of this expansion, with many eastern European states in favor of, but Russia strongly opposed to, the continued existence of what had been an anti-Soviet alliance.

Another important security issue is arms sales. America is by far the world's largest exporter of weaponry, and this is a concern of foreign governments in several respects. For some the goal is to purchase American weaponry on favorable terms. For others the goal is to increase the sales of weaponry produced in their state, thus reducing the dominance of American producers. Still others are concerned that arms sales may be destabilizing in some areas, and they try to reduce American sales to these sectors.

Finally, some treaties that have been signed by most of the world's governments have yet to be ratified in the United States. One international treaty would impose a ban on the use of land mines, which have maimed and killed people all around the world. The United States has resisted the appeals of other countries to support this treaty, on the advice of American military officials who argue that land mines are necessary to defend allies such as South Korea. In addition, the United States resisted appeals to sign the treaty to institute an international court to try war criminals; concerns within the military and among some members of Congress that this court would be used by rogue states such as Iraq to prosecute Americans solidified American opposition to this treaty.

ACTIVITIES

Some of the lobbying activities of foreign governments are direct, including testifying at congressional hearings and establishing personal contacts with legislators and staff members. One interest foreign governments have at the level of local governments is to establish "sister cities," which are perceived as one way to increase American interest in their country. In some cases, public relations firms and law firms that were hired by a foreign government work in direct cooperation with business lobbies, as Mexico's lobby did when the North American Free Trade Agreement was debated.

Other techniques are indirect, including mobilizing the public and contributing to American universities and charities. Ethnic lobbies also engage in activities that keep their group informed of developments in the government and throughout critical areas of the world. Foreign governments are also concerned about how they are portrayed in the media. Islamic countries are concerned about images of Islam as a violent anti-Western movement that poses a threat to America. In 1991 they lobbied Disney against the use of negative stereotypes in the theme song for the movie *Aladdin* and succeeded in altering the lyrics on the home video Disney released of the film.

FUTURE OUTLOOK

As the world heads into the twenty-first century, foreign governments will continue to have an interest in American foreign policy. At the same time, their attempts to lobby for their interests are likely to be increasingly scrutinized by those who are suspicious of their intentions. However, the growth of lobbying by foreign governments is likely to continue.

APPENDIX: OUTSIDE COUNSEL AND CONSULTANTS FOR FOREIGN GOVERNMENTS

China:
  Jones, Day, Reavis and Pogue
  Powell, Goldstein, Frazer, and Murphy, LLP

Cuban exiles:
  Jenkins and Gilchrist
  Ralph Marshall
Japan:
  Manatt, Phelps, and Phillips, LLP
  Dechert, Price, and Rhoads
  Hogan and Hortson, LLP
  Milbank, Tweed, Hadley, and McCloy
  Mullin Communications, Inc.
  Saunders and Co.
  Smith Dawson and Andrews, Inc.
Israel:
  Arnold and Porter
  Ifshin and Friedman, P.L.L.C.
Mexico:
  Manatt, Phelps, and Phillips, LLP
  Burson-Marsteller
  Hon. Jack M. McDonald
  Milbank, Tweed, Hadley, and McCloy
Nigeria:
  Washington World Group, Inc.
Russia:
  Coudert Borthers
Taiwan:
  Bergner Bockorny, Inc.
  Heller and Rosenblatt
  O'Connor and Hannan, LLP
  Oldaker and Harris, LLP
  The Solomon Group, LLC
  Symms, Lehn and Associates, Inc.
  Verner, Liipfert, Bernhard, McPherson and Hand, Chartered
  Gary Wasserman and Associates
Turkey:
  Arnold and Porter
  Ahmet Ural Duvak
  IMPACT, LLC
  Patton Boggs, LLP
  Law Offices of David L. Simon

Source: *Washington Representatives*. New York: Columbia University Press, 1999.

ALLYSON FORD

Bibliography

Baumgartner, Frank R., and Beth L. Leech. *Basic Interests: The Importance of Groups in Politics*. Princeton, NJ: Princeton University Press, 1998.

Birnbaum, Jeffrey. *The Lobbyists: How Influence Peddlers Get Their Way in Washington*. New York: Times Books, 1992.

Center for Responsible Politics: www.crp.org

Cigler, Allan, and Bardett Loomis. *Interest Group Politics*, 5th ed. Washington, DC: Congressional Quarterly Press, 1998.

Goldberg, David Howard. *Foreign Policy and Ethnic Interest Groups: American and Canadian Jews Lobby for Israel*. New York: Greenwood Press, 1990.

Kollman, Ken. *Outside Lobbying: Public Opinion and Interest Group Strategies*. Princeton, NJ: Princeton University Press, 1998.

Rozell, Mark J., and Clyde Wilcox. *Interest Groups in American Campaigns: The New Face of Electioneering*. Washington, DC: Congressional Quarterly Press, 1999.

Tierney, John T. "Interest Group Involvement in Congressional Foreign and Defense Policy." In *Congress Resurgent: Foreign and Defense Policy on Capitol Hill*, edited by Randall B. Ripley and James M. Lindsay. Ann Arbor, MI: University of Michigan Press, 1993.

Wantanabe, Paul Y. *Ethnic Groups, Congress, and American Foreign Policy: The Politics of the Turkish Arms Embargo*. Westport, CT: Greenwood Press, 1984.

★★★★★★
CHINA

Since the recognition of the People's Republic of China (PRC) in the 1970s, U.S.-Chinese relations have alternated between positive and critical. With the end of the Cold War the logic of triangulation, or relations with China to check Soviet power, has faded; in the aftermath of the incident in Beijing's Tiananmen Square in 1989, China's image within the United States has been a negative one. Nevertheless, the U.S. policy of constructive engagement with China ensures that China's voice will be heard, if not always heeded.

China has four major objectives in international politics: first, to maintain national security, national unity, and protect its sovereignty; second, to obtain access to foreign markets and secure technology, natural resources, and capital for economic growth; third, to participate in international organizations, which increases China's status and affects its fate; and fourth, to use the international arena to enhance its domestic power.

To pursue these goals, China has relied on the lobbying efforts of its embassy and of several public relations firms, which in the past included Kissinger Associates (formed by former secretary of state Henry Kissinger). It relies on Chinese-Americans as a source of capital, technology, and policy advice. The scandals after the 1996 U.S. presidential election, with revelations that Chinese nationals illegally contributed to political campaigns of both Democrats and Republicans, generated discussion of whether the Chinese lobby was trying to buy American foreign policy. Although the investigation found no link, suspicion remains high.

HISTORY

On October 1, 1949, Mao Zedong, the leader of the Chinese revolution, proclaimed the founding of the People's Republic of China. The United States refused to recognize Mao's Communist government as the legitimate governing body of China, however recognizing the Taiwan-based Republic of China instead. After its founding, the PRC initially focused on establishing ties with the Soviet Union and other Communist nations. In the Korean War, China sent the People's Liberation Army to North Korea to halt the UN offensive (led by the United States) that was approaching the Yalu River. However, by the late 1960s divisions between China and the Soviet Union became increasingly apparent—particularly in 1969, when the two nations engaged in military clashes along their border.

Under the Nixon administration the United States began to open relations with the PRC. In 1969 the United States took measures to relax trade restrictions with China, and America officially met with Chinese leaders in 1972. The United States granted formal diplomatic recognition to China in 1979. Since then, both security and economic concerns have been at the forefront of Chinese issues with the United States.

In the 1980s China tried to combine central planning with market-oriented reforms to increase economic productivity, living standards, and technical capabilities. It tried to do so without increasing unemployment, inflation, and budget deficits. One way China attempted to achieve these goals was by increasing foreign financing and Chinese exports, and the United States was an important partner in this venture. During the 1980s China's annual growth rate averaged an increase of 11 percent per year, and rural incomes doubled. By the late 1980s, however, inflation became a problem and the government instituted an austerity program. In the 1990s China's economy has enjoyed an average annual growth rate of 8 percent per year. China was relatively untouched by the 1998 economic recession that affected other Asian nations.

Security concerns have been matters of contention at times. In 1981 China objected to American arms sales to Taiwan. In response Secretary of State Alexander Haig visited China in June to try to resolve unanswered questions about America's relationship with Taiwan, and in August 1982 the United States and China signed a joint communiqué on the issue. Under this communiqué the United States pledged to reduce arms sales to Taiwan, while China pledged that it would make it a fundamental Chinese policy to strive for a peaceful resolution to the Taiwan question.

One historical event that continues to affect U.S.-Chinese relations is the Chinese suppression of demonstrators in June 1989 in Tiananmen Square. Despite Chinese objections, the U.S. took several punitive steps against China, some through Congress and some by executive decisions. These included the suspension of new activities by the Trade and Development Agency and Overseas Private Insurance Corporation and opposition to International Monetary Fund credits, except for projects that meet basic human needs. One of China's main goals in lobbying the United States is to repair its image from this event, both with policy makers and the general public.

ACTIVITIES: CURRENT AND FUTURE

China places a very high value on maintaining its sovereignty. The Chinese perceive that their country has been exploited and humiliated throughout its history by outside aggressors; thus, vigilance is necessary to protect China. This applies to maintaining internal stability as well as external security; consequently, China perceives any attempt by others to shape internal Chinese politics as a threat. China has been willing to forgo gains from trade if conditions for this trade impose on its domestic policies.

Therefore, China's priority in the 1990s has been to prevent the United States from imposing sanctions or removing most-favored-nation (MFN) trade status because of China's human rights record. Since China has a large nonmarket economy, its normal trade status must be renewed annually by a presidential waiver stipulating that China meets the freedom of emigration requirements set forth in the Jackson-Vanik amendment to the Trade Act of 1974. After Tiananmen, Congress exerted pressure to oppose MFN status for China. In 1991 and 1992 Congress voted to place restrictions on normal trade status renewal for China. However, China was successful at convincing the Bush administration to veto these restrictions.

In 1994 the Chinese lobby won a big victory with President Bill Clinton's decision to delink the annual normal trade status process from China's overall human rights record. In 1998 China had a trade surplus of $58 billion with the United States: it values the gains from trade and places a high priority on keeping the American market open.

Currently China is actively lobbying to get into the World Trade Organization (WTO) and is negotiating the terms of entry with the United States. The United States rejected Beijing's initial suggested terms in April 1999, when President Clinton acted under his advisors' suggestions that a better deal could be obtained. The issue for the United States has been whether China offers sufficient market access for both goods and services, full trading rights for all potential Chinese consumers, nondiscrimination between foreign and local commercial operations in China, the reduction of monopolistic state trading practices, and the elimination of nonscientific technical standards.

Some observers speculate that China is anxious to join the WTO in order to overcome domestic objections to further liberalization of the economy. Hence, China is working very hard to obtain United States approval of its entry, making cuts in tariffs and quotas that would make its terms of trade more liberal than those of many WTO members. Once presidential support for China's entry is granted, Congress will not need to vote on a final deal, but will have to pass legislation granting China normal trade relations with the United States on a permanent basis. In November 1999, the two nations signed an historic trade agreement that paved the way for China's entry into the WTO.

In security affairs Beijing's sense of international vulnerability has increased since the late 1980s: the collapse of the Soviet Union, the Gulf War, developments of democracy in Taiwan, and the reinforcement of the U.S.-Japanese security alliance all make China uneasy. In addition, China is wary of the growth of regional and multilateral forums in Asia. China distrusts international security organizations as the instruments of dominant powers.

One recent loss for Chinese lobbying efforts was the American decision to sell F-16 airplanes to Taiwan; this tests the limits of the U.S.-China arms sales agreement. Meanwhile, China is resisting American attempts to make it cut down or eliminate its sales of weapons and dual-use technology. However, China relies on arms sales to get foreign exchange for needed purchases of technology and supplies.

In 1996 China conducted military exercises in waters close to Taiwan in an apparent effort at intimidation. The United States responded by dispatching two aircraft carrier battle groups to the region, and tensions in the area subsided. In 1999, however, the United States openly repudiated Taiwan's statement that it wanted to be treated as an independent state and reaffirmed its commitment to a "one China" position, under which it recognizes Chinese sovereignty over Taiwan. Beijing praised this U.S. reaffirmation of its "one China" policy.

During the Kosovo crisis of 1999, the United States accidentally bombed the Chinese embassy in Belgrade, Yugoslavia. China successfully demanded that the United States fund the costs of repairing the embassy building; however, Chinese suspicions remain high. There are tensions on the U.S. side as well, with recent allegations of Chinese spying at the Los Alamos research laboratory in New Mexico. In June 1999 the House adopted measures to counter alleged Chinese espionage, including tightening security at Department of Energy nuclear laboratories, strengthening monitoring of overseas satellite launches, and controls of high-technology imports. Together with lingering suspicions about the Chinese lobby after the 1996 scandals, these incidents are likely to lead to a lower profile for China in the future.

ALLYSON FORD

Bibliography

Oksenberg, Michel, and Elizabeth Economy. *Shaping U.S.-China Relations*. New York: Council of Foreign Relations, 1997.

Sutter, Robert G. *Shaping China's Future in World Affairs: The U.S. Role*. Carlisle Barracks, PA: Strategic Studies Institute, 1996.

www.state.gov

CUBAN EXILES

Since the 1959 Cuban revolution, opponents of Fidel Castro's regime have lobbied the United States to exert pressure on the Cuban state to change its government. In service of this goal the Cuban American National Foundation (CANF) was established in 1981 by Cuban exiles in the United States. It has offices in Washington, D.C., Los Angeles, the New York metropolitan area, Chicago, Texas, Georgia, Puerto Rico, Miami and several other cities in Florida, Venezuela, and Spain. In 1991 CANF's Exodus Relief Fund opened an office in Moscow. The fundamental mission of CANF is, first, to generate support in the United States and elsewhere to resisting Castro's regime and replacing it with a democratic system in Cuba. In addition, it seeks to serve as a voice to unite the Cuban exiles.

CANF states that it is in favor of nonviolent change and does not condone the use of force to promote change in Cuba. However, the organization also opposes negotiations with Castro. CANF argues that there is nothing to be gained from meeting with the current Cuban government, as it will not negotiate its own demise. Consequently, CANF's goal is to isolate and weaken the Castro regime, with the eventual result of forcing a change of government in Cuba.

HISTORY

CANF has been effective in maintaining American opposition to the Castro regime. During the Cold War this was not difficult, since Cuba was widely perceived as a Soviet puppet state. However, CANF has continued to be successful in the post–Cold War era in its main goal of preventing the establishment of normal relations between the United States and Cuba.

In the 1980s CANF lobbied for official U.S. and public support for the Union for the Total Independence of Angola (UNITA) rebels in Angola, who were fighting a Marxist government backed by 50,000 Cuban troops. Longtime CANF president Jorge Mas Canosa was a close personal friend of UNITA's Jonas Savimbi, and he tried to counter the negative image of Savimbi as a brutal despot.

In 1984 CANF formed the Cuban Exodus Relief Fund, which provided humanitarian aid to Cuban refugees without legal status who are in other countries waiting for entry into the United States. This organization was incorporated as an independent nonprofit organization in March 1991.

CANF has been particularly active within the Republican Party and established close ties to the Reagan administration. During the Iran-Contra hearings CANF helped fund the legal expenses of Oliver North. When Bill Clinton came to office, however, this partisanship may have worked against CANF's interests. In 1993, after the Clinton administration blocked a black Cuban nominee for the post of chief policy maker on Latin America, its policies tilted toward a moderate approach. The president hosted 100 Cuban-Americans at the White House to celebrate Cuban Independence Day, but did not include CANF officeholders.

CANF was able to establish closer relations with the Clinton administration in 1994, however, when it convinced the administration to take a tough line against a wave of Cuban refugees. At the explicit urging and support of Jorge Mas Canosa, who intended to place the Castro regime under greater pressure, the Clinton administration put the refugees in detention and sent them back to Cuba.

CANF has also been effective in lobbying for its interests outside the United States. In 1989 CANF lobbyists visited Russia and met with President Boris Yeltsin; Russian aid to Cuba was later revoked. CANF also meets regularly with leaders of other Latin American states, though it has a mixed record there.

One success of CANF lobbying was the establishment of TV Marti in 1991. This was a complement to Radio Marti, a media outlet managed by the U.S. Information Agency and broadcast to Cuba, transmitting uncensored news, information, and entertainment in an attempt to stir popular resentment of the Castro regime within Cuba. However, in the mid 1990s budget problems led Congress to reduce funding for Radio Marti by half and to abolish TV Marti.

ACTIVITIES: CURRENT AND FUTURE

One of the major goals of CANF is public education. It formed the Foundation for Human Rights in Cuba, which maintains daily telephone contact with opposition and human rights groups within that country. The foundation publishes a free publication, the *Cuban Human Rights Monitor*.

CANF also promotes its interests through involvement in American education. In 1989 it established an endowment for Cuban studies in Florida universities, for the purpose of supporting scholarly research and publications on Cuba. Under this endowment CANF pledged to raise funds in the private sector to match, dollar for dollar, funds allocated for this purpose by the Florida state legislature.

CANF also has written over 60 monographs, reports, and analyses on subjects such as Cuba's involvement in narcotics trafficking, Cuban ties to terrorist organizations in Latin America and elsewhere, and Cuban economic and human rights problems. CANF distributes issue briefs, newsletters, and news updates; it also hosts press conferences, briefings, and seminars on conditions within Cuba. In preparation for the hoped-for regime change, CANF has established a Blue Ribbon Commission on the Economic Reconstruction of Cuba. This multilateral panel of economic and political leaders gathers to formulate strategies for the economic revival of Cuba after the Castro regime.

CANF's most recent lobbying success in Washington was obtaining passage of the Cuban Liberty and Democratic Solidarity Act, or the Helms-Burton Act. In early 1996, relations between the United States and Cuba appeared to be improving despite CANF's opposition; however, on February 24, 1996, the Cuban army shot down two small planes flown by unarmed Cuban Americans. On March 11, 1996, Helms-Burton was signed into law. The purpose of the act is to increase pressure on the Castro regime and to discourage investment in expropriated properties in Cuba, the claims to which are owned by American nationals. The law permits Americans with these claims to bring suit in American courts against persons who traffic in such property, and any foreign national who invests in these properties can be barred from entry into the United States.

Another strategy of CANF that has proved to be more controversial is to boycott Cuban entertainers. In 1994 an employee of the Spanish-language network of MTV organized a private tour to Havana to see a Cuban singer in concert; she claimed that CANF subsequently pressured MTV to fire her. In 1995 a federal investigation into Radio Marti found that Jorge Mas Canosa improperly tried to intervene with the station's operations and fire his critics. Gloria Estefan was attacked by the organization in 1997 when she supported a Miami concert by Cuban performers.

The main policy goal of CANF currently is to resist congressional moderates who seek to lift the American embargo on sales of food and medicine to Cuba. U.S. law forbids the sale of food and permits the sale of medicine and medical equipment only to nongovernmental organizations. The 1999 Cuban Humanitarian Trade Act of 1999 would exempt necessary medical supplies and food from the embargo, and defeating this bill, sponsored by Senator Christopher Dodd (D-CT) is CANF's priority.

CANF's future is mixed. On the one hand it continues to enjoy the support of many Cuban Americans. Since it was founded, it claims to have received contributions from seven out of ten Cuban families in the United States. Over 54,000 families contribute each month, making CANF by far the largest Cuban-American organization in the United States. One Miami poll found that of those Cuban Americans with a preference, three out of four selected CANF as the most effective and trustworthy Cuban-American organization.

However, other public opinion polls find that, particularly among young Cuban Americans, differences of opinion exist regarding what America's policy toward Cuba should be. One survey of Cuban Americans in 1995 found that 68 percent favored negotiation with Castro regarding the future of Cuba, and a Spanish-language radio station in Miami broadcasts a talk show with a host who regularly criticizes CANF and other hard-liners. These divisions within the Cuban-American community may reduce the long-term effectiveness of CANF as the voice of the Cuban exile community.

In addition, many view the November 1998 death of Jorge Mas Canosa as a setback for the organization, given his effective leadership within CANF: he was described by one Washington observer as "the most significant individual lobbyist in the country." To the extent that CANF's success depended on the talents of his leadership, it may suffer in the future. Nevertheless, CANF is the best organized and most established Cuban-American organization in Washington and is likely to continue to be influential over the short term.

FINANCIAL FACTS

CANF receives monthly donations from over 54,000 donors. In addition, CANF has 100 directors, each of whom contributes $10,000 to the organization; CANF trustees contribute $500. CANF also runs a political action committee (PAC) called Free Cuba, which contributes to political campaigns. In 1998 it contributed $102,500: $53,500 to Democratic candidates and $49,000 to Republicans.

ALLYSON FORD

Bibliography

Cigler, Allan, and Bardett Loomis. *Interest Group Politics*, 5th ed. Washington, DC: Congressional Quarterly Press, 1998.

www.canfnet.org

www.us.net/cip

EUROPEAN UNION

The European Union (EU) is a supranational government concerned with promoting European unity and cooperation whose origins date to the end of the Second World War. One of the American preconditions of Marshall Plan aid to Europe was regional cooperation among recipient countries; generally, the United States has encouraged the development of the EU and has enjoyed good relations with it. Though European integration has not been a story of linear progress, the EU has made great strides in the 1990s after the Maastricht Treaty and has an elected parliament in Brussels. It consists of 15 states: Austria, Belgium, Denmark, Finland, France, Germany, Greece, Ireland, Italy, Luxembourg, the Netherlands, Portugal, Spain, Sweden, and the United Kingdom. The EU has a delegation to the United States, with full ambassadorial status, in Washington, D.C. The EU also has an office in New York that serves as a delegation to the United Nations (UN).

The EU is a diverse community, and its members have different interests and perspectives. There are more differences between Germany and Greece than there are between Maine and Mississippi. Nevertheless, union members have some regional interests in common, and the EU actively lobbies the U.S. government to promote these. As a supranational organization, it has no ethnic lobby; few Americans identify themselves as European Union Americans. The EU also does not register lobbying organizations under the Foreign Agents Registration Act, and had no outside counsel listed in *Washington Representatives*. However, EU representatives visit American federal, state, and local officials on a regular basis.

HISTORY

The story of the EU's lobbying efforts in the United States begins when its predecessor, the European Coal and Steel Community, suffered a setback with France's rejection of the European Defense Community. The "founding father" of the EU, Jean Monnet of France, contacted George Ball, later an influential figure in the Kennedy and Johnson administrations. Ball arranged for Leonard Tennyson to set up an office in Washington in 1954. The purpose was to convince policy makers that the process of European integration was not defeated by this setback. These efforts were successful, though during the 1960s not one official was detailed full time to Congress. The Nixon administration marked a decline in U.S.-EU relations, as Nixon was openly cynical about the prospects for European integration. Nevertheless, the Cold War context made for generally good relations between the EU and the United States.

In the post–Cold War era, the EU has become more powerful within Europe. At the end of 1993 the Maastricht Treaty on European Union came into effect. The goal of the Maastricht Treaty was to create a large market without borders, set a single currency—the euro—for use by member nations, and open trade markets within the union. The treaty also provided for the establishment of a Common Foreign and Security Policy (CFSP). Twice yearly the presidents of the EU and the United States hold summit meetings.

The CFSP was intended to give member nations one voice with which to pursue their interests. However, so far the effectiveness of the CFSP is mixed. As Representative Lee Hamilton (D-IN) stated: "We meet often enough with members of the European parliament. But there is a mismatch between that body and ours—we do not know with whom to deal." Or as Henry Kissinger famously put it, "When I want to talk to Europe, whom do I call?"

Whether the EU will develop a centralized foreign-policy establishment in the future is difficult to predict: most member states wish to preserve state sovereignty in an issue area central to the independent life of member states. At the same time, they also seek the advantages of mutual consultation, support, and coordinated diplomatic action. Future development of the CFSP will depend on the management of national differences within the EU.

ACTIVITIES: CURRENT AND FUTURE

Most of the issues that concern the EU are economic: together, the United States and the EU compose half the world's economy and have the world's largest bilateral trading and investment relationship. Almost 40 percent of world trade, around $1 billion a day, is exchanged between them. However, the EU has had several issues with the United States regarding economic interests in the 1990s. Its record in these issues is mixed, but generally, by the end of the 1990s, trade issues were increasing frictions between the EU and the United States. Both the United States and the EU support multilateral management of international trade; however, they differ on specific sectoral issues. Disputes arose in agricultural trade, aircraft manufacturing, steel products, import quotas, and state subsidies. Another issue the EU is concerned about is state and local government procurement laws that establish "buy-local" requirements: the EU actively lobbies against these, but has had mixed results.

One issue of contention between the EU and the United States is the enactment of secondary trade boycotts in the United States. The Helms-Burton Act and the Iran-Libya Sanctions Act were both written to penalize foreign firms that conducted business in Cuba, Libya, or Iran: the EU perceives this as an infringement on its sovereignty and seeks to overturn the laws. Its attempts to lobby Congress to drop the laws have been unsuccessful; however, in May 1998 the EU did reach an agreement with the Clinton administration in which the United States waived sanctions against EU countries.

Two trade issues have added tensions to the relationship. One involves the EU agricultural import regime, which favored banana imports from former colonies in the Caribbean over Latin American imports from U.S. businesses. The EU argued that its policy was a development issue, not a trade issue, but was unable to convince American policy makers. Against EU wishes, the United States took the case to the World Trade Organization (WTO), and in mid 1999 the case was decided in favor of the United States. The EU is trying to find a compromise solution in which it could comply with the ruling but still give some consideration to its former colonies: it is currently working with U.S. trade representatives to develop a policy that the United States will not challenge in the WTO.

Another recent trade issue is the use of hormones in imported agricultural goods. The EU is trying to prevent the United States from exporting hormone-treated beef. In the aftermath of mad cow disease in Britain, many Europeans are not confident in scientific research showing no ill effects from hormone-treated products; however, the United States is not budging from its argument that this is an unfair trade restriction. In fact, in 1999 the United States imposed 100 percent ad valorem duties on EU products in retaliation for the EU's ban on beef produced with growth hormones. The EU is currently challenging these duties at the WTO; the case was pending in mid 1999.

Other economic issues have been resolved more favorably. After six years of negotiations, in July 1992 agreement was reached regarding public aid from EU countries to the European aircraft manufacturer Airbus. The agreement regulates, but does not eliminate, this aid. Since there is no serious trade deficit or investment imbalance on either side, there is relatively little pressure within the United States to enact across-the-board protectionist legislation against EU imports.

In security affairs the North Atlantic Treaty Organization (NATO) alliance promotes overall cooperative relations between the United States and the EU; many, though not all, EU members are also NATO members. However, there have also been disputes. There were differences in the early to mid 1990s regarding how to resolve the Bosnian crisis. Some EU members had troops on the ground in Bosnia and lobbied the United States not to bomb Serbia; at the same time, they encouraged increased U.S. involvement in the region. The 1999 Kosovo crisis saw greater cooperation between the United States and the EU; the United States financed the war and the EU is to finance the peace.

Besides its lobbying efforts, the EU is also beginning to be active in public education. It is funding a new network of ten EU centers in universities in the United States. This effort was launched in the fall of 1998. In their communities and regions the centers will conduct outreach programs to colleges and universities, local businesses, chambers of commerce, and others, to promote knowledge about the EU, its institutions and policies, and to enhance U.S.-EU relations.

With the introduction of a common currency in 1999, the EU appears to be making steady progress toward integration. How far that process will go and how much that will contribute to successful lobbying in the United States is open to question. Nevertheless, it is likely that the EU will increase its lobbying efforts in the United States in the future.

ALLYSON FORD

Bibliography

Barber, Phillippe I. *European Union Handbook.* Chicago: Fitzroy Dearborn, 1996.

Buchan, David. *Europe: The Strange Superpower.* Brookfield, VT: Dartmouth, 1993.

Hill, Christopher. *The Actors in Europe's Foreign Policy.* London: Routledge, 1996.

www.eurunion.org

★★★★★★
ISRAEL

To lobby for its interests, Israel uses a diverse number of organizations, including its embassy and various ethnic lobbies in the United States. However, the one that is most widely recognized is the American-Israel Political Action Committee (AIPAC). Headquartered in Washington, D.C., with ten regional offices in the United States and one in Jerusalem, along with chapters on over 200 college campuses, AIPAC has 55,000 members. Its interest is to promote friendly relations between Israel and the United States. While these relations have generally been good since the founding of the Israeli state, many credit AIPAC for helping to maintain a close relationship with the United States.

HISTORY

American Jewish community leaders founded AIPAC in 1954. Its mission was twofold: first, to lobby the U.S. government to continue to provide economic and military assistance to support the survival of Israel; second, to nurture and advance the U.S.-Israeli relationship in general.

Up to the 1960s U.S.-Israeli relations were generally good. However, Israel did not receive military aid: American officials in the State Department and the Defense Department felt that such aid would potentially set off an arms race and destabilize the area and that the Suez crisis showed that Israel was strong enough to defend itself on its own. U.S. policy shifted in 1962, with the Kennedy administration's sale of HAWK antiaircraft missiles to Israel. By 1968, with the Johnson administration's sale of Phantom jets to Israel, American arms sales gave Israel a qualitative edge over its neighbors.

During the Nixon and Carter administrations, the United States assisted in concluding disengagement agreements between Israel and Egypt and Israel and Syria. Aid to Israel was increased substantially in this period: between 1946 and 1971 Israel received an average of $60 million in aid annually. From 1974 to 1999, however, Israel has received nearly $50 billion in U.S. aid, averaging $2 billion per year. Relations between the United States and Israel were particularly strong in the Reagan era; despite growing criticism about Israeli policies in Lebanon and in the *intifada* (an armed insurrection of Palestinians in the West Bank and other territories under Israeli occupation), two memorandums of understanding were signed in 1981 and 1988. These set up a number of joint planning and consultative bodies in both military and civilian issue areas.

ACTIVITIES: CURRENT AND FUTURE

Generally, AIPAC has been very successful in achieving its goals. Israel has become the number one recipient of U.S. foreign aid, receiving up to $3 billion a year. AIPAC actively promotes this aid and in 1991 organized 1,500 "citizen lobbyists" to go to Capitol Hill. Armed with computer printouts of their legislators' backgrounds, this group lobbied for additional aid to Israel after the Gulf War damage.

One area where AIPAC has had mixed results is in maintaining a positive image of Israel after the *intifada* of the late 1980s. Israeli actions to combat a Palestinian uprising appeared to many as brutal actions inappropriate for a democratic state, and there was some decline in American public opinion polls on the support of Americans for Israel. However, this problem is mitigated by the magnitude of American support for Israel; public opinion polls show that Americans favor the Israeli position by between three and five to one.

Over the years, there has been some variation in AIPAC's commitment to the peace process with Palestinians. In the early 1990s AIPAC's leadership was conservative and hawkish on the issue. This led Israeli Prime

Minister Yitzhak Rabin to appeal to American rabbis to support the peace process; this appeal was widely perceived as a warning to AIPAC. A subsequent power struggle within the organization resulted in the removal of the hard-liners.

AIPAC continues to lobby the United States on its position on the peace process. In the post–Cold War era, the United States remains actively involved in this process, assisting in the 1993 peace accords and the October 1998 Wye-River Agreement between Israel and the Palestinian National Authority. At times, these negotiations have been difficult, and there have been several setbacks in the peace process. However, when the Clinton administration attempted to promote peace terms that Israel perceived to be unfavorable, AIPAC was able to get 81 U.S. senators to sign a letter to the president asking him not to pressure Israel in 1998. AIPAC is also lobbying for the United States to help pay for the implementation of the Wye-River Agreement; $1.9 billion was pledged to Israel at that time, and AIPAC is currently lobbying in Congress for the appropriation of these funds.

AIPAC continues to lobby for American support of Israel's security. Recent achievements include obtaining American funding for Israeli research on the Arrow missile and tactical high-energy lasers. In 1997 Israel linked up to the U.S. missile warning system: this will provide Israel with real-time warning if a missile is launched against it. Its lobbying efforts on the peace process are more mixed: while the United States continues generally to support the Israeli position, American officials are increasingly inclined to sympathize with Palestinian concerns and to prod Israel to compromise. However, this is still a delicate issue, as Hillary Clinton discovered after public outcry forced her to back away from a statement supporting eventual statehood for Palestinians.

Another issue of contemporary concern for AIPAC is the provision of aid for the resettlement of refugees who come to Israel. Recently AIPAC lobbied successfully for $70 million in assistance from the United States for the resettlement of refugees from the former Soviet Union into Israel. In 1999 Israel obtained just under $3 billion in aid—$1.92 billion in military aid and $960 million in economic aid. This was a reduction of $60 million from the previous year, however, and some Israelis such as former prime minister Benjamin Netanyahu have stated publicly that Israel should wean itself away from dependence on American aid.

Generally, AIPAC is very actively involved in several layers of policy making. In 1996 the Democratic Platform Committee held a marathon one-day hearing in Cleveland, at which representatives of various domestic and foreign interests testified. AIPAC was particularly effective in getting its views heard and in influencing the convention. It got strongly pro-Israel activists selected to the drafting and platform committees, which influenced the wording of some sections of the platform document. Yet the issue of American support for Israel has been kept relatively nonpartisan, even though the majority of Jewish Americans vote Democratic.

AIPAC is very active on Capitol Hill. During the 1998 elections it held over 2,000 meetings with members of Congress and met with over 600 congressional candidates, including all of those elected. AIPAC activists are also involved in public education, publishing over 500 letters to editors, op-ed pieces, and articles on U.S.-Israeli relations.

AIPAC is also promoting the 1999 Iran Nonproliferation Act, which would increase congressional oversight of weapons proliferation to Iran. The act would require the president to report to Congress every six months on all foreign entities about which there is credible evidence that they have transferred to Iran goods, services, or technology that would contribute to the development of nuclear, chemical, or biological weapons.

Due to its successes, AIPAC was recognized as America's second most powerful lobby by *Fortune* magazine in 1998. Factors that contribute to its success include the relatively high issue attentiveness, voting rates, and campaign contributions from American Jews. In 1996 26 percent of Jewish Americans contributed money to one of the presidential candidates; only 5 percent of other American citizens contributed money to any 1996 campaign. This level of involvement reinforces the power of AIPAC: even though it does not contribute directly to political campaigns, its perceived influence over Jewish American contributors is an important source of its strength.

However, there has been some backlash against the power of AIPAC. In 1985 former member of Congress Paul Findley wrote a best-seller that was harshly critical of the Israeli lobby in general and AIPAC in particular. His book, *They Dare to Speak Out: People and Institutions Confront Israel's Lobby*, argued that AIPAC was so powerful that policy makers were afraid to resist its wishes, for fear of retribution. Other critics of AIPAC argue that this power makes it an impediment to the peace process: since its clout in Washington is unmatched by Arab lobbies, it is difficult for American negotiators to take a neutral stance.

However, defenders of Israel and AIPAC argue that the U.S. policy of support for Israel is better explained by strategic considerations than by domestic political pressures. Generally, AIPAC's defenders argue that the

Israeli lobby has been consistent, while American foreign policy has varied: consequently, the pressure from AIPAC does not explain American policy toward Israel. For example, they note that the Reagan administration was strongly pro-Israel even though he had relatively little support from Jewish American voters. Nevertheless, throughout its existence AIPAC has played a role in maintaining some stability in the level of American support for Israel.

Whether AIPAC will continue to maintain its successful record depends in part on unity within the American Jewish community, which mirrors recent splits within Israel. Divisions exist regarding the peace process, with the majority of Reform and Conservative Jews in support and the majority of Orthodox Jews in opposition. In trying to represent the interests of the Jewish state, AIPAC may have a very difficult time if common agreement on what constitutes the national interest declines. Nevertheless, the organizational skills of AIPAC remain strong, and its ability to adapt to policy changes in Israel bodes well for its near future.

FINANCIAL FACTS

AIPAC is classified as a 501(c)(4) organization under the Internal Revenue Service code for registered lobbies. Despite its name, it does not maintain a political action committee that makes contributions to candidates for office.

ALLYSON FORD

Bibliography

Cigler, Allan, and Bardett Loomis. *Interest Group Politics,* 5th ed. Washington: Congressional Quarterly Press, 1998.

Findley, Paul. *They Dare to Speak Out: People and Institutions Confront Israel's Lobby.* Chicago: Lawrence Hill Books, 1985.

Lipson, Charles. "American Support for Israel: History, Sources, Limits." In *U.S.-Israel Relations at the Crossroads,* edited by Gabriel Sheffer. Portland, OR: Frank Cass, 1997.

www.aipac.org

JAPAN

Since the end of the Second World War, the Japanese-U.S. relationship has consisted of general cooperation in security affairs but increased friction on economic issues. Concerns about the possibility of an aggressive North Korea or China continue to promote Japanese interest in an American presence in the region. Since the United States is a $130 billion-a-year export market and holds over $400 billion of Japanese assets in U.S. government bonds, American economic policies are a vital interest of the Japanese government.

While the Japanese embassy is also involved in lobbying efforts and Japan hires several public relations and law firms, it is difficult to separate the lobbying of the Japanese government from that of Japanese businesses. According to *Washington Representatives*, there are over 90 Japanese and international businesses that have hired outside counsel and consultants to represent their interests in Washington. Combined, the Japanese spend hundreds of millions of dollars a year to maintain the world's largest, most expensive, and arguably most effective foreign-financed lobbying, commercial intelligence, and public relations operation. Reported total payments to Japanese lobbies in 1995 totaled $56 million: this is more than the combined payments of the second and third largest countries, Great Britain and Canada.

The main goal of these groups is to influence policy development in the U.S. government. Since the late 1970s, many of their activities have involved prevention of protectionist legislation and other punitive actions against Japan. Another goal is to distinguish between American bluster, or bluffs, and a genuine commitment to unilateral action if not appeased by U.S. actions. Finally, these groups seek to promote Japan's image among American officials and citizens.

HISTORY

The development of modern Japan dates back to the Meiji Restoration of the late 1800s, which instituted Westernizing reforms within Japan. During the restoration Japan adopted a Western-style legal system and other political institutions. During the First World War Japan fought on the winning side; this increased its relative power. During the interwar years its power in Asia grew and it engaged in military expansions throughout the region. However, Japan was driven back to its mainland during the Second World War, and the United States got involved with Japanese reconstruction when the country was placed under international control of the allies through the supreme commander, Douglas MacArthur.

After the war, the United States was actively involved in the reconstruction of Japan, giving $2 billion in direct economic aid and going so far as to design its constitution to prohibit a substantial portion of the Japanese budget to be allocated to the military. Lobbying activity on behalf of Japan in the United States can be traced to the late 1940s: the American Council of Japan, a group of Americans sympathetic to Japanese interests, tried to sidetrack MacArthur's reforms. The council was successful in preventing the proposed breakup of *zaibatsu*, or conglomerate, of banks: this set the stage for the Japanese to establish government control of its economy. As the Cold War developed, the United States offered a security guarantee to Japan in the Mutual Defense Treaty.

By the 1970s, however, the combination of rapid growth of Japanese exports to the United States and the relative decline of the American economy led many Americans to question whether U.S.-Japanese economic relations were managed on a fair basis. Generally, Japan perceives itself to be a small country that has to work hard and fight aggressively in order to survive. However, many in the United States argued that Japan was dumping its products at below-market prices and called for protectionist legislation, particularly against Japanese automobiles. This appeal was intensified by comparisons of the relative openness of American markets to the restricted access that American businesses had to the Japanese market. The major goal of the Japanese lobbies has been and remains to resist the enactment of protectionism. They have been only partly successful in this goal.

ACTIVITIES: CURRENT AND FUTURE

In response to pressures within the United States to establish trade protections against Japanese imports, Japan became more active in lobbying the U.S. government. One early failure of the Japanese lobby occurred in 1981, when congressional and corporate pressures persuaded AT&T to reject Fujitsu's low bid and accept a domestic bid on a major optical filter telephone cable link between the major cities of the northeastern United States. However, Japan was able to avoid the imposition of some proposed trade restrictions by agreeing to voluntary restraint agreements. In addition, the Japanese government resisted pressures from the United States to lower its agricultural tariffs and quotas: as they pointed out in their defense, Japan was by far the world's largest importer of American agricultural goods.

Throughout the 1980s, however, the trade imbalance with Japan was an important political issue. Trade concerns were one issue in the 1986 elections, in which the Democrats regained control of the Senate. The next year Congress passed an omnibus trade bill, which contained provisions requiring mandatory retaliation by the president against violations of U.S. trade agreements. Japan denounced this act, as did President Ronald Reagan, and in 1988 Congress passed a modified trade bill that was less protectionist; this bill was enacted over Reagan's veto. Under this act the Reagan administration placed a retaliatory tariff on $300 million of Japanese electronic products.

Nevertheless, Japan scored several important successes in lobbying the United States. One was its defeat of American efforts in 1988 to punish Toshiba Machine Company for selling restricted propeller-silencing military technology to the Soviet Union. The House voted to ban the sale of Toshiba's products in military exchange stores, and it looked as though it might ban sales of Toshiba products throughout America. But after extensive lobbying by both Toshiba and Japan, the response of the Reagan and Bush administrations was limited to deferred enforcement of a two-year ban on sales by Toshiba's machine tool subsidiary.

In the late 1980s the activities of the Japanese lobby became the target for criticism. Author Pat Choate's *Agents of Influence,* published in 1990, discussed numerous instances of Japanese lobbying of the United States and argued that the power of the Japanese lobby was harmful to the interests of the United States. Although the book attracted much criticism for its sensationalist tone, it also reflected the attitude of many Americans against Japan, which was increasingly perceived as a threat to the economic well-being of the United States. After its publication Japan switched lobbying techniques and now depends more on the lobbying efforts of U.S.-based companies that benefit from free trade with Japan, such as those that are dependent on Japanese suppliers of components of American products.

In the 1990s the economic fortunes of Japan declined. The "bubble economy," which at one point led the land under the Japanese palace to be more highly valued than the real estate of all of California, burst dramatically. Currently Japan is in its worst recession since the Second World War, and its real growth rate in 1998 was -2.5 percent. Meanwhile, the American economy has been relatively strong and unemployment has been at historically low levels. These conditions have reduced the tensions between the United States and Japan regarding trade issues, although in early 1995 Japanese interests spent $3 million on ads in the American media to oppose threatened import sanctions against luxury autos.

Japan has been forced to alter one of its lobbying strategies. It used to be quite common for Japanese interests to hire former federal officials, such as former U.S. trade representatives and Commerce Department employees, who would then make public statements and write articles about bilateral trade negotiations without openly revealing this connection. Critics charged that this "revolving door" meant that, while in government, those who hoped for a lucrative lobbying position in the future were less likely to support a tough stance on Japanese trade. Partly in response to this, recent laws in the United States imposed a waiting period on lobbying activities by departing government officials.

Other Japanese activities include funding academic and charitable institutions, in the goal of being good corporate citizens and promoting a positive image of Japanese businesses. Organized major philanthropic efforts are estimated at $500 million annually. However, Japanese funding of academic research has also attracted criticism from those who believe that Japan does so not to promote objective research, but to use American universities to push the Japanese government's interests.

Security issues continue to be more cooperative, and Japan has been largely successful in promoting its security interests in the post–Cold War era. There was an outcry when U.S. servicemen attacked a teenage girl in Okinawa; in response to the outrage within Japan, the United States closed its military base. More recently, however, concerns about possible nuclear proliferation in North Korea have led to greater cooperation between the United States and Japan. In 1999 the Mutual Security Treaty was updated to provide a more explicit military role for Japan in responding to regional crises such as tensions on the Korean peninsula.

Given the aging of the Japanese population, it is open to question whether it will ever regain the strong economy of the 1980s. This may reduce tensions with the United States, as Japan appears to be less threatening; alternatively, it may increase tensions if Japan attempts to regain economic strength by promoting cheap imports. Nevertheless, Japan remains a major economic power, both within its region and internationally, and it will be likely to continue to try to influence American foreign policy.

ALLYSON FORD

Bibliography

Choate, Pat. *Agents of Influence*. New York: Knopf, 1990.

Cohen, Stephen D. *An Ocean Apart: Explaining Three Decades of U.S.-Japanese Trade Frictions*. Westport, CT: Praeger, 1999.

www.state.gov

MEXICO

Throughout the twentieth century U.S.-Mexican relations have been mixed. On the one hand, as its neighbor to the south, Mexico has had many common interests with the United States. On the other hand, there is a perception in Mexico that it is powerless to resist U.S. pressures: as early-twentieth-century Mexican President Porfirio Diaz put it, "Poor Mexico! So far from God, and so close to the United States." Since 1980, however, the United States and Mexico have become increasingly interdependent, particularly in economic affairs, and tensions between the two countries have increased.

Mexico has greatly expanded its lobbying presence in the United States in the 1990s. Its embassy regularly engages in efforts to affect U.S. policy in a number of issue areas, including trade and economic policies, drug control, and immigration. Also lobbying for Mexican concerns are international businesses; there are more than 2,600 American companies with operations in Mexico, and the United States accounts for 60 percent of all foreign direct investment in Mexico. Mexican state and local governments also actively lobby within the United States, particularly with state and local governments of American states that touch on the 2,000-mile border between the United States and Mexico. Ethnic organizations, such as the Mexican-American Legal Defense and Education Fund, focus primarily on conditions within the United States, but also promote some Mexican interests, such as immigration policy preferences.

HISTORY

Mexico proclaimed its independence in 1810 and established itself as a republic in 1824. Early relations with the United States were poor, and during the Mexican War in the 1840s Mexico lost considerable territory in what are now the Southwest and the West Coast of the United States. During the early 1900s Mexico suffered from economic and social problems, and U.S. President Woodrow Wilson intervened in Mexico under the stated purpose of forcing the country to democratize. The Mexican Revolution gave rise to the 1917 constitution, which established a federal republic. Relations with the United States have been mixed since then, with relatively good relations under the Good Neighbor Policy of the 1930s and the Alliance for Progress in the Kennedy administration.

Since 1981 the management of U.S.-Mexican issues has been formalized within the U.S.-Mexico Binational Commission, which consists of several U.S. cabinet members and their Mexican counterparts. The commission holds annual meetings, with subgroups meeting separately, to discuss U.S.-Mexican relations. Currently Mexico's record in promoting its interests in Washington is mixed.

ACTIVITIES: CURRENT AND FUTURE

Until recently Mexico did not engage in significant lobbying activity in the United States. Their strong belief in noninterventionism led Mexicans to believe that if their country stayed out of American politics, the United States would do the same for Mexico. However, this changed when the North American Free Trade Agreement (NAFTA) was developed. Between 1985 and 1991 the Mexican government's lobbying representation jumped from two minor contracts of $67,229 to more than a dozen contracts worth at least $9 million. Unlike many other governments which rely on their private sectors to finance lobbying in Washington, these lobbies were funded by Mexico's public sector.

NAFTA also marked the beginning of an attempt by Mexico to mobilize Mexican Americans as an ethnic lobby, which it had previously shied away from. Efforts to sway public opinion among Mexican Americans included placing advertisements in the mass media, especially Spanish-language television, to urge Mexican-American voters to pressure their representatives to approve the fast-track strategy in 1991. Fast track would have permitted the president to negotiate trade legislation without the input of Congress on specific details. Congress could only vote for or against.

Mexico also lobbied members of Congress through the Mexican embassy in Washington. This effort was described at the time by the Center for Public Integrity as "the most expensive and elaborate campaign ever conducted by a foreign government in the U.S." The center went on to note that Mexico's lobbying effort for NAFTA exceeded the combined cost of the three previous largest lobbying campaigns in Washington. However, the successful effort was perceived as vital to Mexico's economic interests. Mexico had a debt crisis in the 1980s, and the subsequent austerity conditions imposed on the country by the International Monetary Fund led it to pursue an economic strategy based on exporting goods. NAFTA represented a large portion of this strategy; it will phase out all tariffs between the United States, Canada, and Mexico over a 15-year period. While it does include some provisions for labor rights and environmental protection, these standards were not as high as opponents of the accord would have liked, and Mexico was able to prevent them from being toughened during negotiations. Mexico is hoping that NAFTA and internal economic liberalization will strengthen the nation's economy. Mexico is the United States' third-ranked trading partner, accounting for 10 percent of American trade. In 1994, due in part to NAFTA, the Mexican economy grew by 3.5 percent. In 1998 U.S. imports from Mexico grew nearly 140 percent from 1993 levels. Thus, the passage of NAFTA has proved a boon to the Mexican economy and marked a turning point in U.S.-Mexican relations.

Another partial victory in economic issues for the Mexican government was obtaining American aid during the 1995 debt crisis. Heavy congressional opposition to a $40 billion loan guarantee threatened to defeat delivery of assistance, but acting on his own authority, President Bill Clinton offered Mexico a $20 billion package of short-term loans and loan guarantees from the Federal Exchange Stabilization Fund, and Mexico obtained another $20 million from international sources. However, months after the crisis began, Congress considered legislation to cut off the guarantees, thus reducing investor confidence in Mexico. Generally, when it comes to receiving U.S. foreign aid, Mexico's record is mixed. Nevertheless, Mexico was able to repay the loans from the United States more than three years ahead of schedule.

Mexico has been less successful in lobbying on other issues, notably immigration policy. Federal immigration law, which is set by Congress, determines the legal rights, duties, and obligations of aliens in the United States. Immigration to the United States is an informal means by which Mexico can keep a lid on social tensions, poverty, and other potentially destabilizing problems. However, immigration can be an unpopular political issue, as the 1996 approval of a California initiative to eliminate most social services for illegal aliens shows.

In 1986 Congress passed the Immigration Reform and Control Act, which tightened criminal sanctions for employers who hire illegal aliens and denied federally funded welfare benefits to illegal aliens. Mexico was unable to prevent passage of this bill, but that country's supporters were able to include a provision under which some aliens were legitimized through an amnesty program. In 1993 the Border Liaison Mechanism (BLM) was established, and there are nine BLMs chaired by U.S. and Mexican consuls. These deal with issues such as violation of sovereignty by law enforcement officials, charges of mistreatment of foreign nationals, and coordination of port security and public health matters.

In spite of the establishment of BLMs, however, Mexico was unable to prevent Congress from passing newly restrictive immigration laws. In 1996 Congress passed the Illegal Immigration Reform and Immigrant Responsibility Act, which increased border patrol and investigative personnel, increased penalties for alien smuggling and document fraud, and reformed deportation law and procedures. Mexico continues to lobby on immigration affairs: one concern for Mexico is to prevent the use of U.S. troops in controlling immigration, which it perceives as an affront to its sovereignty.

Another issue that has generated tensions in recent years involves certification that Mexico is cooperating on drug-trafficking abatement. Mexico has had to fight accusations in recent years that it is not cooperating in these efforts: if it is not certified as a cooperative state, it will not be eligible for most forms of U.S. foreign aid. Questions about corruption within the Mexican state and the capability of Mexico to resist pressures from those involved in transporting narcotics continue to be raised in Congress. Mexico's lobby points to Mexican internal reforms in 1998 to increase enforcement and reduce corruption, and so far it has been able to prevent decertification. In 1997 the binational alliance developed a U.S.-Mexico Binational Drug Strategy to coordinate anti-drug trafficking efforts.

It is open to question how effective Mexico's lobby was in the NAFTA debate. The vote in Congress was very close, and the remaining undecided members of Congress were swayed not by the efforts of Mexico, but by the Clinton administration's delivery of federal largess, or pork barrel benefits. However, Mexican Americans are a growing portion of the American population: they are 60 percent of U.S. Latinos, who make up 10 percent of the country's population. This could provide Mexico with increased clout in Washington in the future.

ALLYSON FORD

Bibliography

de la Garza, Rudolfo G., and Jesus Velasco, eds. *Bridging the Border: Transforming Mexico-U.S. Relations*. New York: Rowman and Littlefield, 1997.

www.law.cornell

www.state.gov

NIGERIA

Since achieving independence from Britain in 1960, Nigeria has often suffered from corruption and political misrule. It has leaned to the West to varying degrees, and as the regional power of West Africa, it was of strategic importance during the Cold War. Relations with the United States have been strained in the 1990s, however, as a military government repressed the population. Therefore, Nigeria's main goal in lobbying the United States is to repair its image as a repressive state. With the rise of a new government in 1999 and an attempt to democratize the Nigerian state, there is an opportunity to improve relations with the United States. This will depend on Nigeria's success in stabilizing its new regime; in mid 1999 it was difficult to predict the fate of the newly elected government. One hopeful sign is the return of some Nigerians who lived abroad during the military rule. In 1998 the Nigerian writer Wole Soyinka, who had lived in exile during the military regime, visited the country and met with government officials; he has returned to visit Nigeria several times since then. In mid 1999, the writer Chinua Achebe returned to Nigeria after nine years abroad.

Most of the lobbying done for the Nigerian government comes from the Nigerian embassy and its hired public relations firm. There is no ethnic lobby for Nigeria; in fact, the lobbying group TransAfrica and human rights organizations actively spoke out against the military regime. The other important lobby for Nigeria is international oil companies, particularly Shell: they have been very active in the fight to prevent sanctions on Nigerian oil exports.

HISTORY

As a developing country, Nigeria was initially interested in obtaining foreign aid. During the 1970s Nigeria's fortunes appeared to improve under the oil boom. As the sixth-largest producer of oil, it was in a good position to benefit from increased oil prices. By the 1980s, however, the oil glut depressed oil prices, and Nigeria was very hard hit. As an oil producer, Nigeria had been able to run up a large debt on the basis of its projected ability to repay; when oil prices plummeted, Nigeria's debt rose rapidly: between 1987 and 1990 its debt increased by 25 percent, from $28.7 to $36.1 billion. These economic problems have continued throughout the 1990s—annual economic growth has averaged only 1.6 percent, showing the effect of slow growth and lack of investor confidence.

These economic problems led to political instability in Nigeria. In 1993 General Sani Abacha imposed military rule on the country. His regime lasted for five years, drove many Nigerians into exile, permitted little criticism, and imprisoned or hanged many opponents. Nigeria became an international pariah in 1995 after hanging the writer and political critic Ken Saro-Wiwa.

However, the June 1998 death of military dictator Sani Abacha led to the opening up of the repressive military regime in Nigeria by his successor, General Abubakar. Within months Abubakar implemented political, economic, and military reforms to democratize Nigeria. A civilian government took office in May 1999, and attempts to develop democratic institutions are currently under way.

ACTIVITIES: CURRENT AND FUTURE

Within this context, before mid 1999, Nigeria's two main goals in lobbying the United States were to improve its human rights image and to prevent economic sanctions. The United States is by far Nigeria's number-one trade partner, and 95 percent of Nigerian exports consist of oil. Therefore, the Nigerian lobby fought very hard to prevent the imposition of trade sanctions on its oil exports by critics of its human rights record. Nigeria successfully prevented the imposition of sanctions but was not able to improve its image. After the 1995 executions Nigeria was in a tense diplomatic standoff with the United States, but international measures against the Nigerian government were restricted to verbal and symbolic gestures. After waging a well-funded and aggressive lobbying effort in the United States, Nigeria was able to prevent federal sanctions.

However, it was less successful with other bodies of government. In 1997 Alameda County, California, adopted a binding resolution prohibiting the county from contracting with or purchasing from those who do business in Nigeria. The same year the U.S. Conference of Mayors passed a resolution calling for swift restoration of human rights and democracy in Nigeria as well as the release of political prisoners. These issues were supported by TransAfrica and the Free Nigeria Movement—lobbies in the United States that opposed Nigeria's military government.

For the newly established government, obtaining economic aid is the major goal in its lobbying of the U.S. government. Current U.S. investments in Nigeria are estimated at between $8 billion and $10 billion. American aid to Nigeria in 1999 is projected to be $13.2 million, which funds health, child survival, population control, HIV/AIDS programs, civil society, democracy, and governance activities. Except for a brief period between 1995 and 1997, however, Nigeria's economy has been in decline for the last two decades, and 49 percent of its population lives below the poverty line of $8 a month.

Nigeria is a debtor nation: it holds $30 billion in debts, and debt service payments are the major expenditure of the Nigerian budget. This threatens to undermine the new government, and President Olusegun Obasanjo has made it his number-one priority to get the suspension or renegotiation of this debt. The Nigerian Democracy and Civil Society Empowerment Act of 1999, sponsored by Senator Russell Feingold (D-WI), would allocate $10 million in aid to the new government in 2000, $12 million in 2001, and $15 million in 2002. As of mid 1999, the bill had been read twice and referred to the Committee on Foreign Relations; passage of this bill is a top priority for Nigeria.

The future of Nigeria's new government is difficult to predict. Even if the democratic government is able to establish itself, the economic situation in Nigeria has been steadily worsening since 1995. Its vital oil industry has experienced unprecedented difficulties that have included cutbacks in employees and production goals. Nigeria blames foreign oil companies, who in turn blame Nigerian mismanagement of the economy. These divisions between the Nigerian government and foreign oil producers who have been instrumental in promoting Nigeria's interests in Washington may lead to a less effective lobby. In addition, there are still political prisoners in Nigeria, and it is unclear when or if they will be released. However, if Nigeria does democratize its government, it may gain the support of the human rights lobbies that were in opposition to its military government.

ALLYSON FORD

Bibliography

Lewis, Peter M. *Stabilizing Nigeria*. New York: The Century Foundation Press, 1998.
Association of Concerned African Scholars: www.prairienet.org
www.africapolicy.org
www.amnesty.org
www.nigerianews.org
www.usaid.gov

★★★★★★
RUSSIA

When the Cold War first ended, hopes were high that the United States and Russia would enjoy friendlier relations. However, Russia has become more and more critical of American foreign policy. Between 1992 and 1998 the Russian people became increasingly isolated from the West in general and the United States in particular: they blamed the economic shock therapy promoted by the United States for the decline in Russian living standards. Given nationalist pressures within Russia, its leaders have to avoid giving the appearance of taking a strong pro-Western stance; in fact, some observers argue that much of Russia's criticism of America is more for the purpose of placating domestic groups than to alter U.S. actions. Nevertheless, there are real conflicts of interest between the United States and Russia, and Russia has had a difficult time successfully pressing its case in Washington.

Most of the lobbying on behalf of the Russian government is done by its embassy and its public relations firm. While there are some international businesses with interests in Moscow, they have not focused on issues that concern the Russian government. Interestingly, Russia does not have a substantial ethnic lobby within the United States.

HISTORY

During the twentieth century U.S.-Russian relations have varied from attempts to establish close relations to an openly adversarial stance. When the Russian Revolution occurred in 1917 and Russia changed its governmental structure under the Soviet Union, the United States was resisting the rise of communist and socialist movements in America. Consequently, it did not welcome the regime change and did not recognize the Soviet Union until 1933. During the Second World War, however, the United States and the Soviet Union were allies in the fight against Hitler, and there was some discussion between Franklin Roosevelt and Joseph Stalin about the possibility that their nations could continue to cooperate with each other in the postwar era.

However, concerns about Soviet action in Eastern Europe and American opposition to communism led to the development of an adversarial relationship after 1945. During the Cold War the United States and the Soviet Union were the world's two great powers, and they competed for power and influence in Europe and the Third World. Relations began to improve in the 1960s, after the Cuban Missile Crisis frightened policy makers in both countries, and during the 1970s the Nixon administration pursued a policy of détente. However, after the 1979 Soviet invasion of Afghanistan, relations with the Soviets again soured, and President Ronald Reagan famously referred to the Soviet Union as the "evil empire." Relations began to improve when President Mikhail Gorbachev took power and began to change the internal structure of the Soviet Union; this culminated in the dissolution of the Soviet Union by President Boris Yeltsin in 1991.

ACTIVITIES: CURRENT AND FUTURE

Generally, Russia has lobbied against many foreign-policy decisions of the United States but has had to yield on most of its interests. Though it is tactically helpful to demonstrate Russian independence, Russia is too dependent on the benefits it receives from the United States, such as postponements of debt repayments, receiving foreign credits from partners and international financial institutions, and obtaining other forms of aid and business counsel. Russia is not strong enough to risk confrontation with the United States, and after the war in Chechnya, it is not in a position to bluff.

The most important issue, and the source of failure on the part of Russian lobbying, is the attempt to get the United States to understand Moscow's attitude toward the "near abroad." Russia believes that the former Soviet republics are a legitimate sphere of its concern and interest. Consequently, Russia was very opposed to the expansion of the North Atlantic Treaty Organization (NATO) and lobbied very heavily against the inclusion of the Czech Republic, Hungary, and Poland. Russia promoted greater reliance on the Organization for Security and Cooperation in Europe, the only European international organization in which it is an equal member, as an alternative to NATO enlargement. However, this alternative was not seriously considered by NATO. Russia's failure to prevent the United States from promoting the enlargement of what it perceives as an anti-Russian alliance was a severe disappointment. Russia was able to mitigate this loss, however, by obtaining a promise that nuclear weapons would not be deployed on the territories of the new members. In addition, as a reward for its eventual acceptance of NATO expansion, Russia was admitted to the G-7 (now the G-8), an international group of economic great powers, even though it is not itself an economic power.

Another recent source of tension, and a failure of Russian lobbying, took place in 1997 when the U.S. Department of Commerce, acting under the Enhanced Proliferation Control Initiative, added to its list of "entities of concern" several Russian nuclear research laboratories that it identified with weapons proliferation. This action means that no one in America can send exports to these centers without obtaining a special license. Russia stated that this was a policy of double standards and an example of "new Cold War thinking"; nevertheless, the policy stands.

Russia is also trying to get the United States to concede some part of its large international arms market to cash-strapped Russia. In the mid 1990s Russia wanted to sell advanced rocket engines to India in order to gain badly needed funds for its military and space industries. However, the United States wanted to limit the proliferation of long-range missile technology and objected to the sale. Russia tried to convince the United States not to protest the sale but in the end canceled the arrangement. However, another sale, of Russian nuclear reactors and submarines to Iran, went through despite U.S. objections.

Russia has also taken issue with American policy in the Balkans, believing it to be biased against the Serbian side. Its opposition to Western intervention limited, but did not prevent, NATO actions to stop the violence in Bosnia. More recently Russia opposed Western involvement in Kosovo but was successful in obtaining the participation of Russian troops in the peacekeeping force after the 1999 bombing of that region.

A current issue in security affairs that is causing divisions between Russia and the United States is the possibility that the United States will deploy a national defense missile system. Russia believes that the deployment of this system would violate the 1972 Anti-Ballistic Missile Treaty and strongly opposes this plan. The Clinton administration has until June 2000 to make a decision, and Russia is applying pressure on him to act against a system.

Lobbying efforts on behalf of Russian economic interests have been slightly more successful. Russia received a total of $8.7 billion from the United States in aid between 1992 and 1998, plus $40 billion from other countries and international organizations. American aid programs include economic reforms, such as small- and medium-enterprise development, the establishment of alternative credit sources and loan guarantees for small and micro-enterprises, and help for local governments in developing investor-friendly regulations. U.S. funds have also supported the development of political parties and free and fair elections, healthcare programs, and other social services. Recently new emphasis has been placed on funding nonproliferation programs, such as funding scientific research centers and efforts to employ Russian scientists in nonmilitary areas. Still, these funds are minuscule in comparison to Russian needs. In 1999 the U.S. Agency for International Development declared that it wanted to shift funds from the central government in Moscow and concentrate aid toward reform-minded regions, such as the Russian Far East.

Russia's gross national product was halved between 1989 and 1994, and it continues to suffer from economic recession. In August 1998 its situation worsened with the collapse of the Russian banking system; this was the result of heavy borrowing by the Russian government to fund government expenses. Russia has had to lobby very hard to get International Monetary Fund (IMF) funding (and U.S. support for IMF funding) throughout the 1990s, and while it has received some aid, the conditions imposed by the IMF were opposed, but eventually accepted, by Moscow.

Though foreign direct investment is providing some help to Russia, its situation remains bleak. Although Russia engages in trade with the United States, it ranks 30th in the list of American trade partners, between Colombia and the Dominican Republic. In 1999 Russia's federal reserves were projected to be no more than $25 billion; this compares to $35 billion in reserves held by New York City.

American aid to Russia has dropped since the mid

1990s, and recent allegations of corruption in the Russian government—involving a money-laundering scheme through the Bank of New York and allegations that Boris Yeltsin and his daughters made purchases with credit cards that were paid by a Russian business—make improvement in the U.S.-Russian relationship unlikely in the near future. In August 1999 Treasury Department Secretary Lawrence Summers stated that the United States would oppose further aid to Russia until the scandal was investigated thoroughly; Russia's response was to argue that allegations of corruption were exaggerated. Although Russia is investigating the claims, it also resents American pressure to do so.

Russian relations with the United States have been important since the Second World War, and Russia still has the power to affect American interests for better or for worse. Russia sees its meetings with the United States as a symbol of its continued status as a superpower and values its friendship. Therefore, while Russia may object to much of U.S. foreign policy, it is unlikely to take steps to return to a new Cold War. At the same time, however, Russia perceives less friendship on the part of the West and may be more likely to pursue an independent path. In the near future, however, this is unlikely to make its lobbying efforts more successful.

ALLYSON FORD

Bibliography

Kanet, Roger, and Alexander Kozheminkin. *The Foreign Policy of the Russian Federation.* New York: St. Martin's Press, 1997.

Trofimenko, Henry. *Russian National Interests and the Current Crisis in Russia.* Hampshire, UK: Ashgate, 1999.

www.state.gov

TAIWAN

The island of Taiwan is about 14,000 square miles in size—approximately the size of West Virginia—and is located off the southeast coast of China. It continues to resist efforts by the government of the People's Republic of China (PRC) to claim it as territory under its sovereign control, and Taiwan refers to itself as the Republic of China. After the 1949 defeat of the Kuomintang (KMT) in the Chinese revolution, the KMT regime retreated to Taiwan and commenced a diplomatic battle over who was the legitimate government in China. Over two million refugees, mainly from the nationalist government, fled to Taiwan. They established a base in Taiwan and declared that they were the legitimate governmental representatives of China. To this day their ultimate goal is to be recognized as either the legitimate government of China or as a separate sovereign state.

Taiwan has been unsuccessful in achieving either of these goals in the United States; however, it does have unofficial representation in the United States and has received benefits such as U.S. arms sales. The Taipei Economic and Cultural Representative Office (TECRO), which offers unofficial government representation in Washington, carries out lobbying on behalf of Taiwan. There is also an ethnic lobby, the Taiwan Benevolent Association, which fights for recognition of Taiwan as the legitimate government of China.

HISTORY

Taiwan's lobbying effort was very successful in the United States in the early Cold War, with the Committee of One Million lobbying to preserve American recognition of Taiwan. In 1954 a Mutual Defense Treaty was formed between Taiwan and the United States. Although Secretary of State John Foster Dulles did not want America to sign the treaty, he was maneuvered into doing so during the Taiwan Strait Crisis. He agreed to the treaty in exchange for Chiang Kai-Shek's agreement not to veto the U.S. effort to resolve the crisis through the United Nations (UN).

However, once China was perceived as a critical element in the balance of power and a state that could be interested in allying against Russia, Taiwan was unable to prevent the United States from establishing relations with China in the 1970s. The 1978 normalization of American relations with China made it difficult for Taiwan to continue to assert that it was the government of all of China. Following derecognition, the United States terminated its Mutual Defense Treaty with Taiwan. However, it has continued to sell the country arms and military equipment. It also maintains a policy that it will oppose the use of force by China in Taiwan. In 1979 President Jimmy Carter signed the Taiwan Relations Act, which gave domestic and legal authority for the conduct of unofficial relations with Taiwan.

ACTIVITIES: CURRENT AND FUTURE

Taiwan has had a positive image among the American public and has good economic relations with the United States. Nevertheless, its record in lobbying Washington on security concerns is mixed. After criticizing the Carter administration for its official recognition of the PRC, the Reagan administration nevertheless pursued a policy of engagement with that country, despite criticism from administration hard-liners who wanted to take a stronger stand for Taiwan. Subsequent administrations have continued to resist Taiwan's call for support of its independence from the PRC. Questions in the 1990s about whether China would become a great power and whether China would threaten U.S. interests have so far failed to lead American policy makers to offer increased support for Taiwan, though this could change in the future.

The KMT's medium-term goal is to gain recognition as a separate state. However, its attempts to assert this status in 1999 were openly rejected by the U.S. government, which stated that it would stick to its "one China" policy, which recognizes PRC sovereignty over

Taiwan. The "one China" policy rejects both the idea that there are two Chinas and that there is one China and one Taiwan. The United States further responded to Taiwan's effort to gain autonomy by arguing that when relations between the United States and China deteriorate, Taiwan's position becomes more tenuous and thus Taiwan should not take actions that would destabilize U.S.-Chinese relations. This American response was a blow to Taiwanese interests.

The United States also opposes Taiwanese membership in the UN or other organizations where membership is limited to states. It does support Taiwanese membership in other international organizations, however. Taiwan seeks opportunities for nonstate entities substantively to participate in international organizations, such as the Asian Development Bank and Asia-Pacific Economic Cooperative Forum. American pressure helps maintain Taiwan's presence in these organizations. In June 1999, the House Subcommittee on Asia and the Pacific marked up a bill supporting the participation of Taiwan in the World Health Organization (WHO).

In July 1998 when President Bill Clinton visited China and publicly reaffirmed the American commitment to the "one China" policy, Congress responded by passing a resolution reaffirming American commitments to Taiwan. Sponsors of the resolution stated that they intended to counter the president's remarks, which they said represented a new and damaging direction in U.S.-Taiwanese relations.

One victory, one for which Taiwan had lobbied for over a decade, was the decision to sell U.S. F-16 jet fighters to Taiwan. This sale had been rejected as recently as June 1992, before it was approved in September 1992. Although Taiwan would have preferred more advanced models, the sale allowed for up to 150 F-16/A and F-16/B fighter jets to be sold. This contribution to Taiwan's security was strongly opposed by China, and the approval of the sale was a big victory for Taiwan. Overall U.S. sales of arms to Taiwan include F-16s, AWACS planes, M60-A3 tanks, Knox-class destroyers, minesweepers, helicopters, Stinger missiles, and a derivative of the Patriot missile air defense system. However, the 1992 East Asia Strategic Initiative called for a phased reduction in American troops in the Pacific, and it is open to question whether Taiwanese security will continue to be a concern of the United States.

In May 1999 a Pentagon report to Congress argued that Taiwan will require either a sea- or a land-based missile defense system to protect its territory against Chinese short- and medium-range missile attacks. Obtaining this system is one of Taiwan's current priorities.

A symbolic victory for Taiwan took place in 1993, when the president of Taiwan sought permission to enter the United States to attend a college reunion at his alma mater, Cornell. China opposed his entry on the grounds that this was a decision for China to make; however, President Clinton agreed to let him attend the reunion.

Taiwan has had more success pursuing other interests, such as immigration policy. One successful project of the Taiwan lobby was a 1981 congressional initiative under which Taiwan-born people were given a 29,000 annual quota of immigration visas: this quota was separate from the Chinese one, and the Taiwanese-American population has been growing steadily.

Economic ties between the United States and Taiwan have grown since 1979. In the 1950s and early 1960s Taiwan received foreign economic aid from the United States; now it is a donor and investor, especially in Asia. The United States is Taiwan's number-one trade partner, receiving 26 percent of Taiwan's exports and supplying 19 percent of Taiwan's imports. The United States runs a trade deficit with Taiwan, and when this threatened to become an issue, Taiwan reduced its tariffs on American-made goods. Taiwan's 1998 trade surplus was $14.9 billion, a decrease from the 1997 surplus of $17 billion. Taiwan enjoys ready access to American markets.

A 1995 Harris Poll found that only 22 percent of the American public believed that the United States should help defend Taiwan, even though a majority of Americans have a positive image of Taiwan as an ally or a friend. Since China insists that Taiwan is a part of China, there are limits to how much the United States can support Taiwan on issues that the PRC opposes. Generally, the United States has tended to believe that the less it says about Taiwan, the better. Nevertheless, Taiwan maintains relations with the United States and has achieved some success in being recognized as a political entity, if not as a state.

ALLYSON FORD

Bibliography

Sutter, Robert G., and William R. Johnson. *Taiwan in World Affairs*. San Francisco: Westview Press, 1994.
Taiwan Benevolent Association: www.taipei.org
Van Vranken Hickey, Dennis. *Taiwan's Security in the Changing International System*. Boulder, CO: Lynne Rienner, 1997.
www.cia.gov

TURKEY

Turkey was an important North Atlantic Treaty Organization (NATO) ally during the Cold War due to its strategic location near Russia. Its willingness to provide air bases that could be used for out-of-area operations continues to be valuable to the United States; it was a key ally during the Gulf War. Generally, Turkey has pursued a pro-Western policy, and the United States has consistently promoted its integration into Western institutions such as the European Union (EU). Yet opposition to Turkish interests from Greek, Armenian, Cypriot, and Kurdish lobbyists in Washington makes the job of lobbying for Turkey a difficult one.

Turkey does not have a large lobbying presence in Washington. There is an ethnic lobby, the American Friends of Turkey, although since there are only about 180,000 Turkish Americans it is not as powerful as the ethnic lobbies for Israel or the Cuban exiles. Consequently, Turkey depends primarily on efforts of its embassy and of its hired public relations firms.

HISTORY

Turkey's association with the United States began in the late 1800s, but its current relations with the United States date back to 1947, when the Truman Doctrine designated Turkey as the recipient of special economic and military assistance. Since then Turkey has received over $4 billion in economic aid and loans and more than $14 billion in military assistance. In 1952 Turkey became a NATO member, and its strategic location made it a valuable ally.

Until 1974 Turkey had a strong relationship with the United States. This changed after Turkey invaded the island of Cyprus in 1974, violating a 1960 treaty of guarantee for Cyprus. Turkey did so with the aim of protecting Turkish minorities there from Greek oppression following the overthrow of the Cypriot government by mainland Greek officers in the Cypriot national guard. The subsequent hostilities led to Turkish occupation of the northern part of the island, which continues to this day. Turkey used American-made arms during this intervention.

In reaction Greek Americans successfully lobbied to reduce arms aid to Turkey, and for the next four years an embargo was imposed on military shipments to Turkey. In reaction Turkey canceled several U.S. defense activities at joint installations in an effort to increase military aid. By October 1975, however, Turkey was able to obtain a relaxation of the U.S. arms embargo. In March 1976 a new defense agreement was signed, but not approved by Congress. In September 1978 the embargo ended and U.S.-Turkish relations improved, with Turkey lifting restrictions on U.S. activities in late 1978.

The Greek lobby was also successful in imposing a ten to seven ratio on military aid to Turkey: for every $10 in military aid to Turkey, $7 must be sent to Greece. This ratio exists to this day, and Turkey argues that it is an unfair burden on it, given that its population is six times that of Greece and it has a heavier burden of NATO commitments. However, Turkish lobbying to remove this ratio has been unsuccessful. Nevertheless, Turkey is the third-largest recipient of military aid, after Israel and Egypt.

In early 1990 Turkey imposed temporary restrictions on American military activities in response to the U.S. Senate's consideration of a resolution to declare a day of remembrance for what Armenians and others have described as genocide of Armenians by pre-republican Turkey. Turkey lifted these restrictions after it successfully lobbied against passage of the resolution. In 1990 the United States had 10,000 members of its armed forces in Turkey; by 1992 this number was halved.

Turgut Ozal, Turkey's prime minister from 1983 to 1989 and president from 1989 to 1991, developed close personal relations with President George Bush. However, when Bill Clinton was elected president, the economic, political, and military benefits Turkey hoped for did not materialize. Turkey was able to get the United States to double its textile import quota, to $300 million, and the United States did lobby for Turkey's failed bid to join the EU. However, Turkey was unable to obtain the reimbursement it sought for the economic costs it paid for imposing international sanctions on Iraq.

ACTIVITIES: CURRENT AND FUTURE

In the 1990s there have been some tensions regarding Turkey's policy toward the Kurds. Turkey opposes the establishment of a Kurdish state in northern Iraq and Kurdish separatism in general. When the United States appeared to back the Kurds during the Gulf War, Turkey became very concerned. Its fear is that unless tightly controlled, the Kurdish separatist movement, as led by the Kurdish Worker's Party, will push Turkey into a civil war.

There were reports in the Turkish press that arms may have been transferred to Kurds in northern Iraq by allied troops during the Gulf War; this led Turkey to tighten its border patrols. Western reports that Turkey's action was hampering the war effort were not well received in Turkey. Turkey has had mixed feelings about Operation Provide Comfort, which patrolled the no-fly zone above the 36th parallel in northern Iraq. This provided a deterrent to prevent Saddam Hussein from trying to repeat his 1991 stampeding of Kurdish refugees toward the Turkish border, but Turks also feared that the eventual result would be an independent Kurdistan. Since the Gulf War the Turks have intensified repression against the Kurds, despite international criticism for doing so.

This is relevant to Turkish lobbying in the United States, which has linked military aid and support to human rights. America is cutting its aid to Turkey and converting it into loans; in the mid 1990s this aid dropped from $543 million to $450 million. In 1997 Turkey's aid was cut from $49 million to $25 million to protest the Turkish army's campaign against the Kurds. Then, Armenian lobbyists succeeded in chopping off another $3 million unless Turkey opened its border gates to Armenia—Turkey closed these gates to protest Armenian actions in Nagorno-Karabagh, an Armenian region currently seeking autonomy. When Turkey lobbied against these cuts, this provoked threats that aid would be conditioned on a solution to the Kurdish problem. Turkey fears that if it continues to seek guarantees to reverse the downward trend in aid, the United States will close its Turkish bases.

While the United States has been critical of Turkish policy toward the Kurds, Turkey has been able to prevent America from actively coming to the aid of the Kurds. It appears that the United States thinks that the Kurdish problem will be more amenable to a solution once Saddam Hussein is removed from power in Iraq. However, the Turkish lobby has not been able to prevent some punitive actions taken against it. In the 1990s Turkey was unable to prevent Congress from making a 10 percent reduction of funds appropriated for Turkey until the Department of State could verify improvement of that country's human rights record and progress on confidence-building mechanisms in Cyprus. Turkey considered this to be interference with its internal affairs, yet made no effort to have the funds restored.

One other outcome Turkish lobbying seeks to prevent is the passage of congressional resolutions condemning it for the 1915–1916 massacre of Armenians. Turkey claims that Armenian charges of genocide are greatly exaggerated, yet Armenians have increased awareness of this issue, and this is likely to continue to be a challenge to Turkey's lobby in the future.

On economic issues Turkey's main interest is to obtain the route through which oil from the Caspian Sea will be shipped to the West. It is unknown exactly how much oil there is in this area, but there are at least 42 billion barrels of proven oil reserves, and Western businesses want to drill. There are two possible routes: one, the northern route, would extend a pipeline through Russia, across the Black Sea, and through the Bosporus strait to the Mediterranean. The other route, the Mediterranean route, would go across Turkey, bypassing the Black Sea and the Bosporus strait. Turkey is lobbying for the second route, partly for the economic benefits it would receive in compensation but also for environmental reasons. It argues that the route through the Bosporus would increase traffic jams on one of the world's busiest waterways and that the difficulty of navigating this waterway would increase the danger of a collision and an oil spill. Such a collision occurred in the Bosporus in 1979—over 95,000 tons of oil were dumped, some of which burned for weeks.

In early 1995 Washington decided to back the Mediterranean route. However, the company developing the pipeline, the Azerbaijan International Operating Company (AIOC), refused to commit to building the main pipeline to the Mediterranean through Turkey. The AIOC is not scheduled to decide which route to take until 2000.

Turkey seeks help for the devastation it suffered in the August 1999 earthquake in Ismit. It has made successful appeals to the U.S. government and the U.S.

public for donations. The total value of American aid to Turkey for this disaster was $11 million in goods, services, and economic assistance. Two weeks later an earthquake occurred in Greece. Turks and Greeks both came to each other's aid; this offers the potential to lead to improved relations between the two countries. If so, this would decrease opposition to Turkish interests by the Greek-American lobby. In the face of this natural disaster, Turkey appears relatively sympathetic and could have an opportunity to promote its interests more effectively in Washington.

ALLYSON FORD

Bibliography

Aybet, Gulner. *Turkey's Foreign Policy and its Implications for the West: A Turkish Perspective.* Boulder, CO: Westview Press, 1996.

Blank, Steven J. *Turkey's Strategic Position at the Crossroads of World Affairs.* Carlisle Barracks, PA: Strategic Studies Institute, 1993.

Mastny, Vojtech, and R. Craig Nation, eds. *Turkey between East and West.* Boulder, CO: Westview Press, 1996.

Pope, Nicole, and Hugh Pope. *Turkey Unveiled: A History of Modern Turkey.* New York: Overlook Press, 1997.

www.state.gov

PART II
POLITICAL ACTION COMMITTEES AND LOBBYISTS: TABLES AND FIGURES

SECTION ONE
POLITICAL ACTION COMMITTEES

Political action committees (PACs) are organizations that pool campaign contributions from the members of an interest group and donate them to candidates for political office. PAC contributions are part of an interest group's overall effort to gain access to, lobby, and influence elected officials. PACs have existed for several decades, but only since the mid 1970s have they been a major force in political campaigns as well as a target for critics and reformers of campaign finance laws.

As the old saying goes, "money is the mother's milk of politics." Because of the huge expenses of campaigns, candidates must raise large amounts of money to be competitive. Congressional candidates spent more than $765 million in 1995–96, almost double the $391 million spent a decade earlier. They raised $232.9 million in 1997, a record for off-year fund-raising. Ten years earlier, in 1987, Congressional candidates raised half of that amount, $111.5 million. Political action committees accounted for $62.7 million of the 1997 total, or 27 percent; ten years earlier the candidates raised $42.2 million from PACs.

It is ironic that twenty-five years ago PACs were seen as a positive step in the direction of reforming the system of campaign finance. The 1972 Federal Election Campaign Act (FECA) forbade corporations and unions from contributing directly to national campaigns. Instead, it allowed them to establish their own PACs, solicit voluntary contributions for them and pay their expenses. Amendments to FECA, enacted in the wake of the Watergate scandal in 1974, allowed for the expansion of PACs by authorizing more kinds of interest groups to form them. It also imposed new financial disclosure requirements so that the public would know who was giving and receiving PAC contributions.

Each PAC can accept contributions of up to $5,000 a year per person. In any one year no individual may contribute more than a total of $25,000 to PACs, national party organizations, and candidates for federal office. PACs can give up to $5,000 to a candidate for both the primary and general elections, or $10,000 per year. Individuals can contribute only $1,000 on their own to each candidate for each election.

While PACs are limited in the amount of money they can give to candidates directly, as long as they do not coordinate their campaign activities with the candidate or the candidate's campaign committee there is no limit on what they may spend on behalf of a candidate. These "independent" expenditures constitute only a fraction of total PAC spending, but the amounts have been increasing each year. Because independent expenditures enable PACs to skirt the limits on contributions per campaign, critics see them as giving interest groups the very kind of disproportionate influence that the campaign finance laws were intended to guard against. FECA banned independent expenditures, but the Supreme Court reversed this ban in 1976, ruling in *Buckley v. Valeo* that it violated the First Amendment's protection of free speech.

The Federal Election Commission (FEC) monitors and regulates PACs. Soon after they are established and begin receiving contributions, PACs must register with the FEC and report regularly their contributions and expenditures. Congressional candidates must also file with the FEC concerning which PACs are donating to their campaigns and the amounts of the donations.

THE NUMBER AND VARIETY OF PACS

The number of PACs has risen sharply over the past few decades. Although their number has declined somewhat in recent years from a high of 4,268 in 1988, PACs grew from 608 at the end of 1974 to 3,844 at the beginning of 1998. The importance of PACs in campaign finance has grown along with their numbers. In the 1981–82 election cycle, PACs contributed $87.6 million; in 1995–96, they gave $217.8 million.

The two main kinds of PACs are *connected* and *unconnected*. Connected PACs are those affiliated with specific interest groups, like corporations, trade associations, professional associations, and unions. The parent organization uses its own money to pay the expenses of operating and raising money for the PAC, appoints individuals who direct the PAC, and can decide how the PAC will spend its money. The PAC can solicit contributions only from members of the parent organization, such as stockholders, employees, or union members. The parent organization cannot use its own money to fund contributions, however.

Unconnected PACs are not tied to corporations, trade associations, or labor unions. Their fund-raising and operating expenses must be paid out of the PAC's funds. Unlike connected PACs, however, unconnected PACs have no restrictions on where they can solicit contributions.

Business interests representing particular firms and industries compose the largest number of PACs. These PACs contribute more money than labor union and other nonbusiness PACs. Corporate PACs gave $78.2 million to national candidates in the 1995–96 election cycle, as compared to $48 million from labor PACs. Of the top 20 PACs in terms of contributions, 9 were businesses and trade associations. They included the National Automobile Dealers Association, United Parcel Service (UPS), the National Association of Home Builders, Lockheed Martin, the National Association of Realtors, the American Bankers Association, AT&T Corporation, Philip Morris, and Federal Express Corporation.

Nevertheless, unions are major players in the PAC world. Nine of the top 20 PACs that contributed the most money to federal campaigns in 1997 were unions; for the 1995–96 election cycle, the figure was 12 of the top 20. The top PAC contributor in 1997 was the American Federation of State, County and Municipal Employees, which contributed over $925,000. The leading PAC in 1995–96 was the Teamsters, which contributed $2.6 million. Other unions among the top twenty PACs included the International Brotherhood of Electrical Workers, the Laborers' International Union of North America, the United Food and Commercial Workers Union, the United Auto Workers, the Carpenters Union, the United Transportation Union, and the International Association of Machinists and Aerospace Workers Union.

Other important PACs represent professional groups, such as the Association of Trial Lawyers of America, the Airline Pilots Association, the American Medical Association, and the American Dental Association, which were among the top 25 PAC contributors for 1997. There are also "ideological" PACs that promote various causes, principles and policies. Among the major ideological PACs are the National Rifle Association, which has made the largest contributions among these groups, ranking eleventh among all PACs in 1997. Others include the National Committee to Preserve Social Security and Medicare, the Human Rights Campaign (gay rights), the Sierra Club, the Adam Smith PAC (free markets), the Women's Campaign Fund and the National Abortion and Reproductive Rights Action League (NARAL).

Finally, dozens of members of Congress, such as former House Speaker Newt Gingrich (R-GA), Minority Leader Richard A. Gephardt (D-MO), Senator Edward M. Kennedy (D-MA), and Senate Majority Leader Trent Lott (R-MS), have established their own "leadership PACs." "Campaign America," affiliated with former Vice President Dan Quayle, raised over $829,000 in 1995–96. Rep. Gephardt's "Effective Government Committee" raised over $461,000 in those years. Gingrich's "Monday Morning PAC" raised $766,500, and the figure for Majority Leader Dick Armey's PAC was over $737,000. Because of their clout, leaders can easily raise money from donors. They can then funnel the contributions to other candidates or keep the money for their own expenses. PACs, which can give $10,000 every two years to the reelection committees of the leaders, such as Gephardt's and Gingrich's, can then give another $10,000 to Gephardt's and Gingrich's leadership PACs, and these funds can then be used to benefit other candidates to whom the PACs have contributed directly.

PAC STRATEGIES AND WHO GETS THE MONEY

PACs heavily favor incumbent candidates over challengers. In the 1995–96 election cycle, incumbents received 68 percent of PAC contributions ($145.5 million), with only 13 percent going to challengers ($28.5 million) and 18 percent going to candidates in open races ($39.3 million). PACs view giving money to incumbents as similar to betting on horses. They want to spend their money on candidates that are likely to win, which mostly includes incumbents. House candidates rely upon PAC contributions more than those in Senate races. For the average House of Representatives candidate, PACs accounted for 31 percent of the money raised; for Senate seats, the figure was 16 percent. The reason for this is that Senate campaigns are much more expensive than those for the House. The $5,000 limitation on PAC contributions per election means that Senate candidates need to tap other sources of funds in order to raise enough money.

There are clear patterns of PAC contributions to candidates of the two major political parties. Certain PACs favor Republicans and others favor Democrats. This is most clearly the case with business and labor PACs as well as with ideological PACs. Of the top 50 business PAC recipients in 1995–96, 47 were Republicans. The top five contributors to Republican candidates were insurance companies, health professionals, commercial banks, oil and gas interests, and the GOP's own leadership PACs. All of the top 50 labor PAC recipients were Democrats. The top 5 contributors to Democratic candidates were industrial, public sector, transportation, building trades, and miscellaneous unions.

Among the ideological PACs, a similar partisan pattern is evident. The Adam Smith and antiunion National Right to Work Committee PACs, for example, gave 100 percent of their contributions to Republicans. For the conservative Eagle Forum, the figure was 99 percent; for the National Right to Life Committee, it was 91 percent; and for the NRA, it was 83 percent. By contrast, the feminist Emily's List gave 100 percent of its contributions to Democrats. For the Sierra Club, the figure was 97 percent; for Handgun Control, Inc. it was 94 percent; for NARAL it was 91 percent; for the Human Rights Campaign, it was 89 percent; for the National Committee to Preserve Social Security and Medicare, it was 80 percent; and for the Women's Campaign Fund, it was 79 percent.

However, many PACs affiliated with businesses, trade associations, and professional groups give generously to candidates in both parties. A comparison of the top 20 industry and professional groups that contribute to each party shows considerable overlap. Health professionals, lawyers and law firms, insurance companies, commercial banks, telephone utilities, accountants, crop production and basic food processing firms, and electric utilities appear on both parties' lists of top contributors. Furthermore, the apparent partisan tilt of many PACs masks a nonpartisan strategy of giving the most money to whichever party controls Congress and reflects PACs' pro-incumbent preference regardless of party affiliations. Most PACs want to curry favor with the party that controls the agenda and the flow of legislation on the floors of both houses. For instance, although business interests are traditionally allied with Republicans, the Democrats received more contributions from those PACs than the Republicans did when the Democrats controlled Congress up through 1994. In the 1993–94 election cycle, Democrats won 54 percent of corporate PAC donations. When the GOP took over Congress after the 1994 election, business PACs immediately began to support the new Republican majority. AT&T, which had given 61 percent of its PAC money to the Democrats before 1994, gave 80 percent to Republicans in the months following the '94 election. Similarly striking reversals were followed by the United Parcel Service, Northrop Grumman, Merck & Co., Bell Atlantic, and NationsBank.

PACs target legislators whom they think will carry the greatest weight in determining policy outcomes of interest to them. Particular committees in Congress are the focus of much PAC cmoney. The party leaders and main "money committees" are especially important: the House Ways and Means Committee and Senate Finance Committee, which deal with taxation, trade, health and welfare; Appropriations, which deals with spending; Commerce, which has jurisdiction over health, energy and communications; and Banking and Financial Services. Of the top 20 recipients of the most PAC money in 1997, 10 were members of these committees and another five were legislative party leaders. For the 1996 elections, 19 of the top 20 recipients fit these categories.

There is evidence that the contributions of specific PACs rise and fall depending upon whether a specific policy decision is on the agenda. For example, during the first half of 1993, while Congress prepared to consider President Clinton's proposed healthcare plan, PAC contributions from the healthcare industry to members of the House Ways and Means Committee rose by 46 percent, from $671,742 to $981,279. For the 17 new members of this committee, contributions more than tripled. A similar change occurred on the Senate Finance Committee. Once the bill was defeated, contributions from health care interests dropped off. Taking other examples, when the Republican majority proposed deregulating the telecommunications industry, PACs from Bell Atlantic, Ameritech, and other firms in the industry jumped significantly. UPS, the PAC that gave the most money, $2.6 million, in 1992–93, opposed efforts to give the U.S. Postal Service more flexibility in setting its rates and regulations governing ergonomics that the Labor Department could issue. During 1993–94, labor fought to defeat the North American Free Trade Agreement. On the Teamsters' agenda in those years were trade issues and efforts to block Republican attempts to cut highway funding and the Occupational Safety and Health Administration. The trial lawyers' PAC opposed Republican efforts to limit punitive damages in product liability cases and other tort law reforms.

THE INFLUENCE OF PAC MONEY

What evidence is there that PAC activities actually matter? That is, do they influence electoral outcomes and public policy? For many citizens, reformers, and muckraking journalists, the answer to these questions is an unqualified "yes." For example, a few months after the House voted to repeal the ban on certain assault weapons in 1996, which was a top priority of the NRA, the NRA contributed $2,500 to House Majority Leader Dick Armey's leadership PAC. Armey had led the charge to repeal the ban. AT&T contributed nearly $1.4 million to congressional candidates between 1979 and 1986. Over that same period, Congress legislated tax provisions saving the corporation a total of $12 billion. In 1997, Congress debated whether the budget for the Forest Service to build logging roads should be cut. Environmentalists supported the cuts; industry interests opposed them. Senators who voted against the budget cuts received an average of $42,880 from timber companies from 1991 to 1998; those who voted in favor of the cuts averaged $8,565 from those companies. House members who opposed the cuts received an average of $3,873 from the companies; those who favored them received an average of only $606.

The problem with this kind of evidence is twofold, however. It is anecdotal, focusing on particular instances of apparent influence, while telling us nothing about what happens the many other times in which PACs give money and policymakers make decisions affecting them. Second, it assumes that correlation is causation. We observe that a PAC which favors a certain policy gives a generous contribution to certain candidates. Next we see those candidates, or Congress generally, responding favorably by taking, or failing to take, an action consistent with the policy favored by the PAC. The problem is that we cannot be sure that Congress would not have acted in the same way in the absence of the PAC contribution and whatever other influences were operating on congressional behavior at the time. This is not to say that PAC contributions make no difference. Indeed, it would be surprising if they did not. Certainly those who contribute and operate PACs must think they make a difference or they would probably not commit the money and effort that they do. But most political scientists would agree that pinning down the influence of PACs in a systematic manner is no easy matter.

Because PACs favor incumbents over challengers, it is possible they could help to reelect the former. One way this may happen is if incumbents are able to raise large amounts of money early, which could discourage challengers from entering the race in the first place. Incumbents already start with great advantages over challengers. Hence, the early money could be enough to intimidate otherwise highly qualified candidates. Scholars have debated whether incumbents or challengers benefit more from campaign spending once the campaign has begun. Often it is the most vulnerable incumbents who spend the most. It may be that campaign spending from PACs and other sources help challengers more than incumbents. Challengers are almost always far less well known by the voters than incumbents, so money can buy challengers name recognition and familiarity with their campaign's message that incumbents already enjoy. (This benefit accrues from initial expenditures. As more voters become aware of the challenger, the effectiveness of the spending falls.) On the other hand, incumbents may also benefit if more spending increases turnout or prevents them from losing the support of those who previously committed to them. The effect of challengers' expenditures may depend upon larger political trends. If national opinion trends favor the challenger's party, if an unpopular president is of the incumbent's party, and if macro-economic conditions are declining, then the challenger's campaign spending may make a difference.

Political scientists have also explored whether there is a relationship between PAC contributions and the roll-call votes cast in Congress. The evidence is mixed and conflicting. On the one hand, studies of votes on minimum wage legislation, the B-1 bomber, the debt limit, the windfall profits tax, wage and price controls, trucking deregulation, and legislation of interest to doctors and auto dealers suggest that PAC money affects recipients' support for these policies. One study of labor union contributions showed that contributions influence support for labor's preferred legislation, but another showed support in some congressional sessions but not in others. Yet another study found that labor's contributions had a significant impact on 5 of 9 votes on urban issues and 5 of 8 votes on general issues. On the other hand, the same study showed that business contributions were significant in only one issue conflict of each type.

Still other research suggests that campaign contributions were not important in influencing votes on the

Chrysler Corporation's loan guarantee, the windfall profits tax and dairy price supports. Another study that analyzed roll calls over an eight-year period concluded that contributions are hardly ever related to roll-call voting patterns.

CRITICISMS OF PACS AND PROPOSED REFORMS

As the number of PACs has grown and more and more money has been disbursed, critics have charged that they distort the democratic process by giving "special interests" access to elected officials that citizens who are not members of groups do not have. Furthermore, because some PACs are able to give much more money than others, some groups may have more influence. While the evidence is mixed and our knowledge is limited from which to draw firm conclusions about the effects of campaign contributions on the behavior of elected officials, it cannot be denied that the *perception* that money buys elections and influences policy outcomes exists and is a problem. If the current system engenders suspicion and cynicism, that may be reason enough to reform the system. Furthermore, since PACs give most of their money to incumbents, and since incumbents have other advantages over challengers, certain reforms might induce greater competition in congressional elections.

One proposed reform is to limit the total amount of PAC money that candidates may receive. The argument against doing this is that it may make it more difficult for challengers to seek office. Thus, this reform is often coupled with other reforms, such as permitting individuals to make larger contributions to candidates and political parties, and permitting the parties to give more to candidates and spend more on their behalf. Democrats have opposed these reforms because Republicans are able to raise more money from non-PAC sources. Also, increasing the maximum that an individual may give could increase the influence of those who are more affluent. Another proposed reform to reduce candidates' dependence on PAC money is to encourage more individuals to give small contributions by allowing them to deduct part of the contribution from their gross income or the taxes that they owe.

Yet other proposals would seek to limit the amount of money candidates may spend on their campaigns. Because of the Supreme Court ruling in *Buckley,* such limits would have to be voluntary. Therefore, these proposals are typically tied to schemes that induce compliance with the limits by providing public financing. President Clinton proposed that candidates who comply with spending limits be eligible to receive some of their campaign funds from the government. If a candidate accepted the limits but the opponent did not, the candidate would receive more from the fund. This proposal has been criticized by opponents of use of the federal treasury for funding political campaigns, and has also been criticized on the grounds that spending limits could dampen electoral competition, thus helping incumbents. Finally, there are proposals to encourage voluntary spending limits by providing candidates who comply with them free media time or time at a reduced rate.

Campaign finance reform appeared on the congressional agenda frequently during the 1990s, although no major reforms were enacted. In 1995, President Bill Clinton and Speaker of the House Newt Gingrich, pledged to name a blue-ribbon commission to study reforms in the campaign finance system. This never happened. The two parties have differed sharply over the direction that reform should take. Democrats have advocated limiting expenditures, whereas Republicans seek to limit the sources of campaign money. Democrats have been more receptive to public financing of elections as well. Nevertheless, beginning in 1996, a bipartisan coalition led by Senators John McCain (R-AZ) and Russell Feingold (D-WI) introduced a bill to ban PACs and "soft money," and to provide free or discounted television time and reduced mailing rates to candidates willing to limit how much they spend on their campaigns. Soft money, which is money raised by the national party that gets funneled to state party organizations, falls outside federal regulations on donation limits. The McCain-Feingold bill never reached a vote on the floor of the House or Senate, mainly because of Republican opposition. In 1998, a scaled-back version was introduced, proposing to ban soft money and curb issue ads, but leaving PACs alone. Again, Republicans blocked it from coming to the floor for a vote.

GARY MUCCIARONI

Bibliography

Center for Responsive Politics. *Tracking the Cash: Candidate Fund-Raising in the '98 Elections.* Washington, DC: Center for Responsive Politics, 1998.

Congressional Quarterly's Federal PACs Directory. Washington, DC: Congressional Quarterly, 1998.

Conway, M. Margaret, and Joanne Connor Green. "Political Action Committees and Campaign Finance," in Allan J. Cigler and Burdett A. Loomis, eds., *Interest Group Politics*, 5th ed. Washington, DC: Congressional Quarterly, 1998.

Federal Election Commission: www.fec.gov

Lewis, Charles. *The Buying of Congress: How Special Interests Have Stolen Your Right to Life, Liberty and the Pursuit of Happiness.* New York: Avon Books, 1998.

Makinson, Larry. *The Big Picture: Money Follows Power Shift on Capitol Hill.* Washington, DC: Center for Responsive Politics, 1997.

Nugent, Margaret Latus, and John R. Johannes, eds. *Money, Elections and Democracy: Reforming Congressional Campaign Finance.* Boulder, CO: Westview Press, 1990.

Sabato, Larry J. *PAC Power: Inside the World of Political Action Committees.* New York: W.W. Norton, 1984.

Stern, Philip M. *Still the Best Congress Money Can Buy.* Washington, DC: Regnery Gateway, 1992.

HOW TO USE THE POLITICAL ACTION COMMITTEE (PAC) TABLES

The following 69 tables list the contributions made by PACs in 1997 and 1998 for Republican and Democratic candidates for federal office, as listed and published by the Federal Election Commission. As these years represent a Congress-only election cycle, virtually all of the amounts listed are for congressional candidates. In some cases, the figures for contributions to Democratic and Republican candidates do not add up to the figure in the "total" column. This is because some of the contributions went to independent or third party candidates. Also note that many of the tables list industries in different categories than those provided in the entry section of the encyclopedia. A certain portion of the tables are accompanied by a graphic, offering a more visual presentation of the data.

Top Agriculture PACs 1997–1998

PACs	TOTAL	DEMOCRATS	REPUBLICANS
PHILLIP MORRIS	$793,533	$247,471	$546,062
MID-AMERICA DAIRYMEN	691,956	339,500	352,456
RJR NABISCO	527,000	123,000	404,000
FOOD MARKETING INSTITUTE	506,972	74,220	432,752
AMERICAN CRYSTAL SUGAR	473,850	282,500	191,350
AMERICAN VETERINARY MEDICAL	378,100	138,000	240,100
BROWN & WILLIAMSON TOBACCO	350,821	90,000	260,821
US TOBACCO	347,350	84,500	262,850
NATIONAL CATTLEMEN'S BEEF ASSN.	332,046	68,043	264,003
FARM CREDIT COUNCIL	316,452	133,122	183,330
CONAGRA INC.	303,827	73,500	230,327
AMERICAN SUGAR CANE LEAGUE	281,750	140,000	141,750
CHAMPION INTERNATIONAL	279,334	82,500	196,834
INTERNATIONAL PAPER	251,819	25,000	226,819
AMERICAN SUGARBEET GROWERS ASSN.	231,985	120,789	111,196
ALABAMA FARMERS FEDERATION	209,847	71,575	138,272
PEPSICO	205,001	42,900	162,101
ARCHER-DANIELS-MIDLAND	200,500	95,000	105,500
AMERICAN MEAT INSTITUTE	198,473	32,500	165,973
STONE CONTAINER	180,100	7,000	173,100
SOUTHERN MINNESOTA BEET SUGAR CO-OP	178,500	90,000	88,500
NATIONAL COTTON COUNCIL	177,291	80,515	96,776
FLOWERS INDUSTRIES	177,000	0	177,000
CARGILL	175,000	34,500	140,500
ASSOCIATED MILK PRODUCERS	174,500	82,700	91,800

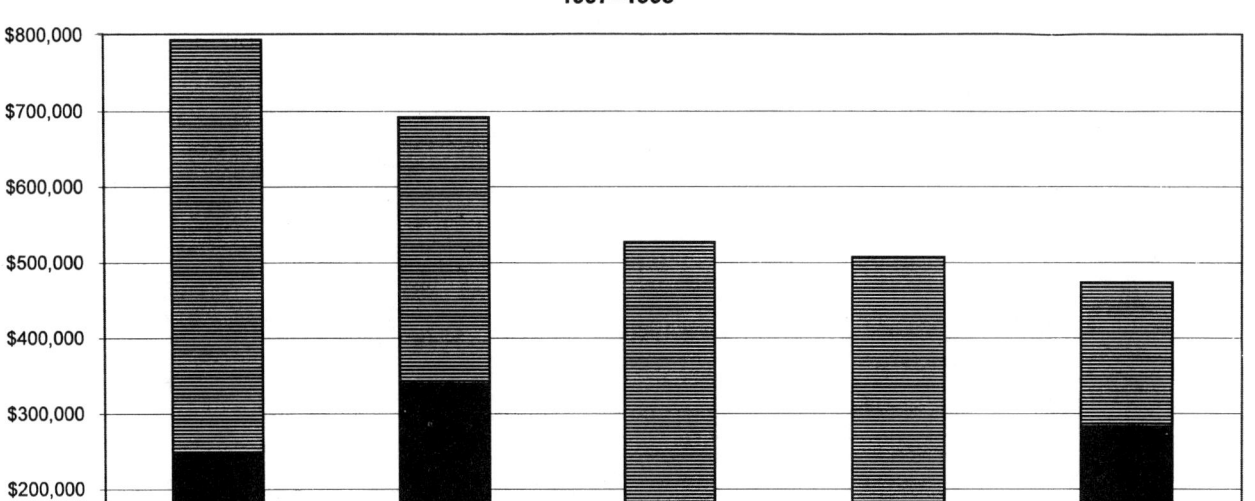

**Top 5 Agriculture Political Action Committees
1997–1998**

	Phillip Morris	Mid-American Dairymen	RJR Nabisco	Food Marketing Institute	American Crystal Sugar
Democrats	~$250,000	~$345,000	~$125,000	~$75,000	~$285,000
Republicans	~$545,000	~$350,000	~$405,000	~$435,000	~$190,000
Total	~$795,000	~$695,000	~$530,000	~$510,000	~$475,000

Top Livestock/Poultry PACs 1997–1998

PACs	TOTAL	DEMOCRATS	REPUBLICANS
AMERICAN VETERINARY MEDICAL ASSOCIATION	$378,100	$138,000	$240,100
NATIONAL CATTLEMEN'S BEEF ASSOCIATION	332,046	68,043	264,003
NATIONAL BROILER COUNCIL	120,000	33,000	87,000
NATIONAL PORK PRODUCERS COUNCIL	109,819	45,549	64,270
UNITED EGG ASSOCIATION	109,000	41,100	67,900
TEXAS CATTLE FEEDERS ASSOCIATION	85,575	15,000	70,575
NATIONAL TURKEY FEDERATION	78,750	31,250	47,500
TYSON FOODS	46,500	17,500	29,000
GOLD KIST	39,768	5,000	34,768
TENNESSEE WALKING HORSE BREEDERS	35,500	24,500	11,000

Top Dairy PACs 1997–1998

PACs	TOTAL	DEMOCRATS	REPUBLICANS
MID-AMERICA DAIRYMEN	$691,956	$339,500	$352,456
ASSOCIATED MILK PRODUCERS	174,500	82,700	91,800
INTERNATIONAL DAIRY FOODS ASSOCIATION	154,413	23,000	131,413
LAND O'LAKES	46,250	28,750	17,500
DAIRYMAN'S CO-OP CREAMERY ASSOCIATION	34,300	8,400	25,900

Top Tobacco PACs 1997–1998

PACs	TOTAL	DEMOCRATS	REPUBLICANS
PHILIP MORRIS	$793,533	$247,471	$546,062
RJR NABISCO	527,000	123,000	404,000
BROWN & WILLIAMSON TOBACCO	350,821	90,000	260,821
US TOBACCO	347,350	84,500	262,850
TOBACCO INSTITUTE	75,000	28,250	46,750

Top Forestry and Paper PACs 1997–1998

PACs	TOTAL	DEMOCRATS	REPUBLICANS
CHAMPION INTERNATIONAL	$279,334	$82,500	$196,834
INTERNATIONAL PAPER	251,819	25,000	226,819
STONE CONTAINER	180,100	7,000	173,100
WILLAMETTE INDUSTRIES	140,000	12,500	127,500
GEORGIA-PACIFIC	138,838	52,585	86,253
WEYERHAEUSER	135,687	21,627	114,060
AMERICAN FOREST & PAPER ASSOCIATION	118,207	11,800	106,407
WESTVACO	100,500	12,500	88,000
MEAD	88,350	13,000	75,350
BOISE CASCADE	55,000	9,000	46,000

Top Business PACs 1997–1998

PACs	TOTAL	DEMOCRATS	REPUBLICANS
NATIONAL BEER WHOLESALERS ASSOCIATION	$1,301,719	$231,500	$1,070,219
NATIONAL FEDERATION OF INDEPENDENT BUSINESSES	1,209,836	86,500	1,123,336
NATIONAL RESTAURANT ASSOCIATION	825,983	157,704	668,279
NATIONAL ASSOCIATION OF CONVENIENCE STORES	573,853	129,956	443,897
OUTBACK STEAKHOUSE	342,000	34,500	307,500
HARRAH'S ENTERTAINMENT	336,150	124,000	212,150
AMERICAN HOTEL & MOTEL ASSOCIATION	315,577	46,750	268,827
INTERNATIONAL COUNCIL OF SHOPPING CENTERS	223,999	54,000	169,999
NATIONAL FRANCHISEE ASSOCIATION	219,500	6,000	213,500
WINE & SPIRITS WHOLESALERS OF AMERICA	210,837	62,233	148,604
BUSINESS INDUSTRY	204,866	13,819	191,047
MCDONALD'S	200,500	47,500	153,000
JC PENNEY	185,500	23,900	161,600
COCA-COLA	168,024	71,074	96,950
NATIONAL FUNERAL DIRECTORS ASSOCIATION	159,150	54,650	104,500
LIMITED	156,000	22,000	134,000
NATIONAL ASSOCIATION OF CHAIN DRUG STORES	152,217	56,667	95,550
OUTDOOR ADVERTISING ASSOCIATION OF AMERICA	150,136	67,298	82,838
COCA-COLA ENTERPRISES	143,566	40,000	103,566
JOSEPH E SEAGRAM & SONS	136,190	56,012	80,178
WAL-MART STORES	135,750	9,250	126,500
BROWN-FORMAN	132,000	31,500	100,500
MAY DEPARTMENT STORES	130,250	40,250	90,000
DIRECT MARKETING ASSOCIATION	127,944	57,550	70,394
MIRAGE RESORTS	127,596	53,096	74,500

Top 5 Business Political Action Committees 1997–1998

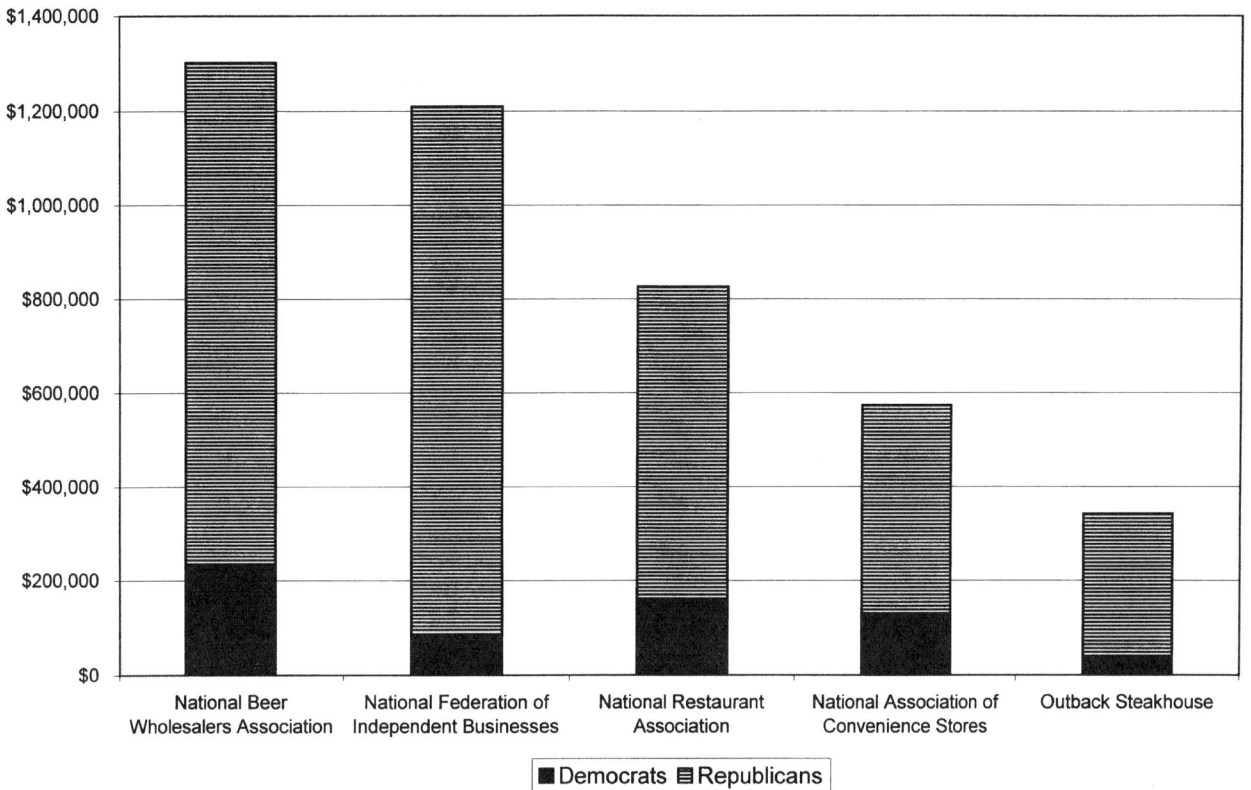

■ Democrats ☰ Republicans

Top Food and Beverage PACs 1997–1998

PACs	TOTAL	DEMOCRATS	REPUBLICANS
NATIONAL BEER WHOLESALERS ASSOCIATION	$1,301,719	$231,500	$1,070,219
NATIONAL RESTAURANT ASSOCIATION	825,983	157,704	668,279
OUTBACK STEAKHOUSE	342,000	34,500	307,500
WINE & SPIRITS WHOLESALERS OF AMERICA	210,837	62,233	148,604
MCDONALD'S	200,500	47,500	153,000
COCA-COLA	168,024	71,074	96,950
COCA-COLA ENTERPRISES	143,566	40,000	103,566
JOSEPH E SEAGRAM & SONS	136,190	56,012	80,178
BROWN-FORMAN	132,000	31,500	100,500
NATIONAL SOFT DRINK ASSOCIATION	117,791	37,791	80,000
ANHEUSER-BUSCH	108,050	35,350	72,700
TACO	98,428	24,100	74,328
BRINKER INTERNATIONAL	84,500	25,000	59,500
DARDEN RESTAURANTS	80,867	19,500	61,367
PIZZA HUT FRANCHISEES ASSOCIATION	80,250	0	80,250

Top Retail PACs 1997–1998

PACs	TOTAL	DEMOCRATS	REPUBLICANS
NATIONAL ASSOCIATION OF CONVENIENCE STORES	$573,853	$129,956	$443,897
INTERNATIONAL COUNCIL OF SHOPPING CENTERS	223,999	54,000	169,999
JC PENNEY	185,500	23,900	161,600
LIMITED	156,000	22,000	134,000
NATIONAL ASSOCIATION OF CHAIN DRUG STORES	152,217	56,667	95,550
WAL-MART STORES	135,750	9,250	126,500
MAY DEPARTMENT STORES	130,250	40,250	90,000
DIRECT MARKETING ASSOCIATION	127,944	57,550	70,394
RITE AID	116,750	43,250	73,500
DAYTON HUDSON	94,788	44,538	50,250

Top Miscellaneous Services PACs 1997–1998

PACs	TOTAL	DEMOCRATS	REPUBLICANS
NATIONAL FUNERAL DIRECTORS ASSOCIATION	$159,150	$54,650	$104,500
OUTDOOR ADVERTISING ASSOCIATION OF AMERICA	150,136	67,298	82,838
EQUIPMENT LEASING ASSOCIATION OF AMERICA	106,800	25,300	81,500
PROFESSIONALS IN ADVERTISING	86,899	22,499	64,400
NATIONAL ASSOCIATION OF TEMPORARY SERVICES	66,250	23,000	43,250
SERVICE CORP. INTERNATIONAL	45,500	24,500	21,000
SERVICEMASTER	44,070	9,250	34,820
ASSOCIATION OF PROGRESSIVE RENTAL ORGANIZATIONS	43,500	18,000	25,500
NATIONAL PEST CONTROL ASSOCIATION	41,405	19,655	21,750
VIAD	35,911	3,400	32,511

Top Gambling/Recreation/Tourism PACs 1997–1998

PACs	TOTAL	DEMOCRATS	REPUBLICANS
HARRAH'S ENTERTAINMENT	$336,150	$124,000	$212,150
AMERICAN HOTEL & MOTEL ASSOCIATION	315,577	46,750	268,827
MIRAGE RESORTS	127,596	53,096	74,500
MARRIOTT INTERNATIONAL	123,500	16,000	107,500
SABRE GROUP	82,499	31,500	50,999
MGM GRAND	73,024	36,000	37,024
PROMUS HOTEL	62,500	8,000	54,500
STARWOOD HOTELS & RESORTS WORLDWIDE	62,304	33,500	28,804
HOLIDAY INNS	53,000	11,000	42,000
BOYD GAMING	52,500	27,000	25,500

Top Miscellaneous Business PACs 1997–1998

PACs	TOTAL	DEMOCRATS	REPUBLICANS
NATIONAL FEDERATION OF INDEPENDENT BUSINESSES	$1,209,836	$86,500	$1,123,336
NATIONAL FRANCHISEE ASSOCIATION	219,500	6,000	213,500
BUSINESS INDUSTRY	204,866	13,819	191,047
NATIONAL ASSOCIATION OF SMALL BUSINESS INVESTMENT COMPANIES	93,000	12,000	81,000
GREATER WASHINGTON BOARD OF TRADE	61,250	21,750	39,500
NATIONAL FEDERATION OF BUSINESS & PROFESSIONAL WOMEN'S CLUBS	33,500	32,750	750

Top Construction PACs 1997–1998

PACs	TOTAL	DEMOCRATS	REPUBLICANS
NATIONAL ASSN. OF HOME BUILDERS	$1,807,240	$517,990	$1,289,250
ASSOCIATED BUILDERS & CONTRACTORS	996,117	21,000	975,117
ASSOCIATED GENERAL CONTRACTORS	778,585	53,750	723,835
MANUFACTURED HOUSING INSTITUTE	362,950	116,500	246,450
NATIONAL ELECTRICAL CONTRACTORS ASSN.	270,000	39,000	231,000
NATIONAL UTILITY CONTRACTORS ASSN.	252,865	45,416	207,449
CATERPILLAR	224,500	12,500	212,000
NATIONAL MULTI HOUSING COUNCIL	200,178	43,394	156,784
NATIONAL ROOFING CONTRACTORS ASSN.	172,250	2,500	169,750
FLUOR	162,750	48,500	114,250
AMERICAN PORTLAND CEMENT ALLIANCE	161,850	51,650	110,200
CH2M HILL	151,965	53,515	98,450
SHEET METAL/AIR CONDITIONING CONTRACTORS	151,114	19,300	131,814
NATIONAL SOCIETY OF PROFESSIONAL ENGINEERS	141,512	41,250	100,262
NATIONAL STONE ASSN.	140,475	27,000	113,475
AMERICAN CONSULTING ENGINEERS COUNCIL	128,356	35,092	93,264
BROWN & ROOT	127,700	4,200	123,500
ICF KAISER INTERNATIONAL	118,625	61,425	57,200
OWENS CORNING	116,356	37,200	79,156
SVERDRUP	106,800	36,300	70,500
PARSONS BRINCKERHOFF	83,617	50,600	33,017
AMERICAN SUPPLY ASSN.	83,000	12,500	70,500
NATIONAL READY MIXED CONCRETE ASSN.	80,017	11,230	68,787
JACOBS ENGINEERING GROUP	71,544	46,044	25,500
NATIONAL LUMBER & BLDG. MATERIALS DEALERS	67,600	15,500	52,100

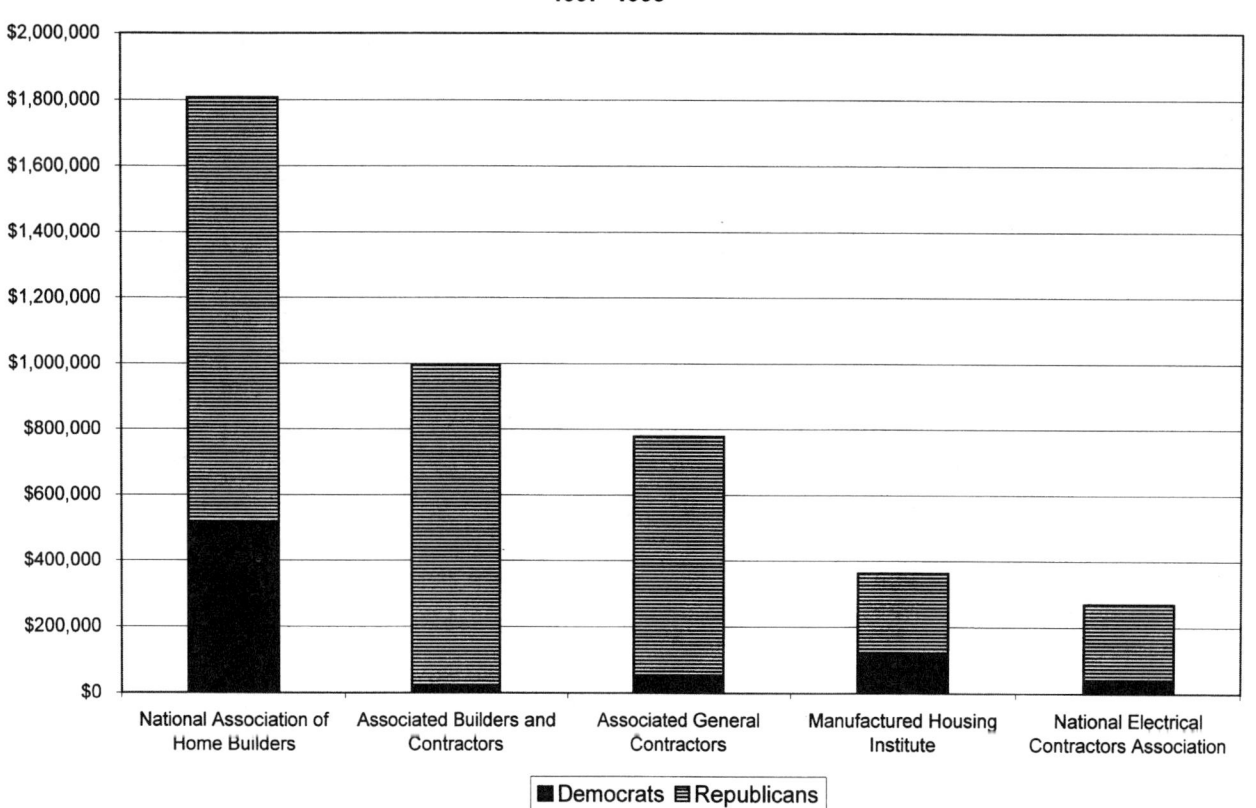

Top 5 Construction Political Action Committees 1997–1998

Top Building Equipment/Materials PACs 1997–1998

PACs	TOTAL	DEMOCRATS	REPUBLICANS
CATERPILLAR	$224,500	$12,500	$212,000
AMERICAN PORTLAND CEMENT ALLIANCE	161,850	51,650	110,200
NATIONAL STONE ASSN.	140,475	27,000	113,475
OWENS CORNING	116,356	37,200	79,156
AMERICAN SUPPLY ASSN.	83,000	12,500	70,500
NATIONAL READY MIXED CONCRETE ASSN.	80,017	11,230	68,787
NATIONAL LUMBER & BLDG. MATERIALS DEALERS	67,600	15,500	52,100
ASSOCIATED EQUIPMENT DISTRIBUTORS	65,000	9,000	56,000
VULCAN MATERIALS	54,100	9,250	44,850
HOLNAM	47,062	13,778	33,284

Top Engineering/Architecture PACs 1997–1998

PACs	TOTAL	DEMOCRATS	REPUBLICANS
CH2M HILL	$151,965	$53,515	$98,450
NATIONAL SOCIETY OF PROFESSIONAL ENGINEERS	141,512	41,250	100,262
AMERICAN CONSULTING ENGINEERS COUNCIL	128,356	35,092	93,264
ICF KAISER INTERNATIONAL	118,625	61,425	57,200
SVERDRUP	106,800	36,300	70,500
PARSONS BRINCKERHOFF	83,617	50,600	33,017
JACOBS ENGINEERING GROUP	71,544	46,044	25,500
PARSONS	47,000	15,000	32,000
AMERICAN INSTITUTE OF ARCHITECTS	38,775	24,275	14,500
STONE & WEBSTER	31,560	15,450	16,110

Top Contractors and Builders PACs 1997–1998

PACs	TOTAL	DEMOCRATS	REPUBLICANS
NATIONAL ASSN. OF HOME BUILDERS	$1,807,240	$517,990	$1,289,250
ASSOCIATED BUILDERS AND CONTRACTORS	996,117	21,000	975,117
ASSOCIATED GENERAL CONTRACTORS	778,585	53,750	723,835
MANUFACTURED HOUSING INSTITUTE	362,950	116,500	246,450
NATIONAL ELECTRICAL CONTRACTORS ASSN.	270,000	39,000	231,000
NATIONAL UTILITY CONTRACTORS ASSN.	252,865	45,416	207,449
NATIONAL MULTI HOUSING COUNCIL	200,178	43,394	156,784
NATIONAL ROOFING CONTRACTORS ASSN.	172,250	2,500	169,750
FLUOR	162,750	48,500	114,250
SHEET METAL/AIR CONDITIONING CONTRACTORS	151,114	19,300	131,814
BROWN & ROOT	127,700	4,200	123,500
AMERICAN ROAD & TRANSPORT BUILDERS ASSN.	64,609	13,500	51,109
MORRISON-KNUDSEN	49,600	17,250	32,350
HB ZACHRY	40,250	14,500	25,750
INDEPENDENT ELECTRICAL CONTRACTORS	38,750	1,100	37,650

Top Defense PACs 1997–1998

PACs	TOTAL	DEMOCRATS	REPUBLICANS
LOCKHEED MARTIN	$1,043,745	$353,478	$690,267
NORTHROP GRUMMAN	456,775	153,750	303,025
RAYTHEON	448,858	150,300	298,558
GENERAL DYNAMICS	436,900	170,650	266,250
NEWPORT NEWS SHIPBUILDING	308,250	105,750	202,500
MARCONI NORTH AMERICA	289,750	102,200	187,550
TENNECO	271,900	84,500	187,400
UNITED TECHNOLOGIES	259,550	106,500	153,050
TRW	236,008	64,983	171,025
SCIENCE APPLICATIONS INTERNATIONAL	227,500	72,250	155,250
TEXTRON	221,550	71,250	150,300
HARRIS	210,999	4,360	206,639
MCDONNELL DOUGLAS	193,250	69,250	124,000
ALLIEDSIGNAL	160,750	55,500	105,250
ALLIANT TECHSYSTEMS	127,750	39,250	88,500
LITTON INDUSTRIES	104,450	32,250	72,200
GENCORP	90,100	37,600	52,500
CUBIC	63,750	10,000	53,750
MANTECH INTERNATIONAL	52,750	29,250	23,500
UNITED DEFENSE	49,500	11,500	38,000
ROCKWELL INTERNATIONAL	48,500	9,500	39,000
THIOKOL	46,850	11,350	35,500
DRS TECHNOLOGIES	41,550	17,250	24,300
ATLANTIC RESEARCH	31,000	8,500	22,500
KAMAN	30,800	13,800	17,000

**Top 5 Defense Political Action Committees
1997–1998**

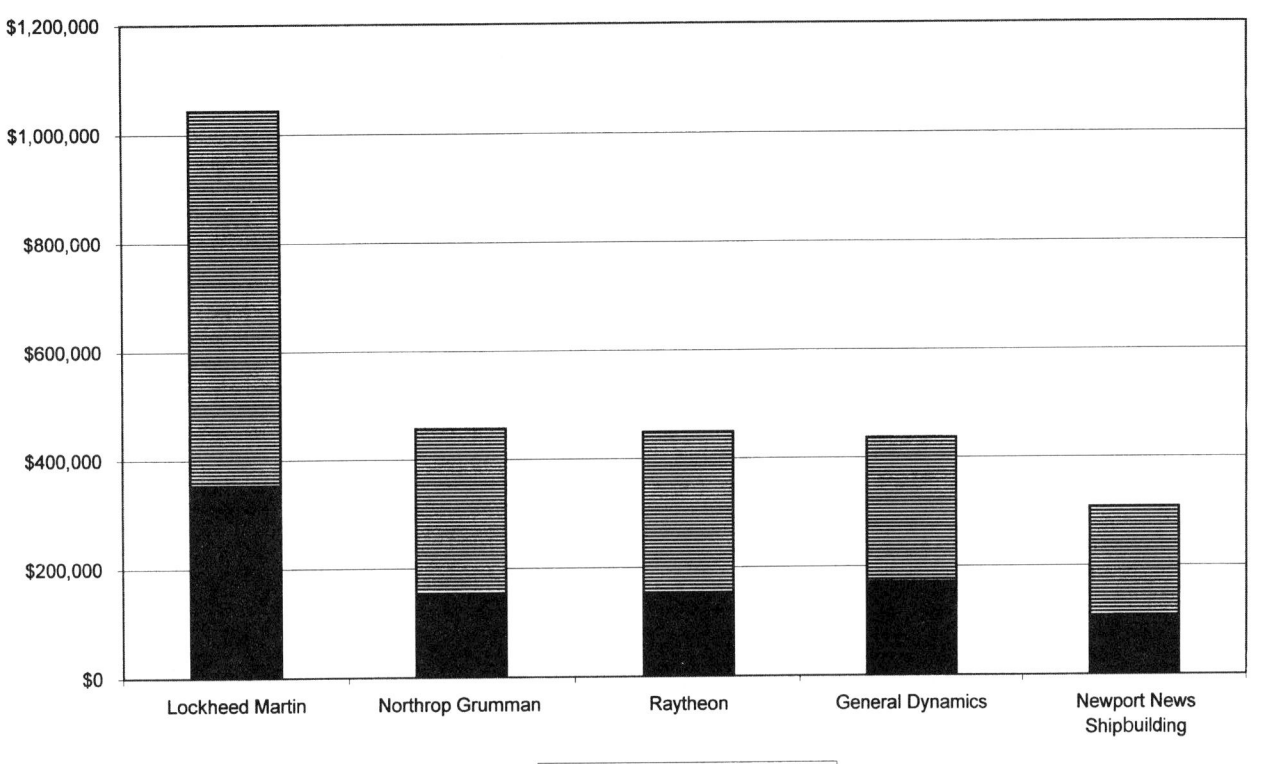

Top Electronics/Communications PACs 1997–1998

PACs	TOTAL	DEMOCRATS	REPUBLICANS
BELL ATLANTIC	$783,495	$288,774	$494,721
AT&T	772,460	335,177	437,283
SBC COMMUNICATIONS	761,071	307,046	454,025
NATIONAL CABLE TELEVISION ASSN.	612,968	249,388	363,580
AMERITECH	610,942	224,939	386,003
GTE	589,429	193,026	396,403
BELLSOUTH TELECOMMUNICATIONS	469,208	188,650	280,558
NATIONAL ASSN. OF BROADCASTERS	456,671	147,367	309,304
MCI TELECOMMUNICATIONS	377,250	155,750	221,500
TIME WARNER	327,073	189,440	137,633
BELLSOUTH	268,200	95,200	173,000
LUCENT TECHNOLOGIES	233,250	81,500	151,750
SPRINT	213,249	98,499	114,750
MICROSOFT	212,000	71,750	140,250
EDS	209,800	96,300	113,500
UNIVERSAL STUDIOS	209,100	89,500	119,600
US WEST	203,365	54,350	149,015
VIACOM INTERNATIONAL	173,038	82,238	90,800
WESTINGHOUSE ELECTRIC	170,600	55,550	115,050
PRINTING INDUSTRIES OF AMERICA	167,100	22,000	145,100
WALT DISNEY	156,986	94,054	62,932
HUGHES ELECTRONICS	144,750	60,000	84,750
ASCAP	130,360	73,610	56,750
LORAL SPACECOM	127,750	85,750	42,000
SONY PICTURES ENTERTAINMENT	109,500	48,750	60,750

Top Electronic/Computer Manufacturing PACs 1997–1998

PACs	TOTAL	DEMOCRATS	REPUBLICANS
MICROSOFT	$212,000	$71,750	$140,250
EDS	209,800	96,300	113,500
WESTINGHOUSE ELECTRIC	170,600	55,550	115,050
INTEL	81,007	16,103	64,904
AMP	80,500	4,000	76,500
COMPUTER SCIENCES	79,500	25,000	54,500
HEWLETT-PACKARD	75,750	20,000	55,750
PHILIPS ELECTRONICS NORTH AMERICA	59,325	11,650	47,675
NCR	58,000	7,500	50,500
HONEYWELL	56,500	11,000	45,500

Top Telephone PACs 1997–1998

PACs	TOTAL	DEMOCRATS	REPUBLICANS
BELL ATLANTIC	$783,495	$288,774	$494,721
AT&T	772,460	335,177	437,283
SBC COMMUNICATIONS	761,071	307,046	454,025
AMERITECH	610,942	224,939	386,003
GTE	589,429	193,026	396,403
BELLSOUTH TELECOMMUNICATIONS	469,208	188,650	280,558
MCI TELECOMMUNICATIONS	377,250	155,750	221,500
BELLSOUTH	268,200	95,200	173,000
SPRINT	213,249	98,499	114,750
US WEST	203,365	54,350	149,015

Top TV/Music/Movies PACs 1997–1998

PACs	TOTAL	DEMOCRATS	REPUBLICANS
NATIONAL CABLE TELEVISION ASSN.	$612,968	$249,388	$363,580
NATIONAL ASSN. OF BROADCASTERS	456,671	147,367	309,304
TIME WARNER	327,073	189,440	137,633
UNIVERSAL STUDIOS	209,100	89,500	119,600
VIACOM INTERNATIONAL	173,038	82,238	90,800
WALT DISNEY	156,986	94,054	62,932
ASCAP	130,360	73,610	56,750
SONY PICTURES ENTERTAINMENT	109,500	48,750	60,750
COMCAST	98,475	52,700	45,775
MOTION PICTURE ASSN. OF AMERICA	89,118	39,771	49,347

Top Telecommunications PACs 1997–1998

PACs	TOTAL	DEMOCRATS	REPUBLICANS
LUCENT TECHNOLOGIES	$233,250	$81,500	$151,750
HUGHES ELECTRONICS	144,750	60,000	84,750
LORAL SPACECOM	127,750	85,750	42,000
MOTOROLA	108,306	35,500	72,806
NORTHERN TELECOM	91,879	45,766	46,113
AIRTOUCH COMMUNICATIONS	91,720	33,898	57,822
CELLULAR TELECOM INDUSTRY ASSN.	87,158	32,539	54,619
COMSAT	76,003	41,250	34,753
GENERAL INSTRUMENT	47,500	4,500	43,000
AT&T WIRELESS SERVICES	45,022	13,489	31,533

Top Printing and Publishing PACs 1997–1998

PACs	TOTAL	DEMOCRATS	REPUBLICANS
PRINTING INDUSTRIES OF AMERICA	$167,100	$22,000	$145,100
HALLMARK CARDS	66,750	15,750	51,000
PHILLIPS PUBLISHING INTERNATIONAL	64,550	100	64,450
RR DONNELLEY & SONS	59,750	6,000	53,750
NEWS AMERICA PUBLISHING	48,000	14,000	34,000

Top Energy/Resource PACs 1997–1998

PACs	TOTAL	DEMOCRATS	REPUBLICANS
NATIONAL RURAL ELECTRIC COOPERATIVE ASSN.	$789,771	$412,345	$377,426
KOCH INDUSTRIES	533,878	105,600	428,278
EXXON	482,900	27,600	454,800
GENERAL ATOMICS	347,977	115,150	232,827
CHEVRON	331,529	53,150	278,379
SOUTHERN CALIFORNIA EDISON	307,224	127,831	179,393
NATIONAL MINING ASSN.	282,949	37,000	245,949
CYPRUS AMAX MINERALS	268,750	45,100	223,650
MOBIL OIL	237,250	29,500	207,750
HOUSTON INDUSTRIES	222,130	71,785	150,345
PG&E	220,952	94,070	126,882
TEXACO	219,200	44,700	174,500
EDISON ELECTRIC INSTITUTE	213,472	65,505	147,967
ENRON	209,893	64,864	145,029
PETROLEUM MARKETERS ASSN.	207,140	38,238	168,902
HALLIBURTON	190,500	6,500	184,000
FLORIDA POWER & LIGHT	182,250	37,000	145,250
AMOCO	172,500	42,000	130,500
CAROLINA POWER & LIGHT	170,500	66,500	104,000
CMS ENERGY	169,333	81,135	88,198
DTE ENERGY	161,400	79,200	82,200
OCCIDENTAL PETROLEUM	161,000	50,000	111,000
UNION PACIFIC RESOURCES GROUP	159,516	33,500	126,016
TEXAS UTILITIES	157,650	72,650	85,000
EL PASO ENERGY	157,250	23,250	134,000

Top 5 Energy/Resource Political Action Committees
1997–1998

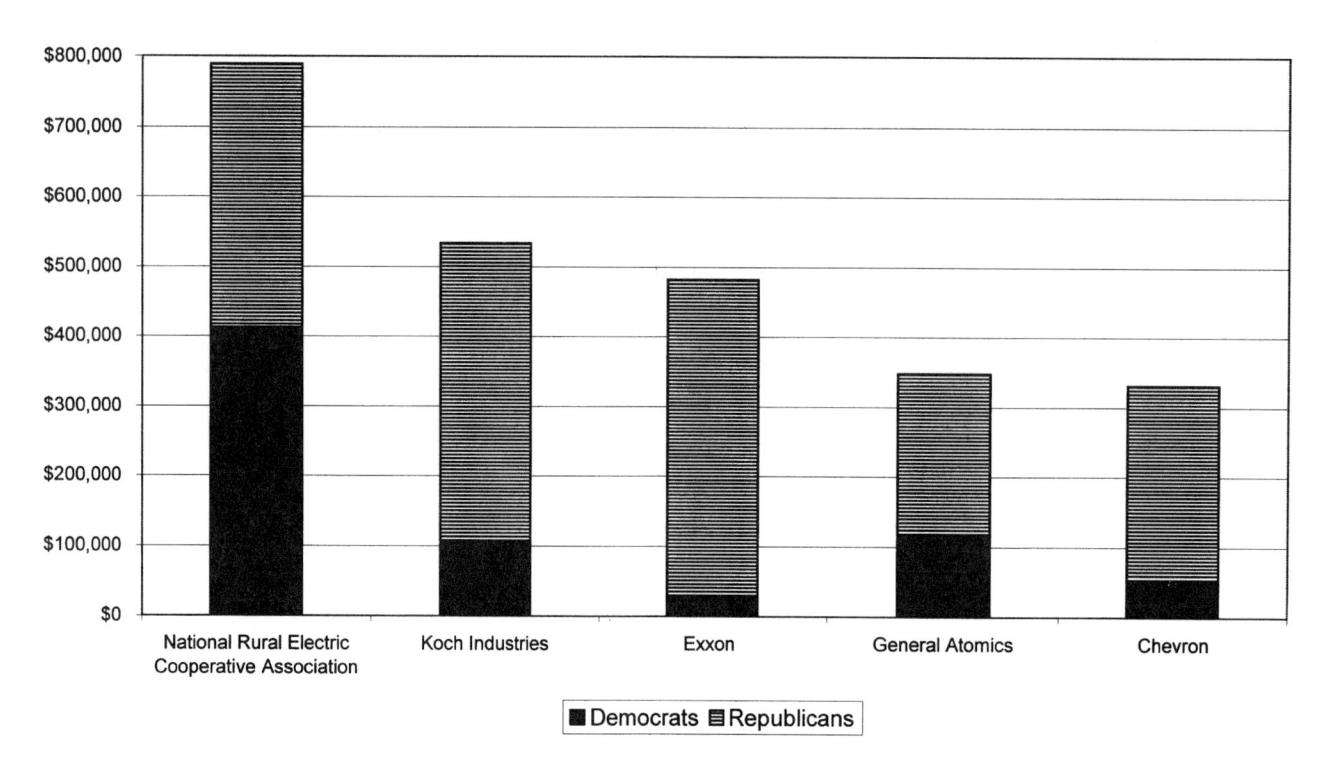

Organization	Democrats	Republicans	Total (approx.)
National Rural Electric Cooperative Association	~$410,000	~$375,000	~$785,000
Koch Industries	~$105,000	~$430,000	~$535,000
Exxon	~$25,000	~$455,000	~$480,000
General Atomics	~$110,000	~$235,000	~$345,000
Chevron	~$45,000	~$280,000	~$325,000

Top Oil and Gas PACs 1997–1998

PACs	TOTAL	DEMOCRATS	REPUBLICANS
KOCH INDUSTRIES	$533,878	$105,600	$428,278
EXXON	482,400	27,600	454,800
CHEVRON	331,529	53,150	278,379
MOBIL OIL	237,250	29,500	207,750
TEXACO	219,200	44,700	174,500
ENRON	209,893	64,864	145,029
PETROLEUM MARKETERS ASSN.	207,140	38,238	168,902
HALLIBURTON	190,500	6,500	184,000
AMOCO	172,500	42,000	130,500
OCCIDENTAL PETROLEUM	161,000	50,000	111,000
UNION PACIFIC RESOURCES GROUP	159,516	33,500	126,016
EL PASO ENERGY	157,250	23,250	134,000
ATLANTIC RICHFIELD	154,814	34,250	120,564
COASTAL	146,521	48,271	98,250
WILLIAMS COMPANIES	143,350	21,600	121,750
PHILLIPS PETROLEUM	132,996	19,500	113,496
SOCIETY OF INDEP. GASOLINE MARKETERS	128,000	35,500	92,500
BP AMERICA	122,361	31,250	91,111
USX	120,792	53,171	67,621
MARATHON OIL	119,250	19,500	99,750

**Top 5 Oil and Gas Political Action Committees
1997–1998**

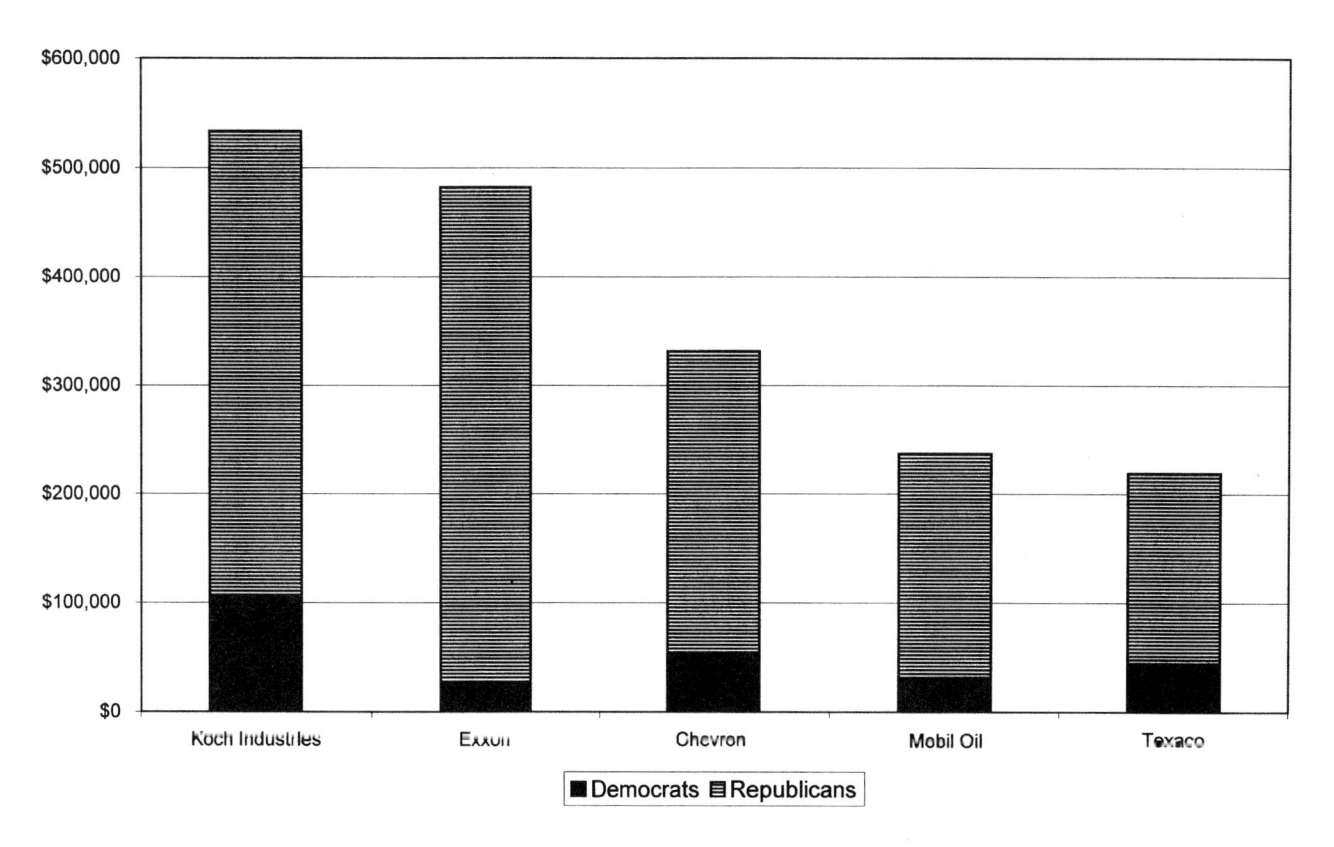

Company	Democrats	Republicans	Total (approx)
Koch Industries	~$110,000	~$425,000	~$535,000
Exxon	~$30,000	~$450,000	~$480,000
Chevron	~$55,000	~$275,000	~$330,000
Mobil Oil	~$30,000	~$205,000	~$235,000
Texaco	~$45,000	~$175,000	~$220,000

Top Mining PACs 1997–1998

PACs	TOTAL	DEMOCRATS	REPUBLICANS
NATIONAL MINING ASSN.	$282,949	$37,000	$245,949
CYPRUS AMAX MINERALS	268,750	45,100	223,650
PHELPS DODGE	100,000	16,500	83,500
OHIO VALLEY COAL	88,700	5,000	83,700
PEABODY COAL	65,500	10,500	55,000
FREEPORT-MCMORAN COPPER & GOLD	62,500	25,000	37,500
DRUMMOND	61,850	21,250	40,600
BARRICK GOLDSTRIKE MINES	59,878	26,128	33,750
CLEVELAND-CLIFFS IRON	49,725	13,300	36,425
KENNECOTT	33,500	8,000	25,500

Top Electric Utility PACs 1997–1998

PACs	TOTAL	DEMOCRATS	REPUBLICANS
NATIONAL RURAL ELECTRIC COOPERATIVE ASSN.	$789,771	$412,345	$377,426
SOUTHERN CALIFORNIA EDISON	307,224	127,831	179,393
HOUSTON INDUSTRIES	222,130	71,785	150,345
PG&E	220,952	94,070	126,882
EDISON ELECTRIC INSTITUTE	213,472	65,505	147,967
FLORIDA POWER & LIGHT	182,250	37,000	145,250
CAROLINA POWER & LIGHT	170,500	66,500	104,000
CMS ENERGY	169,333	81,135	88,198
DTE ENERGY	161,400	79,200	82,200
TEXAS UTILITIES	157,650	72,650	85,000
ENTERGY OPERATIONS	126,300	38,000	88,300
PUBLIC SERVICE ELECTRIC & GAS	112,314	51,735	60,579
AMERICAN ELECTRIC POWER	109,000	29,500	79,500
GENERAL PUBLIC UTILITIES	108,960	37,200	71,760
COMMONWEALTH EDISON	106,250	40,750	65,500

Top Nuclear/Misc. Energy PACs 1997–1998

PACs	TOTAL	DEMOCRATS	REPUBLICANS
GENERAL ATOMICS	$347,977	$115,150	$232,827
BECHTEL GROUP	153,900	65,900	88,000
NUCLEAR ENERGY INSTITUTE	70,819	25,624	45,195
SOUTHERN NUCLEAR	57,000	11,000	46,000
STEWART & STEVENSON SERVICES	51,750	13,750	38,000

Top Waste Management/Environmental Service PACs 1997–1998

PACs	TOTAL	DEMOCRATS	REPUBLICANS
WASTE MANAGEMENT	$129,100	$46,100	$83,000
BROWNING-FERRIS INDUSTRIES	97,475	30,100	67,375
IT GROUP	88,750	23,250	65,500
BATTELLE MEMORIAL INSTITUTE	43,050	15,400	27,650
MONTGOMERY WATSON AMERICAS	42,750	21,500	21,250

Top Finance, Insurance, and Real Estate PACs 1997–1998

PACs	TOTAL	DEMOCRATS	REPUBLICANS
NATIONAL ASSN. OF REALTORS	$2,473,633	$966,159	$1,507,474
NATIONAL ASSN. OF LIFE UNDERWRITERS	1,336,000	481,500	854,500
AMERICAN BANKERS ASSN.	1,205,350	469,750	735,600
AMERICAN INSTITUTE OF CPAs	1,134,414	387,349	747,065
CREDIT UNION NATIONAL ASSN.	1,039,333	448,796	590,537
ERNST & YOUNG	897,241	347,743	549,498
PRICEWATERHOUSE-COOPERS	889,675	300,744	588,931
BANK ONE	776,399	305,750	470,649
DELOITTE & TOUCHE	712,379	234,558	477,821
AFLAC	632,000	272,000	360,000
INVESTMENT CO INSTITUTE	563,687	214,904	348,783
MBNA AMERICA BANK	514,000	113,000	401,000
KPMG LLP	513,785	107,705	406,080
JP MORGAN	502,600	195,550	307,050
INDEPENDENT INSURANCE AGENTS OF AMERICA	500,580	173,354	327,226
AMERICAN COUNCIL OF LIFE INSURANCE	495,780	129,033	366,747
INDEPENDENT BANKERS ASSN.	462,705	211,660	251,045
CITICORP	437,543	177,248	260,295
NATIONSBANK	431,950	232,250	199,700
BANKAMERICA	430,478	138,190	292,288
ARTHUR ANDERSEN	427,586	157,619	269,967
CHICAGO MERCANTILE EXCHANGE	399,700	181,500	218,200
MORTGAGE BANKERS ASSN. OF AMERICA	399,494	123,224	276,270
NATIONAL VENTURE CAPITAL ASSN.	394,000	88,000	306,000
BLUE CROSS & BLUE SHIELD ASSN.	347,114	111,300	235,814
CHICAGO BOARD OF TRADE	310,027	143,054	166,973

**Top 5 Finance, Insurance and Real Estate Political Action Committees
1997–1998**

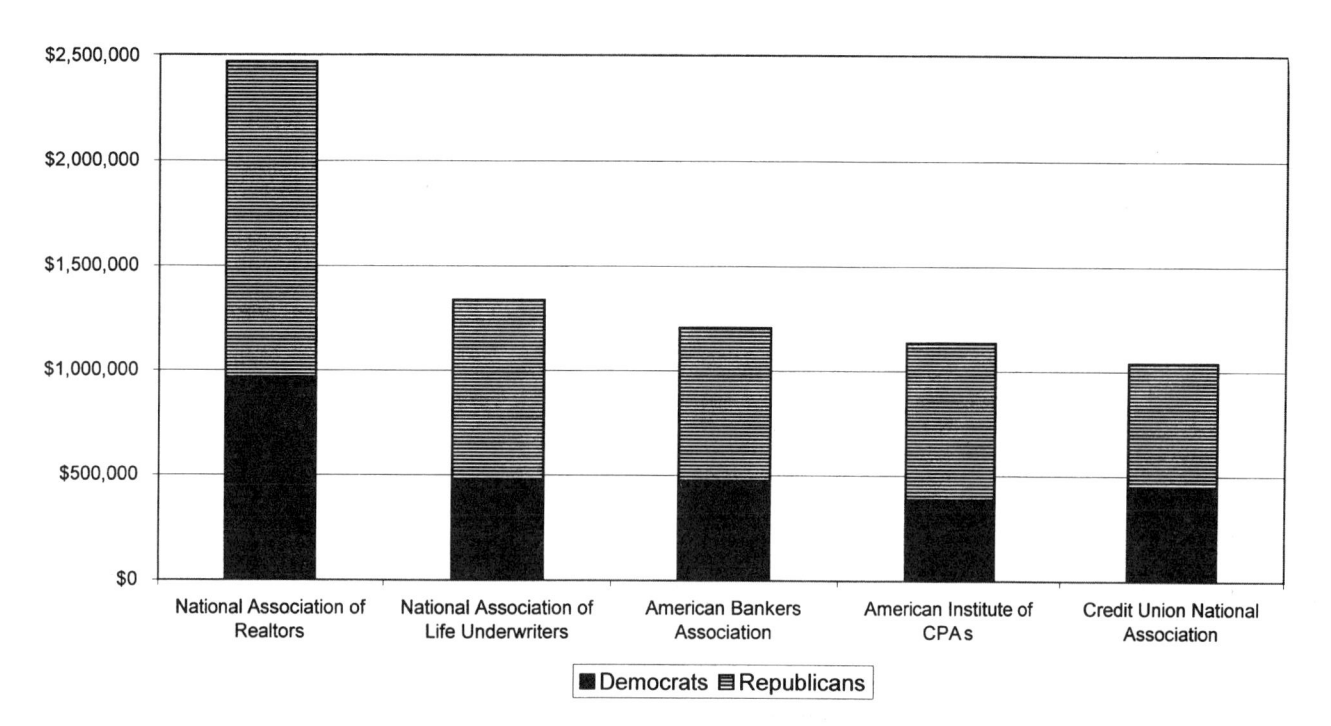

Top Commercial Bank PACs 1997–1998

PACs	TOTAL	DEMOCRATS	REPUBLICANS
AMERICAN BANKERS ASSN.	$1,205,350	$469,750	$735,600
BANK ONE	776,399	305,750	470,649
JP MORGAN	502,600	195,550	307,050
INDEPENDENT BANKERS ASSN.	462,705	211,660	251,045
CITICORP	437,543	177,248	260,295
NATIONSBANK	431,950	232,250	199,700
BANKAMERICA	430,478	138,190	292,288
CHASE MANHATTAN	299,186	102,273	196,913
NORWEST	228,425	101,200	127,225
FIRST UNION	172,499	60,820	111,679
KEYCORP	159,050	55,800	103,250
NATIONAL CITY	116,375	25,600	90,775
BANKERS TRUST	112,500	61,000	51,500
MERCANTILE BANCORP	86,000	27,050	58,950
FLEET FINANCIAL GROUP	72,474	50,474	22,000

**Top 5 Commercial Bank Political Action Committees
1997–1998**

Top Savings and Loan/Credit Union PACs 1997–1998

PACs	TOTAL	DEMOCRATS	REPUBLICANS
CREDIT UNION NATIONAL ASSN.	$1,039,333	$448,796	$590,537
AMERICA'S COMMUNITY BANKERS	202,705	78,285	124,420
WASHINGTON MUTUAL	131,648	51,983	79,665
NATIONAL ASSN. OF FEDERAL CREDIT UNIONS	114,765	53,025	61,740
MICHIGAN CREDIT UNION LEAGUE	102,719	83,629	19,090
HF AHMANSON	83,600	46,000	37,600
CHEVY CHASE SAVINGS BANK	51,600	19,600	32,000
ALABAMA CREDIT UNION ASSN.	38,000	15,000	23,000
SAVINGS BANKS ASSN. OF NY STATE	33,400	16,000	17,400
WESTERN LEAGUE OF SAVINGS INSTITUTIONS	29,000	12,550	16,450

Top Finance/Credit Company PACs 1997–1998

PACs	TOTAL	DEMOCRATS	REPUBLICANS
MBNA AMERICA BANK	$514,000	$113,000	$401,000
HOUSEHOLD INTERNATIONAL	221,970	82,000	139,970
AMERICAN FINANCIAL SERVICES ASSN.	177,132	41,745	135,387
AMERICAN EXPRESS	174,550	72,550	102,000
BENEFICIAL MANAGEMENT	169,038	72,037	97,001
SALLIE MAE	153,500	63,500	90,000
ADVANTA	90,528	28,028	62,500
ASSOCIATED CREDIT BUREAUS	66,471	16,202	50,269

Top 5 Finance/Credit Company Political Action Committees 1997–1998

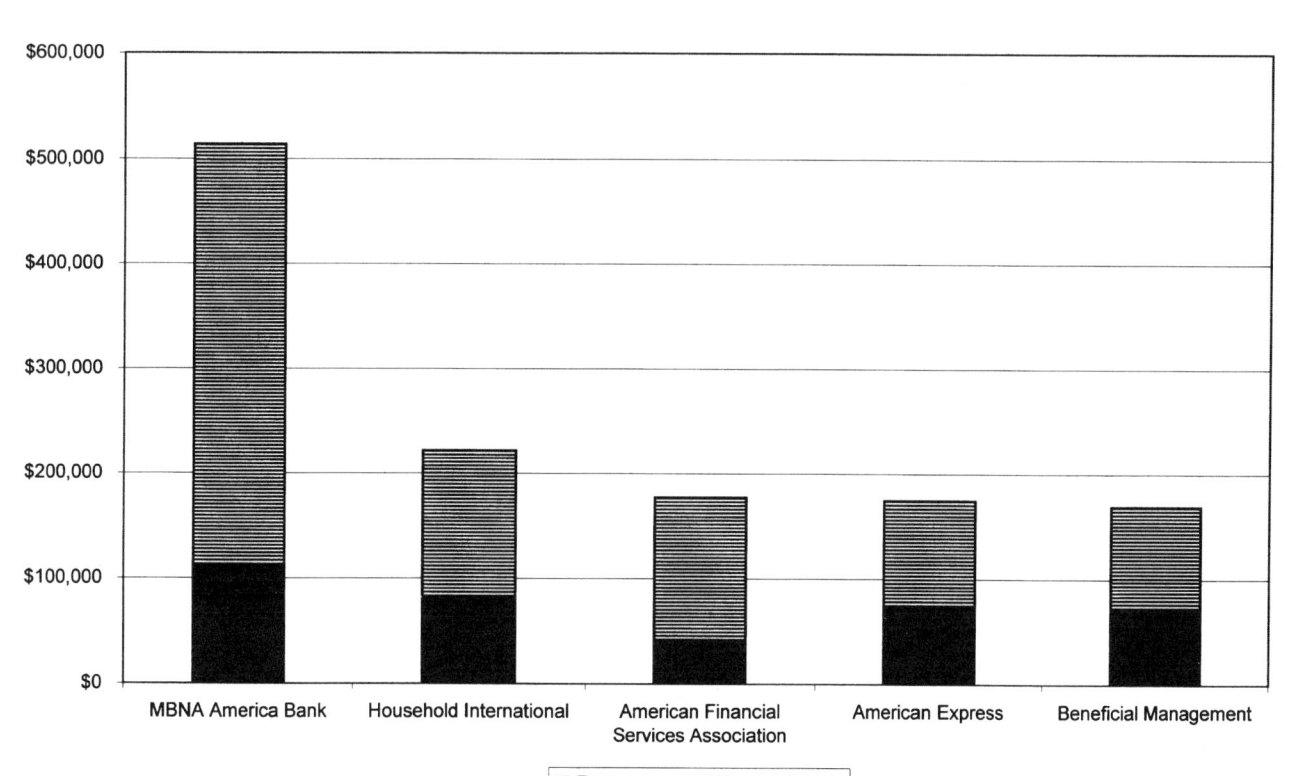

Top Security and Investment PACs 1997–1998

PACs	TOTAL	DEMOCRATS	REPUBLICANS
INVESTMENT CO. INSTITUTE	$563,687	$214,904	$348,783
CHICAGO MERCANTILE EXCHANGE	399,700	181,500	218,200
NATIONAL VENTURE CAPITAL ASSN.	394,000	88,000	306,000
CHICAGO BOARD OF TRADE	310,027	143,054	166,973
SALOMON SMITH BARNEY	293,303	94,675	198,628
GOLDMAN, SACHS	229,233	106,499	122,734
BOND MARKET ASSN.	227,899	81,020	146,879
CHICAGO BOARD OF OPTIONS EXCHANGE	204,499	92,499	112,000
MORGAN STANLEY, DEAN WITTER	200,625	82,500	118,125
CREDIT SUISSE FIRST BOSTON	187,500	89,500	98,000
NEW YORK STOCK EXCHANGE	166,309	69,309	97,000
MERRILL LYNCH	156,300	51,550	104,750
LEHMAN BROTHERS	135,650	73,050	62,600
SECURITIES INDUSTRY ASSN.	134,427	54,652	79,775
SALOMON BROTHERS	130,691	70,691	60,000

Top Insurance PACs 1997–1998

PACs	TOTAL	DEMOCRATS	REPUBLICANS
NATIONAL ASSN. OF LIFE UNDERWRITERS	$1,336,000	$481,500	$854,500
AFLAC	632,000	272,000	360,000
INDEPENDENT INSURANCE AGENTS OF AMERICA	500,580	173,354	327,226
AMERICAN COUNCIL OF LIFE INSURANCE	495,780	129,033	366,747
BLUE CROSS & BLUE SHIELD ASSN.	347,114	111,300	235,814
MASSACHUSETTS MUTUAL LIFE INSURANCE	286,699	114,000	172,699
CNA FINANCIAL	269,550	57,300	212,250
UNITED SERVICES AUTOMOBILE ASSN. GROUP	259,500	30,000	229,500
NATIONAL ASSN. OF INDEPENDENT INSURERS	258,657	16,075	242,582
NEW YORK LIFE INSURANCE	250,770	103,170	147,600
MUTUAL OF OMAHA	236,790	45,000	191,790
COUNCIL OF INSURANCE AGENTS & BROKERS	223,530	44,508	179,022
METROPOLITAN LIFE INSURANCE	220,919	106,973	113,946
CIGNA	212,350	35,800	176,550
LIBERTY MUTUAL INSURANCE	196,000	55,000	141,000
PRUDENTIAL INSURANCE	192,750	81,000	111,750
NATIONAL ASSN. OF PROF INSURANCE AGENTS	189,961	32,599	157,362
NORTHWESTERN MUTUAL LIFE	169,300	70,300	99,000
CHUBB	160,286	59,250	101,036
CITIGROUP	157,524	65,600	91,924

**Top 5 Insurance Political Action Committees
1997–1998**

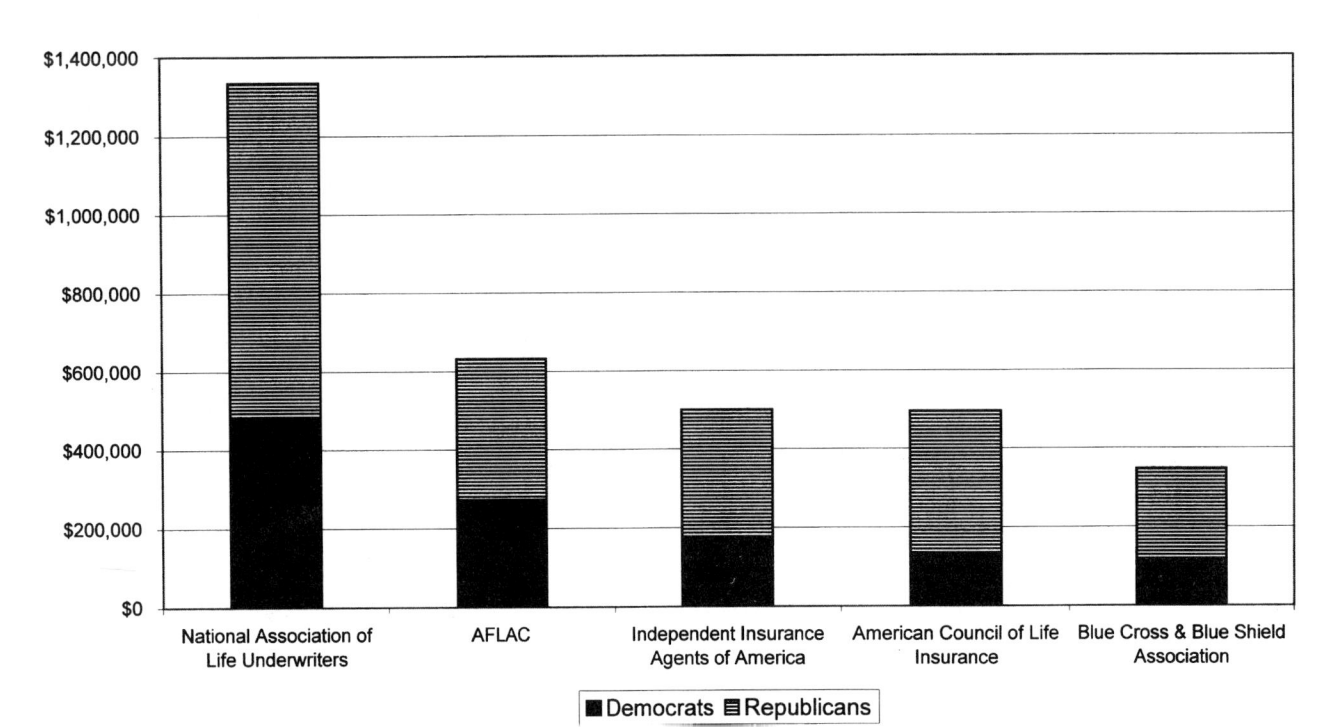

■ Democrats ☰ Republicans

Top Accounting PACs 1997–1998

PACs	TOTAL	DEMOCRATS	REPUBLICANS
AMERICAN INSTITUTE OF CPAs	$1,134,414	$387,349	$747,065
ERNST & YOUNG	897,241	347,743	549,498
PRICEWATERHOUSE-COOPERS	889,675	300,744	588,931
DELOITTE & TOUCHE	712,379	234,558	477,821
KPMG LLP	513,785	107,705	406,080
ARTHUR ANDERSEN	427,586	157,619	269,967

Top Real Estate PACs 1997–1998

PACs	TOTAL	DEMOCRATS	REPUBLICANS
NATIONAL ASSN. OF REALTORS	$2,473,633	$966,159	$1,507,474
MORTGAGE BANKERS ASSN. OF AMERICA	399,494	123,224	276,270
AMERICAN LAND TITLE ASSN.	167,291	64,713	102,578
NATIONAL ASSN. OF MORTGAGE BROKERS	112,555	33,000	79,555
NATIONAL ASSN. OF REITS	99,350	32,500	66,850
COUNTRYWIDE CREDIT INDUSTRIES	77,905	28,400	49,505
ASSN. FOR COMMERCIAL REAL ESTATE	75,800	6,250	69,550
DEL WEBB	50,130	2,750	47,380
NATIONAL HOME EQUITY MORTGAGE ASSN.	48,500	14,500	34,000
OHIO ASSN. OF MORTGAGE BROKERS	42,550	5,500	37,050

Top Health PACs 1997–1998

PACs	TOTAL	DEMOCRATS	REPUBLICANS
AMERICAN MEDICAL ASSOCIATION	$2,323,781	$654,026	$1,669,755
AMERICAN HOSPITAL ASSOCIATION	1,072,868	505,932	566,936
AMERICAN DENTAL ASSOCIATION	908,312	414,483	493,829
AMERICAN NURSES ASSOCIATION	817,848	687,248	130,600
AMERICAN SOCIETY OF ANESTHESIOLOGISTS	751,529	298,725	452,804
AMERICAN HEALTH CARE ASSOCIATION	722,580	338,813	383,767
AMERICAN ACADEMY OF OPHTHALMOLOGY	579,663	323,000	256,663
AMERICAN OPTOMETRIC ASSOCIATION	519,950	310,500	209,450
GLAXO WELLCOME	406,001	110,825	295,176
AMERICAN ASSOCIATION OF NURSE ANESTHETISTS	401,669	172,849	228,820
AMERICAN PODIATRY ASSOCIATION	364,750	216,250	148,500
AMERICAN COLLEGE OF EMERGENCY PHYSICIANS	352,675	194,000	158,675
AMERICAN PHYSICAL THERAPY ASSOCIATION	313,536	162,617	150,919
AMERICAN SPEECH-LANGUAGE-HEARING ASSOCIATION	305,127	241,635	63,492
ELI LILLY	302,800	92,750	210,050
PFIZER	301,800	91,550	210,250
AMERICAN CHIROPRACTIC ASSOCIATION	270,427	135,204	135,223
MERCK	262,437	88,747	173,690
AMERICAN OCCUPATIONAL THERAPY ASSOCIATION	238,445	142,960	95,485
COLLEGE OF AMERICAN PATHOLOGISTS	232,638	100,138	132,500
AMERICAN DIETETIC ASSOCIATION	212,118	101,800	110,318
BRISTOL-MYERS SQUIBB	211,949	68,600	143,349
JOHNSON & JOHNSON	209,350	79,350	130,000
BAYER	187,500	50,250	137,250
ABBOTT LABORATORIES	182,371	54,122	128,249

Top 5 Health Political Action Committees
1997–1998

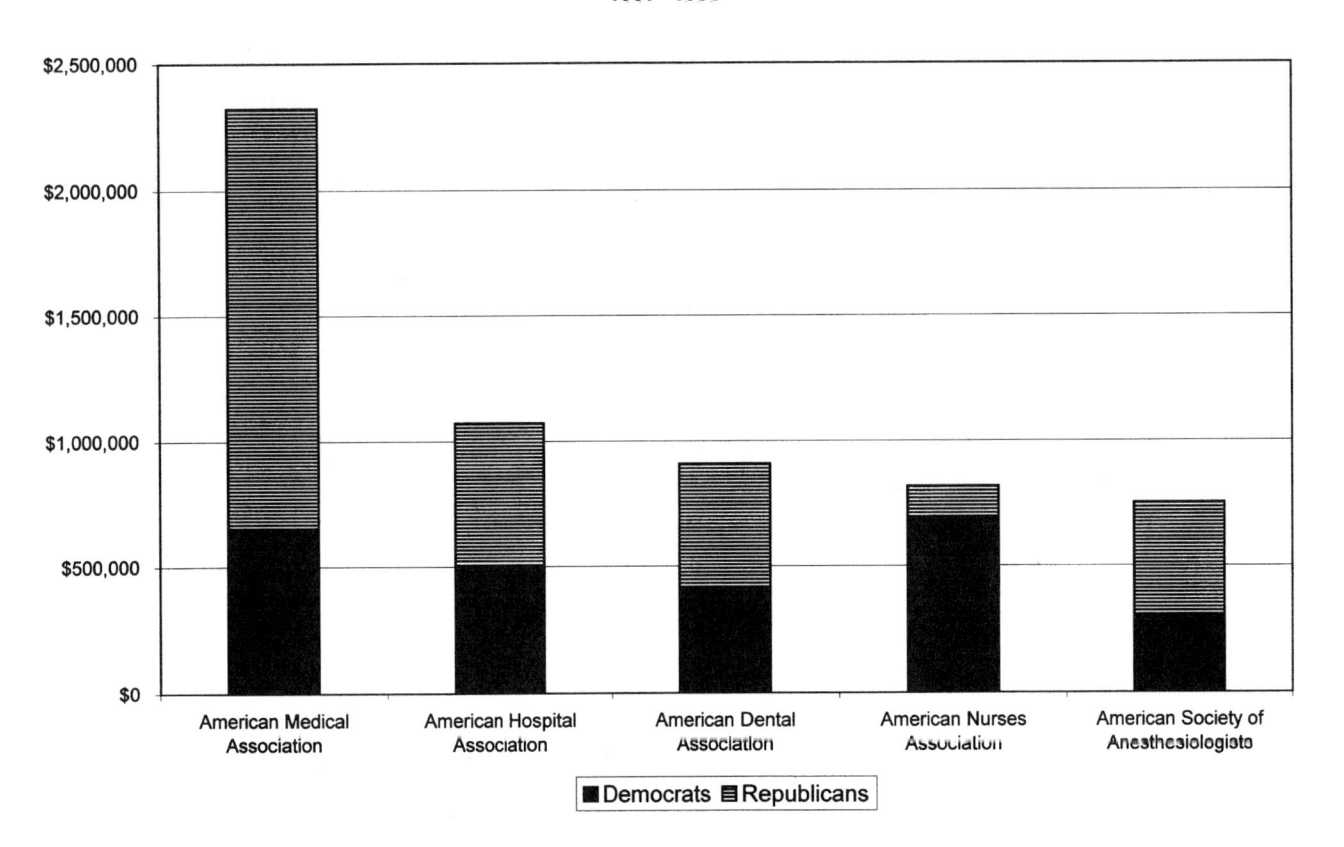

■ Democrats ☰ Republicans

Top Health Professional PACs 1997–1998

PACs	TOTAL	DEMOCRATS	REPUBLICANS
AMERICAN MEDICAL ASSOCIATION	$2,323,781	$654,026	$1,669,755
AMERICAN DENTAL ASSOCIATION	908,312	414,483	493,829
AMERICAN NURSES ASSOCIATION	817,848	687,248	130,600
AMERICAN SOCIETY OF ANESTHESIOLOGISTS	751,529	298,725	452,804
AMERICAN ACADEMY OF OPHTHALMOLOGY	579,663	323,000	256,663
AMERICAN OPTOMETRIC ASSOCIATION	519,950	310,500	209,450
AMERICAN ASSOCIATION OF NURSE ANESTHETISTS	401,669	172,849	228,820
AMERICAN PODIATRY ASSOCIATION	364,750	216,250	148,500
AMERICAN COLLEGE OF EMERGENCY PHYSICIANS	352,675	194,000	158,675
AMERICAN PHYSICAL THERAPY ASSOCIATION	313,536	162,617	150,919
AMERICAN SPEECH-LANGUAGE-HEARING ASSOCIATION	305,127	241,635	63,492
AMERICAN CHIROPRACTIC ASSOCIATION	270,427	135,204	135,223
AMERICAN OCCUPATIONAL THERAPY ASSOCIATION	238,445	142,960	95,485
COLLEGE OF AMERICAN PATHOLOGISTS	232,638	100,138	132,500
AMERICAN DIETETIC ASSOCIATION	212,118	101,800	110,318
ASSOCIATION FOR THE ADVANCEMENT OF PSYCHOLOGY	159,182	97,370	61,812
AMERICAN NEUROLOGICAL SURGERY	136,688	53,000	83,688
COMMITTEE FOR QUALITY ORTHOPEDIC HEALTH CARE	133,119	61,960	71,159
NATIONAL ASSOCIATION OF RETAIL DRUGGISTS	129,750	79,000	50,750
SOCIETY OF THORACIC SURGEONS	124,370	36,000	88,370

Top Hospital/Nursing Home PACs 1997–1998

PACs	TOTAL	DEMOCRATS	REPUBLICANS
AMERICAN HOSPITAL ASSOCIATION	$1,072,868	$505,932	$566,936
AMERICAN HEALTH CARE ASSOCIATION	722,580	338,813	383,767
FEDERATION OF AMERICAN HEALTH SYSTEMS	173,811	45,734	128,077
TENET HEALTHCARE	85,974	31,900	54,074
MANOR HEALTHCARE CORP	85,814	49,565	36,249
COLUMBIA/HCA HEALTHCARE	69,950	31,250	37,700
COLUMBIA/HCA HEALTHCARE-TEXAS	57,650	24,100	33,550
GENESIS HEALTH VENTURES	57,500	26,000	31,500
CALIFORNIA HEALTHCARE ASSOCIATION	40,795	27,495	13,300
NATIONAL ASSOCIATION OF PSYCHIATRIC HEALTH SYSTEMS	35,000	10,000	25,000

Top Pharmaceutical and Health Product PACs 1997–1998

PACs	TOTAL	DEMOCRATS	REPUBLICANS
GLAXO WELLCOME	$406,001	$110,825	$295,176
ELI LILLY	302,800	92,750	210,050
PFIZER INC	301,800	91,550	210,250
MERCK	262,437	88,747	173,690
BRISTOL-MYERS SQUIBB	211,949	68,600	143,349
JOHNSON & JOHNSON	209,350	79,350	130,000
BAYER	187,500	50,250	137,250
ABBOTT LABORATORIES	182,371	54,122	128,249
SCHERING-PLOUGH	169,500	39,000	130,500
NOVARTIS	155,763	44,500	111,263

Top 5 Pharmaceutical and Health Product Political Action Committees 1997–1998

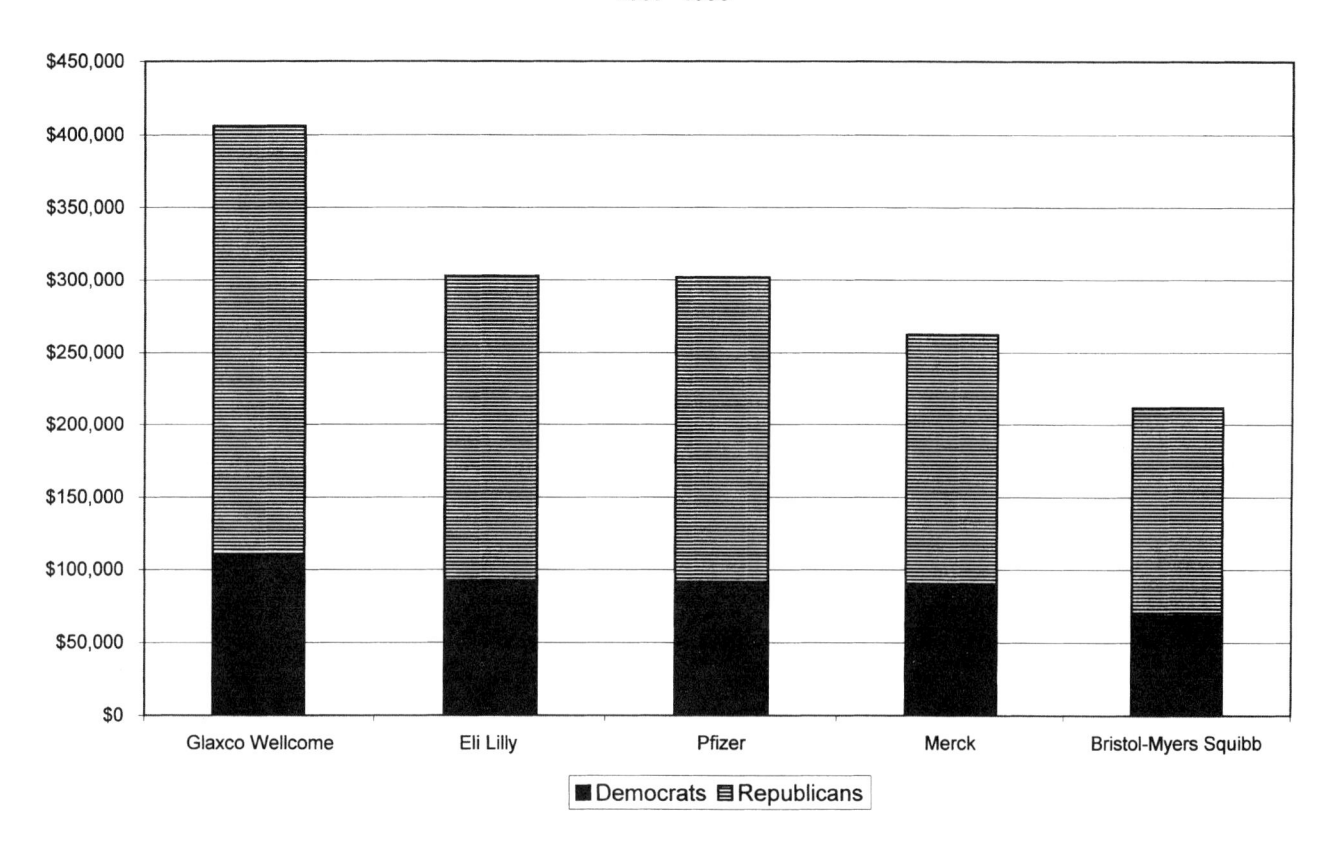

■ Democrats ▤ Republicans

Top Democratic/Liberal PACs 1997–1998

PACs	TOTAL	DEMOCRATS	REPUBLICANS
NATIONAL COMMITTEE FOR AN EFFECTIVE CONGRESS	$927,535	$927,535	$0
NEW DEMOCRAT NETWORK	264,257	264,176	81
BLUE DOG	177,500	177,500	0
PEOPLE FOR THE AMERICAN WAY	139,235	138,235	1,000
AMERICANS FOR DEMOCRATIC ACTION	105,551	104,551	1,000
AMERICA WORKS	84,500	84,500	0
DEMOCRATIC STUDY GROUP CAMPAIGN FUND	43,102	43,102	0
IRISH-AMERICANS FOR A DEMOCRATIC VICTORY	15,000	15,000	0
AGENDA FOR THE 90S	11,000	11,000	0
FIFTH HORSEMAN	11,000	11,000	0

Top 5 Democratic/Liberal Political Action Committees
1997–1998

■ Democrats ▤ Republicans

Top Republican/Conservative PACs 1997–1998

PACs	TOTAL	DEMOCRATS	REPUBLICANS
CAMPAIGN FOR WORKING FAMILIES	$454,847	$16,500	$438,347
RESTORING THE AMERICAN DREAM	170,500	0	170,500
EAGLE FORUM	158,912	1,500	157,412
CONSERVATIVE VICTORY FUND	139,224	0	139,224
CAT	137,000	0	137,000
UNITED SENIORS	125,200	8,250	116,950
BLACK AMERICA'S	103,275	0	103,275
REPUBLICAN LEADERSHIP COUNCIL	87,500	0	87,500
DALENPAC	75,000	0	75,000
CALIFORNIA 2000	45,000	0	45,000

Top 5 Republican/Conservative Political Action Committees 1997–1998

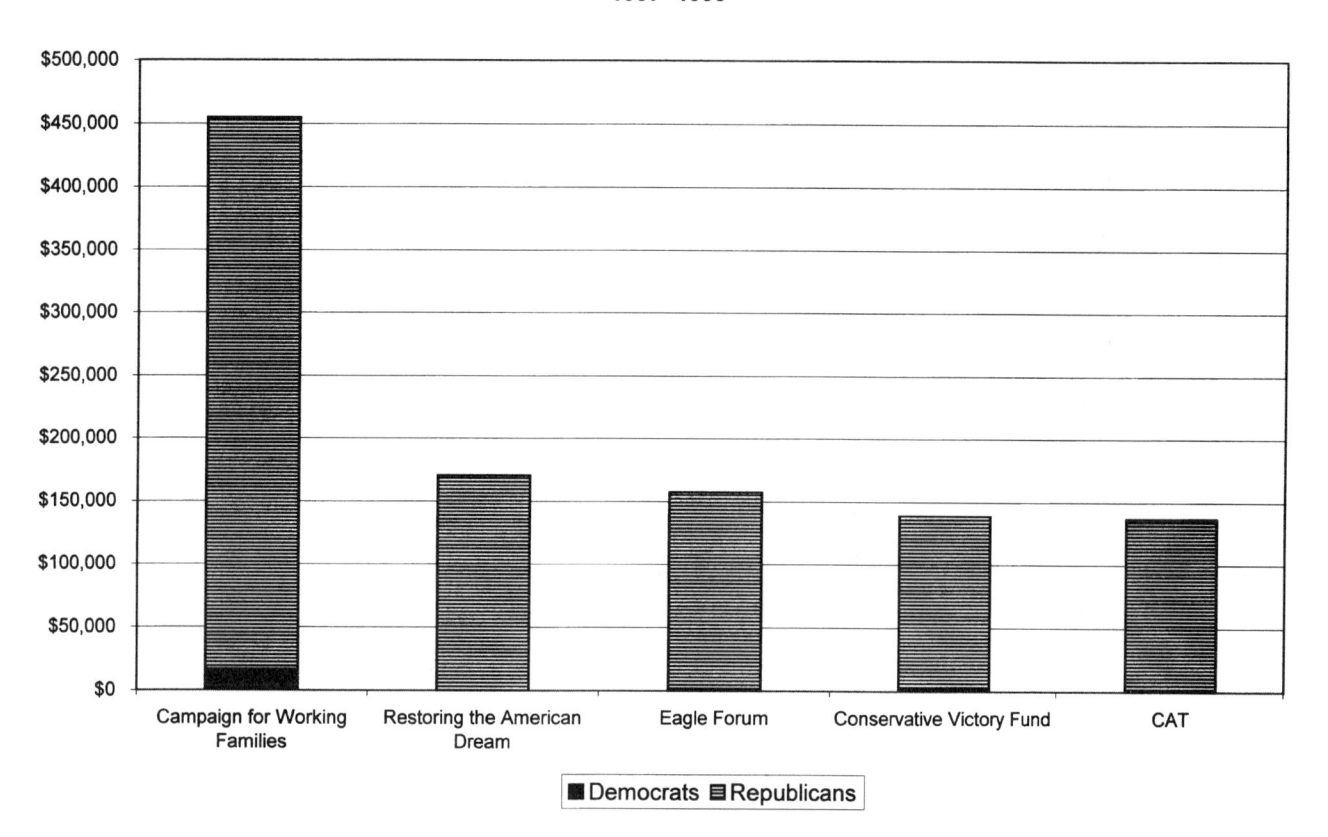

Top Women's Issues PACs 1997–1998

PACs	TOTAL	DEMOCRATS	REPUBLICANS
EMILY'S LIST	$236,221	$236,221	$0
WOMEN'S CAMPAIGN FUND	146,017	116,017	30,000
VALUE IN ELECTING WOMEN	118,250	0	118,250
NATIONAL ORGANIZATION FOR WOMEN	80,385	80,385	0
WOMEN'S POLITICAL COMM.	75,000	75,000	0

**Top 5 Women's Issues Political Action Committees
1997–1998**

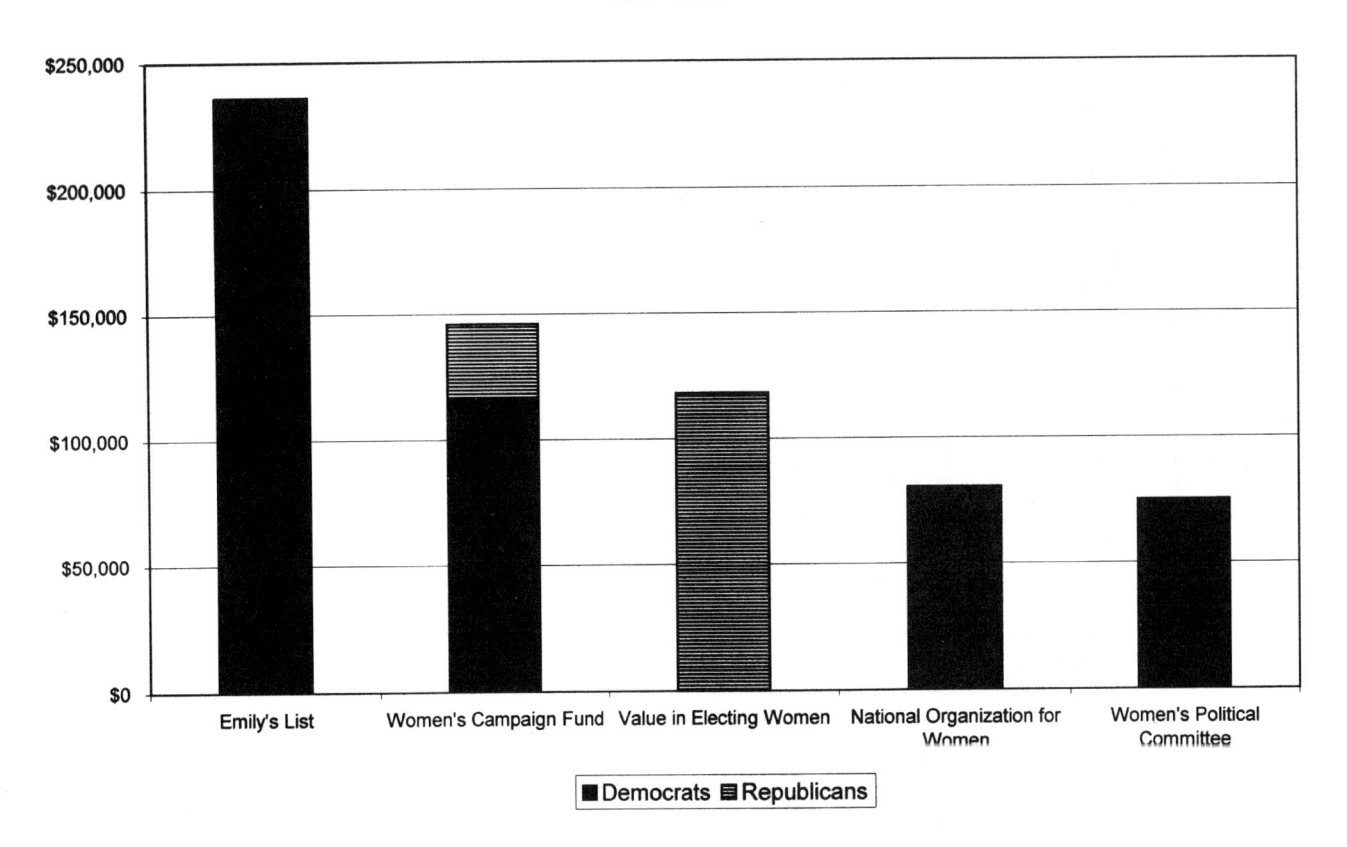

[Bar chart showing:
- Emily's List: ~$238,000 (Democrats)
- Women's Campaign Fund: ~$148,000 (Democrats ~$118,000, Republicans ~$30,000)
- Value in Electing Women: ~$120,000 (Republicans)
- National Organization for Women: ~$83,000 (Democrats)
- Women's Political Committee: ~$79,000 (Democrats)

Legend: ■ Democrats ☰ Republicans]

Top Miscellaneous Human Rights/Identity Group PACs 1997–1998

PACs	TOTAL	DEMOCRATS	REPUBLICANS
HUMAN RIGHTS CAMPAIGN	$801,125	$711,400	$89,725
KIDSPAC	290,500	283,500	6,000
NATIONAL COMMUNITY ACTION FOUNDATION	138,500	105,000	33,500
AMERICAN AIDS	74,586	71,967	2,619
ALBANIAN AMERICAN	42,100	12,600	29,500

Top Law Firm PACs 1997–1998

PACs	TOTAL	DEMOCRATS	REPUBLICANS
ASSN. OF TRIAL LAWYERS OF AMERICA	$2,408,300	$2,091,300	$318,000
AKIN, GUMP ET AL.	384,973	166,738	218,235
VERNER, LIIPFERT ET AL.	268,054	153,358	114,696
VINSON & ELKINS	213,313	134,911	78,402
HOLLAND & KNIGHT	181,727	91,727	90,000
PRESTON, GATES ET AL.	149,782	57,684	92,098
SHAW, PITTMAN ET AL.	140,350	76,350	64,000
MCDERMOTT, WILL & EMERY	135,400	57,400	78,000
GREENBERG, TRAURIG ET AL	120,667	76,500	44,167
HOGAN & HARTSON	111,800	50,550	61,250
WILLIAMS & JENSEN	107,569	37,857	69,712
SKADDEN, ARPS ET AL.	100,500	58,000	42,500
O'MELVENY & MYERS	97,964	39,000	58,964
KING & SPALDING	96,515	39,642	56,873
WINSTON & STRAWN	95,874	44,958	50,916
FULBRIGHT & JAWORSKI	93,462	39,100	54,362
REID & PRIEST	93,055	54,305	38,750
MANATT, PHELPS ET AL.	89,379	53,379	36,000
DICKSTEIN, SHAPIRO & MORIN	88,612	39,712	48,900
POWELL, GOLDSTEIN ET AL.	87,242	52,892	34,350

Top Lobbyist Firm PACs 1997–1998

PACs	TOTAL	DEMOCRATS	REPUBLICANS
WEXLER GROUP	$112,098	$47,498	$64,600
PAUL MAGLIOCCHETTI ASSOC.	104,500	53,500	51,000
R DUFFY WALL & ASSOC.	84,045	27,061	56,984
BURSON-MARSTELLER	70,278	21,375	48,903
HILL & KNOWLTON	54,575	26,325	28,250
LENT & SCRIVNER	38,717	2,250	36,467
JEFFERSON GROUP	38,150	19,650	18,500
FLEISHMAN-HILLARD	37,250	16,750	20,500
SYMMS, LEHN & ASSOC.	35,950	500	35,450
BROWN	33,788	15,750	18,038

Top Manufacturing PACs 1997–1998

PACs	TOTAL	DEMOCRATS	REPUBLICANS
GENERAL ELECTRIC	$663,000	$278,000	$385,000
FMC	224,000	52,750	171,250
DOW CHEMICAL	171,750	48,500	123,250
CORNING	165,257	38,000	127,257
AMERICAN FURNITURE MANUFACTURERS ASSOCIATION	158,750	21,000	137,750
BURLINGTON INDUSTRIES	155,266	54,000	101,266
DUPONT	132,000	31,000	101,000
CHEMICAL MANUFACTURERS ASSOCIATION	125,199	28,829	96,370
AMERICAN TEXTILE MANUFACTURERS INSTITUTE	119,000	40,500	78,500
PROCTER & GAMBLE	117,100	25,500	91,600
INSTITUTE OF SCRAP RECYCLING INDUSTRIES	109,499	60,499	49,000
NATIONAL MACHINE TOOL BUILDERS ASSOCIATION	98,130	17,000	81,130
TIMKEN	91,500	7,000	84,500
HOECHST CELANESE	74,500	29,500	45,000
LTV STEEL	68,250	27,750	40,500

**Top 5 Manufacturing Political Action Committees
1997–1998**

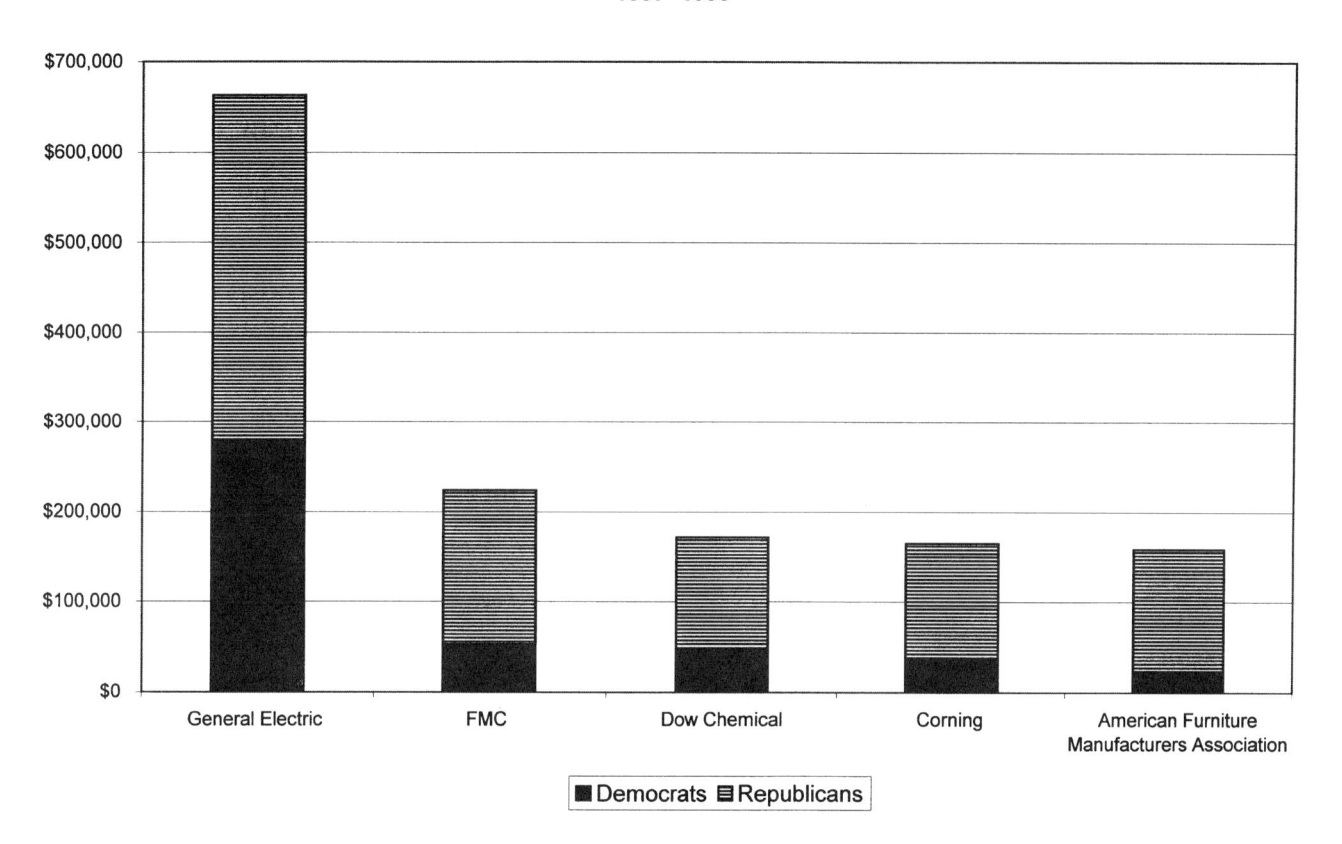

Top Chemical Manufacturing PACs 1997–1998

PACs	TOTAL	DEMOCRATS	REPUBLICANS
FMC	$224,000	$52,750	$171,250
DOW CHEMICAL	171,750	48,500	123,250
DUPONT	132,000	31,000	101,000
CHEMICAL MANUFACTURERS ASSOCIATION	125,199	28,829	96,370
PROCTER & GAMBLE	117,100	25,500	91,600

Top Steel PACs 1997–1998

PACs	TOTAL	DEMOCRATS	REPUBLICANS
LTV STEEL	$68,250	$27,750	$40,500
ALLEGHENY TELEDYNE	$45,600	$15,800	$29,800
BETHLEHEM STEEL	$43,675	$18,175	$25,500
AMERICAN IRON & STEEL INSTITUTE	$31,750	$14,750	$17,000
AK STEEL	$21,700	$3,000	$18,700

Top Textile PACs 1997–1998

PACs	TOTAL	DEMOCRATS	REPUBLICANS
BURLINGTON INDUSTRIES	$155,266	$54,000	$101,266
AMERICAN TEXTILE MANUFACTURERS INSTITUTE	119,000	40,500	78,500
SPRINGS INDUSTRIES	31,000	18,000	13,000
AMERICAN YARN SPINNERS ASSOCIATION	29,750	9,500	20,250

Top Miscellaneous Manufacturing PACs 1997–1998

PACs	TOTAL	DEMOCRATS	REPUBLICANS
GENERAL ELECTRIC	$663,000	$278,000	$385,000
CORNING	165,257	38,000	127,257
AMERICAN FURNITURE MANUFACTURERS ASSOCIATION	158,750	21,000	137,750
INSTITUTE OF SCRAP RECYCLING INDUSTRIES	109,499	60,499	49,000
NATIONAL MACHINE TOOL BUILDERS ASSOCIATION	98,130	17,000	81,130
TIMKEN	91,500	7,000	84,500
HOECHST CELANESE	74,500	29,500	45,000
PRECISION MACHINED PRODUCTS ASSOCIATION	65,000	0	65,000
EMERSON ELECTRIC	64,500	3,500	61,000
PRECISION METALFORMING ASSOCIATION	63,500	0	63,500

Top Single-Issue PACs 1997–1998

PACs	TOTAL	DEMOCRATS	REPUBLICANS
NATIONAL RIFLE ASSOCIATION	$1,633,211	$283,200	$1,350,011
NATIONAL COMMITTEE TO PRESERVE SOCIAL SECURITY	669,246	534,057	135,189
NATIONAL (PRO-ISRAEL)	354,000	153,000	201,000
PLANNED PARENTHOOD	346,757	323,042	23,715
NATIONAL ABORTION AND REPRODUCTIVE RIGHTS ACTION LEAGUE	299,255	271,700	27,555
SIERRA CLUB	235,658	229,950	5,708
SAFARI CLUB INTERNATIONAL	173,846	26,000	147,846
DESERT CAUCUS	168,000	89,000	79,000
HANDGUN CONTROL	146,614	137,114	9,500
WASHINGTON	137,650	84,150	53,500
VOTERS FOR CHOICE/FRIENDS OF FAMILY PLANNING	132,569	130,339	2,230
WOMEN'S ALLIANCE FOR ISRAEL	116,000	73,500	42,500
REPUBLICAN NATIONAL COALITION FOR LIFE	111,488	500	110,988
NATIONAL RIGHT TO LIFE	106,954	10,000	96,954
AMERICANS FOR GOOD GOVERNMENT	100,350	38,350	62,000

**Top 5 Single-Issue Political Action Committees
1997–1998**

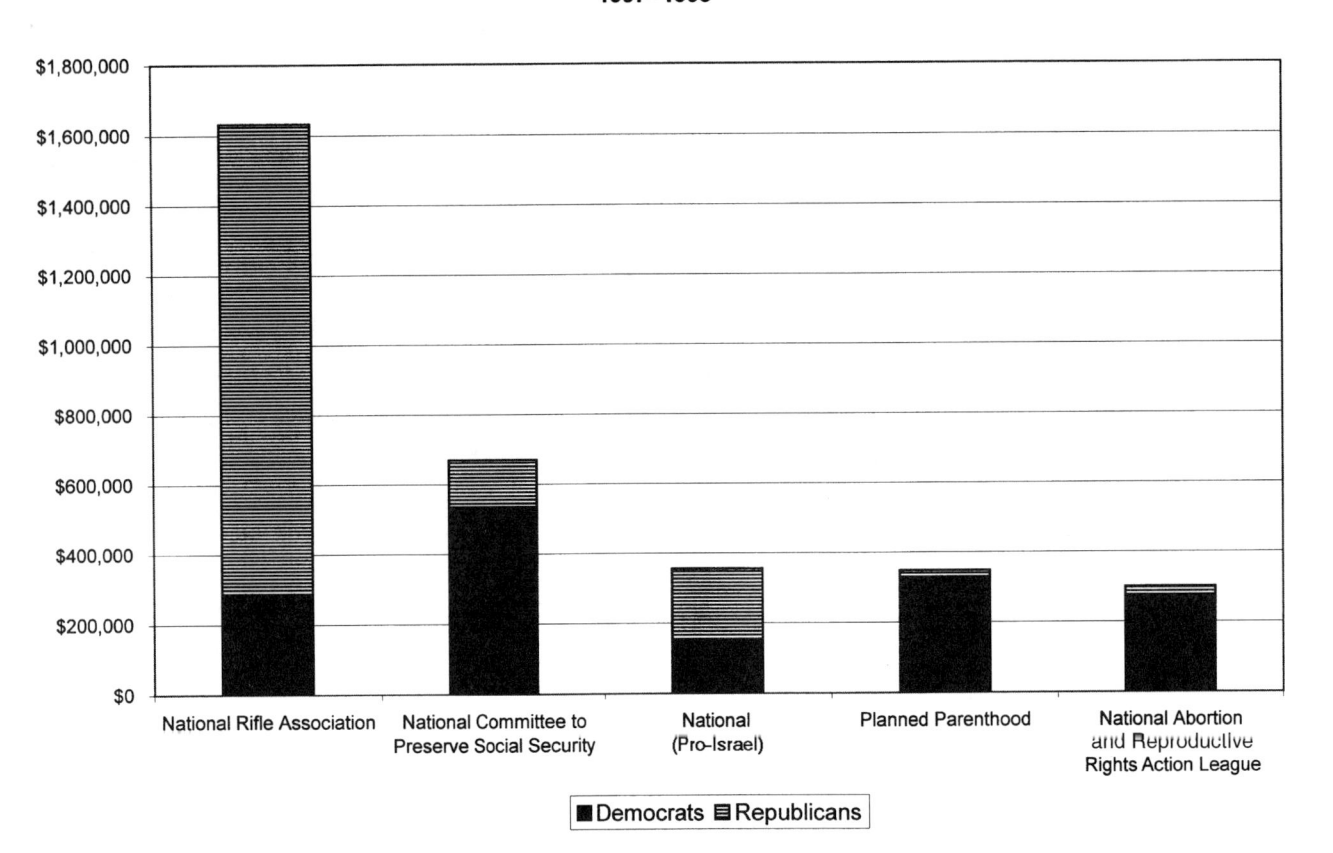

Top Pro-Israel PACs 1997–1998

PACs	TOTAL	DEMOCRATS	REPUBLICANS
NATIONAL	$354,000	$153,000	$201,000
DESERT CAUCUS	168,000	89,000	79,000
WASHINGTON	137,650	84,150	53,500
WOMEN'S ALLIANCE FOR ISRAEL	116,000	73,500	42,500
NATIONAL ACTION COMMITTEE	102,000	67,000	35,000
AMERICANS FOR GOOD GOVERNMENT	100,350	38,350	62,000
MOPAC	90,750	90,750	0
JOINT ACTION COMMITTEE FOR POLITICAL AFFAIRS	86,168	83,141	3,027
CITIZENS ORGANIZED	84,500	58,000	26,500
ST. LOUISIANS FOR BETTER GOVERNMENT	82,000	56,500	25,500

Top Environment PACs 1997–1998

PACs	TOTAL	DEMOCRATS	REPUBLICANS
SIERRA CLUB	$235,658	$229,950	$ 5,708
LEAGUE OF CONSERVATION VOTERS	70,926	53,879	17,047
CALIFORNIA LEAGUE OF CONSERVATION VOTERS	31,163	31,163	0
DUCK	13,500	11,500	2,000
IDAHOANS FOR THE OUTDOORS	10,700	10,700	0

Top Gun and Gun Control PACs 1997–1998

PACs	TOTAL	DEMOCRATS	REPUBLICANS
NATIONAL RIFLE ASSOCIATION	$1,633,211	$283,200	$1,350,011
SAFARI CLUB INTERNATIONAL	173,846	26,000	147,846
HANDGUN CONTROL	146,614	137,114	9,500
GUN OWNERS OF AMERICA	56,843	911	55,932
ARENA	26,932	489	26,443

Top Pro-Choice and Pro-Life PACs 1997–1998

PACs	TOTAL	DEMOCRATS	REPUBLICANS
PLANNED PARENTHOOD	$346,757	$323,042	$23,715
NATIONAL ABORTION AND REPRODUCTIVE RIGHTS ACTION LEAGUE	299,255	271,700	27,555
VOTERS FOR CHOICE/FRIENDS OF FAMILY PLANNING	132,569	130,339	2,230
REPUBLICAN NATIONAL COALITION FOR LIFE	111,488	500	110,988
NATIONAL RIGHT TO LIFE	106,954	10,000	96,954

Top Miscellaneous Single-Issue PACs 1997–1998

PACs	TOTAL	DEMOCRATS	REPUBLICANS
NATIONAL COMMITTEE TO PRESERVE SOCIAL SECURITY	$669,246	$534,057	$135,189
RIGHT TO WORK	61,335	0	61,335
HOWARD JARVIS TAXPAYERS ASSOCIATION	31,200	200	31,000
TERM LIMITS AMERICA	29,750	8,750	21,000
FRIENDS OF HIGHER EDUCATION	28,250	13,250	15,000
CAMPAIGN FOR U.N. REFORM	23,371	23,371	0
KENNEDY SPACE CENTER SUPPORT COMM.	22,182	12,791	9,391
ENGLISH LANGUAGE	17,000	1,000	8,500

Top Transport PACs 1997–1998

PACs	TOTAL	DEMOCRATS	REPUBLICANS
NATIONAL AUTO DEALERS ASSOCIATION	$2,107,800	$609,175	$1,498,625
UNITED PARCEL SERVICE	1,527,149	320,174	1,206,975
FEDERAL EXPRESS	995,750	249,000	746,750
AMERICANS FOR FREE INTERNATIONAL TRADE	908,500	135,500	773,000
UNION PACIFIC	831,268	127,399	703,869
BOEING	660,175	238,800	421,375
DAIMLERCHRYSLER	493,386	192,936	300,450
AMERICAN TRUCKING ASSOCIATION	419,196	78,677	340,519
FORD MOTOR	414,750	103,200	311,550
GENERAL MOTORS	339,490	83,350	256,140
AMERICAN AIRLINES	328,708	149,723	178,985
AIRCRAFT OWNERS & PILOTS ASSOCIATION	287,500	63,500	224,000
NORFOLK SOUTHERN	263,600	86,000	177,600
BURLINGTON NORTHERN RAILROAD	209,042	65,395	143,647
UNITED AIRLINES	198,700	83,700	115,000
CSX TRANSPORTATION	194,400	69,300	125,100
GOODYEAR TIRE & RUBBER	178,763	25,000	153,763
NORTHWEST AIRLINES	177,388	73,500	103,888
INTERNATIONAL COUNCIL OF CRUISE LINES	168,146	79,000	89,146
SEA-LAND SERVICE	165,175	39,675	125,500
CONTINENTAL AIRLINES	129,500	46,000	83,500
ASSOCIATION OF AMERICAN RAILROADS	111,850	32,000	79,850
YELLOW	111,500	21,500	90,000
DELTA AIRLINES	108,317	26,567	81,750
CALIBER SYSTEM	105,250	30,500	74,750

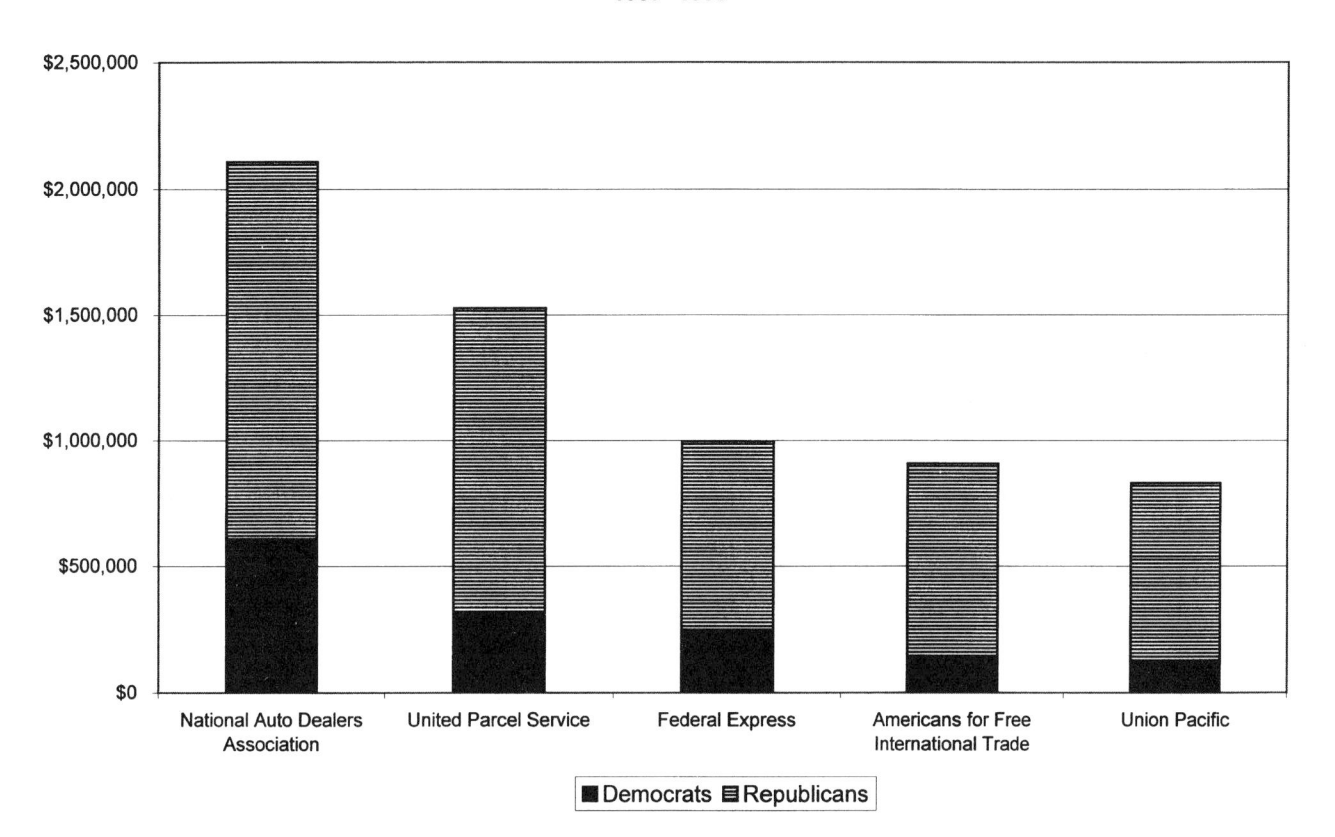

Top 5 Transport Political Action Committees 1997–1998

Top Air Transport PACs 1997–1998

PACs	TOTAL	DEMOCRATS	REPUBLICANS
UNITED PARCEL SERVICE	$1,527,149	$320,174	$1,206,975
FEDERAL EXPRESS	995,750	249,000	746,750
BOEING	660,175	238,800	421,375
AMERICAN AIRLINES	328,708	149,723	178,985
AIRCRAFT OWNERS & PILOTS ASSOCIATION	287,500	63,500	224,000
UNITED AIRLINES	198,700	83,700	115,000
NORTHWEST AIRLINES	177,388	73,500	103,888
CONTINENTAL AIRLINES	129,500	46,000	83,500
DELTA AIRLINES	108,317	26,567	81,750
GENERAL AVIATION MANUFACTURERS ASSOCIATION	82,400	33,200	49,200

Top Automobile PACs 1997–1998

PACs	TOTAL	DEMOCRATS	REPUBLICANS
NATIONAL AUTO DEALERS ASSOCIATION	$2,107,800	$609,175	$1,498,625
AMERICANS FOR FREE INTERNATIONAL TRADE	908,500	135,500	773,000
DAIMLERCHRYSLER	493,386	192,936	300,450
FORD MOTOR	414,750	103,200	311,550
GENERAL MOTORS	339,490	83,350	256,140
GOODYEAR TIRE & RUBBER	178,763	25,000	153,763
ENTERPRISE LEASING	58,650	4,200	54,450
AUTOZONE	52,500	4,500	48,000
TORRINGTON	39,750	26,000	13,750
JM FAMILY ENTERPRISES	39,050	12,250	26,800

Top Trucking PACs 1997–1998

PACs	TOTAL	DEMOCRATS	REPUBLICANS
AMERICAN TRUCKING ASSOCIATION	$419,196	$78,677	$340,519
YELLOW	111,500	21,500	90,000
CALIBER SYSTEM	105,250	30,500	74,750
PACCAR	73,797	8,000	65,797
RYDER SYSTEM	60,203	18,601	41,602

Top Railroad PACs 1997–1998

PACs	TOTAL	DEMOCRATS	REPUBLICANS
UNION PACIFIC	$831,268	$127,399	$703,869
NORFOLK SOUTHERN	263,600	86,000	177,600
BURLINGTON NORTHERN RAILROAD	209,042	65,395	143,647
CSX TRANSPORTATION	194,400	69,300	125,100
ASSOCIATION OF AMERICAN RAILROADS	111,850	32,000	79,850

Top Sea Transport PACs 1997–1998

PACs	TOTAL	DEMOCRATS	REPUBLICANS
INTERNATIONAL COUNCIL OF CRUISE LINES	$168,146	$79,000	$ 89,146
SEA-LAND SERVICE	165,175	39,675	125,500
AMERICAN COMMERCIAL BARGE LINE	73,310	13,500	59,810
SOUTHWEST MARINE	72,134	16,134	56,000
CROWLEY MARITIME	68,583	34,250	34,333

Top Union PACs 1997–1998

PACs	TOTAL	DEMOCRATS	REPUBLICANS
AMERICAN FEDERATION OF STATE, COUNTY, & MUNICIPAL EMPLOYEES	$2,367,450	$2,271,950	$ 95,500
TEAMSTERS	2,178,250	2,026,450	151,800
UNITED AUTO WORKERS	1,905,460	1,885,460	20,000
INTERNATIONAL BROTHERHOOD OF ELECTRICAL WORKERS	1,883,970	1,812,560	71,410
MACHINISTS AND AEROSPACE WORKERS	1,632,300	1,611,800	20,500
UNITED FOOD & COMMERCIAL WORKERS	1,494,951	1,457,651	37,300
LABORERS POLITICAL LEAGUE	1,412,350	1,255,850	156,500
CARPENTERS & JOINERS	1,369,923	1,279,500	90,423
SERVICE EMPLOYEES INTERNATIONAL	1,293,099	1,264,599	28,500
UNITED TRANSPORTATION	1,285,375	1,099,525	185,850
COMMUNICATIONS WORKERS OF AMERICA	1,216,113	1,208,113	8,000
SHEET METAL WORKERS	1,159,900	1,107,400	52,500
IRONWORKERS	1,142,300	1,040,800	101,500
AFL-CIO	1,113,140	1,100,640	12,500
UNITED STEELWORKERS	1,078,462	1,074,462	4,000
INTERNATIONAL ASSOCIATION OF FIRE FIGHTERS	898,400	743,950	154,450
MARINE ENGINEERS DISTRICT 2 MARITIME OFFICERS	860,750	374,500	486,250
NATIONAL ASSOCIATION RETIRED FEDERAL EMPLOYEES	820,150	732,900	87,250
AIR LINE PILOTS ASSOCIATION	816,200	633,500	182,700
PLUMBERS/PIPEFITTERS	757,100	713,600	43,500
TRANSPORT WORKERS	740,100	679,650	60,450
SEAFARERS INTERNATIONAL	686,532	544,902	141,630
AMERICAN POSTAL WORKERS	569,740	558,040	11,700
BOILERMAKERS	550,664	525,664	25,000
NATIONAL AIR TRAFFIC CONTROLLERS ASSOCIATION	541,150	479,050	62,100
AMALGAMATED TRANSIT	509,575	458,875	50,700
INTERNATIONAL LONGSHOREMEN'S ASSOCIATION	477,600	454,150	23,450
UNITED MINE WORKERS	444,550	431,550	13,000

**Top 5 Union Political Action Committees
1997–1998**

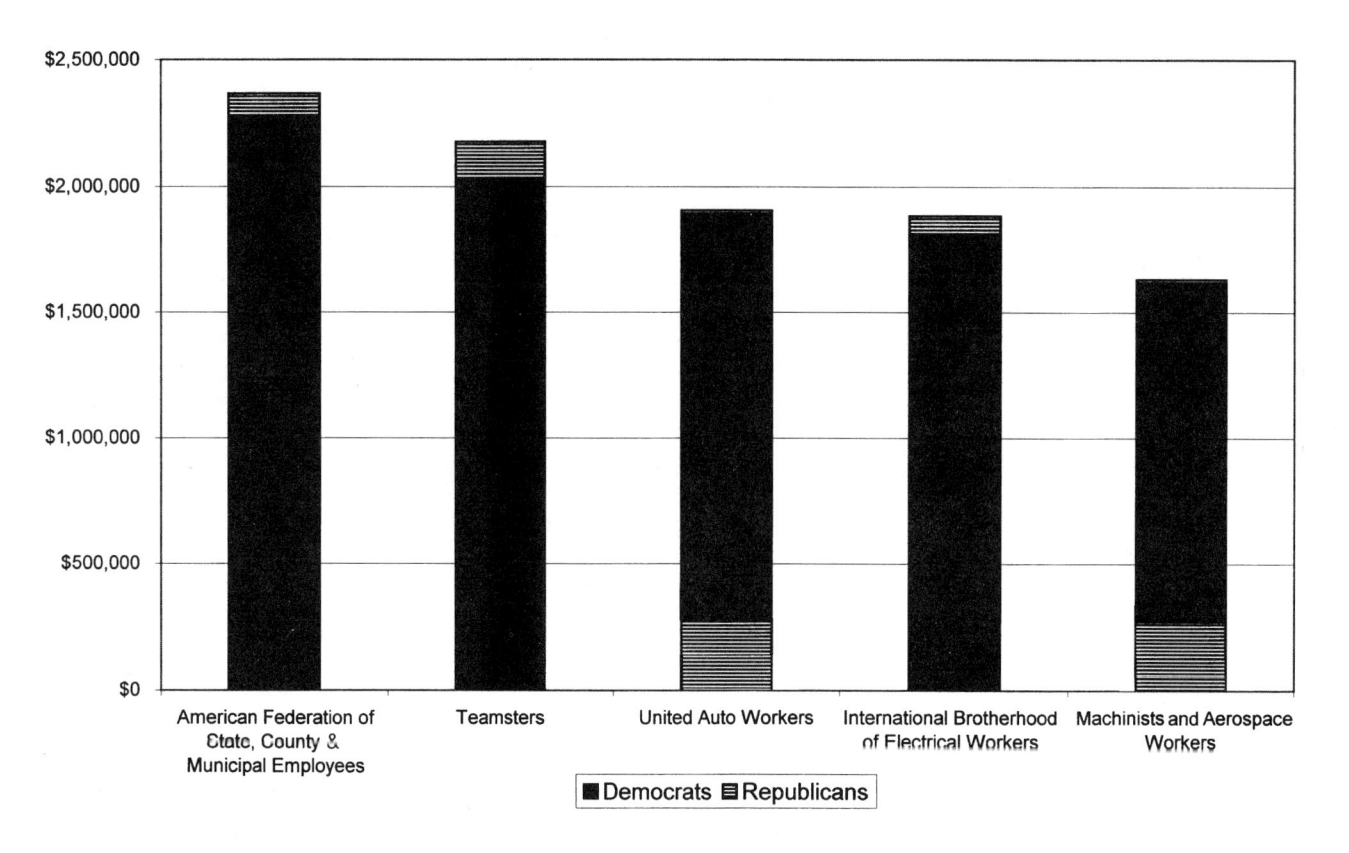

Top Industrial Union PACs 1997–1998

PACs	TOTAL	DEMOCRATS	REPUBLICANS
UNITED AUTO WORKERS	$1,905,460	$1,885,460	$20,000
INTERNATIONAL BROTHERHOOD OF ELECTRICAL WORKERS	1,883,970	1,812,560	71,410
MACHINISTS AND AEROSPACE WORKERS UNION	1,632,300	1,611,800	20,500
COMMUNICATIONS WORKERS OF AMERICA	1,216,113	1,208,113	8,000
UNITED STEELWORKERS	1,078,462	1,074,462	4,000
BOILERMAKERS	550,664	525,664	25,000
UNITED MINE WORKERS	444,550	431,550	13,000
UNITE (UNION OF NEEDLETRADES EMPLOYEES)	361,871	346,371	15,500
ELECTRONIC MACHINE FURNITURE WORKERS	271,125	271,125	0
OIL, CHEMICAL & ATOMIC WORKERS	121,900	121,900	0

Top 5 Industrial Union Political Action Committees 1997–1998

■ Democrats ▤ Republicans

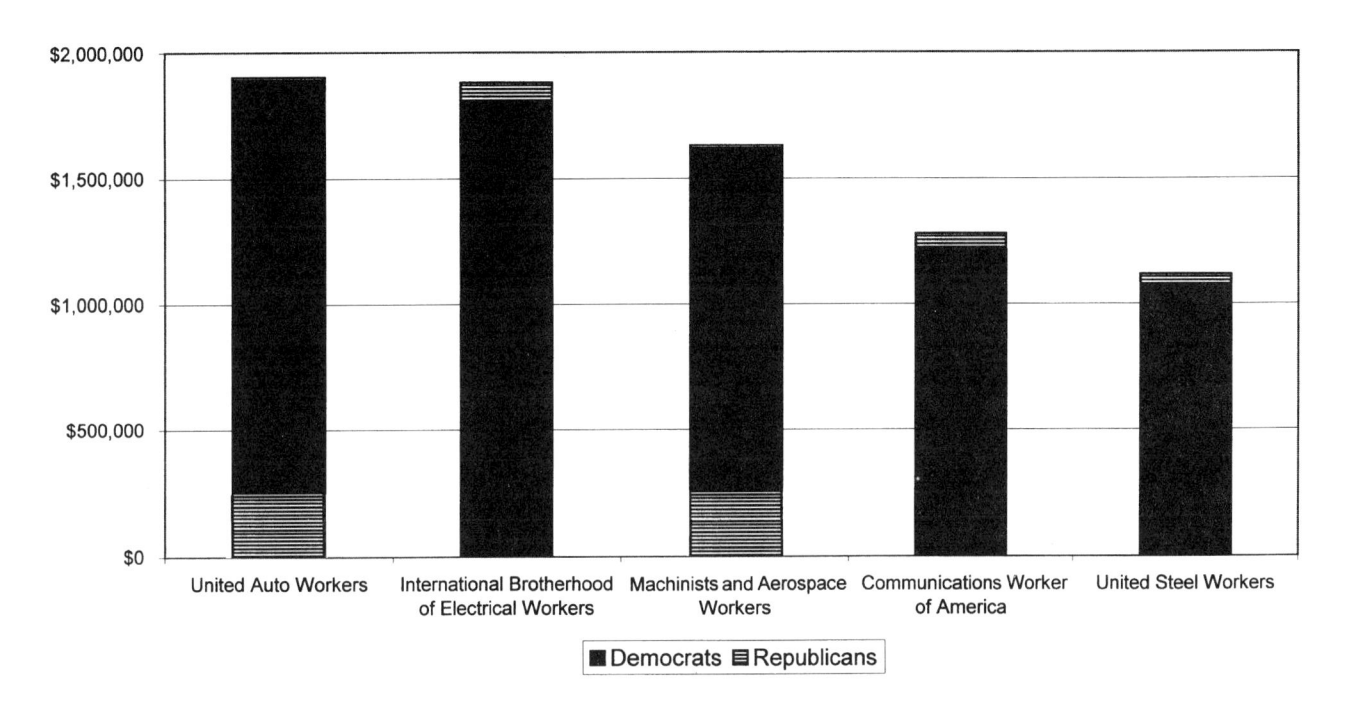

Top Transport Union PACs 1997–1998

PACs	TOTAL	DEMOCRATS	REPUBLICANS
TEAMSTERS UNION	$2,178,250	$2,026,450	$151,800
UNITED TRANSPORTATION	1,285,375	1,099,525	185,850
MARINE ENGINEERS DISTRICT 2 MARITIME OFFICERS	860,750	374,500	486,250
AIR LINE PILOTS ASSOCIATION	816,200	633,500	182,700
TRANSPORT WORKERS	740,100	679,650	60,450
SEAFARERS INTERNATIONAL	686,532	544,902	141,630
NATIONAL AIR TRAFFIC CONTROLLERS ASSOCIATION	541,150	479,050	62,100
AMALGAMATED TRANSIT	509,575	458,875	50,700
INTERNATIONAL LONGSHOREMEN'S ASSOCIATION	477,600	454,150	23,450
MARINE ENGINEERS DISTRICT 1/PACIFIC COAST DISTRICT	416,985	265,285	151,700
BROTHERHOOD OF LOCOMOTIVE ENGINEERS	386,879	363,914	22,965
TRANSPORTATION COMMUNICATION INTERNATIONAL	323,350	291,850	31,500
MAINTENANCE OF WAY EMPLOYEES	255,466	230,166	25,300
ALLIED PILOTS ASSOCIATION	223,500	102,500	121,000
ASSOCIATION OF FLIGHT ATTENDANTS	193,350	185,850	7,500

Top Building Trade Union PACs 1997–1998

PACs	TOTAL	DEMOCRATS	REPUBLICANS
LABORERS POLITICAL LEAGUE	$1,412,350	$1,255,850	$156,500
CARPENTERS & JOINERS UNION	1,369,923	1,279,500	90,423
SHEET METAL WORKERS UNION	1,159,900	1,107,400	52,500
IRONWORKERS	1,142,300	1,040,800	101,500
PLUMBERS AND PIPEFITTERS	757,100	713,600	43,500
PAINTERS & ALLIED TRADES	259,268	253,268	6,000
BRICKLAYERS	229,175	211,675	17,500
LABORERS	111,000	111,000	0
AFL-CIO BLDG/CONSTRUCTION TRADES DEPT	91,650	59,150	32,500
OPERATING ENGINEERS LOCAL 12	71,337	71,337	0

Top Public-Sector Union PACs 1997–1998

PACs	TOTAL	DEMOCRATS	REPUBLICANS
AMERICAN FEDERATION OF STATE, COUNTY & MUNICIPAL EMPLOYEES	$2,367,450	$2,271,950	$95,500
NATIONAL EDUCATION ASSOCIATION	1,853,390	1,751,540	97,850
NATIONAL ASSOCIATION OF LETTER CARRIERS	1,763,496	1,458,996	297,000
AMERICAN FEDERATION OF TEACHERS	1,415,400	1,386,500	23,400
INTERNATIONAL ASSOCIATION OF FIRE FIGHTERS	898,400	743,950	154,450
NATIONAL ASSOCIATION OF RETIRED FEDERAL EMPLOYEES	820,150	732,900	87,250
AMERICAN POSTAL WORKERS	569,740	558,040	11,700
NATIONAL RURAL LETTER CARRIERS ASSOCIATION	378,900	269,150	109,750
NATIONAL ASSOCIATION OF POSTMASTERS	346,433	207,449	138,984
NATIONAL TREASURY EMPLOYEES	308,180	290,180	18,000
AMERICAN FEDERATION OF GOVERNMENT EMPLOYEES	296,735	270,810	25,925
NATIONAL LEAGUE OF POSTMASTERS	192,900	104,500	88,400

Top 5 Public-Sector Union Political Action Committees 1997–1998

- American Federation of State, County & Municipal Employees
- National Education Association
- National Association of Letter Carriers
- American Federation of Teachers
- International Association of Fire Fighters

■ Democrats ▤ Republicans

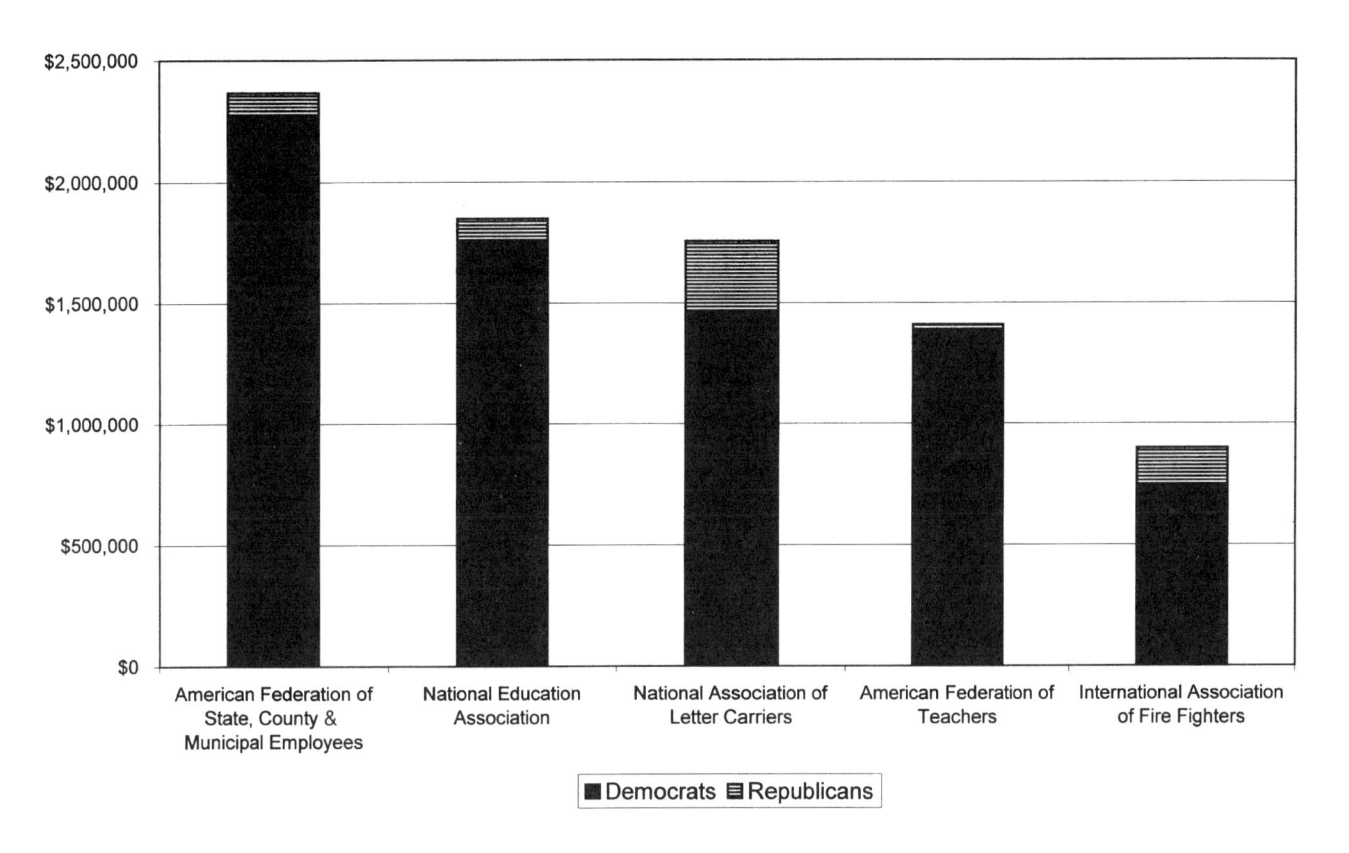

Top Miscellaneous Union PACs 1997–1998

PACs	TOTAL	DEMOCRATS	REPUBLICANS
UNITED FOOD & COMMERCIAL WORKERS UNION	$1,494,951	$1,457,651	$37,300
SERVICE EMPLOYEES INTERNATIONAL	1,293,099	1,264,599	28,500
AFL-CIO	1,113,140	1,100,640	12,500
HOTEL/RESTAURANT EMPLOYEES	371,600	305,300	66,300
HOSPITAL & HEALTH CARE EMPLOYEES 1199	199,600	199,600	0
OFFICE & PROFESSIONAL EMPLOYEES	196,450	196,450	0

Top Soft-Money Donors 1997–98 Election Cycle

DONATING ORGANIZATION	TOTAL	DEMOCRATS	REPUBLICANS
PHILIP MORRIS	$2,446,316	$ 418,564	$2,027,752
COMMUNICATIONS WORKERS OF AMERICA	1,464,250	1,464,250	0
AMERICAN FEDERATION OF STATE, COUNTY & MUNICIPAL EMPLOYEES	1,340,954	1,340,954	0
AMWAY	1,312,500	0	1,312,500
AMERICAN FINANCIAL GROUP	1,210,000	250,000	960,000
MCI WORLDCOM	1,142,390	422,565	719,825
NATIONAL EDUCATION ASSOCIATION	1,139,200	1,105,200	34,000
RJR NABISCO	1,132,922	132,572	1,000,350
AT&T	1,024,493	333,240	691,253
LORAL SPACECOM	1,021,000	1,021,000	0
FEDERAL EXPRESS	927,750	256,500	671,250
BELL ATLANTIC	909,519	255,300	654,219
FREDDIE MAC	875,500	650,500	225,000
WALT DISNEY	854,573	379,775	474,798
AMERICAN FEDERATION OF TEACHERS	854,400	854,400	0
GOLDMAN, SACHS & COMPANY	790,750	622,500	168,250
BUTTENWIESER & ASSOCIATES	783,500	783,500	0
CITIGROUP	774,879	194,300	580,579
MICROSOFT	774,816	145,000	629,816
JOSEPH E. SEAGRAM & SONS	753,846	394,110	359,736
PFIZER	747,050	100,000	647,050
BELLSOUTH	736,560	341,981	394,579
AFL-CIO	721,899	721,899	0
US WEST	719,000	142,000	577,000
ENRON	691,950	112,200	579,750
CSX	678,500	79,000	599,500
SERVICE EMPLOYEES INTERNATIONAL	662,375	632,375	30,000
BLUE CROSS/BLUE SHIELD	657,500	163,375	494,125
SLIM-FAST FOODS/THOMPSON MEDICAL	650,000	610,000	40,000
UNITED FOOD & COMMERCIAL WORKERS	638,833	638,833	0
MA BERMAN	600,000	600,000	0
BRISTOL-MYERS SQUIBB	559,975	140,300	419,675
NORTHWEST AIRLINES	559,727	232,477	327,250
BROWN & WILLIAMSON TOBACCO	559,250	20,000	539,250
ATLANTIC RICHFIELD	547,456	207,500	339,956

Top Soft-Money Donors 1997–98 Election Cycle (Cont.)

DONATING ORGANIZATION	TOTAL	DEMOCRATS	REPUBLICANS
TELE-COMMUNICATIONS	536,000	221,000	315,000
ALFA MUTUAL INSURANCE	532,000	105,000	427,000
JW CHILDS ASSOCIATES	530,000	0	530,000
BOEING	529,000	225,800	303,200
NEWS	523,466	60,000	463,466
ARCHER-DANIELS-MIDLAND COMPANY	518,000	263,000	255,000
ERNST & YOUNG	514,866	277,300	237,566
ANHEUSER-BUSCH	501,907	202,207	299,700
FANNIE MAE	501,350	189,100	312,250
AMR	497,804	171,618	326,186
SPRINT	496,542	273,714	222,828
NOVARTIS	495,604	149,500	346,104
TIME WARNER	471,000	211,000	260,000
SBC COMMUNICATIONS	470,161	161,061	309,100
GALLO WINERY	465,000	465,000	0

SECTION TWO
LOBBYISTS

As the official representatives of interest group organizations, lobbyists communicate information and opinions to government officials in order to influence specific decisions. Rather than acting on their own, citizens who belong to these interest groups rely upon lobbyists to convey their interests to policymakers. The term "lobbyist" is traced to Britain, where it referred to journalists who stood in the lobby of the House of Commons waiting to talk to members of Parliament. In the United States, it was first used in the early nineteenth century to refer disdainfully to privilege seekers in the Capitol lobby in Albany, New York. Lobbyists' negative image in the political culture stems from Americans' suspicion of the motives and influence of "special interests" that began with James Madison's warning about the "mischiefs of faction" in 1787. This suspicion was fueled by muckraking journalists who exposed the role lobbyists played in bribery and other forms of corruption in late-nineteenth- and early-twentieth-century American politics. Although bribery and other illegal practices occur much less frequently than in the past, suspicions about lobbyists still linger.

BACKGROUND AND RECRUITMENT OF LOBBYISTS

"Experience and expertise" are the "common denominators" of the careers of most lobbyists, according to Jeffrey Berry (1989). Lobbyists typically have backgrounds either in government, law, or business, or some combination of these. Many lobbyists are former executive branch officials, members of Congress, legislative aides, corporate managers, and practicing lawyers. Government work provides important experience and connections. In the mid-1980s, the *New York Times* reported that more than 200 former members of Congress made their living as lobbyists.

Following the 1994 elections, more than 20 legislators began lobbying careers, including former senators George J. Mitchell (Democrat, ME) and Steve Symms (Republican, ID), and former Representatives Robert H. Michel (Republican, IL) and Norman Lent (Republican, NY). More former high-ranking officials from the executive branch than from the legislative branch serve as lobbyists. Several of the best-known lobbyists in Washington have held important posts in the White House and key agencies under both Republican and Democratic administrations. Charles E. Walker was a deputy Treasury secretary under President Richard Nixon before he began lobbying for big business interests, and Stuart Eizenstat was President Jimmy Carter's chief domestic policy adviser before becoming a lobbyist for high-technology companies. Others who have gone on to become lobbyists include include Clark Clifford from the Truman administration; Robert Strauss from the Carter administration; Paul Warnke and Michael Deaver from the Reagan administration; and Joseph Califano, who served under presidents Johnson and Carter.

Legal training and experience provide valuable skills and preparation for understanding how bills and regulations are formulated. Lawyer-lobbyists are especially useful because of their ability to collect and deploy information to advocate for clients and analyze how legislative provisions will affect them. Business is a frequent recruitment channel because the majority of lobbyists represent corporations and trade associations, and the knowledge of technical complexity of tax, regulatory, and other issues of interest to the business community is particularly valuable.

Presently there are more male than female lobbyists, and most are highly educated. The majority have graduate degrees, most in law but also in economics, business, and political science. Compared to other Americans, lobbyists are highly paid, though wide disparities in income prevail between those working for trade associations, for instance, and those representing citizens groups. Tommy Boggs, the senior partner in the law firm Patton, Boggs, and Blow, reported income in 1985 of more than $1 million. Lobbyist Clark Clifford reportedly received $1 million ($4 million at 1995 prices) for his advice to the DuPont family involving the divestiture of General Motors stock. Clifford's advice saved the family $500 million. At the other end of the spectrum are Patricia Ireland, President of the National Organization for Women and Fred Wertheimer, former president of Common Cause (a "good government" reform-oriented organization), who made $81,000 and $73,400 in 1994, respectively. The highest-paid lobbyists tend to be attorneys in private practice, former members of Congress with lengthy careers on Capitol Hill, and former high-ranking executive branch officials.

Lobbying has become increasingly professionalized. Schools of "political management" now exist that offer formal academic training in the skills and subject matter relevant to lobbying. Lobbyists today have technical competence in the substantive aspects of their clients' work as well as in modern forms of communication, such as direct marketing.

THE NUMBER AND VARIETY OF LOBBYING ORGANIZATIONS

As the number of interest groups has proliferated, so has the volume of lobbying. Political scientist James Thurber has calculated that, as of the early 1990s, 91,000 lobbyists and individuals associated with lobbying worked in Washington, DC. They represented approximately 23,000 organizations.

Lobbyists represent a wide array of interests in society. Business organizations include individual firms; trade associations that represent entire industries; large umbrella associations; and temporary, ad hoc coalitions of business groups that come together to lobby for or against particular pieces of legislation, administrative rulings, or court decisions. For example, American Airlines is a single corporation that may lobby on its own, or as part of its trade group, the Air Transport Association. It may also belong to a general association like the Chamber of Commerce or Business Roundtable and may participate in loose, temporary coalitions of business interests, such as the Tax Reform Action Committee, which fought in favor of tax reform in 1985 and 1986.

Professional associations include organizations representing professions, such as the American Bar Association and the American Medical Association. Trade unions include particular unions like the Teamsters and the American Federation of Teachers, as well as umbrella organizations like the American Federation of Labor and Congress of Industrial Organizations. Governmental organizations in Washington represent subnational units of government, such as the National League of Cities, the National Association of Counties, and the National Governors Association. Nonprofit sector groups encompass a broad range of interests, including religious (the National Council of Churches), and community and citizens' groups, such as the Veterans of Foreign Wars, the Sierra Club, the National Association for the Advancement of Colored People (NAACP), and the National Rifle Association (NRA).

Lobbyists are either employed directly by clients to be their full-time, in-house lobbyists, or they are employed by law and public relations firms that have interest group clients. The larger interest group organizations establish permanent lobbying departments that work full-time as their political representatives. Most lobbyists fall into this category. Lobbyists that work at law and public relations firms, on the other hand, are "hired guns," who are paid by interest groups on a retainer or fee-for-service basis. The largest customers for these firms are corporations and trade associations, some of which may not have Washington offices, or may not have the resources for undertaking major lobbying campaigns, and who rely upon the lawyers who work in these firms for their government experience and political connections. The largest law firms in Washington include Covington and Burling; Arnold and Porter; Hogan and Hartson; Steptoe and Johnson; Arent, Fox, Kinter, Plotkin and Kahn; Akin, Gump, Strauss, Haver and Feld; Jones, Day, Revis and Pogue; Morna, Lewis and Bockius, and Fried; Frank, Harris, Shriver and Jacobson. Each firm staffs 100 to 200 or more lawyers.

A significant change in recent years has been the rise of huge, full-service lobbying/public relations firms. These firms offer more services to clients than law firms, with specialists not only in lobbying and legal services, but also in advertising and public relations, working with the mass media and planning events, as well as engaging in grassroots lobbying and political fundraising. The largest of these include Black, Manafort, Stone, and Kelly Public Affairs; Burson-Marsteller; Hill and Knowlton Inc.; The Kamber Group; and Ogilvy and Mather Public Affairs. Many of the clients of these firms are among the top corporations, trade associations, financial institutions, universities, and nonprofit organizations in the United States, and foreign interests.

Clients of Akin, Gump, Strauss, Haver and Feld, for example, include AT&T, Dow Jones, and the government of Norway. Arnold and Porter clients include Paine Webber, the Republic of Venezuela, and Stanford University. Covington and Burling work for Proctor and Gamble and the National Football League. Black, Manafort, Stone, and Kelly serve Union Pacific Railroad, the Trump Organization, and Bethlehem Steel.

Some lobbyists and lobbying firms develop expertise in specific areas and represent clients in particular industries or sectors of the economy and society. For example, Wilmer, Cutler and Pickering represents the National Association of Broadcasters, Cable News Network, ABC, CBS, and NBC. Former Senator Mark Andrews represents a variety of Japanese consumer electronic firms, such as Akai, Fuji, Hitachi, JVC, and Sony. Some firms specialize in particular tasks. Burson, Marsteller, for example, the large New York public relations firm, specializes in building images of its clients, using such tools as press kits, telemarketing, direct mailings, media tours, and seminars.

WHAT LOBBYISTS DO

Most lobbyists spend most of their time collecting information about what their clients want and what government officials are planning or doing that could affect them. They act as watchdogs, listening to their contacts in government, keeping tabs on all pending legislation that could affect their clients, and reporting this information to them. Lobbyists also act as advocates for their clients, contacting politicians and bureaucrats, and presenting information, arguments, and opinions to them. They do this through informal contacts, such as meetings, phone calls, receptions, and dining together, as well as through formal channels, such as testifying at committee hearings.

The relationship between lobbyists and government officials is not one-sided. Lobbyists seek favorable treatment from the government, and policymakers seek information and political support from the organizations represented by them. The information that lobbyists provide can be substantive facts and arguments concerning issues and policies that are on the agenda, or that may come on to the agenda, as well as political information concerning the positions of group members, the public generally, and other political actors.

Popular perceptions are that lobbyists mainly work behind the scenes, arm-twisting government officials to do something that they know should not be done. Political scientists view this image as inaccurate most of the time. Far from trying to be invisible, lobbyists seek attention and visibility for their organizations. Moreover, according to Leech and Baumgartner (1998), "the idea that groups are on the outside, pressuring recalcitrant government officials into doing their bidding and against their will, is wholly incomplete. Most major groups, and many small ones, benefit from long-standing relations with government officials who are predisposed to helping them."

Lobbyists are effective when they can develop and sustain relationships with public officials that are built upon trust, and trust is earned only if the lobbyist is credible to the policymaker. If policymakers feel that they have been misled, the credibility of the lobbyist is diminished, trust erodes, and consequently so too will access and effectiveness. Credibility is determined by whether the lobbyist supplies information to the policymaker that is relevant, factual, and accurate. According to Berry, "the optimal role for a lobbyist to play is that of a trusted source of information whom policymakers can call on when they need hard-to-find data. A reputation for credibility and high-quality factual information are prerequisites for becoming a lobbyist from whom government officials request help." Some legislators become so closely identified with specific interests that they are called "inside lobbyists." For example, for many years former Senator Russell B. Long (D-LA) and others from oil-producing states represented oil interests in Congress.

With more special interest groups populating the Washington landscape, especially since the 1970s, more lobbying is taking place and in a greater variety of forms. Lobbying strategies include applying pressure to policymakers who are undecided or in opposition to a group's position, and providing services to policymakers with whom they are allied in mutually reinforcing relationships. Lobbyists pressure policymakers through such tactics as argumentation, letter-writing campaigns, demonstrations of constituency support, and the threat of opposition in the next election. They provide services by cooperating closely with allies and supplying relevant information in order to affect the content of legislation. Whether lobbyists choose to apply pressure or provide services depends on the context. For instance, during the early stages of the legislative process, lobbyists may work with a small set of allies within government and then broaden their targets to undecided or opposing legislators.

Lobbying can be direct or indirect. Direct lobbying brings lobbyists as official representatives of organized groups into direct contact with government officials. It is the most time-honored and conventional approach to seeking access and influence. Classic forms of direct lobbying include writing letters, meeting with government officials, and offering testimony at hearings. Indirect lobbying involves a more circuitous route to influencing government officials, such as stimulating grassroots or third-party efforts.

Lobbying organizations use media campaigns in numerous ways to mold public opinion and alert community leaders. They may use them to induce goodwill, attempting over the long term to create a favorable image for the interest group. For instance, the Atlantic Richfield Oil Company has funded concerts aired by the Public Broadcasting System. Philip Morris, the tobacco company whose holdings include Kraft Foods and Miller Brewing, has run advertisements celebrating the Bill of Rights and emphasizing personal freedom. Other organizations use media campaigns to attain specific policies that will benefit them, such as when Allied Chemical took out a series of ads in magazines and newspapers arguing for various changes in the federal tax laws.

Then there are those groups that work through the mass media to block policy changes they perceive as threats. Perhaps the most famous of these were the "Harry and Louise" advertisements funded by the Health Insurance Association of America in 1994. The ads, intended to create opposition to the Clinton administration's healthcare reform proposal, portrayed a young, middle-class couple puzzled and troubled over provisions that were alleged to raise taxes and deprive Americans of personal choice. Indirect lobbying also includes stimulating the grassroots—mobilizing group members and the general public to write, fax, and e-mail letters to policymakers, as well as to engage in protest demonstrations and boycotts. Through the use of computer-based direct mail techniques, interest groups can send out slick "appeals packets," often using fear and hyperbole, to encourage members to write letters and e-mail messages to officials targeted by the organization, or to send money to the organization to fund lobbying campaigns.

THE IMPACTS OF LOBBYING

The actual impact of lobbying activity upon public policy remains uncertain because of the many other possible influences that exist and the difficulty of trying to "control" scientifically for all of them. Compounding the difficulty is the fact that it is hard, perhaps impossible, to disentangle the effects of lobbying per se from the other activities that interest groups engage in to influence government, such as donating to election campaigns and mobilizing constituents to vote for or against candidates.

Some political scientists discount the importance of lobbying and other forms of active participation in the political process altogether on certain critical issues. Political scientist Charles Lindblom and others have argued that the political power of business interests rests upon the structural position of business in the political system. Public officials can be expected to try their best to help business because they will stay in power only if the economy prospers, and this depends critically upon doing whatever is needed to induce businessmen to invest. In such a system, businesses do not need to exert pressure on policymakers, and thus lobbying is of secondary importance.

The major studies of lobbying, by Milbrath and Bauer, and Pool and Dexter, date back to the 1960s. The first study painted a benign picture of lobbyists contributing positively to the policymaking process. The second claimed that business lobbyists were largely incapable of influencing Congress on trade policy. More recent scholarship has also deemphasized the power of interest groups. A spate of studies have argued that relatively narrow and specific economic interests have fared poorly in making major public policy changes. The deregulation of many industries in the 1970s and 1980s, tax reform in the 1980s, the continued resistance against protectionist pressures in trade policy, and reductions in discretionary spending on subsidy programs for agriculture and "pork barrel" projects for specific localities suggest that the days in which particular interests could capture benefits for themselves at the expense of the larger public may be waning. Formerly formidable interest groups like cigarette manufacturers, tobacco farmers, pesticide producers, and the NRA have been challenged and put on the defensive in ways that years ago would have seemed highly improbable. What is striking about virtually all of these cases is that the interest groups suffering defeats have been resourceful, active, and adamantly opposed to the policy changes brought about by their opponents.

Several reasons may account for what Peterson has called "the decline of special interest politics." First, the demands of many groups have come in conflict with the need for policymakers to maintain budgetary discipline and the dynamism of the economy. Interest groups' demands on the government for benefits and protection may impede progress on those vital issues. In addition, policymaking arenas that were once stable and secure interest group "monopolies" or "subgovernments," such as agriculture, tobacco, and gun ownership, have become much more competitive and conflict ridden as new groups have emerged to counter the groups that once dominated them. The NRA, for instance, must now compete with several gun control advocacy groups. The American Medical Association cannot exert the influence it did in the 1950s and 1960s when it was the overwhelmingly dominant group in healthcare policy. Pesticide manufacturers must now contend with several environmental groups that were virtually nonexistent in decades past. As the interest group field has "thickened" and groups have crowded each other out, it may now be more difficult for particular interests to prevail.

Nevertheless, it would be unwise to conclude that interest groups no longer wield influence in politics. First, most of the literature on the decline of "special interest" influence has focused on relatively narrow economic interests, saying little about other kinds of interest organizations serving larger societal interests and social movements, such as those that represent racial and ethnic minorities, the elderly, the environment, and taxpayers. Second, if one source of the diminished influence of some groups is the mobilization and pressure of others, then what may have changed is not so much the decline of interest groups as powerful political actors, but the decline of particular interests that monopolized policymaking in the past. Finally, the role of health insurance interests in the demise of the Clinton healthcare plan, as well as the fact that many business interests continue to secure favorable legislation for themselves, suggest strongly that groups have influence. Many groups continue to get their way, particularly on what seem to most people arcane and minor provisions in law or regulation, but which prove significant victories for the groups. A slight change in an obscure provision of the tax laws, for instance, can save a corporation millions of dollars but hardly be noticed or understood by the press or public.

Perhaps the safest conclusion is that lobbying can matter, to some degree, depending upon the circumstances. Among the most important of these circumstances is whether the policies that interest groups prefer mirror the policy preferences and political goals of policymakers. The health insurers would have had much less chance of prevailing against the Clinton health plan if Congress had been dominated by liberal, activist legislators rather than conservative ones in the early 1990s. Feminist and labor groups had little chance of getting President George Bush to go along with family and medical leave regulations. They succeeded only when a new president was elected who strongly supported the policy. Cathie Jo Martin has shown that major changes in corporate tax policy occur when partnerships of rising economic forces and political entrepreneurs in government are able to articulate the need for a new policy and forge a coalition of interests and officials to bring it about.

The opportunities for lobbying also vary with the institutional structure of government. Institutions that disperse power among a number of governmental officials, as with those in the United States, make it easier for lobbyists to gain access and exert influence in order to block unwanted policy changes. But the very same institutions make it more difficult to bring about changes in policy that groups want. Committee and agency jurisdictions and decision-making procedures may make it easier or harder for groups to find sympathetic officials and apply pressure. For instance, if a bill proposing to regulate the use of pesticides is referred to the Agriculture Committee instead of the Public Health and Welfare Committee, farm interests are more likely to be invited to testify before the committee and to be accommodated in other ways. A classic example of how institutional venue matters for group influence is the experience of African Americans in securing civil rights in the 1950s and 1960s. Because the elected branches of government were mainly concerned about how white Southern voters would react to civil rights, the NAACP and other civil rights organizations turned to the courts where they made important breakthroughs in cases like *Brown v. Board of Education*.

Two other potentially crucial factors that probably help to determine whether lobbying will have an impact are public opinion and cultural predispositions about groups and their interests. For example, David Vogel argues that the fortunes of business interests seem to wax and wane with public attitudes about the long-term health of the economy. When the public is deeply concerned about economic performance, as it was from the mid 1970s to the mid 1980s, it tends to be more sympathetic to the needs and demands of business. With the public on their side, business lobbyists will have a powerful ally in trying to convince officials to enact policies friendly to business, such as lower taxes and less regulation. Conversely, when the economy prospers and the public is optimistic about economic performance, it will be less concerned about the needs of business, and may even turn toward nonmaterial wants (e.g., a cleaner environment) that entail more regulation. Business lobbyists, as a result, will be in a less advantageous position.

Images of interest groups portrayed through the mass media, which often reflect longstanding cultural myths and symbols, may also help or hinder interest groups' political efforts. For example, because farmers and farming are a venerated part of the American past, lobbyists for farm interests can project an image of their clients as hard-working, small, independent farmers who represent the wholesome virtues of rural life and Jeffersonian democracy. By contrast, because labor unions are often viewed as run by corrupt and undemocratic "bosses," it may be harder for labor lobbyists to persuade the public and policymakers of their arguments.

Finally, we should note that lobbying, as a chief activity of interest groups, has an ambivalent relationship with liberal democracy. On the one hand, lobbying is consistent with such values as free association, free expression, and the right to petition the government for redress. It is a crucial mechanism for citizens to communicate their demands and preferences to government officials, and thus serves as a key form of democratic control between elections. On the other hand, lobbying for group interests requires resources. Modern-day lobbying campaigns at the national level are very expensive. Lobbying thus reflects and exacerbates the political inequality that exists among citizens. If government better attends to the interests of the rich and organizationally sophisticated than to those of the poor and unorganized, then it may be because the former have the wherewithal to compete in an arena in which lobbying plays a major role in what information policymakers receive and what kinds of political pressures they come under.

GARY MUCCIARONI

Bibliography

Bauer, Raymond A., Ithiel De Sola Pool and Lewis Anthony Dexter. *American Business and Public Policy: The Politics of Foreign Trade.* New York: Atherton Press, 1964.

Berry, Jeffrey M. *The Interest Group Society.* 2d ed. Glenview, IL: Scott, Foresman/Little, Brown, 1989.

Birnbaum, Jeffrey H. *The Lobbyists: How Influence Peddlers Get Their Way in Washington.* New York: Random House, 1992.

Cigler, Allan J., and Burdett A. Loomis (eds.). *Interest Group Politics.* 5th ed. Washington, DC: Congressional Quarterly Press, 1998.

Hrebenar, Ronald J. *Interest Groups Politics in America.* 3d ed. Armonk, NY: M.E. Sharpe, 1997.

Leech, Beth L., and Frank R. Baumgartner, "Lobbying Friends and Foes in Washington," in *Interest Group Politics,* edited by Allan J. Cigler and Burdett A. Loomis. 5th ed. Washington, DC: Congressional Quarterly Press, 1998.

Lindblom, Charles E. *Politics and Markets: The World's Political Economic Systems.* New York: Basic Books, 1977.

Martin, Cathie Jo. *Shifting the Burden: The Struggle over Growth and Corporate Taxation.* Chicago: University of Chicago Press, 1991.

Milbrath, Lester W. *The Washington Lobbyists.* Chicago: Rand McNally, 1963.

Mucciaroni, Gary. *Reversals of Fortune: Public Policy and Private Interests.* Washington, DC: The Brookings Institution, 1995.

Peterson, Paul E. "The Rise and Fall of Special Interest Politics," in Mark P. Petreacca, ed., *The Politics of Interests: Interest Groups Transformed.* Boulder, CO: Westview Press, 1992.

Vogel, David. 1989. *Fluctuating Fortunes: The Political Power of Business in America.* New York: Basic Books, 1989.

Wolpe, Bruce C., and Bertram J. Levine, *Lobbying Congress: How the System Works.* 2d ed. Washington, DC: Congressional Quarterly Press, 1996.

HOW TO USE THE LOBBYING TABLES

The following 16 tables list the amounts of money spent on lobbying by various corporations, advocacy organizations, trade associations, law firms, lobbying firms, and labor unions for the years 1997 and 1998. Lobbying expenditures are separate from donations to candidates, as listed in the PAC tables that precede this section. Lobbying expenditures include moneys spent on advocacy, research, entertainment, polling, public relations, advertising, and other activities. The following lobbying tables do not present firms and organizations in the same order that they are presented in the entry section of this encyclopedia.

Top Banking, Security, and Investment Companies Lobbying Expenditures 1997–1998

COMPANY/ASSOCIATION	1998	1997
CITIGROUP	$7,290,000	$9,040,000
CHASE MANHATTAN	5,920,000	4,140,000
AMERICAN BANKERS ASSOCIATION	4,808,000	3,449,000
SECURITIES INDUSTRY ASSOCIATION	4,660,000	5,000,000
BANK OF AMERICA	4,580,000	2,200,000
MERRILL LYNCH	3,800,000	2,880,000
INVESTMENT COMPANY INSTITUTE	3,380,000	3,720,000
BOND MARKET ASSOCIATION	2,591,000	2,392,000
UNIFORM STANDARDS COALITION	2,340,000	1,760,000
JP MORGAN	1,280,000	2,340,000
MORGAN STANLEY, DEAN WITTER	1,220,000	1,820,000
WELLS FARGO	1,200,000	680,000
BANK ONE	1,026,000	680,000
CHICAGO MERCANTILE EXCHANGE	860,000	968,000
INDEPENDENT BANKERS ASSOCIATION	841,000	759,000
CHICAGO BOARD OF TRADE	720,000	1,100,000
SECURITY TRADERS ASSOCIATION	720,000	180,000
PRUDENTIAL SECURITIES	640,000	600,000
FIRST UNION	580,000	440,000
FLEET FINANCIAL GROUP	560,000	500,000

Top 5 Banking, Security, and Investment Companies Lobbying Expenditures 1997–1998

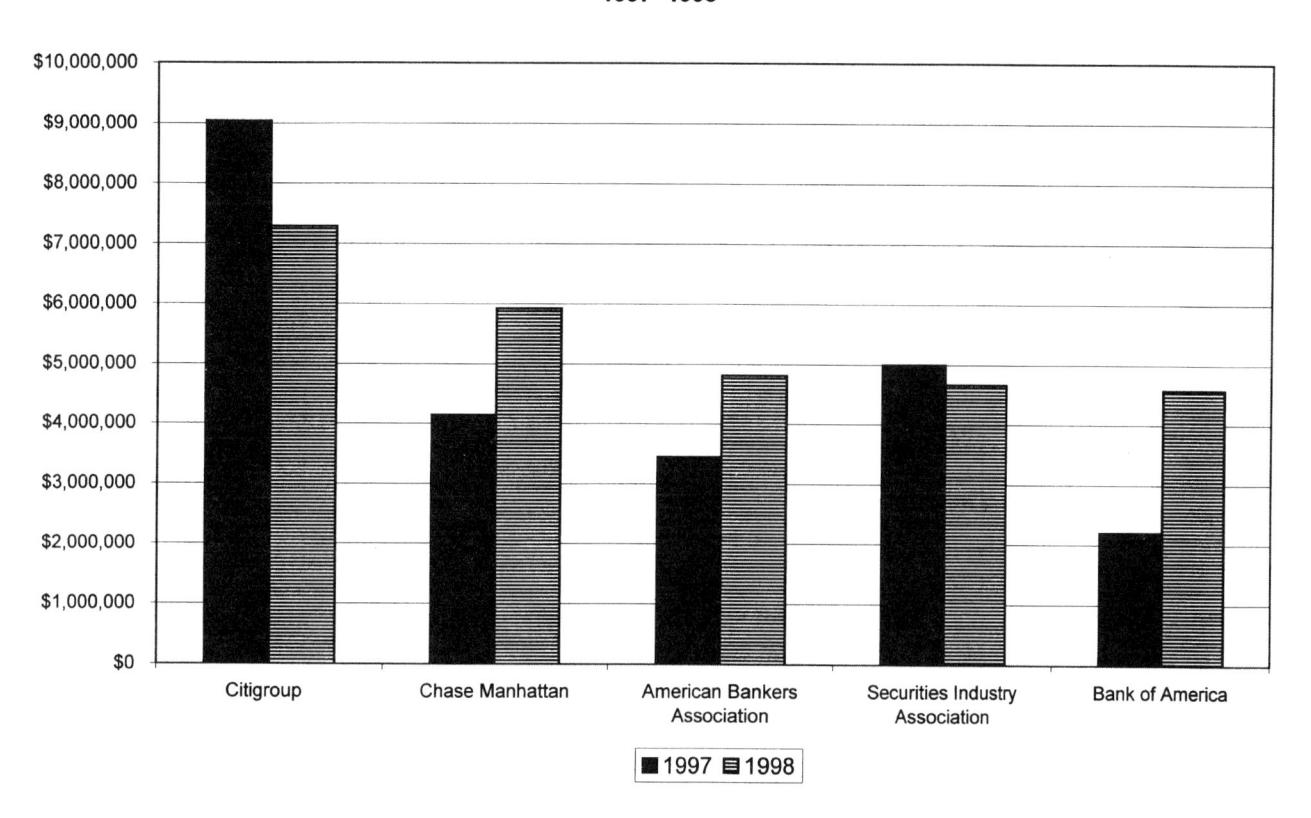

Top Business Associations Lobbying Expenditures 1997–1998

COMPANY/ASSOCIATION	1998	1997
CHAMBER OF COMMERCE OF THE UNITED STATES	$17,000,000	$14,240,000
BUSINESS ROUNDTABLE	11,640,000	9,480,000
NATIONAL FEDERATION OF INDEPENDENT BUSINESSES	4,249,000	2,240,000
NATIONAL FOREIGN TRADE COUNCIL	1,660,000	1,880,000
EMERGENCY COMMITTEE FOR AMERICAN TRADE	660,000	276,000
HONG KONG TRADE DEVELOPMENT COUNCIL	600,000	840,000
SMALL BUSINESS SURVIVAL COMMITTEE	600,000	100,000
CIVIL JUSTICE REFORM GROUP	580,000	360,000
EUROPEAN-AMERICAN BUSINESS COUNCIL	503,000	480,000
LABOR POLICY ASSOCIATION	460,000	840,000

**Top 5 Business Associations
Lobbying Expenditures
1997–1998**

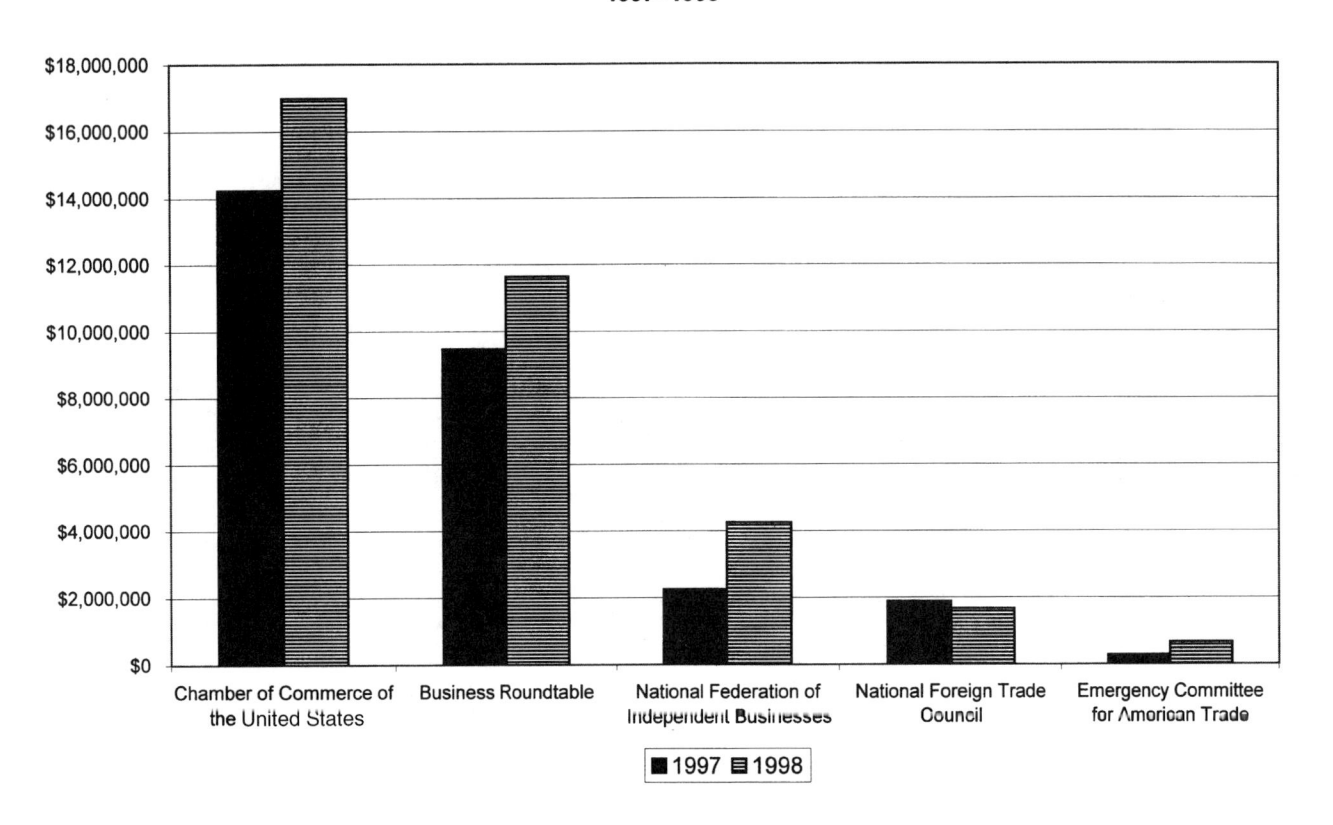

Top Computer Companies Lobbying Expenditures 1997–1998

COMPANY/ASSOCIATION	1998	1997
IBM	$5,552,000	$5,240,000
MICROSOFT	3,740,000	2,120,000
EDS	3,310,000	2,220,000
TEXAS INSTRUMENTS	2,260,000	1,960,000
ORACLE	1,900,000	900,000
COMPAQ COMPUTER	1,462,000	759,000
SUN MICROSYSTEMS	1,180,000	1,220,000
INTEL	1,100,000	600,000
BUSINESS SOFTWARE ALLIANCE	1,020,000	960,000
AMERICA ONLINE	1,020,000	784,000
COMPUTER SYSTEMS POLICY PROJECT	1,020,000	680,000

**Top 5 Computer Companies
Lobbying Expenditures
1997–1998**

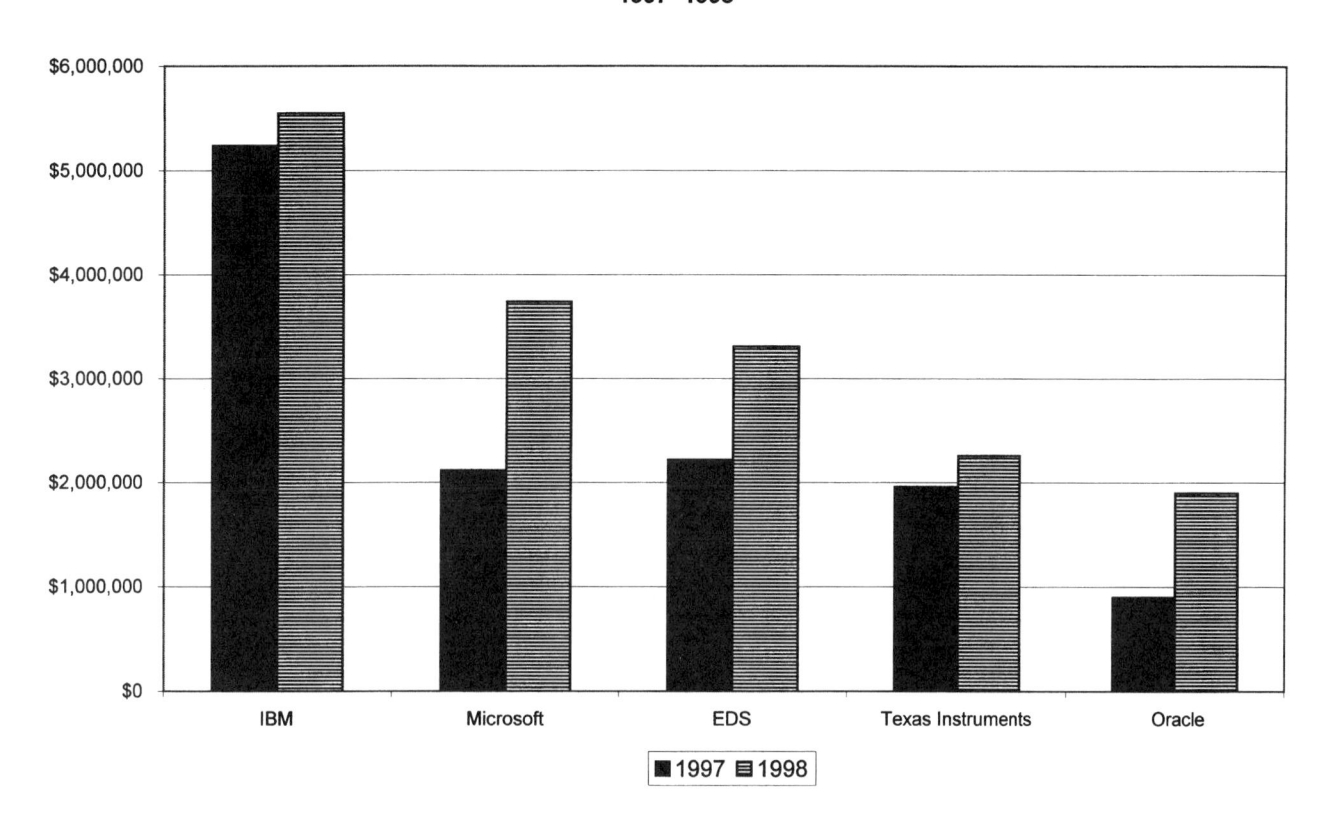

Top Entertainment/Media Institutions Lobbying Expenditures 1997–1998

COMPANY/ASSOCIATION	1998	1997
NATIONAL ASSOCIATION OF BROADCASTERS	$5,200,000	$4,680,000
NATIONAL CABLE TELEVISION ASSOCIATION	4,800,000	3,360,000
TIME WARNER	3,000,000	3,000,000
WALT DISNEY	2,447,000	2,150,000
CBS	1,940,000	1,300,000
TELE-COMMUNICATIONS	1,200,000	1,460,000
BROADCAST MUSIC	1,040,000	800,000
VIACOM	1,000,000	320,000
MOTION PICTURE ASSOCIATION OF AMERICA	980,000	600,000
RECORDING INDUSTRY ASSOCIATION OF AMERICA	820,000	860,000

Top Government Agencies Lobbying Expenditures 1997–1998

COMPANY/ASSOCIATION	1998	1997
COMMONWEALTH OF PUERTO RICO	$4,045,000	$4,335,000
COMMONWEALTH OF THE NORTHERN MARIANA ISLANDS	1,360,000	2,061,000
CITY & COUNTY OF DENVER, COLORADO	840,000	430,000
LOS ANGELES COUNTY, CALIFORNIA	720,000	725,000
MIAMI-DADE COUNTY, FLORIDA	690,000	720,000
CITY OF CHICAGO, ILLINOIS	500,000	405,000
CITY OF SACRAMENTO, CALIFORNIA	470,000	385,000
SAN DIEGO COUNTY, CALIFORNIA	460,000	400,000
ORANGE COUNTY, CALIFORNIA	459,000	470,000
METRO TRANSIT AUTHORITY OF HARRIS COUNTY, TEXAS	420,000	480,000

Top Health Professional Associations Lobbying Expenditures 1997–1998

COMPANY/ASSOCIATION	1998	1997
AMERICAN MEDICAL ASSOCIATION	$16,820,000	$17,280,000
AMERICAN ASSOCIATION OF NURSE ANESTHETISTS	1,735,000	670,000
AMERICAN SOCIETY OF ANESTHESIOLOGISTS	1,537,015	400,000
AMERICAN COLLEGE OF PHYSICIANS	1,200,000	280,000
COLLEGE OF AMERICAN PATHOLOGISTS	1,120,000	725,000
AMERICAN COLLEGE OF EMERGENCY PHYSICIANS	1,021,000	2,001,000
AMERICAN OCCUPATIONAL THERAPY ASSOCIATION	960,000	820,000
AMERICAN ACADEMY OF FAMILY PHYSICIANS	937,000	951,000
AMERICAN SOCIETY OF INTERNAL MEDICINE	908,142	1,702,000
AMERICAN PSYCHOLOGICAL ASSOCIATION	880,000	716,000

**Top 5 Professional Associations
Lobbying Expenditures
1997–1998**

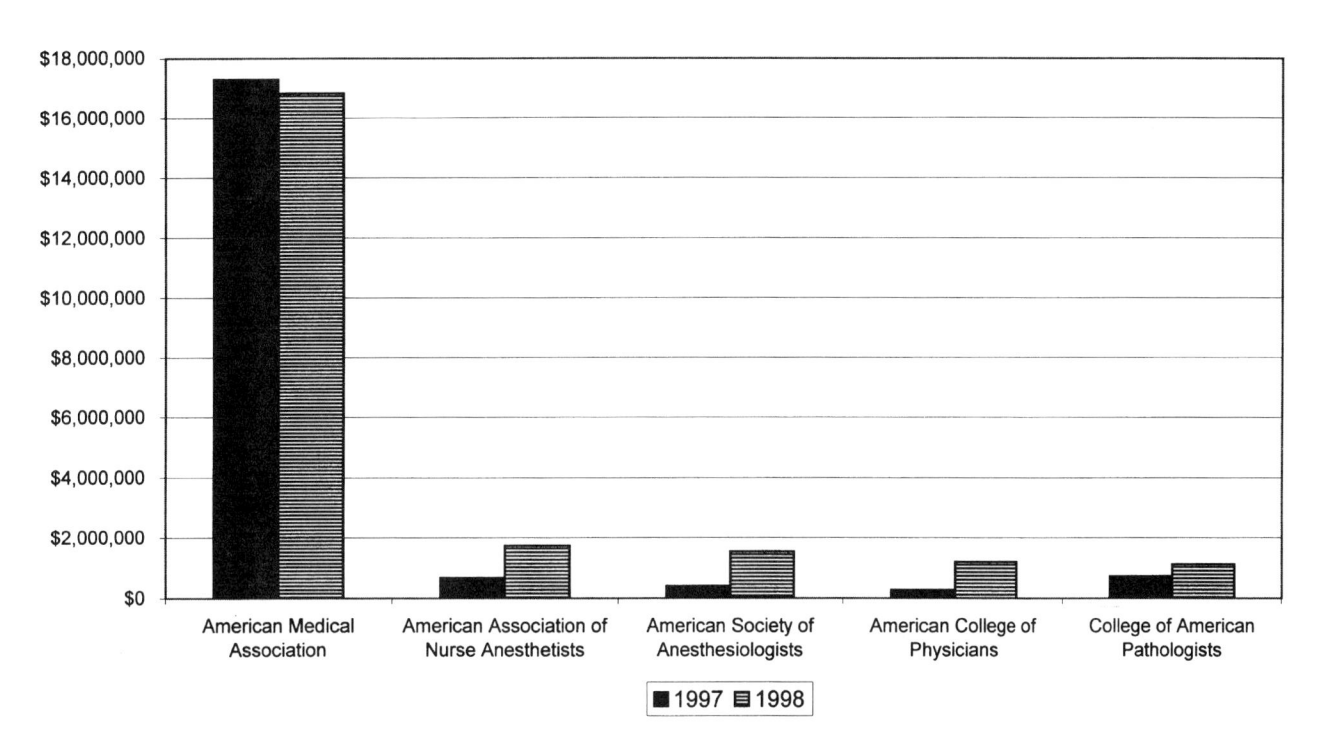

[Bar chart showing lobbying expenditures for 1997 and 1998:
- American Medical Association: ~$17,300,000 (1997), ~$16,800,000 (1998)
- American Association of Nurse Anesthetists: ~$700,000 (1997), ~$1,700,000 (1998)
- American Society of Anesthesiologists: ~$500,000 (1997), ~$1,600,000 (1998)
- American College of Physicians: ~$300,000 (1997), ~$1,200,000 (1998)
- College of American Pathologists: ~$800,000 (1997), ~$1,100,000 (1998)]

Top Insurance Companies Lobbying Expenditures 1997–1998

COMPANY/ASSOCIATION	1998	1997
BLUE CROSS/BLUE SHIELD	$8,132,000	$8,762,000
AMERICAN COUNCIL OF LIFE INSURANCE	7,050,000	4,935,000
AMERICAN INTERNATIONAL GROUP	6,940,000	3,400,000
HEALTH INSURANCE ASSOCIATION OF AMERICA	4,495,000	4,800,000
UNITED SERVICES AUTOMOBILE ASSOCIATION GROUP	3,520,000	3,560,000
PRUDENTIAL INSURANCE	3,200,000	2,877,000
AMERICAN INSURANCE ASSOCIATION	3,062,000	2,637,000
NATIONAL ASSOCIATION OF INDEPENDENT INSURERS	3,007,000	2,806,000
AFLAC	2,580,000	920,000
NEW YORK LIFE INSURANCE	1,920,000	1,180,000

**Top 5 Insurance Companies
Lobbying Expenditures
1997–1998**

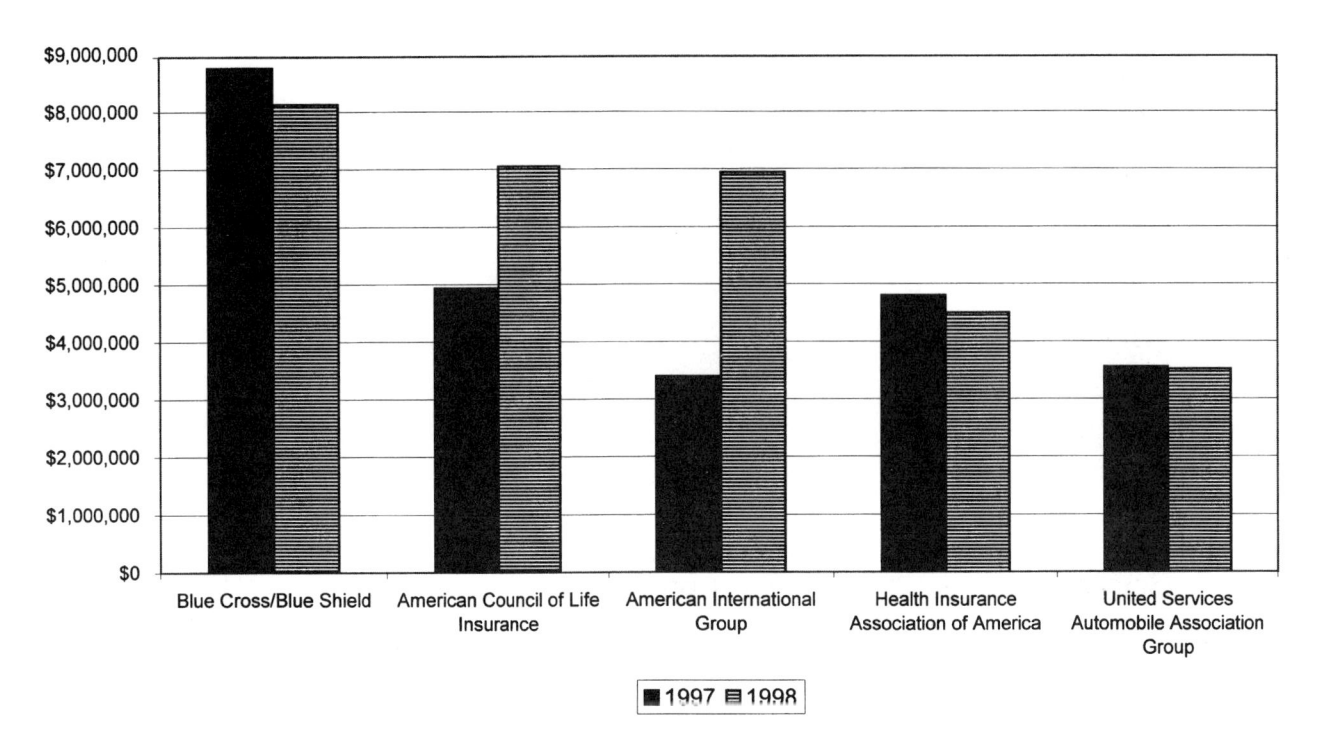

Top Oil and Gas Companies Lobbying Expenditures 1997–1998

COMPANY/ASSOCIATION	1998	1997
MOBIL OIL	$6,160,000	$5,240,000
EXXON	5,620,000	5,215,000
USX	4,300,000	4,060,000
TEXACO	4,229,000	5,629,000
SHELL OIL	3,720,000	2,940,800
ATLANTIC RICHFIELD	3,000,000	5,500,000
AMERICAN PETROLEUM INSTITUTE	2,982,000	3,680,000
CHEVRON	2,970,000	3,999,000
AMOCO	1,760,000	3,380,000
BP AMERICA	1,712,000	1,834,000

**Top 5 Oil and Gas Companies
Lobbying Expenditures
1997–1998**

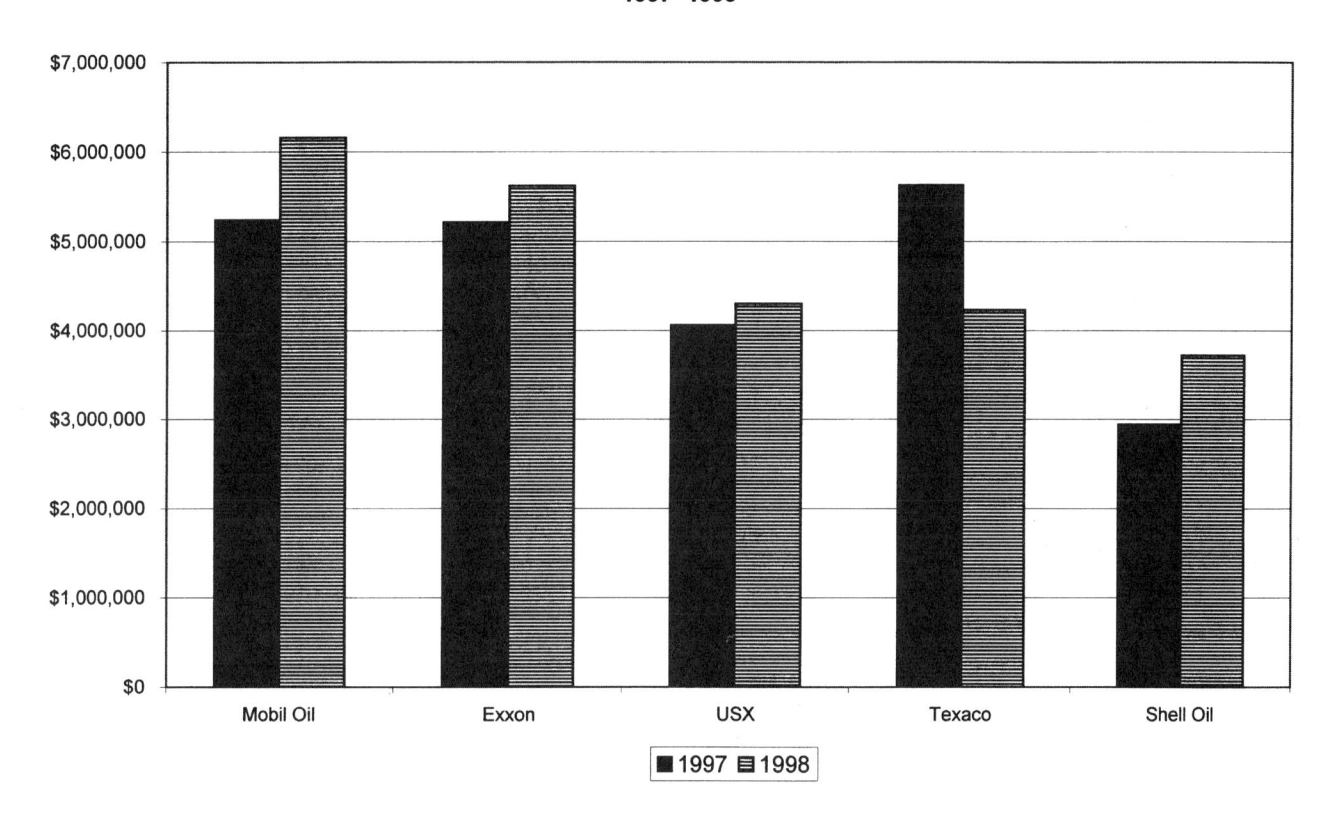

[Bar chart showing lobbying expenditures for Mobil Oil, Exxon, USX, Texaco, and Shell Oil for 1997 and 1998]

Top Pharmaceutical/Health Product Companies Lobbying Expenditures 1997–1998

COMPANY/ASSOCIATION	1998	1997
PFIZER	$8,000,000	$10,000,000
ELI LILLY	5,160,000	3,836,000
MERCK	5,000,000	5,140,000
SCHERING-PLOUGH	4,268,000	2,683,000
BIOTECHNOLOGY INDUSTRY ORGANIZATION	3,704,000	1,277,000
GLAXO WELLCOME	3,120,000	3,774,000
PHARMACEUTICAL RESEARCH & MANUFACTURERS OF AMERICA	3,120,000	6,320,000
BRISTOL-MYERS SQUIBB	2,821,000	3,780,000
SMITHKLINE BEECHAM	2,680,000	2,600,000
HEALTH INDUSTRY MANUFACTURERS ASSOCIATION	2,470,000	3,392,000

**Top 5 Pharmaceutical/Health Product Companies
Lobbying Expenditures
1997–1998**

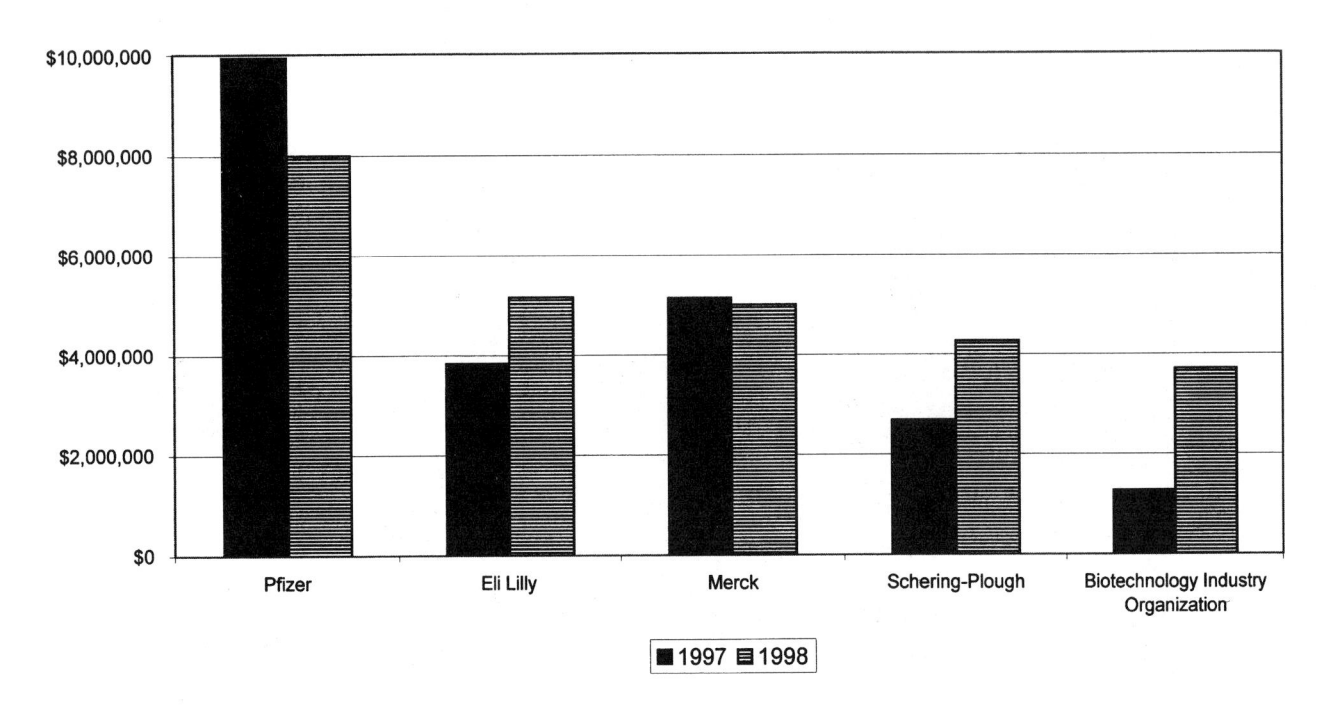

Top Single Issue/Identity Groups Lobbying Expenditures 1997–1998

COMPANY/ASSOCIATION	1998	1997
NATIONAL COMMITTEE TO PRESERVE SOCIAL SECURITY	$6,780,000	$7,660,000
SENIORS COALITION	6,290,000	6,183,000
AMERICAN ASSOCIATION OF RETIRED PERSONS	3,720,000	6,120,000
60 PLUS ASSOCIATION	3,000,000	2,500,000
CAMPAIGN FOR AMERICA	2,850,000	720,000
NATIONAL RIGHT TO WORK COMMITTEE	2,520,000	2,600,000
HUMANE SOCIETY OF THE UNITED STATES	1,200,000	820,000
MULTINATIONAL TAX COALITION	840,000	0
TAXPAYERS AGAINST FRAUD	800,000	40,000
ENGLISH FIRST	780,000	780,000

Top Tobacco Companies Lobbying Expenditures 1997–1998

COMPANY/ASSOCIATION	1998	1997
BRITISH AMERICAN TOBACCO	$25,180,000	$ 4,060,000
PHILIP MORRIS	23,000,000	15,800,000
RJR NABISCO	5,368,000	5,606,000
LOEWS	2,900,000	2,610,000
TOBACCO INSTITUTE	2,360,000	2,080,000
SMOKELESS TOBACCO COUNCIL	2,320,000	1,834,000
UST	2,110,000	920,000
BROOKE GROUP	1,880,000	780,000
CIGAR ASSOCIATION OF AMERICA	660,000	180,000
CONWOOD	560,000	200,000

Top 5 Tobacco Companies Lobbying Expenditures 1997–1998

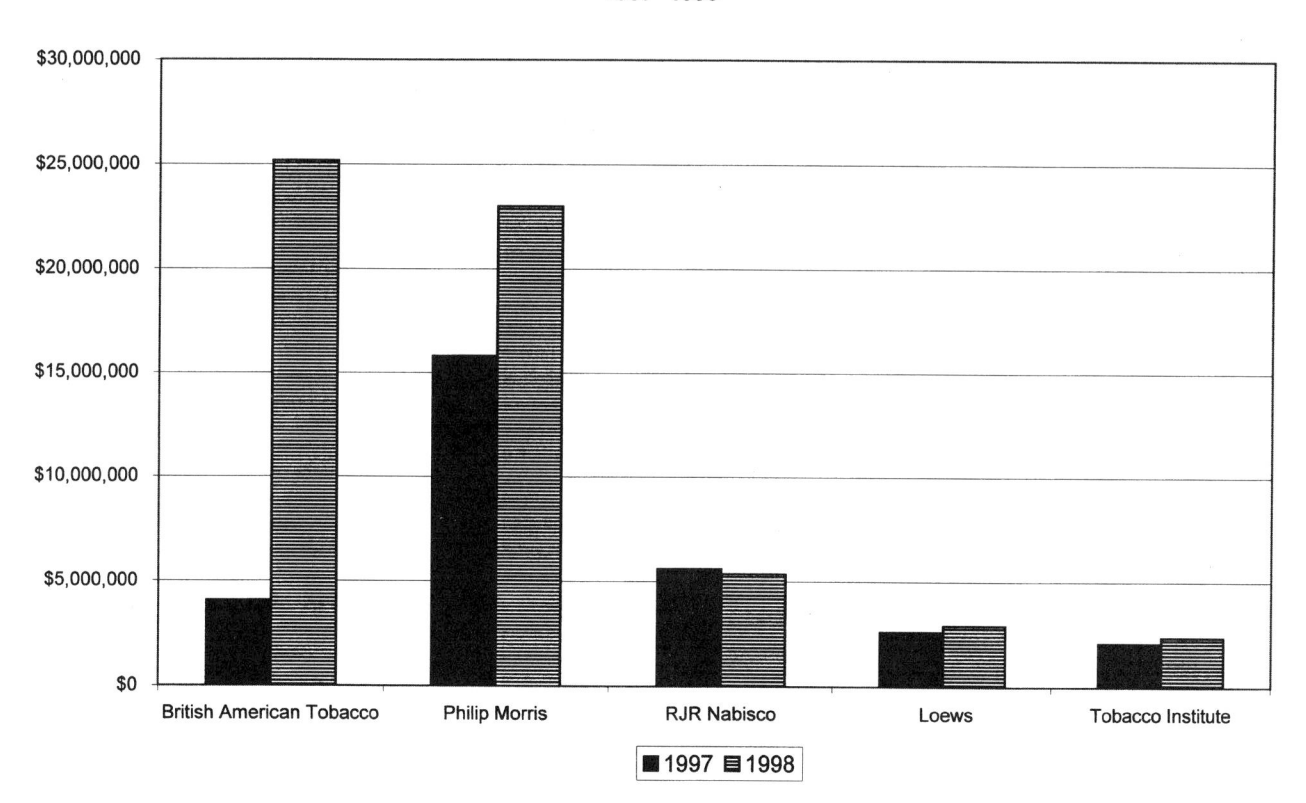

Top Corporations/Associations Lobbying Expenditures 1997–1998

CORPORATION/ASSOCIATION	INDUSTRY	1998	1997
BRITISH AMERICAN TOBACCO	TOBACCO	$25,190,000	$ 4,060,000
PHILIP MORRIS	TOBACCO	23,000,000	15,800,000
BELL ATLANTIC	TELEPHONE/UTILITIES	21,260,000	15,673,000
CHAMBER OF COMMERCE OF THE UNITED STATES	BUSINESS	17,000,000	14,240,000
AMERICAN MEDICAL ASSOCIATION	HEALTH PROFESSIONALS	16,820,000	17,280,000
FORD MOTOR	TRANSPORTATION	13,807,000	7,343,000
BUSINESS ROUNDTABLE	BUSINESS	11,640,000	9,480,000
EDISON ELECTRIC INSTITUTE	TELEPHONE/UTILITIES	11,020,000	10,020,000
AMERICAN HOSPITAL ASSOCIATION	HEALTH	10,520,000	7,880,000
BLUE CROSS/BLUE SHIELD	INSURANCE	9,172,000	8,762,000
CITIGROUP	BANKING/SECURITIES	8,710,000	9,040,000
BOEING	TRANSPORTATION	8,440,000	10,020,000
GENERAL MOTORS	TRANSPORTATION	8,415,000	10,600,000
PFIZER	PHARMACEUTICALS	8,000,000	10,000,000
AT&T	TELEPHONE/UTILITIES	7,740,000	7,800,000
SPRINT	TELEPHONE/UTILITIES	7,399,000	6,740,000
GENERAL ELECTRIC	MISCELLANEOUS MANUFACTURING	7,280,000	7,220,000
AMERITECH	TELEPHONE/UTILITIES	7,254,000	6,800,000
AMERICAN COUNCIL OF LIFE SURANCE	INSURANCE	7,050,000	4,935,000
AMERICAN INTERNATIONAL GROUP	INSURANCE	6,940,000	3,400,000
NATIONAL COMMITTEE TO PRESERVE SOCIAL SECURITY	SINGLE ISSUE	6,780,000	7,660,000
LOCKHEED MARTIN	DEFENSE	6,601,000	3,600,000
CHRISTIAN COALITION	IDEOLOGICAL	6,380,000	7,980,000
SENIORS COALITION	IDENTITY GROUP	6,290,000	6,183,000
DAIMLERCHRYSLER	TRANSPORTATION	6,280,000	4,340,000
MOBIL OIL	OIL AND GAS	6,160,000	5,240,000
NORTHROP GRUMMAN	DEFENSE	6,118,000	5,880,000
NATIONAL ASSOCIATION OF REALTORS	REAL ESTATE	6,040,000	6,320,000
CHASE MANHATTAN	BANKING/SECURITIES	5,920,000	4,140,000
EXXON	OIL AND GAS	5,620,000	5,215,000
IBM	COMPUTERS	5,552,000	5,240,000
FANNIE MAE	BANKING/SECURITIES	5,550,000	4,960,000

Top Corporations/Associations Lobbying Expenditures 1997–1998 (Cont.)

CORPORATION/ASSOCIATION	INDUSTRY	1998	1997
RJR NABISCO	TOBACCO	5,448,000	5,762,000
SBC COMMUNICATIONS	TELEPHONE/UTILITIES	5,280,000	6,220,000
NATIONAL ASSOCIATION OF BROADCASTERS	ENTERTAINMENT/MEDIA	5,200,000	4,680,000
AMERICAN BANKERS ASSOCIATION	BANKING/SECURITIES	5,196,000	4,148,000
ELI LILLY	PHARMACEUTICALS	5,160,000	3,836,000
MOTOROLA INC.	MISCELLANEOUS MANUFACTURING	5,153,000	5,660,000
MERCK	PHARMACEUTICALS	5,000,000	5,140,000
BELLSOUTH	TELEPHONE/UTILITIES	4,940,000	5,126,000
CHEMICAL MANUFACTURERS ASSOCIATION	MISCELLANEOUS MANUFACTURING	4,849,000	5,020,000
NATIONAL CABLE TELEVISION ASSOCIATION	ENTERTAINMENT/MEDIA	4,800,000	3,360,000
SECURITIES INDUSTRY ASSOCIATION	BANKING/SECURITIES	4,660,000	5,000,000
ASSOCIATION OF AMERICAN LROADS	TRANSPORTATION	4,580,000	5,790,000
BANK OF AMERICA	BANKING/SECURITIES	4,580,000	2,200,000
CELLULAR TELECOM INDUSTRY ASSOCIATION	TELEPHONE/UTILITIES	4,570,000	1,549,000
AMERICAN FARM BUREAU ERATION	AGRICULTURE	4,560,000	3,000,000
HEALTH INSURANCE ASSOCIATION OF AMERICA	INSURANCE	4,495,000	4,800,000
USX	OIL AND GAS	4,400,000	4,060,000
AMR (AMERICAN AIRLINES)	TRANPORTATION	4,320,000	5,638,000

Note: Industry affiliation concerns main business of company. For example, Boeing is involved in defense but most of its business concerns commercial aircraft.

**Top 5 Corporations/Associations
Lobbying Expenditures
1997–1998**

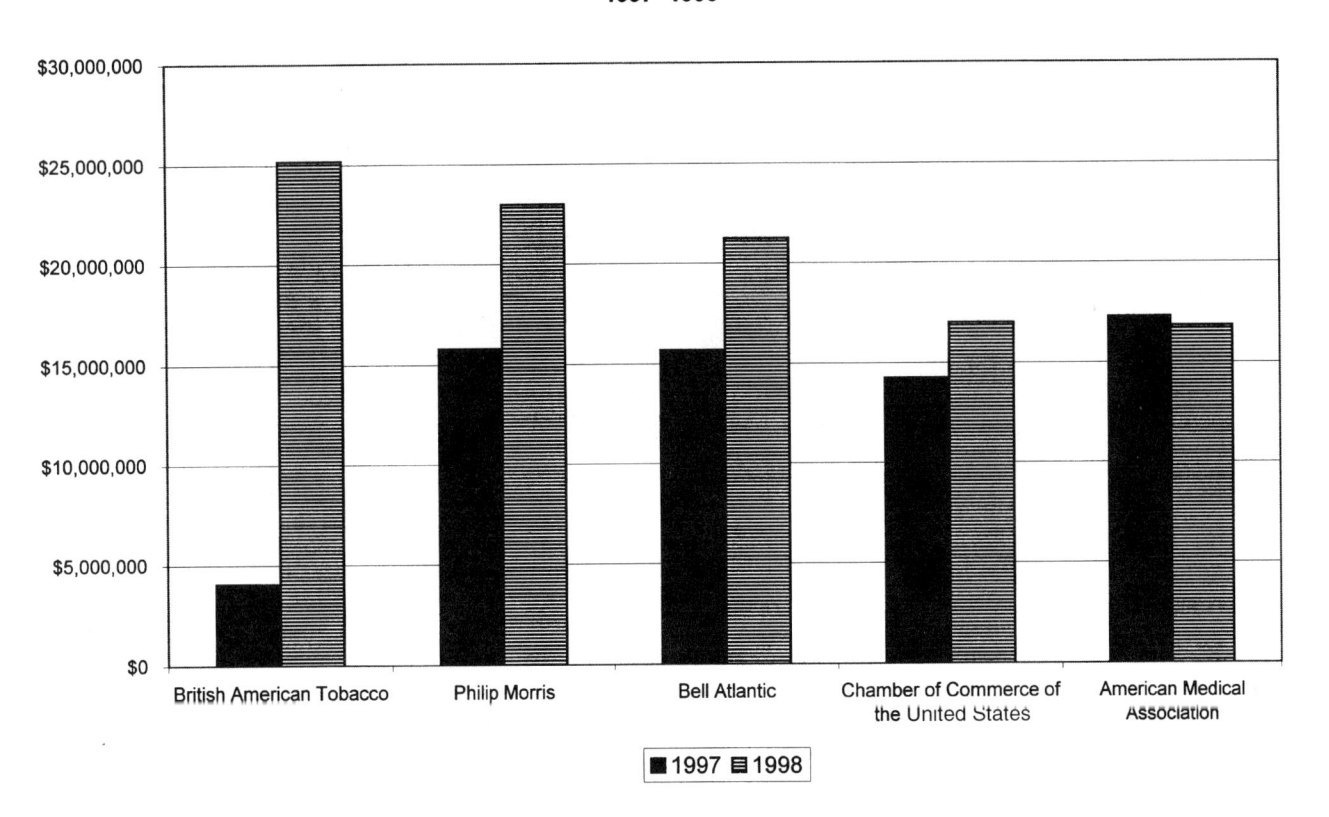

Top Industries—Lobbying Expenditures 1997–1998

INDUSTRY	1998	1997
INSURANCE COMPANIES	$77,206,908	$64,098,955
PHARMACEUTICAL/HEALTH PRODUCT COMPANIES	73,799,855	74,832,930
TELEPHONE COMPANIES	67,943,819	62,345,284
TOBACCO COMPANIES	67,367,172	38,240,340
ELECTRIC UTILITIES	63,666,873	54,785,778
OIL AND GAS COMPANIES	57,696,393	62,328,028
HEALTH PROFESSIONALS	45,839,289	43,233,423
BUSINESS ASSOCIATIONS	44,848,823	37,828,943
SINGLE ISSUE/IDENTITY GROUPS	39,744,183	37,434,551
COMPUTER COMPANIES	38,992,707	24,917,944
AIR TRANSPORT	38,659,484	33,853,401
AUTOMOTIVE	38,179,000	38,726,094
MISCELLANEOUS MANUFACTURING	35,848,576	37,932,955
GOVERNMENT AGENCIES	35,009,695	28,939,110
COMMERCIAL BANKS	32,995,164	29,823,287
ENTERTAINMENT/MEDIA INSTITUTIONS	29,685,424	27,687,454
EDUCATION	29,148,273	26,269,335
SECURITIES AND INVESTMENT	28,019,985	31,098,287
DEFENSE AEROSPACE	27,633,085	28,512,200
HOSPITALS/NURSING HOMES	26,348,997	23,228,170
REAL ESTATE	25,632,099	23,327,239
CHEMICAL AND RELATED MANUFACTURING	25,492,611	26,224,810
TELECOM SERVICES AND EQUIPMENT	25,284,839	18,426,976
FINANCE/CREDIT COMPANIES	20,669,850	10,424,222
AGRICULTURAL SERVICES/PRODUCTS	18,198,500	15,012,887
RAILROADS	16,550,950	17,958,527
HEALTH SERVICES	15,699,175	14,449,464
LAWYERS/LAW FIRMS	15,469,903	9,661,168
PRINTING AND PUBLISHING	13,102,867	8,917,462
CASINOS/GAMBLING	12,175,099	8,234,125
FORESTRY AND FOREST PRODUCTS	11,700,804	11,962,052
MISCELLANEOUS DEFENSE	11,478,417	11,058,353
FOOD PROCESSING AND SALES	11,044,518	9,431,655
HUMAN RIGHTS	10,772,841	9,555,021
ELECTRONICS MANUFACTURING AND SERVICES	10,602,773	8,781,160
DEFENSE ELECTRONICS	9,597,000	8,361,500

Top Industries—Lobbying Expenditures 1997–1998 (Cont.)

INDUSTRY	1998	1997
RETAIL SALES	9,487,041	7,605,224
MINING	9,229,100	8,803,100
MISCELLANEOUS TRANSPORTATION	8,938,698	7,678,848
SEA TRANSPORT	8,895,011	9,959,248
TRANSPORTATION UNIONS	8,657,900	5,873,980
REPUBLICAN/CONSERVATIVE	8,004,000	9,364,000
BUILDING MATERIALS AND EQUIPMENT	7,935,028	5,933,107
MISCELLANEOUS NONPROFIT INSTITUTIONS	7,547,735	6,760,679
BUSINESS SERVICES	7,541,124	6,010,899
BEER, WINE, AND LIQUOR	7,473,754	7,124,512
FOOD AND BEVERAGE	7,297,943	5,860,620
ACCOUNTING FIRMS/ASSOCIATIONS	6,676,297	7,645,000
CROP PRODUCTION AND BASIC PROCESSING	6,597,733	7,345,143
MISCELLANEOUS BUSINESS	6,122,250	4,788,076

**Top 5 Industries
Lobbying Expenditures
1997–1998**

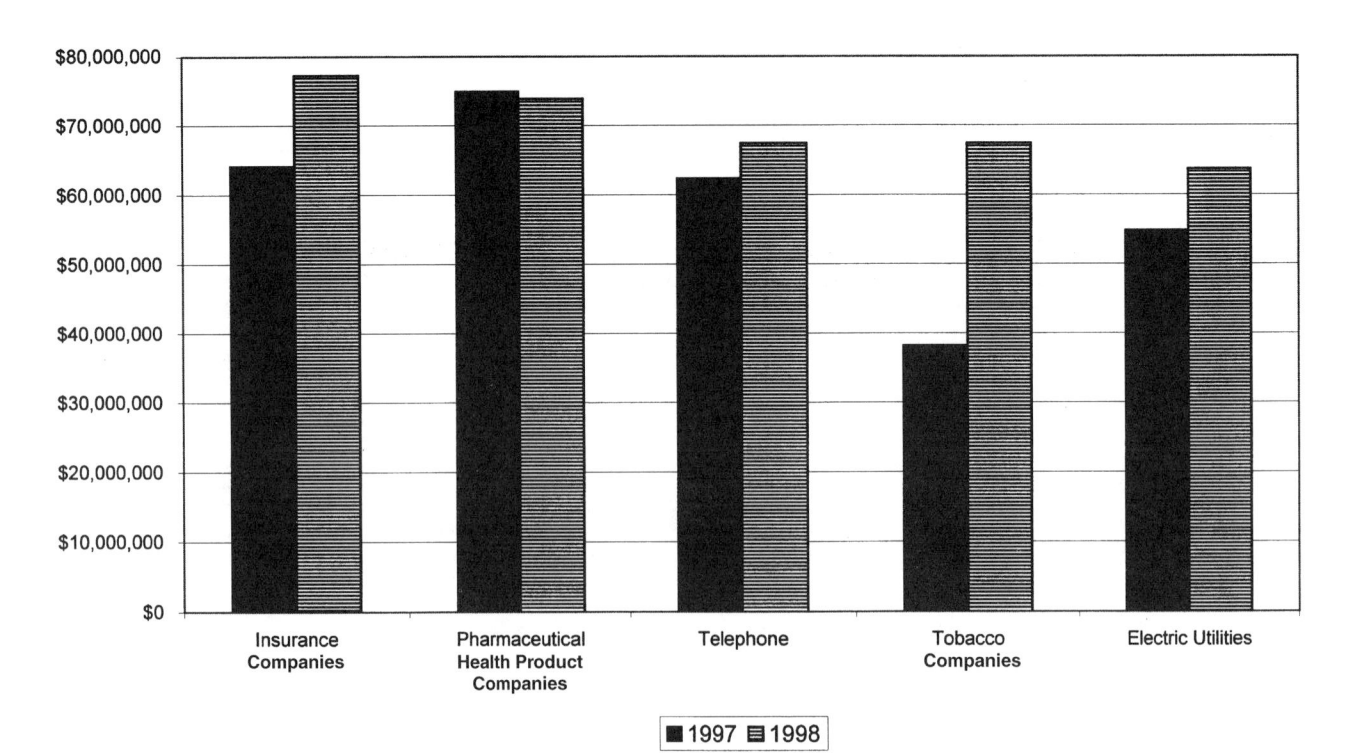

Top Telephone Companies/Utilities Lobbying Expenditures 1997–1998

COMPANY/ASSOCIATION	1998	1997
BELL ATLANTIC	$21,260,000	$14,300,000
EDISON ELECTRIC INSTITUTE	11,020,000	10,020,000
AT&T	7,740,000	7,800,000
SPRINT	7,399,000	6,740,000
AMERITECH	7,254,000	6,800,000
SBC COMMUNICATIONS	5,280,000	6,220,000
BELLSOUTH	4,940,000	5,125,700
GTE	4,200,000	3,880,000
FLORIDA POWER & LIGHT	3,220,000	2,180,000
ENTERGY	3,060,000	3,940,000
US WEST	3,020,000	4,100,000
MCI WORLDCOM	2,924,000	3,268,000
SOUTHERN	2,600,000	2,200,000
DTE ENERGY	2,514,000	2,610,000
PG&E	2,260,000	978,000
PACIFICORP	1,737,000	625,000
PUGET SOUND ENERGY	1,590,000	1,519,000
TEXAS UTILITIES	1,500,000	1,470,000
SOUTHERN CALIFORNIA EDISON	1,320,000	1,180,000
US TELEPHONE ASSOCIATION	1,320,000	1,100,000

Top Transportation Companies Lobbying Expenditures 1997–1998

COMPANY/ASSOCIATION	1998	1997
FORD MOTOR	$13,080,000	$6,880,000
BOEING	8,440,000	6,560,000
GENERAL MOTORS	7,360,000	9,300,000
DAIMLERCHRYSLER	6,280,000	4,340,000
AIR TRANSPORT ASSOCIATION OF AMERICA	3,820,000	2,570,000
AMERICAN AIRLINES	3,800,000	5,560,000
FEDERAL EXPRESS	3,320,000	3,300,000
NORTHWEST AIRLINES	2,880,000	2,251,000
DELTA AIRLINES	2,240,000	1,340,000
AMERICAN AUTOMOBILE MANUFACTURERS ASSOCIATION	2,200,000	9,916,000
UNITED AIRLINES	1,660,000	1,200,000
UNITED PARCEL SERVICE	1,300,000	880,000
TOYOTA MOTOR SALES USA	1,200,000	720,000
HONDA NORTH AMERICA	1,043,000	846,000
GOODYEAR TIRE & RUBBER	900,000	820,000
CONTINENTAL AIRLINES	900,000	660,000
AMERICAN INTERNATIONAL AUTO DEALERS ASSOCIATION	900,000	600,000
AIRCRAFT OWNERS & PILOTS ASSOCIATION	800,000	940,000
ALLIANCE FOR RAIL COMPETITION	460,000	100,000
NATIONAL AUTO DEALERS ASSOCIATION	400,000	407,000

Top Lobbying Firms 1997–1998

LOBBYING FIRM	1998	1997
CASSIDY & ASSOCIATES	$19,890,000	$17,754,000
VERNER, LIIPFERT ET AL.	18,775,000	18,798,000
PATTON BOGGS LLP	14,390,000	9,980,000
AKIN, GUMP ET AL.	11,800,000	10,165,000
PRESTON, GATES ET AL.	10,150,000	9,517,000
BARBOUR, GRIFFITH & ROGERS	7,410,000	5,200,000
WASHINGTON COUNSEL	7,251,000	6,377,000
WILLIAMS & JENSEN	7,060,000	6,340,000
BAKER, DONELSON ET AL.	6,820,000	3,848,000
HOGAN & HARTSON	6,546,000	6,439,000
PRICEWATERHOUSECOOPERS	6,500,000	2,440,000
VAN SCOYOC ASSOCIATES	6,480,000	5,170,000
TIMMONS	5,940,000	5,260,000
PODESTA.COM	5,360,000	3,590,000
ALCALDE & FAY	4,720,000	3,653,000
ARNOLD & PORTER	4,660,000	2,860,000
DUTKO GROUP	4,632,000	4,177,000
BLACK, KELLY ET AL.	4,625,000	5,181,000
CAPITOL ASSOCIATES	4,350,000	3,690,000
MAYER, BROWN & PLATT	4,260,000	3,400,000
BOLAND & MADIGAN	4,200,000	3,800,000
GRIFFIN, JOHNSON ET AL.	4,180,000	5,290,000
MCDERMOTT, WILL & EMERY	4,109,000	3,568,000
ARTER & HADDEN	4,100,000	4,106,000
WEXLER GROUP	4,080,000	2,900,000

**Top 5 Lobbying Firms
Lobbying Expenditures
1997–1998**

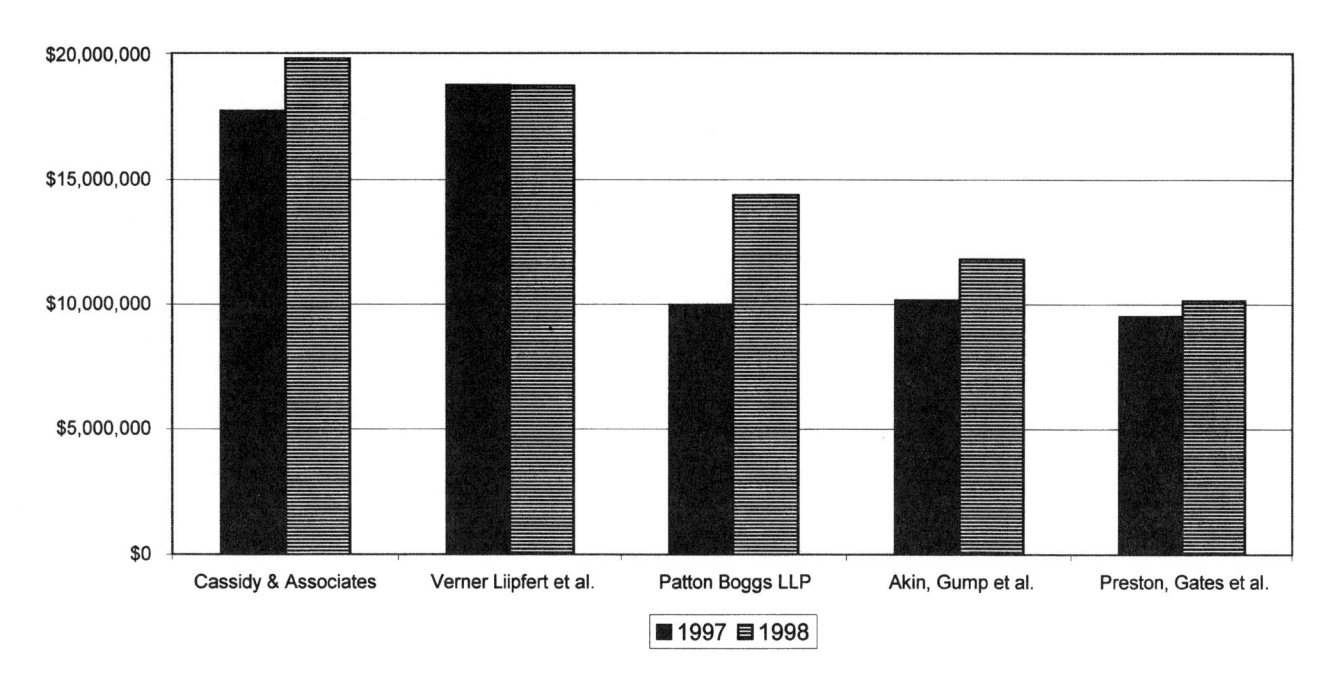

Top Clients of Top Lobbying Firms 1997–1998

LOBBYING FIRM	CLIENT	1998 RECEIPTS
CASSIDY & ASSOCIATES		
	BOSTON UNIVERSITY	$ 760,000
	HUNTON & WILLIAMS	720,000
	LINCOLN ELECTRIC	600,000
	UNITED SPACE ALLIANCE	460,000
	GENERAL DYNAMICS	440,000
	MONTEFIORE MEDICAL CENTER	440,000
	RUSH-PRESBYTERIAN-ST LUKES MEDICAL CENTER	440,000
	MERHAV GROUP OF COMPANIES	420,000
	BOEING	400,000
	NORTHWESTERN UNIVERSITY	400,000
VERNER, LIIPFERT ET AL.		
	PHILIP MORRIS	3,620,000
	RJR NABISCO	1,910,000
	BROWN & WILLIAMSON TOBACCO	1,260,000
	STARWOOD HOTELS & RESORTS WORLDWIDE	1,000,000
	LORILLARD	660,000
	AMERICAN FINANCIAL SERVICES ASSOCIATION	645,000
	NORTHWEST AIRLINES	520,000
	PUERTO RICO ECONOMIC DEVELOPMENT ADMINISTRATION	400,000
	PUERTO RICO INDUSTRIAL DEVELOPMENT	400,000
	SBC COMMUNICATIONS	340,000
PATTON BOGGS LLP		
	SMOKELESS TOBACCO COUNCIL	960,000
	ASSOCIATION OF TRIAL LAWYERS OF AMERICA	700,000
	MARS	700,000
	PACIFIC LUMBER & SHIPPING	380,000
	CHARLES E. SMITH COMPANIES	360,000
	INTERNATIONAL SWAPS & DERIVATIVES DEALERS ASSOCIATION	340,000
	DFS GROUP	280,000
	I-69 MID-CONTINENT HIGHWAY COALITION	240,000
	SIERRA MILITARY HEALTH SERVICE	240,000
	CFFE LLC	220,000

Top Clients of Top Lobbying Firms 1997–1998 (Cont.)

LOBBYING FIRM	CLIENT	1998 RECEIPTS
AKIN, GUMP ET AL.		
	CITIZENS EDUCATIONAL FOUNDATION	1,060,000
	MOBIL OIL	700,000
	MOTION PICTURE ASSOCIATION OF AMERICA	660,000
	MORTGAGE INSURANCE COMPANIES OF AMERICA	480,000
	AT&T	440,000
	METRO TRANSIT AUTHORITY OF HARRIS COUNTY, TEXAS	420,000
	AMERICAN LEGION	400,000
	AMERICAN AIRLINES	320,000
	MILLER & CHEVALIER	320,000
	AMERICA ONLINE	300,000
PRESTON, GATES ET AL.		
	MISSISSIPPI BAND OF CHOCTAW INDIANS	1,400,000
	COMMONWEALTH OF THE NORTHERN MARIANA ISLANDS	1,360,000
	PITNEY BOWES	800,000
	FUTURE OF PUERTO RICO	760,000
	MICROSOFT	600,000
	AMERICAN SEAFOODS	560,000
	AMERICAN CLASSIC VOYAGES	400,000
	NEPTUNE ORIENT LINES	400,000
	US MARITIME COALITION	400,000
	TATE & LYLE NORTH AMERICAN SUGARS	340,000

CONTACT INFORMATION

Section 1: Banking, Finance, Insurance, and Real Estate

American Bankers Association
1120 Connecticut Avenue NW
Washington, DC 20036
Phone: 202-663-5000
Fax: 202-828-4547
Website: www.aba.com

American Council of Life Insurance
1001 Pennsylvania Avenue NW, #500-S
Washington, DC 20004
Phone: 202-624-4000
Fax: 202-624-2319
Website: www.acli.com

Independent Insurance Agents of America
127 South Peyton Street
Alexandria, VA 22314
Phone: 703-683-4422
Fax: 703-683-7556
Website: www.iiaa.iix.com

Mortgage Bankers Association of America
1125 15th Street NW, #700
Washington, DC 20005
Phone: 202-861-6500
Fax: 202-861-0734
Website: www.mbaa.org

National Association of Independent Insurers
2600 River Road
Des Plaines, IL 60018
Phone: 847-297-7800
Fax: 847-297-5064
Website: www.naii.org

National Association of Professional Insurance Agents
400 North Washington Street
Alexandria, VA 22314
Phone: 703-836-9340
Fax: 703-836-1279
Website: www.pianet.com

National Association of Realtors
430 North Michigan Avenue
Chicago, IL 60611-4087
Phone: 312-329-8200
Fax: 312-329-8576
Website: www.realtor.com

Securities Industry Association
120 Broadway, 35th floor
New York, NY 10271
Phone: 212-608-1500
Fax: 212-608-1604
Website: www.sia.com

Section 2: Service, Trade, and Professional

American Bar Association
750 Lake Shore Drive
Chicago, IL 60611
Phone: 1-800-285-2221
Fax: 312-988-5528
Website: www.abanet.org

American Gaming Association
555 13th Street NW, #1010-E
Washington, DC 20004
Phone: 202-637-6500
Fax: 202-637-6507
Website: www.americangaming.org

American Hotel and Motel Association
1201 New York Avenue NW, #600
Washington, DC 20005
Phone: 202-289-3100
Fax: 202-289-3199
Website: www.ahma.com

American Library Association
50 East Huron Street
Chicago, IL 60611
Phone: 1-800-545-2433
Fax: 312-440-0901
Website: www.ala.org

American Association of Advertising Agencies
405 Lexington Avenue
New York, NY 10174
Phone: 212-682-2500
Fax: 212-682-8391
Website: www.aaaa.org

Association of Trial Lawyers of America
1050 31st Street NW
Washington, DC 20007
Phone: 202-965-3500
Fax: 202-342-5484
Website: www.atlanet.org

Food Marketing Institute
800 Connecticut Avenue NW, #500
Washington, DC 20006
Phone: 202-452-8444
Fax: 202-429-4519
Website: www.fmi.org

Fraternal Order of Police
1410 Donaldson Pike A-17
Nashville, TN 37217
Phone: 615-399-0900
Fax: 615-399-0400
Website: www.grandlodgefop.org

National Association of Convenience Stores
1605 King Street
Alexandria, VA 22314
Phone: 703-684-3600
Fax: 703-836-4564
Website: www.nacsnet.org

National Association of Retired
Federal Employees
606 North Washington Street
Alexandria, VA 22314
Phone: 703-838-7760
Fax: 703-838-7782
Website: www.narfe.org

National Association of Social Workers
750 1st Street NE, #700
Washington, DC 20002
Phone: 202-408-8600
Fax: 202-336-8310
Website: www.naswdc.org

National Automobile Dealers Association
8400 Westpark Drive
McLean, VA 22102-3591
Phone: 703-821-7000
Fax: 703-821-7075
Website: www.nadanet.com

National Beer Wholesalers Association
1100 South Washington Street
Alexandria, VA 22314
Phone: 703-683-4300
Fax: 703-683-8965

National Federation of Independent Business
600 Maryland Avenue SW, #700
Washington, DC 20024
Phone: 202-554-9000
Fax: 202-554-9496
Website: www.nfib.org

National Funeral Directors Association
11121 West Oklahoma Avenue
Milwaukee, WI 53227
Phone: 414-541-2500
Fax: 414-541-1909
Website: www.nfda.org

National Restaurant Association
1200 17th Street NW, #800
Washington, DC 20036
Phone: 202-331-5900
Fax: 202-331-2429
Website: www.restaurant.org

Petroleum Marketers Association of America
1901 Fort Myers Drive, #1200
Arlington, VA 22209
Phone: 703-351-8000
Fax: 703-351-9160
Website: www.pmaa.org

United States Chambers of Commerce
1615 H Street NW
Washington, DC 20062
Phone: 202-659-6000
Fax: 202-463-3190
Website: www.uschamber.com

Section 3: Media, Entertainment, and Information

Accuracy in Media
4455 Connecticut Avenue NW, #330
Washington, DC 20008
Phone: 202-364-4401
Fax: 202-364-4098
Website: www.aim.org

American Council on Education
One Dupont Circle NW
Washington, DC 20036
Phone: 202-939-9300
Fax: 202-833-4760
Website: www.ace.nche.edu

Association of American Publishers
71 Fifth Avenue
New York, NY 10003
Phone: 212-225-0200
Fax: 212-225-7007
Website: www.publishers.org

Fairness and Accuracy in Reporting
130 West 25th Street
New York, NY 10001
Phone: 212-633-6700
Fax: 212-727-7668
Website: www.fair.org

Magazine Publishers of America
919 Third Avenue, 22nd floor
New York, NY 10022
Phone: 212-872-3700
Fax: 212-888-4217
Website: www.magazine.org

Motion Picture Association of America
1600 I Street NW
Washington, DC 20006
Phone: 202-293-1966
Fax: 202-293-7410
Website: www.mpaa.org

National Association of Broadcasters
1771 N Street NW
Washington, DC 20036
Phone: 202-429-5300
Fax: 202-429-5343
Website: www.nab.org

National Cable Television Association
1724 Massachusetts Avenue, NW
Washington, DC 20036
Phone: 202-775-3550
Fax: 202-775-3695
Website: www.ncta.com

Newspaper Association of America
1921 Gallows Road, #600
Vienna, VA 22182
Phone: 703-902-1600
Website: www.naa.org

Recording Industry Association of America
1330 Connecticut Avenue NW, #300
Washington, DC 20036
Phone: 202-775-0101
Fax: 202-775-7253
Website: www.riaa.com

Software and Information Industry Association
1730 M Street NW, #700
Washington, DC 20036
Phone: 202-452-1600
Fax: 202-223-8756
Website: www.siia.net

Section 4: Health and Medical

American Academy of Ophthalmology
655 Beach Street
San Francisco, CA 94109
Phone: 415-561-8500
Fax: 415-561-8533
Website: www.eyenet.org

American Cancer Society
1599 Clifton Road
Atlanta, GA 30329
Phone: 1-800-227-2345
Website: www.cancer.org

American Chiropractic Association
1701 Clarendon Boulevard
Arlington, VA 22209
Phone: 703-276-8800
Fax: 703-243-2593
Website: www.amerchiro.org

American College of Emergency Physicians
P.O. Box 619911
Dallas, TX 75261-9911
Phone: 972-550-0911
Fax: 972-580-2816
Website: www.accp.org

American Dietetic Association
216 West Jackson Boulevard
Chicago, IL 60606
Phone: 312-899-0040
Fax: 312-899-1758
Website: www.eatright.org

American Federation for AIDS Research
120 Wall Street, 13th Floor
New York, NY 10005
Phone: 212-806-1600
Fax: 212-806-1601
Website: www.amfar.org

American Healthcare Association
1201 L Street NW
Washington, DC 20005
Phone: 202-842-4444
Fax: 202-842-3860

American Heart Association
National Center
7272 Greenville Avenue
Dallas, TX 75231
Phone: 1-800-242-8721
Website: www.americanheart.org

American Hospital Association
1 North Franklin Street
Chicago, IL 60606
Phone: 202-422-3000
Fax: 312-422-4700
Website: www.aha.org

American Medical Association
515 North State Street
Chicago, IL 60610
Phone: 312-464-5000
Fax: 312-464-4184
Website: www.ama-assn.org

American Nurses Association
600 Maryland Avenue SW, #100
Washington, DC 20024
Phone: 202-651-7000
Fax: 202-651-7001
Website: www.nursingworld.org

American Occupational Therapy Association
4720 Montgomery Lane, P.O. Box 31220
Rockville, MD 20824
Phone: 301-652-2682
Fax: 301-652-7711
Website: www.aota.org

American Psychiatric Association
1400 K Street NW, #300
Washington, DC 20005
Phone: 202-682-6000
Fax: 202-682-6114
Website: www.psych.org

American Society of Anesthesiologists
520 North Northwest Highway
Park Ridge, IL 60068
Phone: 708-825-5586
Fax: 708-825-1692
Website: www.asahq.org

Blue Cross and Blue Shield Association
225 North Michigan Avenue
Chicago, IL 60690
Phone: 312-440-6000
Fax: 312-440-6609
Website: www.bluecares.com

Section 5: Agriculture

American Farm Bureau Federation
225 Touhy Avenue
Park Ridge, IL 60068
Phone: 312-399-5700
Fax: 312-399-5896
Website: www.fb.com

American Meat Institute
1700 North Moore Street, #1600
Arlington, VA 22209
Phone: 703-841-2400
Fax: 703-527-0938
Website: www.meatami.org

American Sugarbeet Growers Association
1156 15th Street NW #1101
Washington, DC 20005
Phone: 202-833-2398
Website: www.member.aol.com/sugar.html

International Dairy Foods Association
1250 H Street NW
Washington, DC 20005
Phone: 202-296-4250
Fax: 202-331-7820
Website: www.idfa.org

National Association of Wheat Growers
415 2nd Street NE, #300
Washington, DC 20005
Phone: 202-547-7800
Fax: 202-546-2638
Website: www.wheatworld.org

National Cattlemen's Beef Association
5420 South Quebec Street, P.O. Box 3469
Englewood, CO 80155
Phone: 303-694-0305
Fax: 303-694-2851
Website: www.cowtown. org

National Chicken Council (formerly National Broiler Council)
1155 15th Street NW, #614
Washington, DC 20005
Phone: 202-296-2622
Fax: 202-293-4005
Website: www. eatchicken. com

National Cotton Council of America
1918 North Parkway
Memphis, TN 38112
Phone: 901-274-9030
Fax: 901-725-0510
Website: www.cotton. org

National Council of Farmer Cooperatives
50 F Street NW, #900
Washinton, DC 20001
Phone: 202-626-8700
Fax: 202-626-8722
Website: www.access. digex.net/~ncfc

National Farmers Organization
2505 Elwood Drive
Ames, IA 50010
Phone: 515-292-2000
Fax: 515-292-7106
Website: www.nfo.org

National Farmers Union
10065 East Harvard Avenue
Denver, CO 80231
Phone: 303-337-5500
Fax: 303-695-4518
Website: www.nfuic.com

National Grange
1616 H Street NW
Washington, DC 20006
Phone: 202-628-3507
Fax: 202-347-1091
Website: www.nationalgrange.org

National Pork Producers Council
1776 NW 114th Street
Clive, IA 50322
Phone: 515-223-2600
Fax: 515-223-5265
Website: www.nppc.org

Organic Trade Association
50 Miles Street
P.O. Box 1078
Greenfield, MA 01302
Phone: 413-774-7511
Fax: 413-774-6432
Website: www.ota.com

United Egg Association
1 Massachusetts Avenue NW, #800
Washington, DC 20001
Phone: 202-789-2499
Fax: 202-682-0775
Website: www.unitedegg.org

Section 6: Environment

Environmental Defense Fund
257 Park Avenue South
New York, NY 10010
Phone: 1-800-684-3322
Website: www.edf.org

Friends of the Earth
1025 Vermont Avenue NW, #300
Washington, DC 20005
Phone: 202-783-7400
Fax: 202-783-0444
Website: www.foe.org

Greenpeace
1436 U Street NW
Washington, DC 20009
Phone: 202-462-1177
Fax: 202-462-4507
Website: www.greenpeace.org

Izaak Walton League
707 Conservation Lane
Gathersburg, MD 20878
Phone: 301-548-0150
Fax: 301-548-1046
Website: www.iwla.org

League of Conservation Voters
1707 L Street NW, #550
Washington, DC 20036
Phone: 202-785-8683
Fax: 202-835-0491
Website: www.lcv.org

National Audubon Society
700 Broadway
New York, NY 10003
Phone: 212-979-3000
Website: www.audubon.org

National Wildlife Federation
8925 Leesburg Pike
Vienna, VA 22184
Phone: 703-790-4000
Website: www.nwf.org

Rainforest Action Network
221 Pine Street, #500
San Francisco, CA 94104
Phone: 415-398-4404
Fax: 415-398-2732
Website: www.ran.org

Sierra Club
730 Bush Street
San Francisco, CA 94109
Phone: 415-981-8634
Fax: 415-776-0350
Website: www.sierraclub.org

Wise Use Movement
Center for the Defense of Free Enterprise
12500 NE Tenth Place
Bellevue, WA 98005
Phone: 425-455-5038
Fax: 425-451-3959
Website: www.cdfe.org

Section 7: Industry, Construction, and Transport

Aerospace Industries Association
1250 "I" Street NW, #1200
Washington, DC 20005
Phone: 202-371-8400
Fax: 202-371-8470
Website: www.aia-aerospace.org

CONTACT INFORMATION

Air Transport Association
1301 Pennsylvania Avenue NW, #1100
Washington, DC 20004
Phone: 202-626-4000
Fax: 202-626-4081
Website: www.air-transport.org

American Forest and Paper Association
1111 19th Street NW, #800
Washington, DC 20036
Phone: 202-463-2700
Fax: 202-463-2785
E-mail: INFO@afandpa.org
Website: www.afandpa.org

American Furniture Manufacturers Association
918 16th Street NW, #402
Washington, DC 20036
Phone: 202-466-7362
Fax: 202-429-4915
Website: www.afmahp.org

American Textile Manufacturers Institute
1130 Connecticut Avenue NW, #1200
Washington, DC 20036
Phone: 202-862-0500
Fax: 202-862-0570
Website: www.atmi.org

American Trucking Associations
430 1st Street SE
Washington, DC 20003
Phone: 202-544-6245
Fax: 202-675-6568
Website: www.truckline.com

Associated Builders and Contractors
1300 North 17th Street
8th Floor
Arlington, VA 22209
Phone: 703-812-2000
Fax: 703-812-8203
Website: www.abc.org

Business Round Table
1615 L Street NW, #1100
Washington, DC 20036
Phone: 202-872-1260
Website: www.brtable.org

Chemical Manufacturers Association
1300 Wilson Blvd.
Arlington, VA 22209
Phone: 703-741-5000
Fax: 703-741-6000
Website: www.cmahq.com

Distilled Spirits Council of the U.S.
1250 "I" Street, #400
Washington, DC 20005
Phone: 202-628-3544
Fax: 202-682-8888
Website: www.discus.health.org

Edison Electric Institute
701 Pennsylvania Avenue NW
Washington, DC 20004
Phone: 202-508-5000
Fax: 202-508-5794
Website: www.eei.org

National Association of Home Builders
1201 15th Street NW
Washington, DC 20005
Phone: 202-822-0200
Fax: 202-822-0559
Website: www.nahb.com

National Association of Manufacturers
1331 Pennsylvania Avenue NW
Washington, DC 20004-1790
Phone: 202-637-3000
Fax: 202-637-3182
E-mail: manufacturing@nam.org
Website: www.nam.org

National Mining Association
1130 17th Street NW
Washington, DC 20036
Phone: 202-463-2625
Fax: 202-463-6152
Website: www.nma.org

Nuclear Energy Institute
1776 "I" Street, #400
Washington, DC 20006
Phone: 202-739-8000
Fax: 202-785-4019
Website: www.nei.org

Pharmaceutical Research and Manufacturers
of America
1100 15th Street NW, #900
Washington, DC 20005
Phone: 202-835-3400
Fax: 202-835-3413
Website: www.phrma.org

Printing Industries of America
100 Daingerfield Road
Arlington, VA 22314
Phone: 703-519-8100
Fax: 703-548-3227
Website: www.printing.org

Semiconductor Industry Association
181 Metro Drive, #450
San Jose, CA 95110
Phone: 408-436-6600
Fax: 408-436-6646
Website: www.semichips.org

The Technology Network
101 University Avenue, #240
Palo Alto, CA 94301
Phone: 650-463-1510
Fax: 650-463-1501
Website: www.technetwork.org

Section 8: Labor

Air Line Pilots Association
535 Herndon Parkway
Herndon, VA 22070
Phone: 703-689-2270
Fax: 703-689-4370
Website: www.alpa.org

American Federation of Labor-Congress
of Industrial Organizations (AFL-CIO)
815 16th Street NW
Washington, DC 20006
Phone: 202-637-5000
Fax: 202-637-5058
Website: www.aflcio.org

American Federation of State, County
and Municipal Employees (AFSCME)
1625 "L" Street NW
Washington, DC 20036
Phone: 202-429-1000
Fax: 202-429-1293
Website: www.afscme.org

American Federation of Teachers
555 New Jersey Avenue NW, #1000
Washington, DC 20001
Phone: 202-879-4400
Fax: 202-879-4556
Website: www.aft.org

American Postal Workers Union
1300 "L" Street NW
Washington, DC 20005
Phone: 202-842-4200
Fax: 202-842-4297
Website: www.apwu.org

Communications Workers of America
501 3rd Street NW, #1102
Washington, DC 20001
Phone: 202-434-1320
Fax: 202-434-1318
Website: www.cwa-union.org

Hotel Employees and Restaurant Employees
International Union
1219 28th Street NW
Washington, DC 20007
Phone: 202-393-4373
Fax: 202-333-0468
Website: www.hereunion.org

International Association of Fire Fighters
1750 New York Avenue NW, #300
Washington, DC 20006
Phone: 202-737-8484
Fax: 202-737-8418
Website: www.iaff.org

International Association of Machinists and
Aerospace Workers
9000 Machinists Place
Upper Marlboro, MD 20772
Phone: 301-967-4500
Fax: 301-967-4586
Website: www.iamaw.org

International Brotherhood of Electrical Workers
1125 15th Street NW
Washington, DC 20005
Phone: 202-833-7000
Fax: 202-728-6316
Website: www.ibew.org

International Brotherhood of Teamsters
25 Louisiana Avenue NW
Washington, DC 20001
Phone: 202-624-6800
Fax: 202-624-2918
Website: www.teamster.org

International Union of Operating Engineers
1125 17th Street NW
Washington, DC 20036
Phone: 202-429-9100
Website: www.iuoe.org

Laborers' International Union of
North America
905 16th Street NW
Washington, DC 20006
Phone: 202-942-2246
Fax:202-638-4398
Website: www.liuna.org

National Education Association
1201 16th Street NW
Washington, DC 20036
Phone: 202-822-7300
Fax: 202-822-7292
Website: www.nea.org

Seafarers International Union
of North America
5201 Auth Way
Camp Springs, MD 20746
Phone: 301-899-0675
Fax: 301-899-7355
Website: www.seafarers.org

Service Employees International Union
1313 L Street NW
Washington, DC 20005
Phone: 202-898-3200
Fax: 202-898-3438
Website: www.seiu.org

Transport Workers Union of America
80 West End Avenue, 6th floor
New York, NY 10023
Phone: 212-873-6000
Fax: 212-724-5826
Website: www.twu.org

Union of Needletrades, Industrial, and
Textile Employees
1710 Broadway
New York, NY 10019
Phone: 212-265-7000
Fax: 212-265-3415
Website: www.uniteunion.org

United Automobile Workers
8000 East Jefferson Avenue
Detroit, MI 48214
Phone: 313-926-5200
Fax: 313-824-5750
Website: www.uaw.org

United Food and Commercial Workers Union
1775 "K" Street NW
Washington, DC 20036
Phone: 202-223-3111
Fax: 202-466-1462
Website: www.ufcw.org

United Steelworkers of America
5 Gateway Center
Pittsburgh, PA 15222
Phone: 412-562-2442
Fax: 412-562-2445
Website: www.uswa.org

United Transportation Union
14600 Detroit Avenue
Cleveland, OH 44107
Phone: 216-228-9400
Fax: 216-228-5755
Website: www.utu.org

Section 9: Civil and Human Rights

ACORN
21015 Main Street
Little Rock, AR 72204
Phone: 501-376-7151
Fax: 501-376-3952
Website: www.acorn.org

American Civil Liberties Union
125 Broad Street, 18th Floor
New York, NY 10004-2400
Phone: 212-549-2500
Website: www.aclu.org

Anti-Defamation League
823 United Nations Plaza
New York, NY 10017
Phone: 212-889-7970
Website: www.adl.org

Freedom House
1319 18th Street NW
Washington, DC 20036
Phone: 202-296-5101
Fax: 202-296-5078
Website: www.freedomhouse.org

Human Rights Watch
350 Fifth Avenue, 34th Floor
New York, NY 10118
Phone: 212-290-4700
Fax: 212-736-1300
Website: www.hrw.org

League of Women Voters of
the United States
1730 M Street NW
Washington, DC 20036
Phone: 202-429-1965
Fax: 202-429-0854
Website: www.lwv.org

Legal Services Corporation
750 First Street NE, 10th Floor
Washington, DC 20002-4250
Phone: 202-336-8800
Website: www.ltsi.net/lsc.html

National Coalition for the Homeless
1012 14th Street NW, #600
Washington, DC 20005
Phone: 202-737-6444
Fax: 202-737-6445
Website: www.nch.ari.net

National Lawyers Guild
126 University Place, 5th Floor
New York, NY 10003
Phone: 212-627-2656
Fax: 212-627-2404
Website: www.nlg.org

Section 10: Political, Religious, and Ideological

American Conservative Union
1007 Cameron Street
Alexandria, VA 22314
Phone: 703-836-8602
Fax: 703-836-8606
Website: www.conservative.org

American Enterprise Institute
1150 Seventeenth Street NW
Washington, DC 20036
Phone: (202) 862-5800
Fax. (202) 862-7178
Website: www.aei.org

Americans for Democratic Action
8124 West Third, #102
Los Angeles, CA 90048
Phone: 323-651-4440
Website: www.411web.com

Americans for Tax Reform
1320 18th Street NW, #200
Washington, DC 20036
Phone: 202-785-0266
Fax: 202-785-0261
Website: www.townhall.com/atr

Brookings Institution
1775 Massachusetts Avenue NW
Washington, DC 20036
Phone: 202-797-6000
Fax: 202-797-6004
Website: www.brook.edu

Cato Institute
1000 Massachusetts Avenue NW
Washington, DC 20001-5403
Phone: 202-842-0200
Fax: 202-842-3490
Website: www.cato.org

Center for Public Integrity
910 17th Street NW
7th Floor
Washington, DC 20006
Phone: 202-466-1300
Website: www.publicintegrity.org

Center for Responsive Politics
1320 19th Street NW, #620
Washington, DC 20036
Phone: 202-857-0044
Fax: 202-857-7809
Website: www.opensecrets.org

Christian Coalition
1801-L Sara Drive
Chesapeake, VA 23320
Phone: 757-424-2630
Fax: 757-424-9068
Website: www.cc.org

Citizens for a Sound Economy
1250 H Street NW, #700
Washington, DC 20005
Phone: 202-783-3870
Fax: 202-783-4687
Website: www.cse.org

Economic Policy Institute
1660 L Street NW, #1200
Washington, DC 20036
Phone: 202-775-8810
Website: www.epinet.org

Heritage Foundation
214 Massachusetts Avenue NE
Washington, DC 20002-4999
Phone: 202-546-4400
Fax: 202-546-8328
Website: www.heritage.org

Hudson Institute
Washington DC Office
1015 18th Street, #300
Washington, DC 20036
Phone: 202-223-7770
Fax: 202-223-8537
Website: www.hudson.org

John Birch Society
P.O. Box 8040
Appleton, WI 54912
Phone: 920-749-3780
Fax: 920-749-5062
Website: www.jbs.org

National Council of the Churches of Christ
475 Riverside Drive
New York, NY 10115
Phone: 212-870-2227
Fax: 212-870-2030
Website: www.ncccusa.org

National Taxpayers Union
108 North Alfred Street
Alexandria, VA 22314
Phone: 703-683-5700
Fax: 703-683-5722
Website: www.ntu.org

Public Citizen
1600 20th Street NW
Washington, DC 20009
Phone: 202-588-1000
Website: www.citizen.org

United States Catholic Conference
3211 4th Street NE
Washington, DC 20017
Phone: 202-541-3000
Website: www.nccbuscc.org

U.S. Public Interest Research Group
218 D Street SE
Washington, DC 20003
Phone: 202-546-9707
Fax: 202-546-2461
Website: www.pirg.org

Section 11: Single Issue

Americans United for the Separation of Church and State
518 C Street NE
Washington, DC 20002
Phone: 202-466-3234
Fax: 202-466-2587
Website: www.au.org

Citizens Flag Alliance
P.O. Box 7197
Indianapolis, IN 46207
Phone: 317-630-1384
Fax: 317-630-1385
Website: www.cfa-inc.org

Council for a Livable World
20 Park Plaza
Boston, MA 02116
Phone: 617-542-2282
Fax: 617-542-6695
Website: www.clw.org

Handgun Control
1225 I Street NW, #1100
Washington, DC 20005
Phone: 202-898-0792
Fax: 202-371-9615
Website: www.handguncontrol.org

Mothers Against Drunk Driving
P.O. Box 541688
Dallas, TX 75354
Phone: 1-800-438-6233
Website: www.madd.org

National Abortion and Reproductive Rights Action League
1156 15th Street NW, #700
Washington, DC 20005
Phone: 202-973-3000
Website: www.naral.org

National Committee to Preserve Social Security and Medicare
2000 K Street NW, 8th Floor
Washington, DC 20006
Phone: 202-822-9459
Fax: 202-822-9619
Website: www.ncpssm.org

National Rifle Association
11250 Waples Mill Road
Fairfax, VA 22030
Phone: 703-267-1000
Fax: 703-352-6408
Website: www.nra.org

National Right to Life Committee
419 7th Street NW, #500
Washington, DC 20004
Phone: 202-626-8820
Website: www.nrlc.org

People for the Ethical Treatment of Animals
501 Front Street
Norfolk, VA 23510
Phone: 757-622-7382
Fax: 757-622-0457
Website: www.peta-online.org

Planned Parenthood Federation of America
810 Seventh Avenue
New York, NY 10019
Phone: 212-541-7800
Fax: 212/245-1845
Website: www.plannedparenthood.org

Union of Concerned Scientists
Two Brattle Square
Cambridge, MA 02238
Phone: 617-547-5552
Fax: 617-864-9405
Website: www.ucsusa.org

U.S. English
1747 Pennsylvania Avenue NW, #1100
Washington, DC 20006-4604
Phone: 202-833-0100
Fax: 202-833-0108
Website: www.us-english.org

U.S. Term Limits
10 G Street NE, #410
Washington, DC 20005
Phone: 202-379-3000
Fax: 202-379-3010
Website: www.termlimits.org

Zero Population Growth
1400 Sixteenth Street NW, #320
Washington, DC 20036
Phone: 202-332-2200
Fax: 202-332-2302
Website: www.zpg.org

Section 12: Identity Groups

American Association of Retired Persons
601 E Street NW
Washington, DC 20049
Phone: 1-800-424-3410
Website: www.aarp.org

American Indian Movement
P.O. Box 13521
Minneapolis, MN 55414
Phone: 612-721-3914
Fax: 612-721-7826
Website: www.aimovement.org

American Legion
700 North Pennsylvania Street
P.O. Box 1055
Indianapolis, IN 46206
Phone: 317-630-1200
Fax: 317-630-1223
Website: www.legion.org

Congress of Racial Equality
817 Broadway, 3rd Floor
New York, NY 10003
Phone: 212-598-4000
Fax: 212-598-4141
Website: www.coreonline.org

Emily's List
805 15th Street NW, #400
Washington, DC 20005
Phone: 202-326-1400
Fax: 202-326-1415
Website: www.emilyslist.org

Human Rights Campaign
1101 14th Street NW, #1000
Washington, DC 20005
Phone: 202-628-4160
Fax: 202-347-5323
Website: www.hrcusa.org

National Association of the Advancement of Colored People
1025 Vermont Street NW, #1120
Washington, DC 20005
Phone: 202-638-2269
Website: www.naacp.org

National Gay and Lesbian Task Force
2320 175th Street NW
Washington, DC 20009
Phone: 202-332-6438
Fax: 202-332-0207
Website: www.ngltf.org

National Organization of Women
1000 16th Street NW, #700
Washington, DC 20036
Phone: 202-331-0066
Fax: 202-785-8576
Website: www.now.org

GLOSSARY

A

Accuracy in Media. Conservative media watchdog group.

Advertising Council. Public service association of the advertising industry.

Airline Pilots Association. International union representing airline pilots in the United States.

America's Community Bankers. Formerly the Community Bankers of America, a trade association representing savings and loan associations, mutual savings banks, cooperative banks, and other financial institutions that are not commercial banks or credit unions.

American Bankers Association. Interest group representing commercial banks and trust companies.

American Council of Life Insurance. Umbrella trade association for life insurance companies in the United States.

American Enterprise Institute. Conservative think tank.

American Farm Bureau Federation. Founded in 1920 with the support of land-grant colleges, the organization is the largest agricultural general interest group in the United States. Although the federation is a national organization, most of its membership is rooted in the Midwest and South.

American Federation of Labor—Congress of Industrial Organizations. Leading national federation of American labor unions.

American Federation of State, County, and Municipal Employees. International union representing state, county, and municipal public service workers in the United States.

American Federation of Teachers. The second largest international teachers union in the United States.

American Financial Services Association. National trade association for the financial services industry.

American Gaming Association. Trade association for the gambling industry.

American Healthcare Association. Leading trade association for the nursing home industry.

American Institute of Certified Public Accountants. Professional association of accountants certified by the states and territories to practice accounting.

American Legion. Major organization of American veterans.

American Postal Workers Union. Largest postal workers union in the United States.

Americans for Democratic Action. Liberal advocacy and lobbying organization.

amicus curiae. "Friend of the court," referring to briefs presented by interest groups in support of a specific cause during a case on trial.

B

Blue Cross and Blue Shield. Nation's largest federation of nonprofit health insurers.

Brookings Institution. Centrist think tank.

C

Cato Institute. Libertarian think tank.

Center for Public Integrity. Progressive research and advocacy organization that investigates lobbyist and corporate influence over the federal government, among other issues.

Center for Responsive Politics. Progressive research organization that researches and publicizes campaign contributions.

Christian Coalition International. Lobbying and political action committee arm of the Christian Coalition.

Christian Coalition. Conservative and fundamentalist advocacy organization; recently, under pressure from government, the group was forced to form a separate lobbying arm, the Christian Coalition International.

Citizens Flag Alliance. Conservative interest group promoting a constitutional amendment to ban desecration of the American flag.

Citizens for a Sound Economy. Conservative think tank and advocacy organization that backs market solutions to public policy issues.

Commodity Credit Corporation. U.S.-government-owned corporation founded in 1933 by President Franklin Roosevelt that allowed farmers to use their farms as collateral to obtain government loans. The organization was incorporated in 1948.

Common Cause. Progressive lobbying and advocacy organization that emphasizes more open and accountable government policies.

Communications Act. 1934 legislation defining government role in regulating airwaves; superseded by Telecommunications Act of 1996.

Communications Workers of America. Largest international union representing workers in the American telecommunication industry.

Congress of Racial Equality. Conservative civil rights organization.

Copyright Act. 1978 legislation protecting copyrights on written materials; passed in response to widespread use of photocopying machines.

Council for a Livable World. Organization dedicated to ridding the world of weapons of mass destruction and protecting the environment.

Credit Union National Association. Federal trade association that represents local credit unions.

D

Department of Health and Human Services. Federal agency in charge of health and welfare issues.

Dietary Reference Intakes. Proposed federal standard for the dietary content of foods, recommended by American Dietetic Association.

E

Economic Policy Institute. A pro-labor think tank that focuses on economic issues.

Emily's List. Organization established in 1985 to promote and fund the campaigns of Democratic, pro-choice women candidates for federal office.

Environmental Defense Fund. Interest group that monitors and promotes environmental protection.

Environmental Protection Agency. Federal agency seeking to safeguard the environment by monitoring industrial and consumer pollution and enforcing regulations.

F

Fairness and Accuracy in Reporting. Progressive media watchdog group.

Federal Communications Commission. Federal agency that regulates private and public interstate, national, and international broadcasting, telephone, and communications.

Federal Reserve Board. Federal agency that regulates U.S. money supply and other financial affairs.

Federal Trade Commission. Federal agency that regulates trade and business.

Food and Drug Administration. Federal agency that oversees and regulates the commercial marketing of food and drug products.

G

General Agreement on Tariffs and Trade. International negotiations for promoting free trade. The series of negotiations, known as rounds, began in 1947 and culminated in the creation of the World Trade Organization in 1995.

Glass-Steagall Act. Federal law passed in 1932 to separate the banking, insurance, and securities industries.

H

Healthcare Financing Administration. Federal agency that regulates and oversees the health insurance industry.

Heritage Foundation. Conservative think tank.

Higher Education Act. 1965 legislation establishing federal grants, loans, and fellowships for higher education.

Hotel Employees and Restaurant Employees International Union. International union that represents workers employed in the hospitality industry in the United States and Canada.

Hudson Institute. Conservative think tank.

Human Rights Campaign. Largest gay and lesbian advocacy organization in America.

I

Independent Community Bankers of America. Association representing small and mid-sized community banks in the United States.

Independent Insurance Agents of America. Association representing insurance sales agents who sell all types of insurance offered by multiple insurance companies.

Individual Retirement Accounts. Tax-free individual pension savings plans created by the federal government.

International Association of Fire Fighters. International union representing firefighters in the United States.

International Association of Machinists and Aerospace Workers. International union representing workers in the machine tool, metals, aerospace, and spacecraft industries in the United States and Canada.

International Brotherhood of Electrical Workers. International union representing workers employed in electrical, building trades, and communications industries.

International Brotherhood of Teamsters. Union representing workers employed in the trucking and distribution industries in the United States and Canada.

International Monetary Fund. Created in 1944 by Allied powers in the Bretton Woods Conference as a funding vehicle to assist indebted countries in meeting balance of payment problems. To receive funding, the IMF requires debtor countries to meet strict spending and monetary requirements.

International Union of Operating Engineers. Union representing workers employed in maintenance, mechanics, and operation of heavy equipment—particularly in the construction industry.

Investment Company Act. Federal legislation passed in 1940 that provided protections for investors in mutual funds and closed-end investment companies.

Investment Company Institute. National trade association for mutual fund and closed-end investment companies.

Izaak Walton League. Interest group that promotes environmental and wilderness conservation.

J–L

John Birch Society. Conservative, anti-communist advocacy group.

Laborers' International Union of North America. Union representing workers employed in construction and a litany of other industries in the United States and Canada.

Land Grant Universities. Created by the Morrill Act of 1862 to teach agricultural and mechanical sciences. Land grant universities are primarily state-supported institutions.

League of Conservation Voters. Interest group promoting environmental protection.

M

McCarran-Ferguson Act. Federal law passed in 1947 that assigned the regulation of insurance to state governments.

Medicaid. State-administered, federally financed healthcare program for the poor.

Medicare. Federal healthcare program for the disabled and elderly.

Mortgage Bankers Association of America. Trade association representing the real estate finance industry.

N

National Association for the Advancement of Colored People. Oldest and largest civil rights organization in America.

National Association of Independent Insurers. Trade association representing independent property and casualty insurance companies.

National Association of Insurance Commissioners. Association of chief insurance regulatory officials.

National Association of Life Underwriters. Federation of state and local associations of life and health insurance sales professionals.

National Association of Professional Insurance Agents. Trade association representing independent insurance agents and their employees who specialize in auto, home, and business insurance.

National Association of Realtors. National trade association of professional realtors.

National Audubon Society. Organization that promotes the protection and expansion of wilderness and open-space habitats of birds.

National Council of Churches of Christ. Liberal advocacy group that represents mainstream Protestant churches.

National Education Association. Largest union in the United States, representing teachers and educators.

National Endowment for the Humanities. Federal agency that funds the humanities and arts.

National Gay and Lesbian Task Force. Main gay and lesbian interest group promoting pro-gay and lesbian legislation and candidates.

National Grange. Founded in 1867, the oldest farmers' educational and political organization in America.

National Labor Relations Act. 1935 law also known as the Wagner Act that dramatically expanded trade unions' legal rights to organize workers in America.

National Rifle Association. Organization dedicated to preventing gun control legislation and defending the Second Amendment to the Constitution.

National Right to Life Committee. Largest organization dedicated to outlawing abortions.

National Taxpayers Union. Conservative lobbying organization that pushes for lower taxes.

National Venture Capital Association. Trade organization of corporate financiers, venture capital groups, and individual venture capitalists who invest private capital in growth-oriented companies.

North American Free Trade Agreement. 1994 pact allowing for freer trade between Canada, Mexico, and the United States.

O–P

Office of the Controller of the Currency. A U.S. Treasury Department office responsible for regulating the banking industry.

Patients' Bill of Rights. Proposed federal and/or state laws guaranteeing specific rights to health insurance customers, most notably, the right to sue health maintenance organizations and health insurers for denial of services.

People for the Ethical Treatment of Animals. Organization dedicated to stopping the use of animals for scientific and commercial experimentation, banning fur in clothing, and promoting vegetarianism.

Planned Parenthood Federation of America. Reproductive rights advocacy organization that runs birth control clinics.

Political Action Committee. Funding mechanisms established by interest groups and parties to raise money for candidates running for office.

Preferred Provider Organization. Private healthcare programs in which patients choose their own doctors.

Pro-Choice. Supporting the right of women to choose an abortion.

Pro-Life. Opposing the right of women to choose an abortion.

Public Citizen. Progressive, consumer-oriented advocacy organization.

R–S

Recommended Dietary Allowances. Federal standards for dietary content of foods.

Seafarers International Union of North America. Largest union of maritime workers in the United States and Canada.

Securities and Exchange Commission. Federal agency that regulates the securities industry.

Securities Industry Association. Trade association representing investment banks, broker-dealers, and mutual fund companies active in corporate and public finance.

Service Employees International Union. Union representing workers employed in diverse public and private sector industries in the United States and Canada.

State Postsecondary Review for Entities. State accreditation boards for higher education institutions.

T

Taft-Hartley Act. Law passed in 1947 curtailing the ability of unions to organize workers in the United States.

Technology Network. Trade association for software and computer industry.

Telecommunications Act. 1996 law superseding 1934 Communications Act that defines the federal role in regulating the communications industry in the era of digital electronics and the Internet.

Tilman Act. Federal campaign finance law passed in 1907.

Transport Workers Union of America. Union representing public bus, train, air transport, and associated workers in the United States.

Truth in Lending Act. Federal law passed in 1968 that requires lenders to provide simple and accurate information about loans for borrowers to facilitate comparison shopping.

U

U.S. Public Interest Research Group. Progressive, consumer-oriented advocacy organization.

Union of Concerned Scientists. Organization of science professionals dedicated to promoting environmentally friendly technologies.

Union of Needletrades, Industrial, and Textile Employees. International union representing workers primarily employed in the textile and garment production industries.

United Automobile, Aerospace, and Agricultural Implement Workers of America. Union representing workers primarily employed in the automobile industry in the United States.

United Food and Commercial Workers Union. Union representing workers primarily employed in the food processing and retail sales industries.

United States Catholic Conference. Generally liberal advocacy organization of the American Catholic church.

United Steelworkers of America. International union of workers employed in steel, aluminum, copper, tin, plastics, rubber, stone, and glass industries.

United Transportation Union. Union representing railroad, bus, and mass transit workers in the United States and Canada.

US English. Organization dedicated to making English the official language of the United States and to eliminating bilingualism in government and education.

US Term Limits. Organization dedicated to setting term limits for elected officials at the local, state, and federal levels.

W

World Bank. Created as the International Bank for Reconstruction and Development to provide financing for economic growth and development projects in less-developed countries.

World Intellectual Property Organization. Main international organization dealing with copyright and other intellectual property issues.

World Trade Organization. Created in Singapore in 1995 as an international supervisory body to oversee global trade by country participants in the General Agreement on Tariffs and Trade negotiations.

Y–Z

Y2K. Term referring to computer problems that could result from technical difficulties associated with the turning of the year 2000.

Zero Population Growth. Organization dedicated to restraining population growth in the United States and abroad.

BIBLIOGRAPHY

General Works

Adams, James Ring. *The Big Fix*. New York: John Wiley & Sons, 1990.

Ainsworth, Scott. "Regulating Lobbyists and Interest Group Influence. *Journal of Politics* 55 (1993): 41–56.

Ainsworth, Scott, and Itai Sened. "The Role of Lobbyists: Entrepreneurs with Two Audiences." *American Journal of Political Science* 37 (1993): 834–66.

Alexander, Herbert E. *Financing Politics: Money, Elections, Political Reform*. Washington, DC: Congressional Quarterly Press, 1992.

———, ed. *Campaign Money*. New York: Free Press, 1976.

Arnold, Douglas R. *The Logic of Congressional Action*. New Haven, CT: Yale University Press, 1990.

Ashworth, William. *Under the Influence: Congress, Lobbies, and the American Pork-Barrel System*. New York: Hawthorn/Dutton, 1981.

Austen-Smith, David. "Information and Influence: Lobbying for Agendas and Votes." *American Journal of Political Science* 38 (1994): 799–833.

Barone, Michael, and Grant Ujifusa. *The Almanac of American Politics 1998*. Washington, DC: National Journal, 1997.

Baumgartner, Frank R., and Beth L. Leech. *Basic Interests: The Importance of Groups in Politics*. Princeton, NJ: Princeton University Press, 1998.

———. "The Multiple Ambiguities of 'Counteractive Lobbying.'" *American Journal of Political Science* 40 (1996): 521–42.

Baumgartner, Frank R., and Jack L. Walker. "Interest Groups and Political Change." In *New Directions in American Politics*, edited by Bryan D. Jones. Boulder, CO: Westview Press, 1995.

Beck, Deborah, et al. *Issue Advocacy Advertising During the 1996 Election*. Philadelphia: Annenberg Public Policy Center, 1997.

Berg, John C. *Unequal Struggle: Class, Gender, Race, and Power in the U.S. Congress*. Boulder, CO: Westview Press, 1994.

Berry, Jeffrey M. *The Interest Group Society*. 2d ed. Boston: Scott Foresman/Little, Brown, 1989.

———. *Lobbying for the People: The Political Behavior of Public Interest Groups*. Princeton, NJ: Princeton University Press, 1977

———. *The New Liberalism: The Rising Power of Citizen Groups*. Washington, DC: Brookings Institution Press, 1999.

Biersack, Robert, Paul S. Herrnson, and Clyde Wilcox, eds. *After the Revolution: PACs, Lobbies, and the Republican Congress*. Boston: Allyn & Bacon, 1999.

———. *Risky Business: PAC Decisionmaking in Congressional Elections*. Armonk, NY: M.E. Sharpe, 1994.

———. "Seeds for Success: Early Money in Congressional Elections." *Legislative Studies Quarterly* 18 (1993): 535–52.

Birnbaum, Jeffrey. *The Lobbyists: How Influence Peddlers Get Their Way in Washington*. New York: Times Books, 1992.

Birnbaum, Jeffrey H., and Alan S. Murray. *Showdown at Gucci Gulch: Lawmakers, Lobbyists, and the Unlikely Triumph of Tax Reform*. New York: Vintage Books, 1988.

Brown, Clifford, Lynda Powell, and Clyde Wilcox. *Serious Money: Fundraising and Contributing in Presidential Nomination Campaigns*. New York: Cambridge University Press, 1995.

Browne, William P. *Groups, Interests, and U.S. Public Policy*. Washington, DC: Georgetown University Press, 1998.

Business–Industry Political Action Committee. *Rising to the Challenge in 1996: What Business Groups Must Do to Protect Free Enterprise Majorities in Congress*. Washington, DC: Business–Industry Political Action Committee, 1996.

Bykerk, Loree, and Ardith Maney. *U.S. Consumer Interest Groups: Institutional Profiles*. Westport, CT: Greenwood Press, 1995.

Cammisa, Anne Marie. *Governments as Interest Groups: Intergovernmental Lobbying and the Federal System*. Westport, CT: Praeger, 1995.

Choate, Pat. *Agents of Influence*. New York: Alfred A. Knopf, 1990.

Cigler, Allan J., and Burdett A. Loomis. *Interest Group Politics*. 5th ed. Washington, DC: Congressional Quarterly Press, 1998.

Cohen, Richard E. *Washington at Work: Back Rooms and Clean Air*. New York: Macmillan, 1992.

Common Cause. *How Money Talks in Congress: A Common Cause Study of the Impact of Money on Congressional Decision-Making*. Washington, DC: Common Cause, 1979.

———. *Return on Investment: The Hidden Story of Soft Money, Corporate Welfare, and the 1997 Budget and Tax Deal*. Washington, DC: Common Cause, 1998.

Corrado, Anthony. *Creative Campaigning: PACs and the Presidential Selection Process*. Boulder, CO: Westview Press, 1992.

Corrado, Anthony, Thomas E. Mann, Daniel R. Oritz, Trevor Potter, and Frank J. Sorauf, eds. *Campaign Finance Reform: A Sourcebook*. Washington, DC: Brookings Institution Press, 1997.

Costain, Anne N., and Andrew S. McFarland, eds. *Social Movements and American Political Institutions*. Lanham, MD: Rowman & Littlefield, 1998.

Crotty, William, Mildred A. Schwartz, and John C. Green. *Representing Interests and Interest Group Representation*. Lanham, MD: University Press of America, 1994.

Danielian, Lucig, and Benjamin I. Page. "The Heavenly Chorus: Interest Group Voices on TV News." *American Journal of Political Science* 38 (1994): 1056–78.

De Angelis, James J., ed. *Public Interest Profiles, 1998–99*. Washington, DC: Congressional Quarterly Foundation for Public Affairs, 1998.

DeGregorio, Christine, and Kevin Snider. *Networks of Champions: Leadership, Access, and Advocacy in the U.S. House of Representatives*. Ann Arbor: University of Michigan Press, 1997.

Downs, Buck, et al. *National Trade and Professional Associations of the United States*. Washington, DC: Congressional Quarterly Press, 1998.

Drew, Elizabeth. *Whatever It Takes: The Real Struggle for Political Power in America*. New York: Viking, 1997.

Eismeyer, Theodore, and Philip H. Pollock III. "An Organizational Analysis of Political Action Committees." *Political Behavior* 7 (1985): 192–216.

Epstein, Lee. "Courts and Interest Groups." In *American Courts*, edited by John B. Gates and Charles A. Johnson. Washington, DC: Congressional Quarterly Press, 1991.

Etzioni, Amitai. *Capital Corruption: The New Attack on American Democracy*. New Brunswick, NJ: Transaction Books, 1988.

Ferguson, Thomas, and Joel Rogers. *Right Turn: The Decline of the Democrats and the Future of American Politics*. New York: Hill and Wang, 1986.

Fleisher, Richard. "PAC Contributions and Congressional Voting on National Defense." *Legislative Studies Quarterly* 18 (1993): 391–409.

Foundation for Public Affairs. *Public Interest Group Profiles, 1996–1997*. Washington, DC: Foundation for Public Affairs, Congressional Quarterly Press, 1996.

Furlong, Scott. "Interest Group Influence on Regulatory Policy." Ph.D. diss., American University, 1992.

Gais, Thomas. *Improper Influence: Campaign Finance Law, Political Interest Groups, and the Problem of Equality*. Ann Arbor: University of Michigan Press, 1998.

Gale Group. *Encyclopedia of Associations*, 34th ed. Detroit: Gale, 1999.

Ginsberg, Benjamin, Walter R. Mebane, and Martin Shefter. "The Presidency and Interest Groups: Why Presidents Cannot Govern." In *The Presidency and the Political System*, 4th ed., edited by Michael Nelson. Washington, DC: Congressional Quarterly Press, 1995.

Goldstein, Joshua. *PACs in Profile*. Washington, DC: Center for Responsive Politics, 1995.

Gray, Virginia, and David Lowery. "Interest Group System Density and Diversity: A Research Update." *International Political Science Review* 15 (1994): 5–14.

———. *The Population Ecology of Interest Representation*. Ann Arbor: University of Michigan Press, 1996.

Green, Mark, with Michael Waldman. *Who Runs Congress?* New York: Dell Publishing, 1984.

Greenwald, Carol Schwartz. *Group Power: Lobbying and Public Policy*. New York: Praeger Publishers, 1977.

Greider, William. *Who Will Tell the People? The Betrayal of American Democracy*. New York: Touchstone Books, 1992.

Grenzke, Janet M. "PACs and the Congressional Supermarket: The Currency Is Complex." *American Journal of Political Science* 33 (1989): 1–24.

Grier, Kevin B., and Michael C. Munger. "Committee Assignments, Constituent Preferences, and Campaign Contributions." *Economic Inquiry* 29 (1991): 24–43.

Hager, George, and Eric Pianin. *Mirage: Why Neither Democrats nor Republicans Can Balance the Budget, End the Deficit, and Satisfy the Public*. New York: Random House, 1997.

Hall, Richard L. *Participation in Congress*. New Haven, CT: Yale University Press, 1996.

Hall, Richard L., and Frank W. Wayman. "Buying Time: Moneyed Interests and the Mobilization of Bias in Congressional Committees." *American Political Science Review* 84 (1990): 797–820.

Heinz, John P. *The Hollow Core: Private Interests in National Policy Making*. Cambridge, MA: Harvard University Press, 1993.

Heldman, Dan C. *Interest Groups, Lobbying, and Policymaking*. Arlington, VA: Foundation for the Advancement of the Public Trust, 1980.

Herring, Pendleton. *Group Representation Before Congress*. New York: Russell and Russell, 1929.

Herrnson, Paul S. *Congressional Elections: Campaigning at Home and in Washington*, 2d ed. Washington, DC: Congressional Quarterly Press, 1998.

———. "Money and Motives: Party, PAC, and Individual Spending in House Elections." In *Congress Reconsidered*, edited by Lawrence C. Dodd and Bruce I. Oppenheimer. Washington, DC: Congressional Quarterly Press, 1997.

———. "Parties and Interest Groups in Postreform Congressional Elections." In *Interest Group Politics*. 5th ed., edited by Allan J. Cigler and Burdett A. Loomis. Washington, DC: Congressional Quarterly Press, 1998.

Herrnson, Paul S., Ronald G. Shaiko, and Clyde Wilcox, eds. *The Interest Group Connection: Electioneering, Lobbying, and Policymaking in Washington*. Chatham, NJ: Chatham House Publishers, 1998.

Hojnacki, Marie. "Interest Groups' Decisions to Join Alliances or Work Alone." *American Journal of Political Science* 41 (1997): 61–87.

Howe, Russell Warren. *The Power Peddlers*. Garden City, NY: Doubleday, 1977.

Hrebenar, Ronald J. *Interest Group Politics in America*, 3d ed. Armonk, NY: M.E. Sharpe, 1997.

Hrebenar, Ronald J., and Clive S. Thomas, eds. *Interest Group Politics in the American West*. Salt Lake City: University of Utah Press, 1987.

———. *Interest Group Politics in the Midwestern States*. Ames: Iowa University Press, 1993.

———. *Interest Group Politics in the Northeastern States*. University Park: Pennsylvania State University Press, 1997.

———. *Interest Group Politics in the Southern States*. Tuscaloosa: University of Alabama Press, 1992.

Hula, Kevin W. *Lobbying Together: Interest Group Coalitions in Legislative Politics*. Washington, DC: Georgetown University Press, 1999.

Jackson, Brooks. *Honest Graft*. Washington, DC: Farragut Publishing, 1990.

Jackson, John E., and John W. Kingdon. "Ideology, Interest Group Scores, and Legislative Votes." *American Journal of Political Science* 36 (1992): 805–23.

Johnson, Haynes, and David Broder. *The System: The American Way of Politics at the Breaking Point.* Boston: Little, Brown and Company, 1996.

Jones, Bryan D., Frank R. Baumgartner, and Jeffery Talbert. "The Destruction of Issue Monopolies in Congress." *American Political Science Review* 87 (1993): 657–71.

Judis, John. "The Contract with K Street." *New Republic* 4 (1995): 18–25.

Kollman, Ken. "Inviting Friends to Lobby: Interest Groups, Ideological Bias, and Congressional Committees." *American Journal of Political Science* 41 (1997): 519–44.

———. *Outside Lobbying: Public Opinion and Interest Group Strategies.* Princeton, NJ: Princeton University Press, 1998.

Kreml, William P. *Losing Balance: The De-Democratization of America.* Armonk, NY: M.E. Sharpe, 1991.

Kurian, George T. *A Historical Guide to the U.S. Government.* New York: Oxford University Press, 1998.

Laumann, Edward O. *The Organizational State: Social Choice in National Policy Domains.* Madison: University of Wisconsin Press, 1987.

Leech, Beth L. "Lobbying Strategies of Amerian Interest Groups." Ph.D. diss., Texas A&M University, 1998.

Lehman Scholzman, Kay, and John T. Tierney. *Organized Interests and American Democracy.* New York: Harper and Row, 1986.

Levitan, Sar A. *Business Lobbies: The Public Good & the Bottom Line.* Baltimore: Johns Hopkins University Press, 1984.

Lewis, Charles. *The Buying of the Congress: How Special Interests Have Stolen Your Right to Life, Liberty, and the Pursuit of Happiness.* New York: Avon Books, 1998.

———. *The Buying of the President.* New York: Avon Books, 1996.

Mack, Charles S. *Business, Politics, and the Practice of Government Relations.* Westport, CT: Quorum, 1997.

Magleby, David B., and Candice J. Nelson. *The Money Chase: Congressional Campaign Finance Reform.* Washington, DC: Brookings Institution

Makinson, Larry. *The Price of Admission: Campaign Spending in the 1994 Elections.* Washington, DC: Center for Responsive Politics, 1995.

Makinson, Larry, and Joshua Goldstein. *Open Secrets: The Encyclopedia of Congressional Money and Politics.* Washington, DC: Congressional Quarterly Press, 1992–1996.

Maney, Ardith, and Loree Bykerk, *Consumer Politics: Protecting Public Interests on Capitol Hill.* Westport, CT: Greenwood Press, 1994.

Mater, Jean. *Public Hearings, Procedures and Strategies: A Guide to Influencing Public Decisions.* Englewood Cliffs, NJ: Prentice-Hall, 1984.

Maurer, Christine, Tara E. Sheets, and Ian A. Goodhall, eds. *Encyclopedia of Associations.* Vol. 1, *National Organizations of the U.S.* New York: Gale, 1998.

McCarty, Nolan, and Lawrence S. Rothenberg. "Commitment and the Campaign Contribution Contract." *American Journal of Political Science* 40 (1996): 872–904.

McChesney, Fred S. *Money for Nothing: Politicians, Rent Extraction, and Political Extortion.* Cambridge, MA: Harvard University Press, 1997.

McFarland, Andrew S. "Interest Groups and Political Time: Cycles in America." *British Journal of Political Science* 21 (1991): 257–84.

———. "Interest Groups and Theories of Power in America." *British Journal of Political Science* 17 (1987): 129–47.

Meier, Kenneth J. *Regulation: Politics, Bureaucracy, and Economics.* New York: St. Martin's Press, 1985.

Mitchell, William C., and Michael C. Munger. "Economic Models of Interest Groups: An Introductory Survey." *American Journal of Political Science* 35 (1991): 512–46.

Mucciaroni, Gary. *Reversals of Fortune: Public Policy and Private Interests.* Washington, DC: Brookings Institution, 1995.

Mundo, Philip A. *Interest Groups: Cases and Characteristics.* Chicago: Nelson-Hall, 1992.

Neustadtl, Alan. "Interest Group PACsmanship: An Analysis of Campaign Contributions, Issue Visibility, and Legislative Impact." *Social Forces* 69 (1990): 549–64.

Nugent, M., and John Johannes, eds. *Money, Elections, and Democracy.* Boulder, CO: Westview Press, 1990.

Penny, Timothy J., and Major Garrett. *Common Cents.* New York: Avon Books, 1995.

Pertschuk, Michael. *Giant Killers.* New York: Norton, 1986.

Petracca, Mark P., ed. *The Politics of Interests: Interest Groups Transformed.* Boulder, CO: Westview Press, 1992.

Phelps, Timothy M., and Helen Winternitz. *Capitol Games.* New York: Hyperion, 1992.

Phillips, Kevin. *Arrogant Capital: Washington, Wall Street, and the Frustration of American Politics.* Boston: Little, Brown and Company, 1994.

Quinn, Dennis P., and Robert Y. Shapiro. "Business Political Power: The Case of Taxation." *American Political Science Review* 85 (1991): 851–74.

Rassell, Edith. "Health Care Reform." In *Reclaiming Prosperity: A Blueprint for Progressive Economic Reform,* edited by Todd Schafer, and Jeff Faux. Armonk, NY: M.E. Sharpe, 1992.

Rauch, Jonathan. *Demosclerosis: The Silent Killer of American Government.* New York: Random House, 1994.

Renfro, William L. *The Legislative Role of Corporations.* New York: Presidents Association, Chief Executive Officers' Division of the American Management Association, 1983.

Richardson, Jeremy, ed. *Pressure Groups.* New York: Oxford University Press, 1993.

Romer, Thomas, and James M. Snyder, Jr. "An Empirical Investigation of the Dynamics of PAC Contributions." *American Journal of Political Science* 38 (1994): 745–69.

Rosenthal, Alan. *The Third House: Lobbyists and Lobbying in the States.* Washington, DC: Congressional Quarterly Press, 1993.

Rothenberg, Lawrence S. *Linking Citizens to Government: Interest Group Politics at Common Cause.* New York: Cambridge University Press, 1992.

Rozell, Mark J., and Clyde Wilcox. *Interest Groups in American Campaigns: The New Face of Electioneering.* Washington, DC: Congressional Quarterly Press, 1999.

Sabato, Larry J. *PAC Power: Inside the World of Political Action Committees.* New York: W.W. Norton, 1984.

Sabato, Larry J., and Glenn R. Simpson. *Dirty Little Secrets: The Persistence of Corruption in American Politics.* New York: Times Books, 1996.

Schram, Martin. *Speaking Freely.* Washington, DC: Center for Responsive Politics, 1995.

Schlozman, Kay Lehman, and John T. Tierney. *Organized Interests and American Democracy.* New York: Harper and Row, 1986.

Silverstein, Ken. *Washington on $10 Million a Day: How Lobbyists Plunder the Nation.* Monroe, ME: Common Courage Press, 1998.

Smith, Richard A. "Interest Group Influence in the U.S. Congress." *Legislative Studies Quarterly* 20 (1995): 89–139.
Sorauf, Frank. *Inside Campaign Finance*. New Haven, CT: Yale University Press, 1992.
———. *Money in American Elections*. San Francisco: Scott Foresman, 1988.
Stern, Philip M. *Still the Best Congress Money Can Buy*. Updated ed. Washington, DC: Regnery Gateway, 1992.
Stratmann, Thomas. "What Do Campaign Contributions Buy? Deciphering Causal Effects of Money and Votes." *Southern Economic Journal* 57 (1991): 606–20.
Symms, Steven D. *The Citizen's Guide to Fighting Government*. Ottawa, IL: Jameson Books, 1994.
Thomas, Bill. *Club Fed: Power, Money, Sex, and Violence on Capitol Hill*. New York: Charles Scribner's Sons, 1994.
Thompson, Dennis F. *Ethics in Congress: From Individual to Institutional Corruption*. Washington, DC: Brookings Institution Press, 1995.
Trento, Susan B. *The Power House: Robert Keith Gray and the Selling of Access and Influence in Washington*. New York: St. Martin's Press, 1992.
Vogel, David. *Fluctuating Fortunes: The Political Power of Business in America*. New York: Basic Books, 1989.
Watzman, Nancy, and James Youngclaus. *Capital Lobbying: Money Played Its Part in 1995*. Washington, DC: Center for Responsive Politics, 1996.
West, Darrell M., and Burdett A. Loomis. *The Sound of Money: How Political Interests Get What They Want*. New York: W.W. Norton & Co, 1999.
Wilson, Graham, K. *Interest Groups*. Cambridge, MA: Basil Blackwell Ltd., 1990.
Wilson, James Q. *Political Organizations*. Princeton, NJ: Princeton University Press, 1995.
Wolpe, Bruce C., and Bertram J. Levine. *Lobbying Congress: How the System Works*. 2d ed. Washington, DC: Congressional Quarterly Press, 1996.
Wright, John R. *Interest Groups and Congress: Lobbying, Contributions, and Influence*. Boston: Allyn & Bacon, 1996.
Zeigler, Harmon. *Interest Groups in American Society*. Englewood Cliffs, NJ: Prentice-Hall, 1964.
Zuckerman, Edward, ed. *The Almanac of Federal PACs: 1998-99*. Arlington, VA: Amward Publications, 1998.

Banking, Finance, Insurance, and Real Estate

American Institute of Certified Public Accountants. *Annual Report 1997–1998: A Future in the Making*. New York: American Institute of Certified Public Accountants, 1998.
Birnbaum, Jeffrey H., and Alan S. Murray. *Showdown at Gucci Gulch: Lawmakers, Lobbyists, and the Unlikely Triumph of Tax Reform*. New York: Vintage Books, 1988.
Bykerk, Loree G. "Business Power in Washington: The Insurance Exception." *Policy Studies Review* 11(3/4) (1992): 259–79.
———. "Gender in Insurance: Organized Interests and the Displacement of Conflicts." *Policy Studies Journal* 17(2) (1988): 261–76.
Bykerk, Loree, and Ardith Maney. *U.S. Consumer Interest Groups: Institutional Profiles*. Westport, CT: Greenwood Press, 1995.
Cranford, John R. "Marketplace Forces Hold Key to Future Bank Legislation." *Congressional Quarterly Weekly Report*, January 4, 1992.
Gale Group. *Encyclopedia of Associations*. 34th ed. Detroit: Gale, 1999.
Grant, H. Roger. *Insurance Reform: Consumer Action in the Progressive Era*. Ames: Iowa State University Press, 1979.
Hosansky, David. "Taxes, Regulations Sought by Business Lobbyists." *Congressional Quarterly Weekly Report*, April 18, 1998.
Hrebenar, Ronald J., and Clive S. Thomas, eds. *Interest Group Politics in the American West*. Salt Lake City: University of Utah Press, 1987.
———. *Interest Group Politics in the Northeastern States*. University Park: Pennsylvania State University Press, 1997.
Independent Bankers Association of America. *Annual Report*. Washington, DC: Independent Bankers Association of America, 1999.
Independent Insurance Agents of America. "IIAA—A Year in Review," *Independent Insurance Agent* (December 1998).
Maney, Ardith, and Loree Bykerk, *Consumer Politics: Protecting Public Interests on Capitol Hill*. Westport, CT: Greenwood Press, 1994.
Meier, Kenneth J. *The Political Economy of Regulation: The Case of Insurance*. Albany: State University of New York Press, 1988.
———. *Regulation: Politics, Bureaucracy, and Economics*. New York: St. Martin's Press, 1985.
National Association of Insurance Commissioners. *Issues 1999*. Kansas City, MO: National Association of Insurance Commissioners, 1999.
———. *NAIC: Performing in the Public Interest*. Kansas City, MO: National Association of Insurance Commissioners, 1999.
Olson, Walter, ed. *New Directions in Liability Law*. Vol. 37. New York: Proceedings of the Academy of Political Science, 1988
Pertschuk, Michael. *Revolt Against Regulation: The Rise and Pause of the Consumer Movement*. Berkeley: University of California Press, 1982.
Phillips, Kevin. *Arrogant Capital: Washington, Wall Street, and the Frustration of American Politics*. Boston: Little, Brown and Company, 1994.
Rosenthal, Alan. *The Third House: Lobbyists and Lobbying in the States*. Washington, DC: Congressional Quarterly Press, 1993.
Securities Industry Association. *Annual Report: Preparing for the Millennium*. New York: Securities Industry Association, 1999.
Taylor, Andrew. "Glass-Steagall Rewrite Stalls as Industry Foes Do Battle." *Congressional Quarterly Weekly Report*, March 2, 1996.
Taylor, Andrew. "Bill on Interstate Branching Sails Through Senate Panel: What Opponents Seek." *Congressional Quarterly Weekly Report*, February 26, 1994.
———. "Disputes Over Regulatory Relief May Put Bill on Crash Course." *Congressional Quarterly Weekly Report*, June 24, 1995.
West, Darrell M., and Burdett A. Loomis. *The Sound of Money: How Political Interests Get What They Want*. New York: W.W. Norton & Co, 1999.
Wolpe, Bruce C., and Bertram J. Levine. *Lobbying Congress: How the System Works*. 2d ed. Washington, DC: Congressional Quarterly Inc, 1996.
Zuckerman, Edward, ed. *The Almanac of Federal PACs: 1998-99*. Arlington, VA: Amward Publications, 1998.

Service, Trade, and Professional

Abel, Richard. *American Lawyers*. New York: Oxford University Press, 1989.

American Bar Association. "The American Bar Association. One Hundred Years of Service." *The American Bar Association Journal* 64 (July 1978).

———. *Overview.* Washington, DC: American Bar Association, July 1998.

American Bar Association, Division of Media Relations and Public Affairs. *Profile.* (January 1999) Washington, DC: American Bar Association, 1998.

American Library Association. Public Information Office. *Fact Sheet.* Chicago, 1999.

American Trial Lawyers Association. "ATLA: The First Fifty Years." *TRIAL* 32 (7) (July 1996): 23–53.

———. "Chronicles: An Historical Trilogy." *TRIAL* 32 (7) (July 1996): 44–63.

———. "Rumor and Reflection." *The NACCA Journal* (18) (November 1957): 25–38.

Anderson, Brian, and Burdett A. Loomis. "Taking Organization Seriously: The Structure of Interest Group Influence." In *Interest Group Politics,* 5th ed., edited by Allan J. Cigler and Burdett A. Loomis. Washington, DC: Congressional Quarterly Press, 1998.

Biersack, Robert, and Paul S. Herrnson. "Introduction." In *After the Revolution: PACs, Lobbies, and the Republican Congress,* edited by Robert Biersack, Paul S. Herrnson, and Clyde Wilcox. Boston: Allyn & Bacon, 1999.

Biersack, Robert, Paul S. Herrnson, and Clyde Wilcox, eds. *After the Revolution: PACs, Lobbies, and the Republican Congress.* Boston: Allyn & Bacon, 1999.

Donohue, Thomas. "American Business: The Next Agenda." *Vital Speeches of the Day* 64 (4) (December 1, 1997).

Drew, Elizabeth. *Whatever It Takes: The Real Struggle for Political Power in America.* New York: Viking, 1997.

Green, Mark, and Andrew Buchsbaum. "The Corporate Lobbies: Political Profiles of the Business Roundtable & the Chamber of Commerce." *Public Citizen* (February 1980).

Haefele, Edwin T. "Shifts in Business-Government Interactions." In *Government Regulation of Business: Its Growth, Impact and Future.* Council of Trends and Perspectives, Chamber of Commerce of the United States. Washington, DC: Chamber of Commerce of the United States, 1979.

Herrnson, Paul S. *Congressional Elections: Campaigning at Home and in Washington.* 2d ed. Washington, DC: Congressional Quarterly Press, 1998.

———. "Parties and Interest Groups in Postreform Congressional Elections." In *Interest Group Politics.* 5th ed., edited by Allan J. Cigler and Burdett A. Loomis. Washington, DC: Congressional Quarterly Press, 1998.

Herrnson, Paul S., Ronald G. Shaiko, and Clyde Wilcox, eds. *The Interest Group Connection: Electioneering, Lobbying, and Policymaking in Washington.* Chatham, NJ: Chatham House Publishers, 1998.

Horovitz, Samuel B. "NACCA and Its Objectives." In *The NACCA Journal* 10 (November 1952): 18–42.

Owens, James. "Mumia Abu-Jamal: The ABC Hatchet Job." *Covert Action Quarterly* 67 (Spring/Summer 1999).

Robbins, Louise. *Censorship and the American Library. The American Library Association's Response to Threats to Intellectual Freedom. 1939–1969.* Westport, CT: Greenwood Press, 1996.

Shaffer, Butler. *In Restraint of Trade. The Business Campaign Against Competition 1918–1938.* Lewisburg, PA: Bucknell University Press, 1997.

Shaiko, Ronald G., and Marc A. Wallace. "From Wall Street to Main Street: The National Federation of Independent Business and the New Republican Majority." In *After the Revolution: PACs, Lobbies, and the Republican Congress,* edited by Robert Biersack, Paul S. Herrnson, and Clyde Wilcox. Boston: Allyn & Bacon, 1999.

Thomison, Dennis. *A History of the American Library Association 1876–1972.* Chicago: American Library Association, 1978.

Tyack, David. *The One Best System: A History of American Urban Education.* Cambridge, MA: Harvard University Press, 1974.

Weidenbaum, Murray L. *Business, Government and the Public.* Englewood Cliffs, NJ: Prentice-Hall, 1977.

Wilson, Graham K. *Interest Groups.* Cambridge, MA: Basil Blackwell Ltd., 1990.

Wingand, Wayne A. *The Politics of an Emerging Profession. The American Library Association 1876–1917.* New York: Greenwood Press, 1986.

Zuckerman, Edward, ed. *The Almanac of Federal PACs: 1998-1999.* Arlington, VA: Amward Publications, 1998.

Media, Entertainment, and Information

Bagdikian, Ben. *The Media Monopoly.* 5th ed. Boston: Beacon Press, 1997.

Balio, Tina, ed. *The American Film Industry.* Madison: University of Wisconsin Press, 1985.

Baughman, James L. *Television's Guardians: The FCC and the Politics of Programming, 1958–1967.* Knoxville: University of Tennessee Press, 1985.

Browne, William P. *Groups, Interests, and U.S. Public Policy.* Washington, DC: Georgetown University Press, 1998.

Carney, Dan. "Software Firms Seek to End Ban on Exporting Encryption Codes." *Congressional Quarterly* 13 (April 1996): 985–87.

Cook, Constance Ewing. *Lobbying for Higher Education: How Colleges and Universities Influence Federal Policy.* Nashville, TN: Vanderbilt University Press, 1998.

Cook, Timothy E. *Governing with the News: The News Media as a Political Institution.* Chicago: University of Chicago Press, 1998.

Crandall, Robert W., and Harold Furchtgott-Roth. *Cable TV: Regulation or Competition?* Washington, DC: Brookings Institution Press, 1996.

Daly, Charles P., Patrick Henry, and Ellen Ryder. *The Magazine Publishing Industry.* Boston: Allyn & Bacon, 1997.

Dessauer, John P. *Book Publishing: What It Is, What It Does.* New York: R.R. Bowker Company, 1981.

Dolan, Edward V. *TV or CATV? A Struggle for Power.* New York: National University Publications Associate Faculty Press, 1984.

Emery, Edwin. *History of the American Newspaper Publishers Association.* Minneapolis: University of Minnesota Press, 1950.

Fallows, James. *Breaking the News: How the Media Undermine American Democracy.* New York: Vintage Books, A Division of Random House, 1997.

Fink, Michael. *Inside the Music Industry: Creativity, Process and Business.* New York: Schirmer Books, An Imprint of Simon and Schuster MacMillan, 1996.

Foundation for Public Affairs. *Public Interest Group Profiles, 1996–1997.* Washington, DC: Foundation for Public Affairs, Congressional Quarterly, 1996.

Gais, Thomas. *Improper Influence: Campaign Finance Law, Po-*

litical Interest Groups, and the Problem of Equality. Ann Arbor: University of Michigan Press, 1998.
Greco, Albert N. *The Book Publishing Industry.* Boston: Allyn & Bacon, 1997.
Herman, Edward S., and Robert W. McChesney. *The Global Media: The New Missionaries of Corporate Capitalism.* Washington, DC: Cassell, 1997.
Hull, Geoffrey. *The Recording Industry.* Boston: Allyn & Bacon, 1998.
Keller, Bill. "How News Business Lobbyists Put Their Press on Congress . . . But with Mixed Feelings." *Congressional Quarterly* 2 (August 1980): 2176–84.
Kindem, Gorham, ed. *The American Movie Industry: The Business of Motion Pictures.* Carbondale: Southern Illinois University Press, 1982.
King, Lauriston R. *The Washington Lobbyists for Higher Education.* Lexington, MA: Lexington Books, D.C. Heath and Company, 1975.
Kobrak, Fred, and Beth Luey, eds. *The Structure of International Publishing in the 1990s.* New Brunswick, NJ: Transaction Publishers, 1992.
Koughan, Martin. "Easy Money." *Mother Jones* (July/August 1997). www.motherjones.com.
Krasnow, Erwin G., and Lawrence D. Longley. *The Politics of Broadcast Regulation.* 2d ed. New York: St. Martin's Press, 1982.
Litman, Barry R. *The Motion Picture Mega-Industry.* Boston: Allyn & Bacon, 1998.
Mackey, David. "The Development of the National Association of Broadcasters." *Journal of Broadcasting* 1 (1957): 305–25.
Maurer, Christine, Tara E. Sheets, and Ian A. Goodhall, eds. *Encyclopedia of Associations,* Vol. 1, *National Organizations of the U.S.* New York: Gale, 1998.
McChesney, Robert. *Corporate Media and the Threat to Democracy.* Seven Stories, 1997.
Mills, Mike. "Bill Advances to Nudge Industry to Get Schools Online." *Congressional Quarterly* 26 (February 1994): 469–70.
Miracle, Gordon E., and Terence Nevett. *Voluntary Regulation of Advertising: A Comparative Analysis of the United Kingdom and the United States.* Lexington, MA: Lexington Books, D.C. Heath and Company, 1987.
Ota, Alan K. "Casinos Look to Improve Their Odds on Capitol Hill." *Congressional Quarterly* 23 (January 1999): 191–95.
Parsons, Michael P. *Power and Politics: Federal Higher Education Policy Making in the 1990s.* Albany: State University of New York Press, 1997.
Parsons, Patrick, Robert Frieden, and Rob Frieden. *The Cable and Satellite Television Industries.* Boston: Allyn & Bacon, 1998.
Shecter, Jennifer. "Connected: Political Superhighway Links Silicon Valley with Capitol Hill." *Capitol Eye* 5 (December 1998).
Tebbell, John, and Mary Ellen Zuckerman. *The Magazine in America, 1741–1990.* New York: Oxford University Press, 1991.
Walker, James, and Douglas Ferguson. *The Broadcast TV Industry.* Boston: Allyn & Bacon, 1998.
Zuckerman, Edward, ed. and com. *The Almanac of Federal PACs, 1998-1999.* Arlington, VA: Amward Publications, 1998.

Health and Medical

Aaron, Henry, and William B. Schwartz. *The Painful Prescription: Rationing Health Care.* Washington, DC: Brookings Institution, 1984.
Barton, Walter E. *The History and Influence of the American Psychiatric Association.* Washington, DC: American Psychiatric Press, 1987.
Bennefield, Robert L. "Health Insurance Coverage: 1997, Report P60–202." *Current Population Reports.* Washington, DC: U.S. Department of Commerce. Economics and Statistics Administration. Bureau of the Census. September 1998.
Bennett, James T. *Cancer Scam: Diversion of Federal Cancer Funds to Politics.* New Brunswick, NJ: Transaction Publishers, 1998.
Cassell, Jo Anne. *Carry the Flame: The History of the American Dietetic Association.* Chicago: The Association, 1990.
Clements, Colleen. "It's a Mistake to Make Patient Privilege Eternal." *Medical Post* (September 22, 1998): 19.
Coulston, Ann M. "Shaping Health Policy, Influencing Policy Makers." *Journal of the American Dietetic Association* 99 (3) (March 1, 1999): 276.
Cunningham, Robert M. *The Blues: A History of the Blue Cross/Blue Shield System.* DeKalb: Northern Illinois University, 1997.
Gubrium, Jaber F. *Living and Dying at Murray Manor.* Charlottesville: University Press of Virginia, 1997.
Hallan, Kristen. "Government Looks at Nursing Home Fraud." *Modern Healthcare* (February 22, 1999): 8.
Jennings, Marian, ed. *Financing Long-Term Care.* Frederick, MD: Aspen Publishers, 1991.
Johansson, Cynthia. "Quality of Care vs. Profits in HMOs." *OT Week* 13 (28) (July 22, 1999): I, iv.
Johnson, Haynes, and David Broder. *The System: The American Way of Politics at the Breaking Point.* Boston: Little, Brown and Company, 1996.
Johnson, James A., and Walter J. Jones. *The American Medical Association and Organized Medicine: A Commentary and Annotated Bibliography.* New York: Garland Publishing, 1993.
Jonas, Steven. *An Introduction to the U.S. Health Care System.* New York: Springer Publishing Company, 1997.
Kahn, Charles N. III. "Self-Interest Can Serve the Uninsured." *National Underwriter* (July 19, 1999): 33.
Law, Sylvia A. *Blue Cross: What Went Wrong?* New Haven, CT: Yale University Press, 1974.
Marks, Geoffrey, and William K. Beatty. *The Story of Medicine in America.* New York: Charles Scribner's Sons, 1973.
Navarro, Vicente. *The Politics of Health Policy: The U.S. Reforms, 1980–1994.* Oxford: Blackwell, 1994.
Peterson, Mark A. *Healthy Markets?: The New Competition in Medical Care.* Durham, NC: Duke University Press, 1998.
Rassell, Edith. "Health Care Reform." In *Reclaiming Prosperity: A Blueprint for Progressive Economic Reform,* edited by Todd Schafer and Jeff Faux. Armonk, NY: M.E. Sharpe, 1992.
Ross, Walter Stanford. *Crusade: The Official History of the American Cancer Society.* New York: Arbor House, 1987.
Starr, Paul. *The Social Transformation of American Medicine.* New York: Basic Books, 1982.
Steib, Paula A. "Assessing the Changes in Health Care." *O.T. Week* 12 (42) (October 15, 1998): 10.
Stevens, Rosemary. *In Sickness and in Wealth: American Hospitals in the Twentieth Century.* New York: Basic Books, 1989.
Wallerstein, Robert S. *Lay Analysis: Life Inside the Controversy.* Hillsdale, NJ: The Analytic Press, 1998.
Wolinksy, Howard, and Tom Brune. *The Serpant and the Staff: The Unhealthy Politics of the American Medical Association.* New York: Tarcher/Putnam, 1994.
Zelman, Walter A., and Robert A. Berenson. *The Managed Care*

Blues and How to Cure Them. Washington, DC: Georgetown University Press, 1998.

Zuckerman, Edward, ed. *The Almanac of Federal PACs: 1998–99.* Arlington, VA: Amward Publications, 1998.

Agriculture

Albrecht, Don, and Steve Murdock. *The Sociology of U.S. Agriculture.* Ames: Iowa State University Press, 1990.

Ashbridge, Tom. Interview with National Director of the American Agriculture Movement, April 1999.

Blanpied, Nancy A., ed. *Farm Policy: The Politics of Soil, Surpluses, and Subsidies.* Washington, DC: Congressional Quarterly Press, 1984.

Block, William J. *The Separation of the Farm Bureau and the Extension Service.* Urbana: University of Illinois Press, 1960.

Browne, William P. *Cultivating Congress: Constituents, Issues, and Interests in Agricultural Policymaking.* Lawrence: University Press of Kansas, 1995.

———. *Private Interests, Public Policy, and American Agriculture.* Lawrence: University of Kansas Press, 1988.

Browne, William P., and Alan J. Cigler. *U.S. Agricultural Groups.* New York: Greenwood Press, 1990.

Browne, William P., Jerry R. Skees, Louis E. Swanson, Paul B. Thompson, and Laurian J. Unnevehr. *Sacred Cows and Hot Potatoes: Agrarian Myths in Agricultural Policy.* Boulder, CO: Westview Press, 1992.

Butler, Nick. *The International Grain Trade: Problems and Prospects.* New York: St. Martin's Press, 1986.

Greenblatt, Alan. "Farmers Have Whip Hand in Drive for Control of House." *Congressional Quarterly Weekly Report,* August 15, 1998.

Hadwiger, Don. *Federal Wheat Commodity Programs.* Ames: Iowa State University, 1970.

Hansen, John Mark. *Gaining Access: Congress and the Farm Lobby, 1919–1981.* Chicago: University of Chicago Press, 1991.

Heinz, John. "Political Impasse in Farm Support Legislation." In *Interest Group Politics in America,* edited by Robert Salisbury. New York: Harper and Row, 1970.

Herring, Pendleton. *Group Representation Before Congress.* New York: Russell and Russell, 1929.

Ives, Ralph, and John Hurley. *United States Sugar Policy: An Analysis.* Washington, DC: U.S. Department of Commerce, 1988.

Kurian, George T. *A Historical Guide to the U.S. Government.* New York: Oxford University Press, 1998.

Makinson, Larry, and Joshua Goldstein. *Open Secrets: The Encyclopedia of Congressional Money and Politics.* Washington, DC: Congressional Quarterly Press, 1992–1996.

Mooney, Patrick, and Theo J. Majka. *Farmers' and Farm Workers' Movements.* New York: Twayne Publishers, 1995.

Ornstein, Norman J. *The Food Lobbyists: Behind the Scenes of Food and Agri-Politics.* Washington, DC: Congressional Quarterly Press, 1978.

Rapp, David. *How the U.S. Got into Agriculture and Why It Can't Get Out.* Washington, DC: Congressional Quarterly Press, 1988.

Shepherd, Geoffrey S., and Gene A. Futrell. *Marketing Farm Products.* Ames: Iowa State University Press, 1982.

Wolpe, Bruce C., and Bertram J. Levine. "Grazing Rights." In *Lobbying Congress: How the System Works.* 2d ed. Washington, DC: Congressional Quarterly Press, 1996.

Youngberg, Garth. 1978. "Alternative Agriculturalists: Ideology, Politics and Prospects." In *The New Politics of Food,* edited by Don Hadwiger and William Browne. Lexington, MA: Lexington Books, 1984.

Zeigler, Harmon. *Interest Groups in American Society.* Englewood Cliffs, NJ: Prentice-Hall, 1964.

Environment

Allen, Thomas B. *Guardian of the Wild: The Story of the National Wildlife Federation, 1936–1986.* Bloomington: Indiana University Press, 1987.

Bosso, Christopher J. "Adaption and Change in the Environmental Movement." In *Interest Group Politics,* 4th ed., edited by Allan J. Cigler and Burdett A. Loomis. Washington, DC: Congressional Quarterly Press, 1994.

———. "The Color of Money: Environmental Groups and the Pathologies of Fund Raising." In *Interest Group Politics,* 4th ed., edited by Allan J. Cigler and Burdett A. Loomis. Washington, DC: Congressional Quarterly Press, 1994.

Environmental Policy Making: Controversies in Achieving Sustainability. Albany: State University of New York Press, 1997.

Gottlieb, Robert. *Forcing the Spring: The Transformation of the American Environmental Movement.* Washington, DC: Island Press, 1993.

Graham, Frank. *The Audubon Ark: A History of the National Audubon Society.* New York: Alfred A. Knopf, 1990.

Greenpeace. "Declaration of Interdependence, 1976." In *Radical Environmentalism: Philosophy and Tactics,* edited by Peter C. List. Belmont, CA: Wadsworth Publishing Co., 1993.

Helvarg, David. *The War Against the Greens: The 'Wise Use' Movement, the New Right, and Anti-Environmental Violence.* San Francisco: Sierra Club Books, 1994.

Hunter, Bob. "Taking on the Goliaths of Doom." In *Radical Environmentalism: Philosophy and Tactics,* edited by Peter C. List. Belmont, CA: Wadsworth Publishing Co., 1993.

Kamieniecki, Sheldon, George A. Gonzalez, and Robert O. Vos, eds. "Flashpoints." In *First Along the River: A Brief History of the U.S. Environmental Movement,* edited by Benjamin Kline. San Francisco: Acada Books, 1997.

Lacey, Michael J., ed. *Government and Environmental Politics: Essays on Historical Developments Since World War Two.* Washington, DC: Woodrow Wilson Center Press and the Johns Hopkins University Press, 1991.

List, Peter C., ed. *Radical Environmentalism: Philosophy and Tactics.* Belmont, CA: Wadsworth Publishing Company, 1993.

Mundo, Philip A. *Interest Groups: Cases and Characteristics.* Chicago: Nelson-Hall, 1992. Chapter 7, "The Sierra Club," 165–231.

Pepper, David. *Modern Environmentalism: An Introduction.* New York: Routledge, 1996.

Public Disclosure Inc., Suite 1198, 50 F Street NW, Washington, DC 20001. www.tray.com/fecinfo.

Switzer, Jacqueline Vaughn. *Green Backlash: The History and Politics of the Environmental Opposition in the U.S.* Boulder, CO: Lynne Rienner Publishers, 1997.

Vig, Norman J., and Michael E. Kraft, eds. *Environmental Policy in the 1990s: Toward a New Agenda.* 2d ed. Washington, DC: Congressional Quarterly Press, 1994.

Industry, Construction, and Transportation

Adams, Gordon. *The Politics of Defense Contracting: The Iron Triangle.* New Brunswick, NJ: Transaction Books, 1982.

Airozo, Dave. "NEIPAC Pre-Election Spending Adds $14,000 to Contributions." *Nucleonics Week* 40 (1) (January 7, 1999): 13.

———. "Nuclear Industry Election Giving Creates a Tangled Trail of PACs." *Nucleonics Week* 39 (34) (August 20, 1998): 1.

Anason, Dean. "The Lobbyists: 'One Helluva Fight' Over Thrift Charter." *The American Banker* (March 10, 1999): 2.

Angel, David P. *Restructuring for Innovation: The Remaking of the U.S. Semiconductor Industry.* New York: Guilford, 1994.

Baker, Gerard. "Big Labour, Big Fightback: Leaders of Trade Unions in the U.S. Believe They Have Started to Reverse a Generation of Decline." *Financial Times* (London), September 29, 1997, p. 19.

Bang, Hae-Kyong. "Analyzing the Impact of the Liquor Industry's Lifting of the Ban on Broadcast Advertising." *Journal of Public Policy & Marketing* 17 (1) (Spring 1998): 132.

Barber, Wayne. "Nader Group Attacks NEI Ads with 'Greenwashing' Claim to FTC." *Nucleonics Week* 40 (23) (June 10, 1999): 15.

Barett, Joyce. "ATMI Weighs Demonstration Against Africa Free Trade Bill: Textile Workers May Be Bused into D.C. for Capitol Hill Rally." *Daily News Record* 50 (April 27, 1998): 1A.

Bastra, Lisa. *Searching for the Magic Bullets: Orphan Drugs, Consumer Activism, and the Pharmaceutical Development.* New York: Pharmaceutical Products Press, 1994.

Belden, Tom. "Congress Seems Eager to Address Complaints About Airlines." *The Philadelphia Inquirer*, March 14, 1999.

Bellinger, Robert, and George Leopold. "Industry Lauds H-1B Vote; Vows to Aid U.S. Education." *TechWeb News*, October 23, 1998.

Berlau, John. "Does Rule 'Blacklist' Business?" *Investor's Business Daily*, June 18, 1999, p. A1.

Bilstein, Roger E. *The American Aerospace Industry: From Workshop to Global Enterprise.* New York: Prentice-Hall, 1996.

Borland, John. "High-Tech Checkbooks Open for Campaign Season." *TechWeb News*, September 16, 1998.

Bourge, Christian. "Battle Lines Drawn on Mine Noise Proposals." *American Metal Market* 107 (104) (May 31, 1999): 6.

———. "Senate Moves to Block Restriction on Mill Sites." *American Metal Market* 107 (123) (June 28, 1999).

Bridis, Ted. "Congress Agree on New High-Tech Laws." *The Associated Press*, October 16, 1998.

Brown, Steve. "Local-Growth Regulations, Labor Shortages Concern Home Builders." *The Dallas Morning News*, January 18, 1999.

Chambers, Ann. *Power Branding.* Tulsa, OK: Pennwell, 1998.

Chubb, John E. *Interest Groups and the Bureaucracy: The Politics of Energy.* Stanford, CA: Stanford University Press, 1983.

Cleary, Mike. "Survey Finds Home Buyers Oppose Sprawl but Prefer Suburbs." *The Washington Times*, May 12, 1999.

Clune, Ray. "Fabric Makers Get New Tool for Complying with EPA Regs." *Daily News Record*, November 4, 1998, p. 9.

Cohn, Steve. *Too Cheap to Meter: An Economic and Philosophical Analysis of the Nuclear Dream.* Albany: State University of New York Press, 1997.

Cross, Lisa. "Tax Reform Promises Printers a Break: Effects of the 1997 Tax Bill on the Printing Industry. *Graphic Arts Monthly* 69 (9) (September 1997): 79.

Crow, Patrick. "EPA's Agenda." *The Oil and Gas Journal* 96 (49) (December 7, 1998): 48.

Danzon, Patricia. *Pharmaceutical Price Regulation: National Policy Versus Global Interests.* Washington, DC: American Enterprise Institute Press, 1997.

Davis, Mary. "Overreaction on Global Warming Could Prove Costly for Trucking." *Modern Bulk Transporter* (May 1998).

Dekker-Robertson, Donna L., and William J. Libby. "American Forest Policy—Global Ethics Tradeoffs." *BioScience* 48 (6) (June 1998): 471.

Dickinson, James G. "Off-Label Uses: Tiny Concession Splits Industry; Pharmaceutical Industry." *Medical Marketing & Media* 32 (11) (November 1997): 12.

Drake, Donald. *Making Medicine, Making Money.* Kansas City, MO: Andrews and McNeel, 1993.

Dunne, Nancy. "Washington Resumes Annual Battle Over Trade." *Financial Times* (London), July 22, 1998, p. 4.

Durden, Garey C., Jason F. Shogren, and Jonathan I. Silberman. "The Effects of Interest Group Pressure on Coal Strip-Mining Legislation." *Social Science Quarterly* 72 (1991): 237–50.

Environmental Protection Agency. *Profile of the Printing Industry.* Washington, DC: Office of Compliance, Office of Enforcement and Compliance Assurance, U.S. Environmental Protection Agency, 1995.

———. *Profile of the Pulp and Paper Industry.* Washington, DC: Office of Compliance, Office of Enforcement and Compliance Assurance, U.S. Environmental Protection Agency, 1995.

Fagin, Dan. *Toxic Deception: How the Chemical Industry Manipulates Science, Bends the Law, and Endangers Your Health.* Monroe, ME: Common Courage Press, 1999.

Farhi, Paul. "An Ounce or Two of Suspicion; Distillers' TV Spot Has Critics Questioning Industry's Motives." *The Washington Post*, July 28, 1998, p. E01.

Fincham, Jack, and Albert Wertheimer, eds. *Pharmacy and the U.S. Health Care System.* New York: Pharmaceutical Products Press, 1998.

Foster, Andrea. "House Passes MSDS Bill." *Chemical Week* (August 12, 1998).

Green, Paula. "Importers May Yet Be Hemmed In by Whistle-Blower Law." *Journal of Commerce* (January 22, 1998): 1A.

———. "Textiles Group Appeals Ruling on Transshipments: Court Has Turned Down the Case Against Limited Two Times So Far." *Journal of Commerce* (June 10, 1998): 3A.

Haavind, Robert. "Is the Roadmap Losing Its Effectiveness? Semiconductor Industry Association's Technology Roadmap." *Solid State Technology* 42 (2) (February 1, 1999): 12.

Hall, Kevin G. "Border Proviso Remains in Limbo." *Journal of Commerce* (October 14, 1998): 3A.

———. "Customs Agrees to Revisit Border Diversion Plan." *Journal of Commerce* (February 26, 1998): 1A.

———. "Trade Groups Want End to Nafta Dispute Panels." *Journal of Commerce* (January 29, 1998): 3A.

Henderson, Bruce. "Furniture Firms Want to Exempt 85 Carolina Factories from Clean-Air Rules." *The Charlotte Observer*, May 8, 1999.

Hess, Glenn. "Administration's Utility Proposal Receives Guarded Support from CMA." *Chemical Market Reporter* 255 (17) (April 26, 1999).

———. "CMA Cautions EPA on Its Internet Data Plan." *Chemical Market Reporter* (September 21, 1998): 5.

———. "CMA-EPA Study Assesses Reasons Why Companies Fail to Comply with Gov't Environmental Guidelines." *Chemical Market Reporter* 256 (3) (July 19, 1999): 28.

———. "CMA Tentatively Endorses Restrictions on Access to Worst-Case Scenario Data." *Chemical Market Reporter* 255 (22) (May 31, 1999): 1.

———. "PhRMA Takes a Wait-and-See Approach to a Medicare Prescription Drug Plan." *Chemical Market Reporter* 256 (1) (July 5, 1999): 1.

———. "Trade Groups Call for Revisions to Osha's Pels: Occupational Safety and Health Administration's Permissible Exposure Limits." *Chemical Market Reporter* 255 (3) (January 18, 1999): 40.

Hicks, Darryl. "Industry PACs Donate $ 10.8 Million." *National Mortgage News,* February 15, 1999.

Hogan, Dave. "Expected Attempt to Revise Endangered Species Law Sparks Debate." *The Oregonian,* December 28, 1998.

Holm, Erik. "NEI Calls For Overhaul of NRC Enforcement Policy." *The Energy Daily,* July 6, 1998.

Ichniowski, Tom, and Sherie Winston. "Tax-Cut Bills Could Be Vehicles for Construction Breaks." *Engineering News-Record* 242 (8) (February 22, 1999): 11.

Jasper, James. *Nuclear Politics: Energy and the State in the United States, Sweden, and France.* Princeton, NJ: Princeton University Press, 1990.

Karey, Gerald. "EPA Plots Appeal of Court Verdict on Ozone, Soot Regulations." *Platt's Oilgram News* 77 (94) (May 18, 1999): 1.

Kauzlarich, David. *Crimes of the American Nuclear State: At Home and Abroad.* Boston: Northeastern University Press, 1998.

Kertes, Noella. "Mining Joins R&D Initiative." *American Metal Market* 105 (198) (October 13, 1997): 4.

———. "NMA Alleges Assault by Federal Agencies." *American Metal Market* 106 (68) (April 10, 1998): 2.

———. "NMA Urges Speed-Up of Environmental Process." *American Metal Market* 106 (55) (March 24, 1998): 8.

Kjelgaard, Chris. "ATA Protests DOT's Huge Proposed Fee Hikes." *Air Transport Intelligence,* March 23, 1999.

———. "DOT Wants to Widen Safety Audit Net to Foreign Airlines." *Air Transport Intelligence,* August 5, 1999.

———. "FAA to Attack Growing U.S. Flight Delay Problem. *Air Transport Intelligence,* August 13, 1999.

Knee, Richard. "U.S. Health Group Plans Chem Lobby Effort." *Chemical News & Intelligence,* June 4, 1999.

Kochiesen, Carol. "Court Reins in EPA in Clean Air Suit." *Nation's Cities Weekly* 22 (21) (May 24, 1999): 9.

Kwoka, John E. *Power Structure: Ownership, Integration, and Competition in the U.S. Electricity Industry.* Boston: Kluwer Academic Publishers, 1996.

Lewis, Diane. "Judge Overturns Labor Agreement; Says Nonunion Workers Entitled to Work on Project." *The Boston Globe*, April 2, 1998, p. C1.

Lobsenz, George. "Utilities, Coal Groups Float NOx Control Proposal." *The Energy Daily,* February 3, 1998.

Love, Alice Ann. "Campaigns Under Way to Influence Social Security Debate." *The Associated Press,* March 10, 1999.

MacMillan, Robert. "Govt Helps Create Chip Fund." *Newsbytes,* December 10, 1998.

———. "Lobbyists Fan the Senate's Y2K Flames." *Newsbytes,* June 8, 1999.

———. "Some Nuclear Plants Still Not Y2K-Compliant." *Newsbytes,* July 7, 1999.

McManus, Reed. "Taking It to the Streets; Al Gore's Plan to Battle Urban Sprawl." *Sierra* 84 (3) (May 1, 1999): 22.

Moore, W. Henson. "Elimination of Tariff Barriers a Must for Health of the Industry." *Pulp & Paper* 72 (5) (May 1998): 144.

Morrissey, James A. "Congress Eyes Issues Impacting Textiles." *Textile World* 148 (1) (January 1998): 64.

Mosquera, Mary. "Congress Commits to Long-Term R&D Tax Credit." *TechWeb News,* August 2, 1999.

Mottley, Robert. "Rigged? Jury Settlement Has Insurers Crying Foul. ATA Proposal Would Steer Truckers Clear of Liability." *American Shipper* 41 (6) (June 1, 1999): 46.

Niccolai, James. "Chip Industry Distances Itself from Y2K Issue." *InfoWorld Electric,* December 4, 1998.

Owens, Jennifer. "Lobbyists Ready for Reruns in January." *WWD.* November 3, 1998, p. 19.

Pattillo, Donald M. *Pushing the Envelope: The American Aircraft Industry.* Ann Arbor: University of Michigan Press, 1998.

Pope, Carl. "Slugs and Dinosaurs: Why Some Industries Drag Their Feet." *Sierra* 82 (5) (September 19, 1997): 14.

Porstner, Donna. "Manufacturers Spin Off Lobby for Taking Social Security Private." *The Washington Times,* July 21, 1998.

Przybyla, Heidi. "Business Groups to Lobby for China Deal." *Journal of Commerce* (March 30, 1999): 2A.

Quinlan, Tom. "Chip Industry, U.S. Government Commit to Research Effort." *San Jose Mercury News,* December 10, 1998.

Reddy, Tarun. "Computing Bill Emphasizes Basic R&D Funding." *Federal Technology Report* (June 3, 1999): 3.

Robertson, Jack. "SIA Praises Clinton's Trade Extension for China." *Electronic Buyers' News,* June 4, 1999.

———. "SIA to Congress: Scrap Trade Barriers." *Electronic Buyers' News,* August 9, 1999.

———. "SIA Warns Congress About Anti-Dumping." *Electronic Buyers' News,* August 5, 1999.

Robyn, Dorothy L. *Braking the Special Interests: Trucking Deregulation and the Politics of Policy Reform.* Chicago: University of Chicago Press, 1987.

Ryan, Margaret L. "Actions Favoring Nei Raising Fairness Questions in Industry." *Inside N.R.C.* 21 (11) (May 24, 1999): 1.

Salant, Jonathan. "Businesses, Trial Lawyers Square Off Over Y2K." *The Associated Press,* April 24, 1999.

Sanda, Arthur. "NMA Becoming a Force in Washington." *Coal Age* (September 1997): 37.

———. "NMA Perspective; NMA Year in Review." *Coal Age* (September 1998).

Schweitzer, Stuart. *Pharmaceutical Economics and Policy.* New York: Oxford University Press, 1997.

Semiconductor Industry Association. *Status Report & Industry Directory.* Cupertino, CA: The Association, 1997–98.

Semien, John. "Builders' Group, Contractor Sue over Set-Asides for Minorities." *The Commercial Appeal* (Memphis, TN), January 6, 1999, p. B2.

Sidler, Stephen. "U.S. Manufacturers Call for Tax Cut as Fed Holds Interest Rates." *Financial Times* (London), December 23, 1998, p. 14.

Simonsis, Yolanda. "Is There a Kinder and Gentler OSHA?" *Paper, Film & Foil Converter* 72 (11) (November 1998): 6.

Sissell, Kara. "Court Strikes Down OSHA Compliance Program." *Chemical Week* (April 21, 1999): 12.

Smeloff, Ed. *Reinventing Electric Utilities: Competition, Citizen Action, and Clean Power.* Washington, DC: Island Press, 1997.

Sonner, Scott. "Campaign Gifts Said to Help Timber Industry Keep Road Funds." *The Associated Press,* December 16, 1997.

Steelman, Aaron. "Are Trade Sanctions Worth It?" *Investor's Business Daily,* September 23, 1998, A1.

Stern, Christopher. "Booze on Back Burner at FCC. *Daily Variety,* February 2, 1998.

Sullivan, Kevin. "Lobbyists Turn Up the Heat at Global Warming Forum; Industry Makes Its Case Against Proposed Treaty." *The Washington Post,* December 4, 1997, p. A01.

Tong, Kathryn. "Exporters Pour on the Spirits Globally." *Journal of Commerce* (August 4, 1998): 13A.
Ulbrecht, Jaromir, J. ed. *Competitiveness of the U.S. Chemical Industry in International Markets*. New York: American Institute of Chemical Engineers, 1990.
Usdin, Steve. "U.S. House Passes Regs Accountability Bill." *Chemical News & Intelligence* (July 27, 1999).
Watson, Rip. "House Bill Proposes Putting Heftier Trucks on Nation's Highways." *Journal of Commerce* (May 7, 1999): 1A.
———. "Lobby Blasts Federal Regulations." *Journal of Commerce* (June 7, 1999): 17.
———. "Ports Blast Proposal to Blame Terminals." *Journal of Commerce* (August 5, 1999): 14.
———. "TA Supports DOT on Safety, Emissions." *Journal of Commerce* (June 24, 1999): 14.
Wechsler, Jill. "FDA Faces 'Modernization'; FDA to Reform Following Congress Approval of Its Modernization Act of 1997." *BioPharm* (January 1998): 10.
Weil, Jenny. "NEI Calls for Legislative Fixes to Help Industry Be Competitive." *Inside N.R.C.* 20 (6) (December 21, 1998): 13.
Whitmore, Elaine. *Product Development Planning for Health Care Products Deregulated by the FDA*. Milwaukee: ASQC Quality Press, 1997.
Winston, Sherie. "Rules Rile Contractor Groups." *Engineering News-Record* 243 (3) (July 19, 1999): 10.
Winston, Sherie, and Jeff Barber. "Labor: Court Upholds Suspension of Helper Rules." *Engineering News-Record* 239 (7) (August 18, 1997): 7.
Zuckerman, Amy. "Manufacturers Group Official Spending More Time Helping Members Cope with Standards." *Journal of Commerce* (October 15, 1997): 14C.

Labor

American Federation of Labor and Congress of Industrial Organizations. *AFL-CIO American Federationist*. Vols. 84–present (1976–present).
———. *One Hundred Years of American Labor, 1881–1981*. Washington, DC: American Federation of Labor and Congress of Industrial Organizations, 1981.
American Federation of State, County and Municipal Employees. *A Powerful Voice in the Workplace* (pamphlet). Washington, DC: American Federation of State, County and Municipal Employees, n.d.
———. *Public Employee*. Vols. 46–present (1992–present).
American Federation of Teachers. *AFT Convention Reports*. Vols. 1–present (1977–present). Washington, DC: American Federation of Teachers.
———. *American Educator*. Vols. 1–present (Winter 1977–present).
American Postal Workers Union. *The American Postal Worker*. Vols. 1–present (1971–present).
———. *Questions and Answers about the APWU* (pamphlet). Washington, DC: American Postal Workers Union, n.d.
Aronowitz, Stanley. *From the Ashes of the Old: American Labor and America's Future*. Boston: Houghton Mifflin Company, 1998.
Asher, Robert, and Ronald Edsforth, with the assistance of Stephen Merlino. *Autowork*. Albany: State University of New York Press, 1995.
Bahr, Morton. *From the Telegraph to the Internet*. Washington, DC: National Press Books, 1998.
Berube, Maurice R. *Teacher Politics: The Influence of Unions*. New York: Greenwood Press, 1988.
Bronfenbrenner, Kate, Sheldon Friedman, Richard W. Hurd, Rudolph A. Oswald, and Ronald L. Seeber. *Organizing to Win: New Research on Union Strategies*. Ithaca, NY: Cornell University Press, 1998.
Brooks, Thomas R. *Communications Workers of America: The Story of a Union*. New York: Mason/Charter, 1977.
Chaison, Gary N. *Union Mergers in Hard Times: The View From Five Countries*. Ithaca, NY: ILR Press, 1996.
Clark, Paul F., Peter Gottlieb, and Donald Kennedy, eds. *Forging a Union of Steel: Philip Murray, SWOC and the United Steelworkers*. Ithaca, NY: International Labor Review Press, 1987.
Communications Workers of America. *CWA News: Official Journal of the Communications Workers of America*. Vols. 1–present (July–present).
Cowie, Jefferson. *Capital Moves: RCA's 70-Year Quest for Cheap Labor*. Ithaca, NY: Cornell University Press, 1999.
Dark, Taylor. *The Unions and the Democrats: An Enduring Alliance*. Ithaca, NY: Cornell University Press, 1998.
Fraser, Steven, and Joshua B. Freeman. *Audacious Democracy: Labor, Intellectuals, and the Social Reconstruction of America*. Boston: Houghton Mifflin Company, 1997.
Freeman, Richard B., and Joel Rogers. *What Workers Want*. Ithaca, NY: Cornell University Press, 1999.
Goodman, John F. *Working at the Calling*. Hopkinton, MA: New England Laborers' Labor-Management Cooperation, 1991.
Herzenberg, Stephen A., John A. Alic, and Howard Wial. *New Rules for a New Economy: Employment and Opportunity in Postindustrial America*. Ithaca, NY: Cornell University Press, 1998.
Hoerr, John. *We Can't Eat Prestige: The Women Who Organized Harvard*. Philadelphia: Temple University Press, 1997.
Hopkins, George. *The Airline Pilots; a Study in Elite Unionism*. Cambridge, MA: Harvard University Press, 1971.
———. *Flying the Line: The First Half Century of the Air Line Pilots Association*. Washington, DC: Air Line Pilots Association, 1982.
Hotel Employees & Restaurant Employees (HERE) International Union. *Catering Industry Employee* (bimonthly publication).
International Association of Fire Fighters. *International Fire Fighter*. Vols. 1–present (1918–present).
International Association of Machinists. *International Association of Machinists Journal*. Vols. 1–present (1995–present).
International Association of Machinists. *The Machinist*. Vols. 1–49 (April 4, 1946-1994).
International Brotherhood of Electrical Workers. *IBEW Journal*. Vols. 1–present (1902–present).
———. *International Brotherhood of Electrical Workers. History and Structure*. Washington, DC: International Brotherhood of Electrical Workers, n.d.
International Union of Operating Engineers. *Building a Better Tomorrow*. Washington, DC: International Union of Operating Engineers, n.d.
Johnston, Paul. *Success While Others Fail: Social Movement Unionism and the Public Workplace*. Ithaca, NY: ILR Press, 1994.
Juravich, Tom, and Kate Bronfenbrenner. *Ravenswood: The Steelworkers' Victory and the Revival of American Labor*. Ithaca, NY: Cornell University Press, 1999.
Kuttner, Robert. *Everything for Sale. The Virtues and Limits of Markets*. New York: Alfred A. Knopf, 1977.

Laborers International Union of North America. *Innovation at Work* (pamphlet). Washington, DC: n.d.
———. *The Laborer*. Vols. 1–present (1947–present).
Lichtenstein, Nelson. *The Most Dangerous Man in Detroit: Walter Reuther and the Fate of American Labor*. New York: Basic Books, 1995.
Mangum, Garth. *Union Resilience in Troubled Times: The Story of the Operating Engineers, AFL-CIO, 1960–1993*. Armonk, NY: M.E. Sharpe, 1994.
Mantsios, Gregory, ed. *A New Labor Movement for a New Century*. New York: Monthly Review Press, 1998.
Moody, Kim. *Workers in a Lean World: Unions in the International Economy*. London: Verso, 1997.
Mort, Jo-Ann. *Not Your Father's Union Movement: Inside the AFL-CIO*. New York: Verso, 1998.
Mungazi, Dickson A. *Where He Stands: Albert Shanker of the American Federation of Teachers*. Westport, CT: Praeger, 1995.
Murphy, Marjorie. *Blackboard Unions: The AFT and the NEA, 1900–1980*. Ithaca, NY: Cornell University Press, 1990.
National Education Association of the United States. *Handbook*. Washington, DC: National Education Association, 1975–present.
———. *NEA Today: A Newspaper for Members of the National Education Association*. Vols. 1–present (October 1982–present). Washington, DC: National Education Association.
Ness, Immanuel. *Trade Unions and the Betrayal of the Unemployed*. New York: Garland Publishing, 1998.
Palladino, Grace. *Dreams of Dignity, Workers of Vision: A History of the International Brotherhood of Electrical Workers*. Washington, DC: International Brotherhood of Electrical Workers, 1991.
Perusek, Glenn, and Kent Worcester, eds. *Trade Union Politics: American Unions and Economic Change: 1960s–1990s*. Atlantic Highlands, NJ: Humanities Press, 1995.
Pollin, Robert, and Stephanie Luce. *The Living Wage: Building a Fair Economy*. New York: New Press, 1998.
Richardson, George J. *Symbol of Action: A History of the International Association of Fire Fighters, AFL-CIO-CLC*. Washington, DC: International Association of Fire Fighters, 1974.
Rodden, Robert G. *The Fighting Machinists: A Century of Struggle*. Washington, DC: Kelly Press, 1984.
Schafer, Todd, and Jeff Faux. *Reclaiming Prosperity: A Blueprint for Progressive Economic Reform*. Armonk, NY: M.E. Sharpe, 1996.
Seafarers International Union. *Seafarers Log*. Vols. 1–present (1976–present).
Service Employees International Union. *SEIU Leadership News*. Vols. 1–present (May/June 1968–present).
———. *Service Employee*. Vols. 16–46 (February 1957–December 1986).
Sweeney, John J. *America Needs a Raise: Fighting for Economic Security and Social Justice*. Boston: Houghton Mifflin Company, 1996.
Transport Workers Union. *TWU Express: Official Organ of the Transport Workers Union of America, CIO*. Vols. 1–present (December 1948–present).
Tyler, Gus. *Look for the Union Label: A History of the International Ladies' Garment Workers' Union*. Armonk, NY: M.E. Sharpe, 1995.
Union of Needletrades, Industrial and Textile Employees. *The Phony Social Security Crisis* (pamphlet). New York: Union of Needletrades, Industrial and Textile Employees, n.d.
———. *Stop Sweatshops* (pamphlet). New York: Union of Needletrades, Industrial and Textile Employees, n.d.
United Automobile Workers. *Highlights of the History of Organized Labor and the UAW*. Detroit: United Automobile Workers, 1993.
———. *UAW Action Program* (pamphlet). Detroit: United Automobile Workers, 1998.
———. *UAW Resources: A Guide to UAW Services* (pamphlet). Detroit: United Automobile Workers, n.d.
———. *UAW Solidarity*. Vols. 1–present (January 1985–present).
United Food and Commercial Workers. *The Professional's Choice* (pamphlet). Washington, DC: United Food and Commercial Workers, n.d.
———. *UFCW Action*. Vols. 1–present (1979–present).
———. *UFCW: An Introduction* (pamphlet). Washington, DC: United Food and Commercial Workers, n.d.
———. *The Voice of Working America* (pamphlet). Washington, DC: United Food and Commercial Workers, n.d.
United Steelworkers of America. *News from the Steel Workers* (pamphlet). Pittsburgh: United Steelworkers of America, 1998.
———. *Steelabor: The Voice of the United Steelworkers of America*. Vols.1–present (January 1979–present).
United Transportation Union. *Constitution*. Cleveland: United Transportation Union, 1995.
———. *Getting a Message to Congress*. Cleveland: United Transportation Union, n.d.
———. *A History of the United Transportation Union and the American Labor Movement*. Cleveland: United Transportation Union, n.d.
———. *Tranportation Occupation Handbook*. Cleveland: United Transportation Union, n.d.
———. *UTU News*. Vols. 1–present (1969–present). Cleveland: United Transportation Union, 1969–present.
Walsh, John. *Labor Struggle in the Post Office: From Selective Lobbying to Collective Bargaining*. Armonk, NY: M.E. Sharpe, 1992.
West, Allan M. *The National Education Association: The Power Base for Education*. New York: Free Press, 1980.

Civil and Human Rights

ACORN. *ACORN's 25 Year History*. www.acorn.org.
De Angelis, James J., ed. *Public Interest Profiles, 1998–1999*. Washington, DC: Congressional Quarterly Foundation for Public Affairs, 1998.
Duskin, Meg. "Census 2000 Doesn't Add Up." *National Voter* 48 (3) (March/April 1999).
Foxman, Abraham H. *Wall Street Journal*, Op-ed., December 4, 1998.
Freedom House. "Freedom House and National Forum Foundation Join Forces." *Freedom Monitor* 13 (2) (Fall 1997).
Greider, William, "The Hard Fight Against Soft Money." *Rolling Stone* 763 (June 6, 1997).
Griffin Kelley. *Ralph Nader Presents More Action for a Change*. New York: Dembner Books, 1987.
National Lawyers Guild. Informational materials sent upon request: National Lawyers Guild, 126 University Place, 5th Floor, NY, NY 10003. www.nlg.org.
Raymond, John. "Human Rights Watch Member Offers Resignation." *New Amsterdam News* 90 (11) (March 11, 1999).
Richan, Willard C. *Lobbying for Social Change*. New York: Haworth Press, 1991.

Rothenburg, Lawrence S. *Linking Citizens to Government: Interest Group Politics at Common Cause.* New York: Cambridge University Press, 1992.

Tolley, H. "Interest Group Litigation to Enforce Human Rights." *Political Science Quarterly* 105 (4) (Winter 1990): 617–39.

Walker, Jack L. *Mobilizing Interest Groups in America: Patrons, Professions, and Social Movements.* Ann Arbor: University of Michigan Press, 1991.

Political, Religious, and Ideological

American Enterprise Institute. *Annual Report 1999.* Washington, DC: American Enterprise Institute for Public Policy Research, 1999.

———. "The Face of the Future: 1997 Annual Report." Indianapolis, IN: Hudson Institute, 1998.

Bartel, Richard D. "EPI Links Economic Growth with Economic Justice." *Challenge* 35 (1) (January/February 1992): 13-23.

Berry, Jeffrey M. *The Interest Group Society.* 2d ed. Boston: Scott, Foresman/Little, Brown, 1989.

Brock, Clifton. *Americans for Democratic Action: Its Role in National Politics.* Washington, DC: Public Affairs Press, 1962.

Callahan, David. *$1 Billion for Ideas: Conservative Think Tanks in the 1990s.* Washington, DC: National Committee for Responsive Philanthropy, 1999.

Cato Institute. *Cato Handbook for Congress: 105th Congress.* Washington, DC: Cato Institute, 1997.

Cigler, Allan J., and Burdett A. Loomis, eds. *Interest Group Politics.* 4th ed. Washington, DC: Congressional Quarterly Press, 1994.

Critchlow, Donald T. *The Brookings Institution, 1916–1952: Expertise and the Public Interest in a Democratic Society.* DeKalb: Northern Illinois University Press, 1985.

Edsall, Thomas B., and Mary D. Edsall. *Chain Reaction: The Impact of Race, Rights, and Taxes on American Politics.* New York: W.W. Norton and Company, 1992.

Edwards, Lee. *The Power of Ideas: The Heritage Foundation at 25 Years.* Ottawa, IL: Jameson Books, 1997.

Forster, Arnold, and Benjamin Epstein. *Danger on the Right.* New York: Random House, 1964.

Gillon, Steven. *Politics and Vision: The ADA and American Liberalism, 1947–1985.* New York: Oxford University Press, 1987.

Herrnson, Paul S., Ronald G. Shaiko, and Clyde Wilcox, eds. *The Interest Group Connection: Electioneering, Lobbying, and Policymaking in Washington.* Chatham, NJ: Chatham House Publishers, 1998.

Hrebenar, Ronald J. *Interest Group Politics in America.* 3d ed. Armonk, NY: M.E. Sharpe, 1997.

Lanouette, William J. "The Shadow Cabinets—Changing Themselves as They Try to Change Policy." *National Journal* 10 (8) (February 25, 1978): 296–300.

Mundy, Alicia. "Tanks for the Quotes." *Mediaweek* 6 (27) (July 1, 1996): 16–19.

Saunders, Charles. *Brookings Institution: A Fifty-Year History.* Washington, DC: Brookings Institution, 1966.

Solomon, Burt. "Ferment at Brookings." *The National Journal* 29 (42) (October 18, 1997): 2080–89.

Stone, Barbara S. "The John Birch Society: A Profile." *Journal of Politics* 36 (February 1974).

Stone, Peter H. "Grass-Roots Goliath." *National Journal.* (July 13, 1996): 1529–33.

Walker, Jack L. "The Origins and Maintenance of Interest Groups in America." *The American Political Science Review* 77 (2) (June 1983): 390–406.

Wilcox, Derk Arend. *The Right Guide: A Guide to Conservative and Right-of-Center Organizations.* Ann Arbor, MI: Economics America, Inc., 1997.

———, ed. *The Left Guide: A Guide to Left-of-Center Organizations.* Ann Arbor, MI: Economics America, Inc., 1996.

Single Issue

Anderson, Jack. *Inside the NRA: Armed and Dangerous: An Exposé.* Beverly Hills, CA: Dove Books, 1996.

Archer, Glenn, and Albert Menendez. *The Dream Lives On: The Story of Glenn L. Archer and Americans United.* Washington, DC: Robert B. Luce, Inc., 1982.

Batchelor, John Calvin. *Ain't You Glad You Joined the Republicans?* New York: Henry Holt and Company, 1996.

Bruce, John, and Clyde Wilcox, eds. *The Changing Politics of Gun Control.* Lanham, MD: Rowman & Littlefield, 1998.

Chafe, William H. *Never Stop Running—Allard S. Lowenstein and the Struggle to Save American Liberalism.* New York: Basic Books, 1993.

Cigler, Allan J., and Burdett A. Loomis. *Interest Group Politics,* 5th ed. Washington, DC: Congressional Quarterly Press, 1998.

Cole, Wayne S. *Charles A. Lindbergh and the Battle Against American Intervention in World War II.* New York: Harcourt Brace Jovanovich, 1974.

Davidson, Osha Gray. *Under Fire—The NRA & The Battle for Gun Control.* New York: Henry Holt & Co. 1993.

De la Pena, Fernando. *Democracy or Babel? The Case for Official U.S. English.* Washington, DC: U.S. English, 1991.

Goodman, Y.R. "Flag Law on the Front Burner." *Legal Times,* May 10, 1999.

Gorney, Cynthia. *Articles of Faith.* New York: Simon & Schuster, 1998.

Kamber, Victor. *Giving Up on Democracy—Why Term Limits Are Bad for America.* Washington, DC: Regnery Publishing, 1995.

Leddy, Edward. *Magnum Force Lobby: The National Rifle Association Fights Gun Control.* Lanham, MD: University Press of America, 1987.

Leone, Bruno. *The Women's Rights Movement—Opposing Viewpoints.* San Diego, CA: Greenhaven Press, 1996.

Lewin, Tamer. "Founder of Anti-Drunk-Driving Campaign Now Lobbies for Breweries." *New York Times,* June 15, 1994.

Lindeman, Bard. "A Famous Son, An Old Game." *50 Plus* (June 1988).

Loeb, Raul Rogat. *Hope in Hard Times—America's Peace Movement in the Reagan Era.* Lexington, MA: Lexington Books, 1987.

Massie, Robert Kinloch. *Loosing the Bonds—The United States and South Africa in the Apartheid Years.* New York: Doubleday, 1994.

McWilliam, Rita. "The Best and Worst of the Public Interest Groups." *The Washington Monthly* (March 1988).

Pratt, Henry J. *Gray Agendas: Interest Groups and Public Pensions in Canada, Britain, and the United States.* Ann Arbor: University of Michigan Press, 1993.

Sherman, Dianne. "Zero Population Growth." *Environment Magazine* (November 1993).

Slaughter, Thomas P. *The Whiskey Rebellion: Frontier Epilogue to the American Revolution.* New York: Oxford University Press, 1986.

Spindler, Amy. "Calvin Klein Will Stop Making Furs." *New York Times*, February 11, 1994.
Wager, Janet S. "Union of Concerned Scientists." *Environment Magazine* (May 1994).
Young, Amy. "The Money Behind the Movement." *Common Cause Magazine* (Summer 1993).
Zinn, Howard. *A People's History of the United States, 1492–Present.* New York: HarperPerennial, 1995.

Identity Groups

American Association of Retired Persons. *Where We Stand.* www.aarp.org/where.htm.
American Civil Liberties Union. *77 Years, 77 Great Victories.* ACLU Informational material. aclu.org.
American Civil Liberties Union. "Guardian of Liberty: American Civil Liberties Union." *ACLU Briefing Paper*, no. 1. aclu.org.
American Legion. *The American Legion: Who We Are.* www.legion.org/backfact.htm.
Aronowitz, Stanley. *The Politics of Identity: Class, Culture, and Social Movements.* New York: Routledge, 1992.
Birnbaum, Jeffrey. "Washington's Second Most Powerful Man." *Time,* May 12, 1997.
Churchill, Ward. "A Force, Briefly, to Be Reckoned With." *The Progressive* (June 1997).
Cigler, Allan J., and Burdett A. Loomis. *Interest Group Politics.* 3d ed. Washington, DC: Congressional Quarterly Press, 1991.
Congress of Racial Equality. *Congress of Racial Equality.* www.core-online.org.
Craig, Barbara Hinkson, and David O'Brien. *Abortion and American Politics.* Chatham, NJ: Chatham House, 1993.
De Angelis, James, ed. *Public Interest Profiles, 1998–99.* Washington, DC: Congressional Quarterly Foundation for Public Affairs, 1998.
Epstein, Lee. *Contemplating Courts.* Washington, DC: Congressional Quarterly Press, 1996.
Epstein, Lee, and Thomas Walker. *Constitutional Law for a Changing America.* Washington, DC: Congressional Quarterly Press, 1997.
Harrington, Michael. *The Other America.* New York: Simon & Schuster, 1997.
Herrnson, Paul S., Ronald G. Shaiko, and Clyde Wilcox. *The Interest Group Connection.* Chatham, NJ: Chatham House Publishers, 1998.
Hertzke, Allen D. *Representing God in Washington: The Role of Religious Lobbies in the American Polity.* Knoxville: University of Tennessee Press, 1988.
Hofrenning, Daniel J. B. *In Washington But Not of It: The Prophetic Politics of Religious Lobbyists.* Philadelphia: Temple University Press, 1995.
Johnson, Troy. "Roots of Contemporary Native American Activism." *American Indian Culture and Research Journal* 20 (2) (1996).
Kennedy, Michael. "The Law and Native Americans." *Boston Globe,* November. 20, 1997.
Keys, David. "Collective Identity Theory of Social Movements: Development of African American Consciousness and the Congress of Racial Equality, 1942–66." Master's thesis, University of Missouri-Columbia, Columbia, MO, 1994.
Lehman Scholzman, Kay, and John T. Tierney. *Organized Interests and American Democracy.* New York: Harper and Row, 1986.
Lieberman, Alan. "Up from Liberalism." *National Review,* March 1, 1993.
Madison, James. "Federalist No. 10." In *The Federalist Papers,* by James Madison, Alexander Hamilton, and John Jay. New York: Viking/Penguin, 1989.
McArdle, Thomas. "Golden Oldies: American Association of Retired Persons' Liberalism." *National Review* 47 (4) (1995).
Meier, A., and E. Rudwick. *CORE: A Study in the Civil Rights Movement, 1942–1968.* New York: Oxford University Press, 1973.
Morris, Charles. *The AARP: America's Most Powerful Lobby and the Clash of Generations.* New York: Times Books, 1996.
Offe, Claus. "New Social Movements: Challenging the Boundaries of Institutional Politics." *Social Research* 52 (4) (1985).
Pratt, Henry J. *Gray Agendas: Interest Groups and Public Pensions in Canada, Britain, and the United States.* Ann Arbor: University of Michigan Press, 1993.
Rajchman, John, ed. *The Identity in Question.* New York: Routledge, 1995.
Riessman, Frank, and Timothy Bay. "The Politics of Self-Help." *Social Policy* 23 (2) (1993).
Ross, Jeffrey, et al., eds. *The Mobilization of Collective Identity: A Comparative Perspective.* Lanham, MD: University Press of America, 1980.
Rozell, Mark J., and Clyde Wilcox. *God at the Grassroots 1994: The Christian Right in American Elections.* Lanham, MD: Rowman & Littlefield, 1995.
Rumer, Thomas. *The American Legion: An Official History.* New York: M. Evans and Company, 1990.
Slagle, Anthony. "In Defense of Queer Nation: From Identity Politics to a Politics of Difference." *Western Journal of Communication* 59 (2) (1995): 85–103.
Taylor, V., and Whittier, N. "Collective Identity in Social Movement Communities: Lesbian Feminist Mobilization." In *Frontiers in Social Movement Theory,* edited by Aldon Morris and Carol M. Mueller. New Haven: Yale University Press, 1992.
Tolley, H. "Interest Group Litigation to Enforce Human Rights." *Political Science Quarterly* 105 (4) (Winter 1990).
Walker, Jack L. *Mobilizing Interest Groups in America: Patrons, Professions, and Social Movements.* Ann Arbor: University of Michigan Press, 1991.
Waterman, Laura, and Elaine Salinas. *A Brief History of the AIM.* www.tdi.net/Ishgooda/aimhist1.htm.

Foreign

Aybet, Gulner. *Turkey's Foreign Policy and Its Implications for the West: A Turkish Perspective.* Boulder, CO: Westview Press, 1996.
Barber, Phillippe I. *European Union Handbook.* Chicago: Fitzroy Dearborn Publishers, 1996.
Baumgartner, Frank R., and Beth L. Leech, *Basic Interests: The Importance of Groups in Politics.* Princeton, NJ: Princeton University Press, 1998.
Birnbaum, Jeffrey. *The Lobbyists: How Influence Peddlers Get Their Way in Washington.* New York: Times Books, 1992.
Blank, Steven J. *Turkey's Strategic Position at the Crossroads of World Affairs.* Carlisle Barracks, PA: Strategic Studies Institute, 1993.
Buchan, David. *Europe: The Strange Superpower.* Brookfield, VT: Dartmouth Publishing Co., 1993.
Choate, Pat. *Agents of Influence.* New York: Alfred A. Knopf, 1990.

Cigler, Allan, and Burdett A. Loomis. *Interest Group Politics*. 5th ed. Washington, DC: Congressional Quarterly Press, 1998.

Cohen, Stephen D. *An Ocean Apart: Explaining Three Decades of U.S.–Japanese Trade Frictions*. Westport, CT: Praeger Publishers, 1999.

de la Garza, Rudolfo, and Jesus Velasco, eds. *Bridging the Border: Transforming Mexico-US Relations*. New York: Rowman and Littlefield, 1997.

Dresser, Denise. *Mr. Salinas Goes to Washington: Mexican Lobbying in the United States*. New York: Columbia University–New York University Consortium, National Resource Center for Latin American and Caribbean Studies, 1991.

Findley, Paul. *They Dare to Speak Out: People and Institutions Confront Israel's Lobby*. Chicago: Lawrence Hill Books, 1985.

Goldberg, David Howard. *Foreign Policy and Ethnic Interest Groups: American and Canadian Jews Lobby for Israel*, New York: Greenwood Press, 1990.

Hickey, Dennis Van Vranken. *Taiwan's Security in the Changing International System*. Boulder, CO: Lynne Rienner Publishers, 1997.

Hill, Christopher. *The Actors in Europe's Foreign Policy*. London: Routledge, 1996.

Kanet, Roger, and Alexander Kozheminkin. *The Foreign Policy of the Russian Federation*. New York: St. Martin's Press, 1997.

Kegley, Charles W., Jr., and Eugene R. Wittkopf. *The Domestic Sources of American Foreign Policy*. New York: St. Martin's Press, 1988.

Lewis, Peter M. *Stabilizing Nigeria*. New York: The Century Foundation Press, 1998.

Lipson, Charles. "American Support for Israel: History, Sources, Limits." In *US-Israel Relations at the Crossroads*, edited by Gabriel Sheffer. Portland, OR: Frank Cass, 1997.

Mastny, Vojtech, and R. Craig Nation, eds. *Turkey Between East and West*. Boulder, CO: Westview Press, 1996.

Oksenberg, Michael, and Elizabeth Economy. *Shaping U.S.-China Relations*. New York: Council of Foreign Relations, 1997.

Pope, Nicole, and Hugh Pope. *Turkey Unveiled: A History of Modern Turkey*. New York: Overlook Press, 1997.

Rozell, Mark J., and Clyde Wilcox. *Interest Groups in American Campaigns: The New Face of Electioneering*. Washington, DC: Congressional Quarterly Press, 1999.

Sutter, Robert G. *Shaping China's Future in World Affairs: The U.S. Role*. Carlisle Barracks, PA: Strategic Studies Institute, 1996.

Sutter, Robert G., and William R. Johnson. *Taiwan in World Affairs*. San Francisco: Westview Press, 1994.

Tierney, John T. "Interest Group Involvement in Congressional Foreign and Defense Policy." In *Congress Resurgent: Foreign and Defense Policy on Capitol Hill*, edited by Randall B. Ripley and James M. Lindsay. Ann Arbor: University of Michigan Press, 1993.

Trofimenko, Henry. *Russian National Interests and the Current Crisis in Russia*. Hampshire, UK: Ashgate Publishing, 1999.

Wantanabe, Paul Y. *Ethnic Groups, Congress, and American Foreign Policy: The Politics of the Turkish Arms Embargo*. Westport, CT: Greenwood Press, 1984.

INDEX

A

AARP. *See* American Association of Retired Persons
AARP Bulletin, **2**:561
AARP/VOTE, **2**:562
ABA Banking Journal, **1**:10
Abacha, Sani, **2**:507, 609
Abbott Laboratories, **2**:653, 656
ABC, **1**:133; **2**:372, 680
ABC/Disney, **1**:87–88
ABC Today, **1**:315
Abolitionist movement, **2**:506–7
Abortion
    American Civil Liberties Union, **2**:434
    American Conservative Union, **2**:461–62
    Americans for Democratic Action, **2**:458, 467
    Cato Institute, **2**:458
    Christian Coalition, **2**:458, 481, 482
    Global Gag Rule, **2**:554
    John Birch Society, **2**:458, 495
    National Abortion and Reproduction Action League, **2**:526–28, 622, 623, 665, 667
    National Organization for Women, **2**:583–85
    National Right to Life Committee, **2**:536–38, 623, 665, 667
    Pro-Choice and Pro-Life PACs, **2**:665, 667
    Supreme Court Rulings, **2**:543
    United States Catholic Conference, **2**:458, 503
    Zero Population Growth, **2**:554
    See also Family planning; *Roe v. Wade*
Abraham, Spencer, **1**:91, 348
Abubakar, **2**:609
Mumia, Abu-Jamal, **1**:87–88
Accounting
    leading PACs, **2**:652
    lobbying expenditures, **2**:698
    See also under Specific group
Accreditation Council for Graduate Medical Education, **1**:202
Accuracy in Media, **1**:125–26, 133
ACEP News, **1**:172
ACLU. *See* American Civil Liberties Union
ACORN. *See* Association of Community Organizations for Reform Now
ACT-SO, **2**:559, 579

Action alerts
    American Meat Institute, **1**:221
    Center for Responsive Politics, **2**:479
    Christian Coalition, **2**:481
    Council for a Livable World, **2**:518
    Rainforest Action Network, **1**:284
    Securities Industry Institute, **1**:60
    U.S. Public Interest Research Group, **2**:504
Actiongram, **1**:32
Active Ballot Club, **2**:413, 415
Ad Tax Coalition, **1**:136
ADA. *See* Americans for Democratic Action
ADA Today, **2**:466
ADAction News & Notes, **2**:466
Adam Smith PAC, **2**:622, 623
Adams, Ansel, **1**:288
Addiction on the Streets: Homelessness and Substance Abuse in America, **2**:451
Adolph Coors Foundation, **2**:457
Advanta, **2**:649
Advertising
    Ad Tax Coalition, **1**:136
    Advertising Council, **1**:78
    alcohol, **1**:120, 122, 323–24
    American Association of Advertising Agents, **1**:78–79
    classified, **1**:151
    costs, **1**:136
    FCC regulations, **1**:142–43
    Freedom to Advertise Coalition, **1**:136
    off-label information dissemination, **1**:342
    prescription drugs, **1**:136
    tobacco, **1**:120, 122, 136, 168, 185
    Wal-Mart investigation, **2**:415
    See also Advertising campaigns
Advertising campaigns
    Americans for Tax Reform, **2**:471
    Anti-Defamation League, **2**:436
    anti-fur, **2**:539
    Christian Coalition, **2**:481
    Citizens Flag Alliance, **2**:516
    Common Cause, **2**:485
    lobbying organizations, **2**:681
    National Cattlemen's Beef Association, **1**:233
    Sierra Club, **1**:288

Advertising Council, **1:**78
Advisory Commission on Consumer Protection and Quality in the Healthcare Industry, **1:**43
Aeronautical Chamber of Commerce of America. *See* Aerospace Industries Association
Aerospace
　International Association of Machinists and Aerospace Workers, **2:**381–83, 622
　lobbying expenditures, **2:**697
Aerospace Industries Association, **1:**296, 298–99
Affirmative action
　American Civil Liberties Union, **2:**433, 434
　American Conservative Union, **2:**461
　American Enterprise Institute, **2:**464
　Americans for Democratic Action, **2:**468
　Association of Community Organizations for Reform Now, **2:**428
　backlash against, **2:**558
　Congress of Racial Equality, **2:**570
　National Association for the Advancement of Colored People, **2:**579
　National Lawyers Guild, **2:**452
　National Organization for Women, **2:**584, 585
Afghanistan, treatment of women, **2:**585
AFL–CIO. *See* American Federation of Labor–Congress of Industrial Organizations
AFL–CIO BLDG/Construction Trades Dept., **2:**674
AFLAC, **2:**646, 651, 689
Africa
　free-trade, **1:**309, 310
　Nigeria, **2:**570, 609–10
　Rainforest Action Groups in, **1:**285
African American civil rights groups, **2:**557, 569–71, 682
　See also under Specific group
Agency for Healthcare Policy Research, **1:**184
Agenda 2020 Sustainable Forestry Request, **1:**305
Agenda for the 90s, **2:**657
Agents of Influence, **2:**604
Agnew, Spiro, **2:**460
Agricultural Adjustment Act, **1:**215
Agricultural Fair Practices Act, **1:**234
Agricultural interest groups
　leading PACs, **2:**627–29
　lobbying expenditures, **2:**697, 698
　lobbyists, **2:**683
　overview of, **1:**209–14
　See also under Specific group
Agriculture Committee, **2:**682
AIDS
　American Federation for AIDS Research, **1:**163, 178–79
　Human Rights Campaign, **2:**575–76
　National Gay and Lesbian Task Force, **2:**582
　Ryan White Comprehensive AIDS Resources Emergency Act, **2:**575–76
AIM Report, **1:**126
AIMNet, **1:**125
Airbags, **1:**51, 99, 100, 168
Air Canada, **1:**300
Air Cargo Council, **1:**301
Air pollution
　American Trucking Associations, **1:**312
　Environmental Defense Fund, **1:**262
　Izaak Walton League, **1:**273, 274
　National Association of Furniture Manufacturers, **1:**308

Air pollution *(continued)*
　U.S. Public Interest Research Group, **2:**505
　See also Clean Air Act
Air-traffic control, **1:**301; **2:**351
Air Transport Association, **1:**296, 300–303; **2:**679
　lobbying expenditures, **2:**700
Air transportation
　leading PACs, **2:**669
　lobbying expenditures, **2:**697
　See also under Specific group
Airbus, **2:**598
Aircraft Industries Association of America. *See* Aerospace Industries Association
Aircraft Manufacturers' Association. *See* Aerospace Industries Association
Aircraft Owners & Pilots Association, **2:**668, 669
　lobbying expenditures, **2:**700
Aircraft safety, **1:**301; **2:**356–57, 383, 478
Airline carriers, **1:**300–303
Airline Clearing House, **1:**296, 300
Airline Inventory Redistribution Systems, **1:**296, 300
Airline Pilots Association, **2:**356–58, 622, 671, 673
Airline safety. *See* Aircraft safety
Airline Scheduling Committees, **1:**296, 300
Airlines Reporting Corporation, **1:**301
Airport Improvement Program Act, **2:**405–6
AK Steel, **2:**663
Akai, **2:**680
Akin, Gump, Strauss, Haver and Feld, **2:**661, 679, 680, 701, 704
ALA Bulletin, **1:**76
Alabama Credit Union Association, **2:**648
Alabama Farmers Federation, **2:**627
Aladdin, **2:**589
Alaska Airlines, **1:**300
Alaska Arctic National Wildlife Refuge, **1:**279
Alaska Fish Cannery Workers Union, **2:**399
Alaskan oil pipeline, **2:**391
Albanian American, **2:**660
Albanians, **2:**442
Alcalde & Fay, **2:**701
Alcatraz, **2:**565
Alcoa, **1:**318
Alcohol Beverage Labeling Act, **2:**524
Alcohol industry
　advertising, **1:**78, 120, 122, 143, 323–24
　Blood Alcohol Concentration level, **1:**112, 323; **2:**525
　blue laws, **2:**377
　Distilled Spirits Council of the United States, **1:**295, 323–25
　drinking age, **1:**102–3, 104
　ignition interlock devices, **2:**525
　lobbying expenditures, **2:**698
　Prohibition, **1:**63; **2:**508
　regulation of sale, **1:**64, 102–3, 104
　sobriety checkpoints, **2:**524
　taxes, **1:**65, 89–90, 323; **2:**506
　United Food and Commercial Workers Union, **2:**413
　warning labels, **1:**323; **2:**524
　Wine & Spirits Wholesalers of America, **2:**630, 631
　See also Beer industry; Mothers Against Drunk Driving
Alfa Mutual Insurance, **2:**677
Aliens. *See* Immigration legislation
Allard, Wayne, **1:**106–7
Allegheny Teledyne, **2:**663
Alliance for America, **1:**291

Alliance for Environmental Innovation, **1**:263
Alliance for Progress, **2**:606
Alliance for Rail Competition, **2**:700
Alliant Techsystems, **2**:636
Allied and Technical Workers, **2**:416
Allied Chemical, **2**:681
Allied Pilots Association, **2**:673
Allied Signal, **1**:298; **2**:636
Allstate, **1**:39
Aloha Airlines, **1**:300
Alternative Minimum Tax, **1**:295, 343
Aluminum, Brick, and Glass Workers international Union, **2**:417
Aluminum Workers America, **2**:416
Alzheimer's disease research, **1**:94
Amalgamated Association of Iron, Steel, and Tin Workers, **2**:416
Amalgamated Clothing and Textile Workers Union, **2**:407
Amalgamated Clothing Workers of America, **2**:407
Amalgamated Meat Cutters, **2**:413
Amalgamated Transit, **2**:671, 673
Amazon forest, **1**:265
Amchitka Island, **1**:269
America Financial Services Association, **2**:649
America First Committee, **2**:509
America Online, **2**:686, 704
"America Reads," **1**:131
America Works, **2**:657
American Academy of Family Physicians, **2**:688
American Academy of Ophthalmology, **1**:162, 164–66; **2**:653, 655
American Academy of Ophthalmology and Otolaryngology, **1**:164
American Accounting Association, **1**:23
American Agriculture Movement, **1**:209, 218–19, 242
American Aids, **2**:660
American Airlines, **1**:300; **2**:356, 404, 679, 704
  leading PAC, **2**:668, 669
  lobbying expenditures, **2**:695, 700
American Association of Advertising Agents, **1**:78–79, 136
American Association of Hispanic CPAs, **1**:21
American Association of Nurse Anesthetists, **2**:653, 655, 688
American Association of Nursing Homes, **1**:181
American Association of Nursing Homes Journal, **1**:181
American Association of Port Authorities, **1**:313
American Association of Retired Persons, **1**:9; **2**:557–59 *passim,* 561–63
  lobbying expenditures, **2**:692
American Automobile Manufacturers Association, **2**:700
American Bankers Association, **1**:8–10; **2**:684
  attack on client base of credit unions, **1**:24
  campaign contributions, **1**:6
  fellowships, **1**:7
  leading PAC, **2**:622, 646, 647
  lobbying expenditures, **2**:695
American Bar Association, **1**:64, 67–69, 80; **2**:425
American Bar Association Fund for Justice and Education, **1**:68
American Bar Association Journal, **1**:69
American Bar Endowment, **1**:68
American Bar Foundation, **1**:68
American Birth Control Conference, **2**:542
American Birth Control League, **2**:542
American Board of Anesthesiology, **1**:202
American Book Publishers Council, **1**:130
American Cancer Society, **1**:163, 167–68
American Chiropractic Association, **1**:163, 169–71; **2**:653, 655
American Civil Liberties Union, **2**:423–27 *passim,* 433–34

American Civil Liberties Union Foundation, **2**:434
American Classic Voyages, **2**:704
American College of Emergency Physicians, **1**:162, 172–74
  leading PAC, **2**:653, 655
  lobbying expenditures, **2**:688
American College of Physicians, **2**:688
American Commercial Barge Line, **2**:670
American Conservative Union, **2**:455, 456, 458, 460–62
American Consulting Engineers Council, **2**:633, 635
American Cotton Manufacturers Association, **1**:309
American Council of Life Insurance, **1**:4, 15–17, 45
  leading PAC, **2**:646, 651
  lobbying expenditures, **2**:689, 694
American Council on Education, **1**:123, 127–29
American Crystal Sugar, **2**:627
American Dental Association, **1**:162; **2**:622, 653, 655
American Dietetic Association, **1**:162–63, 175–77; **2**:653, 655
American Educational Institute, **1**:130
American Electric Power, **2**:645
American Electronics Association, **1**:22
American Enterprise, The, **2**:463
American Enterprise Institute for Public Policy Research, **2**:456–59 *passim,* 463–65, 472
American Entrepreneurs for Economic Growth, **1**:55, 56
American Express, **1**:18; **2**:649
American Farm Bureau Federation, **1**:209, 215–17; **2**:695
American Federation for AIDS Research, **1**:163, 178–79
American Federation of Government Employees, **2**:363, 674
American Federation of Labor. *See* American Federation of Labor–Congress of Industrial Organizations
American Federation of Labor–Congress of Industrial Organizations, **2**:353–54, 359–62
  leading PAC, **2**:671, 675
  opponents of, **1**:63, 111, 113
  opposition to NAFTA, **2**:351
  soft money donations, **2**:676
American Federation of State, County, and Municipal Employees, **2**:363–53
  leading PAC, **2**:622, 671, 674
  soft money donations, **2**:676
American Federation of Teachers, **1**:97; **2**:366–68, 674, 676
American Financial Group, **2**:676
American Financial Services Association, **1**:4, 6, 18–20; **2**:703
American Financial Skylink, **1**:10
American Forest and Paper Association, **1**:295, 304–5; **2**:629
American Forest Council, **1**:304
American Furniture Manufacturers Association, **1**:295, 307–8; **2**:662, 664
American Gaming Association, **1**:70–72, 73
American Healthcare Association, **1**:163, 181–83; **2**:653, 656
American Heart Association, **1**:163, 184–85
American Heritage Act, **2**:514
American Home Economics Association, **1**:175
American Hospital Association, **1**:163, 186–88
  leading PAC, **2**:653, 656
  lobbying expenditures, **2**:694
American Hotel and Motel Association, **1**:73–74; **2**:630, 632
American Hotel Foundation, **1**:74
American Indian Movement, **2**:556–59 *passim,* 564–66
American Industrial Bankers Association. *See* American Financial Services Association
American Institute of Architects, **2**:635
American Institute of Banking, **1**:10

American Institute of Certified Public Accountants, **1:**4, 6, 21–23; **2:**646, 652
American Institute of Cooperation, **1:**240
American Insurance Association, **2:**689
American International Automobile Dealers Association, **1:**100; **2:**700
American International Group, **2:**689, 694
American Iron & Steel Institute, **2:**663
American-Israel Political Action Committee, **2:**588, 600–602
American Journal of Insanity, **1:**199
American Journal of Nursing, **1:**193
American Journal of Psychiatry, **1:**199
American Land Title Association, **2:**652
American Legion, **2:**516–17, 557–59 *passim*, 567–68, 704
American Legion Auxiliary, **2:**567
American Library Association, **1:**64, 75–77
American Life Insurance Association, **1:**15
American Meat Institute, **1:**220–22; **2:**627
American Meat Packers Association. *See* American Meat Institute
American Medical Association, **1:**162, 189–92; **2:**682
    acceptance of birth control, **2:**542
    and assisted suicide, **1:**204
    boycotts, **1:**170
    collaboration with AOTA, **1:**196
    leading PAC, **2:**622, 653, 655
    lobbying expenditures, **2:**688, 694
    physician unionization, **1:**161, 188, 190, 206, 207
American Mining Congress, **1:**335
American Movers Conference, **1:**312
American National Cattlemen's Association. *See* National Cattlemen's Beef Association
American National Livestock Association, **1:**231
American Neurological Surgery, **2:**655
American Newspaper Publishing Association, **1:**150–51
American Nuclear Energy Council, **1:**338
American Nurses Association, **1:**162, 193–95; **2:**653, 655
American Nurses Credentializing Center, **1:**193
American Occupational Therapy Association, **1:**162, 196–98; **2:**653, 655, 688
American Opinion, **2:**495
American Opinion Books, **2:**458, 494, 495
American Optometric Association, **1:**162; **2:**653
American Osteopathic Association, **1:**202
American Outlook, **2:**492, 493
American Paper Institute, **1:**304
American Petroleum Institute, **2:**690
American Physical Therapy Association, **2:**653, 655
American Podiatry Association, **2:**653, 655
American Portland Cement Alliance, **2:**633, 634
American Postal Workers Union, **2:**369–71, 671, 674
American Psychiatric Association, **1:**162, 199–201
American Psychological Association, **2:**688
American Railway Union, **2:**419
American Road & Transport Builders Association, **2:**635
American Seafoods, **2:**704
American Society for the Control of Cancer. *See* American Cancer Society
American Society of Anesthesiologists, **1:**162, 202–4; **2:**653, 655, 688
American Society of Anesthetists. *See* American Society of Anesthesiologists
American Society of Association Executives, **1:**99
American Society of Composers, Authors, and Publishers, **1:**65

American Society of Internal Medicine, **2:**688
American Society of Magazine Editors, **1:**136
American Speech-Language-Hearing Association, **2:**653, 655
American Stores, **2:**413
American Sugar Cane League, **2:**627
American Sugarbeet Growers Association, **1:**223–24; **2:**627
American Supply Association, **2:**633, 634
American Textile Foundation, **1:**309
American Textile Manufacturers Institute, **1:**295, 309–11; **2:**662, 664
American Textile Manufacturers Institute Committee for Good Government, **1:**311
American Trans Air, **1:**300
American Trucking Association, **1:**296, 312–14; **2:**668, 670
American Veterinary Medical Association, **2:**627, 628
American Victims of Abortion, **2:**536
American Volunteers in International Development, **2:**439
American West Airlines, **1:**300
American Woman Suffrage Association, **2:**444
American Wood Council, **1:**304
American Yarn Spinners Association, **2:**664
Americans Against Unfair Family Taxation, **1:**90
Americans for Democratic Action, **2:**455–58 *passim*, 466–68, 509, 657
Americans for Free International Trade, **2:**668, 670
Americans for Good Government, **2:**665, 666
Americans for Tax Reform, **1:**64; **2:**455, 456, 458, 469–71
Americans for Tax Reform Foundation, **2:**471
Americans United for the Separation of Church and State, **2:**513–15
Americans with Disabilities: Accessibility for Older Persons, **2:**562
Americans with Disability Act, **2:**576
America's Community Bankers, **1:**12–14; **2:**648
America's Road Team, **1:**312
Americas Watch. *See* Human Rights Watch
Ameritech, **2:**623, 638, 639, 694, 699
AmFAR. *See* American Federation for AIDS Research
Amman, Arthur J., **1:**178, 179
Amnesty International, **2:**424, 497
Amoco, **2:**641, 643, 690
Amortization periods, **1:**53
AMP, **2:**639
AMR, **2:**677, 695
Amtrak, **2:**406, 419
Amtrak Reform and Accountability Act, **2:**420
Amway, **2:**456, 491, 676
Anderson, Craig B., **2:**497
Andrews, Mark, **2:**680
Anesthesiologists, American Society of Anesthesiologists, **1:**162, 202–4; **2:**653, 655
Anesthesiology, **1:**202
Angola, **2:**594
Anheuser-Busch, **2:**631, 677
Animal Liberation, **2:**540
Animal testing, **2:**539, 540–41
Animal trapping, **2:**281
Animal welfare
    People for the Ethical Treatment of Animals, **2:**539–41
    United Egg Association, **1:**254
Animal Welfare Act, **2:**539
Annals of Emergency Medicine, **1:**172
Annual Financial Review, **1:**84
Annual Voting Record, **2:**466

Anti-Ballistic missile system, **2**:519
Anti-Ballistic Missile Treaty, **2**:462, 491, 545, 612
Anticommunist organizations. *See* John Birch Society
Anti-Defamation League, **2**:423, 424, 427–28, 435–37
Anti-Defamation League Foundation, **2**:435
Antidiscrimination groups
    Human Rights Campaign, **2**:575–76
    Human Rights Watch, **2**:442
    League of Women Voters of the United States, **2**:445
    National Association of Social Workers, **1**:95
    National Lawyers Guild, **2**:452, 453
    National Organization for Women, **2**:585
    See also Discriminatory practices
Anti-Semitism. *See* Anti-Defamation League
Anti-sodomy laws, **2**:582
Antiwar activists, National Lawyers Guild's defense of, **2**:452
Antiwar movements, **2**:455, 509
"Antidumping" bill (nursing home), **1**:182
Antidumping legislation (trade)
    American Textile Manufacturers Institute, **1**:309
    Economic Policy Institute, **2**:488
    National Cattlemen's Beef Association, **1**:232
    Semiconductor Industry Association, **1**:347
    United Steelworkers of America, **2**:417
Anti-environmental movement, **1**:257, 259
Antimonopolies, **1**:247
Antipiracy. *See* Copyright
Antitrust legislation, **1**:63, 83, 154
A&P, **2**:413
Apartheid, **2**:497, 509, 511–12
Archer Daniels Midland, **1**:8, 210, 223; **2**:627, 677
Architecture, leading PACs, **2**:635
Arent, Fox, Kinter, Plotkin and Kahn, **2**:679
Arizona Farm Bureau PACs, **1**:215
Arkansas Community Organizations for Reform Now, **2**:424, 430
Arkansas Power and Light company, **2**:430
Armacost, Michael, **2**:472, 473
Armani, Giorgio, **2**:539
Armenia, **2**:617
Armey, Richard, **1**:30; **2**:490
    leadership PAC, **2**:622, 624
Arms control, **2**:510–11
    Americans for Democratic Action, **2**:457, 467
    Council for a Livable World, **2**:518–20
    League of Women Voters of the United States, **2**:445
    Union of Concerned Scientists, **2**:545–46
    United States Catholic Conference, **2**:503
    See also Anti-Ballistic Missile Treaty; Arms sales; Defense budget; Nuclear weapons
Arms sales, **2**:589
    India, **2**:612
    Iran, **2**:601, 612
    Israel, **2**:600
    Soviet Union, **2**:604
    Taiwan, **2**:591–92, 615
Army Air Corps. *See* U.S. Army Air Corps
Army Corps of Engineers. *See* U.S. Army Corps of Engineers
Army War College, **1**:301
Arnold & Porter, **2**:679, 680, 701
Arnold, Ron, **1**:291, 292
Arrest Now, **1**:442
Arter & Hadden, **2**:701
Arthur Andersen, **2**:646, 652
Aryan Nations, **2**:477

ASCAP, **2**:638, 639
Ashbrook, John, **2**:460
Ashburton, Lord, **2**:587
Asia, Human Rights Watch and, **2**:442
Asia-Pacific Economic Cooperative Forum, **2**:615
Asian Development Bank, **2**:615
Asian markets, **1**:234, 254, 309, 346; **2**:493
Ask Sybil Liberties, **2**:434
Aspinal, Wayne, **1**:275
Assault Weapons Ban, **2**:521
Assisted suicide, **1**:204
Associated Builders and Contractors, **1**:296, 315–17; **2**:633, 635
Associated California Loggers, **1**:291
Associated Credit Bureaus, **2**:649
Associated Equipment Distributors, **2**:634
Associated General Contractors, **2**:633, 635
Associated Milk Producers, **1**:227; **2**:627, 629
Association for Advanced Life Underwriting, **1**:45
Association for Commercial Real Estate, **2**:652
Association for the Advancement of Psychology, **2**:655
Association of American Law Schools, **1**:67
Association of American Publishers, **1**:130–32
Association of American Railroads, **2**:668, 670, 695
Association of Community Organizations for Reform Now, **2**:423–28 *passim*, 430–32
Association of Finishers of Textile Fabrics, **1**:309
Association of Flight Attendants, **2**:673
Association of Health Insurance Agents, **1**:46
Association of Hospital Superintendents, **1**:186
Association of Mutual Fund Plan Sponsors. *See* Investment Company Institute
Association of Newspaper Classified Advertising Managers, **1**:150
Association of Progressive Rental Organizations, **2**:632
Association of Publicly Traded Investment Funds. *See* Investment Company Institute
Association of Stock Exchange Firms, **1**:58
Association of Trial Lawyers of America, **1**:62, 64, 80–82; **2**:622, 661, 703
Astroturf lobbying, **1**:147–48
ATLA Law Reporter, **1**:82
Atlantic Research, **2**:636
Atlantic Richfield, **2**:643, 676, 681, 690
ATM. *See* Automated teller machines
Atomic Energy Act, **1**:338
AT&T, **1**:60; **2**:372, 384, 604, 680, 704
    leading PAC, **2**:622, 623, 638, 639
    lobbying expenditures, **2**:694, 699
    soft money donations, **2**:676
AT&T Wireless Services, **2**:640
Attica Prison uprising, **2**:452
Audio Home Recording Act, **1**:154
Audubon, John Jay, **1**:278
Audubon Expedition Institute, **1**:279
Audubon Magazine, **1**:278, 279
Audubon Society. *See* National Audubon Society
Authors League, **1**:130
Auto Choice Reform Act, **1**:50
Automated teller machines, **1**:28
Automobiles & automobile legislation
    electric, **2**:546
    excise taxes, **1**:99, 100
    Independent Insurance Agents of America, **1**:31
    leading PACs, **2**:670
    lobbying expenditures, **2**:697

Automobiles & automobile legislation *(continued)*
   National Association of Independent Insurers, **1:**39, 40, 41
   National Association of Professional Insurance Agents, **1:**49, 51
   National Automobile Dealers Association, **1:**66, 99–101; **2:**668, 670
   purchase of, **1:**257
   safety, **1:**99, 100, 168
   United Automobile Workers, **2:**350, 381, 410–12, 671, 672
   See also under Specific group
Autozone Inc., **2:**670
Aviation taxes, **2:**405–06
Aviation Trust Fund, **1:**301
Avon, **2:**539
Azerbaijan International Operating Company, **2:**617

B

B-52 Stealth Bomber program, **2:**545
B-52s (musicians), **2:**540
Babbit, Bruce, **1:**232, 259, 260
Backyard Wildlife Habitat program, **1:**283
Bair, Jeanette, **1:**198
Baker, Donelson et al., **2:**701
Bakker, Jim, **2:**455
Balanced Budget Act, **1:**198; **2:**484
Balanced Budget Amendment, **2:**470, 495, 499
Baldwin, Roger, **2:**433
Baldwin, Simeon Eben, **1:**67
Baldwin, Tammy, **2:**577
Ball, George, **2:**597
Bank insurance fund, **1:**27
Bank of America, **2:**684, 695
Bank of the United States, **1:**8
Bank One, **2:**646, 647, 684
BankAmerica, **2:**646, 647
Bankers Trust, **2:**647
Banking system, duel, **1:**13
BankPac, **1:**10
Bankruptcy laws, **1:**5, 13, 25, 154
Banks
   expansion into securities business, **1:**58
   Farm Credit system, **1:**240
   lobbying expenditures, **2:**684
   sale of insurance, **1:**30, 39, 45–46, 47, 49–50
   See also Financial interest groups
   See also under Specific bank or group
Banks, Dennis, **2:**564, 565
Barbers, Beauticians, and Allied Industries Association, **2:**414
Barbour, Griffith & Rogers, **2:**701
Baroody, William J., Sr., **2:**463–64
Barr, Bob, **1:**87
Barrick Goldstrike Mines, **2:**644
Bartenders and Waiters Unions, **2:**375
Bartenders Union Local 165, **2:**376
Battle Memorial Institute, **2:**645
Bayer, **2:**653, 656
Bechtel Group, **2:**645
Beck, Dave, **2:**387
Becker, George, **2:**418
"Beef, It's What's For Dinner," **1:**233
Beef Business Bulletin, **1:**231
Beef industry. *See* Meat industry

Beer industry
   advertising, **1:**323
   lobbying expenditures, **2:**698
   National Beer Wholesalers Association, **1:**62–66 *passim,* 90, 102–4; **2:**630, 631
   taxes, **1:**89–90, 91, 103, 104
   See also Alcohol industry
Bell Atlantic, **1:**60
   leading PAC, **2:**623, 638, 639
   lobbying expenditures, **2:**694, 699
   soft money donations, **2:**676
Bell Curve, The, **2:**463
Bellagio Resort Hotel and Casino, **2:**376
Bellecourt, Clyde, **2:**564
Bellecourt, Vernon, **2:**564
Bellsouth, **2:**638, 639, 676, 695, 699
Bellsouth Telecommunications, **2:**638, 639
Benedict XV (Pope), **2:**502
Beneficial Corporation, **1:**18
Beneficial Management, **2:**649
Berman, Jay, **1:**154, 156
Bernadin, Joseph, **2:**496
Berosini, Bobby, **2:**539
Beryllium, **1:**262
Best Congress Money Can Buy, The, **2:**479
Best of Extra!, The, **1:**133
Bethlehem Steel, **2:**663, 680
Better Bonds proposal, **1:**279
Beverage industry
   leading PACs, **2:**631
   Licensed Beverage Industries, **1:**323
   lobbying expenditures, **2:**698
   soft drink taxes, **1:**83
Biennial Wilderness conference, **1:**288
Big Six, **1:**127, 128, 153
Bill Emerson English Empowerment Act, **2:**547
Bill Tally, **2:**498
Binding Industries of America, **1:**343
Bingaman, Jeff, **2:**518
Biological Weapons Convention, **2:**520
Biomaterials Access Assurance Act, **1:**56
Biotechnology, **1:**57, 211
Biotechnology Industry Organization, **2:**691
Birch, Elizabeth, **2:**575
Birch, John, **2:**494
Bird Lore, **1:**278
Birds, protection of. *See* National Audubon Society
Birth control. *See* Family planning
Birth Control Clinic Research Bureau, **2:**542
Birth Control Federation of America, **2:**542
Bissonette, Pedro, **2:**565
Black, Kelly et al., **2:**701
Black, Manafort, Stone, and Kelly Public Affairs, **2:**679, 680
Black Americans for Life, **2:**536
Black America's, **2:**658
Black Panther Party, **1:**88
Blacklisting, **1:**315–16
Blass, Bill, **2:**539
Block grants, **2:**365, 367, 373, 397–89
Blood Alcohol Concentration level. *See* Alcohol, Blood Alcohol Concentration level
Bloomingdale's, **2:**540
Blue Cross, **1:**186

Blue Cross and Blue Shield Association, **1:**161–62, 205–8
    leading PAC, **2:**646, 651
    lobbying expenditures, **2:**689, 694
    soft money donations, **2:**676
Blue Cross Association, **1:**205–6
Blue Dog, **2:**657
Blue Ribbon Coalition, **1:**291
Blue Ridge Environmental Defense League, **1:**308
Bluestone, Barry, **2:**487
Blunt, Roy, **1:**113
BMG, **1:**153
Boeing, **1:**298; **2:**668, 669, 677, 694, 700, 703
Boer War, **2:**532
Boggs, Tommy, **2:**679
Bohlen, James, **1:**269
Boilermakers, **2:**671, 672
Boise Cascade Corp., **1:**304; **2:**629
Boland & Madigan, **2:**701
Bond, Julian, **2:**578
Bond Market Association, **2:**650, 684
Bonior, David, **1:**97; **2:**487
Bonnisky, Mark, **2:**521
Books, electronic, **1:**131
Border Liaison Mechanism, **2:**607
Bork, Robert, **2:**433, 464
Bosnia, **2:**438, 442, 476, 598, 612
Boston Society for Encouraging Trade and Commerce, **1:**294
Boston University, **2:**703
Bourbon Institute, **1:**323
Bower, Charles, **2:**553
Bowles, Erskine, **1:**107
Boxer, Barbara, **2:**577
Boy Scouts, **2:**559, 568
Boycotts, **2:**540, 595, 598
Boyd Gaming, **2:**632
BP America, **2:**643, 690
Brady, James, **2:**521
Brady, Sarah, **2:**521
Brady Bill, **2:**521, 533
Brand Chairman's Committee, **1:**115
Braun Holocaust Institute Jewish Foundation for Christian Rescuers, **2:**435, 436
Brazil, **1:**285; **2:**417
Breen, Joseph, **1:**138
Brennan, Donald, **2:**492
Bricklayers, **2:**674
Brief Bank Index, **2:**453
Brinker International, **2:**631
Bristol-Myers Squibb, **2:**653, 656, 676, 691
British American Tobacco, **2:**693, 694
Broadcast Music, **2:**687
Broadcast Music Incorporated, **1:**65
Broadcasting industry
    overview of, **1:**120–23
    See also under Specific group
Broiler industry, National Chicken Council, **1:**234–36; **2:**628
Broken Lives: Denial of Education to Homeless Children, **2:**451
"Broker-dealer lite," **1:**60
Broker-dealers, **1:**58–61
Brooke Group, **2:**693
Brookings, Robert S., **2:**472–73
Brookings Institution, **2:**454–58 *passim*, 472–74
Brookings Papers on Economic Activity, **2:**472

Brookings Policy Brief Series, **2:**472, 473
Brookings Policymaker series, **2:**472
Brookings Quarterly Newsletter, **2:**472
Brookings Review, **2:**472
Broomfield, William, **2:**432
Brotherhood of Locomotive Engineers, **1:**419; **2:**673
Brotherhood of Locomotive Firemen and Enginemen, **2:**419
Brotherhood of Railroad Trainmen, **2:**419
Brower, David, **1:**265, 266, 275, 284, 288
Brown, Lewis H., **2:**463
Brown & Root, **2:**633, 635
Brown & Williamson Tobacco, **2:**627, 629, 676, 703
Brown-Foreman, **2:**630, 631
Brown v. Board of Education, **2:**433, 435–36, 578, 682
Brownfields Redevelopment, **1:**40
Browning-Ferris Industries, **2:**645
Bryan, William Jennings, **1:**114; **2:**422, 507–8
Brzezinski, Zbigniew, **2:**438
Buchanan, Patrick, **2:**477
Buckely, William F., **2:**460
Buckley v. Valeo, **2:**621, 625
Build PAC of the National Association of Home Builders, **1:**329, 331; **2:**633, 635
Building codes, **1:**329
Building equipment/materials
    leading PACs, **2:**634
    lobbying expenditures, **2:**698
Building industry. *See* Construction industry
Building trade union PACs, **2:**674
Bulcao, Doug, **1:**310
Bureau of Indian Affairs, **2:**565
Burger King, **1:**111, 284
Burlington Industries, **2:**662, 664
Burlington Northern Railroad, **2:**668, 670
Burnside, Ambrose, **2:**532
Burson-Marsteller, **2:**661, 679, 680
Bush, David, **1:**315
Bush, George, **1:**147, 257, 292; **2:**511
Business
    leading PACs, **2:**623, 630–31, 633
    lobbying expenditures, **2:**685, 697, 698
Business Industry, **2:**630, 633
Business Roundtable, **1:**65, 318–20; **2:**685, 694
Business services, lobbying expenditures, **2:**698
Business Software Alliance, **2:**686
Butcher-Forde, **2:**529
Butcher Workmen of North America, **2:**413–14
Buttenwieser & Associates, **2:**676
Butterball, **2:**413
Buyers Up, **2:**501
"Buying of Congress," **2:**478
"Buying of the President," **2:**478
Byline, **2:**475
Byrd, James Jr., **2:**558, 570, 579
Byrne, Ethel, **2:**542
Byrne Foundation, **2:**439

C

Cable Act, **1:**144
Cable Communications Policy Act, **1:**147
Cable News Network, **2:**680
Cable television, **1:**121, 139, 143

Cable television *(continued)*
    National Cable Television Association, **1:**122, 146–49; **2:**638, 639, 687, 695
Cable Television Consumer Protection and Competition Act, **1:**139, 147
Cabotage laws, **2:**400
Calculated Compassion: How the Ex-gay Movement Serves the Right's Attack on Democracy, **2:**581
Caliber System, **2:**668, 670
Califano, Joseph, **2:**678
California
    airborne lead standards, **1:**262
    Charter Public Schools Legislation, **1:**348
    Long Beach, **1:**285
    Los Angeles County, **2:**688
    Orange County, **2:**688
    proposition 13, **2:**510, 529
    San Diego County, **2:**688
    Sierra Club, **1:**287–88
    vehicle emissions regulations, **1:**101
California 2000, **2:**658
California Desert Coalition, **1:**292
California Grocers Association, **1:**83
California Healthcare Association, **2:**656
California League of Conservation Voters, **2:**667
California Protection Act, **1:**292
Calvin Klein, **2:**539
Cammermeyer, Margarethe, **2:**577
"Campaign America," **2:**622
Campaign contributions
    agriculture, **1:**212
    bundling, **2:**572
    illegal, **2:**388, 586, 587
    leading soft money donors, **2:**676–77
    See also Political action committees
Campaign finance laws
    Federal Election Campaign Act, **2:**621
    Tilman Act, **2:**422
Campaign finance reform, **2:**625
    American Conservative Union, **2:**461
    American Meat Institute, **1:**221
    Americans for Democratic Action, **2:**467
    Center for Public Integrity, **2:**477
    Center for Responsive Politics, **2:**479–80
    Christian Coalition, **2:**482
    Common Cause, **2:**486
    International Association of Machinists and Aerospace Workers, **2:**383
    International Union of Operating Engineers, **2:**391
    Laborers International Union of North America, **2:**394
    League of Women Voters of the United States, **2:**445
    Public Citizen, **2:**501
    U.S. Public Interest Research Group, **2:**505
Campaign for America, **2:**692
Campaign for Human Development, **2:**502
Campaign for U.N. Reform, **2:**667
Campaign for Working Families, **2:**658
Campbell, Carroll A., **1:**17
Campbell, Joan Brown, **2:**497
Campbell, Naomi, **2:**539
Canada
    bilingualism in, **2:**548
    clear-cutting protests, **1:**270
    healthcare system, **1:**159

Canadian Airlines International, **1:**300
Canadian Brewery, Flour, Cereal, Soft Drink, and Distillery Workers, **2:**414
Canadian Broadcasting Corporation, **2:**372
Canadian Printing Industries Association, **1:**343
Cancer, American Cancer Society, **1:**163, 167–68
Cannon, Christopher, **1:**104
Canosa, Jorge Mas, **2:**594, 595
Capital Cities, **1:**133
Capital Eye, **2:**479
Capital Gains and Losses: A State by State Review of Gay, Lesbian, Bisexual, Transgender, and HIV/AIDS-related Legislation in 1998, **2:**581
Capital Gains Coalition, **1:**56
Capital gains tax
    Grange, **1:**248
    National Association of Realtors, **1:**53
    National Venture Capital Association, **1:**56
    Printing Industries of America, **1:**295, 343
    Securities Industry Association, **1:**58
Capital Ideas, **2:**498
Capitol Associates, **2:**701
Capper-Volstead Act, **1:**240, 254
Capper-Volstead Cooperative, **1:**254
Caps, agricultural, **1:**245
Carbon dioxide emissions. *See* Emissions, regulation of
Card-recognition agreements, **2:**377
Career College Association, **1:**127
Carey, Ron, **2:**387–88
Cargill, **1:**210; **2:**627
Cargo services, **1:**301
Cargo Theft Deterrent Act, **1:**313
Caribbean, **1:**309, 310
Carlisle, Belinda, **2:**540
Carnegie, Andrew, **1:**75
Carnegie Corporation, **2:**480, 488
Carolina Biological Supply Company, **2:**539
Carolina Power & Light, **2:**641, 645
Carpenters & Joiners, **2:**671, 674
Carpenters Union, **2:**622
Carson, Rachel, **1:**256, 279
Carter, Jimmy
    agricultural policies, **1:**218
    Americans for Democratic Action and, **2:**467
    Association of Community Organizations for Reform Now and, **2:**431
    LWV's presidential debate, **2:**445
    Small Business Administration Loan, **1:**100
Carthage Foundation, **2:**439
Case Against the Death Penalty, The, **2:**434
Casinos. *See* Gaming industry
Cassidy & Associates, **2:**701, 703
Castro, Fidel, **2:**594, 595
CAT, **2:**658
Catering Industry Employee, **2:**375
Caterpillar, **2:**633, 634
Catholic News Service, **2:**502
Cato Handbook for Congress, **2:**475, 476
Cato Institute, **2:**455, 456, 458, 475–76
Cato Journal, **2:**475
Cato Policy Report, **2:**475
Cato's Letters, **2:**475
Catt, Carrie Chapman, **2:**444
Cattle ranchers, **1:**231–33

CauseNet, **2**:485
CBS, **2**:680, 687
Cellular phones, and 911 emergency system, **2**:379
Cellular Telecom Industry Association, **2**:640, 695
Censorship
  Internet, **1**:122, 131
  V-chip, **1**:141
Censorship opponents
  American Civil Liberties Union, **2**:434
  American Library Association, **1**:76
  Association of American Publishers, **1**:131
  Cato Institute, **2**:476
  Magazine Publishers of America, **1**:135
  media industry, **1**:120
  Motion Picture Association of America, **1**:138–39, 140
  Recording Industry Association of America and, **1**:153, 154
Centers for Disease Control, **1**:186
Center for Entrepreneurial Leadership, **1**:57
Center for Financial Studies, **1**:14
Center for Global Food Issues, **2**:492
Center for Policy Analysis, **1**:128
Center for Public Integrity, **2**:458, 477–78
Center for Public Policy Education, **2**:473–74
Center for Religious Freedom, **2**:439
Center for Responsive Politics, **2**:458, 459, 479–80
Center for the Defense of Free Enterprise, **1**:291, 292–93
Center for the Study of Market Processes, **2**:483
Center for Workforce Success, **1**:333
Center to Prevent Handgun Violence, **2**:521
CFFE LLC, **2**:703
Chafee, John, **2**:517
Chamber of Commerce. *See* U.S. Chamber of Commerce
Champion International, **1**:304; **2**:627, 629
Chapman, Frank, **1**:278
Charitable Choice, **2**:514
Charles E. Smith Companies, **2**:703
Charles Stewart Mott Foundation, **2**:457
Chartbook on Entitlements, **2**:498
Charter Public Schools Legislation, **1**:348
Charter schools, **2**:397
Chase Manhattan, **2**:647, 684, 694
Chechnya, **2**:611
Checkoffs, marketing, **1**:209, 249, 253
Chemical industry
  agricultural dependence on, **1**:252
  fertilizer, **1**:238
  leading PACs, **2**:663
  lobbying expenditures, **2**:697
Chemical Manufacturers Association, **1**:295, 321–22
  leading PAC, **2**:662, 663
  lobbying expenditures, **2**:695
Chemical pollution, **1**:257
Chemical Weapons Convention, **2**:519
Chemical Weapons Treaty, **2**:462, 518
Chemicals, high production volume, **1**:304
Chevron, **2**:641, 643, 690
Chevy Chase Savings Bank, **2**:648
Chiang Kaishek, **2**:614
Chicago Board of Options Exchange, **2**:650
Chicago Board of Trade, **2**:646, 650, 684
Chicago Mercantile Exchange, **2**:646, 650, 684
Child care, **2**:365
Child Care Access Act, **2**:405
Child Custody Protection Act, **2**:527, 538

Child labor laws
  exemption from, **1**:150
  League of Women Voters of the United States, **2**:445
  violation of, **1**:100
Child safety seats, **1**:100
Childbirth, denial of epidurals, **1**:203
Children of the Dream, **2**:436
Children's Gun Violence Prevention Act, **2**:397
Children's Miracle Network, **1**:19
Children's Television Act, **1**:143
Children's welfare
  Anti-Defamation League, **2**:436
  Human Rights Watch, **2**:441
  League of Women Voters, **2**:445
  Legal Services Corporation, **2**:448
  National Coalition for the Homeless, **2**:450
Chile, **2**:490–91
China, **2**:591–93
  contributions scandal, **2**:586, 587
  importer/exporter of cotton, **1**:237
  "most favored nation," **1**:295, 333; **2**:592
  trade relations, **1**:59, 347; **2**:462, 484, 488
  transshipping, **1**:310
  and World Trade Organization, **1**:319; **2**:473, 488
  See also Taiwan
Chiropractic interest groups, American Chiropractic Association, **1**:163, 169–71; **2**:653, 655
CH2M Hill, **2**:633, 635
Choate, Pat, **2**:604
Christian Coalition, **2**:481–82
  annual budget, **2**:457
  lobbying expenditures, **2**:694
  membership, **2**:456
  revocation of tax exempt status, **2**:458, 481, 482, 514
  scorecards, **2**:458
  support of GOP, **1**:63; **2**:105
  voter education pamphlets, **2**:514
Christian Coalition International, **2**:482
Christian Coalition of America, **2**:482
Christian Identity Movement, **2**:477
Christian movement
  Christian Identity Movement, **2**:477
  Freedom House, **2**:439
  National Council of the Churches of Christ, **2**:496–97
  schools, **2**:455–56
  See also Christian Coalition
"Christian Right," **2**:457
Christian Rural Overseas Program, **2**:496
Christian Voice, **2**:456
Chrysler, **2**:411
CHUBB, **2**:651
Church, Frank, **2**:479
Church World Service, **2**:496
Cigar Association of America, **2**:693
Cigarette Labeling Act, **1**:78
Cigarettes. *See* Tobacco
CIGNA, **2**:651
Cisneros, Henry, **2**:431, 432
Citicorp, **2**:646, 647
Citigroup, **2**:651, 676, 684, 694
Citizen Action, **2**:455, 457
Citizen Agenda, **2**:504
Citizen groups
  definition of, **2**:456

Citizen groups *(continued)*
  overview of, **2:**555–59
Citizens Educational Foundation, **2:**704
Citizens Flag Alliance, Inc., **2:**516–17, 568
Citizens for a Sound Economy, **2:**455–59 *passim,* 483–84
Citizens for a Sound Economy Foundation, **2:**484
Citizens for Congressional Reform, **2:**550
Citizens Organized, **2:**666
Civil Aeronautics Act, **1:**301
Civil Aeronautics Authority, **1:**301
Civil Aeronautics Board, **1:**301
Civil disobedience, **1:**258, 270, 284
Civil Justice Digest, **1:**82
Civil Justice Foundation, **1:**82
Civil Justice Reform Group, **2:**685
Civil Reserve Air Fleet, **1:**296, 300, 301
Civil Rights Act, **2:**436, 467, 509, 578
Civil rights groups
  overview of, **2:**422–28
  See also under Specific group
Civil Service Employees Association of New York State, **2:**363
Civil Service Retirement System, **1:**92
Civil War, **1:**65, 89; **2:**506
Clark, Dick, **2:**536–37
Clark, Mark, **2:**513
Class-action litigation
  American Council of Life Insurance, **1:**17
  American Financial Services Association, **1:**18
  American Institute of Certified Public Accountants, **1:**22
  America's Community Bankers, **1:**13
  Association of Trial Lawyers of America, **1:**81
  Chemical Manufacturers Association, **1:**321, 322
  National Association of Manufacturers, **1:**333
  National Venture Capital Association, **1:**56
  Securities Industry Association, **1:**59
  Technology Network, **1:**348
  See also Liability law reform
Claybrook, Joan, **2:**500
Clayton Anti-Trust Act, **1:**294
Clean Air Act, **1:**100, 257
  American Forest and Paper Association, **1:**304
  Citizens for a Sound Economy, **2:**483
  National Mining Association, **1:**335, 336
  and right-to-know, **1:**322
  Sierra Club Legal Defense Fund, **1:**289
  U.S. Circuit Court of Appeals ruling on, **1:**313
  See also Air pollution
Clean Water Act, **1:**257
  National Wildlife Federation, **1:**282
  Sierra Club Legal Defense Fund, **1:**289
  violation of, **1:**282
Clean Water Action plan, **1:**279
Cleveland, Grover, **2:**507
Cleveland-Cliffs Iron, **2:**644
Client privacy. *See* Customer privacy
Clifford, Clark, **2:**678, 679
Climate. *See* Global warming
Clinch River, Tennessee, **2:**501
Clinical trials Community-Based Clinical Trials, **1:**178
Clinton, Bill
  impeachment, **2:**458, 468, 482, 495, 584
  Lincoln bedroom scandal, **2:**477
  as speaker/guest, **1:**60, 349; **2:**576
Clinton, Hillary, **2:**601

Cloning, **1:**211, 342; **2:**503
Close to Home, **1:**267
Clot-busting drugs, **1:**184
Clothing, toxic materials on, **1:**262
CMS Energy, **2:**641, 645
CN Tower, **2:**391
CNA Financial, **2:**651
Coalition—Americans Working for Real Change, The, **1:**63, 106, 111
Coalition building
  Council for a Livable World, **2:**518
  environmental groups and, **1:**260
"Coalition to Fix Medicare Now," **1:**181–82
CoalPAC, **1:**335, 336
Coast Seaman's Union, **2:**399
Coastal, **2:**643
Coca-Cola, **2:**630, 631
Coca-Cola Enterprises, **2:**630, 631
Cockfighting, **2:**540
Cohen, Jeff, **1:**133
Cold War, **1:**298; **2:**476, 511, 587, 611
Collective bargaining, **2:**351
  American Federation of State, County, and Municipal Employees, **2:**365
  American Nurses Association, **1:**193, 194
  International Association of Fire Fighters, **2:**378, 379
  National Farmers Organization, **1:**242, 243
  public safety officers, **1:**87
  United Automobile Workers, **2:**410
College of American Pathologists, **2:**653, 655, 688
Collier Trophy, **1:**301
Colorado, City & County of Denver, **2:**688
Colorado Association of Home Builders PAC, **1:**329
Colorado River, **1:**288
Columbia/HCA Healthcare, **2:**656
Columbia/HCA Healthcare-Texas, **2:**656
Columbia University School of Journalism, **1:**60
Combest, Larry, **1:**100
Combined Federal campaign, **2:**451
COMCAST, **2:**639
Commercial banks
  leading PACs, **2:**647
  lobbying expenditures, **2:**697
Committee for Quality Orthopedic Health Care, **2:**655
Committee of One Million, **2:**614
Committee on National Defense and Industrial Mobilization, **1:**332
Committee to Aid Southern Lawyers, **2:**452
Commodity agricultural groups, **1:**209, 212, 215
  American Sugarbeet Growers Association, **1:**223–24; **2:**627
  defined, **1:**253
  National Cotton Council, **1:**209, 237–39; **2:**627
  National Pork Producers Council, **1:**249–51; **2:**628
Commodity Credit Corporation, **1:**211, 213
Commodity prices, **1:**218
Common Cause, **2:**456–59 *passim,* 485–86
Common Cause, **2:**485
Common Foreign and Security Policy, **2:**597–98
Common Ground Award, **2:**496
Commonwealth Edison, **2:**645
Communication Alerts, **1:**221
Communication Workers of America, **2:**671
Communications Act, **1:**121, 142

Communications industry. See Telecommunications industry
Communications Workers of America, **2**:372–74, 676
Communist, **2**:494, 495
Community bank interest groups, Independent Community Bankers of America, **1**:27–29
Community Banking Network, **1**:28, 29
Community-Based Clinical Trials, **1**:178
Community Nursing Organizations, **1**:194
Community Reinvestment Act, **1**:8, 40
Community reinvestment requirements, **1**:5, 8, 27
Compaq Computer, **2**:686
Compensation bills, **1**:282
Competition: Dealing with Japan, The, **2**:493
Competitiveness Center, **2**:492
Compleat Angler, The, **1**:272
Comprehensive School Reform Demonstration, **2**:367
Comprehensive Test Ban Treaty, **2**:462, 503, 519
Computer industry, **1**:295, 346–47
　computer manufacturing PACs, **2**:639
　lobbying expenditures, **2**:686, 697
　Software and Information Industry Association, **1**:157–58
　Technology Network, **1**:295, 348–49
　See also Encryption; Technology
Computer Sciences, **2**:639
Computer Systems Policy Project, **2**:686
COMSAT, **2**:640
Comstock laws, **2**:542, 543
ConAgra, **2**:413, 627
Concealed Carry Law for Law Enforcement Officers, **1**:87
Concerned Citizens Action Network, **2**:545
Conference of State Banking Supervision, **1**:43
Conference on the Commission on the Status of Women, **2**:583
Congress of Industrial Organizations. See American Federation of Labor–Congress of Industrial Organizations
Congress of Racial Equality, **2**:556–59 *passim*, **2**:569–71
Congress Watch, **2**:500
Connecticut, birth control laws, **2**:543
Connecticut Bar Association, **1**:67
Connerly, Ward, **2**:569–70
Conrail, **2**:419
Conservation Issues Forum, The, **1**:274
Conservation Newsletter, **1**:273
Conservation programs, **1**:273, 281
Conservation Reserve, **1**:210, 211, 212, 279
Conservative PACs, **2**:658
Conservative Political Action Conference, **2**:460
Conservative Victory Fund, **2**:460, 658
Conspiracy theories
　Accuracy in Media, **1**:125
　Communist, **2**:494, 495
Construction industry
　leading PACs, **2**:633–34, 635
　overview of, **1**:294–96
　See also under Specific group
Construction Legal Rights Foundation, **1**:315
Construction Users Anti-Inflation Roundtable, **1**:318
Consumer education
　Association of Retired Persons, **2**:562
　food handling, **1**:84
　National Chicken Council, **1**:234
Consumer Nutrition Hotline, **1**:175
Consumer packaging legislation, **1**:83–84
Consumer Price Index, seniors only, **2**:530
Consumer Product Safety Commission, **1**:308

Consumer protection, **1**:5, 37
Consumer rights, **2**:500–501
Consumer safety, **2**:458
　Consumer Product Safety Commission, **1**:308
　Public Citizen, **2**:500–501
　U.S. Public Interest Research Group, **2**:505
Containerboard and Kraft Paper, **1**:304
Continental Airlines, **1**:300; **2**:356, 668, 669, 700
Contingency fees, **1**:81
Contraception. See Family planning
"Contract With America," **1**:258; **2**:482, 550
Contractors. See Construction industry
Contractors for Free Enterprise, **1**:315
Contractors Referral Service, **1**:315
Control Data, **2**:512
Convenience stores
　National Association of Convenience Stores, **1**:64, 65, 83, 89–91; **2**:630, 632
　See also Grocery store industry
Convention of the Elimination of All Forms of Discrimination Against Women, **2**:585
Conwood, **2**:693
Cooperative Extension Service, **1**:213, 215–16, 247, 252
Cooperatives
　Grange, **1**:247
　National Council of Farmer Cooperatives, **1**:240–41
　National Farmers Union, **1**:244–46
Coors, **1**:114
Coors, Joseph, **2**:491
Copyright, **1**:65, 120, 121
　Association of American Publishers, **1**:130–31
　"fair use," **1**:130
　"First Sale Doctrine," **1**:153
　Magazine Publishers of America, **1**:135, 136
　Motion Picture Association of America, **1**:138, 140
　National Association of Broadcasters, **1**:153
　National Cable Television Association, **1**:147
　National Funeral Directors Association's Group Music License, **1**:110
　Newspaper Association of America, **1**:150, 151
　Printing Industries of America, **1**:343, 344
　Recording Industry Association of America, **1**:153–54, 155
　Software and Information Industry Association, **1**:157–58
　See also Intellectual property; Internet, copyright issues
Copyright Act, **1**:130–31
Copyright Act, Record Rental Amendment, **1**:153
Copyright Damages Improvement Act, **1**:65, 113
Copyright Music (AHMA committee), **1**:73
Copyright Protection Fund, **1**:158
Corn sweetener industry, **1**:223
Corning, **2**:662, 664
Corporate bookkeeping, **1**:319
Corporate taxation, **1**:15; **2**:501
Corporate welfare, **2**:486
Corporation for American Banking, **1**:10
Corporations, lobbying expenditures, **2**:694–96
Correction officers, **2**:365
Corrigan, Wilfred, **1**:346
Cosmetic companies, animal testing, **2**:539
"Cost of Government Day," **2**:469
Cost of living adjustments, **1**:93–94
Cote, Paul, **1**:269
Cotton Foundation, **1**:237

Cotton industry
  American Cotton Manufacturers Association, **1**:309
  Cotton Textile Institute, **1**:309
  National Cotton Council, **1**:209, 237–39; **2**:627
Cotton Textile Institute, **1**:309
Coughlin, Charles E., **1**:244
Council for a Livable World, **2**:518–20
Council of Insurance Agents & Brokers, **2**:651
Council on Postsecondary Education, **1**:197
Counterspin, **1**:134
Countrywide Credit Industries, **2**:652
Covington and Burling, **2**:679, 680
Cox, Archibald, **2**:467, 485
CPA Client Bulletin, **1**:23
Crane, Edward H., **2**:475, 476
Creating Change conference, **2**:581
"Creating the Future," **1**:175–76
Credentialization, of occupational therapists, **1**:198
Credit card disclosures, opposition to, **1**:8, 19
Credit companies
  leading PACs, **2**:649
  lobbying expenditures, **2**:697
Credit history, **1**:41
Credit reports, **1**:43
Credit Suisse First Boston, **2**:650
Credit Union Legislative Action Council, **1**:26
Credit Union Membership Access Act, **1**:24, 25
Credit Union National Association, **1**:24–26; **2**:646, 648
Credit unions
  attack on client base of, **1**:13, 24
  expansion, **1**:10, 27
  leading PACs, **2**:648
  National Credit Union Administration, **1**:22
  See also under Specific credit union
Crime
  highway, **1**:312, 313
  juvenile crime bills, **1**:96
  Violent and Repeat Juvenile Offender Act, **1**:97
  Violent Crime Control and Law Enforcement Act, **2**:521
Crisis Magazine, **2**:579
Critical Mass Bulletin, **2**:500
Critical Mass Energy Project, **2**:500
Crop insurance, **1**:27, 31
Crop production/processing, lobbying expenditures, **2**:698
Cross-border trucking, **1**:313
Crowley Maritime, **2**:670
CSE Sentinel, **2**:483
CSX Transportation, **2**:668, 670, 676
Cuba, **1**:229; **2**:503
Cuba Democracy Project, **2**:439
Cuban American National Foundation, **2**:594
Cuban Exiles, **2**:594–96
Cuban Exodus Relief Fund, **2**:594
Cuban Human Rights Monitor, **2**:595
Cuban Humanitarian Trade Act, **2**:595
Cuban Independence Day, **2**:594
Cuban Liberty and Democratic Solidarity Act, **2**:595
Cuban Missile Crisis, **2**:611
Cubic, **2**:636
Culinary Workers Union Local 226, **2**:376
CUNA Mutual Group, **1**:25
Curtiss, Glen, **1**:298
Customer privacy, **1**:5
  American Civil Liberties Union, **2**:434

Customer privacy *(continued)*
  America's Community Bankers, **1**:13
  Independent Community Bankers of America, **1**:29
  National Association of Life Underwriters, **1**:47
  Securities Industry Association, **1**:59–60
  See also Electronic data; Patient privacy
"Cut Out Dissection," **2**:540
Cutler-Hammer, **2**:384
Cuyahoga River, **1**:257
Cyprus, **2**:616
Cyprus Amax Minerals, **2**:641, 644

D

Daimler Chrysler, **2**:410, 668, 670, 694, 700
Dairy industry, **1**:240, 242
  Dairy compacts, **1**:226, 248
  Dairy farmers, **1**:226
  International Dairy Foods Association, **1**:226–28; **2**:629
  leading PACs, **2**:629
  Mid-American Dairymen, **1**:227; **2**:627, 629
  National Dairy Food Association, **1**:210
Dairyman's Co-op Creamery Association, **2**:629
DALENPAC, **2**:658
D'Amato, Alphonse, **2**:577
Danger on the Right, **2**:427, 436
Darden Restaurants, **2**:631
Darling, Jay, **1**:272, 281
Darrow, Clarence, **2**:433
Daschle, Tom, **1**:63, 93, 349
David H. Koch Charitable Foundation, **2**:457
Davidson, James D., **2**:498
Davis, Nathan Smith, **1**:189
Davis-Bacon Bill, **2**:390
Daytime Broadcasters Association, **1**:142
Dayton Hudson, **2**:632
D.C. Environmental Agenda 99, **1**:267
DDT. *See* Pesticides
Dealers Election Action Committee of the National Automobile Association, **1**:99
Dean Witter Reynolds Financial Group, **1**:35
Dearborn Independent, **2**:424
Death tax. *See* Estate tax
Deaver, Michael, **2**:678
Debs, Eugene, **2**:419
Debs, Horace, **2**:561
Deere & Company, **2**:410
Defense budget
  American Conservative Union, **2**:461
  American Enterprise Institute, **2**:464
  Americans for Democratic Action, **2**:468
  Brookings Institution, **2**:473
  Common Cause, **2**:486
  Council for a Livable World, **2**:518–20
  Heritage Foundation, **2**:457, 491
  lobbying expenditures, **2**:697
  reduction of, **2**:588
  Union of Concerned Scientists, **2**:545–46
  See also Arms control; Arms sales
Defense Credit Union Council, **1**:25
Defense PACs, **2**:636–37
Defense Research Institute, **2**:80
Deforestation. *See* Logging
Del Webb, **2**:652

Deloitte & Touche, **2**:646, 652
Delta Air Lines, **1**:300; **2**:356, 668, 669, 700
Democratic/Liberal PACs, **2**:623, 657
Democratic Study Group Campaign Fund, **2**:657
Demonstrations
    environmental groups, **1**:260, 270
        logger, **1**:291
        property owners, **1**:291
DeMuth, Christopher C., **2**:464
Dentists, American Dental Association, **2**:653, 655
Denton, James S., **2**:438
Deposit insurance, **1**:27
Desegregation, **2**:579
Desert Caucus, **2**:665, 666
DeSilver, Albert, **2**:433
Developing countries, environmental issues, **1**:267
Dewey, Melvil, **1**:75
DFS Group, **2**:703
DHL Airways, **1**:300
Diabetes, National Diabetes Month, **1**:166
Diablo Canyon, **1**:288
Diagnostic Statistical Manual of Mental Disorders, **1**:199
Diaz, Porfirio, **2**:606
Dickstein, Shapiro & Morin, **2**:661
Diesel standards, **1**:313
Dietary Reference Intakes, **1**:177
Digital Millennium Copyright Act, **1**:344
Digital Performance Right in Sound Recordings Act, **1**:154
Digital recording devices, **1**:154
Digital revolution, **1**:121, 148
    National Association of Broadcasters, **1**:143–44
    Recording Industry Association of America, **1**:155
Dilg, Will, **1**:272
Dingell-Norwood bill. *See* Patient's Bill of Rights
Dinkins, David, **2**:570
Dinosaur National Monument, **2**:288
Direct action organizations
    Greenpeace, **2**:270
    Rainforest Action Network, **2**:284–86
Direct credit lending, **1**:18
Direct-mail campaigns, **2**:270, 457
Direct Marketing Association, **2**:630, 632
Directory of National, State, and Local Homeless and Housing Advocacy Organizations, **2**:451
Dirty Dozen, **1**:276, 277
Disability income insurance, **1**:15–16
Discriminatory practices
    National Funeral Directors Association, **1**:108
    Petroleum Market Association of America, **1**:115
Disney. *See* Walt Disney
Distilled Spirits Council of the United States, **1**:295, 323–25
Distilled Spirits Institute, **1**:323
Distillery, Wine, and Allied Workers, **2**:414
Dodd, Christopher, **2**:595
Dole, Bob, **2**:469
Dole, Elizabeth, **1**:103
Dollars and Sense, **2**:498
Domestic Violence Offender Gun Ban. *See* Lautenberg Law
Domestic violence victims, legal assistance for, **2**:448
Donahue, Thomas, **2**:361, 401
Don't Make a Wave committee, **1**:269
Douglass, John, **1**:298, 299
Dow Chemical, **2**:512, 662, 663
Dow Jones, **2**:680

Dr. Seuss Foundation, **2**:443
Draft resisters, legal assistance to, **2**:452
Drake University, **1**:43
Dreier, David, **1**:30
Driver's License law. *See* Graduated Driver's License law
DRS Technologies, **2**:636
Drug legislation, **2**:476
Drug trafficking
    Cuba, **2**:595
    Mexico, **2**:607–8
Drugs. *See* Pharmaceutical industry; Prescription drugs
Drummond, **2**:644
DSM, **1**:199
D'Souza, Dinesh, **2**:463
DTE Energy, **2**:641, 645, 699
Du Bois, W.E.B., **2**:578
Du Pont, Lammot, **1**:321
Dual banking system, **1**:13
Dubinsky, David, **2**:407
Dulles, John Foster, **2**:614
DuPont, **2**:662, 663, 679
Dutko Group, **2**:701
Dwight D. Eisenhower Professional Development Program (Title II), **1**:96

E

E. Coli, **1**:177, 221, 235
E-mail
    American Conservative Union, **2**:460
    Americans for Democratic Action, **2**:468
    Center for Responsive Politics, **2**:479
    Christian Coalition, **2**:481
    Common Cause, **2**:485
    environmental interest groups, **1**:259, 260
    Greenpeace, **1**:270
    League of Conservation Voters, **1**:275–76
    National Audubon Society, **1**:279
    National Wildlife Federation, **1**:283
    Public Citizen, **2**:500
    service interest groups, **1**:65
    U.S. Public Interest Research Group, **2**:504
    wise use movement, **1**:292
Eagle Forum, **2**:623, 658
Early Detection and Control of Breast Cancer, **2**:562
Earth Day, **1**:240, 256, 257
Earthlist, **1**:276, 277
Earthshare, **2**:504
East Asia Strategic Initiative, **2**:615
Eastman, Crystal, **2**:433
Eastman Kodak, **2**:512
Economic assistance
    Americans for Democratic Action, **2**:457
    Heritage Foundation, **2**:457
    National Council of the Churches of Christ, **2**:497
    See also Foreign aid
Economic-based interest groups
    overview of, **1**:422–28
    See also under Specific group
Economic development
    European Union, **2**:598, 599
    Friends of the Earth's position on, **1**:265, 266
Economic Policy Institute, **2**:455, 457, 487–89

*Numbers in **bold** indicate volume.*

Economic sanctions
    foreign governments, **2**:588
    National Council of the Churches of Christ, **2**:497
Ecuador, **1**:285
Edey, Marion, **1**:266, 275
Edison Electric Institute, **1**:295, 296, 326–28, 338
    leading PAC, **2**:641, 645
    lobbying expenditures, **2**:694, 699
EDS, **2**:638, 639, 686
Education
    adult, **2**:373
    environmental groups and, **1**:260, 270–71
    funding cuts, **1**:121–22
    funding for, **1**:131
    higher. *See* Higher education
    lobbying expenditures, **2**:697
    prisoner, **2**:453
    public. *See* Schools
    vocational, **2**:332, 373
Education and Research Foundation, **1**:43
Education Excellence Center, **2**:492
Education Savings Account and School Excellence Act, **2**:514
Educational Institute, **1**:74
Educational Rights project, **2**:450
Educational vouchers. *See* School vouchers
"Effective Government Committee," **2**:622
Egg industry, United Egg Association, **1**:254–55; **2**:628
EggPAC, **1**:255
Eighteenth Amendment, **2**:508
Eisenhower, Dwight, **2**:433, 494
Eizenstat, Stuart, **2**:678
El Paso Energy, **2**:641, 643
Eldercare, **1**:189
Elderly
    assistance for, **2**:448, 502, 503
    See also American Association of Retired Persons
Election laws, **1**:64
Electric industry
    leading PACs, **2**:645
    lobbying expenditures, **2**:697
    See also Electric industry deregulation
    See also under Specific group
Electric industry deregulation, **1**:295–96, 326–27
    Chemical Manufacturers Association, **1**:321–22
    Citizens for a Sound Economy, **2**:484
    National Grange, **1**:248
    and nuclear energy deregulation, **1**:338
Electronic commerce, **1**:157–58
Electronic/computer manufacturing PACs, **2**:639
Electronic data, privacy concerns, **1**:29, 151, 188, 200–201, 206–7
Electronic Machine Furniture Workers, **2**:672
Electronic media
    books, **1**:131
    magazines, **1**:136
    National Association of Broadcasters, **1**:142
    Newspaper Association of America, **1**:150, 151
    real estate listings, **1**:53
Electronic reservation systems (airline), **1**:301
Electronics industry
    leading PACs, **2**:638
    lobbying expenditures, **2**:697
Elementary and Secondary Education Act, **1**:96; **2**:367, 398, 514
Eli Lilly, **2**:653, 656, 691, 695

Emancipation Proclamation, **2**:506
Embassies, **2**:588
Emergency Committee for American Trade, **2**:685
Emergency Council on Education, **1**:127
Emergency medicine. *See* American College of Emergency Physicians
Emergency Medicine Foundation, **1**:172
Emergency Planning and Community Right-to-Know Act, **1**:295
Emergency system, 911, **2**:379
Emerging Japanese Superstate, The, **2**:492
Emerson Electric, **2**:664
Emery Worldwide Airlines, **1**:300; **2**:370
Emily's List, **2**:556–59 *passim,* 572–74, 623, 659
Emissions, regulation of, **1**:101, 256, 259, 312, 319, 336
Emory University, **1**:57
Employee Retirement Income Security Act, **1**:84
Employee wages. *See* Minimum wage legislation
Empowerment Directory, 1997, **2**:451
Encouraging Environmental Excellence program, **1**:311
Encryption
    National Venture Capital Association, **1**:57
    Securities Industry Association, **1**:60
    Software and Information Industry Association, **1**:157
    TechNet, **1**:349
End of Racism, The, **2**:463
Endangered Species Act
    AF&PA opposition to, **1**:305
    Environmental Defense Fund, **1**:263
    establishment of, **1**:257
    National Audubon Society, **1**:278, 279
    National Cattlemen's Beef Association, **1**:231
    supporters of reauthorization of, **1**:248, 279
    U.S. Public Interest Research Group, **2**:505
Endangered Species List, **1**:260, 262, 292
Energy/resource PACs, **2**:641–42
Engineering industry
    International Union of Operating Engineers, **2**:390–92
    leading PACs, **2**:635
Engineers' Political Education Committee, **2**:392
English as a Second Language, **2**:547
English First, **2**:692
"English for Children," **2**:547
English Language, **2**:667
English Language Fluency Act, **2**:547
Enhanced Proliferation Control Initiative, **2**:612
Enron, **2**:641, 643, 676
Entergy, **2**:699
Entergy Operations, **2**:645
Enterprise Leasing, **2**:670
Entertainment industry
    lobbying expenditures, **2**:687, 697
    overview of, **1**:65, 120–23
    See also under Specific group
EnviroAction, **1**:283
Environmental Defense Fund, **1**:259, 260, 262–64
Environmental interest groups
    leading PACs, **2**:667
    overview of, **1**:256–60
    See also under Specific group
Environmental issues & legislation
    American Forest & Paper Association, **1**:304, 305
    American Textile Manufacturers Institute, **1**:310–11
    automobile industry, **1**:99, 100
    Business Roundtable, **1**:318, 319

Numbers in **bold** *indicate volume.*

Environmental issues & legislation *(continued)*
    Citizens for a Sound Economy, **2**:483–84
    construction industry, **1**:296
    credit plans, **1**:333
    current issues, **1**:259
    Distilled Spirits Council of the United States, **1**:324
    eco-friendly homebuilding, **1**:296, 329, 330
    Environmental Defense Fund, **1**:263
    exemptions from, **1**:308
    GOP's banning/questioning of, **1**:63
    Grange, **1**:248
    Hudson Institute, **2**:493
    International Union of Operating Engineers, **2**:391
    League of Women Voters, **2**:445
    market-based solutions, **2**:473
    National Cattlemen's Beef Association, **1**:231, 232, 233
    National Chamber Litigation Center, **2**:118
    National Chicken Council, **1**:234
    National Cotton Council, **1**:238
    National Council of the Churches of Christ, **2**:497
    National Mining Association, **1**:335–36
    National Pork Producers Council, **1**:249
    real estate developers, **1**:5
    Union of Concerned Scientist, **2**:545–46
    United Egg Association, **1**:254
    U.S. Public Interest Research Group, **2**:505
Environmental Policy Institute, **1**:265, 266
Environmental Protection Agency
    American Forest & Paper Association, **1**:304
    American Meat Association, **1**:221
    American Trucking Associations, **1**:312–13
    Associated Builders and Contractors, **1**:315
    Chemical Manufacturers Association, **1**:321
    construction industry's interest in, **1**:296
    establishment of, **1**:257
    failure to enforce Great Lakes regulations, **1**:282
    Laborers International Union of North America, **2**:395
    litigation, **1**:260, 293
    manufacturing industry's interest in, **1**:295
    National Association of Furniture Manufacturers, **1**:308
    National Mining Association, **1**:335–36
    praise of American Textile Manufacturers Institute, **1**:311
    Superfund, **1**:40, 304, 391, 505
    target of environmental groups, **1**:256
    United Egg Association, **1**:254
"Environmental scorecard," **1**:275, 276–77
EPI Journal, **2**:487
Epidurals, denial of, **1**:203
Equal Rights Amendment, **2**:445, 485
    John Birch Society's opposition to, **2**:495
    National Organization for Women and, **2**:583
Equal Time and Fairness Doctrine, **1**:133
Equal Time Provision, **1**:143
Equality Begins at Home, **2**:581
Equipment Leasing Association of America, **2**:632
Equitable, **1**:17
Ergonomics regulations, **1**:104, 113
Ehrlich, Paul, **1**:256; **2**:553, 554
Ernst & Young, **1**:57; **2**:646, 652, 677
ESL, **2**:547
Esquire, **1**:136
Estate Tax Rate Reduction Act (HR-8), **1**:304
Estate taxes
    America Trucking Association, **1**:296

Estate taxes *(continued)*
    Grange, **1**:248
    Heritage foundation, **2**:490
    National Association of Convenience Stores, **1**:90
    National Association of Wheat Growers, **1**:229
    National Cattlemen's Beef Association, **1**:231
    Newspaper Association of America, **1**:151
    Printing Industries of America, **1**:295, 343
Estée Lauder, **2**:539
Estefan, Gloria, **2**:595
Ethics
    agricultural, **1**:211
    legal, **1**:68
    medical, **1**:191
    outdoor, **1**:272, 274
    political, **2**:477–78
Eurasia Foundation, **2**:439
European-American Business Council, **2**:685
European Coal and Steel Community, **2**:597
European Defense Community, **2**:597
European Economic Community, **1**:229
European Union, **1**:43, 59, 270, 299; **2**:597–99
Euthanasia. *See* Assisted suicide
Evergreen International Airlines, **1**:300
Everybody's Money, **1**:25
Ewing Marion Kauffman Foundation, **1**:57
Ex-Gay movement, **2**:576–77, 582
Excise taxes
    automobile, **1**:99, 100
    beer, **1**:104
    distilled spirits, **1**:323
    Federal Excise Tax, **1**:323
    first, **2**:506
    hunting & fishing equipment, **1**:272, 282
    meat, fish, poultry, **2**:540
Executions, **2**:442
Experimental Negotiating Agreement, **2**:417
Explosion of Hate, **2**:436
Export Administration Act, need for, **1**:299
Exports. *See* International trade
Extra!, **1**:134
Extra Update!, **1**:134
Exxon, **1**:114; **2**:512
    leading PAC, **2**:641, 643
    lobbying expenditures, **2**:690, 694
Eye care, **1**:162, 164–66

F

Factory farming, **1**:211
Facts About Store Development, **1**:84
Fahrenkopf, Frank J., Jr., **1**:70
Fair Housing Act, **1**:329
Fair Housing Rights Act, **2**:578
Fair Labor Standards Act, **1**:97, 100; **2**:365, 379, 394
Fair Minimum Wage Act, **1**:97
Fair Reader: Press and Politics, **1**:133
Fair Share program, **2**:579
Fairness and Accuracy in Reporting, **1**:123, 133–34
Fairness Doctrine, **1**:143
Fallon, George, **1**:275
False Claims Act, **1**:182, 187
False Disparagement of Perishable Food Products Act, **1**:233
Falwell, Jerry, **2**:455

Family and medical leave, **2:**682
Family and Medical Leave Act, **1:**113, 402; **2:**352, 503
Family planning
　birth control laws, **2:**542, 543
　contraception, **2:**527, 542
　Planned Parenthood Federation of America, **2:**542–44
　voluntary, **2:**554
　　See also Abortion; Population
Family Planning and Choice Act, **2:**527
Family Planning International Assistance, **2:**543
Fannie Mae. *See* Federal National Mortgage Association
Faris, Jack, **1:**107
Farm Bill
　American Agriculture Movement, **1:**218
　American Farm Bureau Federation, **1:**216
　American Sugarbeet Growers Association, **1:**223, **1:**224
　National Cotton Council, **1:**239
　National Farmers Union, **1:**245
　overview of, **1:**210, 211–12, 214
Farm Bloc, **1:**244
Farm Bureau. *See* American Farm Bureau Federation
Farm commodity marketing programs, **1:**245
Farm cooperatives. *See* Cooperatives
Farm Credit Council, **2:**627
Farm Credit system, **1:**28, 240
Farm safety net, **1:**245
Farm Security Administration, **1:**215, 244
Farmer, James, **2:**569
Farmers' Alliance, **1:**244
Farmers Educational and Cooperative Union of America. *See* National Farmers Union
Farmers Holiday Movement, **1:**244
Farmland legislation. *See* Property rights
Farrakhan, Louis, **2:**436, 579–80
Fast-food industry. *See* Food industry
Fatal Accident Reporting System Statistics, **2:**524
Faulkner, Daniel, **1:**87
Faux, Jeff, **2:**487, 488
Faxes, **1:**65, 270, 292; **2:**468
Fazio, Vic, **1:**103
FBI. *See* Federal Bureau of Investigation
FCC. *See* Federal Communications Commission
FEC. *See* Federal Election Commission
Federal Aviation Act, **1:**300, 301
Federal Aviation Administration, **1:**301; **2:**356–57
　Airport Improvement Program Act, **2:**405–6
Federal Bureau of Investigation, **1:**154
Federal Communications Commission, **1:**133, 152, 153
　advertising-time regulations, **1:**142–43
　cable television, **1:**146–47, 148
　establishment of, **1:**121, 123, 142
　Financial Interest and Syndication Rule, **1:**139, 140
　Internet access fees, **1:**53
　media, information, & entertainment interest groups and, **1:**120
　National Association of Broadcasters, **1:**123, 142–43
　Prime-Time Access rule, **1:**139, 140
Federal Deposit Insurance Corporation, **1:**10, 40, 47
　America's Community Bankers liaison with, **1:**14
Federal Election Campaign Act, **2:**621
Federal Election Commission, **2:**479, 559, 621
　lawsuit against Christian Coalition, **2:**481
Federal Emergency Management Agency, **1:**282
Federal employees. *See* National Association of Retired Federal Employees

Federal Exchange Stabilization Fund, **2:**607
Federal Excise Tax, **1:**323
Federal Express, **1:**55, 300
　leading PACs, **2:**622, 668, 669
　lobbying expenditures, **2:**700
　soft money donations, **2:**676
Federal Home Loan Bank System, **1:**14, 38
Federal Home Loan Mortgage Corporation (Freddie Mac), **1:**36, 38, 330; **2:**676
Federal Housing Authority, **1:**53–54
Federal Judiciary Retirement System, **1:**92
Federal Labor Relations Authority, **1:**87
Federal Meat Inspection Act, **1:**220
Federal National Mortgage Association (Fannie Mae), **1:**36, 38, 330; **2:**677, 694
Federal Radio Commission, **1:**142
Federal Reserve, **1:**5
　American Banker's Association and, **1:**10
　Credit Union National Association and, **1:**25
　Independent Community Bankers of America and, **1:**28
　Mortgage Bankers Association of America and, **1:**38
　National Association of Realtors and, **1:**53
　Securities Industry Association and, **1:**60
　See also Thrift Institutions Advisory Council
Federal Reserve Board, **1:**8, 43
Federal thrift charter. *See* Thrift charter
Federal Trade Commission
　on advertising, **1:**136, 323
　establishment of, **1:**63
　media, information, & entertainment interest groups and, **1:**120, 123
　National Association of Furniture Manufacturers and, **1:**308
　Wal-Mart investigation, **2:**415
Federal Trade Commission Act, **1:**78
"Federalist No. 10," **2:**422, 424
Federation of American Health Systems, **2:**656
Federation of Organized Trades and Labor Unions of the United States and Canada, **2:**359
Feingold, Russell, **2:**577, 610, 625
Feldman, Sandra, **2:**367
Feminism groups. *See* Women's rights
Fidelity Ventures, **1:**55
Field and Stream, **1:**278
Fifth Horseman, **2:**657
Fight BAC™, **1:**84
Fighting Police Abuse: A Community Action Manual, **2:**434
Filenes, Albert E., **1:**117
Fillmore, Millard, **2:**507
Film, Air and Package Carriers Conference, **1:**312
Film industry
　copyright issues, **1:**121
　leading PACs, **2:**639
　See also under Specific group
Financial Accounting Standards Board, **1:**22, 56–57, 349
　Independent Community Bankers of America and, **1:**28
Financial Interest and Syndication Rule, **1:**139, 140
Financial interest groups
　leading PACs, **2:**646, 649
　lobbying expenditures, **2:**697
　overview of, **1:**3–7
　See also under Specific group
Financial service restructuring, **1:**4–5
　American Council of Life Insurance, **1:**15
　Independent Insurance Agents of America, **1:**30

Financial service restructuring *(continued)*
   National Association of Independent Insurers, **1**:39
   National Association of Insurance Commissioners, **1**:42–43
   National Association of Life Underwriters, **1**:46
   National Association of Professional Insurance Agents, **1**:49
   National Association of Realtors, **1**:52
   Security Industry Association, **1**:58–59
Findley, Paul, **2**:601
Fineran, Lawrence, **1**:333
Fink, Matthew P., **1**:34
Fink, Richard H., **2**:483
Fire fighters, International Association of Fire Fighters, **1**:378–80; **2**:671, 674
FIRE PAC, **1**:380
Firearms. *See* Gun control
First Amendment, **1**:138–39; **2**:514
First Freedom, The, **2**:427, 439
"First Sale Doctrine," **1**:153
First Union, **2**:647, 684
Fiscal policy
   Business Roundtable, **1**:319
   National Association of Manufacturers, **1**:332
Fishermen & fishing
   Environmental Defense Fund on, **1**:262
   environmental interest groups on, **1**:259
   excise taxes, **1**:282
   Fishermen's Union of America, **2**:399
   Greenpeace on, **1**:269
   Izaak Walton League, **1**:258; 272–74
   PETA on, **2**:540
501(c)(3) & 501(c)(4) status, defined, **2**:458, 557
Flag protection, **2**:516–17, 568
Flag Protection Act, **2**:516
Flat tax
   American Conservative Union, **2**:461
   Americans for Tax Reform, **2**:470
   Citizens for a Sound Economy, **2**:484
   Heritage Foundation, **2**:490
   Printing Industries of America, **1**:295, 343–44
   United Automobile Workers, **2**:412
Fleet Financial Group, **2**:647, 684
Fleishman-Hillard, **2**:661
Flore, Edward, **2**:375
Florence and John Schumanm Foundation, **2**:457, 478, 480
Florida, Miami-Dade County, **2**:688
Florida Power & Light, **2**:641, 645, 699
Flowers Industries, **2**:627
Fluor, **2**:633, 635
FMC, **2**:662, 663
Food, Drug and Cosmetic Act, **1**:84
Food-aid programs, **1**:211, 229, 232
Food and Drug Administration
   American Federation for Aids Research, **1**:178–79
   American Heart Association, **1**:185
   American Meat Institute, **1**:221
   Citizens for a Sound Economy, **2**:484
   establishment of, **1**:175
   Magazine Publishers of America, **1**:136
   media, information, & entertainment interest groups and, **1**:123
   Petroleum Marketers Association of America, **1**:115
   Pharmaceutical Research and Manufacturers of America, **1**:341–42
   RU-486, **2**:527, 528, 544, 554
   tobacco sales regulation, **1**:91, 185

Food and Drug Administration Modernization Act, **1**:341–42
Food industry
   leading PACs, **2**:631
   lobbying expenditures, **2**:698
   See also Food and Drug Administration; Food labeling; Food safety
   See also under Specific group
Food Information Service, **1**:84
Food labeling, **1**:163, 177, 220
Food Marketing Industry Speaks, The, **1**:84
Food Marketing Institute, **1**:64, 83–85, 177; **2**:627
Food Marketing Institute Foundation, **1**:64, 83, 84
Food safety, **1**:211
   American Meat Institute, **1**:220, 221
   Center for Public Integrity, **2**:478
   Food Marketing Institute, **1**:83, **1**:84
   Hazard Analysis and Critical Control Points, **1**:221
   National Cattlemen's Beef Association, **1**:231, **1**:233
   National Pork Producers Council, **1**:249–50
   United Egg Association, **1**:254
Food Stamps, **1**:210, 211, 212; **2**:497
Food store interest groups. *See* Grocery store industry
Food subsidy programs. *See* Food-aid programs; Food stamps
Forbes, Steve, **2**:438
Ford, **2**:410, 411
   disinvestment from South Africa, **2**:512
Ford, Gerald, **2**:445, 464
Ford, Henry, **2**:424, 435
Ford, Tom, **2**:540
Ford Foundation, **1**:262, 263; **2**:439, 443, 478
Ford Motor, **2**:668, 670, 694
   lobbying expenditures, **2**:700
Foreign Agents Registration Act, **2**:587
Foreign aid, **2**:588
   Israel, **2**:600
   Mexico, **2**:607
   Nigeria, **2**:610
   Russia, **2**:612, 613
   Turkey, **2**:616, 617, 618
Foreign governments, **2**:586–90
Foreign imports. *See* International trade
Foreign policy
   Americans for Democratic Action, **2**:457, 467
   Anti-Defamation League, **2**:428
   Cato Institute, **2**:476
   NAACP, **2**:579
   United States Catholic Conference, **2**:503
Foreign Sales Corporation benefit, **1**:157
Foreign Service Retirement System, **1**:92
Foreign trade. *See* International trade
Forest Industries PAC, **1**:305
Forest Resources, **1**:304
Forestry and paper
   forest preservation, **1**:269, 281
   leading PACs, **2**:629
   lobbying expenditures, **2**:697
   See also Land management & development; Logging
Fort Howard Corporation, **1**:304
Fort Pitt Lodge No. 1, **1**:86
Forum 500, **1**:17
Foster, Vincent, **1**:125
Foster Farms, **2**:413
Foundation for Human Rights in Cuba, **2**:595
Fowler, Mark, **1**:133

Foxman, Abraham H., **2:**435, 436–37
Frances Boyers Award, **2:**463
Frank, Harris, Shriver and Jacobson, **2:**679
Frank, Leo, **2:**424, 435
Franklin Delano Roosevelt Memorial, **2:**529
Fraternal Order of Police, **1:**62, 64, 86–88
Fraternal Order of Police v. United States, **1:**87
Freddie Mac. *See* Federal Home Loan Mortgage Corporation
Free Cuba, **2:**596
Free-market solutions, **1:**259, 262, 263
Free markets
    American Enterprise Institute, **2:**463
    American Textile Manufacturers Institute, **1:**309
    Brookings Institution, **2:**473
    Cato Institute, **2:**475, 476
    Center for the Defense of Free Enterprise, **1:**291, 292–93
    Citizens for a Sound Economy, **2:**457, 483, 484
    Economic Policy Institute, **2:**488
    Freedom House, **2:**428, 439
    Heritage Foundation, **2:**490
    National Chicken Council, **1:**234
    Printing Industries of America, **1:**343
    Public Citizen, **2:**501
    Semiconductor Industry Association, **1:**346–47
    United Egg Association, **1:**254
    See also Global Agreement on Tariffs and Trade; International trade; North American Free Trade Agreement
Free Nigeria Movement, **2:**610
"Free of E. Coli" label, **1:**177
Free Silver movement, **2:**507–8
Free Soil Party, **2:**506
Free trade. *See* Free markets
Free Trade in the Americas, **1:**282
Freedom Forum, **2:**439
Freedom House, **2:**422–28 *passim*, 438–40
Freedom in the World, **2:**427, 438, 439
Freedom Monitor, **2:**427, 439
Freedom of Access to Clinical Entrances Act, **2:**544
Freedom of information, **2:**485
Freedom of Information Act, **1:**151
Freedom of speech & press, **1:**130, 133, 139, 151; **2:**433
Freedom Review, **2:**439
Freedom to Advertise Coalition, **1:**136
Freedom to farm legislation, **1:**249
Freedom to Read, The, **1:**76
Freedom to Read Foundation, **1:**76
Freeman, **1:**245
Freemasons, **1:**247
Freeport-Mcmoran Copper & Gold, **2:**644
Friedan, Betty, **2:**583, 584
Friedman and Hayek on Freedom, **2:**475
Friends of Higher Education, **2:**667
Friends of the Earth, **1:**258, 262, 265–68, 275, 288
Friends of the Earth Newsmagazine, **1:**267
"Friends of the Taxpayer," **2:**469
Friendship Food Ships, **2:**496
Friendship Food Trains, **2:**496
Frito-Lay, **2:**413
FTC. *See* Federal Trade Commission
Fugitive Slave Law, **2:**506
Fuji, **2:**680
Fujitsu, **2:**604
Fulbright & Jaworski, **2:**661

Fund for America's Libraries, **1:**77
Funeral organizations
    Funeral Service Credit Union, **1:**110
    National Funeral Directors Association. *See* National Funeral Directors Association
Funeral Service Credit Union, **1:**110
Furniture industry, American Furniture Manufacturers Association, **1:**295, 307–8; **2:**662, 664
Furniture Political Action Committee, **1:**308
Future of Puerto Rico, **2:**704

G

Gaboury, Jennifer, **2:**441
Gag Rule, **2:**554
Galbraith, John Kenneth, **2:**466
Gallagher, Ann, **1:**176
Gallo, **2:**413
Gallo Winery, **2:**677
Gambling. *See* Gaming industry
Gaming industry
    American Gaming Association, **1:**70–72, 73
    Christian Coalition on, **2:**482
    copyright issues, **1:**121
    image of, **1:**123
    leading PACs, **2:**632
    lobbying expenditures, **2:**697
    minimum wage issues, **1:**121
    tax proposal, **1:**70
    unions, **2:**376
Gandhi, Indira, **2:**569
Gannett, **1:**150
Garcyznski, Gary, **1:**331
Gardner, John, **2:**485
Gasoline
    consumption of, **1:**257
    convenience store sales, **1:**89
    lead free, **1:**262
    See also Petroleum industry
Gateway to Education Materials, **2:**396
Gay and lesbian rights
    American Civil Liberties Union, **2:**434
    Cato Institute, **2:**476
    Christian Coalition, **2:**481, 482
    Common Cause, **2:**486
    Human Rights Campaign, **2:**556–59 *passim*, 575–77
    National Council of the Churches of Christ, **2:**497
    National Gay and Lesbian Task Force, **2:**556–59 *passim*, 581–82
    National Lawyers Guild, **2:**453
    National Organization for Women, **2:**585
GE Capital Corporation, **1:**18
GEICO, **1:**39
Gencorp, **2:**636
Genentech, **1:**55
General Accounting Office, **1:**182
General Atomics, **2:**641, 645
General Aviation Manufacturers Association, **2:**669
General Dynamics, **1:**298; **2:**636, 703
General Electric, **1:**8, 298, 318; **2:**384, 390
    disinvestment from South Africa, **2:**512
    leading PAC, **2:**662, 664
    lobbying expenditures, **2:**694
General Instrument, **2:**640

General Motors, **2:**410, 411, 546, 679
  leading PAC, **2:**668, 670
  lobbying expenditures, **2:**694, 700
General Motors Acceptance Corporation, **1:**18
General Public Utilities, **2:**645
Genesis Health Ventures, **2:**656
Genetic engineering
  agricultural, **1:**211, 238, 270
  environmental concerns, **1:**256, 259
  Greenpeace's position on, **1:**270
Genetic testing, **1:**16
Genocide, **2:**438, 442
Georgia-Pacific Corp., **1:**304; **2:**629
Gephardt, Richard A., **1:**103; **2:**622
German-American Bund, **2:**435
Germany, labor union, **2:**350
"Get Caught Reading" Month, **1:**131
G.I. Bill, **1:**127; **2:**567
G.I. Bill of Health, **2:**567, 568
Giant, **2:**413
Gibbons, James, **2:**502
Gideon v. Wainwright, **2:**433, 447
Gillette, **2:**539
Gingrich, Newt, **1:**27, 30; **2:**470, 622, 625
Ginnie Mae. *See* Government National Mortgage Association
Gitlow v. New York, **2:**433
Glass-Steagall Act, **1:**4–5, **1:**8, **1:**59
Glasser, Ira, **2:**433
Glaucoma Awareness Month, **1:**166
Glaxo Wellcome, **2:**653, 656, 691
Glenn, John, **2:**517
Glickman, Daniel, **1:**218
Global Agreement on Tariffs and Trade
  American Sugarbeet Growers Association, **1:**223–24
  Economic Policy Institute, **2:**488
  Heritage Foundation, **2:**490
  manufacturing groups and, **1:**295
  National Association of Manufacturers, **1:**332
  Public Citizen, **2:**501
Global Gag Rule, **2:**554
Global Trade Watch, **2:**500–501
Global warming, **1:**256, 319
  Greenpeace's interest in, **1:**269
  Izaak Walton League's interest in, **1:**273
Global Warming Treaty. *See* Kyoto Global Climate Change Treaty
"Go Ask Alice," **1:**77
Gold Kist, **2:**628
Golden Gate Bridge, **1:**291
Goldman, Emma, **2:**508
Goldman, Sachs & Company, **1:**61; **2:**650, 676
Goldwater, Barry, **2:**492, 509
Gompers, Samuel, **2:**351, 359, 393
Good Neighbor Policy, **2:**606
Goodyear Tire & Rubber, **2:**668, 670
  lobbying expenditures, **2:**700
GOP. *See* Republican Party
Gorbachev, Mikhail, **2:**611
Gore, Albert, **1:**258, 277, 315, 330, 349; **2:**576
Gottlieb, Alan, **1:**291, 292
Gould, **2:**384
Government Affairs Update and Regulatory Update, **1:**315
Government agencies, lobbying expenditures, **2:**688, 697

Government agency retirement programs, **1:**92–94
Government National Mortgage Association (Ginnie Mae), **1:**36, 38
Governmental Affairs Conference, **1:**220–21
Governmental Affairs Office, **1:**68
Grace Foundation, Inc., **2:**439
Graduated Driver's License law, **1:**31, 39
Graduated income taxes, **1:**245
Grain bank, **1:**242
Grange, **1:**209, 215, 240, 247–48
Graphic Arts Employers of America, **1:**343
Graphic arts industry
  Graphic Arts Employers of America, **1:**343
  Printing Industries of America, **1:**295, 343–45
Graphic Arts Marketing Information Service, **1:**343
Graphic Arts Technical Foundation, **1:**343
Graphic Communications Association, **1:**343
Grassroots Action Information Network, **1:**119
Grazing rights, **1:**231, 232, 233, 259
  Izaak Walton League, **1:**273
  National Wildlife Federation, **1:**281, 282
  wise use movement's in, **1:**291, 293
Great Lakes, **1:**282
Great Washington Board of Trade, **2:**633
Greece, Turkish invasion of Cyprus, **2:**616
Green, Gene, **1:**100
Green Mountain Energy, **2:**546
Greenbert, Traurig et al., **2:**661
Greenpeace, **1:**63, 258, 260, 262, 269–71
Greenpeace, **1:**269
Greenspan, Alan, **1:**29
Grenada, **2:**567
Gresham, Isaac, **1:**244
Griffin, Johnson et al., **2:**701
Grinnell, George Bird, **1:**278
Grocery store industry
  Food Marketing Institute, **1:**83–85
  United Food and Commercial Workers Union, **2:**413–15
  See also Convenience stores
Group Music License, **1:**110
Group of Ten, **1:**257
Growth hormones, agricultural, **1:**211
Gruenebaum, Jane, **2:**444
GTE, **2:**372, 384, 638, 639, 699
Guatemala, **2:**441
Guenther, Kenneth A., **1:**28
Gulf Coast Retailers, **1:**83
Gulf War
  American Legion, **2:**567
  Cato Institute, **2:**476
  Common Cause, **2:**486
  National Council of the Churches of Christ, **2:**497
  Turkey and, **2:**617
Gulfstream, **1:**298
Gun control
  Brady Bill, **2:**521, 533
  Cato Institute, **2:**458
  Children's Gun Violence Prevention Act, **1:**397
  Christian Coalition, **2:**458
  Concealed Carry Law for Law Enforcement Officers, **1:**87
  Congress of Racial Equality, **2:**570
  excise taxes, **1:**281
  Fraternal Order of Police, **1:**86–87
  Handgun Control, Inc., **2:**521–23

*Numbers in **bold** indicate volume.*

Gun control *(continued)*
  Lautenberg Law, **1:**86–87
  leading PACs, **2:**667
  League of Women Voters of the United States, **2:**445
  National Association for the Advancement of Colored People, **2:**579
  National Council of Churches, **2:**458
  United States Catholic Conference, **2:**503
  U.S. Catholic Conference, **2:**458
  See also National Rifle Association
Gun Control Act, **2:**533
Gun Owners of America, **2:**667

H

Hague v. CIO, **2:**433
Haig, Alexander, **2:**591
Halliburton, **2:**641, 643
Hallmark Cards, **2:**640
Hamilton, Alexander, **1:**3, 8
Hamilton, Lee, **2:**597
Hancock, John, **1:**15
Handgun Control, Inc., **2:**521–23
  leading PAC, **2:**623, 665, 667
Handgun Control Voter Education Fund, **2:**522
Hanley, Edward T., **2:**376
Hanson, Justine, **2:**441
Harbor Maintenance Tax, **2:**399
"Harbor Services Fund," **2:**399
Harding, Warren, **2:**508
Harrah's Entertainment, **2:**630, 632
Harrington, Michael, **2:**467
Harris, **2:**636
"Harry and Louise" advertisements, **2:**681
Hatano, Darryl, **1:**347
Hatch Human Life Federalism Amendment, **2:**543
Hate Crimes: ADL Blueprint for Action, **2:**436
Hate Crimes Laws, 1999, **2:**436
Hate crimes legislation
  Anti-Defamation League, **2:**427–28, 436, 437
  Human Rights Campaign, **2:**575
  NAACP, **2:**579
  National Gay and Lesbian Task Force, **2:**582
  National Lawyers Guild, **2:**453
Hate Crimes Sentencing Enhancement Acts, **2:**576
Hate Crimes Statistics, **2:**576
Hawaiian Airlines, **1:**300
Hayakawa, S.I., **2:**547
Hayek, Friedrich A., **2:**475
Hayes, Randall, **1:**284
Hays, Will, **1:**138
Hazard Analysis and Critical Control Points, **1:**221
HB Zachry, **2:**635
HBO, **1:**147
Head Start, **1:**96
Healthcare interest groups
  overview of, **1:**159–63
  See also under Specific group
Health Industry Manufacturers Association, **2:**691
Health insurance, **2:**682
  American College of Emergency Physicians, **1:**172–73
  lack of universal, **2:**350
  National Association of Retired Federal Employees, **1:**93

Health insurance *(continued)*
  payment for contraception, **2:**527–28
  See also Health maintenance organizations; Healthcare reform; Managed care; Medicaid; Medicare; Patient's Bill of Rights
  See also under Specific group
Health Insurance Association of America, **1:**161; **2:**681, 689, 695
Health Letter, **2:**500
Health maintenance organizations, **1:**159, 161, 186
  American Occupational Therapy Association, **1:**198
  American Psychiatric Association, **1:**200
  American Society of Anesthesiologists, **1:**203–4
  Blue Cross and Blue Shield Association and, **1:**205, 206
  guidelines & restrictions, **1:**206
  National Association of Retired Federal Employees, **1:**93
  See also Managed care
Health products & services
  leading PACs, **2:**653–54, 656
  lobbying expenditures, **2:**697
Health professionals
  leading PACs, **2:**655
  lobbying expenditures, **2:**688, 697
Health Research Group, **2:**500
Healthcare Financing Administration, **1:**43, 161, 171, 203
Healthcare reform
  American Federation of State, County, and Municipal Employees, **2:**365
  American Legion, **2:**567, 568
  American Nurses Association, **1:**162, 193–95
  American Postal Workers Union, **2:**371
  Americans for Democratic Action, **2:**466, 467
  Americans for Tax Reform, **2:**458
  Association of Community Organizations for Reform Now, **2:**430
  Business Roundtable, **1:**319
  Cato Institute, **2:**475
  Citizens for a Sound Economy, **2:**483
  employee benefits, **1:**65
  Independent Insurance Agents of America, **1:**30, 31
  insurance interest groups, **1:**5
  International Association of Machinists and Aerospace Workers, **2:**381, 382–83
  labor union support of, **2:**352
  League of Women Voters of the United States, **2:**445
  National Association of Insurance Commissioners, **1:**43
  National Association of Life Underwriters, **1:**45, 46
  National Association of Retired Federal Employees, **1:**93
  National Coalition for the Homeless, **2:**451
  National Federation of Independent Business, **1:**106
  National Restaurant Association, **1:**112–13
  National Taxpayers Union, **2:**458
  Printing Industries of America, **1:**343
  Public Citizen, **2:**500
  Service Employees International Union, **2:**401–3
  Transport Workers Union of America, **2:**405
  Union of Needletrades, Industrial, and Textile Employees, **2:**408
  United Food and Commercial Workers Union, **2:**413, 415
  United States Catholic Conference, **2:**503
  U.S. Chamber of Commerce, **1:**119
  See also Health insurance; Health maintenance organizations; Long-term care; Managed care; Medicaid; Medicare; Patient's Bill of Rights
Healthcare Worker Protection Act, **1:**194

Healthcare workers
  Service Employees International Union, **2:**401–3
  United Food and Commercial Workers Union, **2:**413
Hearst, **1:**130, 135
Heart disease prevention. *See* American Heart Association
Heinz, **2:**413
Helms, Jesse, **2:**481
Helms-Burton Act, **2:**595, 598
Helping Disadvantaged Children Meet High Standards (Title I), **1:**96, **2:**367
Helsinki Watch. *See* Human Rights Watch
Henry J. Kaiser Family Foundation, **2:**457
Henry J. Kaiser Institute, **2:**488
Heritage Foundation, **2:**353, 455–59 *passim,* 490–91
Herman, Alexis, **2:**487
Herman Kahn Center, **2:**492
Herrera, Carolina, **2:**539
Herrnstein, Richard, **2:**463
Hershey Foods, **2:**413
Hetch Hetchy Valley, **1:**287
Hewlett-Packard Company, **1:**55; **2:**639
HF Ahmansion, **2:**648
Hidden Child Foundation, **2:**435
Higgins, Fred, **1:**91
High Performance Work Organization, **2:**381
Higher education
  American Council on Education, **1:**123, 127–29
  Council on Postsecondary Education, **1:**197
  funding cuts for, **1:**121–22, 127
Higher Education Act, **1:**127–28
Higher Education and National Affairs, **1:**128
Higher Education Facilities Act, **2:**514
Highway safety legislation
  American Trucking Associations, **1:**312, 313
  Mothers Against Drunk Driving, **2:**524–25
  National Automobile Dealers Association, **1:**99
Highway Traffic Safety Administration, **1:**313
Highway Watch, **1:**312
Highways. *See* Road systems
Hill, Anita, **2:**584
Hill & Knowlton, **2:**661, 679
Hill, Rick, **1:**50
Hillhaven, **2:**413
Hillman, Sidney, **2:**407
Hisgen, Thomas L., **1:**114
Hispanic Outreach program of the NRLC, **2:**536
Hitachi, **2:**680
HIV. *See* AIDS
HMO. *See* Health maintenance organizations
Hodgson v. Minnesota, **2:**537
Hoechst Celanese, **2:**662, 664
Hoffa, James P., **2:**388, 389
Hoffa, James R. (Jimmy), **2:**387
Hogan & Hartson, **2:**661, 679, 701
Holiday Inns, **2:**632
Holland & Knight, **2:**661
Holley, Rick R., **1:**305
Hollywood Production Code, **1:**138
Holmer, Alan, **1:**341, 342
HOLNAM, **2:**634
Holocaust awareness programs, **2:**436
Holocaust victim claims, **1:**43
Home Box Office, **1:**147
Home Builders Association of Central Arizona, **1:**329

Home Builders Association of Louisville PAC, **1:**329
Home Builders Institute, **1:**329
Home Depot, RAN's campaign against, **1:**286
Home equity loans, **1:**18, 19
Home mortgages, **1:**36–38
Homebuilding, eco-friendly, **1:**296, 329, 330
Homebuyers assistance, **2:**428, 430, 431–32
Homelessness. *See* National Coalition for the Homeless
Homosexuality. *See* Gay and lesbian rights
Honda North America, lobbying expenditures, **2:**700
Honeywell, **1:**298; **2:**639
Hong Kong, transshipping, **1:**310
Hong Kong Trade Development Council, **2:**685
Hope, Clifford, **1:**229
Hormel, **2:**413
Horovitz, Samuel, **1:**80, 81
Hospital & Health Care Employees 1199, **2:**675
Hospital corporations, private, **1:**159
Hospital Service Plan Commission, **1:**186
Hospitalists, **1:**207
Hospitals
  American Hospital Association. *See* American Hospital Association
  leading PACs, **2:**656
  lobbying expenditures, **2:**697
  spot investigations, **1:**187
Hotel and Restaurant Employees National Alliance, **2:**375
Hotel Employees and Restaurant Employees International Union, **2:**375–77, 675
Hotel industry. *See* Lodging industry
Hour laws, **1:**73
House Agriculture Committee, **1:**212
House Appropriation Committee, **2:**448
House of Representatives Resources Committee, **1:**273
House Resolution No. 10, **1:**49
House Resources Committee, **1:**281
House Un-American Activities Committee, **1:**139
House Ways and Means Committee, **2:**623
Household Finance, **1:**18
Household International, **2:**649
Housing and Urban Development. *See* U.S. Department of Housing and Urban Development
Housing finance bills, **1:**305
Housing industry. *See* Construction industry
Houston Industries, **2:**641, 645
Hove, Skip, **1:**29
"How to Drive" press conference, **1:**312
Howard Jarvis Taxpayers Association, **2:**667
HRC News, **2:**575
HRC Quarterly, **2:**575
Hubbell Lighting Co., **1:**114
HUD. *See* U.S. Department of Housing and Urban Development
Hudson Institute, **2:**492–93
Hughes Electronics, **1:**298; **2:**638, 640
Hughes Space and Communications, **1:**298
Human Life Amendment, **2:**536
Human rights
  American Textile Manufacturers Institute, **1:**310
  Americans for Democratic Action, **2:**457
  Amnesty International, **2:**424
  Cuban Exodus Relief Fund, **2:**595
  Freedom House, **2:**424–28 *passim,* 438–40
  Human Rights Watch, **2:**424–27 *passim,* 441–43

Human rights *(continued)*
  leading PACs, **2:**622, 660
  lobbying expenditures, **2:**697
  National Council of the Churches of Christ, **2:**497
  National Lawyers Guild, **2:**423–26 *passim,* 452–53
  Nigeria and, **2:**609–10
  overview of, **2:**422–28
  Turkey and, **2:**617
  United States Catholic Conference, **2:**503
Human Rights Campaign, **2:**556–59 *passim,* 575–77
  leading PAC, **2:**622, 623, 660
Human Rights Watch, **2:**424–27 *passim,* 441–43
Human Rights Watch California, **2:**441
Humane Society of the United States, **2:**692
Humphrey, Hubert, **2:**466, 510
Hunting equipment, excise taxes, **1:**272, 282
Hunting interest groups. *See* Izaak Walton League
Huntington, Samuel, **2:**438
Hunton & Williams, **2:**703
Hussein, Saddam, **2:**617
Hyde, Henry, **1:**90
Hyde Amendment, **1:**65, 90; **2:**526, 536, 554
Hydropower projects, **1:**327
Hynde, Chrissie, **2:**540

I

I-69 Mid-Continent Highway Coalition, **2:**703
IBM, **2:**686, 694
ICBA Compliance Deskbook and Compliance Bulletin, The, **1:**29
ICF Kaiser International, **2:**633, 635
Idahoans for the Outdoors, **2:**667
Identity groups
  leading PACs, **2:**622, 623, 660
  lobbying expenditures, **2:**692, 697
  overview of, **2:**555–59
Ideological interest groups, overview of, **2:**454–59
Illegal Immigration Reform and Immigrant Responsibility Act, **2:**607
Illinois, City of Chicago, **2:**688
Illinois Dissection Alternative Act, **2:**540
Immigration and Naturalization Service, **1:**313
Immigration and Refugee Program, **2:**496
Immigration legislation
  American Civil Liberties Union, **2:**433
  Association of Community Organizations for Reform Now, **2:**428
  Cato Institute, **2:**475
  Communications Workers of America, **2:**374
  foreign governments and, **2:**588
  Illegal Immigration Reform and Immigrant Responsibility Act, **2:**607
  Immigration and Naturalization Service, **1:**313
  Immigration and Refugee Program, **2:**496
  Immigration Reform and Control Act, **2:**607
  legal assistance, **2:**448
  National Council of the Churches of Christ, **2:**496
  National Lawyers Guild, **2:**452, 453
  Semiconductor Industry Association, **1:**347
  Technology Network, **1:**348
  United Automobile Workers, **2:**412
  United States Catholic Conference, **2:**503
Immigration Newsletter, **2:**453

Immigration policy
  Mexico, **2:**607
  Taiwan, **2:**615
Immigration Reform and Control Act, **2:**607
Imports. *See* International trade
In-office surgery, **1:**204
Income Inflation: The Myth of Affluence Among Gay, Lesbian, and Bisexual Americans, **2:**581
Income maintenance programs, **1:**95
Independence Standards Board, **1:**22
Independent Agent, **1:**32
Independent Banker: The National Voice of America's Independent Bankers, **1:**29
Independent Bankers Association of America. *See* Independent Community Bankers of America
Independent Community Bankers of America, **1:**27–29
  leading PAC, **2:**646, 647
  lobbying expenditures, **2:**684
Independent Counsel law, **2:**468, 485, 501
Independent Electrical Contractors, **2:**635
Independent Insurance Agents of America, **1:**30–32, 39, 47
  leading PAC, **2:**646, 651
Independent Order of B'nai B'rith, **2:**435
Independent Petroleum Marketers Association. *See* Petroleum Marketers Association
Independent Statistical Service, **1:**41
India, bilingualism in, **2:**548
Indianapolis, Hudson Institute and, **2:**493
Indigenous populations, protection of, **1:**267, 285
Indigo Girls, **2:**540
Individual Retirement Accounts, **1:**32, 34, 58
Individuals with Disabilities Education Act, **2:**397
Industrial Professional Technical Workers International Union, **2:**399
Industrial union PACs, **2:**672
Industry, lobbying expenditures, **2:**697–98
Industry Audit Program, **1:**296, 300
Industry Services Department, **1:**296, 300
Information industry
  overview of, **1:**120–23
  See also under Specific group
Information Industry Association, **1:**157, 158
Information Reporting Program Advisory Committee, **1:**25
Information Resource Center, **1:**151
Inheritance taxes. *See* Estate taxes
Innis, Roy, **2:**569, 570
Insecticides. *See* Pesticides
Inspection laws, meat
  American Meat Institute, **1:**220, 221
  National Cattlemen's Beef Association, **1:**231
Institute for Government Research, **2:**472
Institute of American Meat Packers. *See* American Meat Institute
Institute of Economics, **2:**472
Institute of Scrap Recycling Industries, **2:**662, 664
Institution of Life Insurance, **1:**15
Insurance Broadcast System, **1:**51
Insurance industry
  leading PACs, **2:**646, 651
  lobbying expenditures, **2:**689, 697
  overview of, **1:**3–7
  See also Health insurance
  See also under Specific group
Insurance Industry's Citizen Action Network, **1:**16

Numbers in **bold** *indicate volume.*

Insurance Regulatory Information Network, **1**:43
Insurance Workers International Union, **2**:414
Insurance Youth Golf Classic, **1**:32
InsurBanc, **1**:32
Intel, **1**:55; **2**:639, 686
Intellectual Freedom Roundtable, **1**:76
Intellectual property
  Association of American Publishers, **1**:130
  Magazine Publishers of America, **1**:136
  Motion Picture Association of America, **1**:139
  Motion Picture Export Association, **1**:139
  National Association of Manufacturers, **1**:332
  National Venture Capital Association, **1**:57
  World Intellectual Property Organization, **1**:122, 131, 139, 151, 154, 157
  See also Copyright
Interest groups
  categorization of, **2**:456–57
  single, **2**:506–12
  worst public, **2**:530
Interest on Lawyer Trust Accounts, **2**:449
Interest rates, disclosure of, **1**:18, 19
Interest tax deductions, **1**:330
Interfaith relations, Anti-Defamation League interest in, **2**:436
Intermodel Surface Transportation Efficiency Act, **2**:524
Internal Revenue Service
  Independent Community Bankers of America and, **1**:28
  International Brotherhood of Electrical Workers and, **2**:385–86
  reform of, **1**:21
  Sierra Club and, **2**:288
  See also Information Reporting Program Advisory Committee; Tax codes
International Accounting Standards Committee, **1**:23
International Association of Fire Fighters, **2**:378–80, 671, 674
International Association of Fire Fighters Interested in Registration and Education, **2**:380
International Association of Insurance Supervisors, **1**:44
International Association of Machinists and Aerospace Workers, **2**:381–83, 622
International Brotherhood of Electrical Workers, **2**:372, 384–86
  leading PAC, **2**:622, 671, 672
International Brotherhood of Teamsters, **2**:387–89, 623–24
  leading PAC, **2**:622, 671, 673
International Builders' Show, **1**:329
International Building Code, **1**:305
International Chemical Workers Union, **2**:414
International Circulation Managers Association, **1**:150
International Climate Network, **2**:546
International Compressed Air and Foundation Workers, **2**:393
International Conference on Population, **2**:542
International Consortium of Investigative Journalists, **2**:477
International Council of Cruise Lines, **2**:668, 670
International Council of Shopping Centers, **2**:630, 632
International Criminal Court, **2**:442
International Dairy Foods Association, **1**:226–28; **2**:629
International Federation of Accountants, **1**:23
International Harvester, **2**:410
International Hod Carriers and Building Laborers Union of America. *See* Laborers' International Union of North America
International Holocaust Commission, **1**:43
International Ice Cream Association, **1**:226

International Ladies' Garment Workers' Union, **2**:407
International Longshoremen's Association, **2**:671, 673
International Monetary Fund
  China and, **2**:592
  Economic Policy Institute, **2**:488
  Friends of the Earth, **1**:267
  National Council of Farmer Cooperatives, **1**:240
  Russia and, **2**:612
  Semiconductor Industry Association, **1**:347
  United Egg Association, **1**:254
International Network of Engineers and Scientists for Global Responsibility, **2**:546
International Newspapers Advertising and Marketing Executives, **1**:150
International Paper Co., **1**:304; **2**:627, 629
International Planned Parenthood Committee, **2**:542
International Religious Freedom Act, **2**:439
International Seaman's Union of North America, **2**:399
International Supermarket Industry Convention, **1**:84
International Swaps & Derivatives Dealers Association, **2**:703
International Thermographers Association, **1**:343
International trade
  American Agriculture Movement, **1**:218
  American Conservative Union, **2**:462
  American Council of Life Insurance, **1**:16
  American Forest and Paper Association, **1**:304, **1**:305
  American Meat Institute, **1**:220, **1**:221
  American Sugarbeet Growers Association, **1**:223
  American Textile Manufacturers Institute, **1**:309–10
  Americans for Democratic Action, **2**:457
  Business Roundtable, **1**:318, 319
  Cato Institute, **2**:457, 476
  China as "Most Favored Nation," **1**:295, 333; **2**:592
  Citizens for a Sound Economy, **2**:484
  European Union, **2**:598
  foreign governments, **2**:587–88
  International Dairy Foods Association, **1**:226–27
  Japan, **2**:603–4
  manufacturing industry, **1**:295
  Mexico, **2**:606–7
  National Association of Manufacturers, **1**:332
  National Association of Wheat Growers, **1**:229
  National Chicken Council, **1**:234, 235
  National Cotton Council, **1**:237, 238
  National Venture Capital Association, **1**:57
  National Wildlife Federation, **1**:282
  Securities Industry Association, **1**:59
  Semiconductor Industry Association, **1**:346–47
  of sophisticated technology, **1**:299
  Taiwan, **2**:615
  United Egg Association, **1**:254
  United Steelworkers of America, **2**:417–18
  U.S. Catholic Conference, **2**:457
  U.S. Chamber of Commerce, **1**:119
  Webb-Pomerence Export Trade Act, **1**:138
  See also Free markets; Trade agreements; World Trade Organization
International Trade Commission, **1**:308
International Typographers Union, **2**:372
International Union of Life Insurance Agents, **2**:414
International Union of Mine, Mill, and Smelter Workers, **2**:416
International Union of Operating Engineers, **2**:390–92
International Union of Pavers, **2**:393

International Union of Petroleum and Industrial Workers, **2:**399
International Union of Steam and Operating Engineers. *See* International Union of Operating Engineers
International Whaling Commission, **1:**269
International Wildlife, **1:**283
Internet
    access fees, **1:**53
    alcohol sales, **1:**104
    censorship, **1:**122, 131
    civil, economic, and human rights interest groups' use of, **2:**427
    commerce, **1:**5
    commercialization of, **1:**133
    copyright issues, **1:**120, 122, 130, 136, 155, 344
    Digital Performance Right in Sound Recordings Act, **1:**154
    disaster information, **1:**322
    gambling, **1:**70, 71–72
    identity groups' use of, **2:**559
    insurance marketing, **1:**43
    rural access, **1:**248
    in schools, **2:**397
    service interest groups' use of, **1:**65
    service providers, **1:**148, 157
    taxes, **1:**157; **2:**470
    See also E-mail; World Wide Web
Internet Tax Freedom Act moratorium, **1:**54, 59
Interstate Carriers Conference, **1:**312
Interstate Class Action Jurisdiction Act, **1:**333
Interstate Commerce Act, **1:**63, 247, 294
Interstate Commerce Commission, **1:**312
Interstate Theft Union, **1:**313
InVest, **1:**32
Investigative reporting, **1:**221; **2:**477–78
Investment Bankers Association of America, **1:**58
Investment Company Act, **1:**33
Investment Company Institute, **1:**6, 33–35
    leading PAC, **2:**646, 650
    lobbying expenditures, **2:**684
Investment firms
    leading PACs, **2:**650
    lobbying expenditures, **2:**684
Investor margin requirements, **1:**60
Iran-Contra, **2:**594
Iran-Libya Sanctions Act, **2:**598
Iran Nonproliferation Act, **2:**601
Iraq, **2:**491
    National Council of the Churches of Christ, **2:**497
    trade embargo, **1:**229
Ireland, Patricia, **2:**584, 585, 679
Irish-Americans for a Democratic Victory, **2:**657
Ironworkers, **2:**671, 674
Irradiation, food, **1:**177, 220
IRS. *See* Internal Revenue Service
Irvine, Reed J., **1:**125
Islam, portrayal of, **2:**589
Israel, **2:**588, 600–602
    ADL's U.S. foreign policy, **2:**435
    American support for, **2:**436
    pro-Israel PACs, **2:**666
Issues 98: The Candidate's Briefing Book, **2:**490
IT Group, **2:**645
IT&T, **2:**384
IT&T Industries, Defense and Electronics, **1:**298
Izaak Walton League, **1:**258, 272–74
Izaak Walton League Monthly, **1:**272

J

Jackson, Andrew, **2:**506
Jackson, Jesse, **1:**60; **2:**431, 576
Jackson-Vanik amendment, **2:**592
Jacobs, Karen, **1:**197
Jacobs Engineering Group, **2:**633, 635
Japan, **2:**588, 603–05
    AF&PA's interest in, **1:**305
    antidumping, **1:**347; **2:**603
    Hudson Institute's interest in, **2:**493
    Pearl Harbor, **2:**509
    steel imports from, **2:**417
    trade with, **1:**43; **2:**603–04
Japanese Challenge, The, **2:**493
Jarvis, Howard, **2:**510
JBS Bulletin, **2:**494, 495
JC Penny, **2:**630, 632
Jefferson, Thomas, **1:**3
Jefferson Award, **2:**483
Jefferson Group, **2:**661
Jepsen, Roger, **2:**536
Jewell, Jesse, **1:**234
Jim Beam, **2:**413
JM Family Enterprises, **2:**670
John Birch Society, **2:**455–58 *passim*, 494–95
John D. and Catherine T. MacArthur Foundation, **2:**457, 478
John Hancock, **2:**413
John M. Olin Foundation, **2:**456, 457, 464, 476, 491, 493, 499
Johnson, Gregory, **2:**516
Johnson & Johnson, **2:**653, 656
Johnson, Lyndon, **2:**509–10, 514, 564
Johnson, Robert Underwood, **1:**287
Johnson Controls, **2:**512
Johnston, Eric, **1:**139
Joint Action Committee for Political Affairs, **2:**666
Joint Commission on Accreditation of Healthcare Organizations, **1:**187
Joint Forum on Financial Conglomerates, **1:**44
Jones, Day, Revis and Pogue, **2:**679
Joseph E Seagram & Sons, **2:**630, 631, 676
Journal of the American Dietetic Association, **1:**175
Journal of the American Medical Association, **1:**189
Journalists, investigative reporting, **2:**477–78
Joyce Foundation, **2:**457
J.P. Morgan, **1:**35; **2:**646, 647, 684
Jungle, The, **1:**175
Jury system, **1:**80
Just in Time, **1:**333
Juvenile crime bills, **1:**96, 97
JVC, **2:**680
JW Childs Associates, **2:**677

K

K Street Project, **2:**469
Kahn, Herman, **2:**492
Kaiser Permanente, **2:**413
Kamali, Norma, **2:**539
Kaman, **2:**636
Kamber Group, The, **2:**679

Kansas City Federal Reserve Board, **1**:28
Karatnycky, Adrian, **2**:438
Katz, Marc, **1**:90
Kehoe, Christine, **2**:577
Keller, Helen, **2**:508
Kelley, Oliver Hudson, **1**:247
Kemp-Roth tax bill, **2**:510
Kennecott, **2**:644
Kennedy, Edward, **1**:97, 112–13; **2**:487
    Americans for Democratic Action support for, **2**:467
    on flag burning, **2**:517
    leadership PAC, **2**:622
Kennedy, James, **2**:481
Kennedy, John F., **2**:466, 514, 533
Kennedy, Robert, **2**:510
Kennedy Space Center Support Comm., **2**:667
Kentucky Fried Chicken, **1**:111
Kerrey, Robert, **2**:517
"Key Vote" program, **2**:483
Keycorp, **2**:647
Khrushchev, Nikita, **2**:494
KIDSPAC, **2**:660
Kildee, Dale, **1**:87
King & Spalding, **2**:661
Kings Canyon National Park, **1**:287
Kirkland, Lane, **1**:63; **2**:353, 361
Kirkpatrick, Jeane J., **2**:438
Kissinger, Henry, **2**:492, 597
Kissinger Associates, **2**:591
KIWI International Air Lines, **1**:300
Klatsky, Bruce, **2**:441
KLM-Royal Dutch Airlines, **1**:300
Kmart, **1**:83
Knight-Ridder, **1**:150
Knights of Columbus, **2**:516
Knights of Labor, **2**:359
Knopf, Alfred, **1**:288
"Know-Nothing" Party, **2**:507
Koch, Charles, **2**:475, **2**:483
Koch, David, **2**:483
Koch family, **2**:456
Koch Industries, **2**:484, 641, 643
Koonan, Karen Jo, **2**:452
Korean War, **2**:567, 591
Kosovo, **1**:299; **2**:593, 612
    Brookings Institution, **2**:473
    Cato Institute, **2**:476
    European Union and, **2**:598
    John Birch Society, **2**:495
KPMG LLP, **2**:646, 652
Kraft, **2**:413
Kraft Foods, **2**:681
Krese, Jennifer, **1**:333
Kroger, **1**:83; **2**:413
Ku Klux Klan, **2**:423, 434, 435
Kuhn, Thomas, **1**:327
Kunstler, William, **2**:565
Kuomintang, **2**:614
Kurdish Worker's Party, **2**:617
Kuttner, Robert, **2**:487
Kyoto Protocol and Global Climate Change Treaty
    American Conservative Union, **2**:462
    American for Tax Reform, **2**:470

Kyoto Protocol and Global Climate Change Treaty *(continued)*
    Business Roundtable, **1**:319
    Citizens for a Sound Economy, **2**:484
    National Council o Farmer Cooperatives, **1**:240
    National Council of the Churches of Christ, **2**:497
    National Mining Association, **1**:335
    United States Catholic Conference, **2**:503

L

La Croix, Christian, **2**:539
La Follette, Robert, **1**:244
Labatt's, **2**:413
Label Printing Industries of America, **1**:343
Labeling practices, textile, **1**:310
Labor Law Study Committee, **1**:318
Labor laws & rights
    AFL–CIO, **2**:359–62
    Air Transport Association, **1**:302
    American Federation of State, County, and Municipal Employees, **2**:363–65
    Business Roundtable, **1**:319
    Communications Workers of America, **2**:372–74
    compensation lawsuits, **1**:62
    Farm Bureau, **1**:215
    Fraternal Order of Police, **1**:87
    Hotel Employees and Restaurant Employees International Union, **2**:376–77
    International Association of Fire Fighters, **2**:379–80
    International Association of Machinists and Aerospace Workers, **2**:381
    International Brotherhood of Electrical Workers, **2**:385
    International Brotherhood of Teamsters, **2**:389
    International Union of Operating Engineers, **2**:390, 391
    Laborers International Union of North America, **2**:394–95
    National Association of Home Builders, **1**:330
    National Association of Manufacturers, **1**:333
    National Lawyers Guild, **2**:452–53
    Seafarers International Union of North America, **2**:399–400
    Service Employees International Union, **2**:402
    Transport Workers Union of America, **2**:404–5
    Union of Needletrades, Industrial, and Textile Employees, **2**:408–9
    United Automobile Workers, **2**:412
    United Food and Commercial Workers Union, **2**:413, 415
    violation of child, **1**:100
    See also Labor unions; Minimum wage legislation; Worker safety
Labor Policy Association, **2**:685
Labor practices, illegal
    American Textile Manufacturers Institute's denouncement of, **1**:310
    Food Marketing Institute affiliates and, **1**:85
Labor unions
    leading PACs, **2**:622, 671–75
    overview of, **2**:350–54
    See also Labor laws & rights; Specific union
Laboratory animals, humane treatment of, **1**:185
Laborers, **2**:674
Laborers International Union of North America, **2**:393–95, 622
Laborers' Political League, **2**:394, 395, 671, 674
LaHaye, Beverly, **2**:481
"Land and hold short" operations, **2**:357

Land grant universities, **1**:213, 215
Land management & development
　American Forest and Paper Association, **1**:305
　Izaak Walton League, **1**:272
　Nationwide Permit program, **1**:282
　Sierra Club, **1**:287, 289
　Yosemite National Park, **1**:291
　See also Property rights
Land O'Lakes, **2**:629
Land-mine abolition, **2**:589
　Council for a Livable World, **2**:520
　Human Rights Watch, **2**:442
　United States Catholic Conference, **2**:503
lang, k.d., **2**:540
Laramie Treaty, **2**:565
Las Vegas, hotel industry, **2**:376
Laser surgery, eye, **1**:165
Latin America, Human Rights Watch and, **2**:442
Lautenberg Law, **1**:86–87
Law schools, **1**:67–68
LAWbriefs, **2**:575
Lawson, Richard L., **1**:335, 336
Lawyers & law firms
　leading PACs, **2**:661
　lobbying expenditures, **2**:697
Le Conte, Joseph, **1**:287
Lead, **1**:262
Leadership Conference on Civil Rights, **2**:578
Leadership PACs, **2**:622
League Leader, **1**:273
League of Conservation Voters, **1**:259, 266, 275–77; **2**:667
League of Conservation Voters Action Fund, **1**:277
League of Women Voters, **2**:423, 424, 428, 444–46
League of Women Voters Education Fund, **2**:444–45, 446
League of Women Voters of the United States. *See* League of Women Voters
Leave Us Alone Coalition, **2**:469
Lebanon, **2**:567
Lee, Percy Maxim, **2**:444
Lee Apparel, **2**:413
Legal Alert, **1**:60
Legal ethics, **1**:68
Legal interest groups. *See* American Bar Association; Association of Trial Lawyers of America; Legal Services Corporation
Legal Rights Center, **2**:565
Legal Services Corporation, **2**:423–28 *passim*, 447–49
Legion of Decency, **1**:138
Legislative Alerts, **1**:60
Lehman Brothers, **2**:650
Lent, Norman, **2**:678
Lent & Scrivner, **2**:661
Leon and Marilyn Klinghoffer Memorial Foundation of the Anti-Defamation League, **2**:435
Lesbian and Gay Families project, **2**:582
Letter-writing campaigns
　American Postal Workers Union, **2**:371
　Americans United for the Separation of Church and State, **2**:513
　Greenpeace, **1**:270
　National Audubon Society, **2**:279
　National Wildlife Federation, **1**:282
　Public Citizen, **2**:500
　Rainforest Action Network, **1**:285

Letter-writing campaigns *(continued)*
　wise use movement, **1**:292
Levi Strauss, **2**:413
Levin, Carl, **2**:518
Levitt, Arthur, **1**:60
Lewis, Charles, **2**:477
Lewis, John L., **2**:359, 416
Liability law reform
　Citizens for a Sound Economy, **2**:484
　Public Citizen, **2**:501
　See also Class action litigation
Liberal interest groups, **2**:456
Liberal PACs, **2**:657
Libertarianism, **2**:475
Liberty Mutual Insurance, **2**:651
Liberty Party, **2**:506
Librarians
　American Library Association, **1**:64, 75–77
　Association of American Publishers and, **1**:130, 131
Library Journal, **1**:75
Licensed Beverage Industries, **1**:323
Lieberman, Joseph, **1**:50, 91
Life and Health Insurance Foundation for Education, **1**:47
Life Association News, **1**:47
Life-line rates, **1**:9
Life Underwriters Political Involvement Committee, **1**:46
Life Underwriting Training Council, **1**:47
Lightner, Candy, **2**:525
Lilly Endowment, Inc., **2**:439
Limbaugh, Rush, **1**:133
Limited, **2**:630, 632
Limited Test Ban Treaty, **2**:519
Lincoln, Abraham, **2**:506, 507
Lincoln bedroom scandal, **2**:477
Lincoln Electric, **2**:703
Lindbergh, Charles, **2**:509
Line Item Veto Act, **2**:501
Literacy promotion & programs, **1**:65, 131, 151
Litton Industries, **1**:298; **2**:636
Livestock industry
　leading PACs, **2**:628
　National Cattlemen's Beef Association, **1**:231–33
　National Chicken Council, **1**:234–36; **2**:628
　National Farmers Organization, **1**:242
　National Pork Producers Council, **1**:249–51; **2**:628
Livingston, Sigmound, **2**:424, 435
Lloyd, Henry Demarest, **2**:507–8
Loans, farm, **1**:211, 212
Lobbyists & lobbying
　activities, **2**:680–81
　astroturf, **1**:147–48
　background & recruitment, **2**:678–79
　direct/indirect defined, **2**:680–81
　effective, **1**:6–7
　impacts of, **2**:681–83
　"insider"/"outsider" defined, **1**:93
　leading PACs, **2**:661
　lobbying expenditures, **2**:701–2
　methods, **1**:65; **2**:680
　organization categories, **2**:679–80
　top clients, **2**:703–4
Lobel, Kerry, **2**:581
Lockheed Martin, **1**:298; **2**:622, 636, 694

*Numbers in **bold** indicate volume.*

Lodging industry
    American Hotel and Motel Association, **1:**73–74; **2:**630, 632
    copyright issues, **1:**121
    Hotel and Restaurant Employees National Alliance, **2:**375
    Hotel Employees and Restaurant Employees International Union, **2:**375–77, 675
    minimum wage issues, **1:**121
Loeb, James, Jr., **2:**466
Loews, **2:**693
Logging legislation, **1:**259
    Greenpeace, **1:**269, 270
    International Association of Machinists and Aerospace Workers, **2:**383
    Izaak Walton League, **1:**273
    logger protests, **1:**291
    old-growth, **1:**260, 285–86
    spotted owl, **1:**260, 292
London, Herbert, **2:**493
Long, Russell B., **2:**680
Long-term care, **1:**181–82
    American Council of Life Insurance, **1:**15, 16, 17
Loral Spacecom, **2:**638, 640, 676
Lord, Bette Bao, **2:**438
L'Oreal, **2:**539
Lorillard, **2:**703
Los Angeles County, California, **2:**688
Lott, Trent, **1:**97, 101, 349; **2:**383, 394, 582
    leadership PAC, **2:**622
Lowenstein, Allard K., **2:**509
LTV Steel, **2:**662, 663
Lucent Technologies, **2:**638, 640
Ludwig, Gene, **1:**29
Lugar, Richard, **1:**519
Lutheran World Relief, **2:**496
LWH Family Foundation, Inc., **2:**439
Lynde and Harry Bradley Foundation, **2:**439, 457, 464

M

Maastricht Treaty, **2:**597
MacArthur, Douglas, **2:**603
Macau, transshipping, **1:**310
Machinists and Aerospace Workers, **2:**671, 672
Machinists Nonpartisan Political League, **2:**383
Macy's, **2:**540
Mad cow disease, **1:**221, 233; **2:**598
MADD. *See* Mothers Against Drunk Driving
Made in the USA Foundation, **2:**418
Madison, James, **2:**422, 454, 678
Magazine Publishers of America, **1:**135–37
    RIAA liaison with, **1:**153–54
Mail Handlers Union, **2:**393
Mailers Council, **1:**136
Maintenance of Way Employees, **2:**673
Makah tribe, **1:**270–71
Makinson, Larry, **2:**479
Malcolm, Ellen, **2:**572
Malpractice, **1:**82
Managed care, **1:**160–63
    American Academy of Ophthalmology, **1:**165–66
    American College of Emergency Physicians, **1:**172–73
    American Medical Association, **1:**189–91
    American Nurses Association, **1:**193
    American Occupational Therapy Association, **1:**198

Managed care *(continued)*
    Service Employees International Union, **2:**402
Manatt, Phelps, et al., **2:**661
Mandela, Nelson, **2:**512
Manor Healthcare Corp, **2:**656
Mantech International, **2:**636
Manufactured Housing Institute, **2:**633, 635
Manufacturing Chemists Association. *See* Chemical Manufacturers Association
Manufacturing industry
    leading PACs, **2:**662, 664
    lobbying expenditures, **2:**697
    overview of, **1:**294–95
    See also under Specific group
Manufacturing Institute, **1:**333
Mao Zedong, **2:**591
Maquiladoras, **2:**441, 442
Marathon Oil, **2:**643
March Group, **1:**318
March to Fight the Right, **2:**585
Marconi North America, **2:**636
Marcus, Ben, **1:**80
Marine Engineers District 2 Maritime Officers, **2:**671, 673
Marine Engineers District 1/Pacific Coast District, **2:**673
Marine Fireman's Union, **2:**399
Maritime Security Program, **2:**400
Marketing checkoffs. *See* Checkoffs, marketing
Marriage penalty tax, **2:**405
Marriage rights, same-gender, **2:**582
Marriot International, **2:**632
MARS, **2:**703
Marshall, Paul, **2:**439
Marshall, Ray, **2:**487
Marshall Plan, **2:**438, 466, 472, 587, 597
Martin, Cathie Jo, **2:**682
Martinez, Matthew, **1:**100
Massachusetts Audubon Society, **1:**278
Massachusetts Mutual Life Insurance, **2:**651
Master Printers of America, **1:**343
May Department Stores, **2:**630, 632
Mayer, Brown & Platt, **2:**701
MBNA America Bank, **2:**646, 649
MCA, **1:**153
McBride, Ann, **2:**485
McCaffrey, Barry, **1:**179
McCain, John, **1:**50, 168; **2:**517, 625
McCain-Feingold finance reform, **2:**394, 538, 625
McCarran-Ferguson Act, **1:**15, 30, 42, 45, 49
McCarthy, Eugene, **2:**509–10
McCarthy, Frank, **1:**100
McCarthy, Joseph, **2:**444
McCarthyism
    American Federation of Teachers, **2:**366
    American Library Association, **1:**76
    Motion Picture Association of America, **1:**139
    National Lawyers Guild, **2:**452
McClure-Volkmer Act, **2:**533
McConnell, Mitch, **1:**50
McCullum v. Board of Education, **2:**435
McDermott, Will & Emery, **2:**661, 701
McDonald, Charles, **1:**167
McDonald, Eugene, **1:**142
McDonald, Larry, **2:**495
McDonald, Steve, **2:**431

*Numbers in **bold** indicate volume.*

McDonald's, **1:**263; **2:**630, 631
McDonnell Douglas, **2:**636
MCI Telecommunications, **2:**638, 639
MCI Worldcom, **2:**676, 699
McKay, John, **2:**447, **2:**448
McKinley, William, **2:**422, 508
McKinney, Cynthia, **2:**576
McKinney Act. *See* Stewart B. McKinney Homelessness Assistance Act
McMahon, Douglas, **2:**404
Mead, **1:**304; **2:**629
Means, Russell, **2:**565
Meany, George, **2:**411
Meat industry
   American Meat Institute, **1:**220–22; **2:**627
   National Cattlemen's Beef Association, **1:**231–33; **2:**627, 628
   National Pork Producers Council, **1:**249–51; **2:**628
   See also Poultry industry
Media Beat, **1:**134
Media Coalition, **1:**136
Media industry
   cross-ownership of, **1:**151
   and environmental issues, **1:**257
   Fraternal Order of Police and, **1:**87–88
   interest groups' use of, **1:**32, 92, 94, 134; **2:**459, 518
   investigative reporting, **1:**221; **2:**477–78
   lobbying expenditures, **2:**687, 697
   lobbying groups' use of, **2:**681
   National Cattlemen's Beef Association and, **1:**233
   overview of, **1:**120–23
   perceived bias in, **1:**125, 126, 133–34
   See also under Specific group
Media Monitor, The, **1:**126
Medicaid
   American Dietetic Association, **1:**176–77
   anesthesia, **1:**203
   Blue Cross and Blue Shield Association, **1:**162
   history of, **1:**159, 160, 189
   labor union support of, **2:**352
   long-term care, **1:**182
   zero funding for abortions, **2:**526, 536, 554
Medical ethics, **1:**191
Medical interest groups, **1:**162
   See also under Specific group
Medical malpractice, **1:**82
Medical nutrition, **1:**176
Medical records, privacy issues, **1:**188, 200–201, 206–7; **2:**405
Medicare
   American Academy of Ophthalmology, **1:**165
   American Association of Retired Persons, **2:**561
   American Chiropractic Association, **1:**170–71
   American Conservative Union, **2:**458
   American Dietetic Association, **1:**176–77
   American Healthcare Association, **1:**181–82
   American Hospital Association, **1:**186–87
   American Medical Association, **1:**191
   American Nurses Association, **1:**194
   American Occupational Therapy Association, **1:**198
   Americans for Tax Reform, **2:**458
   anesthesia, **1:**203
   Blue Cross and Blue Shield Association, **1:**162, 207
   Brookings Institution, **2:**473
   "Coalition to Fix Medicare Now," **1:**181–82
   Communications Workers of America, **2:**372, 373

Medicare *(continued)*
   Economic Policy Institute, **2:**488
   fraud, **1:**187, 201
   Grange, **1:**248
   Healthcare Financing Administration, **1:**43
   Heritage Foundation, **2:**491
   history of, **1:**159, 160, 186, 189
   International Union of Operating Engineers, **2:**390, 391
   labor unions and, **2:**352
   Laborers International Union of North America, **2:**395
   National Committee to Preserve Social Security and Medicare, **2:**529–31, 665, 667
   National Council of the Churches of Christ, **2:**497
   National Tax Payers Union, **2:**499
   National Taxpayers Union, **2:**458
   Pharmaceutical Research and Manufacturers of America, **1:**341
   Union of Needletrades, Industrial, and Textile Employees, **2:**407, 408
   United Automobile Workers, **2:**412
Medicare Act, **2:**509
"Medicare Beneficiaries Freedom to Contract Act," **2:**373
Medicare Medical Nutrition Therapy Act, **1:**176
Medigap, **1:**207
Meiji Restoration, **2:**603
Mental health
   American Occupational Therapy Association, **1:**197
   American Psychiatric Association, **1:**162, 199
   American Restaurant Association, **1:**112
   National Association of Social Workers, **1:**95
Mercantile Bancorp, **2:**647
Merchant banking, **1:**8, 10, 12
Merck, **2:**512, 623, 653, 656, 691, 695
Mercury, **1:**262
Mergers
   airline, **1:**302
   book publishing, **1:**130
   media, entertainment, & information, **1:**121, 133
Merhav Group of Companies, **2:**703
Merrill Lynch, **2:**650, 684
Merrill Lynch Asset Management, **1:**35
MetLife Insurance Corporation, **1:**182
Metro Transit Authority of Harris County, Texas, **2:**688, 704
Metropolitan Life, **2:**413
Metropolitan Life Insurance, **2:**651
Mexican-American Legal Defense and Education Fund, **2:**588, 606
Mexican American Trucking Associations, **1:**313
Mexican Manufacturing Week, **1:**333
Mexican Revolution, **2:**606
Mexico, **2:**606–08
   American Forest and Paper Association's interest in, **1:**305
   automobile industry, **2:**412
   National Cattlemen's Beef Association's interest in, **1:**232
   See also North American Free Trade Agreement
Meyer, Frank, **2:**460
Mfume, Kweisi, **2:**578, 579
MGM Grand, **2:**632
Miami Beach Hotel Association, **2:**375
Miami-Dade County, Florida, **2:**688
Mica, Daniel A., **1:**25
Michel, Robert H., **2:**678
Michigan Credit Union League, **2:**648
Microsoft, **1:**55, 157; **2:**704
   leading PAC, **2:**638, 639

Numbers in **bold** *indicate volume.*

Microsoft *(continued)*
    lobbying expenditures, **2**:686
    soft money donations, **2**:676
Mid-American Dairymen, **1**:227; **2**:627, 629
Middle East
    Brookings Institution, **2**:473
    Cato Institute, **2**:476
    peace process, **2**:600–601
Midwest Express Airlines, **1**:300
MIGIZI, **2**:565
Migrant workers, **2**:447
Mikulski, Barbara, **2**:572
Military spending. *See* Defense budget
Milk Industry Foundation, **1**:226
Milk products. *See* Dairy industry
Millennium March, **2**:559, 577
Miller & Chevalier, **2**:704
Miller, Ellen, **2**:479
Miller, James, III, **2**:483
Miller Brewing, **2**:681
Million-Man March, **2**:436
Mills, C. Wright, **2**:466
Mindel, Fania, **2**:542
MinePAC, **1**:335
Minimum-wage legislation
    American Conservative Union, **2**:461
    American Federation of Labor–Congress of Industrial
        Organizations, **2**:361
    American Federation of State, County, and Municipal
        Employees, **2**:365
    Americans for Democratic Action, **2**:466, 467
    exemption from, **1**:120, 150
    Fair Minimum Wage Act, **1**:97
    Farm Bureau, **1**:215
    Food Marketing Institute, **1**:84, 85
    Heritage Foundation, **2**:353
    Hotel Employees and Restaurant Employees International
        Union, **2**:377
    media, information, and entertainment interest groups and,
        1:121
    National Association of Convenience Stores, **1**:91
    National Association of Social Workers, **1**:96, 97
    National Farmers Union, **1**:245
    National Federation of Independent Business, **1**:106
    National Restaurant Association, **1**:111–12
    small-business interest groups and, **1**:65
    Transport Workers Union of America, **2**:405
    United Food and Commercial Workers Union, **2**:413, 415
    United States Catholic Conference, **2**:503
Mining industry
    leading PACs, **2**:644
    lobbying expenditures, **2**:698
    National Mining Association, **1**:295, 335–36; **2**:641, 644
    National Wildlife Federation, **1**:281, 282
    Office of Surface Mining, **1**:336
    United Mine Workers of America, **1**:335; **2**:416, 671, 672
    Western States Public Lands Coalition, **1**:291
    wise use movement, **1**:293
Minneapolis Patrol, **2**:565
Mirage Resorts, **2**:630, 632
Mississippi Band of Choctaw Indians, **2**:704
Mississippi River national preserve, **1**:272
Missouri Farm Bureau PACs, **1**:215
Mitchell, George, **2**:564, 678

Mitsubishi Corporation, **1**:285, 286
Mobil, **1**:114; **2**:539, 641, 643, 690, 694, 704
Modern Maturity, **2**:561
Modern Red School House program, **2**:493
Mogen David, **2**:413
Molson, **2**:413
"Monday Morning PAC," **2**:622
Monnet, Jean, **2**:597
Monsanto, **1**:210
Montefiore Medical Center, **2**:703
Montgomery Watson Americas, **2**:645
Moore, W. Henson, **1**:305
MOPAC, **2**:666
Moral Majority, **2**:456
Morgan Stanley, **1**:61
Morgan Stanley, Dean Witter, **2**:650, 684
Morisson's Hospitality Group, **1**:111
Morna, Lewis and Bockius, and Fried, **2**:679
Morrill Act, **1**:213
Morrison-Knudsen, **2**:635
Mortgage Bankers Association of America, **1**:6, 36–38; **2**:646,
    652
Mortgage Banking: The Magazine of Real Estate Finance, **1**:38
Mortgage bills, American Forest and Paper Association, **1**:305
Mortgage Insurance Companies of America, **2**:704
Mortgages
    buyers of, **1**:36
    class action suits, **1**:13, 18
    interest deductions, **1**:37
    interest payments, **1**:12
    National Association of Home Builders, **1**:329, 330
Mortuary Employees Union, **2**:399
Mosley-Braun, Carol, **2**:577
Mothers Against Drunk Driving, **2**:524–25
Motion Picture Association of America, **1**:122, 138–41; **2**:704
    leading PAC, **2**:639
    lobbying expenditures, **2**:687
Motion Picture Export Association, **1**:138, 139
Motion Picture Producers and Distributors of America, **1**:138
Motor Carrier Act, **1**:312
Motor Voter Bill. *See* National Voter Registration Act
Motorola, **2**:640, 695
Movie ratings system, **1**:139, 140
Moynihan, Daniel Patrick, **1**:50; 112
MTV, **2**:595
Muir, John, **1**:287
Mujica, Mauro, **2**:548
Multinational Tax Coalition, **2**:692
Munitions Carriers Conference, **1**:312
Murray, Charles, **2**:463
Murray, Patty, **2**:577
Murray, Pauli, **2**:583
Music industry
    copyright issues, **1**:65, 121. *See also* Copyright
    leading PACs, **2**:639
    Parents Music Resource Center, **1**:154
    Recording Industry Association of America, **1**:153–55; **2**:687
    U.S. Hispanic, **1**:154
    warning labels, **1**:154
Mutual Defense Treaty, **2**:603, 614
Mutual fund interest groups
    Investment Company Institute, **1**:33–35
    Securities Industry Association, **1**:58–61
Mutual of Omaha, **2**:651

Mutual Security Treaty, 2:605
Myanmar, 1:285, 286

N

NAACP. *See* National Association for the Advancement of Colored People
Nabisco. *See* RJR Nabisco
Nader, Ralph, 1:266; 2:500, 504
NAFTA. *See* North American Free Trade Agreement
Nagle, Delbert, 1:86
NAIC Reporter, 1:41
Nambikwara people, 1:285
NARAL. *See* National Abortion and Reproductive Rights Action League
NARFENET, 1:93
Nation at Risk, A, 2:396
National, 2:665, 666
National Abortion and Reproductive Rights Action League, 2:526–28
    leading PAC, 2:622, 623, 665, 667
National Action Committee, 2:666
National Air Traffic Controllers Association, 2:671, 673
National American Woman Suffrage Association, 2:444
National Association for the Advancement of Colored People, 2:556–59 *passim*, 2:578–80, 682
    Legal Defense Fund, 2:427
National Association for the Repeal of Abortion Laws, 2:526
National Association for the Support of Long-Term Care, 1:182
National Association of Audubon Societies, 1:278
National Association of Black Accountants, 1:21
National Association of Blue Shield Plans, 1:206
National Association of Broadcast Employees and Technicians, 1:372
National Association of Broadcasters, 1:120–21, 142–45; 2:680
    Ad Tax Coalition member, 1:136
    competition with NCTA, 1:146
    exempt from paying royalties, 1:153
    influence over FCC, 1:123
    leading PAC, 2:638, 639
    lobbying expenditures, 2:687, 695
National Association of Chain Drug Stores, 2:630, 632
National Association of Claimant's Compensation Attorneys, 1:80
National Association of Convenience Stores, 1:64, 65, 83, 89–91
    leading PAC, 2:630, 632
National Association of Counties, 2:679
National Association of Evangelicals, 2:497
National Association of Federal Credit Unions, 2:648
National Association of Food Chains, 1:83
National Association of Furniture Manufacturers, 1:308
National Association of Home Builders, 1:296, 329–31; 2:622, 633, 635
National Association of Home Builders National Research Center, Inc., 1:329
National Association of Home Manufacturers, 1:330
National Association of Independent Insurers, 1:6, 39–41
    leading PAC, 2:651
    lobbying expenditures, 2:689
National Association of Insurance Agents. *See* Independent Insurance Agents of America
National Association of Insurance Commissioners, 1:6, 15, 31, 41, 42–44, 47
National Association of Investment Companies. *See* Investment Company Institute
National Association of Letter Carriers, 2:674
National Association of Life Underwriters, 1:6, 45–47; 2:646, 651
National Association of Local Fire Insurance Agents. *See* Independent Insurance Agents of America
"National Association of Magazine Publishers." *See* Magazine Publishers of America
National Association of Manufacturers, 1:106, 111, 294, 295, 332–33
    opposition to labor unions, 2:353
    U.S. Chamber of Commerce's liaison with, 1:119
National Association of Mortgage Brokers, 2:652
National Association of Mutual Insurance Agents. *See* National Association of Professional Insurance Agents
National Association of Mutual Savings Banks, 1:12
"National Association of Periodical Publishers." *See* Magazine Publishers of America
National Association of Post Office and General Service Maintenance Employees, 2:369
National Association of Postmasters, 2:674
National Association of Professional Insurance Agents, 1:49–51; 2:651
National Association of Psychiatric Health Systems, 2:656
National Association of Radio and Television Broadcasters. *See* National Association of Broadcasters
National Association of Real Estate Boards. *See* National Association of Realtors
National Association of Real Estate Exchanges. *See* National Association of Realtors
National Association of Realtors, 1:6, 52–54
    leading PAC, 2:622, 646, 652
    lobbying expenditures, 2:694
National Association of Reits, 2:652
National Association of Retail Druggists, 2:655
National Association of Retired Federal Employees, 1:63, 64, 66, 92–94, 98
    leading PAC, 2:671, 674
National Association of Small Business Investment Companies, 2:633
National Association of Social Workers, 1:62–65 *passim*, 95–98
National Association of Special Delivery Messengers, 2:369
National Association of State Boards of Accountancy, 1:22
National Association of Temporary Services, 2:632
National Association of Wheat Growers, 1:229–30
National Association of Wholesaler-Distributors, 1:106, 111
National Association of Wool Manufacturers, 1:309
National Audubon Society, 1:258, 278–80
    coalition building, 1:260
    plumage restrictions, 1:272
National Automobile Dealers Association, 1:66, 99–101; 2:670
    leading PAC, 2:622, 668
    lobbying expenditures, 2:700
National Automobile Dealership Insurance Trust, 1:99
National Automobile Dealership Retirement Trust, 1:99
National Automobile Transporters Association, 1:312
National Ballistic Missile Defense, 2:518
National Bank Act, 1:50
National Beer Wholesalers Association, 1:62–66 *passim*, 1:90, 102–4; 2:630, 631
National Board for the Promotion of Rifle Practice, 2:532
National Board of Trial Advocacy, 1:82
National Broiler Council. *See* National Chicken Council
National Brotherhood of Electrical Workers, 2:384
National Cable Television Association, 1:122, 146–49

National Cable Television Association *(continued)*
  leading PAC, **2:**638, 639
  lobbying expenditures, **2:**687, 695
National Catholic War Council, **2:**502
National Catholic Welfare Council, **2:**502–3
National Catholic Welfare Program, **2:**496
National Cattle and Horse Growers Association, **1:**231
National Cattlemen, **1:**231
National Cattlemen's Beef Association, **1:**231–33; **2:**627, 628
National Center for Construction Education and Research, **1:**315
National Center for Nutrition and Dietetics, **1:**175
National Chamber Foundation, **1:**118
National Chamber Litigation Center, **1:**118
National Cheese Institute, **1:**226
National Chicken Council, **1:**234–36; **2:**628
National City, **2:**647
National Civil Aviation Review Commission, **2:**356–57
National Coal Association, **1:**335
National Coalition for the Homeless, **2:**423–28 *passim*, 450–51, 455
National Coming Out Day, **2:**576
National Coming Out Project, **2:**575
National Committee for an Effective Congress, **2:**657
National Committee for Responsive Philanthropy, **2:**456
National Committee to Preserve Social Security and Medicare, **2:**529–31
  leading PAC, **2:**622, 623, 665, 667
  lobbying expenditures, **2:**692, 694
National Community Action Foundation, **2:**660
National Community Television Association. *See* National Cable Television Association
National Conference of State Legislatures, **1:**42
National Consumer Finance Association. *See* American Financial Services Association National Convention of Insurance Commissioners. *See* National Association of Insurance Commissioners
National Cooperative Council, **1:**240
National Cotton Council, **1:**209, 237–39; **2:**627
National Council of Automobile Workers Unions, **2:**410
National Council of Catholic Bishops, **2:**502
National Council of Churches, **2:**456, 458
National Council of Community Bankers, **1:**12
National Council of Farmer Cooperatives, **1:**240–41
National Council of Savings Institutions, **1:**12
National Council of the Churches of Christ, **2:**496–97
National Credit Union Administration, **1:**10, 22, 24, 25
National Credit Union Share Insurance Fund, **1:**24
National Dairy Food Association, **1:**210
National defense. *See* Defense budget
National Diabetes Month, **1:**166
National Education Association, **2:**396–98, 674
National Electric Light Association, **1:**326
National Electrical Contractors Association, **2:**633, 635
National Endowment for Democracy, **2:**439
National Endowment of the Arts, **2:**462, 481, 482
  funding cuts, **1:**122, 128
National Endowment for the Humanities, funding cuts, **1:**122, 128
National Farmers Organization, **1:**209, 242–43
National Farmers Organization PAC, **1:**243
National Farmers Union, **1:**209, 213, 215, 240, 242, 244–46, 248, 276
National Farmers Union Insurance Company, **1:**244
National Federation of Beet Growers, **1:**223

National Federation of Business & Professional Women's Clubs, **2:**633
National Federation of Community Development Credit Unions, **1:**25
National Federation of Independent Business, **1:**62–66 *passim*, 105–7, 111, 113
  leading PAC, **2:**630, 633
  lobbying expenditures, **2:**685
  opposition to labor unions, **2:**353
  PMAA compared with, **1:**114–15
  support of GOP, **1:**102
National Federation of Independent Business Free Enterprise PAC, **1:**108
National Federation of Independent Business/Save America's Free Enterprise Trust, **1:**105, 106, 107
National Federation of Motor Vehicle Employees, **2:**369
National Federation of Telephone Workers, **2:**372
National Federation of Textiles, **1:**309
National Flag Conference, **2:**568
National Flood Insurance program, **1:**282
National Football League, **2:**680
National Foreign Trade Council, **2:**685
National Forest Products Association, **1:**304
National Forum Foundation, **2:**438
National Franchise Association, **2:**630, 633
National Funeral Directors Association, **1:**63, 64, 65, 108–10
  leading PAC, **2:**630, 632
National Gambling Impact Study Commission, **1:**70–71
National Gay and Lesbian Task Force, **2:**556–59 *passim*, 581–82
National Governors Association, **1:**42, 49; **2:**679
National Grange. *See* Grange
National Green Building Conference, **1:**296, 329
National Highway Traffic Safety Administration, **1:**51
National Highway Transportation Safety Administration, **2:**524
National Home Equity Mortgage Association, **1:**19; **2:**652
National Homeless Civil Rights Organizing project, **2:**450
National Homeless Person's Memorial Day, **2:**450
National Ice Cream Manufacturers, **1:**226
National Immigration Project, **2:**428, 453
National Independent Meat Packers Association, **1:**220
National Industrial Council, **1:**332
National Institutes of Health, **1:**184, 186, 195
National Institutes of Health AIDS/HIV research, **1:**179
National Korean-American Grocers Foundation, **1:**83
National Labor Relations Act
  Communications Workers of America, **2:**372
  Hotel Employees and Restaurant Employees International Union, **2:**376
  International Brotherhood of Electrical Workers, **2:**385
  overview of, **2:**351, 354
  United Automobile Workers, **2:**412
  United Food and Commercial Workers, **2:**414–15
National Labor Relations Board
  overview of, **2:**351, 354
  Public Safety Employer-Employee Cooperation Act's affect on, **1:**87
  Union of Needletrades, Industrial, and Textile Employees, **2:**408, 409
National Lawyers Guild, **2:**423–26 *passim*, 452–53
National League of Cities, **1:**147; **2:**679
National League of Postmasters, **2:**674
National Legal Assistance Support Project, **2:**562
National Library on Money and Politics, **2:**479
National Live Stock and Meat Board/Beef Industry Council, **1:**232

*Numbers in **bold** indicate volume.*

National Lumber & Building Materials Dealers, **2**:633, 634
National Machine Builders Association, **2**:662, 664
National Manufacturing Week Expo, **1**:333
National Marine Engineers' Beneficial Association, **2**:399
National Maritime Union, **2**:399
National Mining Association, **1**:295, 335–36; **2**:641, 644
National Motor Vehicle Theft Law, **1**:99
National Multihousing Council, **2**:633, 635
National NOW Times, **2**:585
National Oil Heat Research Alliance, **1**:115
National Oil Jobbers Council, **1**:114
National Organization for Women, **2**:556–59 *passim*, 583–85, 659
National Park Service, **1**:292
National Pest Control Association, **2**:632
National Pork Producers Council, **1**:249–51; **2**:628
National Postal Union, **2**:369
"National Publishers Association." *See* Magazine Publishers of America
National Radio Broadcasters Association, **1**:142
National Ready Mixed Concrete Association, **2**:633, 634
National Recovery Administration, **1**:118
National Restaurant Association, **1**:63, 83, 91, 106, 111–13
 copyright lawsuits against, **1**:65
National Restaurant Association PAC, **1**:90; **2**:630, 631
National Rifle Association, **1**:62, 63, 103; **2**:532–35
 Center for Responsive Politics' interest in, **2**:480
 challengers & competitors, **2**:681, 682
 Lautenberg Law amendment, **1**:87
 leading PAC, **2**:622, 623, 665, 667
 National Wildlife Federation's clash with, **1**:281
 support of GOP, **1**:105
National Rifle Association Political Victory Fund, **2**:534–35
National Right to Life Committee, **2**:536–38, 623, 665, 667
National Right to Life Convention, **2**:536
National Right to Life News, **2**:537
National Right to Work Act, **2**:353
National Right to Work Committee, **2**:353, 623, 692
National Roofing Contractors Association, **2**:633, 635
National Rural Electric Cooperative Association, **2**:641, 645
National Rural Letter Carriers Association, **2**:674
National Safety Council, **1**:332
National Savings and Loan League, **1**:12
National School of Banking, **1**:14
National Securities Markets Improvement Act, **1**:35
National Silver Party, **2**:507
National Society for the Promotion of Occupational Therapy. *See* American Occupational Therapy Association
National Society of Professional Engineers, **2**:633, 635
National Soft Drink Association, **2**:631
National Stone Association, **2**:633, 634
National Students Association, **2**:509
National Summit on Homelessness, **2**:451
National Swine Growers Council, **1**:249
National Tax Payers Union, **2**:455, 458, 498–99
National Tax Payers Union Foundation, **2**:498, 499
National Transportation Safety Board, **1**:301
National Treasury Employees, **2**:674
National Truck Carriers, **1**:312
National Truck Driver Appreciation Week, **1**:312
National Turkey Federation, **2**:628
National Union of Steam Engineers. *See* International Union of Operating Engineers National Utility Contractors Association, **2**:633, 635
National Venture Capital Association, **1**:4, 22, 55–57

National Venture Capital Association *(continued)*
 leading PAC, **2**:646, 650
National Volunteer Fire Council, **2**:379
National Voter Registration Act, **2**:423, 428, 432, 445
National Welfare Monitoring and Advocacy Partnership, **2**:450
National Welfare Rights Organization, **2**:424, 430
National Wildlife, **1**:281, 283
National Wildlife Federation, **1**:258, 272, 281–83
National Wildlife Refuge system, **1**:278
National Wildlife Week, **1**:281
National Woman Suffrage Association, **2**:444
Nations in Transition, **2**:427, 439
NationsBank, **2**:428, 432, 623, 646, 647
Nationwide Permit program, **1**:282
Native Americans
 American Indian Movement, **2**:556–59 *passim*, 564–66
 discrimination against, **1**:115
 gambling, **1**:72
 Legal Services Corporation interest in, **2**:447
 Tax Treatment of Native Americans, **1**:115
NATO. *See* North Atlantic Treaty Organization
Natural disasters, **1**:30, 31, 40
Navy Seabies, **2**:390
NBC, **2**:372, 680
NCC Washington Report, The, **1**:234
NCR, **2**:639
NEAPAC, **2**:398
Needle exchange programs, **1**:179
Neeld, John, **1**:204
Neiman Marcus, **2**:540
Neo Nazis, **2**:423, 434
Neotropical Migratory Bird Habitat Enhancement, **1**:279
Neptune Orient Lines, **2**:704
Netanyahu, Benjamin, **2**:601
Nevada, Yucca Mountain, **1**:339; **2**:386
New American, The, **2**:494, 495
New Deal, **1**:213, 215, 231, 237, 244; **2**:472
New Deal agencies, National Recovery Administration, **1**:118
New Democratic Network, **2**:657
New England Anti-Slavery Society, **2**:506
New Jersey, Wildwood, **1**:285
New Orleans, hotel industry, **2**:376
New Revised Standard Version of the Bible, **2**:496
New Unionism, **2**:396
New York
 birth control laws, **2**:542
 Congress of Racial Equality fundraising, **2**:569
 Stonewall Riots, **2**:558
New York Life Insurance, **1**:17; **2**:651, 689
New York Society of Anesthetists. *See* American Society of Anesthesiologists
New York Stock Exchange, **2**:650
New York Times
 Christian Coalition advertisements, **2**:481
 Sierra Club advertisements, **1**:288
New York Times v. United States, **1**:151
Newkirk, Ingrid, **2**:540
Newmont Mining, **2**:512
Newport News Shipbuilding, **2**:636
NEWS, **2**:677
News America Publishing, **2**:640
News industry. *See* Media industry
Newspaper Advertising Bureau, **1**:150
Newspaper Advertising Co-op Network, **1**:150

*Numbers in **bold** indicate volume.*

Newspaper Association of America, **1:**122, 136, 150–52
Newspaper Guild, **2:**372
Newspaper Preservation Act, **1:**150
Newspaper Research Council, **1:**150
Next 200 Years, The, **2:**492
"Next Agenda, The," **2:**493
Ney, Bob, **1:**87
NGO News: A Regional Newsletter for Non-Governmental Organizations, **2:**439
Niagara Falls, **1:**270
Nicaragua, **2:**452, 491
Niebuhr, Reinhold, **2:**466
Nigeria, **2:**570, 609–10
Nigerian Democracy and Civil Society Empowerment Act, **2:**610
Nineteenth Amendment, **2:**423, 444, 508
Nixon, Richard, **2:**447, 510
 American Conservative Union's support of, **2:**460
 NFO on enemy list of, **1:**242
 pardoning of Hoffa, **2:**387
No Electronic Theft Act, **1:**130–31
No Ifs, Ands or Butts: Tobacco's Not For Kids, **1:**90–91
"Nonmember" interest groups, **2:**456
Nonpartisan League, **1:**244
Nonprint trade associations, **1:**122
Nonprofit institutions, lobbying expenditures, **2:**698
Norfolk Southern, **2:**668, 670
Norquist, Grover, **2:**469, 470
North, Oliver, **2:**594
North American Free Trade Agreement, **2:**623
 AFL–CIO, **2:**351, 361, 362
 American Council of Life Insurance, **1:**16
 American Sugarbeet Growers Association, **1:**223–24
 American Textile Manufacturers Institute, **1:**310
 American Trucking Associations, **1:**313
 Business Roundtable, **1:**319
 Economic Policy Institute, **2:**488
 Heritage Foundation, **2:**490–91
 International Brotherhood of Teamsters, **2:**389
 manufacturing interest groups, **1:**295
 Mexico and, **2:**606–7, 608
 National Association of Independent Insurers, **1:**40
 National Association of Manufacturers, **1:**332–33
 Public Citizen, **2:**501
 United Food and Commercial Workers Union, **2:**415
 United Steelworkers of America, **2:**418
North American Log Homes Council, **1:**330
North American Securities Administrators Association, **1:**42
North Atlantic Treaty Organization, **2:**587, 589
 Cato Institute, **2:**476
 Council for a Livable World, **2:**520
 European Union, **2:**598
 Freedom House, **2:**438
 Human Rights Watch, **2:**442
 John Birch Society, **2:**495
 Russia's opposition to, **2:**612
 Turkey and, **2:**616
North Korea, **2:**605
Northeast Dairy Compact, **1:**226
Northern Mariana Islands, Commonwealth of, **2:**688, 704
Northern Telecom, **2:**640
Northrop Grumman, **1:**298; **2:**623, 636, 694
Northwest Airlines, **1:**300; **2:**356, 357, 703
 leading PAC, **2:**668, 669
 lobbying expenditures, **2:**700

Northwest Airlines *(continued)*
 soft money donations, **2:**676
Northwestern Mutual Life, **2:**651
Northwestern University, **2:**703
Norway, **2:**680
Norwest Venture Capital, **1:**55; **2:**647
Norwood, Charles, **1:**65
Not Man Apart, **1:**266
Novartis, **2:**656, 677
Noyce, Robert, **1:**346
Nuclear Energy Institute, **1:**295, 296, 338–39; **2:**645
Nuclear Freeze Movement, **2:**510–11
Nuclear Management and Resources Council, **1:**338
Nuclear power industry
 cleanup funds, **1:**327
 Council for a Livable World, **2:**518–20
 Friends of the Earth, **1:**266
 leading PACs, **2:**645
 Nuclear Energy Institute, **1:**295, 296, 338–39; **2:**645
 Nuclear Freeze Movement, **2:**510–11
 Nuclear Management and Resources Council, **1:**338
 Public Citizen, **2:**501
 safety issues, **2:**386
 Union of Concerned Scientists, **2:**546
 waste storage, **1:**339
Nuclear power plants, Diablo Canyon, **1:**288
Nuclear Regulatory Commission, **1:**266, 338; **2:**546
Nuclear Test Ban Treaty, **2:**519
Nuclear testing, **1:**260; **2:**269, 503
Nuclear Testing Moratorium, **2:**519
Nuclear weapons
 American Conservative Union, **2:**462
 North Korea, **2:**605
 Russia, **2:**612
 See also Arms control; Arms sales
Nunn, Sam, **2:**519
Nuppomo Dunes, **1:**288
Nuremberg Trials, **2:**425, 452
Nurses
 American Association of Nurse Anesthetists, **2:**653, 655, 688
 American Nurses Association, **1:**162, 193–95; **2:**653, 655
 as anesthetists, **1:**203
Nursing home industry
 American Healthcare Association, **1:**163, 181–83
 leading PACs, **2:**656
 lobbying expenditures, **2:**697
Nutrition
 American Dietetic Association, **1:**162–63, 175–77; **2:**653, 655
 American Heart Association, **1:**184, 185
 National Cattlemen's Beef Association, **1:**231, 233
 National Center for Nutrition and Dietetics, **1:**175
Nutrition InfoCenter, **1:**175
Nutritional education, United Egg Association, **1:**254
NWP 26, **1:**282

O

Obasanjo, Olusegun, **2:**610
Occidental Petroleum, **2:**641, 643
Occupational hazards, **1:**194
Occupational Safety and Health Administration, **2:**624
 American Federation of State, County, and Municipal Employees, **2:**365
 American Meat Institute, **1:**221

Occupational Safety and Health Administration *(continued)*
    American Postal Workers Union, **2:**371
    Associated Builders and Contractors, **1:**315, 316
    Chemical Manufacturers Association, **1:**322
    construction industry, **1:**296
    International Association of Fire Fighters, **2:**379–80
    International Association of Machinists and Aerospace Workers, **2:**382–83
    Laborers International Union of North America, **2:**395
    manufacturing industry, **1:**295
    National Association of Furniture Manufacturers, **1:**308
    National Association of Manufacturers, **1:**333
    National Beer Wholesalers Association, **1:**104
    National Restaurant Association, **1:**113
    Petroleum Marketers Association of America, **1:**115
    Printing Industries of America, **1:**344
    United Automobile Workers, **2:**412
    United Food and Commercial Workers Union, **2:**415
Occupational therapy
    American Occupational Therapy Association. *See* American Occupational Therapy Association
    Occupational Therapy Association, **1:**182
Occupational Therapy Association, **1:**182
Ocean Shipping Reform Act, **1:**304
Oceanic Society, **1:**266
Offe, Claus, **2:**555
Office & Professional Employees, **2:**675
Office of International Justice and Peace, **2:**502
Office of Surface Mining, **1:**336
Office of the Comptroller of the Currency, **1:**5, 8, 43
    ABA on advisory committees of, **1:**10
    insurance regulation, **1:**15, 42, 45, 49–50
Office of the U.S. Trade Representative
    American Council of Life Insurance, **1:**16
    American Meat Institute, **1:**221
    Center for Public Integrity, **2:**477
    National Association of Furniture Manufacturers, **1:**308
    National Association of Insurance Commissioners, **1:**43
    National Cattlemen's Beef Association, **1:**232
Office of Thrift Supervision, **1:**10, 14, 43
Ogilvie, Donald G., **1:**10
Ogilvy and Mather Public Affairs, **2:**679
Oglala, **2:**565
Ohio Association of Mortgage Brokers, **2:**652
Ohio Valley Coal, **2:**644
Oil, Chemical, & Atomic Workers, **2:**672
Oil Field Haulers Association, **1:**312
Oil industry. *See* Petroleum industry
Oil pollution, **1:**260
Oil spills, **1:**256, 257
Old-growth lumber. *See* Logging, old-growth
Olive Garden, The, **1:**111
Oliver, Wilbert Jean, **1:**108
O'Melveny & Myers, **2:**661
Omnibus Anti-Drug Abuse Act, **2:**524
Omnibus Budget Reconciliation Act, **1:**104
On Thermonuclear War, **2:**492
Online databases, protection of. *See* Electronic data, privacy concerns
Online service providers. *See* Internet, service providers
Open Secrets: The Encyclopedia of Congressional Money and Politics, **2:**479
Open Secrets projects, **2:**479
Operating Engineers Local 12, **2:**674
Operation Desert Shield. *See* Gulf War

Operation Just Cause, **2:**567
Operation Provide Comfort, **2:**617
Operation Respond, **2:**380
Operations Review, **1:**84
Ophthalmologists, AAOP's definition of, **1:**164–65
Ophthalmology, American Academy of Ophthalmology, **1:**162, 164–66; **2:**653, 655
Opticians, AAOP's definition of, **1:**165
Optometrists
    AAOP's concern over, **1:**164–65
    American Optometric Association, **1:**162; **2:**653
Oracle, **2:**686
Orange County, California, **2:**688
Order of Patron of Husbandry, The. *See* Grange
Order of Railway Conductors and Brakemen, **2:**419
Order of Sleeping Car Conductors, **2:**419
Oregon, Snake River, **1:**282
Organic Food Production Act, **1:**252
Organic Food Production Association of North America. *See* Organic Trade Association
Organic Standards Board, **1:**252
Organic Trade Association, **1:**252–53
Organization for Security and Cooperation in Europe, **2:**612
Organization of Economic Cooperation and Development, **1:**44
Organized crime, **2:**387
O'Rourke, P.J., **2:**438
Osborn, Fairfield, **1:**256
Osh Kosh B'Gosh, **2:**413
OSHA. *See* Occupational Safety and Health Administration
Osnos, Susan, **2:**441
Oswald, Lee Harvey, **2:**533
Other America, The, **2:**423, 425, 447
Otolaryngology, **1:**164
Ottawa Treaty. *See* Landmine abolition
Out and Voting: The Gay, Lesbian, and Bisexual Vote in Congressional Elections 1990–96, **2:**581–82
Outback Steakhouse, **2:**630, 631
Outdoor Advertising Association of America, **2:**630, 632
Outdoor America, **1:**272, 273
Outdoor Channel, **1:**293
Outdoor Ethics program, **1:**274
Outdoor recreation
    Blue Ribbon Coalition, **1:**291
    Izaak Walton League, **1:**272
    Sierra Club, **1:**289
Outdoor Recreation conference, **1:**272
Outrage!, **2:**556
OutVote, **2:**559
OutVote Convention, **2:**576
Overseas Private Insurance Corporation, **2:**592
Owens Corning, **2:**633, 634
Ozal, Turgut, **2:**616

P

PACCAR, **2:**670
Pacheco, Alex, **2:**539
Pacific Gas and Electric, **1:**288
Pacific Lumber & Shipping, **2:**703
Paine Webber, **1:**35; **2:**680
Painters & Allied Trades, **2:**674
Palestinian National Authority, **2:**601
Palmer, Daniel David, **1:**169

Palmer Method, **1:**169
Palmer Raids, **2:**433
Pan Am, **2:**404
Panama, **2:**567
Panama Canal, **2:**390, 495
Panara people, **1:**285
Paper industry
  American Forest and Paper Association, **1:**295, 304–5; **2:**629
  Environmental Defense Fund and, **1:**263
  leading PACs, **2:**629
Paper Recycling Awards, **1:**305
Paper Task Force, **1:**263
Paperboard, Paper, and Pulp, **1:**304
Paramount case, **1:**139
Parents Music Resource Center, **1:**154
Parsons, **2:**635
Parsons Brinckerhoff, **2:**633, 635
"Partial Birth" Abortion Ban, **2:**527
Partnership for Drug-Free America, **1:**78
Partnership for Regulatory Innovation and Sustainable Manufacturing, **1:**263
Passengers, airline, **2:**357
  Air Transport Association, **1:**301
  passenger rights bill, **1:**302
Patient privacy, medical record, **1:**188, 200–201, 206–7; 405
Patient rights, decline of, **1:**160
Patient Safety Bill, **1:**194
Patient's Bill of Rights
  American Hospital Association, **1:**187–88
  American Medical Association, **1:**190, 191
  American Nurses Association, **1:**194
  American Psychiatric Association, **1:**200
  Blue Cross and Blue Shield Association, **1:**206
  Business Roundtable, **1:**319
  National Association of Retired Federal Employees, **1:**63, 93, 94
  National Association of Social Workers, **1:**63
  National Restaurant Association, **1:**113
  Service Employees International Union, **2:**402
  Transport Workers Union of America, **2:**405
  Union of Needletrades, Industrial, and Textile Employees, **2:**408
Patients' Cure, **1:**168
Patitz, Tatjana, **2:**539
Patton, James, **1:**244
Patton Boggs LLP, **2:**701, 703
Paul Magilocchetti Association, **2:**661
"Paycheck deception" acts, **2:**364
"Paycheck protection" acts, **2:**409, 470–71
Peabody Coal, **2:**644
PeacePAC, **2:**519
Pearl Harbor, **2:**509
Pell Grants, **1:**127
Peltier, Leonard, **2:**497, 565
Pennsylvania Food Merchants Association, **1:**83
Pennzoil, **2:**539
Pension legislation
  American Council of Life Insurance, **1:**15
  International Association of Fire Fighters, **2:**378
  International Brotherhood of Electrical Workers, **2:**386
  Investment Company Institute, **1:**33, 34
  National Association of Retired Federal Employees, **1:**92
  Securities Industry Association, **1:**58

Pension legislation *(continued)*
  Transport Workers Union of America, **1:**405
  See also Retirement policy
Pentagon Papers case, **1:**151
People for the American Way, **2:**657
People for the Ethical Treatment of Animals, **2:**539–41
People of the Earth, **1:**284
People's Party, **1:**244
Pepperdine University Law School, **1:**126
Pepsico, **2:**627
Percy, Ethel, **2:**561
Perdue, **2:**413
Perfluorocompounds, **1:**347
Perot, Ross, **2:**550
Persian Gulf War. *See* Gulf War
Peru, Shell Oil gas project, **1:**285
Pesticides, **1:**211, 273; **2:**682
  DDT, **1:**257, 262, 279
  insecticides, **1:**238
PETA. *See* People for the Ethical Treatment of Animals
Petroleum industry
  leading PACs, **2:**643
  lobbying expenditures, **2:**690, 697
  Nigeria, **2:**609–10
  See also Gasoline
  See also under Specific group
Petroleum Marketers Association, **1:**63–66 *passim,* **1:**114–16
  leading PAC, **2:**641, 643
Petroleum Marketers Association Small Businessmen's Committee, **1:**90, 114
Pew Charitable Trusts, **1:**263; **2:**439–40, 480, 493, 505
Pfizer, Inc., **2:**491
  leading PAC, **2:**653, 656
  lobbying expenditures, **2:**691, 694
  soft money donations, **2:**676
PG&E, **2:**641, 699
Pharmaceutical industry
  AIDS/HIV, **1:**179
  clot-busting drugs, **1:**184
  Food Marketing Institute and, **1:**84
  leading PACs, **2:**656
  lobbying expenditures, **2:**691, 697
  Pharmaceutical Research and Manufacturers of America, **1:**295, 341–42
  psycho-pharmaceuticals, **1:**199–200
  Public Citizen, **2:**501
  warning labels, **2:**501
  See also Prescription drugs
Pharmaceutical Research & Manufacturers of America, **2:**691
Pharmaceutical Research and Manufacturers of America, **1:**295, 341–42
Phelps Dodge, **2:**644
Philadelphia Bridges, **1:**285
Philip Morris, **1:**212; **2:**681, 703
  leading PAC, **2:**622, 627, 629
  lobbying expenditures, **2:**693, 694
  soft money donations, **2:**676
Philips Electronics North America, **2:**639
Phillips, Wendell, **2:**506
Phillips Petroleum, **2:**643
Phillips Publishing International, **2:**640
Phillips-Van Heusen, **2:**441
Phonograms, **1:**153

Photorefractive keratectomy, **1:**165
Physician unionization, **1:**161, 188, 190, 206, 207
PIA PAC, **1:**51
Pickle Family Circus, **2:**540
Pilots, **1:**302
    Aircraft Owners & Pilots Association, **2:**668, 669, 700
    Airline Pilots Association, **2:**356–58, 622, 671, 673
    Allied Pilots Association, **2:**673
Pinchot, Gifford, **1:**291
Pinochet, Augusto, **2:**442
Piracy. *See* Copyright
Pitney Bowes, **2:**704
Pizza Hut Franchisees Association, **2:**631
PL. 480. *See* Food-aid programs
Planet, The, **1:**289
Planned Parenthood, **2:**497, 665, 667
Planned Parenthood Action Fund, **2:**544
Planned Parenthood Federation of America, **2:**542–44
Planned Parenthood of Central Missouri v. Danforth, **2:**543
Planned Parenthood of Kansas City v. Ashcroft, **2:**543
Planned Parenthood of Southeastern Pennsylvania v. Casey, **2:**543
Playboy, **1:**136
Ploughshares Fund, **2:**488
Plum Creek Timber Co., **1:**304
Plumbers and Pipefitters, **2:**671, 674
Podesta.Com, **2:**701
"Poison pill" amendment, **2:**394
Polar Air Cargo, **1:**300
Police
    American Federation of State, County, and Municipal Employees, **2:**365
    brutality, **2:**565
    Fighting Police Abuse: A Community Action Manual, **2:**434
    Fraternal Order of Police, **1:**62, 64, 86–88
Policy, Hudson Institute, **2:**492–93
Policy Briefs, **2:**472, 473
Policy Review, **2:**490
Polish Solidarity movement, **2:**438
Political action committees
    criticisms & reforms, **2:**625
    influence of, **2:**624–25
    number & types of, **2:**621–22
    overview of, **2:**621
    strategies & finance, **2:**622–24
    See also under Specific group
Political interest groups, overview of, **2:**454–59
PolyGram, **1:**153
Population
    Zero Population Growth, **2:**553–54
    See also Family planning
Population Bomb, The, **2:**553
Population Education Network, **2:**553
Population Union, **2:**542
Populist Party, **1:**244; **2:**507
Pork industry. *See* Meat industry
Pork Industry Congressional Caucus, **1:**249
Postal Rate Commission, **1:**136, 151
Postal rates
    Association of American Publishers, **1:**130, 131
    Magazine Publishers of America, **1:**135–36
    Newspaper Association of America, **1:**150, 151
    print media industry's interest in, **1:**122
    See also United States Postal Service
Postal Reform Act, **2:**370

Postal Reorganization Act, **2:**369
Postal Service. *See* United States Postal Service
Postal workers, American Postal Workers Union, **2:**369–71
Poultry industry
    leading PACs, **2:**628
    National Chicken Council, **1:**234–36; **2:**628
    See also Meat industry
Pound, Roscoe, **1:**81
Poverty
    National Association of Social Workers, **1:**95
    United Food and Commercial Workers Union and, **2:**413
    United States Catholic Conference, **2:**502
Powell, Goldstein et al., **2:**661
Power plants, public education of, **1:**274
PPOs. *See* Preferred provider organizations
Pratt, Larry, **2:**477
"Prayer amendment," **2:**514, 515
Precision Machined Products Association, **2:**664
Precision Metalforming Association, **2:**664
Preferred provider organizations, **1:**161
Premises liability, **1:**82
Prescription drugs
    advertising, **1:**136
    insurance for, **1:**207, 341; **2:**530
"Preserving the American Dream: NAHB Agenda for 1999," **1:**330
Presidential debates, **2:**445
President's Council of Petroleum Marketers Association, **1:**114
President's Council on Small Manufacturers Action Committee, **1:**333
Preston, Gates et al., **2:**661, 701, 704
Price controls, **1:**245
PricewaterhouseCoopers, **1:**57; **2:**646, 652, 701
Prime-Time Access rule, **1:**139, 140
Principal Financial Group, **1:**17
PRINT-PAC, **1:**344
Printing Industries of America, **1:**295, 343–45; **2:**638, 640
Printing industry
    leading PACs, **2:**640
    postal rates, **1:**122
    Printing Industries of America, **1:**295, 343–45; **2:**638, 640
Prison conditions, **2:**441
Prison Law project, **2:**452, 453
Prisoner rights, **2:**365, 452, 453
Privacy
    American Civil Liberties Union, **2:**434
    customer. *See* Customer privacy
    electronic. *See* Electronic data, privacy concerns
    medical. *See* Medical records, privacy issues
Private pension policy, **1:**15
Private Securities Litigation Reform Act, **1:**22
Proctor & Gamble Co., **1:**304; **2:**540, 662, 663, 680
Product liability, **1:**81, 82
Product safety, **2:**458
Product Seller Fair Treatment Law, **1:**91
Production Code Administration, **1:**138
Professional Agent, **1:**51
Professional associations
    lobbying expenditures, **2:**688
    overview of, **1:**62–66
    See also under Specific association
Professional Security Officers Association, **2:**399
Professionals in Advertising, **1:**78; **2:**632
Programs of National Significance: Elementary School Counseling Demonstration Program (Title X), **1:**96–97

Progress and Freedom Foundation, **1**:64, 327
Prohibition, **1**:63
Prohibition Party, **2**:508
"Project Exile," **2**:533
Project Independence, **2**:559, 570
Project labor agreements, **1**:316
Project Learning Tree, **1**:305
Project Vote, **2**:432
Promus Hotel, **2**:632
Property rights, **1**:259
    Cato Institute, **2**:476
    Environmental Defense Fund, **1**:263
    farmer, **1**:248, 331
    National Cattlemen's Beef Association, **1**:231
    National Wildlife Federation, **1**:282
    wise use movement, **1**:293
    Yosemite National Park, **1**:291
Proposition 13, **2**:510, 529
Protecting Children from the Culture of Violence, **1**:90
Protestants and Other Americans United for the Separation of Church and State. *See* Americans United for the Separation of Church and State
Protests. *See* Demonstrations
Protocols of the Elders of Zion, The, **2**:424, 435
Prudential Insurance, **1**:4, 15; **2**:413, 563, 651, 689
Prudential Securities, **1**:61; **2**:684
Psychiatrists, American Psychiatric Association, **1**:162, 199–201
Psycho-pharmaceuticals, **1**:199–200
Commonwealth of Puerto Rico, **2**:688
Public advocacy groups, Fairness and Accuracy in Reporting, **1**:123, 133–34
Public Broadcasting Act, **1**:143
Public broadcasting systems, funding cuts, **1**:122
Public Broadcasting Trust Fund, **1**:143
Public Citizen, **1**:313; **2**:455–59 *passim*, 500–501
Public Citizen Foundation, **2**:500
Public Citizen News, **2**:500
Public Employees Organized to Promote Legislative Equality, **2**:363, 365
Public Health and Welfare Committee, **2**:682
Public Health Smoking Act, **1**:78
Public i, The, **2**:477
Public Interest Research Group, **1**:265
Public lands. *See* Land management & development
Public Law 149, **2**:532
Public Opinion, **2**:464
Public Safety Employer-Employee Cooperation Act, **1**:87
Public School Excellence Act, **2**:405
Public schools. *See* Schools
Public-sector unions, **2**:354, 674
Public Service Electric & Gas, **2**:645
Public television, corporate takeover of, **1**:133
Public transportation
    Economic Policy Institute, **2**:488
    United Transportation Union, **2**:420
Public Utility Holding Company Act, **1**:326–27
Publishing industry
    American Newspaper Publishing Association, **1**:150–51
    Association of American Publishers, **1**:130–32
    leading PACs, **2**:640
    Magazine Publishers of America, **1**:135–37, 153–54
    News America Publishing, **2**:640
    Software Publisher's Association, **1**:157, 158
Puerto Rico, **2**:548, 688

Puerto Rico Economic Development Administration, **2**:703
Puerto Rico Industrial Development, **2**:703
Puget Sound Energy, **2**:699

Q

Quarterly Economic Forecast, **1**:307
Quayle, Dan, **2**:492, 622
Quill, Michael, **2**:404

R

R. J. Reynolds, **1**:114
    See also RJR Nabisco
R Duffy Wall & Associates, **2**:661
Rabin, Yitzhak, **2**:601
Racism. *See* Discriminatory practices
Racketeer Influenced Corrupt Organization, **2**:387
Radio broadcasting industry
    commercialization, **1**:142
    increase in FM stations, **1**:153
    National Association of Broadcasters. *See* National Association of Broadcasters
Radio Marti, **2**:595
Railroads & railroad legislation
    Grange, **1**:247
    leading PACs, **2**:670
    lobbying expenditures, **2**:697
    Transport Workers Union of America, **2**:404, 406
    United Transportation Union, **2**:420
Railway Labor Act, **2**:356
Rainbow Coalition, **2**:431
Rainbow Warrior, **1**:260, 270
Rainforest Action Groups, **1**:284–85
Rainforest Action Network, **1**:258, 284–86
Ranger Rick, **1**:283
Rapid transit, **2**:420
Rathke, Wade, **2**:424, 430
Ratings Board, **1**:140
Ratings system, **1**:139, 140
Ray of Light, **2**:576
Raytheon Company, **1**:298; **2**:636
RCA, **1**:384
Read Across America, **1**:396
Reading Excellence Act, **1**:131
Reading promotion & programs, **1**:131, 151
Reagan, Ronald, **1**:103, 218, 318
    American Conservative Union, **2**:461
    and antienvironmental movement, **1**:257, 258
    arms race, **2**:510–11
    conservatism and, **2**:455
    firing of air traffic controllers, **2**:351
    as governor, **2**:510
"Reagan Ranches," **2**:428, 431
Real Estate Finance Today, **1**:38
Real estate industry
    leading PACs, **2**:646, 652
    lobbying expenditures, **2**:697
    overview of, **1**:3–7
    See also under Specific group
Real estate settlement procedures, **1**:13
Real Estate Settlement Procedures Act
    American Financial Services Association, **1**:18

Real Estate Settlement Procedures Act *(continued)*
  described, **1**:37
    Mortgage Bankers Association of America, **1**:37
    National Association of Realtors, **1**:52
Reardon, Thomas R., **1**:191
Recommended Dietary Allowances, **1**:177
Record Industry Association of America. *See* Recording Industry Association of America
Record Rental Amendment, **1**:153
Recording devices, **1**:154
Recording Industry Association of America, **1**:153–56; **2**:687
Recordings, Gold & Platinum awards, **1**:154
Recreation, leading PACs, **2**:632
  See also Outdoor recreation
Recycle America's Land Act, **1**:53
Recycling
  American Forest and Paper Association, **1**:305
  Distilled Spirits Council of the United States, **1**:324
  Food Marketing Institute, **2**:84
  National Beer Wholesalers Association, **1**:104
  National Wildlife Federation, **1**:282
  programs, **1**:257
  Recycle America's Land Act, **1**:53
Red baiting, **2**:366
Red Cross, **1**:75
Redwood National Park, **1**:291
Reed, Ralph, **2**:469, 481
Reeve Aleutian Airways, **1**:300
Refugees, **2**:496, 601
Regional and Distribution Carriers Conference, **1**:312
Regular Common Carrier Conference, **1**:312
Regulation, **2**:464, 475
Regulatory Action Alerts, **1**:221
Regulatory reform
  Business Roundtable, **1**:319
  Chemical Manufacturers Association, **1**:321
Regulatory relief, **1**:5
  America's Community Bankers, **1**:13
  Credit Union National Association, **1**:25
  Independent Community Bankers of America, **1**:27
Regulatory Right-to-Know Act, **1**:319, 322
Rehr, David, **1**:103, 104
Reich, Robert, **2**:487
Reid, Harry, **2**:577
Reid & Priest, **2**:661
Reiner, Rob, **2**:540
Religious interest groups
  overview of, **2**:454–59
  See also under Specific group
Religious liberty, **2**:439
Religious Rights Watch, **2**:481
Remington, Charles, **2**:553
Republican/Conservative
  leading PACs, **2**:623, 658
  lobbying expenditures, **2**:698
Republican Farm Bureau, **1**:245
Republican Leadership Council, **2**:658
Republican National Coalition for Life, **2**:665, 667
Republican National Committee donations, **2**:471
Republican Party
  business & trade associations and, **1**:295
  position on environmental regulations, **1**:258
Research
  American Enterprise Institute, **2**:463–64

Research *(continued)*
  Brookings Institution, **2**:472–74
  Center for Responsive Politics, **2**:479–80
  Economic Policy Institute, **2**:487–89
  Hudson Institute, **2**:492–93
Resource Guide to Coming Out, **2**:575
Response and Analysis: Teaching Literature in Junior and Senior High Schools, **2**:493
Restoring Broadly Shared Prosperity, **2**:487
Restoring the American Dream, **2**:658
Retail
  leading PACs, **2**:632
  lobbying expenditures, **2**:698
  National Association of Convenience Stores, **1**:89–91
  pricing laws, **1**:83
  Retail, Wholesale, and Department Store Union of Canada, **2**:416–17
  Retail, Wholesale and Department Store Union, **2**:414
  Retail Clerks International Union, **2**:413
Retail, Wholesale, and Department Store Union of Canada, **2**:416–17
Retail, Wholesale and Department Store Union, **2**:414
Retail Clerks International Union, **2**:413
Retirement Accessibility, Security, and Portability Act, **2**:405
Retirement Life, **1**:92, 93
Retirement policy
  American Council of Life Insurance, **1**:15, 16, 17
  Employee Retirement Income Security Act, **1**:84
  Food Marketing Institute, **1**:84
  Investment Company Institute, **1**:33, 34
  National Automobile Dealership Retirement Trust, **1**:99
  Securities Industry Association, **1**:58
  Transport Workers Union of America, **2**:405
  See also American Association of Retired Persons; Medicaid; Medicare; National Association of Retired Federal Employees; Social Security
Reuther, Walter, **2**:411
Review of the News, **2**:495
Revlon, **2**:539
Ribicoff, Abraham, **2**:467
Rich, Howard, **2**:550
Right-to-know, **2**:501
  Chemical Manufacturers Association, **2**:321–22
  Emergency Planning and Community Right-to-Know Act, **2**:295
  Regulatory Right-to-Know Act, **2**:319, 322
Right to Organize campaign, **2**:354
Right to Work, **2**:353, 414, 667
Rights Of . . . (series), **2**:427, 434
Ringen, But Knut, **1**:316
Rite Aid, **2**:632
Riverwood International Corp., **1**:304
RJR Nabisco, **2**:627, 629, 676, 693, 695, 703
Road systems, **1**:304
  funding cuts, **2**:624
  International Association of Machinists and Aerospace Workers, **2**:383
  Laborers' International Union of North America, **2**:395
  opposition to northern Brazil's, **1**:285
  rural, **1**:248
  See also Highway safety legislation
"Road to Victory," **2**:481
Road Warrior award, **1**:267
Robert Brookings Graduate School, **2**:472

Robert Welch University, **2**:494
Robert Welch University Press, **2**:494
Roberts, Pat, **1**:212
Robertson, Pat, **2**:455, 481, 537–38
"Rock against Fur," **2**:540
Rockefeller, Jay, **2**:529
Rockefeller, Nelson, **2**:526
Rockefeller Family Fund, **2**:505
Rockefeller Foundation, **2**:473, 488
Rockwell International, **2**:384, 636
Rodale Institute, **1**:252
Rodale Press, **1**:252
Roe v. Wade, **2**:433, 526, 536, 543, 583
Roll Call, **2**:483
Roman Catholic Church, **2**:455
Romer, Roy, **2**:576
Romer v. Evans, **2**:433
Ronald Reagan Legacy Project campaigns, **2**:469
Roosevelt, Eleanor, **2**:424, 438, 466
Roosevelt, Franklin D., **1**:68, 312, 326; **2**:381, 472, 509
    memorial building, **2**:529
    National Wildlife Week, **1**:281
Roosevelt, James, **2**:529
Roosevelt, Theodore, **1**:287
Root Cause Analysis Pilot Project, **1**:321
Roscoe Pound Foundation, **1**:82
Rosen, Hilary, **1**:154
Roth, Kenneth, **1**:441
RR Donnelley & Sons, **2**:640
RU-486, **2**:527, 528, 544, 554
Rubin, Robert, **1**:60
Ruebhausen, Oscar, **2**:492
Ruma, Charles, **1**:329, 330, 331
Rural areas
    Grange and, **1**:248
    post office facilities, **2**:371
Rural housing mortgage loans, **1**:27
Rush-Presbyterian-St. Lukes Medical Center, **2**:703
Rusher, William, **2**:460
Russia, **2**:611–13
    relations with Cuba, **2**:594
    steel imports from, **2**:417
Russian Revolution, **2**:611
Rwanda, **2**:438, 442
Ryan White Comprehensive AIDS Resources Emergency Act, **2**:575–76
Ryder System, **2**:670

S

Sabo, Albert, **1**:88
Sabre Group, **2**:632
Safari Club International, **2**:665, 667
"SAFE Act," **2**:412
Safe and Drug-Free Schools and Communities (Title IV), **1**:96–97
Safe Schools Act, **2**:405
SAFE Trust, **1**:105, 106, 107
SAFECO, **1**:39
Safeguarding Our Last Link, **1**:84
Safety belts, **1**:100, 168
Safety Network, **2**:450
Safeway, **1**:83; **2**:413

Sailors Union of the Pacific, **2**:399
Saks Fifth Avenue, **2**:540
Sales Planning Guide, **1**:307
Sallie Mae, **2**:649
Salmonella, **1**:221, 235
Salomon Brothers, **2**:650
Salomon Smith Barney, **2**:650
SALT I & II, **2**:519
"Salting," **2**:409
San Diego County, California, **2**:688
Sanders, Bernard, **1**:341
Sanders, W.J. III, **1**:346
Sanger, Margaret, **2**:542
Sarah Scaife Foundation, **2**:440, 457, 464, 476, 491, 493, 499
Sarasin, Ronald A., **1**:102
Saro-Wiwa, Ken, **2**:609
Satellite dishes, home, **1**:147
Saunders, William, **1**:247
Save Our Streams, **1**:273
"Save the City" campaign, **2**:430
Savimbi, Jonas, **2**:594
Saving the Planet with Pesticides and Plastic, **2**:493
Savings and Community Bankers of America. *See* America's Community Bankers
Savings and loan institutions
    leading PACs, **2**:648
    scandals, **1**:12, 14
Savings Banks Association of New York State, **2**:648
SBC Communications, **2**:638, 639, 677, 695, 699, 703
Scaife, Richard Mellon, **1**:126
Scarborough, Joseph, **1**:104
Scarborough, Bill, **1**:104
Schering-Plough, **2**:656, 691
Schlesinger, Arthur, Jr., **2**:466
Schloss Family Foundation, **2**:440
School of Mortgage Banking, **1**:38
School vouchers
    American Conservative Union, **2**:461
    American Enterprise Institute, **2**:464
    American Federation of State, County, and Municipal Employees, **2**:365
    American Federation of Teachers, **2**:367–68
    Americans United for the Separation of Church and State, **2**:514–15
    Anti-Defamation League, **2**:436
    Christian Coalition, **2**:482
    League of Women Voters of the United States, **2**:445
    National Association for the Advancement of Colored People, **2**:579
    National Association of Social Workers, **1**:96
    National Council of the Churches of Christ, **2**:497
    National Education Association, **2**:398
    United Automobile Workers, **2**:412
    United States Catholic Conference, **2**:503
Schools
    charter, **2**:397
    Christian, **2**:455–56
    class-size reduction, **2**:396
    conservation programs, **1**:273
    construction jobs, **2**:394, 397
    lunch programs, **1**:211; **2**:430
    prayer in, **2**:482, 514, 515
    rural, **1**:248
    safety, **2**:397, 405

*Numbers in **bold** indicate volume.*

Schools *(continued)*
    separation of church & state, **2:**513–15
    student & teacher testing, **2:**368
    technology in, **2:**397
    See also School vouchers; Teachers
Schosberg, Paul, **1:**14
Schroeder, Patricia, **1:**131
Schumer, Charles, **2:**577
Schwarzkopf, Norman, **2:**517
Science Applications International, **2:**636
Scientific research funding, **1:**57
Scientists Action Network, **2:**545
Scopes, John T., **2:**433
Scorecards
    American Conservative Union, **2:**458
    Americans for Democratic Action, **2:**466
    Christian Coalition, **2:**481
    Citizens for a Sound Economy, **2:**483
    Heritage Foundation, **2:**490
    National Tax Payers Union, **2:**498
    U.S. Public Interest Research Group, **2:**504
Scorsese, Martin, **2:**540
Scott, Hugh, **2:**479
Scott Paper Company, **1:**304
"Scrap the Code Tour," **2:**484
Scudder Kemper Investments, **1:**35
Sea-Land Service, **2:**668, 670
Sea Shepherd Conservation Society, **1:**270
Sea transport
    leading PAC, **2:**670
    lobbying expenditures, **2:**698
Seafarers Commercial Fishermen's Association, **2:**399
Seafarers International Union of North America, **2:**399–400, 671, 673
Seafarers Political Action Donation Department, **2:**400
Seafarers Union of the Pacific, **2:**399
Seagram, **2:**413
Seal pups, killing of, **1:**269
Sears Tower, **2:**391
Seat belts, **1:**100
Second Amendment, **2:**534
Secret Order of the Star Spangled Banner, **2:**507
Securities and Exchange Commission, **1:**22, 33, 56–57
    charges against NFO, **1:**242
    Investment Company Institute's liaison with, **1:**35
    Securities Industry Association's liaison with, **1:**60
Securities industry, **1:**58–61
    leading PACs, **2:**650
    lobbying expenditures, **2:**684, 697
    See also under Specific group
Securities Industry Association, **1:**6, 7, 22, 58–61
    leading PAC, **2:**650
    lobbying expenditures, **2:**684, 695
Securities Industry Institute, **1:**60
Security affairs, European Union, **2:**598
Security issues, **2:**589
Security Traders Association, **2:**684
SEMATECH, **1:**346
Semiconductor Industry Association, **1:**295, 346–47
Semiconductor Research Corporation, **1:**346
Semiconductor Technology Roadmap, **1:**346
Senate Agriculture, Nutrition, and Forestry Committee, **1:**212
Senate Banking Committee, **1:**28, 46
Senate Finance Committee, **2:**623

Senior Community Service Employment Program, **2:**562
Senior Environmental Employment Program, **2:**562
Seniors Coalition, **2:**692, 694
Sensenbrenner, James, **1:**104
Serbia, **2:**442, 598
Service Corp. International, **2:**632
Service Employees International Union, **2:**401–3
    leading PAC, **2:**671, 675
    soft money donations, **2:**676
Service industry
    leading PACs, **2:**632
    overview of, **1:**62–66
    See also under Specific group
Servicemaster, **2:**632
Setting National Priorities, **2:**473
Shabazz, Betty, **2:**570
Sharpton, Al, **2:**570
Shaw, Pittman et al., **2:**661
Sheet Asphalt Pavers, **2:**393
Sheet Metal/Air Conditioning Contractors, **2:**633, 635
Sheet Metal Workers, **2:**671, 674
Shell Oil, **1:**114, 285; **2:**539, 690
Shepard, Matthew, **2:**582
Sheppard-Towner Act, **2:**428, 444
Sherman Antitrust Act, **1:**63, 294
Shields, N.T., **2:**521
Shop Rite, **1:**83
Shoppers Guide to Long-Term Care Insurance, **1:**43–44
Shoup, Harold A., **1:**78
Sierra, **1:**289
Sierra Club, **1:**63, 258, 259, 269, 287–90
    Brower's resignation, **1:**265
    coalition building, **1:**260
    leading PAC, **2:**622, 623, 665, 667
Sierra Club Committee on Political Education, **1:**288, 289, 290
Sierra Club Legal Defense Fund, **1:**289
Sierra Club Political Committee, **1:**259, 289, 290
Sierra Military Health Service, **2:**703
Sierra Nevada mountains, **1:**287
Silent Spring, **1:**279
Silverstone, Alicia, **2:**540
Simon, William, **2:**464
Sinclair, Upton, **1:**175
Singer, Max, **2:**492
Single interest groups
    leading PACs, **2:**665, 667
    lobbying expenditures, **2:**692, 697
    overview of, **2:**506–12
    See also under Specific group
Single State Registration System, **1:**296
Six Day War, **2:**436
60 Plus Association, **2:**692
Skadden, ARPS et al., **2:**661
Sky Dome, **2:**391
Slamming, **2:**373
Slavery, abolitionist movement, **2:**506–7
Slim-Fast Foods/Thompson Medical, **2:**676
Small and Medium Manufacturers Initiative, **1:**333
Small Business Abuse Protection, **1:**91
Small Business Administration, **1:**28, 100
Small-business interest groups, **1:**64
    National Federation of Independent Business, **1:**62, 105–7
Small Business Lawsuit Protection Act, **1:**91
Small Business Liability Reform Act, **1:**91

Small Business Survival Committee, **2**:685
Small Employer Tax Relief Act, **1**:112
Smith-Leaver Act, **1**:213
Smith Richardson Foundation, Inc., **2**:440, 457, 464
Smithkline Beecham, **2**:691
Smokeless Tobacco Council, **2**:693, 703
Smoking. *See* Tobacco
Snake River, **1**:282
Social protest movements, **2**:455
Social Security, **1**:5
    American Association of Retired Persons, **2**:561
    American Conservative Union, **2**:458
    American Council of Life Insurance and, **1**:15
    American Federation of Labor–Congress of Industrial Organizations, **2**:361
    American Federation of State, County, and Municipal Employees, **2**:364, 365
    American Healthcare Association, **1**:182
    American Institute of Certified Public Accountants, **1**:23
    Americans for Tax Reform, **2**:458, 470
    Brookings Institution, **2**:473
    Business Roundtable, **1**:319
    Cato Institute, **2**:475
    Citizens for a Sound Economy, **2**:484
    Communications Workers of America, **2**:372–73
    Economic Policy Institute, **2**:488
    exemption from, **1**:150
    Fraternal Order of Police, **1**:87
    Heritage Foundation, **2**:491
    International Association of Fire Fighters, **2**:378–79
    International Brotherhood of Electrical Workers, **2**:385
    International Brotherhood of Teamsters, **2**:388
    International Union of Operating Engineers, **2**:390, 391
    Investment Company Institute, **1**:33–34
    labor unions, **2**:352
    National Council of the Churches of Christ, **2**:497
    National Education Association, **2**:396
    National Taxpayers Union, **2**:458, 499
    Service Employees International Union, **2**:402
    Transport Workers Union of America, **2**:405
    Union of Needletrades, Industrial, and Textile Employees, **2**:407–8
    United Automobile Workers, **2**:412
    United States Catholic Conference, **2**:503
    United Transportation Union, **2**:420
    White House Conference on, **1**:33
    See also National Committee to Preserve Social Security and Medicare
Social welfare, **2**:350, 352
    Americans for Democratic Action, **2**:458, 467
    Association of Community Organizations for Reform Now, **2**:430
    Cato Institute, **2**:476
    Citizen Actions, **2**:457–58
    Economic Policy Institute, **2**:457–58
    Food Stamps, **1**:210, 211, 212
    Lyndon Johnson, **2**:509
    National Association of Social Workers, **1**:95–98; **2**:95
    National Council of the Churches of Christ, **2**:497
    Public Citizen, **2**:457–58
    United States Catholic Conference, **2**:502–03
Social workers. *See* National Association of Social Workers
Society of Independent Gasoline Marketers, **2**:643
Society of Thoracic Surgeons, **2**:655

Sodium nitrate, **1**:221
Soft drink taxes, **1**:83
Soft money, **2**:625
    leading donors, **2**:676–77
    nonprint trade associations, **1**:122
Software and Information Industry Association, **1**:157–58
Software Publisher's Association, **1**:157, 158
Soil Bank program, **1**:211
Solidarity with Liberty, **2**:475
Sons of the American Legion, **2**:567
Sony, **1**:153; **2**:680
Sony Pictures Entertainment, **2**:638, 639
Sorauf, Frank J., **2**:514
Sorensen, Theodore, **2**:466–67
Soros Foundation, **2**:440
SOT. *See* Special Occupational Tax
Source taxing, **1**:94
South Africa
    AmFAR, **2**:179
    Apartheid, **2**:509, 511–12
    Boer War, **2**:532
    National Council of the Churches of Christ, **2**:497
South Korea, **1**:347; **2**:587
Southern, **2**:699
Southern California Edison, **2**:641, 645, 699
Southern Environmental Law Center, **1**:274
Southern Furniture Manufacturers Association, **1**:308
Southern Minnesota Beet Sugar Co-op, **2**:627
Southern Nuclear, **2**:645
Southwest Airlines, **1**:300; **2**:356
Southwest Marine, **2**:670
Soviet Union
    arms race, **2**:510–11
    grain sales, **1**:242
Soyinka, Wole, **2**:609
Special Occupational Tax, **1**:65, 89–90, 91
Specialized Carriers & Rigging Association, **1**:312
Sporck, Charles, **1**:346
Sports Eye Safety Month, **1**:166
Sportsmen interest groups. *See* Izaak Walton League
Spotted owl, **1**:260; 292
Springs Industries, **2**:664
Sprint, **1**:60; 638, 639
    lobbying expenditures, **2**:694, 699
    soft money donations, **2**:677
Sputnik 1, **1**:127
Square D., **2**:384
St. Louisians for Better Government, **2**:666
Staley, Oren Lee, **1**:242
Stalin, Joseph, **2**:611
Standard Oil Company, **1**:63, 114
Stanford University, **2**:680
Star Wars, **2**:518, 545, 546
Starr, Kenneth, **1**:126
START II, **2**:518
START III, **2**:518
Starwood Hotels & Resorts Worldwide, **2**:632, 703
State Advertising Coalition, **1**:78
State of Working America, The, **2**:487, 488
"State Postsecondary Review for Entities," **1**:128
Steamship Sailor's Protective Association, **2**:399
Steel industry
    leading PACs, **2**:663
    See also under Specific group

Steel Workers Organizing Committee, **2:**416
Stem cell research, **1:**168
Steptoe and Johnson, **2:**679
Stern, Andrew, **2:**401
Stern, Philip, **2:**479
Stewardship, **1:**281–83
Stewart & Stevenson Services, **2:**645
Stewart B. McKinney Homelessness Assistance Act, **2:**428, 450
Stipe, Michael, **2:**540
Stock Market Game, **1:**60
Stock regulation, **1:**240
Stone, Oliver, **2:**540
Stone & Webster, **2:**635
Stone Container Corp., **1:**304; **2:**627, 629
Stonewall Riots, **2:**558
Stonier Graduate School of Banking, **1:**10
Stop and Shop, **1:**83
Stowe, Irving, **1:**269
"Stranded costs," **1:**296
Strategic Defense Initiative. *See* Star Wars
Strauss, Robert, **2:**678
Street Newspaper project, **2:**450
Strickland, Ted, **1:**106
Students Against Nuclear Extermination, **2:**509
Stupak, Bart, **1:**90
Suffolk County Mosquito Control Commission, **1:**262
Suffrage, women's, **2:**444, 508
Sugar Act, **1:**223
Sugar Alliance, **1:**223
Sugar industry
    American Sugarbeet Growers Association, **1:**223–24; **2:**627
    Sugar Workers Union, **2:**399
Sugar Workers Union, **2:**399
Sullivan, Jere, **2:**375
Summer and Casual Furniture Manufacturers Association, **1:**307
Summer camps, **1:**260; **2:**494
Summers, Lawrence, **1:**29; **2:**613
Sun Microsystems, **2:**686
Super Market Institute, **1:**83
Superfund, **1:**40, 304; **2:**391, 505
Superfund Transformation Act, **1:**40
Supermarket interest groups. *See* Grocery store industry
Supplemental Security Income, **2:**530
Supreme Court, nominations, **1:**68
Surgery, in-office, **1:**204
Survey of Current Business, **1:**307
Susan B. Anthony PAC, **2:**574
Sustainability Education project, **1:**274
Sustainability Newsletter, **1:**274
Sustainable Forestry Initiative, **1:**305
SVERDRUP, **2:**633, 635
Sweatshops, **1:**310, **2:**408; 409
Sweeney, John, **2:**353, 361, 362, 401, 576
Swift, **2:**413
Switchmen's Union of North America, **2:**420
Symms, Lehn & Associates, **2:**661
Symms, Steve, **2:**678
Szilard, Leo, **2:**519

T

Taco, **2:**631
TACT. *See* Truth About Civic Turmoil
Taft, William Howard, **1:**114, 117

Taft-Hartley Act, **2:**351, 354, 360, 361
Taipei Economic and Cultural Representative Office, **2:**614
Taiwan, **2:**614–15
    arms sales, **2:**591–92
    "one China" policy, **2:**593, 613
Taiwan Benevolent Association, **2:**614
Taiwan Relations Act, **2:**614
Taiwan Strait Crisis, **2:**614
Takings legislation, **1:**282, 293
Talk radio, **1:**133
Tame Yourself, **2:**540
Tate & Lyle North American Sugars, **2:**704
Tax Code Termination Act, **2:**461
Tax codes, **1:**5, 12
    501(c)(3) & 501(c)(4) status, defined, **2:**458, 557
    provisions, **2:**456
    See also Taxes
Tax Council-Alcoholic Beverage Industries group, **1:**323
Tax credits, **1:**349; **2:**373
Tax-deductible meals, **1:**111
Tax Reform, **1:**52
Tax Reform Act, **2:**385–86
Tax Reform Act Committee, **2:**679
Tax Reform Immediately, **2:**495
Tax Treatment of Native Americans, **2:**115
Taxes
    American Conservative Union, **2:**458, 461
    American Enterprise Institute, **2:**464
    American Institute of Certified Public Accountants, **1:**21
    American Trucking Associations, **1:**312
    Americans for Democratic Action, **2:**458, 468
    Americans for Tax Reform, **1:**64; **2:**455, 458, 469–71
    Association of American Publishers, **1:**130
    Christian Coalition, **2:**481, 482
    Citizen Action, **2:**457–58
    Citizens for a Sound Economy, **2:**484
    corporate, **1:**15
    Economic Policy Institute, **2:**457–58
    Edison Electric Institute, **1:**327
    exemption, **1:**64, 83, 150, 157; **2:**88
    flat. *See* Flat tax
    Heritage Foundation, **2:**490
    insurance, **1:**45
    International Brotherhood of Electrical Workers, **2:**385–86
    Internet Tax Freedom Act moratorium, **1:**54, 59
    John Birch Society, **2:**495
    manufacturing industry, **1:**295
    National Association of Wheat Growers, **1:**229
    National Council of Farmer Cooperatives, **1:**240
    National Farmers Unions, **1:**245
    National Federation of Independent Business, **1:**106
    National Pork Producers Council, **1:**249
    National Tax Payers Union, **2:**455, 458, 498–99
    Newspaper Association of America, **1:**150
    Printing Industries of America, **1:**343–44
    Public Citizen, **2:**457–58
    Small Employer Tax Relief Act, **1:**112
    trade association income, **1:**52
    Union of Needletrades, Industrial, and Textile Employees, **2:**407
    See also Tax codes; Specific tax
Taxpayer Protection Pledge, **2:**469, 471
"Taxpayer Villains," **2:**469
Taxpayers Against Fraud, **2:**692

Taxpayers Against Frivolous Lawsuits, **1**:56
Taxpayers Bill of Rights, **2**:499
Taxpayers for Common Sense, **1**:265
Teachers
    American Federation of Teachers, **1**:97; **2**:366–68, 674, 676
    competency tests, **2**:368, 473
Team Drivers International Union, **2**:387
Teaming with Wildlife, **1**:282
Teamsters. *See* International Brotherhood of Teamsters
Teamsters for a Democratic Union, **2**:387
Teamsters National Union, **2**:387
Teamwork for Employees and Management Act, **2**:364–65, 414
Technology
    Heritage Foundation's interest in, **2**:457
    opposition to, **1**:265
    See also Computer industry
Technology Network (TechNet), **1**:295, 348–49
Techworld, **1**:29
Teen Endangerment Act, **2**:585
Teenagers, automobile legislation, **1**:100
Tele-Communications, **2**:677, 687
Telecommunications Act, **1**:121, 123, 141, 142
    cable and, **1**:147, 148
    Fairness and Accuracy in Reporting, **1**:133, 134
    overview of, **1**:144
Telecommunications industry
    Communications Workers of America, **2**:372–74
    deregulation of, **1**:121, 147
    leading PACs, **2**:638, 640
    lobbying expenditures, **2**:697
Telephone-cable operations, **1**:148
Telephone companies
    leading PACs, **2**:639
    lobbying expenditures, **2**:697, 699
Telephone Workers Organizing Committee, **2**:372
Teleport, **1**:60
Television Broadcasters Association, **1**:142
Television industry, **1**:51
    campaigns, **1**:32
    leading PACs, **2**:639
Tenet Healthcare, **2**:656
Tenneco, **2**:636
Tennessee-Tombigbee Waterway, **1**:265
Tennessee Valley Authority, **1**:327
Tennessee Valley Authority Retirement System, **1**:92
Tennessee Walking Horse Breeders, **2**:628
Tennyson, Leonard, **2**:597
Term Limits America, **2**:667
Term Limits Declaration, **2**:551
Terrorism, **1**:436; **2**:437
Testing, student & teacher, **2**:368, 473
Tet Offensive, **2**:509
Texaco, **2**:539, 641, 690
Texas, Metro Transit Authority of Harris County, **2**:688, 704
Texas Cattle Feeders Association, **2**:628
Texas Farm Bureau PACs, **1**:215
Texas Food Industry Association, **1**:83
Texas Instruments, **2**:686
Texas Utilities, **2**:641, 645, 699
Texas v. Johnson, **2**:433, 568
Textile industry
    American Textile Manufacturers Institute, **1**:295, 309–11; **2**:662, 664
    leading PACs, **2**:664

Textile industry *(continued)*
    Textile Workers Union of America, **2**:407
    Union of Needletrades, Industrial, and Textile Employees, **2**:407–9, 672
    United Food and Commercial Workers Union, **2**:413
Textile Workers Union of America, **2**:407
Textron, **2**:636
Thanksgiving, protests of, **2**:565
Thatcher, Margaret, **2**:490
They Dare to Speak Out: People and Institutions Confront Israel's Lobby, **2**:601
Think tanks, definition of, **2**:456
Thiokol, **2**:636
This Is Dinosaur, **1**:288
Thomas, Clarence, **2**:482, 490, 570, 584
Thread Institute, **1**:309
Three-tier system, **1**:102, 104, 114
Thrift charter, **1**:9–10, 12
Thrift Institutions Advisory Council, **1**:25
Thurow, Lester, **2**:487
Tiananmen Square, **2**:592
Tilman Act, **2**:422
Timber. *See* Logging
Time Warner, **1**:130, 135
    leading PAC, **2**:638, 639
    lobbying expenditures, **2**:687
    soft money donations, **2**:677
Timken, **2**:662, 664
Timmons, **2**:701
TIP, To Insure Progress, **2**:377
Tip income, **2**:377
Title branding legislation, **1**:101
Title educational programs, **1**:96–97; **2**:367
Tobacco industry, **1**:213
    leading PACs, **2**:629
    lobbying expenditures, **2**:693, 697
    support for growers, **1**:248
    See also Tobacco legislation
Tobacco Institute, **2**:629, 693
Tobacco legislation
    American Cancer Society, **1**:167–68
    American Heart Association, **1**:184, 185
    American Medical Association, **1**:191
    Cigarette Labeling Act, **1**:78
    and drop in sales, **1**:89
    Public Citizen, **2**:501
    public smoking, **1**:112, 185
    sales to minors, **1**:90–91, **1**:115
    taxes, **1**:168, 185
    See also Advertising, tobacco; Tobacco industry
Tobin, Daniel J., **2**:387
Tocqueville, Alexis de, **1**:67
Toll-free phone lines, **1**:65, 115
Tolls, highway, **1**:312
Tom Creek Foundation, **2**:505
"Tombstone Tour," **2**:505
Tongsun Park, **2**:587
Toole, Martin, **1**:86
Toronto
    CN Tower, **2**:391
    Sky Dome, **2**:391
Torricelli, Robert, **2**:533
Torrington, **2**:670
Tort reform, **1**:81

Tort reform *(continued)*
    American Council of Life Insurance, **1:**16
    Business Roundtable, **1:**318, 319
    U.S. Chamber of Commerce, **1:**118
Torture, **2:**442
Toshiba Machine Company, **2:**604
Tourism PACs, **2:**632
Toxic chemicals/materials, **1:**262, **1:**269
Toxics Release Inventory Phase 3, **1:**295
Toyota Motor Sales USA, lobbying expenditures, **2:**700
Toys "R" Us, **1:**77
"Tractorcades," **1:**218
Trade Act, **2:**592
Trade agreements
    affect on environment, **1:**258
    AFL–CIO, **2:**351
    environmental restrictions, **1:**259
    Free Trade in the Americas, **1:**282
    Friends of the Earth, **1:**267
    GATT. *See* Global Agreement on Tariffs and Trade
    International Brotherhood of Teamsters, **2:**389
    NAFTA. *See* North American Free Trade Agreement
    National Association of Insurance Commissioners, **1:**43
    See also Federal Trade Commission; Free markets; International trade
Trade Alert Newsletter, **1:**221
Trade and Development Agency, **2:**592
Trade barriers, **1:**221; **2:**362
Trade embargoes, **1:**229
Trade groups, **1:**62–66, 294
Trade unions, **2:**354
Trail of Broken Treaties, **2:**564
Trans World Airlines, **1:**300
    flight 800, **1:**125, 126
TransAfrica, **2:**609, 610
Transgenic species, **1:**211
Transport Workers, **2:**671, 673
Transport Workers Union of America, **2:**404–6
Transportation Communication International, **2:**673
Transportation Employee Testing Safety Act, **2:**524
Transportation Equity Act, **1:**40
Transportation industry
    interstate transportation, **1:**339
    leading PACs, **2:**668–70
    leading union PACs, **2:**673
    lobbying expenditures, **2:**698, 700
    overview of, **1:**294–96
    See also under Specific group
Transportation Political Education League, **2:**419
Transshipping, **1:**309, 310
Trapping, animal, **2:**281
Treaty on Non-Proliferation of Nuclear Weapons, **2:**546
Trends: Consumer Attitudes and the Supermarket, **1:**84
Trial lawyers. *See* Association of Trial Lawyers of America
TRIAL magazine, **1:**82
TRIM. *See* Tax Reform Immediately
Trucker Shuffle Relief Act, **1:**304
Trucking industry
    American Trucking Associations, **1:**312–14; **2:**668, 670
    leading PACs, **2:**670
"Truckline," **1:**312
Truman, Harry, **2:**354, 360, 513
Truman Doctrine, **2:**466, 616
Trump Organization, **2:**680

Trust companies, **1:**8–10
Trusts, **1:**294
Truth About Civic Turmoil, **2:**494
Truth in Employment Act, **2:**385
Truth in Lending Act
    American Financial Services Association, **1:**18
    described, **1:**37
    Mortgage Bankers Association of America, **1:**37
Truth-in-lending requirements, **1:**8, 13, 18, 24, 25, 27
Truth-in-savings requirements, **1:**8, 27
TRW, **1:**18; **2:**636
Tunnel and Subway Constructors International Union, **2:**393
Tuppling, Lloyd, **1:**266, 275
Turkey, **2:**588–89, 616–18
Turlington, Christie, **2:**539
TV Marti, **2:**594–95
TWA. *See* Trans World Airlines
Two-parent families, **2:**464
Tyson Foods, **2:**413, 628

U

Uganda, **2:**442
UHF, **1:**143
Underwriting, legislation proposals, **1:**15, 16
Unemployed Workers Organizing Committee, **2:**430
Unemployment insurance, **2:**352, 353, 361, 395
Uniform Accountancy Act, **1:**23
Uniform Certified Public Accounting Examination, **1:**21
Uniform National Standards for Securities Litigation, **1:**348
Uniform Standards Coalition, **2:**684
Unilever United States Foundation, Inc., **2:**440
Union Camp Corp., **1:**304
Union for Democratic Action, **2:**466
Union for the Total Independence of Angola, **2:**594
Union of Concerned Scientists, **2:**545–46
Union of Needletrades, Industrial, and Textile Employees, **1:**407–9; **2:**672
Union Pacific, **2:**668, 670
Union Pacific Railroad, **2:**680
Union Pacific Resources Group, **2:**641, 643
Unionization
    nurse, **1:**193
    physician, **1:**161, 188, 190, 206, 207
Unions. *See* Labor unions
Unisys, **2:**512
United Airlines, **1:**300; **2:**356, 668, 669
    lobbying expenditures, **2:**700
United Automobile Workers, **2:**350, 381, 410–12
    leading PAC, **2:**622, 671, 672
United Defense, **2:**636
United Egg Association, **1:**254–55; **2:**628
United Egg Producers, **1:**255
United Federation of Postal Clerks, **2:**369
United Federation of Teachers, **2:**366
United Food and Commercial Workers Union, **2:**413–15
    leading PAC, **2:**622, 671, 675
    soft money donations, **2:**676
United Garment Workers Union, **2:**407
United Industrial, Service, Transportation, Professional, and Government Workers of North America, **2:**399
United Industrial Workers of North America, **2:**399
United Labor Union, Association of Community Organizations for Reform Now and, **2:**431

Numbers in **bold** *indicate volume.*

United Mine Workers of America, **1**:335; **2**:416, 671, 672
United Nations, **2**:587
American Enterprise Institute, **2**:464
American Nurses Association, **1**:195
Americans for Democratic Action, **2**:457
Heritage Foundation, **2**:491
John Birch Society, **2**:495
League of Women Voters of the United States, **2**:444
National Lawyers Guild as co-founder of, **2**:452
U.S. debt, **2**:589
United Nations Population Fund, **2**:554
United Parcel Service, **1**:263, 300; **2**:388
leading PAC, **2**:622, 623, 668, 669
lobbying expenditures, **2**:700
United Presbyterian Women's Missionary Society, **2**:513
United Retail Workers, **2**:414
United Rubber, Cork, Linoleum, and Plastic Workers of America, **2**:417
United Seniors, **2**:658
United Services Automobile Association Group, **2**:651, 689
United Space Alliance, **2**:703
United States Catholic Conference, **2**:502–3
United States Department of Agriculture, **1**:213, 215
American Forest and Paper Association, **1**:305
Farmers Union, **1**:244–45
Grange, **1**:248
National Chicken Council, **1**:234
organic farming, **1**:252
United Egg Association, **1**:254
United States Department of Education, **1**:197
United States League of Savings Institutions, **1**:12
United States Postal Service, **1**:301; **2**:369–71, 623
postal subsidies, **1**:120
See also Postal rates
United States Steel, **1**:318; **2**:416
United Steelworkers of America, **2**:350, 381, 416–18, 671, 672
United Stone and Allied Product Workers of America, **2**:416
United Technologies, **1**:298; **2**:636
United Textile Workers of America, **2**:414
United Transportation Union, **2**:419–21, 622, 671, 673
United Voices, **1**:254
Universal Air Travel Plan, **1**:296, 300, 301
Universal Studios, **2**:638, 639
Unsafe at Any Speed, **2**:500
Upholsterers International Union of North America, **2**:416
Urban League, **2**:570
Urban sprawl, **1**:256, 257, 259, 290, 331
U.S. Agency for International Development, **2**:440, 612
U.S. Airways, **1**:300
U.S. Army Air Corps, **1**:301
U.S. Army Corps of Engineers, **1**:256, 265, 282
U.S. Catholic Conference, **2**:458, 514
U.S. Chamber of Commerce, **1**:64, 81, 106, 111, 113, 117–19
Hudson Institute's liaison with, **2**:493
lobbying expenditures, **2**:685, 694
U.S. Chamber of Congress, opposition to labor unions, **2**:353
U.S. Conference of Mayors, **1**:330
U.S. Council for Energy Awareness, **1**:338
U.S. Department of Agriculture, **1**:221, 232
U.S. Department of Commerce, **1**:43, 221, 254, 256
U.S. Department of Defense, **1**:298, 299, 301; **2**:493
See also Defense budget; Defense PACs
U.S. Department of Health and Human Services, **1**:182, 186, 187, 195, 203
U.S. Department of Housing and Urban Development, **1**:38, 53–54, 330; **2**:431–32
U.S. Department of Interior, **1**:256
U.S. Department of Justice, **1**:221; **2**:493
U.S. Department of Labor, **1**:100, 195
U.S. Department of Social Development and World Peace, **2**:502
U.S. Department of the Treasury, **1**:5, 10, 25, 53
U.S. Department of Transportation, **1**:40, 301, 302, 313
U.S. Department of Veterans Affairs, **1**:36, 184, 186; **2**:568
U.S. English, **2**:547–49
U.S. English Foundation, **2**:547
U.S. Federal Housing Administration, **1**:36
U.S. Flag Code, **2**:568
U.S. Forest Service, **1**:305; **2**:383
U.S. Hide, Skin, and Leather Association, **1**:220
U.S. High-Tech Industry Coalition on China, **1**:347
U.S. Hispanic music industry, **1**:154
U.S. Information Agency, **1**:75; **2**:440, 595
U.S. Maritime Coalition, **2**:704
U.S. Medal of Freedom, **2**:569
U.S.-Mexico Binational Commission, **2**:606
U.S.-Mexico Binational Drug Strategy, **2**:608
U.S. National Highway Traffic Safety Administration, **1**:100
U.S. Postal Service. *See* United States Postal Service
U.S. Public Interest Research Group, **1**:322; **2**:455, 504–5
U.S. Public Interest Research Group Fund, **2**:504, 505
U.S. Telephone Association, **2**:699
U.S. Term Limits, **2**:550–52
U.S. Tobacco, **2**:627, 629
U.S. Trade Representative. *See* Office of the U.S. Trade Representative
U.S. Treasury. *See* U.S. Department of the Treasury
U.S. West, **2**:638, 639, 676, 699
USA Today, Christian Coalition advertisements, **2**:481
USAA, **1**:39
UST, **2**:693
USX, **1**:318; **2**:643, 690, 695
Utilities industry
overview of, **1**:294–96
regulation, **1**:326–27
See also under Specific group

V

V-chip, **1**:141
Valenti, Jack, **1**:138, 139, 140
Value-added tax, **2**:470
Value in Electing Women, **2**:659
Van Scoyoc Associates, **2**:701
Vegetarianism, **2**:541
Vehicle manufacturing, **1**:263
Vehicle safety legislation, **1**:99
See also Automobiles & automobile legislation
Venezuela, Republic of, **2**:680
Venture capital interest groups, **1**:55–57
VenturePAC, **1**:57
Verner, Liipfer et al., **2**:661, 701, 703
Veteran benefits, **2**:399
Veteran groups. *See* American Legion
Veterans Administration insurance centers, **2**:568
Veterans Affairs and Rehabilitation Commission, **2**:568
Veterans Home Loan Guarantee Board, **1**:38
Veterans of Foreign Wars, **2**:679
Veterans rights, **2**:430

VHF, **1**:143
Viacom, **2**:130, 638, 639, 687
VIAD, **2**:632
Victim Assistance Institute, **2**:524
Video industry. *See* Film industry
Vietnam Veteran's Organizing Committee, **2**:430
Vietnam War, **2**:467, 485, 509, 567
    Tet Offensive, **2**:509
    See also Anti-war movements
Vigilante Justice, **2**:436
Vinson & Elkins, **2**:661
Violent and Repeat Juvenile Offender Act, **1**:97
Violent Crime Control and Law Enforcement Act, **2**:521
Virginia Clean Air Now, **1**:274
Visas, **1**:57
Vision, **2**:492
Vocational education, **1**:332, 373
Voluntary Community Action Program, **2**:411, 412
Volunteer training, **2**:459
Vote Tally, **2**:498
Votenet, **2**:468
Voter registration, **2**:445, 569, 578
Voters for Choice/Friends of Family Planning, **2**:665, 667
Voting age, **2**:485
Voting Rights Act, **2**:436, 509, 578
Vouchers. *See* School vouchers
Vulcan Materials, **2**:634

W

Wage laws. *See* Minimum-wage legislation
Wagner Act, **2**:351
Wagner-Hatfield amendment, **1**:142
Wal-Mart, **1**:10, 51, 83; **2**:415
    leading PAC, **2**:630, 632
Walker, Charles E., **2**:678
Wall of Separation: The Constitutional Politics of Church and State, The, **2**:514
Wallace, Henry, **2**:466
Walt Disney, **1**:87–88, 121, 140; **2**:589
    leading PAC, **2**:638, 639
    soft money donations, **2**:676
Wamp, Zack, **1**:90
War
    Air Transport Association and, **1**:301
    aircraft industry and, **1**:298–99
    See also Anti-war activists; Specific war
War Air Service Program, **1**:301
War criminals, **2**:589
War Industries Board, **1**:118; **2**:472
War on Poverty, **2**:467, 564
Warner Music, **1**:153
Warnke, Paul, **2**:678
Warren, Earl, **2**:494
Washington, **2**:665, 666
Washington, George, **2**:422
Washington Council, **2**:701
Washington Letter, The, **1**:68
Washington Mutual, **2**:648
Washington Post
    Christian Coalition advertisements, **2**:481
    Sierra Club advertisements, **1**:288
Washington Summary, The, **1**:68
Washington Weekly Report, **1**:29

Waste Management, **2**:645
Waste managment/environmental service PACs, **2**:645
Water pollution, **1**:262, 272, 273
Water quality, **1**:262, 281
Watson, Paul, **1**:270
Watt, James, **1**:260
Web Offset Association, **1**:343
Web Printing Association, **1**:343
Webb-Pomerence Export Trade Act, **1**:138
Webber, Frederick, **1**:321
Webster, Daniel, **2**:587
Webster v. Reproductive Health Service, **2**:537
WebTrust, **1**:21
Weight-distance taxes, **1**:296
Welch, Robert, **2**:455, 494
Welfare. *See* Social welfare
Wells Fargo, **2**:684
Wells-Barnett, Ida, **2**:578
Wertheimer, Fred, **2**:485, 679
West Virginia v. Barnette, **2**:433
Western League of Savings Institutions, **2**:648
Western States Public Lands Coalition, **1**:291
Westinghouse, **2**:384, 390
Westinghouse Electric, **2**:638, 639
Westvaco Corp., **1**:304; **2**:629
Wetland Reserve program, **1**:279
Wetlands, **1**:259
    Army Corps of Engineers, **1**:282
    Environmental Defense Fund, **1**:262
    Izaak Walton League, **1**:272, 273
    National Association of Home Builders, **1**:331
    National Audubon Society, **1**:279
    National Wildlife Federation, **1**:281
Wetly, John, **1**:346
Wexler Group, **2**:661, 701
Weyerhaeuser Co., **1**:304; **2**:629
Whales & whaling, **1**:259, 260
    Environmental Defense Fund, **1**:262
    Greenpeace, **1**:269, 270
    Makah tribe hunt of, **1**:270–71
Wharton School, **1**:60
Wheat industry, **1**:229–30
WheatPAC, **1**:229
Wheeler-Lea Amendment, **1**:78
Whiskey Rebellion, **2**:506
White House Conference on Social Security, **1**:33
Why Are They Lying to Our Children?, **2**:493
Wilderness Act, **1**:288
Wilderness campaigns, **1**:281, 288
Wilderness Society, **1**:288
Wildlife, PETA, **2**:541
Wildlife habitats, **1**:260
    Environmental Defense Fund, **1**:262
    Izaak Walton League, **1**:272
    National Audubon Society, **1**:278, 279
    National Wildlife Federation, **1**:281
Wildlife Stewardship Awards, **1**:305
Wilhelm, John W., **2**:376
Willamette Industries, **1**:304; **2**:629
Willging, Paul, **1**:182
William and Flora Hewlett Foundation, **2**:473
William and Naomi Gorowitz Institute on Terrorism and Extremism, **2**:435
William H. Donner Foundation, **2**:499

---

*Numbers in **bold** indicate volume.*

Williams & Jensen, **2:**661, 701
Williams Companies, **2:**643
Willkie, Wendell L., II, **2:**438
Wilmer, Cutler and Pickering, **2:**680
Wilson, Richard, **2:**565
Wilson, Woodrow, **1:**63; **2:**435, 606
Windfall Elimination Provision, **1:**87
Wine & Spirits Wholesalers of America, **2:**630, 631
Winfrey, Oprah, **1:**233
Winn-Dixie, **1:**83
Winston & Strawn, **2:**661
Wisconsin Farm Bureau, **1:**215
"Wisconsin Works," **2:**492
Wise use movement, **1:**257, 258, 291–93
Wofford, Harris, **2:**467
Wolfe, Sidney, **2:**500
Wolves, **1:**262, 282
Women Vote!, **2:**572, 573
Women's Alliance of Israel, **2:**665, 666
Women's and Children's Resource Act, **2:**538
Women's Campaign Fund, **2:**622, 623, 659
Women's Field Army, **1:**167
Women's Political Committee, **2:**659
Women's rights, **2:**508
  Emily's List, **2:**556–59 *passim,* 572–74, 623, 659
  Human Rights Watch, **2:**441, 442
  leading PACs, **2:**659
  limited Medicaid coverage, **1:**203
  National Organization for Women, **2:**556–59 *passim,* 583–85, 659
  suffrage, **2:**444, 508
  See also League of Women Voters; Planned Parenthood Federation of America
Wood Library-Museum of Anesthesiology, **1:**202
Woodmen Accident and Life, **1:**4
Woods, Harriet, **2:**572
Worker Advocacy Project, **2:**413
Worker exploitation, grocers and, **1:**85
Worker-related interest groups, **1:**64–65
Worker rights. *See* Labor laws & rights
Worker safety
  American Conservative Union, **2:**458
  American Nurses Association, **1:**194
  American Postal Workers Union, **2:**371
  Americans for Democratic Action, **2:**458
  Americans for Tax Reform, **2:**458
  Chemical Manufacturers Association, **1:**321, 322
  Citizen Actions, **2:**457–58
  Communications Workers of America, **2:**372, 373
  Economic Policy Institute, **2:**457–58
  International Association of Fire Fighters, **2:**378, 380
  International Association of Machinists and Aerospace Workers, **2:**381, 382–83
  International Brotherhood of Teamsters, **2:**389
  International Union of Operating Engineers, **2:**390
  National Association of Manufacturers, **1:**332, 333
  National Chicken Council, **1:**235
  National Cotton Council, **1:**238
  National Education Association, **2:**396
  National Taxpayers Union, **2:**458
  Printing Industries of America, **1:**343, 344
  Public Citizen, **2:**457–58
  Service Employees International Union, **2:**402–3
  Transport Workers Union of America, **2:**404

Worker safety *(continued)*
  United Automobile Workers, **2:**412
  United Food and Commercial Workers Union, **2:**413, 415
  United Transportation Union, **2:**419
Workplace Preservation Act, **2:**113
World Bank, **1:**267, 285
World Council of Credit Unions, **1:**25
World Health Organization, **1:**195; **2:**615
World Intellectual Property Organization treaties, **1:**122, 131, 139, 151, 154, 157
World of Difference Institute, **2:**435, 436
World Population Conference, **2:**542
World Rainforest Report, **1:**284
World Resources in Relation to the Family, **2:**542
World Semiconductor Council, **1:**347
World Trade Organization
  American Council of Life Insurance, **1:**16
  American Federation of Labor–Congress of Industrial Organizations, **2:**362
  Brookings Institution, **2:**473
  Business Roundtable, **1:**319
  China and, **2:**592
  Economic Policy Institute, **2:**488
  European Union, **2:**598
  Friends of the Earth, **1:**267
  International Brotherhood of Teamsters, **2:**389
  Semiconductor Industry Association, **1:**347
World Wide Web
  AIMNet, **1:**125
  American Civil Liberties Union, **2:**434
  American Conservative Union, **2:**460
  American Dietetic Association, **1:**175
  American Enterprise Institute, **2:**463
  American Trucking Associations, **1:**312
  Americans for Democratic Action, **2:**466, 468
  Anti-Defamation League, **2:**436, 437
  Brookings Institution, **2:**472
  Cato Institute, **2:**475
  Center for Responsive Politics, **2:**479
  Center for the Defense of Free Enterprise, **1:**292
  Common Cause, **2:**485
  Economic Policy Institute, **2:**487
  Environmental Defense Fund, **1:**263, 264
  environmental groups' use of, **1:**260
  Friends of the Earth, **1:**267
  Greenpeace, **1:**270
  Hudson Institute, **2:**492
  Human Rights Watch, **1:**442
  Independent Insurance Agents of America, **1:**32
  Izaak Walton League, **1:**273, 274
  League of Conservation Voters, **1:**275
  Legal Services Corporation, **2:**448
  National Audubon Society, **1:**279
  National Council of the Churches of Christ, **2:**496
  Public Citizen, **2:**500
  Rainforest Action Network, **1:**284–85
  recording artists', **1:**155
  Sugar Alliance, **1:**223
  U.S. Public Interest Research Group, **2:**504
  WebTrust, **1:**21
Wounded Knee, **2:**452, 565
Wright, Orville, **1:**298
Wye-River Agreement, **2:**601
"Wylie Amendment," **2:**514

X–Y

Xerox, **2**:407
Yannecone, Victor, **1**:262
Year 2000. *See* Y2K
Yellow, **2**:668, 670
"Yellow dog" contracts, **2**:366
Yellowstone National Park, **1**:282, 287
Yellowstone vision document, **1**:291–92
Yeltsin, Boris, **2**:594, 611, 613
Yingling, Edward L., **1**:9
Y2K
    American Institute of Certified Public Accountants, **1**:22, 23
    Credit Union National Association, **1**:22
    Independent Community Bankers of America, **1**:29
    Independent Insurance Agents of America, **1**:32
    Investment Company Institute, **1**:35
    liability, **1**:5
    Securities Industry Association, **1**:60
    Semiconductor Industry Association, **1**:347
    TechNet, **1**:349
    Year 2000 Disclosure Act, **1**:60

Y2K *(continued)*
    Year 2000 Fairness and Responsibility Act, **1**:347
    Year 2000 Readiness and Responsibility Act, **1**:347
Yom Kippur War, **2**:436
Yosemite National Park, **1**:287, 291
You Don't Need a Home to Vote campaign, **2**:450
Young Men Christian Association, **1**:75
Your Big Backyard, **1**:283
Youth for Democratic Action, **2**:466
Youth-related programs, **2**:559, 568, 570
Yucca Mountain, **1**:339; **2**:386
Yugoslavia, former
    Brookings Institution and, **2**:473
    Cato Institute and, **2**:476
    Human Rights Watch and, **2**:442
    John Birch Society and, **2**:495

Z

Zeller, Janet, **1**:308
Zero Population Growth, **2**:553–54
Zero Population Growth Education Network, **2**:553
ZPG Reporter, The, **2**:553